INDUSTRIAL WASTE DISPOSAL AND SEWAGE IRRIGATION
An Annotated Bibliography

CONCEPT'S INTERNATIONAL SERIES IN ENVIRONMENT (CISE)

General Editor : K.V. PALIWAL

CISE-1 Environmental Geography and natural Hazards: Exigencies of Appraisal in Highland – Lowland Interactive Systems by **A.A. Pirazizy**
Rs. 250

CISE-2 Industrial Waste Disposal and Sewage Irrigation: An Annotated Bibliography by **K.V. Paliwal**
Rs. 490

CISE-3 Industrial Pollution Management and Controls – A Directory by **Girish Kumar** and **Priti Anand**
Rs. 300

Concept's International Series in Environment-2

INDUSTRIAL WASTE DISPOSAL AND SEWAGE IRRIGATION

An Annotated Bibliography

Compiled and Edited by

K.V. PALIWAL
Emeritus Professor
Indian Agricultural Research Institute
New Delhi

CONCEPT PUBLISHING COMPANY, NEW DELHI 110059

ISBN 81-7022-455-1

First Published 1993

Published and Printed by
Ashok Kumar Mittal
Concept Publishing Company
A/15-16, Commercial Block, Mohan Garden
NEW DELHI-110059

Lasertypeset by
Microtech Advance Printing Systems (Pvt.) Ltd.
H-13, Bali Nagar
NEW DELHI-110015

PREFACE

Water is life; and purer the water, better the life is of all living creatures. Yet its use and re-use leads into its qualitative deterioration. The continued usage of poor quality water and its disposal on land causes degradation of land resources however great shock absorber the land may be.

In addition to daily human activity, rapidly growing industrial activity is generating huge quantities of waste water of different, physical, chemical and biological characteristics. Such variedly waste waters either through the process of recycling or as a means of irrigation in areas where no other source of good quality water is available, are disposed on land. Under all situations the land resources are more and more contaminated by polluted waters leading to the stage of complete deterioration in soil health.

Crop plants and trees grown on such contaminated soils are likely to reflect poor quality in their produce. Hence the nutritive quality of grains, vegetables, fruits, and food materials obtained from the contaminated lands is bound to be of inferior quality; and in extreme cases such materials become unsuitable for human and animal consumption if they possessed toxins beyond permissible limits.

Innumberable water-soil-plant-food chain processes are operative under contaminated systems. These are not only complex in nature but are of multi-components with widely varying conditions. Hence the laws and predictive approaches meant for single component systems are not usually operative in contaminated systems.

Serious efforts are being made by scientists of various disciplines to simulate the field conditions or studying them *in situ* first to understand the integrated effect of the environment and then to develop a suitable management technology.

Environment science is a fast growing, need-based area of research, and in recent years voluminous literature has been contributed by scientists in view of the local environmental conditions either singly or as a team. A sincere attempt has been made by the author to compile all available information on waste-water-soil-heavy metal plant-relationships covering various aspects namely:

(i) Chemical characteristics of sewage water, sludges, industrial wastes and effluents;

(ii) Chemical, physical and biological properties of contaminated soils,
(iii) Adsorption-desorption of heavy metals on soils, clay minerals and oxides;
(iv) Heavy metals-sludge interaction in soils;
(v) Transformation and transport of heavy metals, nutrients, and organics in sludge/waste treated soils;
(vi) Microbiological behaviour in heavy metal-sewage sludge/waste amended soils;
(vii) Disposal of industrial wastes on soils;
(viii) Reclamation of mine spoiled areas;
(ix) Response of field, fodder, vegetable crops and grasses to sewage water, industrial effluent irrigation and application of sludges and industrial waste materials to soils;
(x) Response of forest trees to Municipal sewage water sludges, industrial wastes and waste waters;
(xi) Absorption of nutrients/heavy metals by crop plants, grasses and trees;
(xii) Crop tolerance to heavy metals;
(xiii) Land and crop management with sewage/industrial waste contaminated soil systems.

It is envisaged that this annotated bibliography will not only provide the latest scientific information on the subject, but will also generate new dimensions of research in the area of waste water irrigation, crop management, soil health, land disposal of wastes and utilization of sludges in agriculture and forestry. And in view of its international coverage and vividity in topics of current interest in the field of environment, it has been accepted to be one of the volumes of the International Series on Environment.

15th Oct., 1992

K.V. Paliwal

CONTENTS

GUIDELINES/STANDARDS/REPORTS

(Central Pollution Control Board, East Arjun Nagar, Delhi-32)

A. MINIMAL NATIONAL STANDARD FOR DIFFERENT INDUSTRIES

1. Oil Refineries
2. Man-made Fibre Industry
3. Caustic Soda Mercury Cell Industry
4. Sugar Industry
5. Fermentation Industry
6. Pesticide Industry
7. Straight Phosphate Fertilizer Industry
8. Straight Nitrogen Industry
9. Straight Nitrogen and Phosphorus Industry
10. Complex Fertilizer Industry
11. Thermal Power Plants
12. Small Pulp and Paper Industry
13. Pharmaceutical Industry
14. Petrochemical Industry
15. Liquid Effluent-Paint Industry
16. Dyes and Dye Intermediate Industry
17. Pollution Control Acts-and Rules with Amendments.
18. Standards for Liquid Effluents, Gaseous Emissions, Automobile Exhaust and Noise

B. REPORTS

1. Industrial Pollution due to small Textile Printing and Dyeing Units of Jodhpur, Pali and Balotara in Rajasthan
2. Impact of Auto Exhausts
3. Water Quality Statistics of India
4. Water Quality of India – Aquatic Resources
5. Status and Trend of Water Quality of River Ganga
6. Report on Pollution Control Implementation in Cement Industry
7. Impact of Auto Exhaust and Land Pollution on Vegetation in Union Territory of Delhi

8. Dust Pollution from Stone Crushers
9. Characteristics and Treatment of Waste Water from an Electric Bulb Manufacturing Unit
10. National Inventory of Water Polluting Industry
11. Characteristics of Waste Water from Wazirpur Industrial Area (Delhi)
12. Guidelines for Cooling Water Management
13. Recycling of Sewage and Industrial Effluent on Land-Monitoring and Surveillance Report
14. Status of Water Supply and Waste Water Collection Treatment and Disposal in Class I cities
15. Status of Waste Water Treatment of Class II Towns

SOME BOOKS ON POLLUTED SOIL-WATER-PLANT ENVIRONMENT MANAGEMENT

A. Water Pollution and Management

Chapman, D.T., El-Shaarawi, A.H. (Eds.), Statistical Methods for the Assessment of Point Source Pollution: Environmental Monitoring and Assessment 13: p. 461.

Mishra, S.G., Prasad, D., 1992, Environmental Pollution: Water, Venus Pub. House, New Delhi.

Sinha, U.K., 1990, Ganga Pollution and Health Hazard, Inter-India Pub., Raja Garden Extension, New Delhi.

Moore, J.W., 1990, Inorganic Contaminants of Surface Water, Springer Books, Delhi.

Hastam, S.M., 1990, River Pollution – An Ecological Perspective, Belhaven Press, London, p. 253.

Harrison, R.M. (Ed.), 1990, Pollution Causes, Effects and Control. 2nd Ed. U.K. Royal Soc. Chemistry Information Service, p. 393.

Hammer, P.J.C., Leeds-Harrison, P.B., 1990, Nitrates and Irrigation, Silose, U.K.

Srivastava, Y.N., 1989, Environmental Pollution, Ashish Publishing House, New Delhi.

Lijklema, *et al*, 1989, Water Pollution Research and Control, Brighton Parts 5. Pergamon/IAWPRC. Oxford, U.K.

Laikari, H. (Ed.), 1989, River Basin Management, 5 Pergamon/ IAWPRC, Oxford, U.K.

Jousma, G., Bear, J., Haimes, Y.Y. Walter, F., 1989, Ground Water Contaminations: Use of Models in Decision-making, Dordrecht. Kluwer Acad. Pub., Netherlands.

Huntley, M.E., 1989, Biotreatment of Agricultural Waste Water, Boca. Raton, CRC, Press Inc., Florida.

Weltre, E., Szabolcs, I. (Eds.), 1988, Protection of Water from Harmful Emission with Special Regard to Nitrate and Heavy Metals, Proc. 5th International Symp. CIEC.

Patrick, R., Ford, E., Quarles, J., 1987, Ground Water Contamination in the United States, 2nd Ed. Penn. Univ. Press.

ICID, 1987, Toxic Substances in Agricultural Water Supply and Drainage, ICID, USA Division.

Powli, P.P., 1986, Proc. International Conference on Environmental Pollution Control, Sri Venkateswara Univ. Tirupati, A.P., India.

Moore, J.W., Ramamoorthy, S., 1984, Heavy Metals in Natural Waters – Applied Monitoring and Impact Assessment, Springer, Verlag, New York.

Varshney, C.K. (Ed.), 1983, Water Pollution and Management, Wiley Eastern Limited, New Delhi.

Devik, O. (Ed.), 1976, Harvesting Polluted Waters, Plenum Press, London.

Hynes, H.B.N., 1971, The Biology of Polluted Waters, Liverpool University Press, Liverpool.

B. Soil Pollution, Land Disposal of Wastes and Environment Management

Prasad, D., Khan, E., 1992, Environmental Pollution: Land, Venus Pub. House, New Delhi.

Mishra, S.G., Prasad, D., 1992, Environmental Pollution: Solid Waste, Venus Pub. House, New Delhi.

Wooldridge, R. (Ed.), 1991, Proc. Techniques for Environmentally Sound Water Resources Development. African Regional Symp., Pentech Press, London.

Tamm, C.O., 1991, Nitrogen in Terrestrial Eco-Systems, Springer Books, Delhi.

Nath, B., Robinson, J.P. (Eds.), 1991, Proc. International Conf. on Environmental Pollution. Inter-Science, Enterprises, Geneva.

Mishra, S.G., Mani, D., 1991, Soil Pollution, Ashish Pub. House, New Delhi.

Lal, R., Pierce, F.J. (Eds.), 1991, Soil Management for Sustainability, Soil & Water Cons. Soc., Ankeny, USA.

Corell, R.W., 1991, Global Environmental Change, Springer Verlag, Vienna.

Buckley, R., 1991, Perspectives in Environmental Management, Springer Verlag, Vienna.

Patnaik, L.N., 1990, Environmental Impacts of Industrial and Mining Activities, Ashish Pub. House, New Delhi.

Murlidhara, H.S. (Ed.), 1990, Solid Liquid Separation Waste Management and Productivity Enhancement. Pub. Battle Press, Columbus, Ohio.

Mishra, P.C., 1990, Fundamentals of Air and Water Pollution, Ashish Pub. House, New Delhi.

Hutzinger, O., 1990, The Hand Book of Environmental Chemistry, Vol. 1 Part. E., The Natural Environment and the Biogeochemical Cycles. Vol. 2 Reactions and Processes, Vol. 3, Anthropogenic Compounds, Vol. 4, Air Pollution, Springer Verlag, Vienna.

Cheng, H.M. (Ed.), 1990, Pesticides in the Soil Environment Processes Impacts and Modelling, Vol. 23. Am. Soil Sci. Soc. Madison Wisconsin, p. 530.

Biswas, A.K., Khoshoo, T.N., Khosla, Ashok, 1990, Environmental Modelling for Developing Countries, Tycooly Pub., London.

Wahi, S.K., Agnihotri, A.K., Sharma, J.S. (Eds.), 1989, Environmental Management in Petroleum Industry, Wiley Eastern Ltd., Delhi.

UNEP, 1989, Environmental Data Report, 2nd Edition, Gems Montoring and Assessment Research Centre, London, p.192.

Sawhney, B.L., Brown, K. (Eds.), 1989, Reactions and Movement of Organic Chemicals in Soils, Vol. 22, Am. Soil Sci. Soc. Madison, Wisconsin.

Pol Prasert, C., 1989, Organic Waste Recycling, Chickester, West Sussex/Johnwiley & Sons Ltd.,

Kostecki, P.T., Calabrese, E.J., 1989, Petroleum Contaminated Soils – Remediation Techniques and Environmental Fate Risk Assessment, Vol. I, Lewis Pub. Inc., Chelsa, Michigan.

Javour, B.J., 1989, Hyper Saline Environment, Springer Verleg, Vienna.

Jacobs, L.W., 1989, Selenium in Agriculture and the Environment. Soil Sci. Soc. Am. Madison, Wisconsin.

Hansen, J.A., Henriksen, K. (Eds.), 1989, Nitrogen in Organic Wastes Applied to Soils, Academic Press, San Diego.

Baccini, P., 1989, The Land Fill, Springer Books Delhi.

Tarradells, J., Albaiges, J., Frei, R.W. (Eds.), 1988, Analysis and Fate of Pollutants, Gordon & Breach, Sci. Pub. 564, Montriau Switzerland.

Steffan, W.L., 1988, Flow and Transport in the Natural Environment, Springer Verlag, Vienna.

Frimmel, F.H., Christman, R.F. (Eds.), 1988, Humic Substances and Their Role in the Environment, Chickester, Sussex/Johnwiley & Sons Ltd.

Calabrese, E.J., Kostecki, P.T., Fleischer, E.J. (Eds.), 1988, Soil Contaminated by Petroleum – Environmental and Public Health Effects, Vol. 2, John. Wiley & Sons Inc. p. 458.

Welte, E., Szabolcs, I. (Eds.), 1987, Agricultural Waste Management and Environment Protection, 4th International CIEC, Symp.

Pawlowski, L., Mentasi, E., Lacy, W.J., Sarzanini, C., 1987, Chemistry for Protections of the Environment, Elsevier Sci. Pub., Amstersdam.

Nriagu, J.O., Spragua, J.B., 1987, Cadmium in the Aquatic Environment, Vol. 19, Adv. In Environment Sci & Technology. Wiley Inter Sci., New York.

Jorgenson, S.E., Johnson, I., 1987, Principles of Environmental Science and Technology, 2nd. Ed. Elsevier, Sci. Pub., Amsterdam.

Winteringham, F.P. (Ed.), 1986, Environment and Chemicals in Agriculture, Elsevier App. Sci. Pub., London.

Sly, P.G., 1986, Sediments and Water Inter-actions. Springer Verlag, Vienna.

Runge, E.C.A. (Ed.), 1986, Utilization, Treatment and Disposal of Waste on Land. Soil Sci. Soc. Am., Madison, Wisconsin.

Pawlowski, L., Alaerts, G., Lacy, W.J. (Eds.), 1986, Proc. 5th International Conf. on Chemistry for Protection of the Environment, Elsevier, Sci. Pub., Amsterdam.

De, A.K., 1986, Environmental Chemistry, Wiley Eastern Ltd., Delhi.

Sastry, C.A., Madhav Krishna, W., 1984, Pollution Problems in Leather Industries in India, Deptt. of Environment, Govt. of India, Delhi.

Rogoshewski, P., Bryson, N., Wagner, K., 1983, Remedial Action Technology for Water Disposal Sites, Noyes Data Corporation, Mill Road, Park Ridge, NJ, USA. p. 495.

Woolfe, J. (Ed.), 1982, Waste Management, D. Reidel Publ. Co., Holland, p. 277.

Ure, A.M., Berrow, M.L., 1982, Environmental Chemistry, Vol. 2, Royal Society of Chemistry, London.

Jordan, R.E., Payne, J.R., 1980, Fate and Weathering of Petroleum Spills in the Marine Environment, Ann. Arbor Sci., Pub., Ann Arbor Mi.

Raychaudhary, S.P., Gupta D.S., 1977, Environmental Pollution and Toxicology, Proc. International Symp., Jagmander Book Agency, New Delhi.

Patel, B. (Ed.), 1960, Management of Environment, Wiley Eastern Ltd., Delhi.

C. Heavy Metals and Other Elements

Izmeror, N.F. (Ed.), Scientific Review of the Soviet Literature on the Toxicity and Hazards of Chemicals. Thallium. U.N. Environmental Programme 17, Moscow.

Fulkerson, W., Goeller H.E. (Eds.), 1973 Cadmium — The Dissipated Element, Oak Ridge National Laboratory, Oak Ridge, Tennessee.

Cannon, H.L., Connally, G.G., Epstin, J.B., Porker, J.G., Thornton, I., Wixson, B.G., Geochemistry and the Environment Vol. 3, National.

Bodik, I., Lyman, W.J., Rechl, W.T., Rosenblatt, D.H. (Eds.), Environmental Inorganic Chemistry, Properties, Processes and Estimation Methods, Pergamon Press, New York.

Mishra, S.G., Mani, D., 1992, Metallic Pollution, Ashish Pub. House, New Delhi.

Worthing, C.R., Hancer, J. (Eds.), 1991, The Pesticide Manual: A World Compendium, Ninth edn. Pub. British Crop Production Council Survey, U.K.

Shaw, A.J. (Ed.), 1990, Heavy Metals Tolerance in Plants Evolutionary Aspects, CRC Boca Raton. Florida, p. 335.

Manahan, S.E., 1990, Environmental Chemistry. Levis Pub. 4th Edn., Chelsa, Mi.

Glaser, U. (Ed.), 1990, Proc. 4th IUPAC Cadmium, Workshop, Toxicol Environ Chem. 27: (1-3)

Ferfusson, J., 1990, The heavy Elements : Chemistry, Environmental Impact and Health Effects, Pergamon Press, New York, p. 614.

Blume, H.D. (Ed.), 1990, Soil Protection, Manual, Soil Ecology and Pollution Preventive and Remedial Measures, Landsberg/Lech.

Alloway, B.J. (Ed.), 1990, Heavy Metals in Soils, John Wiley and Sons, New York, p. 339.

Wendel, A., 1989, Selenium in Biology and Medicine, Springer Verlag, Vienna.

Sposito, G. (Ed.), 1989, The Environmental Chemistry of Aluminium, CRC Boca Razion, Florida.

Lewis, T.E. (Ed.), 1989, Environmental Chemistry and Toxicology of Aluminium. Lewis Pub. Chelsa, Mi.

Krishna Murti, C.R., Vishvanathan, P., 1989, (Eds.), Toxic Metals in the Indian Environment, Tata McGraw-Hill Pub. Comp. Ltd., p. 280.

Fred, Singer, S., 1989, Global Climatic Change: Human and Natural Influences, Pergamon House, New York.

Coler, R.A., Rockwood, J.P., 1989, Water Pollution Biology: A Laboratory/Field Hand Book, Technomic Pub., Lancaster, PA.

Bar-yosef, B., Barrow, N.J., Goldsmid, J. (Eds.), 1989, Inorganic Contaminants in the Vadose Zone, Springer Verlag.

Safe, S., 1988, Cadmium, Springer Verlag, Vienna, Vienna.

Nriagu, J.O., Nieboer, E., 1988, Chromium in the Natural and Human Environmental Adv. in Environmental Science & Technology, Vol. 20: John Wiley & Sons, New York.

Itamer Bodex, et al., 1988, Environmental Inorganic Chemistry, Pergamon Press, New York.

Graham, R.D., Hannam, R.J., Unen, N.C. (Eds.), 1988, Manganese in Soils and Plants, Dordrecht. Kluwer, Acad. Pub., Netherland.

Robert, L., Tate, III, 1987, Soil Organic Matter: Biological and Ecological Effects, Johnwiley & Sons, New York.

Lepparol, G.G. (Ed.), 1987, Trace Element Speciation in Surface Waters and its Ecological Implications, Plenum Pub., New York.

Hutchinson, T.C., Meena K.M. (Eds.), 1987, Lead, Mercury, Cadmium and Arsenic in the Environment, John Wiley and Sons, Chickester, England.

Nath, R., 1986, Environmental, Pollution of Cadmium-Biological, Physiological and Health Effects, Inter Print, New Delhi.

Craig, P.J., 1986, Organometallic Compounds in the Environment — Principles and Reactions, Longman-Harlow.

Besidits, S., Netzer, A., 1986, Removal of Heavy Metals from Waste Waters. B & L Information Service, Toronto.

Adriano, D.C., 1986, Trace Elements in the Terrestrial Environment, Springer-Verlag, Heidelberg.

Sigel, H. (Ed.), 1985, Circulation of Metals in the Environment, Marcel Dekker, New York.

Kabata-Pendias, A., Pendias, H., 1984, Trace Elements in Soils and Plants, CRC Press, Boca Raton, Florida.

Davis, R.D., 1983, Heavy Metals in the Environment, CEP Consultant, Edinburgh.

Lepp, N.W. (Ed.), 1982, Effect of Heavy Metals Pollution on Plants, Vol. 2, Applied Sci. Publ., London.

Langard, S. (Ed.), 1982, Biological and Environmental Aspects of Chromium, Elsevier, Amsterdam.

Kontze, H., 1982, Iron Clogging in Soils and Pipes, Pitman Publish. Inc., Marshfield, p. 148.

Mellanby, K., 1981, Effect of Heavy Metals Pollution on Plants. Vol. 1, Applied Sci. Publ., London.

Loneragan, J.F., Robson, A.D., Graham, R.D. (Eds.), 1981, Copper in Soils and Plants, Academic Press, Sydney.

Kitagishi, K. and **Yamane. I.** (Eds.), 1981, Heavy Metal Pollution in Soils of Japan, Scientific Societies Press, Tokyo.

Nriagu, J.O. (Ed.), 1980, Zinc in the Environment, Part I: Ecological Cycling, John Wiley and Sons, New York.

Nriagu, J.O. (Ed.), 1980, Nickel in the Environment, John Wiley and Sons, New York.

Nriagu, J.O. (Ed.), 1980, Cadmium in the Environment, Part 1: Ecological Cycling, John Wiley and Sons, New York.

Erian, E., Davies, B.E. (Eds.), 1980, Applied Soil Trace Elements, John Wiley and Sons, New York.

Davis, R.D., Calton, Smith, C., 1980, Crops as Indicators of the Significance of Contamination of Soils by Heavy Metals, WRC, Stevenage T.R. p. 140.

Davies, B.E., 1980, Inorganic Pollution and Agriculture, MAFF Reference Book, HMSO, London, p. 325.

Nriagu, J.O. (Ed.), 1979, The Biochemistry of Lead in the Environment, Elsevier, North Holland, Amsterdam.

Nriagu, J.O. (Ed.), 1979, Copper in the Environment, Part 1: Ecological Cycling, John Wiley and Sons, New York.

Friberg, L., Nordberg, G.F., Vouk, V.B. (Eds.), 1979, Chromium Handbook on the Toxicology of Metals, Elsevier, North Holland, Amsterdam.

Bowen, H.J.M., 1979, Environmental Chemistry of the Elements, Academic Press, London.

Smith, I.C., Carson, B.L., Hoffmeister, F., 1978, Trace Metals in the Environment, Vol. I, Ann Arbor Sci., Pub. Inc., Ann Arbour, Mi.

Nriagu, J.O. (Ed.), 1978, The Biochemistry of Mercury in the Environment, Elsevier, North Holland, Amsterdam.

Leeper, G.W., 1978, Managing the Heavy Metals on the Land, Marcel Dekker, Inc. New York.

Smith, I.C., Carson, B.L., 1977, Trace Metals in the Environment, Vol. II. Silver, Ann Arbor Science Pub., Michigan.

Harmsen, K., 1977, Behaviour of Heavy Metals in Soils, Centre for Agricultural Publishing and Documentation, Waginingen.

Drucker, H., Wildung, R.E., 1977, Biological Implication of Metals in the Environment, National Technical Information Service, U.S. Department of Commerce, Spring-field, Virginia.

Chappell, W.R., Peterson, K.K. (Eds.), 1977, Molybdenum in the Environment, Vol. 1, Marcel Dekker, New York.

Boggers, W.R. (Ed.), 1977, Lead in the Environment, National Science Foundation, Washington, D.C.

Aubert, H., Pinta, M., 1977, Trace elements in soils. Elsevier Sci. Publ. Company. Amsterdam.

Bisbjerg, B., 1972, Studies on Selenium in Plants and Soils, Danish Atomic Energy, Comm, Res. Estab. Ris. Rep. No. 200.

Clarke, R.J.H., 1968, The Chemistry of Titanium and Vanadium, Elsevier, New York.

D. Municipal Waste Water and Sewage Sludge

Treatment of Sewage Sludge: The Thermopilic Aerobic Digestion and Processing Requirements of Land Filling, 1989, Elsevier Applied Sci. Pub. Ltd., Amsterdam.

Feigin A., Ravina, I., Shalhevet J., 1991, Irrigation with Treated Sewage Effluent, Springer Verlag, Vienna.

Dirkzwager, A.H., Hermite, R.L. (Eds.), 1989, Sewage Sludge, Treatment and Use, Elsevier App. Sci., London.

Page, A.L., Logan, T.J. Ryan, J.A. (Eds.), 1987, Land Application of Sludge Food Chain Implications, Lewis Pub. Inc., Chelsa, Michigan. p. 168.

Nielsen, V.C., Voorburg, J.H., Hermite, R.L. (Eds.), 1986, Odour Prevention and Control in Organic Sludge and Live Stock Farming, Elsevier Applied Science Pub., London.

Gomez, A., Leschhber, R.L., Hermite, R.L. (Eds.), 1986, Sampling Problems for Chemical Analysis of Sludges, Soils and Plants, Elsevier Sci. Pub. Con. New York.

Leschhber, R., Davis, R.D., Hermite, R.L. (Eds.), 1985, Chemical Methods for Assessing Bio-available Metals in Sludges and Soils, Elsevier Applied Sci. Publishers, New York.

Bruce, A. (Ed.), 1985, Sewage Sludge Stabilization and Disinfection, Ellis Harwood Limited, Chichester, England.

Staff of Biocycle Magazine, 1984, Managing Sludge by Composting, The JG Press, Emmaus, PA. USA.

L'Hermits, P., Otto, H. (Eds.), 1984, Processing and Use of Sewage Sludge. D., Riedel Publ. Co., Dordrecht, Holland.

Connor, E.S., Bruce, A.M., 1984, Stabilisation, Disinfection and Odour Control in Sewage Sludge Treatment — An Annotated Bibliography 1950-1963, Ellis Harwood Limited, Chichester, England.

Ganezarczyk, J.J., 1983, Activated Sludge Process — Theory and Practice, Marcel Dekker Inc., New York, p. 270.

Catroux, G., L'Hermits, P., Suess, E. (Eds.), 1983, The influence of Sewage Sludge Applications on the Physical and Biological Properties of Soils, D. Reidel Publishing Company, Boston, Mass.

Sopper, W.E., Seaker, E.M., Basttan, R.K. (Eds.), 1982, Land Reclamation and Biomass Production with Municipal Waste Water and Sludge, The Pennsyl, Press, Pennsylvania, USA, p. 534.

Hucker, T.W.G., Catroux, G. (Eds.), 1981, Phosphorus in Sewage Sludge and Animal Waste Slurries, D. Reidel Publ. Co., London, p. 443.

Eckenfelder, W.W., Santhanam, Jr. C.J. (Eds.), 1981, Sludge Treatment, Marcel Dekker Inc., New York, NY, p. 501.

Borchardt, J.A., Redman, W.J., Jones, G.E., Sprague, T.R. (Eds.), 1981, Sludge and its Ultimate Disposal, Butter-Worths, Woburn.

Beszedicts, S., Lugowski, A., 1981, Utilizing Waste Activated Sludge for Animal Feeding. B and L Information Services, Toronto. p. 21.

Chaney, R.L., Hornick, S.B., Simon, P.W., 1977, Heavy Metal Relationship during Land Utilization of Sewage Sludge in the Northeast, Ann Arbor Sci. Ann., Arbor, Michigan.

E. Forest Soils and Acidic Precipitation

Taylor, G.E., 1991, Ecological Genetics and Air Pollution, Springer Books, Delhi.

Longhurst, J.W. (Ed.), 1991, Acid Deposition: Sources, Effects and Controls, U.K. Technical Communication.

Ulrich, B., 1990, Soil Acidity, Springer Verlag, Vienna.

Smith, W.H., 1990, Air Pollution and Forests, 2nd Edn., Springer, Verlag.

Cunningham, W.P., Saigi, B.W., 1990, Environmental Science: A Global Concern, Dubuque, Iowa.

Xchloz, F., 1989, Genetic Effects of Air Pollutions in Forest Tree Populations, Springer Verlag, Vienna.

Schulze, E.D., 1989, Forest Decline and Air Pollution, Springer Verlag, Vienna.

Norton, S.A., Lindberg, S.E., Page, A.L., 1989, Acidic Precipitation Vol. IV, Soils, Aquatic Processes, and Lake Acidification. Springer Verlag, New York.

Lindberg, S.E., Page, A.L., Norton S.A. (Eds.), 1989, Acidic Precipitation: Vol. III, Sources, Deposition and Canopy Interactions. Springer Verlag, New York.

Binkley, D., 1989, Acidic Deposition and Forest Soils, Springer Books, Delhi.

Adriano, D.C., Johnson, A.H. (Eds.), 1989, Acid Precipitation Vol. II, Biological and Ecological Effects, Springer Verlag, New York.

Adriano, D.C., Havas, M. (Eds.), 1989, Acid Precipitation, Vol. I, Case Studies, Springer Verlag, New York.

Rodhe, H., Herrara, R., 1988, Acidification in Tropical Countries, Chichester, West Sussex, U.K.

Budyko, M., 1988, Global Climate Catastrophes, Springer Verlag, Vienna.

Cole, D.W., Herry, C.I., Nutter, W.L. (Eds.), 1986, The Forest Alternatives for Treatment and Utilization of Municipal and Industrial Wastes, John Wiley & Sons, New York.

Murray, F., 1982, Fluoride Emissions: Their Monitoring and Effect on Vegetation and Ecosystem, Academic Press, London.

F. Biology and Micro-organisms

Biotechnology, 1990, Applications in Hazardous Waste Treatment, Engineering Foundation, New York.

Ulrich, W.R., 1990, Inorganic Nitrogen in Plants and Micro-organisms, Springer Verlag, Vienna.

Duerre, H.D., 1990, Adaptation of Micro-organisms to Extreme Environments, Sprinter Verlag, Vienna.

Munawar, M., Dixon, G., May-Field, C.T., Reymoldson, T., Sadar, M.M. (Eds.), 1989, Environmental Bioassay Techniques and Their Applications. Pub. Hydrobiologia, p. 188-189.

Mishra, P.C. (ed.), 1989, Soil Pollution and Soil Organisms, Ashish Pub. House, Delhi.

Kamelay, D., Chakrabarty, A., Omenn, G.S. (Eds.), 1989, Biotechnology and Biodegradation, Gulf. Pub. Comp, Houston, Texas.

Forstner, U., 1989, Drinking Water Microbiology, Springer Books, Delhi.

Zehnder, A.J.B., 1988, Biology of Anaerobic Micro-Organisms, John Willey & Sons, New York, p. 872.

Rao, V.C., Melnick, J.L. (Eds.), 1987, Human Viruses in Sediments, Sludges and Soils. CRC Inc. Boca. Raton Florida.

Carlisle, D., Berry, W.L., Kaplin, I.R., Vatterson, J.R. (Eds.), 1985, Mineral Exploration; Biological Systems and Organic Matter, Rubey Series, Vol. 5, Prentice-Hall, Englewood Cliffa, N.J.

Krumbein, W.F. (Ed.), 1978, Environmental Biogeo-Chemistry and Geomicro-Biology Vol. I, Aquatic Environment, Vol. II Terrestrial Environment; Vol. III Methods, Metals & Assessment, Ann. Arbor Sci. Pub. Ann Arbor, Michigan.

G. Water Treatment and Waste Management

Bouman, A.F., 1990, Soils and Greenhouse Effect, Johnwiley & Sons., New York.

Tillman, D.A., Rossi, A.J., Vick, K.M., 1989, Incineration of Municipal and Hazardous Solid Wastes, Acad. Press Inc., San Diago.

Robert, J., 1989, Meyers and Associates and Research Planning Institute, Inc., Noyes Data Corporation, New Jersey.

Hammer, D.A. (Ed.), 1989, Constructed Wet Lands for Waste Water Treatment: Municipal, Industrial and Agricultural, Lewis Pub., Chelsa Michigan.

Guidelines for Hazardous Management, 1989, Ministry of Environment, CGO Complex, New Delhi.

Czupyrana, G., Levy, R.D., Maclean, A.I., Gold H., 1989, Noyes Data, Corporation, New Jersey.

Batstane, R., Smith, J.E., Jr., Wishan, D. (Eds.), 1989, The Safe Disposal of Hazardous Wastes. The Special Needs and Problems of Developing Countries. World Bank Technical Paper No. 93, WB, WHO & UNEPE, Vol. I, II & III.

Wise, D.L., 1988, Biotreatment Systems. Vol. II, CRC Inc., Boca Raton, Florida.

Use and Disposal of Wastes from Phosphoric Acid and Titanium Oxide Extraction, 1988, Economic Commission for Europe, Geneva.

Raghavan, K.V., Thyagarajan, G. (Eds.), 1988, Hazard and Risk Analysis in Chemical Process Industries, Committee on Science & Technology in Developing Countries, CSIR, Adyar, Madras.

Freeman, H.M., 1988, Standard Handbook of Hazardous Waste Treatment and Disposal, McGraw-Hill Book Company, New York.

Bolto, B.A., Pawlowski, L., 1988, Waste Water Treatment by Ion Exchange, E & F.N. Spon Ltd., London.

Abbon, R., 1988, Hazardous Waste: Detection, Control and Treatment (2 Volumes), Elsevier Sci. Pub., Amsterdam.

Bell, J.M. (Ed.), 1987, Proc. Industrial Waste Conference, Perdue Univ. Lewis Pub. Inc., Chelsa, Mi.

ASAE, 1987, On Site Waste Water Treatment, Vol. 5, ASAE Publication.

Bhatt, H.G., Sykes, R.M., Sweeny, T.L., 1985, Management of Toxic and Hazardous Wastes, Lewis Pub. Inc., Chelsa, Mi.

Irving Sax, N., 1984, Dangerous Properties of Industrial Materials, Von Nostrand Reinhold Company, New York.

EPA, 1984, Methodologies for Screening and Evaluation of Remedial Technologies, Proc. Management of Uncontrolled Hazardous Waste Sites, USEPA.

Thornton, I. (Ed.), 1983, Applied Environmental Geochemistry, Academic Press, London.

Murray, Moo-Young, Robinson, C.W., Farquhar, G.J. (Eds.), 1982, Waste Treatment and Utilization: Theory and Practice of Waste Management. Vol II, Pergamon Press, New York.

Muckey, Y.D., Hamzal, A. (Eds.), 1982, Management of Industrial Waste Water in Developing Nations, Pergamon Press, Inc. New York, p. 500.

Arceivale, S.J., 1982, Waste Water Treatment and Disposal Engineering and Ecology in Pollution Control, Marcel Dekker, Inc., New York, p. 892.

Walters, J.K., Wint, A. (Eds.), 1981, Industrial Effluent Treatment, Vol. 1, Water and Solid Wastes, Vol. 2, Air and Noise, Applied Sci., Publ. Ltd., Essex, England.

Middlebrooks, E.J., 1979, Industrial Pollution Control, Vol. I. Agro-Industries, John Wiley and Sons, New York, p. 445.

Kalley, A.G., Forster, C.F., Stefford, D.A., 1977, Treatment of Industrial Effluents, Hodder & Stonghton, London.

ABSTRACTS

1 **Abata-Pendias, A.K., Wiacek, K.,** 1986. Effects of sulphur deposition on trace metal solubility in soils. Environ. Geochem. Health. 8 (4) : 95-98.

Concentrations of Fe, Mn, Zn, Pb, Cu and Cd in soil solutions taken in the vicinity of a sulphur mine range from 354 to 9080μML^{-1}, and exceeded the concentrations measured in solutions from light acid arable soils. The content of each metal was a negative function of either the solution pH or of Ca concentration. Reclamation of S-contaminated soil by an application of 2000 tonnes/ha of limestone did not significantly affect the solubility of trace metals, whereas equilibration of soil samples with $CaCO_3$ in the laboratory decreased solubility of metals, especially in the soil under moist conditions. Sulphur deposition may modify the natural cycling of metals in soils.

2 **Abbasi, S.A., Soni, R.,** 1990. Nickel in environment. J. IAEM. 17: 95-108.

A state-of-the-art review is presented on the occurrence of nickel in the environment, nickel pollution, nutritional role of nickel, and nickel toxicity. The present status of the environmental quality criteria of nickel is also reviewed.

3 **Abboud, S.A., Faught, R.L.,** 1989. The use of lime sludge (by-product of the heavy oil industry) for liming of acid agricultural soils in Alberta, Canada. Proc. Annual Alberta Soil Sci. Workshop : 126-130.

In a 5-year experiment in cold lake area of Alberta after applications of lime sludge changes in soil properties were consistent with those observed after adding agricultural lime. No increases in the soil content of heavy metals and oils and no reductions in yield of barley and lucerne were observed.

4 **Abdel Nain, M., Elawady, R.M.,** 1989. Studies on heavy metal removal from sewage water used in sandy soils in 'Toxic Substances in Agril. Water Supply and Drainage' : 219-230.

Field trials on citrus were conducted on sandy soil during 1984-87 at Giza, Egypt, Conc. of Zn, Mn, Cu and Fe increased in irrigated soils on irrigation with sewage water. However, Conc. of Cu, Cr, Ni, Cd and Pb were slightly increased. However, the Conc. of Zn, Cu, Mn and Fe in citrus leaves was increased, but these conc. were not toxic both in plants and soils. During this study, no nutritive or morphological problems were observed in citrus trees.

5 **Abdelouahab, C., Ait-Amar, H., Obretenov, T.A., Gaid, A.,** 1987. Fixation of metal ions by bentonite clays with Cd (II) and Zn (II). Rev. Int. Sci.

Eav. 3; (2) : 33-40.

The removal of Cd(II) and Zn(II) by adsorption on four bentonite clays has been found to depend on concentration, pH and mass of clays particles. The kinetics of adsorption indicates the process to be diffusion controlled. The Freundlich and Langmuir constants have been calculated at 20°C. The maximum removal was observed at pH 7.5 for Cd(II) and at pH 6.5 for Zn(II), and variation in adsorption with pH has been explained on the basis of surface ionisation.

6 **Abdul, A.S., Gibson, T.L., Rai, D.M.,** 1990. Laboratory studies of the flow of some organic solvents and their aquous solutions, through Bentonite and Kaolinite clays. Ground-water 28(4) : 574-583.

The effect of 9 organic solvents and their aquous solutions was studied on hydraulic properties of these clays. In general, the more hydrophobic solvents caused the clays to shrink, producing distinct large vertical cracks, the hydro-pholic solvents typically caused the clays to aggregate and fractuure, forming network of cracks. The physical changes in the clays and the rapid flow of the neat solvents through them, are attributed to the greater swelling of the clays in water than in the neat organic solvents.

7 **Abdul, A.S., Gibson, T.L., Rai, D.M.,** 1990. Selection of surfactants for the removal of petroleum products from shallow sandy aquifers. Groundwater: 28(6): 920-926.

A laboratory study was conducted to evaluate the relative suitability of 10 commercial surfactants for washing residual levels of automatic transmission and fluid from sandy material. The surfactants included examples from each main group of commercial surfactants: (1) ethoxylated alcohols (non-ionic), (2) ethoxylated non-ylphenols (non-ionic), (3) sulfates (anionic), and (4) sulfonates (anionic). Several properties of aqueous solutions of the surfactants were measured and used in evaluating their suitability. These comprised: the extent of dispersion of soil colloids, the detergency of the surfactant solutions and the critical micelle concentration. The amount of fluid removed from the sand ranged from about 23 per cent by washing with water to more than 80 per cent by washing with ethoxylated alcohol surfactants. The paper presents the detailed results of the comparisons.

8 **Acher, A.J., Boderie, P., Yaron, B.,** 1989. Soil pollution by petroleum products: I multiphase migration of kerosine components in soil columns. J. Contam Hydrology. 4(4) : 333-345.

The contribution of different kerosene components to the adsorption, volatilisation and transport processes is described. The increase in soil moisture content increased the rate and depth of kerosene downward penetration. It topped, however vapour movement (at 4%) and upward liquid movement (at 12%). Among the properties of kerosene components, volatility seems to be the prime factor which determines kerosene movement once liquid phase movement has ceased.

9 **Adamec, V., Sanka, M., Rouchovanska, J.,** 1989. The influence of industrial pollutants from Ostrava region on contamination of agricultural land and crops by lead and cadmium. Vedecke prace vyz kumn. Ustav Pro. Zurodent Zemed. Pud. Praha Nob. : 11-16.

Contamination of agricultural land and crops by lead and cadmium was evaluated. Pb and Cd contents of feeds did not exceed the permitted levels except in some cases.

10 **Adebayo, A.O., Wade, J.W.,** 1984. Effects of effluents from a sewage treatment plant on the aquaticorganisms. Water Air Soil Pollut, 23 : 309-316.

The effect of sewage pollution on the distribution and abundance of some organisms over a period of 4 months at the Kubanni river were studied. Physico-chemical parameters such as dissolved oxygen, temperature, hydrogen ion concentration (pH), electrical conductivity and chemical oxygen demand influenced by pollution were measured with respect to the population of aquatic organisms. The organisms were used as biological indices to monitor the ecological imbalance caused by the effluent. The variations in concentrations of some heavy metals were also measured.

The studies revealed that at the source of pollution there were no organisms except for some insect larva such as Eristails, Psychoda, and some microscopic algae like oscillantoria, Anaebaena, and Poly-systis. A location (site 5) on Kubanni river just before the confluence of the sewage effluent and the river was taken as the control. There was a wide variety of organisms (*crustaceans, rotifers, and fish*) at the control point.

11 **Adema, D.M.M., Henzen, L.,** 1989. A comparison of plant toxicities of some industrial chemicals in soil culture and soilless culture. Ecotoxicol. Environ, Saf. 18(2) : 219-229.

The toxicities of 10 industrial chemicals to three types of plants were determined. It was found that in soilless culture the EC_{50} values obtained were much lower than those in soil culture. Soilless culture of terrestrial plants and tests with aquatic plants yielded about the same results. Absorption of the chemicals to soil particles is the main factor governing the results. In an additional experiment with Cd, it was demonstrated that the Cd content of reacting plants was about the same in tests carried out in soil and in nutrient solution, pointing to the obvious fact that the amount of chemical taken up is the basis for the toxic effect.

12 **Ademoroti, C.M.A.,** 1986. Model to predict BOD from COD values. Effluent Water Treat. J. 26(3-4): 80-84.

The BOD_5 and the COD values for domestic, poultry and brewery waste waters were determined and their values compared. A linear relationship was established : COD = a. BOD+b where 'a' and 'b' were constants.

The values of 'a' were found to be 1.64, 1.45 and 2.32 for domestic, poultry and brewery waste waters, respectively and the corresponding 'b' values were 11.36, 55.7 and 46.2 mg/1. The equation was found useful for predicting BOD from the corresponding COD values.

13 **Adhikary, S.P., Sahu, J.,** 1986. Effect of distillery effluent and the blue-green algea Anabaena on the growth and development of rice seedlings. Environ, Ecol. 4(1) : 36-43.

The diluted effluent of a molasses distillery (1-10% vol/vol) supported the seedling growth of the upland variety of the rice (*Oryza sativa CRM 13*). When 10 per cent neutralized distillery effluent and the nitrogen fixing blue green algae Anabaena sp. were supplemented in different combinations, they could significantly increase the vegetative growth of paddy. The results indicated the beneficial effect of nitrogen fixing blue-green algae on rice plants.

14 **Agarwal, G.D.,** 1989. Environmental impacts of industrial units : assessment how and by whom. Ecology, 3 (8) : 19-29.

Industrial operations results in the disposal of certain amounts of materials into the environment either as planned or unavoidable discharges or as unintentional or accidental escapes. The location time, notice and quantity of the pollutants released into the environment thus become key factors in assessing or even discussing environmental impact of industries and the approach to impact assessment has to take these basic features of the releases adequately into account.

15 **Aggett, J., Simpson, J.D.,** 1976. Chromium, copper, and lead in Manukau Harbour sediments. N.Z.J. Mar. Freshwat. Res. 20(4) : 661-663.

A limited survey was undertaken to determine the concentrations of Cu, Pb & Cr in sediments of the upper Manukau Harbour, New Zealand. The conc. of Cu and Cr (33-70 and 70-107 $\mu g\ g^{-1}$ soil respectively) were of the same order of magnitude as those reported for other New Zealand harbours. However, lead concentrations (98-247 $\mu g\ g^{-1}$) were higher than those found for the other harbours. This may be a consequence of higher traffic densities in the surrounding areas.

16 **Ahmad, S.,** 1990. Cleaning the river Ganga-rhetoric and reality, Ambio. 19(1) : 42-44.

The main pollutant in Ganga is urban sewage. So treatment of sewages is emphasised. At Varanasi some 30 million dead human bodies are burnt annually resulting into 100 tonnes of ashes being dumped in the river per month. An electric cretamatorium was built but had to close down after 6 months of operation due to air pollution problem.

17 **Aichberger, K., Eibelhuber, A., Hofer, G.F.,** 1986. In Sampling problems for the chemical analysis of sludge, soils and plants. A. Gomez. R. Leschber, R.L'Hermite (eds.). Elsevier Sci. Publ. Company, Inc., New

York, 94p.

The variability of the acid soluble heavy metals of a field fertilized with sewage sludge was tested and from this the number of sub-samples were statistically estimated. For this experiment from area of one hundred and ten thousand square metre 100, 50, 25, 16 and 9 sub-samples were taken systematically and analysed for copper, zinc, nickel, chromium, lead and cadmium. Taking the averages of the heavy metal levels as 100 per cent the sub-samples varied between 35 and 200 per cent. But the variability for 100 and for one square metre was much less.

18 **Aichberger, K., Hofer, G.F.,** 1989. Contents of arsenic, mercury and selenium in agricultural soils of Upper Austria. Bodenkulter 40:1-12.

From 398 randomly taken surface soils and different soil profiles of Upper-Austria, contents and distribution of As, Hg and Se were investigated. After a sample digestion with perchloric acid the elements were determined by hybrid atomic absorption (As, Se) and cold vapor technique (Hg.). The contents of the top soils ranged from 1-39 (av 6.2) ppm for As, 0.04-1.8, (av 0.1) ppm for Hg and 0.02-1.2 (av 0.2) ppm for Se. There was a close correspondence to the normal levels known from literature and the tolerable contents were exceeded in only one case by arsenic.

19 **Ajlec, R., Cop, M., Stupar, J.,** 1988. Interferences in the determination of chromium in plant materials and soil samples by flame AAS. Analyst 113(4) : 585-590.

A method is described for the determination of Cr in plant materials and soil samples by flame AAS. Factors influencing the sensitivity of the method for Cr and cationic interferences were investigated in air-acetylene and dinitrogen oxide-acetylene flames.

20 **Ajmal, M., Ahmad, A., Hasan, M.A., Nomani, A.,** 1980. Detrimental effects of pharmaceutical industrial waste on micro-organisms. Water Air Soil Pollut. 13:447-452.

Pharmaceutical industrial waste was collected from Ghaziabad (Cooper Pharma Ltd.) and analyzed. The detrimental effects of industrial waste on microorganisms were studies in the system with lower and higher volumes of the waste with 0.5-12 ml using glucose substrate as a source of carbon for microorganisms. The cultures of saprophytic and nitrifying bacteria were grown from sewage and pea gravel respectively, and tested for their nature. Results show that wastes are harmful to microorganisms which cause pollution in the environment.

21 **Ajmal, M., Khan, A.U.,** 1985. Effect of electroplating factory effluent in the germination and growth of hyacinth, bean and mustard. Environ. Res. 38(2) : 248-255.

The effect of electroplating factory effluent in different concentrations (0.1 to 4%) on the germination and growth of hyacinth beans and mustard seeds was studied. The germination of seeds was delayed with the increase of effluent concentrations and the germination of mustard seeds was totally inhibited at 1.5% while hyacinth bean seeds tolerated the effluent up to 2.5% concentration. The metal content in the hyacinth bean plants increased with increasing effluent concentration but after 1.0% effluent concentration, the concentration of all the metals (Ca, Mg, Na, K, Cu, Zn, Fe) decreased in the plants except Cr, which increased throughout. Percentage germination, fresh weight, dry weight, root length, and shoot length of the plants were also analyzed. Cd, Ni, Co, Mn, and Pb were not detectable in the hyacinth bean plants.

22 **Akabane, T., Nose, K.,** 1980. Leaching of dichromate, phosphate, phosphate esters, and nitrobenzenes in soil. Pesti Sci. 5 (2) : 207-213.

Partition ratio, adsorption ratio, theoretical plate number, and soil weight per unit plate of tested soil column are listed for the following chemicals: potassium dichromate, potassium phosphate monobasic dimethylphosphate, dimethoate, trichlorfon, p-nitrophenol, p-nitrobenzaldehyde, and p-nitroanisole. Dichromates, PO_4^{-3} and dimethyl hydrogen phosphate did not give any physically insignificant plate numbers. Adsorption of dimethoate was too small to give a physically significant plate number. trichlorfon showed a normal leaching curve but the plateau was low, implying the loss during the leaching test. The soil weight per unit plate was 12 g for elution of trichlorfon. The leaching curve of p-nitrophenol, p-nitrobenzaldehyde, and p-nitroanisole were normal, and the soil weight per unit plate was 4-6 g. The theoretical formulae were not always satisfied in all cases, because these had many factors other than physical adsorption.

23 **Akhter, M.S.,** 1990. Trace metal analysis of sewage sludge and soil in Bahrain, Water Air Soil Pollut. 51(1-2) : 147-152.

Trace metals such as Pb, Zn, Cu, Ni, Cd and Fe were determined in sewage sludge produced at a sewage treatment plant in Bahrain (Tubli) area used for agricultural purposes. The trace metals level showed the following range ($\mu g\ g^{-1}$ dry weight), Pb, 242 to 609, Zn, 704 to 836, Cu 329 to 512; Ni, 23 to 41; Cd. 1.8 to 3.9 and Fe, 1867 to 4284. The data show the degree to which untreated soils have already been contaminated with trace elements. The level of trace elements found in sludge showed the following range ($ug\ g^{-1}$ dry weight): Pb 140 to 186; Zn; 597 to 836; Cu, 348 to 449: Ni 47 to 53; Cd 5.7 to 9.2 and Fe, 5950 to 8520. Mean levels were generally close or lower than mean concentration reported in the United Kingdom and United States for sludge.

24 **Al-Attar, A.F., Nickless, G.,** 1988. Response surface methodology for an investigation of the influence of selenium, cadmium and mercury on the growth of *Lolium perene* seedlings. Chemosphere 17(9) : 1851-1861.

The growth of Lolium perene seedlings at the concentrations of Se(VI), Cd & Hg was monitored by measuring their root and shoot lengths and biomasses after three weeks in a controlled environment. Toxicity curves were constructed using a three factors central composite experimental design. The response surface between any two spiked elements was studied by displaying the surfaces. Hg was observed to be most toxic element, while although Cd is toxic and very close in value to mercury; Se appears less toxic than Hg or Cd. Analysis of variance (ANOVA) was used to test for the significance of each of the computed parameters.

25 **Albasel, N., Pratt, P.F.,** 1989. Guidelines for molbydenum in irrigation waters. J. Environ. Qual. 18(2) : 259-264.

Mo in relatively high conc. has been found in saline-sulphate dominated agricultural drainage water of California. The unique conditions of alkaline soils favouring Mo mobility, the high leaching fraction required to control salinity in the root zone and the effect of sulphate conc. in reducing Mo absorption by plants, suggested the guidelines of 10 µg/litre for this area. Assuming the use of 10,000 of water per Ha, the Mo input will be 0.5 kg/ha.

26 **Albasel, N., Pratt, P.F., Westcot, D.W.,** 1989. Guidelines for selenium in irrigation waters. J. Environ. Qual. 18(2) : 253-258.

The specific conditions that justified a reassessment were: (i) the Se in the drainage waters of the West Side is largely in the selenate (SeO_4) form which is not appreciably absorbed by soils and is thus readily leached from the root zone, (ii) the waters containing high concentrations of Se have substantial concentrations of sulfate (SO_4) that dramatically reduce SeO_4 absorption by plants. (iii) the salinity of the waters that contain high Se concentration demand teaching fractions (LF) that insure that Se is also leached from the root zone, and (iv) kinetics of Se-species transformations.

27 **Al-Bashir, B.A.L., Cseh, T. Leduc, R., Samson, R.,** 1990. Effect of soil/contaminant interactions on the biodegradation of naphthalene in flooded soil under denitrifying conditions. Appl. Microbiol. Biotechnol. 34(2-3): 414-419.

The mineralisation of C^{14}-labelled naphthalene was studied in pristine and oil contaminated soil slurry (30% solids) under denitrifying conditions using a range of concentrations from below to above the aqueous phase saturation level. Results from sorption/desorption experiments indicated that naphthalene desorption was highly irreversible and decreased with an increase in the soil organic content, thus influencing the availability for microbiol consumption. Under denitrifying conditions, the mineralisation of naphthalene to CO_2 occurred in parallel with the consumption of nitrate and an increase in pH from 7.0 to 8.6. When the initial substrate concentration was 50 ppm (i.e. close to the aqueous phase saturation level), about 90% of the total naphthalene was mineralized within 50 days. and a maximum mineralisation rate of 1.3 ppm day^{-1} was achieved after a lag period of approx. 18 days.

28 **Albert, L.A., Badillo, F.,** 1991. Environmental lead in Mexico. Rev. Bull. Environ. Contam. & Toxic. 117: 1-50.

Lead in Air, water, soil sediments, animals and man have been reviewed.

29 **Aldag. R.,** 1990. Agricultural use of partly decontaminated wastes. Verbiend. Deut. Land. Unter. Lund For-sching Rethe kongress, 33: 79-92.

The use for agricultural purposes of wastes is discussed on the basis of data from long-term experiments at various German universities. While the use of sewage sludge or refuse compost which satisfy the criteria of the German Sewage Sludge Act is possible, there are restrictions on the use of wastes containing polychlorinated biphenyls and phthalates. If these substances are incorporated into the soil, their uptake by plant roots will be unlikely. They should not be applied, however, where direct contamination of the crop or the ingestion of soil by animals is possible.

30 **Al-Ghazali, M.R., Al-Azawi, S.K.,** 1990. *Listeria monocytogenes* contamination of crops grown on soil treated with sewage sludge cake. J. Appl. Bacteriol. 69(5): 642-647.

Listeria monocytogenes was found in the sewage sludge cake which is commonly used as an agricultural fertilizer in Iraq. Soils treated with this material were contaminated with the organism. Pot and field experiments showed that crops grown on treated soil became contaminated with L. *monocytogenes* and when alfalfa plant was grown on farmland soil treated with sewage cake, *listerias* were found on 10% of 50 plants, sampled at harvest, but the organisms was detected only in low numbers on these crops ($\geq$ 5 cells/g). This could add to the risk to animals and man.

31 **Al-Nahidh, S.** 1991, Effect of frequency of irrigation on sewage sludge amended soil and corn nutrition. Arid Soil Res. Rehab. 5(2) : 137-146.

A greenhouse experiment was conducted to evaluate yield, nutrient uptake, and concentration of nutrients in corn (Zea mays L), tissue under different irrigation frequencies in sludge-amended soil. Sewage sludge was applied at four rates (0.20, 40 and 80 t ha^{-1}). Pots were watered either once or twice a week with the same amount of water. Six sequential harvests of corn were made. Frequent irrigation (twice a week) was more effective in increasing dry weight and nutrient uptake by the shoot than once a week irrigation. The increase in dry weight was 54, 66 and 100% at 20, 40 and 80 t sludge ha,$^{-1}$ respectively. The uptake of N, P, K, Fe, Zn, Mn and Cu was also more than doubled at the highest rate of sludge application (80 t ha^{-1}). Concentrations of nutrients in the plant and the soil were not affected by the frequency of irrigation.

32 **Al-Nahidh, S., Gomah, A.H.M.,** 1991. Response of wheat to dual inoculation with Vamycorrhiza and Azospirilium. fertilized with NPK and irrigated with sewage effluent. Arid Soil Res. Rehab. 5(2): 83-96.

A study was performed to investigate the dual effect of inoculation with Azospirillum and VA-mycorrhiza on wheat growth and nutrition. The effects of irrigation with sewage water & NPK fertilization were determined. Potted wheat plants in a greenhouse were used. The highest increase of dry matter production and N and P content was recorded for NPK and VA-mycorrhiza + Azospirillum treatment. Inoculation with either VA-mycorrhiza or Azospirillum had similar effects on wheat growth, while inoculation with both organisms resulted in higher growth increase than either of them alone. The percentage increase of shoot dry matter over the control group was 56.7, 16.2, 21.6, and 37.8% for NPK, VA-mycorrhiza, Azospirillum, & VA-mycorrhiza + Azospirillum treatment, respectively.

33 **Al-Solaimani, S.G.,** 1987. Effect of sewage sludge borne cadmium on crop production and on soil and plant composition. Dis:- Abst. Int. Pt.B Sci & Eng. 47: No. 9.

Teller sandy loam and Vorge loam were used in a greenhouse study with Cadmium (Cd) in sewage sludge. Two sewage sludges were mixed to produce a range of Cd treatments of 7 to 120 mg Cd kg^{-1} in a 44 mt ha^{-1} sludge treatment rate. Sorghum (Sorghum bicolar) and soybean (*Glycine max*) for two successive crops were included as experimental variables. Fresh and dryweights of plants materials were determined and analyzed for total content of Fe, Mn, Zn and Cd after digestion.

34 **Amir, H., Rouquerol, T., Amir, A.,** 1987. Spreading effect of soil residues from refineries on the evolution of organic matter and microbial density of an agricultural soil. Rev. Ecol. Biol. Sol. 24(2): 137-156.

The present study shows some pedological and microbiological changes due to the practice of adding residues at a cultivated land level. These effects are favourable especially in a rice field where the residues are degraded more quickly.

35 **Anbazhagam, M., Krishnamurthy, R., Bhagwat, K.,** 1989. The performance of three cultivars of rice grown near to and distant from, a fertilizer Plant. Environl. Pollut. 58(2-3): 125-137.

Three rice varieties were grown in pots away and near the fertilizer factory with daily peak conc. of 144 μg SO_2 and 210 μg NO_2/m^3 air. Growth was reduced close to factory.In unpolluted site grain accounted 30% of total grain + straw yield. At polluted site grain accounted for 1, 23 and 31% of the total yield of CV. Co 43, TKMG and GR3, respectively. Pollution significantly enhanced the number of panicles in GR3 whereas in Co43, 98% of grains failed to develop.

36 **Angehern-Bettinazzi CT., Honi, L., Hertz, J.,** 1989. An attempt to evaluate some factors affecting the heavy metal accumulation in a forest stand. Internal. J. Environ. Analy. Chem. 35(2) : 69-79.

The accumulation of heavy metals in the organic layer and in the mosses within the forest stand are shown to be dependent on the pollution level, the type of vegetation as well as on the metal under consideration. Greater accumulation has been noted in spruce than in beech stands due to difference, in interceptions. Pb and Cu are more readily accumulated in the forest ecosystem than Cd and Zn.

37 **Angelakis, A.N.,** 1982. Transient movement and transformations of insoluble, soluble, and gaseous carbon in soil. Diss. Abs. Int. Pt. B. Sci. & Eng., 42(8) : 256.

The interrelated series of transformational processes known collectively as the C cycle control the transport and distribution of C species and various other elements in soil. Studies of these transformational processes under dynamic conditions of soil-water movement, soil-air content and C-species concentrations will contribute not only to the basic understanding of the C cycle, but will ultimately contribute to improve waste treatment, crop production, environmental protection and health standards. The transport and transformation of C-species in soil following primary waste water application were mathematically described by assuming convective and convective-despersive transport for insoluble and soluble C, respectively, first-order kinetics for transformation, linear equilibrium adsorption for insoluble and soluble C, gas-transport by diffusion and a constant gas solubility.

38 **Anon.** 1987. Reclaiming 2,000 acres with waste water. Biocycle 28(4) : 32.

A waste water reuse project in Midland, Texas has turned into productive crop-producing land. The cropping systems are balanced in rotation to allow the application of all of the effluent with minimum irrigation return flow and complete utilization of the nitrogen and phosphorus materials in the water. Wheat production of 106.8 bushels per acre and cotton of 2.5 bales per acre during the first year of operation were more than double the dry land yield in the area.

39 **Anvar Batcha, S.M.,** 1986. Studies on tannery waste waters and related environmental pollution problems. J. Indian Indust. Pollut. Control. 2(2) : 55-62.

The ecology of a fresh water rivulet with reference to environmental parameters like temperature, pH, dissolved oxygen content and salinity has been studied in comparison with tannery waste water effluents from different stations. The type of chemicals and acids in tanning industry and the values of ecological parameters found in different tannery waste waters have been compared with the same parameters of the rivulet of Uyyakhandan channel.

40 **Aprill W., Sims, R.C.,** 1990. Evaluation of the use of Prairie grasses for simulating polycyclic aromatic hydrocarbon treatment in soils. Chem-

sophere. 20 : 253-265.

Eight types of Praire grasses were evaluated in the treatment of four polycyclic aromatic hydrocarbons (PAHs) in a sandy soil. The extent of PAH disappearance in vegetated soil was significantly greater than in the unvegetated soil.

41 **Arar A.,** 1991. Waste water reuse for irrigation in the Near East Region. Water Sci. Technol. 23(10-12) : 2127-2134.

In several countries of the Near East Region, waste water reuse in agril. is well accepted, with considerable social and political commitment. Intensive and direct reuse is being practised in Kuwait, Saudi Arabia, Libya, United Arab Emirates and Tunisia. Direct, but unsupervised reuse is being practised in Yemen Arab Republic, Morocco and Syria. All forms of waste water reuse are practised in Egypt. Indirect and direct restricted reuse is practised in Jordan. However, given the health and environmental hazards associated with reuse of waste water, the strict control of waste water treatment and reuse in all countries, is urgently needed. Further more, in most countries poor coordination amongst the different agencies concerned with water supply, waste treatment, irrigation, public health and the environment is a key constraint for further waste water reuse.

42 **Armbruster, A., Mulchi, C.L.,** 1984. Response of corn and soybeans to soil vs. foliar applied salts of cooling tower origin. J. Environ. Qual. 3(2) : 278-283.

Field studies were conducted on corn (*Zea mays* L.) and soybeans (*Glycine max. L. Merr.*) during 1976 and 1977 to acquire information on the response of crops to saline aerosol deposition near brackish water cooling towers in combination with salt accumulation in the soil.

43 **Arsikere, K.S., Lowry, G.L.,** 1990. Guidelines for environmentally sound surface mined land reclamation in India. Asian Environ. 12(3): 11-27.

A study of ten mining sites in four different climatic regions of the state showed a deficiency in the application of land reclamation techniques. The article explains the different factors that form a successful reclamation effort, based on studies in USA and recommends a guideline for the disturbed land reclamation operations in Karnataka State.

44 **Artiola, F.J., Fuller, W.H.,** 1979. Effect of crushed limestone barriers on chromium attenuation in soils. J. Environ. Qual. 8(4) : 503-510.

The influence of agricultural limestone as a low-cost landfill liner to retard the migration rate of Cr in municipal solid waste leachate through soils was studied. A limestone layer, 2 cm thick over a 10-cm depth of soil in a column, delayed the break-through concentration of the Cr in the effluent many-fold over that without limestone. Crushed limestone was more effective in retaining Cr (III) than the anion (Cr VI). The retention of Cr (III) in soils due to the presence of a limestone liner is much greater than that for other metals tested (Be, Cd, Fe, Ni, and Zn). There appears to be a combined influence on the retention of Cr between the limestone liner and soil not apparent when municipal leachate was passed through the limestone barrier and soil independently. Usefulness of limestone depends primarily on pH and volume of the solution passed through the limestone.

45 **Artiola, F.J., Fuller, W.H.,** 1982. Phenols in municipal solid waste leachates and their attention by clay soils. Soil Sci. 133(4): 218-227.

Municipal solid waste (MSW) landfill leachates retain large quantities of natural phenols in solution, whether they are young or old. Their levels fluctuate as a function of solution pH and total organic carbon (TOC) content. Natural phenols migrate through 10 cm of clay soils in seven pore volume displacements or fewer, especially when accompanied by large TOC levels and low pH values. Aeration of solid waste leachates proved to be effective for lowering the levels of phenols, whether natural or enriched. Humic and fulvic acids in leachates may be responsible for the apparent selective disappearance of enriched phenols from MSW leachate solution.

46 **Artiola, J.F., Zabcik, D., Johnson, S.H.,** 1990. In situ treatment of arsenic contaminated soil from a hazardous industrial site: Laboratory studies, Waste Manage. 10(1) : 73-78.

Addition of ferrous sulfate proved to be effective in reducing water soluble As and its leachability in arsenic-contaminated soil from a pesticide manufacturing industrial site. Soil samples containing up to 4.2% total As, and more than 2.5g L^{-1} water soluble and readily leachable As forms significantly reduced after just three 24-hour wet-dry cycles.

47 **Arvik, H.J., Robert, Z.L.,** 1974. The Influence of temperature, pH and metabolic inhibitions on uptake of lead by plant roots. J. Environ. Qual. 3(4) : 374-376.

Excised roots of selected crop plants were exposed of 10 μg/ml of lead nitrate in the presence of 2, 4-dinitrophenol or radium azide at 10^{-4} and 10^{-5} molar concentration. Additionally roots were exposed to lead nitrate at pH 4.5, 5.5, and 7.0 and at temperatures, of 4 and 24°C. Lead uptake was not influenced bymetabolic inhibitors or low temperature, but was dependent on solution pH, suggesting that the process does not require energy expenditure by the plant.

48 **Asano, T., Pettygrove, G.S.,** 1987. Using reclaimed municipal waste water for irrigation. Calif. Agric. 41 : 15-18.

There are several reasons for the growing use of reclaimed municipal waste water, including: (1) the lack of fresh water at a competitive price, (2) the potential use of plant nutrients in reclaimed municipal waste water, (3) the availability of high-quality effluents; (4) a need to establish comprehensive water resource planning, including water conservation and reuse; and (5) the avoidance of more stringent water pollution control requirements, including advanced waste water treatment.

49 **Asano, T., Tchobanoglous, G.,** 1991 The role of waste water reclamation and reuse in the USA. Water Sci. Technol. 23 : 2049-2059.

After outlining available water resources in the United States, the role of waste water reclamation and reuse is discussed in terms of planning and implementation. Major waste water reuse categories are identified and discussed. This paper emphasizes the benefits to waste water resources management rather than water pollution control measures. The overriding importance in waste water reclamation and reuse is to protect public health and to mitigate health risks. Waste water reclamation criteria for health protection are, therefore, presented.

50 **Asha Juwarkar, Dutta, S.A.,** 1990. Impact of distillery effluent application to land on soil micro-flora. Environl. Monit. Assess. 15(2) : 201-210.

The effects of different treatments of treated diluted and raw distillery waste water mixed with domestic waste stability pond effluent (1:1) on populations of bacteria, fungi, actinomycetes and N_2-fixing bacteria were evaluated. Pot experiment data show that raw waste water decreased the population of bacteria, fungi and actonomycetes. The growth rate of Rhizobium and Azotobacter was also reduced by raw waste water. Raw waste water toxicity was minimised on mixing it with stabilisation pond effluent and there was increase of microbial population. When groundnut was irrigated with raw distillery waste, no fruits were produced and there was less nodulation.

51 **Ashotosh Gautam, Singh, N., Juyal, C.P.,** 1989. On chemical parameters and role of sewage as pollutant in river Bhagirathi at Uttarkashi (Garhwal Himalaya). Himalayan J. Env. Zoo. 3(2) : 262-264.

The study reveals the chemical characteristics of sewage (pH, BOD, COD, humate alkalinity, relative stability, total hardness, bicarbonates, DO, chlorides; phosphates and nitrates) and water quality of river Bhagirathi at Uttarkashi.

52 **Assche, F. Van, Clijsters, H.,** 1990. A biological test system for the evaluation of the phytotoxicity of metal contaminated soil. Environl. Pollut. 66(2) : 157-172.

The potential soil phytotoxicity around an old zinc smelter, closed in 1966, was evaluated by a biological test system. Comparison was made between the biological results and soil and plant metal content. More than 20 years after closure of factory, the soils were still potentially phytotoxic. Zinc was principal, but not the only, phytotoxic element. The effect of contamination extended upto a distance of 3 km. from the industrial site in the direction of prevailing wind.

53 **Asthana, R.K., Pandey, P.K., Singh, S.P.,** 1990. Nickel regulation of

photoautotrophy in a cyanobacterium. Water Air Soil Pollut. 53(3-4) : 263-276.

Ni inhibited photoautotrophic growth, nitrogenase activity. oxygenic photosynthesis (O_2evolution, $C^{14}O_2$uptake) and respiratory O_2 uptake in the diazotrophic cyanobacterium, Nostoc muscorum. $C^{14}O_2$ uptake was more sensitive to Ni compared to nitrogenase activity, O_2 evolution or respiratory O_2 uptake. Lower Ni concentrations (1 µM and 5µM) stimulated N_2ase as well as PuBPcase (ribulose bisphosphate carboxylase) activity. It is proposed that Ni inhibition is mainly through the regulation of PuBPcase activity in the cyanobacterium.

54 **Atalay, A., Blanchar, R.W.,** 1988. Urease activity in soil amended with methane-generator sludge. Biol. Wastes. : 26(1) 49-58.

Sludge obtained from a methane-generator unit charged with fescue hay (*Festuca arundinacea Schreb*) was air-dried and mixed with a sample from the surface horizon of a Mentro silt loam soil to give 0, 40 and 80 g/kg sludge by weight. The sludge-soil mixtures were assayed for urease activity, then used in CO_2-evolutiaon or plant growth studies and again assayed for urease activity. Urease activity was not altered by the addition of sludge when measured 1 h after addition. Urease activity in soil-sludge mixtures upon which plants had been grown for 42 days at -33k Pa water potential and 25°C, was increased by sludge addition. Urease activity measured in soil-sludge mixtures incubated at -20 k Pa water potential and 25°C was increased significantly with increasing sludge.

55 **Aulenbach, D.B., Clesceri, N.I.,** 1980. Monitoring for land application of waste water. Water Air Soil Pollut. 14 : 81-94.

The monitoring system for the Lake George Village Sewage Treatment Plant land application system is described, including suction lsyimeters, observation wells and tracer studies.

56 **Auxt, T.L.,** 1982. Effectiveness of four soil amendments in controlling toxic levels of aluminium and manganese in orchard subsoils. Diss. Abst. Int. Pt. B. Sci. & Environ. 42(10) : 147.

The use of rock phosphate for controlling Al and Mn toxicities in orchard acid soils was investigated. Rock phosphate was compared to a limestone, superphosphate and lime plus superphosphate. Rock phosphate was effectively acidulated in Hagerstown silt loam (pH 5.0-5.5), Berks channery silt loam (pH 3.5-4.0) and Lehew channery fine sandyloam (pH 4.0-4.5). Soil pH, exchangeable Ca and Mg, and available P were significantly increased, and exchangeable Al and Mn were decreased to non-toxic levels. Root and shoot growth were enhanced, and the incidence and seventy of internal bark necrosis (IBN) were decreased. Rock phosphate was less effective than lime or lime plus phosphorus at increasing pH and decreasing Mn and Al. Exchangeable Al and available Mn in rock phosphate-treated soils were well below the toxic range, however, levels of essential nutrients were optimal.

57 **Azpiazu, M.N.,** 1989. Problems of irrigation with polluted waters in green houses. Acta Horticultl 246: 97-104.

Loluim multiforum was grown on perlite to which 100 mg/l Cu, Zn, Ni Cd, As and Pb were added and 1250 mg/1 as Na. In all cases, As was most toxic. Data on uptake of elements in roots and tops are presented.

58 **Azzari, A.S.,** 1985. The effects of the application rates and soils on heavy metals uptake by plants. Diss Abst. Int. Pt. B. Sci. & Engg. 45(9) : 239.

The effects of sludge on plant uptake was measured on two slyghtly acidic soils (Sinks and Franklin Basin) and one calcareous soil (Millville) in field plots and large cylindrical lysimeters. A Chicago sludge high in selected metals and two Utah area sludges were measure. There was no evidence of metal movement downward from the incorporated depth five years after an initial $100t/ha^{-1}$ application. Extraction by DTPA-solution was selective towards the metals tested and removed, from greatest to least, Cd > Cu > Zn> Ni. The percentage of total metal extracted was about 43% from the calcareous soil and about 50 per cent from the slightly acidic soils.

59 **Baath, E.,** 1989. Effects of heavy metals in soil on microbial processes and population – a review. Water Air Soil Pollut. 47(3-4) : 335-379.

The effect of Cd, Cu, Zn and Pb on soil microorganisms and microbially mediated soil processes are reviewed. The sensitivity of different measurement is discussed and data compiled to compare relative toxicity of different metals (on a µg/g soil basis) decreased in the order: Cd > Cu > Zn > Pb, but differences between investigations were found. The influence of abiotic factors on metal toxicity is briefly discussed and especially examplified by different soil organic mater contents. Evidence of tolerance and adaptation in the soil environment and the time scale involved in the evolution of a metal tolerant microbial community after metal exposure are also considered.

60 **Badamchian, B.,** 1986. Heavy metal availability and uptake by barley and Swiss chard from a calcareous soil fertilized with sewage sludges. Abst. Int. Pt. B. Sci. & Engg. 46(8): 176.

Barley (*Hordeum vulgare L.*) and Swiss chard (*Beta vulgaris L.*) were grown on calcareous Millville silt loam in field plots to determine mainly: (1) the effects of single and repeated sludge applications on the plant accumulation of Cd, Zn, Cu, Ni, Pb, and Cr, and (2) the extent of the hazard of heavy metal uptake. A Chicago sludge high in selected metals, a Salt Lake sludge and an Idaho Falls sludge were used. Of the three sludges, only the Idaho Falls sludge with its low metal and high P and K contents was considered suitable for use. Lower rates of the other sludges could allow them to be used. After 5 years of sludge application there was no significant metal movement below the incorporated depth.

61 **Badrinath, S.D., Kaul, S.N., Gadkari, S.K.,** 1987. Environmental impact assessment of fertilizer industries in India. 2nd Natl, Conv. Environ Engrs. and Natl. Semin. on Impact of Environ Prot. Future Dev. of India. Techl. papers II Nainital, : 31-42.

The purpose of environmental impact assessment of fertilizer industries in India is to highlight the potential impact arising from fertilizer projects, and discuss the approach to environmental assessment for siting industry along with the concept test model approach for waste water management.

62 **Baek, N.H., Clesceri, L.S. and Clesceri, N.L.,** 1989. Modelling of enhanced biodegradation in unsaturated soil zone. J. Environ. Eng. 115(1) : 150-172.

To stimulate the mitigation of chemical contamination by microbial enrichment in existing unsaturated soil systems, two important characteristics, i.e. the influence of micro-organisms on soil water flow and chemical removal rates, were incorporated into a mathematical model (BIOSOIL). The resulting mathematical model described the behaviour of the biosoil system under varying input conditions and the following conclusions were drawn: (1) the depth of the unsaturated soil zone, seems to be less crucial under bioremediation than generally thought; and (2) microbial distribution in a vertical column of soil is as important as the total population size of soil micro-organisms. Results suggest a guideline for the development of vertically well distributed biosoil systems; apply a limiting substrate at high concentration, at fast rates, and in infrequent cycles.

63 **Baham, J., Ball, N.B., Sposito, G.,** 1978. Gel filtration studies of trace metal fulvic acid solutions extracted from sewage sludges. J. Environ. Qual. 7(2) : 181-188.

Trace metal fulvic acid solutions extracted with NaOH from two chemically different sewage sludges and separated from humic acid using HCl were fractioned. Fe and Cu showed concentration maxima that followed closely those in both the organic and inorganic fractions, while Cd, Ni and Zn tended to show maxima following the inorganic fraction peak and only one or two of the organic maxima. The data indicated that Cu and Fe formed complexes with sludge derived fulvic acid (FA) under the conditions of the experiment. Cd, Ni and Zn were associated with the Fa only weakly, in a manner dependent on the nature of the sludge, and in the relative orders of affinity: Zn>Ni>Cd. Infrared spectra of the eluted organic fractions indicated that protein decomposition products and polysaccharide components appear in the fractions of relatively large molecule size, as do the components containing SO_3H group. The COOH and SO_3H functional groups are involved in metal FA interactions. An important organic fraction of sludge derived FA was identified that appears to be an aliphatic, carboxylic acid mixture which can complex only Cu significantly.

64 **Baham, J., Sposito, G.,** 1986. Proton and metal complexation by water soluble legends extracted from anaerobically digested sewage sludge. J. Environ. Qual. 15(3) : 239-243.

A water soluble extract (WSE) of an anaerobically-digested sewage sludge containing 19.5 mM total soluble carbon (CTS) was acidified to pH 3 and titrated with NaOH to pH 11 in a 50 mM $NaClO_4$ background at 25°C. Conditional protonation constants were determined from the formation function computed from the titration data. The common logarithms of the average protonation constants for functional groups titrated between pH 3 and 11 were 4.2, 7.2 and 9.6. Trace metal — WSE complexes were chromatographed on a molecular size exclusion gel. Copper formed the more stable complexes with the legends in the WSE when compared to Ni or Cd. Cadmium was present predominately as the free metal ion or in inorganic complexes. Adsorption of Cu by montmorillonite was significantly reduced in the presence of the WSE. Since most of the organic carbon present in the WSE remained in solution during the adsorption experiments, the primary factor controlling Cu solubility was concluded to be the formation of soluble organo-Cu complexes.

65 **Baker, B.L., Amacher, M.C., Leach, R.M.,** 1979. Sewage sludge as a source of cadmium in soil-plant-animal systems. Environl. Health Perspectives. 28 : 45-49.

Natural abundance of Cd in soils, reported as 0.5 µg/g, is higher than the background level of 0.2 µg/g found in soils studied in Pennsylvania. The plant availability of Cd is decreased by liming to increase soil pH. Cd salts or sewage sludge Cd cannot be added without significantly increasing plant uptake. Land application of sewage sludge increased the Cd concentration of corn leaves from a range of 0.05-0.1 µg/g. Two years after the last application of sludge, which totalled 10 ppm Cd to the surface soil, corn grain, sorghum, wheat grain, and potatoes showed a 10- to 15-fold increase in Cd over background levels. Studies with chicks, laying hens, and meadow voles (Microtus pennsylvanias) assessed the impact of this increase in plant Cd upon the food chain. Corn and sorghum plants were grown on soils with inorganic or sludge fertilizer to produce herbage for use in feeding trails with meadow voles. Eight diets and a synthetic control were formulated to study the effect of source (plant vs. inorganic) of Cd on tissue accumulation. Significant accumulation of Cd occurred in kidney and liver, but not muscle, of voles fed direct containing sludge-fertilized corn (1.09 µ/g) or sludge-fertilized sorghum (2.76 µg/g). The source of Cd had little influence on tissue accumulation. In studies with broiler chicks and laying hens, natural diets containing 0.2 ppm Cd were supplemented with 3 ppm of Cd. Cadmium readily accumulated in liver and kidney. Although the results were not statistically significant, 3 ppm dietary Cd doubled muscle Cd content. There was no transfer of Cd to egg in a 12-month experiment with laying hens. Soil management programmes were developed to maintain animal dietary levels of Cd at 100 μg/g from the use of sewage sludge on land in Pennsylvania. This level over time may cause a significant accumulation of Cd in animal tissues.

66 **Balsberg-Pahlsson, A.M.,** 1989. Effects of heavy metal and SO_2 pollution of the concentrations of carbohydrates and nitrogen in tree leaves. Can. J. Bot. 67(7) ; 2106-2113.

The concentrations of carbohydrates and nitrogen in leaves or needles of *Betula pubescens Ehrh., Betula pendula Roth, Piecea abies,* (L). *Karst,* and *Pinus syivestris* L. were studied in two industrial areas in Sweden. One of the sites, the Gusum brass foundry is polluted by Cu & Zn, the other site, the Roennskaer smelter by SO_2 in addition to several heavy metal elements. Leaves and needles were sampled during the main growing season at different distances from the sources and analysed for starch, sugars, total nitrogen, and heavy metals. In most leaf or needle samples nearest to the sources, the concentrations of starch and total sugars were significantly higher than in the controls. Of the sugars, sucrose concentrations was usually elevated, while glucose and fructose were lower than in the controls.

67 **Banasova, V., Holub, Z., Zelenakova, E.,** 1987. The elyanamic, structure and heavy metal accumulation in vegetation under longterm influence of Pb and Cu emissions. Ecology. CSSR : **6** : 101-111.

The smelter at the border of the town Banska Stiavanica worked for about 200 years. Fifteen years after-ward it had stopped at the enterprise, and investigation was made in the transect at different distances from the source of emission. First stadia of secondary succession were found with the dominating species Agrostis tennis. With an increasing distance from the smelter work Pb, Zn, Cu, As and S contents decreased in the soil and in the plant of the communities. Species diversity, overground biomass increased, together with germination of *Agrostis tenuis* seeds.

68 **Banin., A., Navrot, J., Noi, Y., Yoles, D.,** 1981. Accumulation of heavy metals in arid zone soils irrigated with treated sewage effluents and their uptake by Rhodes grass. J. Environ. Qual. 10(4): 536-540.

Prolonged irrigation with treated sewage effluents from rural sources resulted in accumulation of heavy metals in the top 10-15 cm layer of the soil in three commercial fields. Statistically significant difference were found for total content and extractable fractions of Cd in all three soils and for Cu, Ni and Pb in clay soils by comparing these fields and adjacent one irrigated with normal water. Chromium concentration differences were not statistically significant. As a result, there was some increase in the concentration of these elements in Rhodes grass grown in the fields irrigated with normal water. The increase, although statistically significant, was slight, in the field that had been irrigated with sewage effluents for up to 28 years. The uptake of the various metals as assessed by the enrichment factor (EF = µg elements/g plant/µg element/g soil) tended to diminish with an increase in the specific surface area of the soil. This was particularly pronounced with the more labile of the elements studied Cd, Cu and Ni and less of for Pb and Cr. The uptake of a given element appears to be largely determined by its solubility in the soil solution and can be generally predicted by its ionic potential. The relative magnitude of the enrichment factor established for Rhodes grass is in the following order: Cu> Cd > Pb > Ni >>Cr.

69 **Bank., S., Bank., J.F., Marchetti, P.S., Ellis, P.D.,** 1989. Solid state cadmium-113 nuclear magnetic resonance study of cadmium speciation in environmentally contaminated sediments. J. Environ. Qual. 18 (1): 25-30.

Solid State-^{113} Cd nuclear magnetic resonance (NMR) spectroscopy was used to analyse five soil samples taken from an environmental site that is heavily contaminated with Cd and other metals. Not all of the Cd present was observed by the NMR experiments likely due to the presence of paramagnetic species as indicated by the magnetic susceptibilities of the samples. Four cadmium species are indicated; the carbonate as the major component, a carbonate-like species but in a soil-like matrix, a mixed hydroxycarbonate species, and a species in a soil-like environment. Dynamics is considered as a possibility for the larger linewidths of the species in the soil-matrix.

70 **Banks, P.A.,** 1991. Waste water reuse-case studies in the Middle East. Water Sci. Technol. 23: 2141-2148.

The use of effluent in some Middle Eastern countries is reviewed. The features of reuse, the processes used and the standards adopted are described. Tabulated information and operational results are compared and the effect of reuse on the local environment is discussed.

71 **Banuelos, G., Schrale, G.,** 1989. Plants that remove Selenium from soils. Calif. Agric., 43: 19-20.

Initial results from greenhouse experiments suggest that some plants are able to absorb lower selenium concentrations in soils by upto 50%. Use of these plants species may reduce concentrations to acceptable levels in problem soils.

72 **Barbari, C.K.A., Workman, S.M.,** 1987. Ammonium bicarbonate-DTPA and DTPA extractions of sludge-amended soils. J. Environ. Qual. 16: 125-130.

A DTPA solution is typically used to extract sludge-amended soils to determine the relationship between soil concentration and plant levels of certain trace elements. Studies were conducted to compare the standard DTPA soil test method with the ammonium biocarbonate (NH_4HCO_3 - DTPA (AB-DTPA) procedure for extraction of trace elements, and to correlate extractable levels with elemental concentration in leaf to Swiss chard (*Betal vulgaris* L., cv. Fordhood Glant) grown in the greenhouse and in the grain and straw of hard red winter wheat (Triticum aestivum L. Cv. Vona) grown in the field. AB-DTPa was found suitable to assess metal status of soils amended with sludge.

73 **Barber, L.B., Steele, K.F.,** 1981. Variability of mercury concentrations of Mid-Continent soils, USA. Baseline data for a coal fired power plant in Trace Substances in Environ. Health XV. Univ. Missouri, Columbia Mo.: 317-322.

A baseline study of Hg in soils within 80 km radius of the flint creek power plant, Gentry, AR was conducted before the plant went into operation. This plant will release approximately 286 kg of Hg annually. If all this Hg is concentrated in the upper 2.54 cm of soil within the 80 km radius, values will be elevated by 0.003 ppm within 5 years. One hundred and twenty soil samples were collected and analysed for Hg. Mean result of the analysis was 0.036 ppm Hg.

74 **Barcelo, J., Gunse, B., Poschenrieder, C.,** 1986. Chlorophyll and carotenoid content of *Phasedus vulgaris* L. in relation to mineral nutrition disorders induced by chromium (VI) supply. Photosynthetica 20(3) : 249-255.

The contents of chlorophyll-a, chlorophyll-b, total carotenoids and trace elements of initial and Ist trifolicate leaves of *Phaselus valgaris* Cr. contender plants grown with or without CRVI in the nutrient solution were determined in the Ist trifoliate but not the initial leaves. There was a good negative liner relation between chlorophyll/carotenoid contents and that of Cr. High correlation coefficients were also obtained between pigment contents and Fe or Zn contents. Cr-induced inhibition of Fe and Zn transport was considered to cause Cr (VI) induced chlorosis.

75 **Barth, C.L., Kroes, J.,** 1985. Livestock waste lagoon sludge characterisation. Am. Soc. Agr. Eng. Pub. Sp.: 13-85; 660-671.

A conceptual model of sludge accumulation in a livestock waste lagoon is presented. Explanation of inert sludge accumulation in lagoons must account for the deposition of a large fraction of FS (sometimes more than 50% of the total sludge solids) and the non-biodegrable VS. Data collected from measurements of long term accumulations of inert sludge in animal and poultry lagoons are now the best estimates for designing lagoons for waste treatment and sludge storage. Maximum inert sludge accumulation in livestock waste lagoons should be limited to 60% of the operating volume of moderately loaded lagoons to insure continuing efficient operation. A significant added FS load on the dairy lagoon, as much as 100% of the manure FS load, results from soil carried to the cowyard on bodies of dairy animals having access to pastures and paddocks and from free stall litter and base materials.

76 **Bartlett, R., James, B.,** 1979. Behaviour of chromium in soils: III. Oxidation. J. Environ. Qual. 8(1) : 31-35.

Added trivalent Cr oxidizes readily to the hexavalent form under conditions prevalent in many field soils. The presence in the soil of oxidized Mn, serves as the electron acceptor in the reaction. The relative ability of a soil to oxidize Cr maybe predicted by measuring the Mn reducible by hydroquinone or by a quick test in which Cr^{+3} is added to a fresh moist soil sample. Plants were severely damaged by Cr^{+6} formed from Cr^{+3} added to fresh soil samples. Hexavalent Cr still was present in a soil stored moist at 25°C for 5 months.

77 **Bartone, C.R.,** 1991. International perspective on water resources management and waste water reuse — appropriate technologies. Water Sci. Technol. 23 : 2039-2047.

This paper describes research and development carried out in several developing countries on appropriate technologies for implementing waste reuse, as well as coordinated international efforts to provide recommended guidelines and policies for safe waste water reuse in agriculture and aquaculture.

78 **Bar-Yosef, B.,** 1979. pH-Dependent zinc adsorption by soils. J. Soil Sci. Soc. Am., 43(6) : 1095-1099.

A simple equation relating the adsorption of Zn to its solution concentration and pH was derived using the competitive Langmair adsorption isotherm. Experimental results obtained for 5 different soils in bach experiments were compared with results computed for each soil according to fitted parameters. Three criteria for the adequacy of the equation were tested-an acid titration curve in the absence of Zn, Zn adsorption as a function of its solution concentration at a given pH, and Zn solution concentration at a fixed total amount of Zn as a function of pH. Close agreement between calculated and experimental results was obtained for the analyzed soils in all tests.

79 **Basalas, R.K., Singh, S.,** 1978. Atomic absorption spectrophotometric studies on Cu and Zn in textile effluents and soils. Res. J. Natl. Soc. Pollut. Free Environ. 1 (1&2) : 26-30.

The concentration of Cu and Zn in textile effluents, effluent irrigated soil and tube-well water irrigated soil were recorded as 17.2-42.0, and 8.9-25.5 mg/kg and 9.0-22.2 mg/kg, 3.2-6.4, mg/kg and 1.3-4.3 mg/kg respectively. In addition soil samples were analysed for pH, calcium carbonate content, organic-matter, phosphorus and potassium. The effects of irrigation by the effluents on shoot and root length of crop plant, productivity of the soil and energy value, have been discussed.

80 **Bates, M.H.,** 1988. Land farming of reserve pit fluids and sludges: fates of selected contaminants. Water Res. 22(6): 793-797.

This project studied the fates of Zn, Cr, Ba and Cl in a silt loam and a sandy loan as a result of land farming slurried reserve pit waste. Their uptake by bermuda grass, soils and/or the transport of the ions through the soil column were investigated. Results showed that contaminants were taken up by vegetation and/or transported through the soil column.

The extent of transport of Zn and Cr appeared to be a function of soil type, whereas the mobility of barium was probably affected by the presence of chloride. Chloride added to the soil was readily transported.

81 **Bates, M.H., Devries, R.N.,** 1980. Control of pollution in waters containing heavy metals. NTIS Springfield. 97.

An integrated set of experiments were carried out on the fate of chromium and copper in biological waste water treatment processes, aqueous environments, and soil systems. A rotating biological contractor and activated sludge were used as the waste water treatment processes; Stillwater, Oklahoma area lake and river water and sediments, as the aqueous environments; and sandy and red silty clay soils, as the soil systems. While it was determined that chromium was removed by the lake and river sediments but not generally removed by biological treatment processes or by algae, it was found that copper was removed by all systems. Removal efficiencies of the metals were highly dependent upon operating and environmental conditions. Sediments and soils had strong affinities for copper, and uptake could be correlated with soil type.

82 **Battista, J., Connelly, J.P.,** 1988. VOC contamination at selected municipal and industrial land fills in Wisconsin sampling results and policy implications. Proc. Annual Madison Waste Conf. 11 : 59-83.

Volatile organic compounds (VOC) contamination at 25 land fill sites was studied. The reability of inorganic parameters in predicting VOC presence was evaluated. It was shown that : (1) Land fills with natural attenuation designs are more likely to have VOC contaminated groundwater than those designed with the contaminant and leachate collection. (2) Land fills of municipal waste are more likely to have VOC contamination than with industry waste land fills. (3) Land fills <50,000 cubic yards are less likely to have VOC contamination than those of greater volume. (4) VOC monitoring ranged from quarterly at all sites to none. (5) Inorganic parameters are good predictors of VOC contamination.

83 **Bauer, J.W.,** 1981. Waste water spray irrigation at army installations. J. Environ., Eng. Div. ASCE, 107: 435-453.

An evaluation is presented of pretreament aspects, operation, and performance of five currently existing domestic waste water spray irrigation systems at U.S. Army reservations. All are viewed as operating successfully, posing no significant threat to water supply source, and they are capable of complying with applicable State and Federal regulations and permits. Some systems were found to require supplemental disinfection and additional effluent or ground-water surveillance. A few significant problems identified at specific land treatment sites include: A build-up of soil salinity, soil saturation conditions, and drainage problems.

84 **Beauchamp., E.G., Kidd, G.E., Thurtell, G.,** 1978. Ammonia volatilisa-

tion from sewage sludge applied in the field. J. Environ. Qual. 7(1) : 141-146.

Volatilisation of ammonical nitrogen from newly applied anaerobically digested sewage sludge was measured in the field in May and Oct. for 5 and 7 days periods, respectively. Sludge was applied at rates of 116-480 Kg/ha. Fluxes generally followed a diural pattern with maximyms occurring at mid-day. Flux generally decreased with time in an expential manner. Thus, the half life of ammonical N applied in the sludge was 3.6 and 5.0 days for the May and Oct. experimental periods respectively. Of several meteorological variable measures, air temperature appeared to be most closely related to flux rate especially in two or three days following application. It was estimated that, during the 5 days period in May, 60% of the 150 kg ammonial N/ha applied in sludge was volatilized, and during the 7 days period in Oct. 56% of the 89 kg ammonical N/ha applied was volatilized. Sampling the sludge layer and soil beneath it during and after the Oct. experimental period resulted in considerable variability in ammonical N estimates and hence, in volatilization estimates.

85 **Beauchamp, E.G., Kidd, G.E., Thurtell., G.,** 1992. Ammonia volatilization from liquid dairy cattle manure in the field. Can. J. Soil. Sci. 62(1): 11-19.

The volatilisation of ammonia from applied liquid dairy cattle manure was measured in the field during 6-7, day periods in early May of 4 Yr. An "Open" system involving an aerodynamic diffusion method was employed for these measurements. Ammonia flux flowed a diurnal pattern with maxima occurring shorty after mid-day and minima occurring during the early morning hours. The magnitude of daily flux values tended to decrease with time. However, both temperature and rainfall influenced the magnitude of ammonia flux. Generally, ammonia flux values increased with temperature, but were suppressed by rainfall. Over periods of 6 or 7 days following the time of manure application, between 24 and 33% of the ammonical N applied in the manure was lost by volatilization.

86 **Beauchamp, E.C., Soon, Y.K., Moyer, J.R.,** 1979. Nitrate production from chemically treated sewage sludges in soils. J. Environ. Qual. 8(4): 557-560.

Chemicals such as $Ca(OH)_2$, $Al_2(SO_4)_3$ and $FeCl_3$ are used to precipitate and prevent phosphorous from escaping in effluents from sewage plants. Nitrate production of six anaerobically digested sewage sludges differed considerably when incubated with soil but not in a manner related to the chemical treatment of the sewage. Reduced nitrate production from whole sludge from one source was possibly attributable to relatively high liquid and petroleum hydrocarbon contents. With the exception of the their sludge, 17 to 30% of the sludge N was nitrified in 16 weeks under laboratory conditions. Nitrate production lag periods if present, when reconstituted sludges (ammonium and soluble organic N removed) were incubated with soil was one week with the exception of the one sludge which probably had high lipid and petroleum hydrocarbon contents. Incubation of reconstituted sludges in soil resulted in 28 to 32% nitrification of the organic N during the first 16 weeks. Nitrate production was relatively rapid in the early part of the 49 weeks incubation period but slowed substantially latter.

87 **Beckett, P.H.T.,** 1989. Sources and distribution of pollution elements in the environment with particular reference to sewage sludge, in 'Inorganic contaminants in the Vadose zone' (Ed. Baryosef, B. *et al*): 159-175, Springer Verlag, Berlin.

The chemistry of polluted elements in waste water and sludge to a great extent depends upon the sources. The principal sources of the sources and path ways of eight elements are presented. Of the sources that contribute pollutant elements to land sewage and sludge are most amenable. Their chemistry and assessment of their toxicity are discussed.

88 **Beckett, P.H.T.,** 1989. The use of extractants in studies on trade metals in soils, sewage sludges and sludge treated soils. Adv. Soil Sci. 9: 143-176.

Various extractants including water, acids, salt solutions, buffers and salt mixtures have been reviewed for other suitability to sludge and heavy metal amended soils. There is an urgent need for selective extractants to estimate different forms of combinations of trace metals in soils treated with sludges.

89 **Beek, J., De, Haan, F.A.M., Van Riemsdijk, W.H.,** 1977. Phosphates in soils treated with sewage water : 1. General information on sewage farm, soil and treatment, J. Environ. Qual. 6 (1): 4-7.

A sewage farm which has been used during the past 50 years for treatment of raw sewage water of domestic and industrial origin was studied. The Farm (100 ha) is situated on sandy soil and is in use as permanent pasture. Intermittent flooding of the soil with sewage water results in 98% decrease of the biochemical oxygen demand (BOD) by passing it through the soil; phosphates are removed to the extent of 96%. These phosphates accumulate in the top 50-cm layer of the soil. Removal of the nitrogeneous compounds is less effective. The sewage water raised soil pH and increased the organic matter content.

90 **Beek, J. De., Haan, F.A.M., Van Riemsdijk, W.H.** 1977. Phosphates in soils treated with sewage water : II Fractionation of accumulated phosphates. J. Environ. Qual. 6(1): 7-12.

Three different soil phosphate fractionation methods have been applied to samples of different soil layers. Two soil treatments were involved viz. 30 and 50 years sewage water flooding. Accumulated phosphates mainly consisted of inorganic phosphate forms (80 to 85%). These inorganic phosphates are constituted particularly of aluminium-bound phosphates; thus indicating the dominant role of aluminium related reactions in the phosphate-bonding mechanism in this case.

91 **Behera, B.K., Misra, B.N.,** 1985. The effect of sugar mill effluent on enzyme activities of rice seedling. Environ. Res. 37(2) : 390-398.

The effect of sugar mill effluent on the activities of peroxidase, amalyse and nitrate reductase of rice seedlings have been investigated. An attempt was also made to investigate effluent-induced changes in the activities of mitochoridecial enzymes, such as succinate dehydrogenase, during germination of rice seedlings. The effects were studied in relation to both concentration of effluent and time of exposure. The activity of all enzymes tested except succinate dehydrogenase, decreased during effluent treatment. A marked increase in succinate dehydrogenase activity was noticed at various concentrations of effluent treatment. When time dependent changes in succinate dehydrogenase activity were followed a nearly threefold increase was found with 12 hr of treatment with a rapid loss. A correlation was established between the retardation of growth and development of effluent treated rice seedlings with the activities of some key enzymes regulating growth and development.

92 **Bekker, P.H., De, A.M., Van Den, Berg II., J.,** 1989. Land filling with sewage sludge in Treatment of sewage sludge. Thermophillic aerobic digestion and processing requirements for land filling, 72-79. Elsevier Applied Sci. Pub. Ltd., Amsterdam.

Various aspects of sewage sludge filling the land are reviewed.

93 **Beles, N., Montil, A., Husson, G.P., Vilagines, R.,** 1989. Different forms of heavy metals in sewage sludges. Tribune del'Eau. 41(5): 24-31.

Data on content and forms are presented for Cd, Cr, Co, Cu, Pb, Mn, Fe. Al, As, Ni, Zn and Sn, for each stage of sludge treatment. Apart from Fe, Al, and Zn, the treatment had no appreciable effect on the conc. of metals. Fe increased from 27 to 75% in the filter cake, but Al & Zn decreased correspondingly.

94 **Bell, R.G.,** 1976. Persistence of Fecal Coliform Indicator Bacteria on alfalfa irrigated with municipal sewage lagoon effluent. J. Environ. Qual. 5, (1): 39-42.

Fecal Coliform on alfalfa plants irrigated with sewage lagoon effluent were completely destroyed by exposure to 10 hours bright sunlight. No decrease in numbers was observed in the absence of bright sunlight under cool, damp, overcast conditions. Exposure to 10 hours bright sunlight was adequate to destroy all the fecal coliforms present in raw sewage. In the event that sewage treatment failures while alfalfa was being irrigated with sewage effluent in the semiarid Prairie region, livestock would be adequately protected from possible salmonella and enterpathogonic Escherichia coli infection if at least 2 sunny days elapse between the cessation of effluent irrigation and consumption of the forage.

95 **Bell, R.G., Bole, J.B.,** 1976. Elimination of Fecal coliform bacterial from Reed canary grass irrigated with municipal sewage lagoon effluent. J. Environ. Qual. 5, (4): 417-418.

The survival characteristics of fecal coliform bacteria on Reed canary grass (*Phalanis anendinalco* L.) irrigated with Municipal sewage effluent were determined using the most probable number (MPN) technique to develop a recommendation for sunlight de-contamination of Gramineae species. The grass was recontaminated during rainfall because contaminated soil was splashed onto the forlage and the number of fecal coliforms was not reduced during cool, damp periods. Exposure to 50 hours bright sunlight under semiarid Prairie conditions was sufficient to destroy virtually all those fecal coliforms present on the grass after irrigation with sewage effluent containing about 3.2×10^4 fecal coliforms/100 ml. This was considerably longer than the 10 hours previously shown to be adequate to eliminate fecal coliforms from alfalfa (*Medicago Sativa* L.). This difference between species is due to the presence of leaf sheaths on the grass in which effluent could collect and be protected from the bacteriocidal effects of bright sunlight.

96 **Bell, R.G. Bole, J.B.,** 1978. Elimination of fecal coliform bacteria from soil irrigated with municipal sewage lagoon effluent. J. Environ. Qual. 7(2): 193-196.

Unchlorinated sewage lagoon effluent was applied to a stand of reed canary grass (*Phalaris arundinacea* L.) each week at a rate equal to the weekly difference between evapotranspiration and precipitation of the preceeding week, about 4.5 cm. Most of the fecal coliforms applied in the effluent were retained in the surface of 8 cm of the brown caovendish loamy sand. During two growth periods preceding first and second harvests, when effluent was applied at weekly intervals, no build up of coliforms occurred in the surface soil nor did they penetrate the profile below 69 cm. Die-off of the fecal coliforms occurred in two phases; an initial rapid phase in which 90% of the bacterial died within 48 hours of irrigation and a subsequent lower decline in about 2 weeks as the remaining 10% were eliminated. This indicates that the soil no longer constitute a serious public health hazard for eneteric diseases of bacterial etiology 2 weeks after irrigation with sewage lagoon effluent.

97 **Bell, P.F., James, B.R., Chaney, R.L.,** 1991. Heavy metal extractability in long term sewage sludge and metal salt amended soils. J. Environ. Qual. 20(2) : 481-486.

To determine the long term change in forms of Cd added to a soil, Cd and other heavy metals were extracted with several solutions from a Christiana fine sandy loan (Typic Paleudu clayey, kaolinitic, mesic) Ap horizon 8 or 9 year after application of sewage sludge of $CdCl_2$. Cadmium was applied at the rate of 21 kg/ha either as a component of sewage sludge or as $CdCl_2$ in 1978 and 1979, respectively.

98 **Bellin, C.A., Connor, G.A.O.,** 1990. Plant uptake of pentachlorophenol from sludge amended soils. J. Environ. Qual. 19(3): 598-602.

A green-house study was conducted to determine the effects of sludge on plant uptake of C-pentachlorophenol (PCP). Plants included tall fescu (*Festuca arundinacea* Schreb)., lettuce (*Latuca sativa* L.) carrot (*Dauc carota* L)., and chile pepper (*Capsicum annum* L.). Minimal intact PCP was detected in the fescue and lettuce. No intact PCP was detected in the carrot tissue extracts. Chile pepper was not analyzed for intact PCP because methylene chloride extracts contained minimal C. The analysis of soil extracts at harvest suggests a half life of PCP of about Iod independent of sludge rate or PCP loading rate. Rapid degradation of PCP in the soil apparently limited PCP availability to the plant. Bioconcentration factors (dry plant wt/initial soil PCP concentration) based on intact PCP were <0.01 for all crops, suggesting little PCP uptake. Thus, food chain crop PCP uptake in these alkaline soils should not limit land application of sludge.

99 **Belore., R.L., Mcbean, E.A.,** 1987. Modelling of the spreading of chemical spills on grass and impermeable surfaces in Proc. 4th Technical Seminar on Chemical Spills, Sheraton Centre, Toronto. Pub. by Environment. Canada, Ottawa, 1-20.

Two or three dimensional spill models of the spread of liquids on land are developed. Physical modelling results are used to demonstrate the validity of the computer model. Sensitivity tests of the model are provided.

100 **Belyuchenko, I.S., Dronov, A.V.,** 1988. Control of nitrate nitrogen and heavy metals in soil and plants irrigated with sewage water. Dokladey Vsesoyuznoi ordena ienina 1. ordena. Trudovogo. Krasnogo Znameni Akademi Sel. Skikh, Nauk. Imeni U.I. Lenina vol. 11 : 15-17.

Drymatter yield and NO_3 content in dry matter are presented for *panicum antidotale*. NO_3 content decreased with increase of age. Data on heavy metal content in plants are also presented.

101 **Bender, J., Grunhage., L., Jager, H.J.,** 1989. Uptake and effects of heavy metals on trees : soil contamination study with Cd, Pb and Ni. Ange Wandte Botanik, 63 (1-2) : 81-93.

Three years old cuttings of Norway spruce, silver fir and beech were grown for 30 months on soil contaminated with different conc. of Cd, alone or in combination with different conc. of Pb and / or Ni. Cd uptake by roots was greatest on soils contaminated with Cd alone. On soil contaminated with Cd alone, Cd conc. in foliage were significantly increased, while they were only slightly high on soils treated with metal combinations. All treatments caused reduced K conc. in roots of Norway spruce and sliver fir, whereas Ca concs. were mainly affected by the metal combinations. At the end of the experiment the plants did not show visible injuries or growth reductions, but needle dry wt was reduced, specially in Norway spruce.

102 **Benefield, L.D., Randall, C.W., King, P.H.,** 1975. The stimulation of filamentous micro-organisms in activated sludge by high oxygen concentration. Water Air Soil Pollut. 5 : 113-123.

A laboratory study was conducted to compare the response of an activated sludge culture proliferating in an environment where the DO concentration was maintained between 8-9 mgl^{-1} to that of a culture in an environment where the DO concentration was 2 mgl^{-1} when both systems were subjected to identical loading fluctuations. In the high DO system, filamentous micro-organisms became the predominant form when the suspended solids concentration dropped below a value near 4000 mgl^{-1}. However, no filamentous growth appeared in the alternate system until the suspended solids level dropped below 500 mgl^{-1}. A model is developed to explain this observation.

103 **Bengtsson, G., Gunnarsson, T., Rundgren, S.,** 1986. Effects of metal pollution on the earthworm *Dendrobaena rubida* in acidified soils. Water Air Soil Pollut. 28 : 361-383.

Survival of adult Dendroba ha rubida, cocoon production, cocoon viability, and growth of juveniles were examined in laboratory experiments when the worms were reared in acidified and metal polluted soils. Solutions of Cu, Cd and Pb were added to give total concentrations of 10, 100 and 500 μgg^{-1} in soils with a pH of 4.5, 5.5 and 6.5, Adult tissues, hatchings and cocoons were analysed for metals. *D. rubida* survived poorly in soils with low pH, especially in combination with Pb or Cd, which accumulated in seminal vesicies and cerebral ganglion. Cocoon production was halved when pH was lowered from 6.5 to 4.5 and metals reduced the concoon number even more in the most acid soils. Hatching success was lower than 20% in acid field soils in contrast, the number of hatchings increased when pH decreased and peaked in soils polluted with Cd. While low pH reduced the embryonic development time, metals prolonged it. Juveniles grew slowly and died early at low pH.

104 **Bergback, B., Anderberg, S., Lohm, U.,** 1989. A reconstruction of emission flow and accumulation of chromium in Sweden 1920-1980. Water Air Soil Pollut. 48 : 391-407.

A simple model was used to calculate amounts of Cr accumulated in soil and sediment at different times. The importance of production emissions from tanneries and ferrochrome and steel plants is obvious, but in the future, diffuse emissions of the same magnitude may occur from Cr products within urban areas.

105 **Berrow, M.,** 1982. Heavy metals in sewage sludges and possible hazards from disposal on land. Proc. 3rd. Environ. & Safety Conf., London. Int.

Environ. 2 Safety, Labmate Ltd. St. Herts, Al, England.

Sewage sludges vary greatly in total heavy metal content, because their composition is highly dependent on the specified nature of local domestic and industrial effluents. Despite this wide range in contents, reaching to the percentage level for the elements Cr, Cu, Ni, Pb and Zn, and median contents of sludges in industrialized countries are very similar, suggesting that high metal contents arise from similar, domestic sources and industrial processes. About 40 per cent of the sewage sludge produced in England and Wales is utilized in agriculture, while in Scotland much is disposed off at sea, a practice likely to be restricted in the future. The disposal of sludge on land has caused problems of crop growth due to the uptake of large amounts of metals such as Ni and Zn, while excessive uptake of Mo from sludge has caused problems in grazing animals. Field experiments laid down in conjunction with ADAS at two Experimental Horticulture Stations, where sludges with high contents of Zn, Cu, Ni and Cr were applied in 1968, are described.

106 **Bergkvist, B.,** 1987. Soil solution chemistry and metal budgets of spruce forest ecosystems in S. Sweden. Water Air Soil Pollut. 33(1-2) : 131-154.

The fluxes of metals (Na, K, Ca, Mg, Fe, Mn, Al, Cu, Zn, Pb, Cd, Cr, and Ni) in two spruce forest soils in S. Sweden were quantified during the lysimeter technique. Amounts in precipitation (dry and wet), throughfall, litterfall and annual accumulation in biomass were also quantified, as well as stored in soil and biomass. The metal concentrations of the soil solutions varied greatly according to season. The leaching of some metals (Fe, Cu, Pb, Cr, and organic forms of Al) was associated with the leaching of organic matter. These compounds were leached from the A horizon in considerable amounts. They precipitated in the upper B horizon and only small amounts transported further downward. By contrast, the leaching of Na, Ca, Mn, Cd, Zn, Ni and inorganic forms of Al increased with soil depth. The concentrations of these metals also increased with increasing soil solution acidity. The highest concentrations were found at the transition to the C. horizon.

107 **Berrow, M.L., Burridge, J.C.,** 1990. Persistence of metal residues in sewage sludge treated soils over seventeen years. Internatl. J. Environ. Analyt. Chem. 39(2) : 173-177.

Sewage sludge contaminated with Cr, Cu, Ni, or Zn and a relatively uncontaminated sludge were applied at the same rates and metal content in 1968. The Cr rich sludge had high Cd also. Soil samples were collected in 1972, 1976, 1981 and 1985 and total extractable metals were analysed. Metals added in sewage sludge may change other form but persist in soils in an extractable and plant available form for many years. There is little difference in soil extractable contents or plant uptake of Cr and Zn whether sludges are applied as one single application or as four separate annual doses of one quarter the amount. The percentage of the total chromium contents extractable by both EDTA and acetic acid were small and this was reflected in the uptake of this element by herbage. (<0.3 mg Cr/kg DM).

108 **Berry, C.R.,** 1979. Slit application of fertilizer tablets and sewage sludge impure initial growth of lobiolity pine seedlings in the Terrace Copper Basin. Reclamation Review 2(1) : 33-38.

Forest starter fertilizer tablets (9 and 21 g) and dried sewage sludge (30, 60 and 90 g) were placed in slits in soils near recently planted lobiolity pine seedlings in the Terrace Copper Basin. Survival was not affected by treatment. However, by the end of the 3rd yr, the 21g fertilizer tablets increased seedling volume by 20- and 9-fold, and the 90-, 60- and 30-g sludge treatments also increased volume over control — non-fertilized seedlings. Slow-released fertilizer, a commercially produced fertilizer tablet or dried sewage sludge can be useful in emulating those in the Copper Basin. Slit application of nutrients offers several advantages over broadcast.

109 **Berteigne, M., Lefevre, Y., Rose, C.,** 1988. Accumulations of organic pollutants (PAH) in organic layers of soils: Possible relation with forest decline. Eur. J. Pathol. 18(5) : 310-318.

Analysis of the upper levels of the organic layers of forest soils demonstrate a new kind of bioaccumulation leading to high level of contamination with polycyclic aromatic hydrocations (PAH).

110 **Beveridge, A., Pickering, W.F.,** 1980. Influence of humate-solute interactions on aqueous heavy metal Ion levels. Water Air Soil Pollut. 14 : 171-185.

The extent to which heavy metal ions (Cu, Pb, Zn, Cd) are removed from aqueous solution by humic acid suspensions varies with solution pH, concentrations of competing cations, nature of the organic material, and the complexing power of any legends present. The amount adsorbed in acid media increased with pH used, the threshold value required for partial dissolution of the solid, and formation of sodium metal humates, was exceeded. The adsorption maximum pH, and the apparant capacity at lower values, varied with the substrate used and cation being sorbed. The affinity order sequence, as derived from adsorption isotherm studies was Pb > Cu > Cd > Zn > Ca > Mg.

111 **Bewlewy, R.J.F., Ellis, B., Rees, J.F.,** 1990. Development of a microbiological treatment for restoration of oil contaminated soil. Land Degrad. Rehab. 2(1) : 1-11.

This paper describes the laboratory development of a microbial treatment for soil contaminated with oil hydrocarbon residues at a disused refinery site and the application of this technology in a pilot scale treatment bed in the field. Micro-organisms isolated from the site capable of utilizing a number of normal and branched chain alkanes were tested in a series of soil microcosms, together with various permutations of commercially available surfactants and nutrients for stimulating the activities of hydrocarbon utilizing micro-organisms.

112 **Bidwell, A.M., Dowdy, R.H.,** 1987. Cadmium and zinc availability to corn following termination of sewage sludge applications. J. Environ. Qual. 16 : 138-442.

To assess the availability of sludge-borne Cd, and Zn over time, corn (Zea mays L.) and soil (Typic Haplludoll slit loam) were sampled for 6 yr following termination of the annual applications of sewage sludge. Cumulative sludge applications totalled 0,60,120 and 180 Mg ha^{-1}. Sludge treatments consistently resulted in greater Cd and Zn accumulation in stover than did the control treatment for each of the 6 yr following the final sludge application. Cadmium and Zn concentration in stover increased linearly within treatment levels for all years. Concentrations of Cr, Cu, Ni and Pb in stover and grain fluctuated annually, with no predictable effect of sludge rate. Of the metals measured in stover and grain, only stover Cd exceeded suggested tolerance level of 0.5 mg kg^{-1} in animal feed for all sludge treatment in all years. Cadmium uptake decreased over time at all sludge rates, and was inversely related (P > 0.01) to time in years following terminal application. Zinc uptake declined slightly over time, although not to the same degree or with the same predictability as Cd uptake. Soil Cd and Zn extractable with DTPA and I M NHO_3 were highly correlated with plant metal uptake within years. However, metal uptake diminished with consecutive croppings for constant levels of extractable Cd and Zn. Hence the reliability of either DTPA or I M HNO_3 in the prediction of Cd and Zn uptake in subsequent croppings is questionable.

113 **Bielorai, H., Vaisman, I., Feigin, A.,** 1984. Drip irrigation of cotton with treated municipal effluents : I. Yield response. J. Environ. Qual. 13(2) : 231-234.

A long-term drip irrigation experiment was conducted on a grumusol soil at Zor'a Israel in 1978, 1979 and 1980 to study the influence of municipal effluent on growth, yield and line quality of drip-irrigated cotton (*Gossypium hirsutum* L.) var. "Acala SJ-2". Two sources of irrigation water were used: (i) municipal effluent was about 50 mg/l during the 3 years of experimentations. The treatment included three seasonal amounts of effluent and fresh water application: 350, 440, 515 mm; and five levels of N:O, 90, 150, 180 and 230 kg ha^{-1}, added to the fresh water only, via the drip system. The cotton plants irrigated with effluent grew taller, with more vegetative growth than did the plants irrigated with fresh water.

114 **Bingham, F.T.,** 1979. Bioavailability of Cd to food crops in relating to heavy metal content of sludge-amended soils. Environl. Health Perspectives 28 : 39-43.

21 economic crops were grown in pots filled with a calcareous soil

treated with increasing amounts of Cd. yields vs. Cd addition rate relations showed yield reductions to occur with Cd sensitive plants (spinach, soybean, curlycress, and lettuce) at addition rates varying from 5 to 15 µg Cd/g soil, whereas tolerant crops (tomato, squash, cabbage and rice) did not suffer a yield reduction when treated at rates < 150 µg Cd/g soil. Nutrient solution experiments revealed marked differences in growth of crops. Cron, turnip, beets, bean and tomato plants grown in solution cultures containing 0.1 µg Cd/ml accumulated different amounts of Cd in leaf tissue depending on crop species; leaf Cd concentrations ranged from a low of 9µg Cd/g leaf for beans to 200 µg Cd/g leaf for beets. Large differences also occurred with regard to distribution of Cd with the plant. Fruit and seed tissue contained less Cd than leaves. Experiments comparing the toxicity of Cd to Cu, Ni and Zn in an acid soil±lime showed Cd to be the most phytotoxic, while interactive effects occurred with regard to metal uptake and accumulation by plants. Cd uptake essentially depended on the Cd concentration of the soil. Studies of chemical speciation of Cd in relation to Cd availability indicated that the free Cd^{+2} concentration correlates better with Cd uptake than Cd total of the soil solution.

115 **Bingham, F.T., Page., A.L., Mitchel, G.A., Strong, J.E.,** 1979. Effect of liming on acid soil amended with sewage sludge enriched with Cd, Cu, Ni and Zn on yield and Cd content of wheat grain. J. Environ. Qual. 8(2): 202-207.

An acid soil (pH 5.2) was treated ± lime and 1 per cent sewage sludge enriched with three concentrations each of Cd, Zn, Cu and Ni. These treated soils were placed in pots and cropped with wheat. Analysis of variance, revealed significant main effects on grain yield from all metal additions to the acid soil and from Cd and Cu only in the limed soil. Significant main effects on the concentration of Cd in grass occurred with all metals added in the limed soil. But only from Cd, Zn and Ni on the acid soil, significant multiple inter-actions occurred in all cases. Multiple regression equations were developed for estimating grain yield and Cd content from soil metal additions and saturation extract metal content. Grain Cd concentrations were highly correlated with soil metal additions (R^2 = 0.978 and 0.988 for limed and unlimed soils, respectively and saturation extract metals, (R^2 = 0.879 and 0.950 for limed and unlimed soils). The best fit equations were used to calculate metal equivalent column from soil metals added (SME) which were then used to develop regression equations and graphs relating grain yield to SME.

116 **Birch, L., Bachoten, R.,** 1990. Complexing agents from micro-organisms. Experientia 46(8): 827-834.

The majority of extracellular complexing ligands produced by micro-organisms are summarised as being of low molecular mass (<10,000 daltons) and are usually released as part of metal detoxification processes. These exudates appear to exhibit strong metal binding characteristics, often reducing metal toxicity. Under certain conditions microbes produce metal specific compounds of low molecular mass called siderophores. Although these are normally specific for iron they also have relatively high affinities for radionuclides such as Pu and facilitate their uptake into cells. The occurrence of specific actinide complexing agents has been recorded. The breakdown of lignins and cellulosic material produces large macromolecular compounds called humates. Humates also considerably influence absorption of metals to substrate surface and at high pH may compete with OH-ions for metal binding. As well as with extracellular ligands metals can interact directly with micro organisms.

117 **Blais, J.S., Doige, C.A., Marshall, W.D., Knowles, R.,** 1990. Persistence and toxicity of alkyllead salts to anaerobic nitrogen transformations in soil. Arch. Environ. Contam. Toxicol. 19(2): 227-234.

Using acetylene blockage and acetylene reduction techniques as parameters of denitrification and nitrogen fixation respectively, four alkyllead chlorides (Me_3PbCl Me_2PbCl_2, Et_3PbCl Et_2PbCl_2; Me = CH_3, Et = C_2H_5) were separately tested at 0.01, 0.1, 1.0, 5.0 or 10.0 μg/g) for their inhibitory properties against these nitrogen transformations in an agril. soil. In the presence of added nitrate, glucose, and acetylene, alkyllead salts only marginally inhibited nitrous oxide, ethylene, and carbon dioxide accumulation in the head space above soil slurries which were incubated anaerobically up to ten days. In contrast, the same levels of alkyllead toxicants appreciably modified the accumulation of these gases above incubations of supernatant from soil water suspension.

118 **Blais, J.S., Marshall, W.D.,** 1986. Determination of alkyllead salts in run off soils and street dusts containing high levels of lead. J. Environ. Qual. 15: 255-259.

A modified procedure has been developed in which alkyllead salts are selectively extracted complexometrically from samples which contain up to 1000 mg Pb kg^{-1}. This procedure was applied to rainwater run off, soils, and street dusts from urban environments. Ethyllead salts but not methyllead salts were detected in all samples. Concentrations of these analyses were significantly correlated with levels of extractable Pb^{2+} in these samples but no with total Pb.

119 **Blais, J.S., Marshall, W.D., Knowles, R.,** 1988. Toxicity of alkyllead salts to anaerobic nitrogen transformations in sediment. J. Environ. Qual. 17(3): 457-462.

Four alkyllead chlorides were separately tested (at 0.1, 1.0, 5.0 and 10.0 μg/L) for their inhibitory properties against denitrification and N_2 fixation in a lake sediment. In the presence of added nitrate, glucose and acetylene, alkyllead salts only moderately inhibited nitrous oxide, ethylene and carbon dioxide accumulation by whole slurry incubations. These effects were more pronounced in supernatant from sediment. In general, ethylleads were more toxic than methyllead salts and dialkyl leads were more inhibitory than their trialkyl lead homologues to these transformations. Successive incubations indicated that microbes adopted to the presence of these toxicants, a phenomenon also observed with other heavy metals. At the highest concentrations reported in sediments, no serious hazard to N transformations exists.

120 **Bles, N., Montiel, A., Husson, G.P., Vilagines, R.**, 1989. Different forms of heavy metals in sewage sludges. Tribunede, l' Fau. 41(5): 24-31.

Data on forms and contents of Cd, Cr, Cu, Pb, Mn, Fe, Al Co, As, Zn, Ni and Sn for each state of sewage sludge treatment are presented. Apart from Fe, Al and Zn, the treatment had no appreciable effect on the conc. of metals. Fe increased from 27 to 75 per cent in the filter cake but Al and Zn decreased correspondingly. Conc. were compared with European Standards.

121 **Blincoe, C., Theisen, M.O., Stoddard-Gilbert, K.**, 1987. Sample oxidation procedures for the determinations of Cr and Ni in biological material. Commun. Soil Sci. Plant Analy. 18(6): 687-697.

Sample preparation methods for atomic absorption spectro-photometric analysis of Cr and Ni in biological materials were examined. Radiotracer recover, precision of analysis and analysis of NBS reference samples were the criteria used. Cr and Ni in biological materials can be successfully prepared for AAS by dry ashing with nitric acid treatment of the partially oxidised sample.

122 **Boekhold, A.E., Van, Derzee, S.E.A.T.M.**, 1991. Long-term effects of soil heterogeneity on cadmium behaviour in soil. J. Contam. Hydrol. 7(4): 371-390.

A deterministic model for long term behaviour of contaminants in the rootzone is developed that includes sorption, leaching, and plant uptake. The model is applied to cadmium accumulation in a sandy soil and uptake of cadmium by barley. Analysis showed that the sensitivity of the leaching rate to changes in soil chemical and physical parameters decreases as a function of time, and becomes zero when steady state is reached. In contrast, accumulation of cadmium in soil and the plant uptake rate of barley are increasingly sensitive to soil chemical and physical parameters as time preceeds. To analyse cadmium behaviour in a field that is heterogeneous with respect to soil physical properties, the interstitial flow velocity was assumed to be a random, lognormally distributed variate. Using Monte Carlo simulation, the average plant uptake rate appeared to be much higher in the stochastic analysis than in the deterministic approach. Steady state is reached after a very long period of time.

123 **Bohmer, B.M.**, 1989. Leaching of Cd and Ni from the plant-efficacious layer of uncontaminated arable soils. Archiv fur Ackere-and pflanzenban

und Bodinkunde, 33(8): 475-482.

Leaching of Cd and Ni was investigated in nine contaminated soils (sand to clay) under grass using vacuum lysimeters. Depending on the kind of soils, leaching averaged 1.8 to 12.4g Cd and 9 to 71g Ni/ha/yr with the highest values found in clay soil. There was no correlation between heavy metal concentration of the percolating water and texture or heavy metal contents of the soil for the other soil types tested. Cd and Ni concentrations in percolating water varied between 0.8 and 1.9 µg/litre and between 8 and 21 mg/l, respectively. Hence metal leaching was closely correlated with the amount of water. No correlation was found between the amount of leached heavy metals and the heavy metal concentration in percolating water.

124 **Bohn, H.L., Seekamp, G.,** 1979. Beryllium effects on potatoes and oats in acid soil. Water Air Soil Pollut. 11: 319-322.

Potatos (*Salanum tuberosum*) and Oats (*Avena sativa*) were grown in greenhouse pots of a strongly acid soil treated with 0 to 300 ppm Be and 0 to 1000 ppm $CaCO_3$. Germination and yield decreased, and plant Be content increased, with increasing soil Be content. The Be content of the potato tubers appeared to be low and unaffected by the soil Be content. Liming the soil and increasing the time between Be contamination and crop planting lessened the effect of Be.

125 **Bokade, S.S., Thergaonkar, V.P., Deshkar, A.M.,** 1990. Spoiled alumina as an adsorbent. Indian J. Environ. Health. 32(4): 383-388.

Spoiled alumina from aluminium hydroxide manufacturing industry was activated at 400°C and was used for adsorption studies on waste water from paper mill and dairy industry. Results have shown that COD and colour removal are 84 and 99 per cent, respectively.

126 **Bole, J.B., Bell, R.G.,** 1978. Land application of municipal sewage waste water : Yield and chemical composition of forage crops. J. Environ. Qual. 7(3): 222-226.

Alfalfa out yielded four grass species when the forages were irrigated with sufficient lagooned municipal sewage waste water (about 50 cm per year). The yields were increased and the yield differential between the alfalfa and the grasses was reduced when additional N was added as fertiliser or by doubling the amount of waste water. The grasses with the exception of tall wheatgrass, outyielded the alfalfa when fertiliser was added at the high waste water level. Since water did not limit growth, yields were controlled by the N supply. Waste water-N-and fertiliser-N were equally effective in stimulating forage production. Nitrogen yield of alfalfa was double that of the grasses with the unfertilized waste water treatment, and considerably greater than the N yield of the grasses with the other treatments. Nitrogen uptake by all the forages, except tall wheatgrass, exceeded N application by waste water and fertiliser. Phosphorus application, in the waste water or as fertiliser P, exceeded plant uptake. The P content of the forage was unaffected by the treatment; and P uptake was determined by the yield. Alfalfa was the most suitable forage crop when the system was operated for optimum utilization of the waste water.

127 **Bole, J.B. Carefoot, J.M., Chang, G. Oosterveld, M.,** 1981. Effect of waste water irrigation and leaching percentage on soil and ground water chemistry. J. Environ. Qual. 10: 177-183.

Irrigation with sewage waste water for six seasons produced greater salinity under alfalfa than under reed canary grass or fallow. Irrigation rates were designed to produce high and low leaching percentage (L.P.). The high irrigation rate (I_2) was double the low irrigation rate (I_1). Leaching percentages were estimated from the soluble Na concentration at the 90 to 150 cm depth of the soil profile. Na reached a steady state for the conditions of the irrigation season by the fall of each year in the first 2 crop years and by the end of the second irrigation season in the last four crop years. Sodium and Ca+Mg approached equilibrium during the final 3 crop years. High LP (> 34%) in the first 2 years reduced original salinity levels (EC 3.99 to 1.39 mmhos/cm). When irrigation rates were reduced in the last 4 years, salinity increased but the salt levels were well below those (EC < 2.13 mmhos/cm) that would significantly reduce crop yield. Ground-water calculations at low $CaCO_3$ (LP < 10%) showed that EC and SAR values were high, but precipitation was balanced by gypsum dissolution.

128 **Bollag, J.M., Bollag, W.B.,** 1990. A model for enzymatic binding of pollutants in the soil. Internatl. Environ. Analy. Chemistry 39(2): 147-157.

Pollutants released into the environment may be bound to humic acid through abiotic or biological processes. Complex formation can occur by an oxidative coupling reaction leading to oligomeric and polymeric products. The effects of phenoloxidases (monophenol monoygenases) Peroxidases, tyrosinases, and laccases) on the binding of substituted phenols and stromatic amines to humus monomers as well as to humic substances were investigated based on a large number of isolated and identified cross-compiling products; the sites and mecliasions of binding were identified and also the efficiency of some compiling reactions determined. Copolymerization largely seeds on the chemical reactivity of the substrates involved. Certain phenolic humus constituents, such as guaiacol or ferulic acid are very reactive in the presence of phenoloxidases. When of these compounds was incubated together with a phenoloxidase with less or even non reactive phenols, anilines or other chemicals, a synesegistic reaction took place, resulting in increased formation of bound residues of these compounds.

129 **Bona Zountas, M.,** 1988. Mathematical pollutant fate modelling of petroleum products in soil systems in "Soil Contaminated by Petroleum: Environment and Public Health Effects", John Willey & Sons: 31-111.

Information on modelling of contaminants in soil system is presented covering sources, fats chemistry and modelling concepts. The categories of a dissolved pollutant, an immiscible contaminant and a metal are discussed. An evaluation of critical para-meters affecting contaminant migration through soil is appended.

130 **Bordas, Valls, V.; Lillo Puig, P.; Recatala Boix, L.** 1991. Identification and characterization of areas with a high or very high environmental hazard in the topographic sheet of Castellon de la Plana and the Columbretes Islands at a scale of 1:100 000 in XVIII reunion nacional de suelos. Communiccciones. La Laguna, Tenerife; Universidad de La Laguna: 241-248.

Thirty-six units identified as areas at high or very high environmental risks are mapped and their main characteristics are shown in tables.

131 **Borden, R.L., Yanoschak, T.M.,** 1990. Ground and surface water quality impacts of North Carolina sanitary land fills. Water Resources Bull. 26(2): 269-277.

Analysis of 322 surface and 411 groundwaters shows that significant increases in the average concentrations in groundwater and downstream surface water as compared to upstream due to land fills. Largest increases were for zinc, turbidity, total organic carbon, EC, TDS and Pb. The most common heavy metal violations were for Pb (18%), Cr (18%), Zinc (6%), Cd, (16%), As (6%). A comparison of data from sanitary land fills and secondary treatment of waste water suggested that the concentration of heavy metals and organic pollutants discharged tó surface waters from these sources are similar.

132 **Borgegaard, O., Rydin, H.,** 1989. Biomass, root penetration and heavy metal uptake in birch in a soil cover over copper tailings. J. Appl. Ecol. 26(2): 585-595.

A 10-year old soil deposit on copper tailings was used to study the effect of variations in soil thickness on vegetation establishment and on heavy metal contamination of the soil and of Betula leaves. Contamination of the covering soil indicated that upward transport of metals from the spoil had occurred. Even with a 1 m thick soil layer, fine roots of brich trees mostly less than 4 years old had penetrated into the spoil. Leaf contents of Zn, Pb and Cd were higher than, and of Cu similar to, published values for uncontaminated soils.

133 **Bouchard, D.C., Mravik, S.C., Smith, G.B.,** 1990. Benzene and naphthalene sorption on soil contaminated with high molecular weight residual hydrocarbons from unleaded gasoline. Chemosphere, 21(8): 975-989.

For complex non-aqueous phase liquids (NAPLs), the composition of the NAPL retained in the pore space of geological material weathers until the residual NAPL no longer acts as a liquid and exists as discrete regions of hydrocarbon (termed residual hydrocarbons) in association with the geological media (water and media), or as thin film coatings on the media (NAPL wet media). The residual hydrocarbons were found to resist separation from the soil solids even when subjected to shaking in batch reactors. The magnitude of solute sorption was significantly greater for a low organic carbon soil contaminated with residual hydrocarbons than for natural soil organic carbon.

134 **Bourdeau, P.,** 1989. Chemicals in the environment. Pontificae Academiae Scientiarum Scripta Varia 75: 457-476.
Anthropogenic emissions of chemicals and their consequences on the environment are discussed.

135 **Boutin, P., Racault, Y.,** 1986. Natural lagooning. Present situation of a purification technique in France. Tech. Sci. Methods. 81(6): 273-284.
A national survey was conducted in 1983-84 on the actual practice of waste water stabilization by "natural" ponds (lagoons) in France, including an almost exhaustive inventory of plants then in service. Through the statistical interpretation of collected data, it was allowed to analyse the spreading of this technique, to evidence modes of planning and regional features and to suggest models for further investigations.

136 **Boutron, C., Lorius, C.,** 1979. Trace metals in Antarctic snows since 1914. Nature, 277: 551-554.
The concentrations of Pb, Cd, Cu, Zn, Ag, Na, Mg, K, Ca, Fe, Al, and Mn in snow deposited from 1914 to 1974 at an uncontaminated site in east Antarctica were determined. Thirteen successive snow samples were collected from the surface to a depth of 5.35 m in a hand-dug pit at Dome C. The age of the snow samples was determined by stratigraphy, stable isotope composition, and radioactive fallout horizons from nuclear tests. Lead, Cd, Cu, Zn, and Ag were already strongly enriched 60 year ago at levels comparable to present ones. Background atmospheric concentrations of these metals are not strongly influenced by global pollution but are related to natural phenomena, possibly volcanism.

137 **Bouwer, H.,** 1991. Groundwater recharge with sewage effluent. Water Sci. Technol. 23(10-12): 2099-2108.
Before sewage effluent can be used for unrestricted irrigation, it is needed that water meets agronomic, public health, and aesthetic requirements. This involves reduction of nitrogen concn. to < 10 mg/litre, complete removal of pathogenic organisms, suspended solids and biodegradable organic carbon. This can often be achieved, with a ground-water recharge system, using the soil and aquifer materials as natural filters. Studies in Arizona showed that such systems can reduce nitrogen concn. from 20 mg/litre to 7 mg/litre, faecal coliform concn. from 3500 per 100 ml (chlorinated secondary effluent) to 0.3 per 100 ml, viruses from 21 plaque-forming units/litre to 0, suspended solids from 15 mg/litre to 1 mg/litre, and total organic carbon from 20 mg/litre to 2 mg/litre. Hydraulic loading rates for sandy soils were about 300 ft/yr.

Thus, 1 acre of infiltration basin can renovate about 300 acre feet/year of sewage effluent. The renovated water should be removed from the aquifer to avoid its spread into high-quality native ground-water.

138 **Boyle, M.,** 1990. Biodegradation of land applied sludge. J. Environ. Qual. 19(4): 640-644.

There is a need to increase the rate of decomposition during and after sludge formation. Sludge formation determines which environmental factors and enzymatic reactions are effective in further degrading this complex susbtrat. From activated waste treatment through anaerobic digestion to land application, there is a decrease in the volume but an increase in the stabilisation of the remaining organic materials.

139 **Boyle, M., Fuller, W.H.,** 1987. Effect of municipal solid waste leachate composition on zinc migration through soils. J. Environ. Qual. 16: 357-360.

Four Zn enriched leachates of different TOC and TSS composition were perfused through five soils. The effluents from the 20 soil columns were analysed for Zn. Solution displacement continued until the concentration of the Zn in the effluent equalled that of the influent (100 mg L^{-1}). In general, higher TOC and TSS levels in the leachate facilitated the migration of Zn through soil. The soil properties associated with Zn retention were, in order of importance, surface area, cation exchange capacity, and per cent clay content. The TOC and TSS content of the MSW leachate studied were found to be more important in determining Zn attenuation behaviour than soil characteristics.

140 **Boyle, M., Paul, E.A.,** 1989. Nitrogen transformation in soil previously amended with sewage sludge J. Soil Sci. Soc. Am. 53 : 740-744.

This short-term (10_d) incubation experiment established the rates of nitrogen (N) transformations occurring in sludge-amended and non-amended soil. Utilising a nitrification block (C_2H_2) with $(^{15}NH_4)_2SO_4$, first order rate constants were calculated for N immobilisation, ammonification, nitrification and denitrification. These rate constants were compared to values obtained after a long-term (87-wk) incubation performed on soils sampled from the same field plots. The short-term rates of ammonification were still higher than the controls 4 yr after the last sludge audition. Sludge applications over an 8-yr period (180-Mg/ha/yr) reduced soil nitrification potential compared to the controls when spiked with 15_N. Denitrification did not cause a significant loss of N during either a short or long-term incubation period. The microbial biomass in the sludge-amended soil contained more N, which resulted in a microbial C/N ratio of approximately 4:1 vs. 5:1 for the controls. Initial (short-term) N immobilisation rate constants were 0.43 for the sludge-amended and 0.35 for the non-amended soil.

141 **Bradford, G.R., Bakhtar, D., Westcot, D.,** 1990. Uranium, vanadium and

molybdemium in saline waters of California. J. Environ. Qual. 19 : 105-108.

Mean concentration of U, V and Mo were considerately elevated in agricultural drainage and evaporation ponds of the San Joaquan valley compared to saline waters of Salton sea and Mono lake. Relative high correlation coefficient were observed between U, Mo and salinity.

142 **Breimer, R.E., Vogel, J., Otto, J.C.G.,** 1989. Fluorine contamination of soils and earth-worms (Lambricus spp). near site of long term industrial emission in Southern Germany. Biology Fertility Soil 7(4): 297-302.

The HCl soluble fraction of soils was a better indicator of anthropogenic F accumulation than the total and water extractable F fraction. A map of 88 sampling sites showed 3 zones of pollution. In calcareous soils, F accumulation was restricted to the upper 40-50 cm, due to CaF_2 formation. Total F in earth worms either with or without the gut was correlated with soil F. F was higher n linings of earthworm burrows than in the soil mass. This may be a mechanism of soil contamination.

143 **Brewer, A.J.,** 1990. Irrigation and the disposal of farm wastes. In Nitrates and Irrigation (Eds. Hamer, P.J.C., Leeds-Harrison. P.B.)., Silsoe, UK: 58-66.

There has been a steady increase in the number of water pollution incidents caused by farm wastes over the last ten years. Data for 1978 indicate that about 25 per cent of these incidents result from inadequate slurry storage, 25 per cent from dirty yard water and a further 25 per cent from silage effluent Undiluted slurry can be 100 times more polluting than raw sewage, and silage effluent is typically up to 200 times more polluting.

144 **Bridges, E.M.,** 1989. Polluted and contaminated soils. in "Annual Rept. Internatl. Soil Reference and Information Centre. Wageningen 6:27.

Soil Pollution, diffuse contamination, nature and source of contaminants and vulnerable targets are briefly discussed. Methods of dealing the problem are discussed under the sheedings, stabilisation, barriers thermal techniques, microbiological, chemical methods, physical methods, dealing with gases and criteria for contamination. Standards adopted in Netherland for soils are tabulated.

145 **Brockway, D.G., Nguyen, P.V.,** 1986. Municipal sludge application in forests of Northern Michigan--a case study in D.W. Cole, C.I. Herry, and W.L. Nutter (Eds): "The Forest Alternative for Treatment and Utilisation of Municipal and Industrial Wastes". 477-496.

Field trials in four forest types (aspen, oak, pine, northern hardwoods) were of a completely random design covering 54 ha of which 18 ha were treated with nearly 4 million litres of anaerobically digested sludge. Average solids loading ranged from 8 to 10 Mg/ha. Preliminary findings indicate an enhanced nutritive quality of forage on fertilised plots and a resulting increase in use by both deer and elk. Increases in plant growth were related to elevate levels of soil nitrogen, phosphorus, calcium and magnesium. Slight increases of nitrate-N were observed in soil percolate within one year of application, but these rapidly returned to near background concentrations.

146 **Brown, K.W.,** 1986. Use of soils to retain waste in landfills and surface impoundments. J. Soil Sci. Soc. Am. 50 : 279-300.

Laboratory studies of conductivities using a range of organic liquids including both polar and nonpolar solvents, waste solvents, and commercial petroleum products indicated that the hydraulic conductivities of compacted soils to organic liquids were one to five orders of magnitude greater than those of water. Observation of the soils permeated with dye labeled organic liquids revealed the formation of platy structural units near the surface. The dye stains in the soil revealed that the organic liquids moved through cracks that penetrated the soil, which originally had a massive structure. Field test cell liners were constructed using three clays had two organic waste liquids. The conductivity measurements in the test cells confirmed the laboratory findings. The nonpolar solvent waste containing xylene which was used to permeate the 1.5m square and 15 cm thick field test section of compacted clay, broke through many of the replications within two weeks. The acetone waste took as long as two years to break through the test sections; however, in the end, sections of each type of clay were also permeated by the acetone waste. Field data and observations collected at active landfills and surface impoundments suggest that organic liquids have moved 10 to 1000 times faster than anticipated based on laboratory measurements made using water. These data suggest that organic liquids, which are only sparingly soluble in water or water soluble liquids in concentrations greater than about 50 per cent, will desiccate clays causing them to shrink and crack. The liquids are then able to flow through the newly formed macropores in the soil much more rapidly than when the soils are wetted with water.

147 **Broman, D., Naf, C., Rolff, C., Zebohr, Y.,** 1990. Analysis of polychlorinated dibenzo-p-dioxins (PCDD) and polychlorinated dibenzofurans (PCDF) in soil and digested sewage sludge from Stockholm, Sweden. Chemosphere 21, (10-11): 1213-1220.

The content of PCDDs and PCDFs in sewage sludge samples and toposoil from fields situated in the country of Stockholm was investigated and the contribution of PCDDs and PCDFs to fields treated with sewage sludge was compared with the contribution from two non-point emission sources i.e. road traffic and the urban area of the city of Stockholm. The mean concentration in four sludge samples was 79 μg TEQ/g (toxic equivalents/g organic matter). Soil samples taken close to major roads contained 9-32 μg TEQ/g. The results indicate that both road traffic and outputs from the urban area influence the PCDD and PCDF concentrations in arable soil. Fertilisation with sludge (1t DM/ha/year) raised the initial soil concentrations of PCDD and PCDF in the fields by approx. 2-3 per cent.

148 **Brown, K.W., Thomas, J.C., Donnelly, K.C.,** 1991. Mutagenic potential of plants grown on municipal sewage sludge amended soil. Arch. Environ. Contam. Toxicol. 20(3): 385-390.

The Salmonella/microsome assay was used to monitor the mutagenic potential of the organic extract of plants grown on municipal sewage sludge amended soils. The solvent extractable organic chemicals from sewage sludge, unamended Padina fine sand, sludge amended Padina fine sand, and two forage crops, alfalfa and coastal bermudagrass were tested with Salmonella strain TA98 with and without metabolic activation. The mutagenic potential of the sludge amended soil was greater than that of the unamended soil. Fractions extracted from the sludge amended soil over a 154 day period displayed an increase in mutagenicity. None of plant extracts, whether collected from plants grown on sludge amended or unamended soil, induced a positive response (doubling of revertants at two consecutive dose levels) in the bioassay.

149 **Brown, K.W., Thomas, J.C., Slowey, J.F.,** 1983. The movement of metals applied to soils in sewage effluent. Water Air Soil Pollut. 19: 43-54.

The secondary treated sewage effluent amended to contain slightly less than 1 mg L^{-1} each of Cd, Cu, Ni, Pb and Zn. The effluent was applied weekly for a period of one year on large undisturbed monoliths of four diverse soils enclosed in lysimeters. Leachate water and periodic soil samples were collected. Soil samples collected after one year of effluent reveated that increase in the concentration of metals were greatest at the surface and decreased sharply with depth so that in most cases increases below 25 cm were insignificant. The depth of movement appeared to be independent of the soil characteristics. Mobility evaluation from the pe cent of that applied remained in the surface (0 to 2.5 cm) was as follows Cd > Zn = Ni = Pb > Cu. The movement of metals was sufficiently slow however, so that the leachate water collected at 1.5 m below the surface remained free of the applied metals throughout the study.

150 **Browne, C.L., Wong, Y.M., Buhler, D.R.,** 1984. Predictive model for the accumulation of cadmium by container-grown plants. J. Environ. Qual. 13(3): 184-188.

Research into the dietary availability of Cd, a toxic heavy metal, called for prediction of Cd accumulation by edible crop species to be grown to maturity under greenhouse conditions.

151 **Bruch, J.C. Jr., Smith, P.,** 1973. The dispersion of pollutants beneath open channels. Water Air Soil Pollut. 2: 23-24.

An experiment and a numerical scheme which combine previously given methods for the dispersion and seepage phenomena have been presented to describe the dispersion of a pollutant in porous media beneath a triangular channel. The combine effect of longitudinal and lateral dispersion was considered. Numerical concentration profiles are given along with a comparison of experimental and numerical data. The technique suggested here in can be extended to other channel shapes and flow fields accounting for the capillary fringe.

152 **Brune, H., Schaaf, H.,** 1991. Organic pollutants in soil and food chain , in "International Conf. on Environmental Pollution". B. Nath (Ed.) : 335-343.

This work concentrates showing results of chlorinated hydrocarbons (CHC's), polychlorinated biphenyls (PCB's) and polycycled aromatic hydrocarbons (PAH's). In soils and feed stuff we still have detectable concentrations of CHC's and PCB's but we can expect a decline in human fat, because of the low entry rate of PAH's in plants and food, the potential danger for men is rather low.

153 **Bunzi, K., Schimmack, W.,** 1989. Associations between the fluctuations of the distribution coefficients of Cs, Zn, Sr, Co, Cd, Ce, Ru, Tc and I in the upper two horizons of a podzol forest soil. Chemosphere 18 (11-12): 2109-2120.

Within the O and E horizon of a podzol forest soil, several significant associations were observed between the distribution coefficients for the sorption of 9 ions along a transact of 150 m in intervals of 3m. The presence of these associations was investigated by the Spearman correlation test and a sign test for the comparison of point to point fluctuations. They give some information which ions respond with respect to their sorption in a similar (or opposite) way to fluctuations of the soil properties.

154 **Burge, W.D., Marsh, P.B.,** 1978. Infectous diseases hazards of land spreading sewage wastes. J. Environ. Qual. 7(1): 1-9.

Processed sewage wastes often contain residual pathogenic viruses, bacteria, cysts of protozoa and ova of helminths, but most sewage related disease out breaks have been attributed to use of raw sewage waste water, ram sludges, or night soils on food crops consumed raw, to contamination of drinking water from septic tanks or to consumption of raw shell fish from sewage polluted waters. Although subject to relatively high levels of exposure to pathogens in aerosols, waste water treatment plant workers appear to be unaffected, but data on this are limited. Percolation of waste water at a moderate rate through soils of medium to fine texture removes most bacteria and viruses. Pathogen movement in surface runoff water may present a greater hazard for spreading disease. Technique that completely disinfect sludges may fail to stabilise them to that perfection is a problem. Properly conducted composting stabilises raw sludge and destroys most pathogens. Certain fungi and actinomycets generated during composting may have allergenic potentialities of import for workers at sludge composting sites.

155 **Burton, T.M., Hook, J.E.,** 1979. A mass balance study of application of municipal waste water to forests in Michigan. J. Environ. Qual. 8 (4): 589-596.

A mass balance study of the effects of secondary municipal waste water on phosphorus and nitrogen cycling was conducted in 1976 and 1977 on three 1.2 ha plots in a late successional, sugar mapli (*Acer Saccharum* Marsh)-buch (*Fagus-grandifolia* Ehrh.) forest in Southern Michigan. The treatments included an unirrigated control plot and 5 and 10 cm week waste water application plots. About 96 per cent of the added inorganic nitrogen from 5 cm/week of waste water application leached past the root zone. Application of 10 cm/week waste water increased inorganic nitrogen from 5 cm/week of waste water application leached past the root zone. Application of 10 cm/week waste water increased inorganic nitrogen 'retention' on a mass balance basis to 69 per cent of input apparently as a result of denitrification. The 10 cm/week application also resulted in death of trees in the lower areas. Phosphorus retention by the system was 96.5 per cent at an application rate of 5 cm/week and 66 per cent at 10 cm/week. Charges in soils included increased available phosphorus and exchangeable magnesium and potassium in the top 15 cm of soil and increased sodium and chloride concentration throughout the 150 cm depth sampled.

156 **Bustamante, I. De.,** 1990. Land application, its effectiveness in purification of urban and industrial waste waters in La-Mancha, Spain. Environl. Geology Water Sci. 18(3): 179-185.

The effectiveness of land application in the treatment of urban and industrial waste water was studied in the river Guadiana basin. All parameters viz. EC, N, P, COD, tannin, lignins and total coliforms organisms were decreased as a result of land application.

157 **Byers, R.A., Zoiders, K.E.,,** 1976. Effect of spray irrigation with municipal sewage effluent on the cereal leaf beetle and the first fly infesting reed canary grass. J. Environ. Qual. 5 (2): 205-206.

Twelve cloves of reed Canary grass that were spray irrigated with Municipal sewage effluent had a mean of 0.03 larvae per clone of cereal leaf beetle on 7 June 1974. Similar unirrigated cloves had a mean of 3.2 larvae per clone on the date. Also, the irrigated clones had fewer culins killed by the frot fly than unirrigated clones on 7 June and 12th August 1974. Therefore, Reed Canary grass as a receptor of sewage effluent, already the most acceptable species because of its floods tolerance, is even more desirable because there should be fewer members of these two important pests.

158 **Cabrera-Guzman, D., Swartzaugh, J.T., Weisman, A.W.,** 1990. The use of electrokinetics for hazardous waste site remediation Air Waste

Manag. Assoc. 40(2): 1670-1676.

Electrokinesis, the phenomena occurring when a DC electric field is applied to a soil water system, can aid the removal of some hazardous wastes from soils. The electrochemistry of the process is described. Good results have been obtained with inorganic pollutants in clayey soils where traditional removal techniques are less effective.

159 **Cala, V., Sanchi-Drian, J.R.,** 1989. Evaluation of some heavy metals extractants in soils as indicators of the plant available forms. Annales de Edefologia Y. Agrobiologia 48: 11-21.

Some extraction solutions (0.1 M, HCl, IMHCl, 0.5 MHAC, NH_4 ACe 5M + EDTA 0.02 M + HAC 0.5M, pH 4.65) were used to soils to evaluate the biologically active fractions of heavy metals. Despite of variations between themselves, HCl1M and pH 4.65 mixture (Lankamen Ervio solution) provide the greatest extraction of the most available metal forms in plants.

160 **Calder, L.M.,** 1988. Chromium contamination of ground-water. In "Advances in Environmental Science and Technology", Vol. 20: Chromium in the Natural and Human Environment (Eds. J.O. Nriagu, E. Nieboer) John Wiley and Sons : 215-229.

Chromium (VI) is moderately to highly mobile in most shallow groundwaters where as chromium (III) is relatively immobile in most groundwaters. Three case studies are described.

161 **Calderone, S.J., Frankenberger, W.T., Jr.,** 1990. Influence of organic amendments on the mobilisation of molybdenum in soils. Bull. Environl. Contam. Toxicol. 45(2) : 228-231.

The effect of various organic materials on the solubilisation and mobilisation of molybdenum in soils was studied.

162 **Cargo, O.A., Rovers, H. Valadares, J.M.A.S.,** 1989. Nickel adsorption in soils of Sao Paulo State Brazil. Revista Brasileria deciencia do solo 13(2): 125-129.

Ni adsorption on Ca-saturated soils was studied. The adsorption isotherm fitted well in all soils. Specific adsorption was low. Maximum adsorption by Langmuir equation did not reach 40 per cent of the CEC at pH 7, but correlated well with pH and O.C. content.

163 **Carlson, R.W., Rolfe, G.L.,** 1979. Growth of rye grass and fescue as affected by lead-cadmium-fertiliser interaction. J. Environ. Qual. 8(3): 348-352.

Rye grass (Lolium perenne) and red fescue (Festuca rubra) were grown from seed in fertilised and unfertilised Flangan silt loam soil treated with Pb (0, 10, 100, 1000, 5,000, 10,000 μg/g). Cd (0, 0.1, 1, 10, 50, 100 μg/g), or a combination of Pb plus Cd at a ratio of 100 Pb:1 Cd. Plant growth and heavy metal content of plants were measured at the end of 3, consecutive, 10-d periods. Growth of Pb treated plants did not begin to decrease until treatment concentrations reached ≥1,000 µg/g. Above a treatment concentration of 1,000 µg pb/g with or without added Cd, growth was reduced sharply in a log-linear fashion with increasing treatment concentrations. Some reduction in growth of plants treated with Cd alone occured for fertilised fescue > 10 µg/g Cd but not for rye until treatments > 50 µg/g. No reduction in growth was found for nonfertilised plants treated with Cd alone at the highest soil concentration (100 µg/g). Reduction in growth for plants treated with Pb + Cd was no lower than that of plants treated with Pb < 1,000 µg/g, it did not ameliorate the effects of Pb at higher concentrations. Fertilisation reduced Pb content and uptake in rye but not in fescue. The Cd content of fertilised plants was greater than that of nonfertilised plants. Cadmium content of plants treated with Pb + Cd was greater than that of plants treated with Cd alone, while there was no difference in Pb content between Pb and Pb + Cd treatments.

164 **Cash, R.C., Leone, I.A.,** 1987. Effects of foliar applied nickel on tomato plants. J. Environ. Sci. Health 22A (1):11-26.

Shoot-applied nickel treatments produced symptomatology, foliar Ni accumulation, and cytological changes in tomato similar to those caused by treatments with root-applied nickel. Leaf damage resulting from 100 mg/L foliar Ni-treatments consisted of intervenial chlorosis and spotting necrosis which appeared histalogicaally as tissue collapse, cell clumping, and chloroplast disintegration. Shoot-treated plants accumulated more Ni in leaves than in roots; whereas the reverse was true in root-treated plants. Interference with root-to-shoot manganese translocation was attributed to attenuated vascular tissue and phloem blockage.

165 **Cervelli, S., Petruzzelli, G., Perna, A.,** 1987. Fly ashes as an amendment in cultivated soils. I. Effect on mineralisation and nitrification. Water Air Soil Pollut. 33 : 331-338.

The effect of two fly ashes derived from the combustion of coals from Poland (PO) and Southern Africa (SA), on organic N mineralisation and nitrification in two soils, was investigated. Following the addition of 2.5, and 10 per cent (W/W), N mineralisation constant decreased on the soil low in organic matter content. The addition of the same percentages of the two fly ashes to the soil higher in organic matter content gave contrasting results. The nitrification constant increased following the additions of fly ashes to the soils except the addition of 10 per cent SA to the soil, low in organic matter content, where it decreased.

166 **Chaer, A., Wollum, A.G. II,** 1980. A field study of a soil soyabean plant Rhizobium system amended with cadmium. J. Environ. Qual. 9: 420-423.

Soyabean plants were cropped over a period of 3 years, under field conditions in a soil amended with Cd (0 to 22.8 kg Cd/ha) in order to evaluate the effect of Cd on seed yield, Cd accumulation in seeds and the distribution of indigenous Rhizobium Japonicum strains. Cadmium migration from the cultivated layers to the sub soil during 3 years was not significant. Soyabean seed yields were affected significantly only when DTPA-TEA extractable Cd was >1.57 µg Cd/gm in the cultivated layers of the soils. Cadmium content of seeds increased from year to year. Grain yield decreased only in the high Cd treatments. DTPA-TEA extractable soils Cd does not accurately measure the readily available pool of Cd for soyabean plants. Rather Cd content of seeds appears to be a better indicator of the extent of Cd contamination. Rhizobium Japonicum strain distribution was not affected by the presence of Cd in the soil.

167 **Chaer, A., Wollum, A.G. II.** 1981. Effect of cadmium on symbiotic soyabean plants. J. Environ. Qual. 10 (2): 216-221.

A study was conducted to investigate (i) the existence of Rhizobium Japonicium strains tolerant to Cd, (ii) the Cd effect on the symbiosis between host soyabeans plants and R. Japonicum strains and (iii) interactions and distribution of Cd and other elements in the host. The existence of R. Japonicum strains was assessed by comparing growth curves of 10 different strains with increasing Cd (0, 3.5, 7, 14 and 28 µg/ml). Strain 110 (tolerant) and 123 (susceptible) were used to inoculate plants growing in nutrient solution to evaluate in presence of 0, 2.2, 6.7, 10.1 and 20.2 µg Cd/ml, respectively. Plants were harvested and analysed 23 days after starting Cd application. Cadmium decreased dry matter production of tops, roots and nodules. Plants inoculated with strain 123 accumulated significantly more dry matter in nodules than those with strain 110. However, in the presence of 0 and 2.2 µg Cd/ml, Plants inoculated with strain 110 accumulated significantly more N than plants inoculated with strain 123. Nutrient imbalances were observed in the presence of Cd. The interactions of Cd with some nutrients may contribute to Cd toxicity in soyabean plants and the most pronounced Cd effect was on Fe and Mn nutrition, rather than on Zn.

168 **Chakrabarty, A.K.,** 1989. Non-industrial pollution problems in developing countries: an example of urban India- a view point. Internatl. J. Environ. Studies 33 : 205-212.

Some aspects of non-industrial pollution related to the rapidly rising population are examined.

169 **Chakrabarti, C., Chakrabarti, T.,** 1988. Effect of irrigation with raw and differentially diluted sewage and application of primary settled sewage sludge on wheat plant growth, crop yield, enzymatic changes and trace element uptake. Environl. Pollut. 51(3): 219-235.

An increase in the conc. of Cu, Zn, Cr and Mn and a decrease in the activities of aspirate amino transferase, alanine aminotransferase and peoxidase were observed in the different parts of wheat plant, following raw, different diluted (50 and 66%) sewage irrigation and dry primary settled sludge amendment of soils. The grain enrichment efficiency for Cr was low under all sewage irrigation conditions. Only grain yields were not reduced. However, following sewage irrigation and sludge applications metabolic activity in wheat plant parts was reduced.

170 **Chakraborti, D., Ghosh, D., Niyogi, S.,** 1987. Calcutta pollutants I, Appraisal of some heavy metals in Calcutta city sewage and sludge in use for fisheries and agriculture. Internatl. J. Environ. Analyt. 30(4): 243-253.

The conc. of Pb, Zn, Cu, Cd, Co, Ni, Mn, Fe and Cr were determined in Calcutta sewage and sludge. Their conc. was relatively less as compared to some cities of other countries.

171 **Chakraborti, D., Racymaekers, B.,** 1988, Calcutta pollutants. II Toxic metals in dust and characterisation of individual aerosol particles. Internatl. J. Environl. Analyt. Chem. 32(2): 121-133.

Heavy metals viz. Cr, Co, Cu, Cd, Mn, Zn, Ni and Pb in dust of street household, restaurant, top of leaves and 5 soil samples were examined. Dust samples showed higher metal content than, soil samples with Pb and Zn showing the highest values.

172 **Chandra, N., Sriniwas, T., Sharma, A.K., Bandra, T.R.,** 1988. Impact of commercial detergent on *Pisum Sativum* and *Crotalaria Juncia*. Environ Ecol. 6(3): 176-178.

The detergent 'Nirma' inhibited the seed germination and seedling growth of both plants: germination was reduced to 15 per cent in *P. Sativum* and to 26 per cent in *C. Juncia* at 1 per cent level of the detergent. The length of hypocotyl and radicle was also decreased with increase of detergent.

173 **Chaney, R.L.,** 1989. Toxic elements accumulation in soils and crops: protecting soil fertility and agricultural food chains in "Inorganic Contamination in the Vadose Zone" (Ed. B. Bar Yosef et al). Springer Verlag : 140-158.

This review includes hazards of toxic elements in sludge amended soils, possible path ways including transfer of trace elements to animals. Crops can also transfer elements to feeds and fonds. Fe, Pb, Hg, Al, Ti and Cr are among the elements not translocated to plant foliage in sufficient amount to be toxic while Zn, Cd, Mn, Be, Se and B are very easily absorbed and translocated to food chain plants. Interactions between dietary and sludge constituents and their impact on the micro-nutrient behaviour in the food chain is discussed. The application of the non-linear model for plant response to sludge applied metals to risk assessment for Cd, Zn and Cu is described.

174 **Chaney, R.L., Beyer, W.N., Gifford, C.H., Sileo, L.,** 1988. Effects of zinc smelter emissions on farms and gardens at Palmerton, PA, in Trace Substances in Environmental Health-XXII : 263-280.

Whether Zn or Cd contamination of forage or soils from Zn smelter could be providing potentially toxic levels of Zn or other elements in the diets of young horses. The metals in forages, soils, and faces of grazing livestock on two farms near Palmerton were measured.

175 **Chang, F.H., Broadbent, F.E.,** 1980. Effect of nitrification on movement of trace metals in soil columns, J. Environ. Qual. 9(4): 587-591.

Soil column experiments were conducted with sludge-treated and untreated samples of two soils, Omni silty clay and Delhi loamy sand to determine whether protons generated during the nitrification process would affect the mobility of the trace metals. Columns were leached bi- or tri-weekly. Trace metals in effluents from the columns were analysed after each application of leaching solution. The columns were sectioned and the vertical distribution of 2N HCl-extractable metals determined. There was evidence of nitrification affecting movement of several of the metals, particularly in the cases of Mn, Zn, Cu and Cd in the untreated Delhi soil. The presence of sludge had a pronounced stabilizing influence of Cd and Zn.

176 **Chang, A.C., Page, A.L., Warneke, J.E.,** 1987. Long-term sludge application on cadmium and zinc accumulation in Swiss chard and radish. J. Environ. Qual. 16: 217-221.

Swiss chard and radish were grown twice annually on a Romona sandy loam soil treated with 0 to 180 Mg $ha^{-1}yr^{-1}$ of composted sludge. The soil received two sludge inputs of equal amounts each year. Cd and Zn accumulation of the plant tissue from 1976 to 1985 was examined. Results from the analysis of variance indicated that effects due to sludge application rates, seasons plants were grown, number of year of sludge application, and their interactions were all significant. If the data sets were partitioned according to sludge application rates and seasons, metal conc. of the plant tissue may be expressed as a non-linear regression model. The deviations of the observed values from the prediction of the regression model indicated that other factors might have also affected the metal uptake by plants. Stepwise multiple regression analysis of the partitioned data sets indicated that pH, salinity, temperature, of soil and length of growing season influenced the metal accumulation in plant tissue.

177 **Chang, C., Sommerfeldt, T.G., Entz, I.,** 1991. Soil chemistry after eleven annual applications of cattle feedlot manure. J. Environ. Qual 20(2): 475-480.

In a long term experiment at Lethbridge. AB, the effects of cattle (Bos sp) manure on soil characteristics were determined after 11 annual applications. Manure, incorporated by cultivating, rototilling or plowing was applied annually from 1973 to 1983 at 30, 60 and 90 Mg ha^{-1} (wet wt) and 60, 120 and 180 Mg ha^{-1} respectively to non-irrigated and irrigated dark brown chemozemic (Typic Haploborolls) clay loam soil. On both the non-irrigated and irrigated soil, the effects from manure, applied annually at greater than recommended rates for 11 yr. were minimal on

Cu and NH_4 content and substantial on other parameters determined. There were no significant effects on these soil parameters extended to greater depths under irrigation than under non-irrigation.

178 **Chanmugathas, P., Bollag, J.M.,** 1987. Microbial mobilisation of cadmium in soil under aerobic and unaerobic conditions. J. Environ. Qual. 16: 161-167.

Soil treated with Cd and washed to remove readily soluble Cd were suspended in a nutrient medium (at a ratio of 1:20 wt/v) and incubated (aerobically or anaerobically) for a period of 160 d. While no Cd was released from gamma-irradiated sterile soils under aerobic or anaerobic conditions, a significant amount of "strongly bound" or "fixed" Cd was mobilised from nonsterile samples of all soils. The rate and extent of microbial Cd mobilisation was dependent on the soil type, aeration, and moisture content. Among the four soils tested, Morrison sandy loam and Morrison loam soils (Ultic Hapludalfs) showed aerobically and anaerobically a greater degree and a faster rate of microbial Cd mobilisation compared to Hagerstown silt loam soils (Typic Hapludalfs). In all soils but the Morrison sandy loam soil, the amount of Cd released was considerably, greater under anaerobic than aerobic conditions. Although soil moisture content did not have a distinct effect in anaerobic experiments, under aerobic conditions dried field soils exhibited a significantly greater rate and extent of microbial Cd mobilisation than did fresh soils that had been kept moist at 5°C. Cadmium release was much more rapid during anaerobic incubation, but upon prolonged incubation (up to 3 weeks) a continued removal of Cd from the aqueous phase occurred in anaerobic, but not in the aerobic samples. In many instances, the pH of the soil suspensions decreased to an acidic level (near pH 5.5) with a concurrent release of Cd.

179 **Charak, V.S., Tripathi, B.R.,** 1989. Studies on selenium and iodine distribution in some soils of Kangra valley. J. Indian Soc. Soil Sci. 37: 167-170.

Total Salenium (0.09 to 0.26 ppm) and iodine (0 to 22.5 ppm) for some soil profiles of Kangra valley, HP are reported.

180 **Charley, R.C., Hooper, D.C., Mclee, A.G.,** 1980. Nitrification kinetics in activated sludge at various temperatures and dissolved oxygen concentrations. Water Res. 14(10): 1387-1396.

Activated sludge from a domestic sewage works was enriched with nitrifying bacteria by running a laboratory fermenter on NH_3 supplemented sewage. This enriched culture was used to determine, the kinetics of microbial nitrification. The reaction fits the Michaelis-Menten model for temperature from 10° to 35°C, having a temperature optimum at 15°C (saturation constant of 0.72 mg/l NH_3). Nitrification is unaffected by high DO concentrations (38 mg/l, 0_2 at 30°C) after acclimatisation. Nitrite concentrations > 20 mg/l are inhibitory to the reaction.

181 **Chattopadhyay, D.N., Konar, S.K.,** 1989. Removal of detergent toxicity through adsorption by soil particles. Environ. Ecol. 7(2): 441-445.

Two types of soils (sandy loam and sandy clay loam) were added and stirred separately in the solution of three detergents (*Cryptoanionic, non-ionic* and *anionic*) and after 24 hours of settling of these soils the toxicity test of upper clean water was done on Diaptomous forbesi for 24 hours. Generally, both the soils reduced the toxicity of the three detergents tested. The amount of soil was significantly inversely correlated with mortality but the duration of stirring was not significantly correlated with mortality. The detoxification possibly resulted due to simple physical adsorption of detergents on soil surface.

182 **Chaturvedi, A.N.,** 1986. Trees and shrubs for control of tannery waste water in India. Environ. Conserv. 13(2): 164-165.

Twelve species of trees and shrubs — *azadirachta indica (Neem), Pinus roxburghii (Chir), Ficus bengalensis (Bargad), Syaygium cumini (Jamun), Terminalia arjuna (Arjun), Ficus religiosa (Pipal), Pongamia pinnata (Kanji), Baplophragma adenophyllum (Kathsagon), Acacia nilotica (Babul), Cordia dichotoma (Lisora), Cassia auriculata (Awaram), Adhatoda vasica (Arusa)* — were tested for their tolerance to such water at the Forest Researchg Centre, Kanpur (U.P.).

183 **Chaturvedi, Rashmi, Dubey, P.S.,** 1990. Pollutant interaction bioassay employing wheat cultivars. Asian Environ. 12(4): 74-78.

An attempt has been made to study the growth performance of two *Triticum aestivum* cultivars (LOK-1 and WH-147) under individual and combined stress of liquid effluent, sulphur dioxide and 2.4-Dichlorophenoxy acetic acid. The results depict Lok-1 as better equipped cultivar to suit to microclimatic zones with such pollutants in the ambient environment.

184 **Chaturvedi, A.K., Yadava, D.P., Pathak, K.C., Singh, V.N.,** 1990. Defluoridation of water by absorption on fly ash. Water Air Soil Pollut. 49: 51-61.

The ability of fly ash to remove fluoride from water and waste waters has been studied at different concentrations, times, temperatures and pH of the solution. The rate constants of adsorption intraparticle transport, mass transfer coefficients and thermodynamic parameters have been calculated at 30°, 40° and 50°C. The empirical model has been tested at various concentrations for the present system. The removal of fluoride is favourable at low concentration, high temperature and acidic pH.

185 **Chen, Z.S.,** 1989. Cadmium and lead contamination of soils, rice plants and surface water in the Northern Taiwan. Soils Fertilizers Taiwan: 39-47.

Cd and Pb contamination of paddy soils and plants in northern Taiwan are caused by stabilizing materials for plastics produced from 2 chemical plants. Contents of Cd and Pb in paddy soils, brown rice, surface water and sediments are given. Cd was formed mainly in the exchangeable and organic fraction of the polluted soils. Almost equal content (25-30% of total) of Pb occur in the exchangeable, residual and free oxide fractions of the polluted soils, but higher contents of Pb occur in residual (48% of total) than in the other soil fractions of the polluted paleudult soil. Only trace amounts of Cd and Pb were found in brown rice. Correlations of Cd or Pb in the brown rice and soils were not significant.

186 **Chen, Y.Z., Yinmel, Y. Keneng, Z.X.,** 1988. Specific adsorption of copper on soils and clay minerals, Huanjing Kexue Xuebao, 8(4): 411-419.

Adsorption of Cu^{2+} on soils (latosol, yellow brown earth, and volcanic ash soil), kaolinite, montmorillonite, and Fe_2O_3 followed the Langmuir and Freundlich equations. Specific adsorption constants are given. The presence of ionizable Fe in soil samples decreased Cu^{2+} adsorption. The variable electronic charge on Fe_2O_3, volcanic ash soil, and latosol resulted in high adsorption capacities. High pH enhanced the adsorption. Montmorillonite has a constant surface charge and thus showed low adsorption capacity for Cu^{2+}. Its adsorption was not effected by pH. The maximal adsorption capacity is discussed.

187 **Chen, R.L., Patrick, W.H.,** 1980. Nitrogen transformation in a simulated overland flow waste water treatment system. Water Res. 14(8): 1041-1046.

Applications of waste water containing NH_4-N to a simulated overleaf flow model led to the disappearance of NH_4-N and the formation of NO_3. The N balance in simulated overland flow system was estimated by using labeled N^{15}. The amount of N removed in the system depend upon denitrification rates. Nitrogen was adsorbed by soil, and applied NH_4-N was assimilated by the vegetation. The adsorbed NH_4-N of the aerated surface soil mass was nitrified and converted to oxidised forms of N. The nitrogen form diffused downward to the reduced zone subsequent to waste water application. Some of the NO was denitrified in gaseous forms of N or was reduced to organic forms by assimilatory processes. Thus, the net loss of N in an overland flow system was less than that would have been predicted from non-labelled N mass balance calculation.

188 **Chen, C.Y., Roth, J.A., Eckenfelder, W.W., Jr.** 1980. Response of dissolved oxygen to changes in influent organic loading to activated sludge system. Water Res. 14(10): 1449-1457.

A modified laboratory scale activated sludge unit was used to continuously measure the ambient DO Level. The change of DO concentration responded to variations in the influent composition of the waste water. The system was maintained at steady state, and system variables were measured for soluble TOC, MLVSS and O_2 uptake rate. The organic shock loading was induced by increasing or decreasing the baseline feeding of TOC concentration. As soon as a transient loading occurred, the DO levels in the system were continuously monitored with the DO analyser. A simplified material balance equation for DO in the system was developed, and the dynamic behaviour of O_2 uptake rate was examined. Under transient conditions, the change in the DO concentration reflected the variations in the exogenous respiration rate of the biomass in the system due to fluctuations in the influent waste characteristics. Based upon the rapid response to the shock loading and the correlation of the change in the DO level to the magnitude of the shock loading, the DO concentration and O_2 uptake rate generated from this biological monitor showed potential as a control variable for the activated sludge process.

189 **Chen, Yingxu, Zhu, Yinmei, Yuan, Keneng, Zhu, Zuxiang**, 1989. Chemical behaviour in soil. II. Adsorption and reduction of chromium (VI) in soils. Huanjing Kexue Xuebao. 9(2): 137-143.

Adsorption of Cr (VI) to soil particles was satisfactory described by 2 first-order kinetic equations. The adsorption rate was correlated with content of soil organic matter. The maximal amount of Cr adsorbed was related to the content of free Fe_2O_3 and increased markedly after removing the soil organic matter. The adsorption kinetics may be described by the Elorich equation, the porabolic diffusion cquation, and a two constant rate equation. The amounts of Cr adsorption were: dry-land red earth > yellow earth > yellow brown earth > blue-purple soil. It is possible that some of the Cr (VI) in the soil could have been reduced to Cr (III).

190 **Cheng, A.H.D., Hisieh, K.H., Huang, C.P.**, 1989. An interactive microcomputer program for one dimensional solute transport in saturated soil water systems in 'National Water Conference' : 350-357.

This paper presents a microcomputer program for one-dimensional solute transport in saturated soil water system. Eight different types of adsorption isotherms, ranging from linear to non-linear, equilibrium to non-equilibrium, and single to multiple components, are modelled.

191 **Cherry, D.S., Guthrie, R.K.**, 1979. The uptake of chemical elements from coal ash and settling basin effluent by primary producers: II. Relation between concentration in ash deposits and tissues of grasses grown on the ash. Sci. Total Environ. 13(1): 27-31.

The uptake by tissue bioaccumulation of 15 chemical elements within broom sedge (*Andmpogon Virginicus*) and nut grass (*Cyperus retrofractus*) growing in the drainage system of a coal ash basin was studied. Biomagnification of these elements by the grasses was compared to that found in duckweed (*Lemma perpusilla*) within the same system. Aluminum, As, Ba, Cd, Co, Cr, Cu, Fe, Mg, Mn, Mo, Se, Sr, Ti, and Zn were measured in roots, stems, leaves, and fruit of the grasses which grew in sediments within the effluent. Mercury and Zn were biomagnified in both grasses and *durckweed* to a level exceeding the concentration in sediment. All elements were biomagnified above the water concentration in all parts of the plants. Bioaccumulation of elements in the leaves and fruit of these plants provides a concentrated source of potentially toxic chemical elements for passage to animals which may consume these plants.

192 **Cherry, D.Ş., Guthrie, R.K., Singleton, F.L., Harvey R.S.**, 1977. Recovery of aquatic bacterial populations in a stream after cessation of chemical pollution. Water Air Soil Pollut. 7: 95-101.

Times Branch was studied for 1 yr. to determine the effects of an annual loading of about 229900 kg of various chemicals on the bacterial populations of a small fast flowing stream. The 10 yr. discharge of chemical waste to this steam was terminated in 1973 and a yr. study of the streams recovery was begun. Diversity in both systems was more affected by seasonal temperatures than the presence of chemical pollution. Mean total counts dropped from 187×10^3 in the polluted stream to approximate those of the control stream (170×10^3) following cessation of pollution. In the chemically affected stream, per cent chromogens increased from 15% during pollution to 25% approximately 1 yr. after pollution was stopped. The latter percentage was comparable to that of the control stream (28%) during the period of study.

193 **Cheung, T.H., Wong, M.H., Tam, N.F.Y.**, 1989. Root and shoot elongation as an assessment of heavy metal toxicity and Zn equivalent value of edible crops. in Environmental Bioassay Techniques and their Applications. M. Munawar, G. Dixon, C.I. Mayfield. T. Reynoldson, M.H. Sadar. (eds) 377-383.

Seeds of thirteen edible plant species were tested for their response to heavy metals during their early development. It was found that a short term root elongation test of six days could be used to evaluate the degree of toxicity of aqueous samples containing heavy metals. Shoot elongation was found to be less sensitive to metals than root elongation.

194 **Chhabra, R.**, 1989. Sewage water utilization through Forestry, Bull. CSSRI, Karnal : p. 19.

Chemical characteristics of sewage waters of Haryana are presented, Sewage water application increases organic matter, available N, P and K and DTPA extractable Fe, Mn, Zn and Cu. A technology for raising trees with sewage water is presented.

195 **Chhabra, R.**, 1990. Preventing sewage pollution of water bodies through afforestation. J. Instn. Publ. Hlth. Engrs., India. (2): 1-14.

This paper describes a system based on forestry wherein by utilizing the irrigation and nutrient potential of sewage waters right in the area of their production, pollution of lakes and river bodies can be prevented.

196 **Chin, Y.P.**, 1989. Estimating the effects of dispersed organic polymers on

the sorption of contaminants by natural solids. I. A predictive thermodynamic humic substance organic solute inter-action model. Environ. Sci. Technol. 23: 978-984.

A modified flory-huggins model was applied in conjunction with data on solute aqueous activity coefficient to estimate the association of organic contaminants with humic and other organic polymers in aqueous phase. Predictions based on model calibrations to methyl salicylate agreed well with experimental values, for the binding of 14 target compounds.

197 **Chino, M.**, 1981. Metal stress in rice plants. in Heavy Metal Pollution in Soils of Japan. Sci. Soc. Press, Tokyo, 65-80.

The critical levels of metal concentrations in rice plants compiled are given in. The toxic levels of these metals in the tops and in the roots of rice plants can be summarized. In food plants, the critical levels of some toxic metals like Hg and Cd must be established by considering their effects on human health. The maximum allowable limit of Cd in rice grains was set as 1 ppm, although there have been some criticism on this limit among scientists.

198 **Chona, M.K.**, 1990. A preliminary study on variation in quality of sewage at Chandigarh. Himalayan J. Environ. Zoo. 4(1): 55-57.

Sewage samples from primary treatment plant, Chandigarh were analysed for temperature, pH, DO, BOD, TS, TSS, TDS, total alkalinity, total hardness, chlorides and biological characteristics. It has been observed that values of BOD, TSS and TDS vary with time, as these depend upon the quantity of organic matter.

199 **Chona, M.K.; Vasisth, H.S.**, 1989. Reassessment of Chandigarh waste waters. Himalayan J. Environ. Zoo, 3(2): 255-258.

Effluents of Amrit Flour Mill, nickel plating industry, milk plant, combined industrial and domestic sewage have been analysed for temperature, pH, DO, BOD, suspended solids, nitrites, nitrates, phosphates, chlorides, total hardness and total alkalinity parameters and biological characteristics. There was an overall increase in pollution load since 1976.

200 **Chong, C., Cline, R.A., Rinker, D.L.**, 1988. Use of paper mill sludge in container crop culture.Landscape Trades. 10 (7): 17-18.

Four types of paper mill sludge added at 33% by volume in containers were evaluated: primary; secondary; a mixture of primary and secondary from the Quebec and Ontario Paper Co,: and a mixture of primary and secondary from the Fraser Paper Co. *Spiraea bumalda* grew best in amended secondary sludge, which had the highest initial N content. In contrast, poorest growth occurred in Fraser mixture which had the lowest initial N content. Growth and also initial N content in other sludges were intermediate. Leaf nutrients did not reflect sludge treatments.

201 **Chong, C., Cline, R.A., Rinker, D.K.,** 1987. Spent mushroom and paper mill sludge as soil amendments for containerised nursery crops. Proc. Internatl. Plant Prop Soc. 37: 347-353.

Two sources of mushroom compost were evaluated as soil amendments with bark: (1) unweathered (UMC) in proportions of 25, 50, 75 and 100% by volume, and (2) weathered (WMC) in proportions of 25, 50 and 75%. There was also a 100% bark control treatment. Both red osier dogwood (*Cornus stoloniferasyn. C. sericeal*) and forsythai (*Forsythia x intermedia Lynwood*) grew well in all media. While plant height was little affected by the amount of mushroom compost in the media., top dry weight of the two species was increased in proportion to the amount of both UMC and WMC. Regardless of the media treatment, there was no apparent symptoms of nutrient toxicity or deficiency. Of four types of paper mill sludge (primary, secondary, mixtures of primary and secondary) added at 33% by volume to bark, secondary sludge which has the highest N content provided the best growth of spiraea (Spiraea x bumelda). However foliage of plants was dark blue green in colour reflecting high N. Unacceptably poor growth occurred in Fraser amended media because of low N.

202 **Choudhary, S.K., Jha, A.N., Srivastava, D.K.,** 1987. Effect of paper mill effluent on seed germination and seedling growth of maize. Environ. Eco. 5(2): 285-287.

Maize seeds were kept for germination in petridishes containing equal amount of soil treated with different concentrations of effluent (0, 5, 10, 25, 50, 75, 100%). Up to 25% concentration, both the percent of germination and seedling growth were increased, but it decreased at higher concentration. At 25% concentration, over all growth of seedling was better that in control. The values of total chlorophyll, chlorophyll a and b increased up to 50% concentration. However, the chlorophyll contents were higher in 75% than that in control.

203 **Chris, J.,** 1984. Content and chemical form of mercury and selenium in soil, sludge, and fertiliser materials. Water Air Soil Pollut. 22: 95-104.

The content and chemical form of Hg and Se were determined for several samples of municipal sewage sludge and sludge ash, garden soil having a history of sludge and residential compost application, and selected fertilizer materials (peat moss, cow manure, residential compost, composted municipal refuse and sewage sludge, miloganite). Municipal sewage sludge had the highest level of total Hg (av. 1240 ppb), while sludge ash had the lowest levels (av. 5.6 ppb). Total selenium levels were lowest in compost (av. 225 ppb), while being highest in sludge ash (av. 11550 ppb). The methylmercury percentage was fairly constant for all samples, averaging 6.0% of the total Hg content. Hexavalent Se averaged 24.3% of the total Se content, and was notably higher in sludge and fertilizer samples. Successive annual application of sludge and compost to garden soil resulted in a gradual increase of total Hg and Se in the soil, but had no significant influence on chemical form distribution of both elements.

204 **Christensen, T.H.,** 1985. Cadmium soil sorption at low concentrations: III. Prediction and observation of mobility. Water Air Soil Pollut. 26(3): 255-264.

The applicability of relative solute velocity equations for prediction of migration of low concentrations of Cd under intermittent flow conditions was studied by means of eleven small laboratory soil columns monitored for 600 days in terms of Cd break-through curves. The predicted Cd velocities agreed well with the column observations. The soils studied showed only slightly curvilinear equilibrium isotherms and the use of the Freundlich isotherm based equation in preference for the linear distribution based equation was not justified in this case. The use of the relative solute velocity equations for intermittent flow conditions requires that the relative solute velocity is interpreted as a relative Darcy-velocity and that the water saturated porosity is employed in the equations. The observed relative Cd velocities were 0.0015 to 0.002 indicating a very limited mobility.

205 **Christensen, T.H.,** 1985. Cadmium soil sorption at low concentrations. IV. Effects of waste leachates on distribution coefficients. Water Air Soil Pollut. 26(3): 265-274.

Sorption onto two mineral soils of Cd present at low concentrations in unpolluted soils solution and waste leachates (compost, incinerator slag, sewage sludge) was examined by laboratory batch experiments in terms of kinetics, equilibrium distributions isotherms and the effect of pH. Sorption of Cd from waste leachates is a fast process although slightly slower than from unpolluted soil solution. Both soils exhibited approximately linear sorption isotherms for all solutes. The slope of the isotherms, the Cd distribution coefficient, was 30 to 250 — times smaller from waste leachates than from unpolluted soil solution, indicating a much increased mobility of Cd in waste leachates. The effect of pH on the Cd distribution coefficients was less consistent in waste leachate than in unpolluted soil solution, varying from hardly any effect to a 7-fold increase for a pH increase of approximately one unit.

206 **Christensen, T.H.,** 1989. Cadmium soil sorption at low concentration. VII. Effect of stable solid waste leachate complexes. Water Air Soil Pollut.: 44:43-56.

Soil sorption of Cd in solid waste leachates of land fill, sewage sludge, and incinerator residue was studied in the laboratory. Speciation method was employed to determine free divalent Cd and complexed Cd of various stability. The experiments involved 13 soil types. Speciation of Cd present in solution after exposure to increasing amounts of soil showed that stable Cd complexes did not sorb onto the soil. This was supported by equilibrium isotherms exhibiting similar solute concentration intercepts and by a leaching study of soil columns which resulted in the same concentrations of stable Cd complexes.

207 **Christie, P., Beattie, J.A.M.,** 1989. Grassland soil microbial biomass and accumulation of potentially toxic metals from long-term slurry applications. J. Appl. Ecol., 26(2): 597-612.

A randomized block field experiment compared three application rates (50, 100 and 200 m^3/ha/year) of pig and cow slurries with fertilized and control plots of perennial rye grass for 17 years. Herbage copper and zinc contents were determined at the first cut of 1986. The amounts of carbon and nitrogen in the soil biomass were strongly correlated with soil pH. The highest application rate of pig slurry lowered the soil biomass carbon content and increased soil organic carbon content in the top 5 cm of the profile after 16 years. Slurry application rates did not reduce the size of the soil biomass, lead to phytotoxic concentrations of copper or zinc in the soil, or increase herbage copper or zinc concentration likely to be toxic to grazing animals.

208 **Chu, L.M., Bradshaw, A.D.,** 1990. The effect of pulverized refuse fines (PRF) as a soil material on plant growth. Resources, Cons. Recycling 4(4): 257-269.

A greenhouse experiment was carried out to evaluate the effectiveness of pulverized refuse fines (PRF) as a soil amendment for plant growth. PRF was slightly alkaline and high in organic carbon and soluble salts. Unamended PRF supported significantly higher yields of ryegrass (Lolium perenne) than PRF mixed with a sandy soil at 2 and 10% (w/w), and was comparable to that of sewage sludge and sludge-amended PRF. However, PRF supplemented with inorganic nitrogen or phosphorus resulted in better yields than PRF alone. Despite the high C:N ratio of PRF, nitrogen recovery in ryegrass suggested that mineralisation was sufficiently high to allow adequate plant uptake and sustained plant growth, although there was initial inhibition. Tissue contents of zinc, copper and cadmium from pure PRF treatments were not excessive and were lower than those from sewage sludge. High rate applications of PRF should not cause environmental degradation. Use of PRF as a commercial fertilizer or potting media is not recommended, but it may be an excellent soil substitute in horticulture and land reclamation.

209 **Chung, D.Y., Boyd, S.A.,** 1987. Mobility of sludge-borne 3, 3′-dichlorobenzidine in soil columns. J. Environ. Qual. 16: 147-151.

Fate of the carcinogen 3,3′-dichlorohenqidine (DCB) in sludge-amended soil was evaluated. DCB was shown to be very persistent in soil and sludge-amended soil with < 2% of the added (^{14}C) DCB evolved as CO_2 during a 182-d incubation. Mobility of DCB was evaluated by using soil columns (5 to 45 cm) that were irrigated with 2.54 cm water d^{-1} for 84 d. The total C recovered in leachate water was from 0.16 to 0.063% of the total ^{14}C added to the top 14 cm of the soil column at zero time. The strong binding of DCB to soil constituents rendered it highly immobile despite being placed in a sandy soil that was irrigated with large amounts of water.

210 **Ciavatta, C., Sequi, P.,** 1989. Evaluation of chromium released during the decomposition of leather meal fertilizers applied to the soil. Fertilizer Res. 19(1): 7-11.

Humification of leather meal added to soil as granules, took approximately 300 days for completion, but as a powder took longer humification immediately under aerobic conditions and after about 40 days under anaerobic conditions EDTA-extractable and water soluble Cr present in leather decreased sharply immediately after incorporation of fertilizers in soil, after 40 days of incubation. However, there was a pronounced increase especially of EDTA extractable Cr; thereafter there was a decrease. Chromium is continuously released from leather during the decomposition of organic matter and then becomes insoluble. No detectable amounts of Cr (VI) have been found during the entire period of incubation; addition of Cr(VI) resulted in an immediate transformation to Cr(III). The release of Cr when leather is used as a fertilizer, is of little agronomic or environmental significance.

211 **Clarke, B.B., Brennan, E.,** 1989. Differential cadmium accumulation and phyto-toxicity in sixteen tobacco cultivars J. Air. Waste. Manage, Assoc. 39(10): 1319-1322.

When low levels of $CdC1_2$ (0.25 to 1.0 ppm) were added to the nutrient solution of 16 tobacco cultivars growing in sand culture, the heavy metal was partitioned in the following order: leaves > roots > stems. Because leaves are the commercial products, this pattern of partitioning is highly undesirable. The concentration of Cd accumulated in the tissues varies with plant genotype and level of Cd treatment. The 0.25 ppm Cd treatment, a maximum of 127.6 ppm Cd was found in foliage of the Coker-48 variety, and at the 1.0 ppm Cd treatment a maximum of 382.6 ppm Cd was detected in the foliage of "NC-232". None of the Cd treated tobacco plants exhibited visual foliar symptoms commonly observed in other plant species.

212 **Clarke, B., Harkov, R.; Brennan, E.,** 1982. Tomato root: site of initial alteration in minor elements in cadmium treated plants. J. Air Pollut. Control Assoc., 32 : 84-86.

The cadmium-zinc association in particular has received attention for several reasons: (1) the elements occur together in native rock, (2) they share some common properties as indicated by their adjacent position on the Periodic Table, (3) they compete for adsorption sites on plant roots and (4) both may play a role in iron metabolism. The published results concerning the Cd-Zn relationship have been conflicting in respect to the direction and magnitude of the change in microelement concentration and organ affected.

213 **Claussent, T.,** 1990. Dry ash a better reference base than dry matter for heavy metals and other persistent pollutants. Plant Soil. 127(1): 91-95.

This work demonstrates with the use of heavy metal contaminated poplar leaves that ash of dry matter (dry ash) obviously yields a better reference, as it eliminates the natural variations among organic substance contents. Values of heavy metal concentrations in dry ash of leaves were generally more homogeneous and better correlated with corresponding values in air and soil than those in dry matter. It is further shown that concentration of non-bio-decomposable and non volatile pollutants in the mineral fraction (the same as ash) of, plants and their residues (autumn leaves, mulch compost) can directly be compared with those in soil (nearly 100% mineral), and vice versa. This facilitates the setting of maximally permissible values for pollutant concentrations in plant dry matter or their residues, and in soil, which can be used in the protection of soils against pollutants accumulated in fresh or fallen leaves, mulch or compost.

214 **Cleardin, F, Chabbey, L., Chatenou, X.L., Meylan, G.,** 1990. Heavy metals in composts. Reveue Horticole Suisse. 63: 45-51.

Results are presented on the conc. of heavy metals in the 0-10 mm and 10-40 mm fractions of urban refuse and plant residue composts prepared by with and without sorting process. The high Pb conc. in composts was obtained from materials in the vicinity of roads and high ways.

215 **Clothier, B.E.,** 1988. Root zone processes and water quality: the impact of management, in Proc. Internl. Sympo. on Water Quality Modelling of Agricultural Non-point Sources. Part 2: 658-688.

Better management to minimize the increasing problem of agricultural non- point source pollution will arise from clearer understanding of the small scale processes of water and chemical movement in the root zone of crops. Improved field measurement and analytical description will be required initially. Four critical processes are identified as being poorly understood: (1) the effects of aerial plant parts on controlling the arrival of water and chemical at the soil surface: (2) the effects of the structure of the soil surface on the pattern of water and chemical entry into the root zone; (3) the dynamics and behaviour of plant roots as they extract water and chemicals; (4) the unsaturated redistribution of water within and below the root zone. Computer simulation is one means by which these small scale processes can be synthesized and integrated into models for assessing the impact of agricultural management on water quality.

216 **Cocke, C.L., Brown, K.W.,** 1987. The effect of sewage sludge on the physical properties of lignite overburden. Reclam. Reveg. Res., 6(2): 83-93.

This study was conducted to determine the influence of sewage sludge applications on the physical properties of reclaimed mine spoil. The treatments included controls, plots receiving 0.224 Mg ha^{-1} nitrogen as fertilizer, 0.112 Mg Ha^{-1} as fertilizer plus 0.112 Mg ha^{-1} anticipated mineralisable N as sewage sludge. Adjacent sets of identical plots were prepared 1 year apart, and data were collected during the second year to allow comparisons, under similar climatic regimes. Water infiltration from simulated rainfall, aggregate stability, available soil water and vegetation yields all increased significantly as a result of sludge application. Infiltration on plots receiving only sewage sludge averaged 38% greater than the control plots for both years.

217 **Cohen, J., Hillel, I.S.,** 1973, Galiforms, fecal coliforms, and fecal streptococci as indicators of water pollution. Water Air Soil Pollut. 2: 85-95.
The presence and survival of coliforms, fecal coliforms, and fecal streptococci were studied in sewage treatment plants, heavily polluted rivers, a lake and other drinking water sources. In all cases, the fecal streptococci were generally more resistant to the natural water environment and to purification processes than the other indicator organisms and, at points distant from the original source of pollution were often the only indicators of the fecal nature of the pollution. In two of the systems studied, the survival of the fecal streptococci paralleled the survival of enteric viruses better than the coliforms. The fecal streptococci may thus in certain cases provide a better estimate of the probable virus content in lightly contaminated water than the other two indicators.

218 **Collins, B.J., Sell, N.J.,** 1982. Lead contamination associated with snowmobile trails. Environ. Res. 27(1): 159-163.
Lead associated with one season's use of a snowmobile trail was determined. Pb in the snow and, particularly, in the associated soil/particulate matter was extremely high, ranging upward to 136 μ g-atom Pb/m^2 where the trail narrows to approximately 2m. In comparison to these levels, the lead present in field soil due to automobile traffic on nearby roads was found to be negligible.

219 **Colpaert, J.V., Van Assche, J.A.,** 1987, Heavy metal tolerance in some ectomycorrhizal fungi. Funct. Ecol. 1(4): 415-421.
The metal tolerance of isolates of some common ectomycorrhizal fungi of Pinus and Betula spp, collected on heavily metal polluted sites was compared with that of strains of the same species from non-polluted areas. The strains isolated from carpophores on unpolluted soils were greatly inhibited by the metal whereas most of the strains were still able to grow very well at concentrations of 10000 μgZn/g soil.

220 **Colwell, R.R., Orndoff, S.A.,** 1980. Microbial transformation of Kepone. Appl. Environ. Microbiol. 39(2): 398-406.
Pseudomonas aeruginosa strain KO3 and a mixed aerobic enrichment culture, isolated from sewage sludge lagoon water, aerobically trans-

formed the chlorinated insecticide Kepone, yielding monohydro-Kepone. Identification of the product was confirmed by GC and electron impact MS. The mixed culture and P. aeruginosa strain KO3 produced 4% and 16% respectively, dihydro-Kepone. Reduced amounts of monohydro-Kepone, compared with the mixed and pure culture, were produced by James River sediment micro-organisms. Kepone was not utilised as sole C or energy source by any of the bacteria of mixed cultures examined. Although alteration of Kepone can occur via microbiology action, the rate and extent of transformation are such that microbial action will not cause rapid removal of the compound from the natural environment.

221 **Connor, G.A.O., Knudsten, K.L., Connell, G.A.,** 1986. Phosphorus solubility in sludge-amended calcareous soils. J. Environ. Qual. 15(3): 308-312.

Sludge addition to calcareous soils in New Mexico increased water soluble and $NaHCO_3$ extractiable P as well as plant uptake of P, whereas inorganic fertilizer P has often been ineffectual. Both greenhouse and field data, representing several croppings of amended soils were examined. Ancillary effects, primarily slight pH reductions, associated with sludge additions to the soils were apparently responsible for increased P solubility in amended soils.

222 **Constable, T.W., McBean, E.R.,** 1979. BOD/TOC correlations and their application to water quality evaluation. Water Air Soil Pollut. 11: 363-375.

The predictive capabilities of the derived BOD_5/TOC models are examined for interpolation and extrapolation potentials for augmenting water quality data information bases. Use of the models to reduce the statistical uncertainty associated with BOD measurements is considered.

223 **Cooke, M., Jackson, A., Nickless, G., Roberts, D.J.,** 1979. Distribution and speciation of cadmium in the terrestrial snail, Helix aspersa. Bull. Environl. Contam. Toxicol. 23: 445-451.

Snails from clean and polluted sites were collected and analysed. Cadmium is taken up by terrestrial snails in polluted areas and 95% of the total Cd and Zn is stored in the digestive gland. The Cd binds itself to protein with a molecular weight of 22,000 daltons and although water soluble, the Cd-protein complex is not excreted. The Cd: Zn ratio of the soluble extracts and pellets indicate that Zn is complexed in such a way that it is insoluble or not extractable by water.

224 **Cool, M., Marcoux, F., Paulin, A., Mehra, M.C.,** 1980. Metalic contaminants in streets soil of Moncton, New Braunswick, Canada. Bull. Environl. Contam. Toxicol. 25(3): 409-415.

Soil samples, 2-5cm deep, were collected from 22 sites along streets with high automobile circulation and side streets with limited traffic density. At 9 locations, samples were collected 3.5 and 7.0 m from the asphalted surface. All the samples had Pb, Cd, Zn, Mn, Fe, Cu, Na, and

Ca with Fe having the highest concentration, and Cd the lowest. Lead, Cu and Zn concentrations decreased as distance from the road increased while Fe and Mn concentrations were not affected.

225 **Cooper, A.B., Morgan, H.N.,** 1982. Biodegradation of milk when applied to soil. N.Z. Agric. Res. 25(1): 15-20.

Degradation rates of milk applied to soils were not influenced by soil type but were significantly affected by temperature. Of the major substrates present in added milk, the milk lipids were the most resistant to decomposition. Lipase production by the soil microflora coincided with lipid hydrolysis. Application of more milk to the same soil resulted in a more rapid respiratory response and lipid degradation. When milk fats alone were applied to soil, their hydrolysis was much slower than when the equivalent fat concentration had been applied as milk.

226 **Cordonnier, M.J.,** 1981. Yield and development of soybean (*Glycine Max* L.) as affected by irrigation with Municipal waste water and well water. Diss. Abst. Int. Pt. Sci. & Engg. 42(6): p. 95.

The irrigated plots received a total of 9.8 cm of either well water or waste water as spray irrigation in 1979 and 9.4 cm in 1980. Data were collected for seed yield, agronomic characteristics, dry matter production, apparent photosynthesis and leaf chemical analysis.

227 **Couillard, D., Tran, F.T., Tyagi, R.D.,** 1991. Process for the *in situ* restoration of oil contaminated soils. J. Environ. Manage. 32(1): 19-34.

The study was dealt with the cleaning of beach sand contaminated by an accidental oil spill and the decontamination of bottom sludges from petroleum oil tanks. In the first application, a laboratory feasibility study demonstrated that this extraction process (using pressurized hot water) is capable of yielding solid residues (mostly clean sand) which contain hardly any traces of oil and are therefore safe for disposal. The recovery of heavy oil is almost 100 per cent.

228 **Cranston, G.N., Adams, J.C.,** 1978. Effect of sewage lagoon effluent on the concentration of fluorescent and denitrifying bacteria in a High Plains River. J. Environ. Qual. 7: 377-380.

Fecal coliforms, fluorescent bacteria and denitrifying bacteria were enumerated in a high Plains river and in the effluent from sewage lagoons before and after entrance into the river for a period of 13 months. All bacterial groups increased at least 100-fold during the winter in the effluent from the lagoons. Thirty isolates of denitrifying bacteria obtained during the winter were determined to belong in the genus Pseudomonal. The vast majority of these isolates were psychrophile.

229 **Crawford, R.L., Oreilly, K.T., Tao, H.L.,** 1989. Micro-organism stabilization for in situ degradation of toxic chemicals. In Biotechnology, and Biodegradation, (Eds. Kameley, D. et al) Gulf Pub. Comp. Houston. p.:

203-211.

When pure cultures of bacteria are introduced into natural environments such as soil or subsurface waters, they often do not persist because they are not competitive with natural microbial populations, or these environments are too toxic or oligotrophic to support growth or maintenance requirements of the added cells. To improve prospects for successful in situ bioremediation of aquifers contaminated by toxic chemicals, methods are needed to stabilize microbial cells so that they persist following introduction into hostile natural environment. It was found that immobilization of pollutant degrading bacteria in polymeric matrices such as alginate or polyurethnace stabilized them for introduction into surface soils or waters. This stabilisation is at least partly a result of protection of the immobilized microbial cells from pollutant toxicity.

230 **Crouch, M.S.**, 1990. Check soil contamination easily. Chem. Eng. Prog. 86(9): 41-45.

Soil vapor surveys enable the mapping of soil contamination without sophisticated analyses and instrumentation.

231 **Czaznowska, K., Gworek, B.**, 1992. The effect of urban pollution on the heavy metal content of soils and vegetables in Warsaw allotment garden. Roczniki NaHk Rolniczy ch. A. 107(2): 23-33.

Levels of Mn, Zn, Cu, Ni, Co, Cr, Cd, and Pb were reported for soils, lettuce leaves and red beet and carrot roots on 22 allotments at distance of 30 to 100 m from a road. The metal content of lettuce leaves was higher near the road than away from it. Carrot and beet roots had lower metal content than aerial parts, but the Pb in the roots was above the permitted level.

232 **Czarnowski, W, Krechniak, J.**, 1990. Fluoride in the urine, hair and nails of phosphate fertilizer workers. British J. Industrial Medicine. 47(3): 349-351.

233 **Czuba, M.**, 1987. Methylmercury toxicity in plant cultures. Modification of resistance and cemethylation by light and/or 2, 4 - dichlorophenovyacetic acid. Ecotoxicol. Environ. Saf., 13, 191-201.

Cultures of *Daucus carota*, (Ca-68-10,) and *Lactucasativa*, Le-67) were grown at increasing methyl mercury (MeMg) concentrations ranging from initial doses of 0.05 to 5.0 μg/mL per day for 4 days with or without 0.15 μg/ml 2, 4-dichloro-phenoxyacetic acid (2, 4-D) in the presence or absence of light. The presence of 2, 4-D interacted with light synergistically in the expression of MeHg toxicity within the whole range of concentrations. Demethylation patterns increased or decreased depending on the species, the 2, 4-D concentration in the medium, and methyl mercury concentration used in the treatment. Lettuce was more sensitive to this interaction than carrot. In lettuce, the presence of 2 4-D in the light lowered the concentration of total Hg (or MeHg) required to reduce growth by 50%, about 13 times relative to that in the dark. In the absence or 2, 4-D the pattern was reversed.

234 **Czuba, M., Hutchinson, T.C.**, 1980. Copper and lead levels in crops and soils of the Holland Marsh Area-Ontario J. Environ. Qual. 9(4): 566-575.

A comparison is made between the Pb and Cu concentrations in undrained, uncultivated areas of the Marsh and in the intensively used horticultural areas. Analyses show a marked accumulation of Cu in surface layers of cultivated soils; Undrained areas had elevated Pb levels. Cultivation appeared to have increased Cu, but lowered Pb. Copper and lead levels found in the crops were generally higher in the young spring vegetables. Cultivation procedures, including past pesticide applications and fertilizer additions, appeared to be principal sources of Cu. Mobility from the soil and into the plant for these elements in the marsh soils is discussed.

235 **Dahiya, D.J., Mahendra Singh, Narwal, R.P., Singh, J.P.**, 1990. Effect of chloride and sulphate of copper on salinity, pH and nitrogen mineralisation of soil during growing of wheat. J. Indian Soc. Soil Sci. 38(3): 555-557.

The effects of copper salts on the properties of a Typic Ustochrept growing wheat in a pot experiment were studied. The soil's electrical conductivity increased, while pH decreased with time and increasing concn. of copper salts. At low salt concn., dry matter yields increased, but they were depressed by greater concn. Nitrogen uptake decreased, whereas residual soil N and losses of N increased with increasing concn. of copper salts.

236 **Dalal, T., Bairgai, P.**, 1985. Effect of mercury, arsenic and lead on germination and seedling growth of two jute varieties. Environ. Ecol. 3(3): 403-407.

The effects of mercury, arsenic and lead (5, 10, 20, mg/1) each on jute varieties *corchorus olitorius* L.cv. JRO 524 and *corchorus capsular L. cv. JRC 321* were studied. The treatments (10 & 20 mg/l) of the metal pollutants decreased germination percentage, length of root, shoot and whole seedling chlorophyll content and dry weight, and increased protein content and tissue permeability over control. The effects were most pronounced with 20 mg/l. The harmful effects of the metals were, in general: As> Hg> Pb. There was no marked change in these parameters at 5 mg/l of the metals over control. *C. olitorius* showed more resistance to the metals tested than the other variety.

237 **Dalmau, J.L., Garau, M.A.F., Felipo, M.T.**, 1990. Laboratory prediction of soluble compounds before soil recycling of wastes. Internatl. J. Environ. Analyt Chem. 39(2): 141-146.

To predict the release of available nutrients and potentially toxic elements, a laboratory study was conducted with two wastes i.e. sewage sludge and fly ash. Loading rates of 500t/ha of fly ash increased water soluble compounds in soil solution and the sewage sludge N mineralisation was inhibited.

238 **Danana Goud, H., Parekh, L.J., Ramakrishnan, C.V.**, 1985. Bacterial profile of petrochemical industry effluents. Environl. Pollut. (A)., 39(1): 27-37.

Petrochemical industry effluents contain potential cultures of bacteria which show a capacity to utilise hydrocarbons and also have resistance to heavy metals. Among the 92 isolates, four bacterial cultures, namely *Pseudomonas* spp. P-51, *Bacillus* spp P-69. *Aeromonas* spp P-71 and *Azotobacter* spp P-23, grow well on petrochemicals such as benzene, butanol, ethylene glycol, n-heptane, methanol, acetonitrile, phenol and xylene, and show resistance to heavy metals such as cobalt, copper, lead, mercury, molybdenum and zinc. This suggests that they may play an important role in the purification of petrochemical industry effluents.

239 **Das, D.**, 1989. Kinetics of release of zinc in rice soils. Environ. Ecol. 7(4): 966-968.

The amount of DTPA-extractable Zn was influenced by the application of organic matter (FYM) in different times and the amount of release of Zn was consistently more in the treatment receiving organic matter 28 days before puddling or non-pudding of the soil throughout the period of incubation. The amount of extractable Zn, was also found to be increased at saturated soil moisture as compared to water logged soil moisture regimes. The puddling itself had no significant effect on the extractability of Zn.

240 **Davani, B., Ingram, J., Gardea, J.C., Eiceman, G.H.**, 1986. Organic compounds in soils and sediments from unlined waste disposal pits for natural gas production and processing. Water Air Soil Pollut. 27: 267-276.

Samples of soil in dry waste pits and of sediment from waste pits currently in use for natural gas production in New Mexico were collected for characterization of the presence and concentration of organic compounds. Analysis of hexane extracts of samples showed presence of a complex mixture of 40 to 50 organic compounds in dry soil and in sediments from in-use pits. The range of the size for compounds was C_{10} to C_{25}. Although no compounds were detected in GC analysis of subsequent benzene and methanol extracts of the same soil samples, their extracts were highly colored and contained 5 to 10% of total absorptivity at 254 mm. Total extractable residues in the hexane extracts ranged from 49 to 110 mg g^{-1} of soil. Polycyclic aromatic hydrocarbons were detected in hexane extracts at concentration of 270 to 870 $\mu g\ g^{-1}$ of dry sample.

241 **Davidson, C.I., Chu, L.**, 1981. Scanning electron microscope study of iron-containing particles on Foxtail. Environ. Sci. and Technol. 15, (2): 198-201.

Samples of *Setaria viridis* (Wild foxtail) were collected from the side of a heavily travelled road near a steel manufacturing region in Pittsburgh. The particles were nearly perfect spheres of somewhat uniform diameter. Application of deposition theories from the literature suggests that inertial impaction in low Reynolds number flow is responsible for transport of these particles onto the vegetation.

242 **Davies, B.E.,** 1990. Sources, contents and bio-availability of lead in polluted soils with special reference to Wales, Great Britain in Trans 14th Internl. Cong. Soil Sci. Tokyo, Vol II. 78-83.

The mechanisms whereby lead mining has lead contamination of soils and crops are briefly discussed. The rate of decontaminations varies widely, but can be very low. Recent data have shown the presence of increased lead levels in people living in former lead mining areas of Wales.

243 **Davies, B.E., Ballinger, R.C.,** 1990. Heavy metals in soils in North Somerset England with special reference to contamination from base metal mining in the Mendips. Environ. Geochem. Health 12(4): 291-330.

A2 × 2 km grid survey of surface soils was conducted over 600 km of North Somerset, England to investigate the role of pollution from former base metal mines on soil heavy metal content. Soil contents of Pb, Zn, Cu and Cd were determined by atomic absorption spectrometry after extraction in hot, concentrated nitric acid. Most of the soils were contaminated by lead, zinc and cadmium. Isoline maps and perspective block diagram showed this contamination to be most severe on the Mendip plateau especially in the vicinity of Shipham, Wells and Priddy districts.

244 **Davies, B.E., Crews, H.M.,** 1983. The contribution of heavy metals in potato peel to dietrary intake. Environ. 30: 262-264.

For potatoes grown in soil contaminated by Pb/Zn smelter smoke, it was observed that Cd and Pb accumulated in the peel. When potatoes are baked both skin and tuber to diet, it was concluded that normally when both are eaten together there is no risk to health from ingesting excess of toxic metals.

245 **Davies, B.E., Ginnever, R.C., Lear, J.M.,** 1981. Cadmium and lead contaminated soils in some British Metal Mining Areas. in "Trace Substances in Environment Health-XV Univ. Missouri Columbia, Mo: 323-332.

Heavy metal contamination is common in fields and garden areas where lead was once mined in plain. Cadmium and Pb uptake by radish was investigated in field garden plots. Plots were established both in the limestone and non-limestone mining areas. The edible root of radish accumulated significant amounts of metals in each area. EDTA proved a useful extractant for estimating plant available Cd and Pb; but the relationship for Cd was non-linear. The Halkyn area has the severest Pb problem and the Mendips the severest Cd problem.

246 **Davies, B.E., Wixson, B.G.,** 1987. Use of factor analysis to differentiate pollutants from other trace metals in surface soils of the mineralized area of Madison Country, Missouri, USA. Water Air Soil Pollut. 33(3-4): 339-348.

Barium, Be, Co, Cu, Li, Mn, Pb, Sr, and V concentrations were determined in 97 surface soil samples collected 1000 m apart on a regular grid. Strong correlations were observed between several metals and statistically significant correlations were found between others. The data were then analysed by R mode factor analysis. Three factors satisfactory explained the data variance as follows: factor 1 (55% variance) comprised of a group of elements which contaminated local soils as a consequence of operations connected with non-ferrous metal mining. Factor 2 (33% variance) contained elements which accumulated in soils during weathering. The remaining elements were grouped together in factor 3 (12% variance) and here soil contents appeared to be controlled by rock composition.

247 **Davis, R.D.,** 1980. Uptake of fluoride by ryegrass grown in soil treated with sewage sludge. Environl. Pollut. (Ser. B. Chemical & Physical) 1(4): 277-284.

Italian ryegrass *(Lolium multiflorum)* was grown in pots of soil treated with a F-rich sludge. There was an approximately linear relationship between F applied to soil in sludge and concentration of F in ryegrass tissue. Applications of 8.7 t/ha dry matter of the sludge tested (=290 kg/ha of F) produced potentially toxic concentrations of F in the first cut of ryegrass, but plant tissue concentrations of 'S decreased progressively in 2 later cuts. Every 100 mg/kg increase in the concentration of F in soil resulting from treatment with sludge produced an increase in the concentrations of F in ryegrass of 18 mg/kg dm at cut 1,8 mg/kg at cut 2, and 5 mg/kg at cut 3. In field conditions, direct ingestion of sludge and soil by grazing cattle may be as important a source of dietary F as that ingested in herbage.

248 **Davis, R.D.,** 1989. Agricultural utilisation of sewage sludge in Agril. and the environment: Technical Papers. Institution of Water and Environmental Management. Annual Symposium: 11.

Forty per cent of the UK's sewage sludge production is applied to agril. land. Current practice seeks to maximise benefits to farmers whilst controlling potential problems of public nuisance, water pollution, pathogen transmission and soil contamination. Until now this has carried out under government guidelines but an EC Directive is being implemented. The paper also examines the agricultural value of sludge, pollution control, pathogens and soil contamination.

249 **David, J.W., Madsen, S.S.,** 1991. The biodegradation of methylene chloride in soils. Environ. Toxicol. Chem. 10(4): 463-474.

The aerobic biodegradation of methylene chloride was observed in a variety of surface soils including a sand, a sandy loam and a sandy clay loam, as well as a subsurface clay soil. Degradation was found to occur over concentrations ranging from approximately 0.1 to 5.0 ppm. Degradation at higher concentrations was facilitated by the presence of an exogenous organic carbon source. No products other than carbon dioxide were detected in the biologically active microcosms. The time required for 50% disappearance of the parent compound varied over 100-fold, ranging from 1.3 to 181.4 d. Pre-exposure of the soil to methylene chloride resulted in faster rates of degradation upon subsequent exposures. Methylene chloride degradation was also observed under anaerobic conditions in the sandy loam soil.

250 **Dawson, R.A.**, 1978. Sludge management in the paint and coating industry. Sludge Magazine 2(5): 32-38.

An industry profile prepared indicated that 39 of 129 EPA priority pollutants are present in paint waste water, and BOD and COD occurred at relatively high levels. Although physical/chemical treatment systems removed many conventional and priority pollutants, levels for many remained high in the effluent.

251 **Day, A.D., Abdul Rahman, Katterman, R.R.H., Jensen, V.**, 1974. Effects of treated municipal waste water and commercial fertilizer on growth, fiber, acid-soluble nucleotides, protein and amino acid content in wheat hay. J. Environ. Qual. 3(1): 17-18.

Experiments were conducted to study effects of treated municipal waste water on growth, total fiber, acid soluble nucleotides, total protein and amino acids in hay from wheat. Plant heights and number of culms per plant for Resurgence: polluted from mine drainage, also contaminated soils at the base of the Mendip slopes and over the lowlands, trace element enriched Liassic shales significant local anomalies.wheat grown with waste water were similar to plant heights of a number of culms per plant when wheat was produced with well water and suggested amounts of N, P & K and when it was grown with well water plus N, P & K in amounts equal to those in waste water. Wheat plants grown with waste water had culms with a larger diameter and a higher total fiber content than did plants produced with the other treatments. Highest hay yields were obtained when wheat was grown with waste water followed by hay produced with well water plus N, P & K in amounts present in waste water and hay grown with well water plus suggested amounts of N, P & K in decreasing order. Wheat plants from the three irrigation and fertilizer treatments contained similar amounts of acid-soluble nucleotides. Wheat grown with well water plus N, P & K in amounts equal to those in waste water and hay produced with waste water alone contained similar amounts of total protein and more protein than did hay grown with well water plus suggested amounts of N, P & K. Wheat utilized the N in waste water more efficiently than it used the N in well water plus N, P & K equal to waste water. The amino acids alanine glycine, phenyl alanine and tyrosime were present in higher concentrations in wheat hay grown with waste water than in hay produced with the other two treatments. Hay grown with the three irrigation and fertilizer treatments contained similar amounts of leucine, proline and threonine. When wheat hay was grown with waste water, none of the observed amino acids were decreased below the levels at which they were present in hay produced with suggested cultural practices.

252 **Day, J.P., Fergusson, J.E., Chee, T.M.,** 1979. Solubility and potential toxicity of lead in urban street dust. Bull. Environl. Contam. Toxicol. 23(4-5): 497-502.

Samples consisted of loose surface material collected from road side gutters and pavements and from paved areas in gardens, school yards, and playgrounds. Lead content was determinated by boiling the samples with HNO_3. Acid dependent extractions using HCl concentrations from 1.0 to 10^{-5} M were performed and Ist and 2nd extracts were analyzed separately. Total lead in the samples ranges from 570 to 2,130 μg/g. Lead extractability increases with increasing acidity, from 10% at pH 5 to 90% at pH 1. From a toxicological standpoint, the stomach pH 1 would ensure complete extraction of Pb from ingested dust.

253 **Day, A.H., McFadyen, J.A., Tucker, T.C., Cluff, C.B.,** 1979. Commercial production of wheat grain irrigated with municipal waste water and pump water J. Environ. Qual. 8(3): 403-406.

The effects of irrigating wheat with a mixture of pump water and waste water and with pump water alone on wheat growth, grain yield, grain quality, soil properties and irrigation water quality was studied. Wheat irrigated with the pump water waste water mixture produced taller plants, heavier seeds, higher grain yields, and higher straw yields than did wheat grown with only pump water. When large fields were compared, wheat grown with the pump water-waste water mixture had taller plants, more lodging, lower grain volume-weights, and higher grain yields than did wheat produced with pump water alone or the pump water waste water mixture were similar. Soluble salts and No_3-N were higher in soils irrigated with pump water than they were in soils irrigated with the pump water-waste water mixture; however, the pump water waste water mixture had higher levels of total N and P than did pump water. Extractable P was higher in soils irrigated with pump water.

254 **Day, A.D., Mitchell, G.F., Tucker, T.C., Thames, J.L.,** 1979. Emergence and growth of plant species in coal mine soil. J Environ. Qual. 8: 110-114.

The chemical properties of undistributed soil, surface-mined coal land (coal mine soil) on the Black Mesa Coal MIne, and Gila loam soil were evaluated, and the emergence of 7 plant species in the greenhouse in Gila loam soil and coalmine soil were studied. The N content of coal mine soil was higher than the N content of undisturbed soil or Gila loam.

Emergence percentages for 7 plant species grown in coal mine soil were similar to emergence percentages for the same species grown in Gila loam, Alfalfa, barley and wheat had from 84 to 93 per cent emergence in coalmine soil. Indian rice grass, fourwing saltbush *(Atriplex canescens)* yellow sweetclover *(Melilotus officinalis)*, and winterfat *(Euroti lanata)* emerged < 35% in coal mine soil and Gila loam soil. Plant growth data from forage species grown in the greenhouse indicate that coal mine soil has a lower fertility level than Gila loam soil. When supplied with optimum soil moisture and plant nutrients, coal mine soil produced about the same yields of forage from alfalfa, barley, and wheat as were produced in Gila loam under the same soil-moisture and fertility conditions.

255 **Day, A.D., Tucker, T.C.,** 1977. Effects of treated Municipal waste water on growth, fiber protein, and amino acid content of sorghum grain. J. Environ. Qual. 6(3): 325-327.

Experiments were conducted at Tucson, Arizona, to study effect of treated municipal waste water on growth, fiber, protein and amino acid content of grain sorghum. Sorghum grain was grown in two soil types : Camoro sandy loam and Grabe silt loam. Three irrigation and fertilizer treatments were used (i) well water plus suggested amounts of NPK 112, 35 and one kg/ha of N, P and K, respectively (ii) well water plus N, P, and K from commercial sources in amounts equal to those found in waste water; and (iii) waste water from an activated sludge sewage plant (224, 73 and 140 kg/ha of N, P and K, respectively). When sorghum was grown for grain in Comoro sandy loam, average number of days from planting to maturity, leaf length and grain yield were higher in plots that received waste water than in the plots that received well water and suggested amount of N, P and K. Sorghum grown with waste water produced higher grain yields than when grown with synthetic waste water. The plant growth response of sorghum to waste water, in Grabe silt loam was similar to that in Comoro sandy loam. Sorghum grain grown with all irrigation and fertilizer treatments contained similar amounts of total protein. In sandy loam soil, grain from sorghum grown with simulated waste water and waste water alone contained less cystine-glycine and histidine than did grain produced with suggested culture.

256 **Dean-Ross, D., Mills, A.L.,** 1989. Bacterial community structure and function along a heavy metal gradient. Appl. Environl. Microbiol. 55(8): 2002-2009.

Response of planktonic, sediment and epilithic bacterial communities to increasing conc. of heavy metals was determinated in a pollution related effect on bacterial numbers, heterotrophic activity, resistant to Pb or Cu or species diversity. The lack of correlation between conc. of heavy metals and resistant in the sediment bacterial community was mainly due high pH and the reduction in metal toxicity.

257 **Debnath, R., Mukherji, S.,** 1982. Toxic action of barium chloride on germination, growth and metabolism of rice (*Oryza sativa* L.). Environ. Exp. Bot. 22(2): 203-210.

The effects of brarium chloride on growth and metabolism of rice seedling are noted. Inhibition of seedling elongation began 0.1 mM. Root growth inhibition was more pronounced than shoot growth. Germination declined at 1mM and was completely eliminated at 100mM. Ba-induced elongation inhibition could be totally reversed with transfer to GA_3; partial recovery occurred with IAA, EDTA, cations (K, Ca and Fe) and malate, whereas others were ineffective. Respiration rates were found to decline and were proportional to inhibition of seedling vigour. Coincident with growth inhibition, was a difference in pattern of distribution of sugar and nitrogen in the embryo and the endosperm. As compared to control, there was a predominance of reducing sugar and soluble nitrogen in Ba-soaked embryos. Activities of peroxidase, IAA oxidase and ascorbic acid oxidase on a seedling basis were diminished by Ba treatments; catalase was unaffected. On a dry weight basis, however, considerable stimulation was observed in catalase and ascorbic acid oxidase activities.

258 **Dec. S., Wierzbicka, H., Wozniakowska, A., Maliszewska, W.,** 1985. The influence of various heavy metal compounds on the development and activity of soil micro-organisms. Environl. Pollut. (A. Ecol. Biol.) 37(3): 195-215.

Group of micro-organisms important for soil fertility were considered and the relative toxicity of the compounds was in the following order: Hg (metallic) > $CuSO_4$ > $HgC1_2$ >Hg_2C1_2 > HgO > As_2O_3 > $ZnSO_4$ > Na_2HAsO_4 > Pb $(NO_3)_2$. Of the micro-organisms investigated, fungi and actinomycetes were the most resistant to all the metals used. *Azotobacter* sp. and nitrifiers appeared to be the most sensitive.

259 **Decatanzaro, T., Hutchinson, T.C.,** 1985. Leaching and distribution of nitrogen and nickel in nickel-perturbed jack pine forest microcosms. Water Air Soil Pollut. 26(3): 281-292.

The effects of $NiSO_4$ additions of 100 and 500, μg Nig^{-1}, soil and of stack-dust from a Ni smelter, on the accumulation and leaching of N and Ni in a boreal jack pine (Pinus siana lamb) ecosystem were studied using microcosms in the greenhouse. $NiSO_4$ was found to significantly increase leaching losses of NH_4 and NO_3 at some sampling times. Stack-dust added in a single large dose produced much more dramatic leaching losses of N than did the $NiSO_4$, while gradual additions of stack-dust produced no excess leaching losses relative to controls. At the end of 11 mo there were no significant differences in N concentrations of plants in microcosms receiving different treatments, nor were there differences in inorganic N concentrations in soil. Significant leaching of Ni occurred from all microcosms except those treated weekly with stack-dust. Nickel retained by the microcosms was found to accumulate primarily in the organic soil layers. Nickel concentrations of plants were also increased by the treatments, especially in the moss layer. The 500 µg g^{-1} $NiSO_4$ treatments produced the highest increase in plant concentrations of Ni.

260 **DeGroot, R.C., Popham, T.W., Gjovik, L.R., Forehand, T.**, 1979. Distribution gradients of arsenic, copper, and chromium around preservative-treated wooden stakes. J. Environ. Qual. 8(1): 39-41.

The distribution gradients of As and Cr in soil around and below nominal 50 by 101-mm southern pine stakes treated with chromated copper arsenate (CCA Type I or Type II) or ammoniacal copper arsenate (ACA) and exposed for 30 yr in Poarch fine sandy loam soils in Southern Mississippi indicate that the small amounts of As and Cr moving from the stakes into the soil are sorbed by the soil proximal to the stakes. The distribution gradient for Cu is similar to those for As and Cr but is less precise. CCA- and ACA-treated wood, at least, in acidic fine sandy loams, apparently does not contribute significant amounts of As or Cr into surrounding soils and waters.

261 **Dehut, J.P., Fonsny, K., Myttenaere, C., Deprins, D., Vandecasteele, C.M.**, 1989. Bioavailability of Tc incorporate in plant material. Health Physics. 57(2): 263-267.

Six minilysimeters were filled with soil (pH 6.9; CEC 20 meq/100 gm soil) contaminated with grass mixture containing 32g Tc/kg DW and sown with barley, potatoes, tomatoes or grass. Approx 55% of the Tc present, in the dried grass mixture could be recovered as a water soluble fraction. An important part of the recycled bioincorporated Tc was immediately and highly available to plant, but that barley seeds, potato tubers and tomato fruits contained lower amounts of Tc than the leaves.

262 **De, Jong, E.**, 1978. The movement of sewage effluent through soil columns. The major Ions (Na, Ca, Mg, Cl and SO_4). J. Environ.Qual. 75; (1): 133-136.

Sewage effluent was leached through columns of the A, B and C horizons of a loamy sand, and the A horizon of clay. Neither temperature (7, 13 or 18°C) nor method of application (flood or trickle irrigation) affected the passage of sodium, calcium, magnesium chloride and sulfate ions. The breakthrough curves differed considerably from theoretical curves. The anions appeared much earlier in the leachate of the columns than predicted due to incomplete mixing between the sewage effluent and the soil solution. The breakthrough curves of the cations were affected by the incomplete mixing, initial levels of the exchangeable and soluble cations and the increase in the sum of exchangeable (Na + K + Ca + Mg) ions.

263 **De Jong, E.**, 1980. The effect of a crude oil spill on cereals. Environl. Pollut. (A: Ecol. and Biolog.) 22 (3): 178-196.

A break in an oil pipeline near Moose Jaw, Saskatchewan, Canada, in

Jan. 1974 caused oil to travel underground over a distance of 850 m. Oil moved upwards through cracks in the frozen soil, especially during recovery attempts. The contamination in the affected area varied considerably both horizontally and vertically. Oil contamination and damage to the soil structure due to the cleanup efforts caused serious yield decreases during the next summer. In subsequent growing seasons, oil was the major factor in reducing yields. Even very small amounts of oil (<0.2% by wt) in the 0-30 cm or 0-90 cm depth reduced yields considerably Oil reduced the available N content of the soil and markedly reduced water uptake by wheat from contaminated layers or from below such layers. Problems in reclaiming soils with oil contamination below the toposoil are discussed.

264 **Dennis, L., Callister, M.C., Logan, T.J.,** 1978. Phosphate adsorption – desorption characteristics of soils and bottom sediments in Maumee River basin of Ohio. J. Environ. Qual. 7 (1): 87-92.

Langmuir adsorption isotherms showed that Maumee River basin sediments had adsorption capacities 10 to 20 times greater than Basin soils. The difference is attributed to the higher content of amorphous or low range order iron and aluminium components in the bottom sediments. Equilibrium phosphorus concentration (EPC) and phosphorus desorbed was similar for soils and sediments as well as total P. Correlations between adsorption-desorption parameters and soil-sediment properties are presented. Bray "available" P was highly correlated with EPC and P desorbed in the soil but to a lesser extent in the bottom sediments. CDB and oxalate extractable P was highly correlated with P adsorption capacity in the bottom sediments, but not in the soils.

265 **Dermer, O.C., Curtis, V.S., Leach, F.R.,** 1980. Biochemical indicators of subsurface pollution. Ann Arbor Sci. Publishers: p. 203.

The literature concerning state-of-the-art analyses of subsurface pollution in soil and ground-water is reviewed. The limits of analysis are discussed and examples of the number of bacteria required to give a detectable response are presented. Since many of the standard biochemical analyses are not sensitive enough to detect and few simplifications are enquired; this is offered by both enzyme measurements and enzymatic cycling. A brief account of the determinations of whole microorganisms-viruses and bacteria is presented. The limitations and potentials of biochemical analysis must be recognized.

266 **Deshpande, V.P., Kaul, S.N.,** 1991. Utilization, treatment and disposal of sewage – a review. Asian Environ. 13(1): 20-47.

The paper reviews the findings of experimental/field studies conducted by various researchers on treatment and disposal of domestic sewage.

267 **Deshpande, V.P., Murty Balachandra, Nandy, T., Kaul, S.N.,** 1991. Nitrification studies using rotating biological drum contractor. Asian En-

viron. 13(1): 48-68.

Nitrification studies on bench scale were carried out using a two stage aerobic rotating biological drum contractor, packed with nylon scrubbers as support media. Ammonium chloride was used as ammonia nitrogen supplement which was mixed with domestic sewage in different concentrations and used as feed substrate. Performance of the reactor system was evaluated under various operating variables such as, different ammonia nitrogen concentrations and HRT. Data application through use of various models has been made to determine the relevant design variables and biokinetic parameters.

268 **De, Woo. W.,** 1990. Cadmium in agriculture. in Proc. of the 4th IUPAC Cadmium Workshop. U. Glaser (ed.), Toxicol Environ. Chem. 27(1-3): 55-63

Phosphate fertilizers contain varying amounts of cadmium as contaminants from phosphate rock. Plant uptake of cadmium from fertilized soils could conceivably result in entry of cadmium into the human food chain. To keep the cadmium concentration in agricultural products below the maximum permissible levels, "critical" levels of cadmium-concentrations in top soil are evaluated. Based on a calculated rise of 0.2 mg cadmium/kg soil per hundred years, the "critical" value for cadmium in Dutch soils will be reached in one century in the case of sandy soils and in three centuries in the case of clay soils. However, the observed increase in cadmium in long term fertilizer trials is lower than the calculated amount of 0.2 mg/per kg in hundred years. As a consequence the "critical" date will be delayed even further.

269 **Dierberg, F.E., Ewel, K.C.**. 1984. The effects of waste water on decomposition and organic matter accumulation, in Cyprus Swamps, (Eds) K.C. Ewel & W.T. Odum. University Press, Gainesville. Florida: 164-170.

Cypress leaves decompose more rapidly in a sewage-enriched cypress dome than in an undisturbed cypress dome. A model incorporating both labile and refractory components of cypress leaves was found to produce a better fit to decomposition data than a simple exponential decay model. Simulated litter fall and decomposition rates under natural conditions and with waste water enrichment suggest that increased productivity generated by sewage addition will have no effect on the storage capacity of the dome basin.

270 **Dierberg, F.D., Patrick, L.B.,** 1985. Nitrogen and phosphorus removal by Cyprus swamp sediments. Water Air Soil Pollut. 24: 207-213.

Removal of nutrients from waste water by sediments in Cyprus swamps was studied in laboratory leaching columns filled with wet surface sediments. Columns were leached with low-nutrient groundwater, treated waste water, and treated waste water amended with nitrate (20 to 30 mg NL^{-1}) and phosphate (9.5 mg PL^{-1}) for 21 months. From 99 to 100% of the nitrate/nitrite and P was removed from the amended waste water.

271 **Diercxsens, P.T., Tarradell, J.,** 1988. Soil contamination by some organic micropollutants related to sewage sludge spreading. Internatl J. Environ. Analyt. Chem. 28: 143-159.

Two Swiss soils to which sewage sludge had been applied showed a temporary accumulation (of the month's duration) of low molecular weight polynuclear aromatic hydrocarbons (PAHs), polychlorinated biphenyls (PCBs) diethyl hexyl phthalate and 4-nonyl phenol. Application of pig manure to the two soils over a period of ten years led to an accumulation of PAHs and PCBs equivalent to 1.4 and 38.3% of the corresponding accumulations caused by sewage sludge.

272 **Dikshit, V.P.,** 1989. Removal of chromium by adsorption using saw dust. Natl Acad. Sci. Letters 12(12): 419-421.

The potential of locally available saw-dust to remove hexavalent chromium from waste water has been investigated. The extent of removal is dependent on concentration, pH and contact time of the solution. The applicability of the Langmuir isotherm for the present system has been analysed. Saw-dust can be effectively used for the removal of Cr (VI) from highly acidic effluents like electroplating effluents.

273 **Divya Parekh, Rekha, M., Puranik, Srivastava, H.S.,** 1990. Inhibition of chlorophyll biosynthesis by cadmium in greening maize leaf segments. Biochem. Physiol. Pflanzen, 186: 239-242.

Supply of 0.01 to 1.0 mM $CdC1_2$ to greening maize leaf segments, either in the absence or presence of inorganic nitrogen, inhibited total chlorophyll content. During a time course study, there was not any appreciable effect of Cd upto 4 h, but thereafter it inhibited chlorophyll synthesis. While supply of glycine, succinate, glumate, 2-oxoglutarate, $MgCl_2$, cysteine, dithiothreitol and 5,5϶-dithio-bis-2-nitrobenzoic acid had either no or only partial protective action against Cd toxicity, reduced glutathione, could completely overcome the inhibition of chlorophyll biosynthesis by the metal. It is suggested that Cd interferes biosynthesis through glutathione availability.

274 **Dobel, C., Meyer, N., Burgharsdt, W.,** 1990. Studies to determine the potential damage to road side trees. Soil characteristics, pollutant and nutrient contents, vegetation and fauna. Mitt-eilmgen der Deustsher Bodenkundli Chem. Gesellschaft: 61: 81-84.

The amounts of nutrients in the soil were generally larger on rehabilitated beds, although there were large variations. The treatment of tree beds generally resulted in reduced heavy metal contents. There was a relationship between traffic density and the amounts of Pb, Cu and Zn in the soils. Population density and species diversity of the soil fauna were related to the presence of grasses and herbs. No relationship between heavy metals and population density was observed.

275 **Dobija, J.,** 1985. Evaluation of effects of sulphur compounds on the soil environment, in "Air pollution control and forecasting of environmental damage", J.W. Zwozdziak (ed.) 31-36.

Soil acidification by sulphur compounds and difficulties in determining soil losses due to that process are presented. The most effective method of neutralizing the acidification is liming, i.e. the quantitative indicator of soil degradation rate is characterized. The calcium oxide dose necessary to neutralize sulphuric acid arising in the soil as well as the method of soil losses evaluation, are presented.

276 **Doerr, H., Muennich, K.O., Mangini, A., Schmitz, W.,** 1990. Gasoline lead in West German soils. Naturwissenshaften. 77(9): 428-430.

A very simplified mass balance of atmospheric lead in the Federal Republic of Germany is presented, and the relevance of this environmental pollution study is discussed.

277 **Domingo, J.L.,** 1989. Cobalt in the environment and its toxicological implications. Rev. Environ. Contam & Toxicol. 108: 105-132.

Various aspects of cobalt in nature, nutrition, biochemistry and physiology are reviewed. Toxicity of cobalt and its mutagenecity is also discussed.

278 **Domingues, H., Gusmao, M.R., Sequeira, E.M., Soares, A.M., Silva, Monterio, O.R.,** 1991. Study of soil pollution and phytotoxicity risks of Frielas sewage sludge. in "International Conference on Environmental Pollution". B.Nath (Ed.): 344-350.

The urban sewage sludge from Frielas (near Lisbon) was chemically and mineralogically characterized, showing low contents of heavy metals. A phytotoxicity test in maize, showed high yield results with no detrimental effect. The lixiviation test revealed a low heavy metal solubility. An alluvial soil located near Frielas, fertilized with 90 and 180 t/ha of dry sludge, was tested with ryegrass and lettuce in a pot trial. The yields for both crops were higher with the lower level of sludge. No phytotoxicity symptoms were observed.

279 **Doner, H.E., Traina, S.J., Pukite, A.,** 1982. Interaction of nickel, copper and cadmium with soil manganese in saline solutions. Soil. Sci. 133(6): 369-377.

In study Ni, Cu, and Cd in Na salt solutions of C1 and $C1O_4$ were leached through soil, and the effluents analyzed. Peak or pulse increase in the Mn concentration were coincidental with appearance of Ni, Cu, or Cd in the effluent. Increased Na salt concentrations resulted in increased Mn release, even though the amount of heavy metal sorbed decreased. Copper treatments produced a decreased effluent pH, which probably accounted for some of the released Mn. Nickel and Cadmium treatments, on the other hand, resulted in slight or no significant effluent pH decrease. Several possible mechanisms are introduced that could account for Mn release. It is most probably that proton release with Ni, Cu, or Cd sorption accounts most of the Mn release.

280 **Donker, M., Bogert, K.,** 1990. The mechanism of zinc and cadmium tolerance in the isopod Porcellio Scaber, in Physiological and Biochemical Approaches to the Toxicological Assessment of Environment pollution". Royal Netherlands Chem. Soc. Utrecht.

Populations, caused by metal soil pollution was studied by comparing effects of zinc and cadmium on first generation laboratory animals, isopods from a reference loçation (Spanderswoud), from a smelter (Budel: Zn and Cd concentraminated) and from a mining area (Piombieres: Zn, Pb and Cd contaminated) were cultured on clean food. In experiments isopods were exposed for five weeks to Zn and Cd in the food. Consumption assimilation efficiency of food, assimilation of metals, growth efficiency and metal concentration of the isopods were measured.

281 **Donnelly, K.C., Brown, K., Thomas, J.C.,** 1990. Bacterial mutagenecity of leachate water from municipal sewage sludge-amended soils. Environ. Toxicol. Chem. 9(4): 443-451.

The sludge was applied to 18 barrel-sized lysimeters. While 6 unamended lysimeters served as controls. The leachate was concentrated on a combined XAD-2/XAD-7 resin, and the adsorbed organics were eluted with acetone. The leachate extracts were tested in the standard plate incorporation assay using strain TA98 with and without metabolic activation. Nine of 16 leachate induced a positive response in the bioassay. The maximum specific activity was 207 net revertants per 10 mg induced without metabolic activation in the Westwood soil.

282 **Dotta, P., Genon, G., Marchese, F.,** 1990. Leaching phenomena evaluation for an industrial solid waste landfill. Ingegneria Ambientale 19(7-8): 479-485.

The chemical composition, flow and quality of leachates from a large industrial landfill were monitored. Metals were slightly leached as the pH of the leachates was slightly basic whereas organic matter dissolution was markedly greater. The effect of rain intensity on pollutant leaching was noted in the first few months of the landfills operation. At the end of the study period, percolation throughout the landfill was established.

283 **Dowdy, R.H., Page, A.L., Chang, A.C.,** 1991. Management of agricultural land receiving waste water sludges. In "Soil Management for Sustainability", (Eds. R. Lal & F.J. Pierce). Soil Cons Soc. USA: 85-101.

Processes by which soils assimilate chemical constituents of waste water and sludges are discussed and a case study of plant response, water chemistry and soil chemistry in relation to application of sewage sludge, is presented.

284 **Dreiss, S.J.,** 1986. Chromium migration through sludge-treated soils. Ground-water. 24(3): 312-231.

The EPA to investigate the feasibility of using land treatment to dispose of chromium tanning sludges. These sludges contain high concentrations of Cr, in the range of 21000 to 55000 ppm on a dry wt. basis. Chromium could migrate in soil water at a land treatment site as either a soluble Cr(VI) species, as $HCrO_4^-$ or as Cr(III) or Cr(IV) in soluble complexes with organic or inorganic substances. Field measurements of Cr fluxes at an experimental test site near Santa Cruz, California indicate that Cr in tannery sludges exhibits a very low mobility. Less than 0.1% of the total Cr applied to a test plot was transported through the Upper soil zone during a three-month period. However, the sludge applications introduced high concentrations of nitrates and major cations. Estimates of contaminant fluxes based on measured concentrations in soil water collected with porous cup samples contain large uncertainties. In addition to potential errors in moisture flux computations, chemical reactions in the cups can significantly alter the composition of soil water samples.

285 **Driscoll, C.T., Schecher, W.D.,** 1990. The chemistry of aluminium in the environment. Envirol. Geochem. Health. 12: 28-49.

Various aspects of Al in soil are reviewed. High Al conc. are ecologically important because 1) Al is an important buffer in acidic waters regulating the lower limit of pH following acidification by strong acids; 2) through adsorption and coagulation reactions, Al alters the cycling and availability of important elements as P, organic C, and some trace elements; 3) Al may serve as a coagulant facilitating the removal of light attenuating materials and thereby increasing the clarity and decreasing the thermal stability of lakes and 4) Al is potentially toxic to organisms.

286 **Dubey, P.S., Pawar, K., Shringi, S.K., Trivedi, L.,** 1982. Effects of fly ash deposition on photosynthetic pig and dry matter production of wheat and gram. Agro-Ecosys. 8 (2): 137-140.

Wheat gram were dusted with 2, 4 and 6 gm^2 day^{-1} of fly ash for days. Both crops showed an increase in the height of the plants dry and chlorophyll and carotenoid content. The higher dusting rates alter the photosynthetic pigment contents.

287 **Ducaroir, J., Cambier, P., Leydecker, J.P., Prost, R.,** 1990. Application of soil fraction method to the study of the distribution of pollutant metals. Zeits. Chrift. fur. Pflanzenernah rung and Bodenk-unde.

Three agricultural soils polluted by sewage sludge were dispersed by shaking in water or in organic solvent for particle size and density separations. Only carbonate particles were broken down to fiber size. The pollutant metals were not displaced by the treatments, except perhaps Cd that is partly soluble in water and in other solvents. Enough different fractions were obtained by using ultrasonic and other dispersion treatments. Copper was the only element to be more concentrated in the free organic matter. Other metals were more concentrated within an organic-mineral compartment, containing organic matter, fine clay and hydrous oxides. No pollutant metals were associated with carbonates, feldspars and quartz.

288 **Ducreuse, J., Bocard, C., Muntzer, P., Razakarisoa, D., Zilliox, L.,** 1990. Mobility of soluble and non-soluble hydrocarbons in contaminated aquifer. Water Sci. Technol. 22(6): 27-30.

The residual oil traped in an aquifer following petroleum contamination is a constant source of pollution in ground-water. For soluble aromatic hydro-carbons, the residual air had no effect on mobility. But the liquid/solid exchange was predominant.

289 **Dudas, M.J.,** 1987. Accumulation of native arsenic in acid sulphate soils in Alberta. Can. J. Soil Sci., 67 (2): 317-331.

Acid sulphate soils belonging to the Boundary and Josephine soil series were analysed for As to determine mineral partitioning form, and redistribution of the element. Samples of soil, natrojarosite, and zones enriched in iron oxides were collected from upper and lower slop positions. Levels in bulk samples were two times higher than normal background abundances. Arsenic was partitioned into silt and clay fractions and appeared related to the distribution of iron oxides in the size separates. Microbiologically mediated losses of As had depleted surface horizons of the element. The weathering of pyrite is believed to account for the accumulations of As in acid sulphate soils.

290 **Dudka, S., Chlopecka, A.,** 1990. Effect of soil phase speciation on metal mobility and phyto-availability in sludge-amended soil. Water Air Soil Pollut. 51(1-2): 153-160.

Sequential extraction was utilized for partitioning Cd, Cr, Ni and Zn, in soil and sludge samples into five operationally defined fractions: exchangeable, bound to carbonates, bound to Fe-Mn oxides, bound to organic matter and residual. The highest amounts of Cd, Ni and Zn, expressed as per cent of the total, were found in the Fe-Mn oxide fraction of the sewage sludge. Chromium was significantly associated with the organic fraction to the sludge. The residue was the most abundant fraction for all metals studied in the untreated soil, and for Cd and Ni in the sludge treated soil. The concentration of exchangeable Cd and Cr was relatively low in the untreated soil and did not change much after sludge application, whereas the concentrations of exchangeable Zn increased about 50 times and the concentrations of exchangeable Ni doubled in the sludge-treated soil.

291 **Dudley, L.M., McLean, T.E., Furst, T.H., Jurinak, J.J.,** 1991. Sorption of cadmium and copper from an acid mine waste extract by two calcareous soils: Column studies. Soil Sci 151(2): 121-135.

Cadmium and copper show different sorption mechanism for two calcareous soils. When the activity data from batch studies with Skumpah soil (30% $CaCO_3$) were plotted on a phase diagram, results suggested that mineral tenorite (CuO) controlled activity of Cu in solution. Leaching with the mine waste water reduced the intensity of calcite and dolomite peaks. It appears that exchange reactions most clearly controlled metal transport after the pH value had been reduced to acid range.

292 **Dueck, T.A., Endedjik, G.J., Ikkink, H.G.K.,** 1987. Soil pollution and changes in vegetation due to heavy metals in sinter-pavements. Chemosphere, 16(5): 1021-1030.

The use of heavy metal-contaminated sinters from a zinic smelter for paving roads, has resulted in changes in the species richness and genetic constitution of the roadside vegetation. In time, the heavy metals in the sinters leach out, vertically to ground-water levels as well as horizontally where they are taken up by crops growing beside these roads. Roadside soil from sinter-paved roads definitely constitutes an environmental hazard according to the present legislative standards.

293 **Duffy, S.J., Hay, G.W., Micklethwaite, R.K., Vanloon, G.W.,** 1989. Distribution and classification of metal species in soil leachates. Sci. Total Environ. 87-88: 189-197.

Using an ion-exchange separation procedure, metals in soil leachates from laboratory columns were separated into a portion consisting of simple cationic inorganic forms, and a second portion containing anionic organically-bound forms. Concentrations of Al, Ca, Co, Cu, Fe, Hg, K, Mg, Mn, and Na in each of the separated fractions were determined. A range of behaviour was observed, from metals that are generally present in inorganic forms (Ca, K, Mg, Na) to those that are usually found in association with soluble organic matter (Al, Fe, Hg.).

294 **Dumontet, S., Levesque, M., Mathur, S.P.,** 1990. Limited down ward irrigation of pollutants metals Cu, Zn, Ni and Pb in acidic virgin peat soils near a smelter. Water Air Soil Pollut. 43: 329-341.

The distribution of Cu, Zn, Ni Cd and Pb was determined in 11 acidic virgin peat profiles located along two transets moving away from a smelter plant in Canada. The metal concs. level of all were highest in 0-15 cm layer at the site near the smelter and decreased progressively with distance up to 42 km. Copper had the highest conc. 5525 μg/g followed by Pb and Zn. The maximum levels of total metals built up in the peat surface near the smelter were high, reaching the thresh-hold limits for phyto toxicity in peat soils. The amounts of metals moving down and accumulating in the anaerobic zone of the soil were limited. The distribution and enrichment ratios in the profiles showed that Zn Cu and Cd would have relatively higher mobility than Pb.

295 **Dumontet, S., Mathur, S.P.,** 1989. Evaluation of respiration based methods for measuring microbial biomass in metal-contaminated acidic

mineral and organic soil. Soil Biol. Biochem. 21(3): 431-436.

To select the most suitable method for determining microbial biomass in metal-polluted acidic soils both the chloroform fumigation incubation (F1) method and the substrate-induced response (SIR) method were used on four acidic (pH 2.9-4.4) mineral and four organic soils from sites situated 1-42 km from a Copper Smelter. The F1 biomass was calculated with or without non-fumigated controls by using either the general 0.41 or individual soil K_C values, and through the kinetic model of Chaussod and Nicolardot which does not use a non-fumigated control. As SIR biomass calculated by the standard procedure was found not to correlate with the F1 biomass in the soils, a new calibration was derived on the basis of the respiration rate during the first hour after glucose addition.

296 **Dunn, A.J., Hiliman, P.F.,** 1991. The use of filtration to render waste water safe for the reuse in irrigation, in 'Techniques for Environmentally Sound Water Resources Development Proc. Pentech Press London. 155-164.

Laboratory experiments were conducted to assess the performance of rapid sand filtration in removing helminth eggs from non-industrial waste water to be reused for irrigation supply. Column tests showed that the technique can attain WHO guidelines under certain conditions. The major factors are effective sand size, flow rate and number of eggs. A simple model was developed in order to establish design principles for future use of the rapid sand filtration technique.

297 **Dupont, R.R., Mclean, J.E., Hoff, R.H., Moorew, M.,** 1990. Evaluation of the use of solar redaction for the decontamination of soils containing wood treating wastes. J. Air Waste Manage. Assoc. 40(9): 1257-65.

Degradation due to photo-chemical activity was observed for all tests with compound phenolytic half lives ranging from 7 to app. 180 days. None of the soil amendments were found to improve soil phase photodegradation. Soil type and its characteristics of internal reflectance, proved to be the most significant factor affecting compound degradation rates suggesting the necessity for site specific assessments of soil phase photodegradation.

298 **Duxbury, T., Bicknell, B.,** 1983. Metal-tolerant bacterial populations from natural and metal-polluted soils. Soil Biol. Biochem., 15(3): 243-250.

The toxicity of several metals towards bacterial populations from natural and metal-polluted soils could be described either partially by a single exponential or completely by the sum of two exponential functions. Factorial populations from both soils contained two sub-groups, one of which could tolerate metals over a greater range of concentrations than the other. Most bacteria comprising the more metal-tolerant sub-group were Gram-negative and were multiple drug resistant. Exceptions were organisms, tentatively identified as coryneforms, isolated on nickel-supplemented medium. In general, Gram-negative bacteria are more metal-tolerant than Gram-positive organisms and, in soils containing comparatively low levels of metal pollution, may be able to function without the need for plasmid-mediated metal-tolerance.

299 **Eastcott, L., Wanyingshiu, Mackay, D., Kestecki., P.T.,** 1989. Modelling petroleum products in soils in "Petroleum Contaminated Soils – Remediation Techniques, Environmental Fate and Risk Assessment". Vol. 1. (Eds. Kostecki, P.T., Calabrese, E.J.) Lewis Pub. Michigan. 63-80.

In summary, our purpose is to discuss experimental and modelling approaches and give some illustrative results in the hope that others may follow this approach and thus contribute to an increased understanding of oil behaviour in soil.

300 **Ebers, T., Bischofsherger, W.,** 1990. Waste water treatment by soil absorption systems. Water Sci. Technol. 22: 311-312.

Soil filtration as a means of eliminating pollution from household waste water was studied for 2 years. Lysimeters were filled with silty sand and other 3 by fine gravel sand. Hydraulic load varied from 0.5 to 31 cm/day. Results showed good efficiency for fine ground sand in removal of BOD (98-94%), COD (88 to 93%) and Kjeldahl N (90 to 91.3%). Elimination of phosphate ranged from 5.7 to 86%. Slightly silty soil and anaerobic condition showed the best results in removal of phosphate (86 to 93%) and relatively good elimination rates were achieved for BOD (65 to 98%) and COD (≈76%). Elimination of Kjeldahl nitrogen ranged from 39.6 to 68.4 per cent.

301 **Ebing, W., Schuphan, I.,** 1979. Studies on the behaviour of environmental chemicals in plants and soil quantitatively investigated in closed cultivating systems. Ecotoxicol. Environl. Saf. 3(2): 133-143.

In evaluating the metabolism and degradation of chemicals, the quantities of residues, metabolites, and volatile products need to be determined. In investigating the fate of ((^{14}C) phenyl) — monolinuron in the growth of spinach, cress, and potatoes, an overall recovery of 9% was achieved. Additional studies using the system include ((^{14}C) phenyl) - buturon in winter wheat. ((^{14}C) carbonyl) — diallate in preemergent studies with sugar beets, ((^{14}C) flurodichloro-methylmercapto) — dichlofluanid fungicide on strawberry plants, and ((^{14}C) trichloromethyl) — captan applied to stock-keeping apples.

302 **Edmondo, Canelli,** 1976. Simultaneous automated determination of chloride, nitrite, nitrate and ammonia in water and waste water. Water Air Soil Pollut. 5: 339-348.

An automated system capable of simultaneous determination of chloride, nitrate, and ammonia in about 2 ml fresh water or waste water is described. The four compounds are determined using modifications of established colorimetric procedures.

303 **Eduljee, G., Badsha, K., Price, L.,** 1985. Environmental monitoring for PCB and heavy metals in the vicinity of a chemical waste disposal facility. I. Chemosphere. 14(9): 1371-1382.

Three studies on environmental monitoring for PCB and heavy metals in the vicinity of a chemical waste disposal facilities were conducted for 3 years on a monthly basis in soil and foliage samples collected from 13 sites, generally located within a 2 km radius of a hazardous and toxic waste disposal facility that has been operating for over ten years.

304 **Eduljee, G., Badsha, K., Scudamore, N.,** 1986. Environmental monitoring for PCB and trace metals in the vicinity of a chemical waste disposal facility, II & III. Chemosphere 15: 81-93, 947-957.

PCB and trace metal data are reported for soil and grass samples collected over from July 1984 to January 1985, and in March and June 1985, at 13 sites within a 3.5 km radius of a hazardous and toxic waste disposal facility in Bonnybridge, Scotland. Transient elevations in trace metal levels were observed over the whole of the sampling area, unconnected with a point source in Bonnybridge, and suggests that the area is impacted by air-borne material from external sources. However, even the highest concentrations found in this region appear to be well below the levels at which PCBs, when fed to cattle, have been shown to produce no adverse effects. A long-term environmental monitoring programme was instituted in the vicinity of a hazardous waste disposal facility. A statistical analysis of the results for the period August 1984 to March 1986 indicates that the study area is not affected by significant point source emissions within its boundaries. Concentrations of PCBs and trace metals in soils and grass are generally within background levels established for other locations.

305 **Egginton, G.M., Smith, K.A.,** 1986. Losses of nitrogen by denitrification from a grassland soil fertilized with cattle slurry and calcium nitrate. J. Soil. Sci. 37: 69-90.

Losses of N by denitrification from an imperfectly drained grassland soil were measured over a 1 yr. period, during which applications up to 200 kg ha^{-1} of N as cattle slurry or calcium nitrate were made. The quantities of N lost from nitrate-treated soil were much greater than from slurry-treated areas, and ranged up to 21% of the N applied. The losses occurred predominantly over brief periods following fertilizer application in the spring. Ratio of N released as N_2 to that released as N_2O increased as denitrification rates increased. The highest ratio recorded, 24, may have been a conservative estimate because inhibition of N_2O reduction may not have been complete on all occasions. Increased respiration was observed in the soil profile as a result of adding C_2H_2. This effect should be taken into account in interpreting experiments using the C_2H_2 — inhibition technique.

306 **Elfving, D.C., Bache, C.A., Gutenmann, W.H., Lisk, D.J.,** 1981.

Analysing crops grown on waste amended soils. Biocycle 22(6): 44-47.

A range of vegetable crops as well as apple trees and millet were grown on an acid and a neutral soil which were amended with a combination of fly ash and municipal sewage sludge. The crops were then analyzed for several elements known to be typically present in such waste materials to learn the extent of plant absorption of them.

307 **Elliott, H.A., Brown, G.A.,** 1989. Comparative evaluation of NTA and EDTA for extractive decontamination of Pb-polluted soils. Water Air Soil Pollut. 45(3/4): 361-369.

Nitrilotriaetic acid (NTA) and EDTA were compared for their ability to solubilize Pb from a highly contaminated (Pb=21%) soil collected from a battery recycling facility. For chelant concentrations below 0.04 M (representing a 1: 1 chelent-to-Pb molar ratio) EDTA released 10 to 30% more Pb then NTA. NTA-to-Pb ratio greater than 1:1 reduced Pb recovery because of readsorption of Pb(NTA) onto positively-charged oxide soil components at pH < 8.5. For the EDTA system, however, complexion completely bound all coordination sites of Pb and EDTA, leaving no functions groups available for surface adsorption. Thus, Pb recovery progressively increased with higher EDTA concentration, although the additional Pb release with each EDTA increment became smaller. For pH < 5 and EDTA/Pb of 2:1, Pb recovery exceeded 90 per cent. The addition of 0.5M $NaClO_4$ enhanced Pb recovery by EDTA for pH 5 to 12, but substantially suppressed recovery by NTA for pH 11. Because Pb release by NTA was diminished by high ionic strength and chelant to-metal ratios, NTA may be limited as a soil washing reagent. Stronger complexation and consistent Pb desorption behaviour by EDTA favours its use.

308 **Elliott, H.A., Domprey, B.A., Maille, P.J.,** 1990. Content and fraction of heavy metals in water treatment sludges. J. Environ. Qual. 19: 330-334.

The composition and distribution of Cd, Cu, Cr, Ni, Pb and Zn, in eight alum and $FeC1_3$ coagulation sludges were investigated using a five step chemical fractionation procedure to assess potential impacts following soil incorporation. The mean total metal levels (mg/kg by wt) for these sludges were Cd (2), Cu (234), Cr (187), Ni (102), Pb (230), and Zn (557), which are well below maximum available levels for land applied wastes. Two individual $FeC1_3$ sludges had Ni levels slightly above maximum allowable concentrations. Mean total Cr and Ni concentrations in the $FeC1_3$ sludges, were respectively 5.4 and 3.1 times corresponding alum sludges levels, reflecting elevated concentrations in the $FeC1_3$ coagulant. The Cu, Cr, Ni, Pb, and Zn in sludges were predominantly bound within the oxide or slicate components. A small portion of the sludge Cd was in a readily exchangeable form, whereas the dilute acid extractable and organically bound fractions contamined the majority of non-residual Cd. Fractionation results suggested sludge Cd would potentially be mobile under acidic soil conditions, but the total Cd levels were very low (1-2 mg/kg) compared with on allowable maximum of 25 mg/kg. Although fractionation data must be interpreted cautiously, the results suggest that most metals in water treatment sludges occur predominantly in weakly mobile, non-bioavailable forms.

309 **Elliot, H.A., Liberati, M.R., Huang, C.P.,** 1986. Competitive adsorption of heavy metals by soils. J. Environ. Qual. 15(3): 214-219.

The competitive adsorption of Cd, Cu, Pb, and Zn from 0.025 M $NaClO_4$ solution into four soils was investigated. For two mineral soils, adsorption under acidic conditions (pH 5.0) followed the sequence Pb > Cu > Zn > Cd, which corresponds to the order of increasing pK for the first hydrolysis product (e.g. $PbOH^+$) or the metal ions. In contrast, the order of selectivity for two soils containing 20 to 40 g kg^{-1} organic C was Pb > Cu > Zn, suggesting that organic matter increased Cd retention preferentially over that of Zn. When accompanied by a sizable reduction in CEC, extraction of soil OM markedly reduced adsorption all four metals. However, only Cd and Cu adsorption were appreciably smaller for a soil that maintained a sizable CEC, following OM removal. Lead, and possibly Zn, adsorption by soils with substantial inorganic exchange sites may be unresponsive to organic waste amendments. For Cd and Cu, increased soil OM should restrict mobility and bioavailability, at least under acidic conditions where soluble metal complex formation is limited.

310 **Elrashidi, M.A.,** 1986. Chemical equilibria of fluorine in soils as related to contamination in the environment. Diss. Abst. Int. Pt. B. Sci. & Eng. 47 (2).

Thermodynamic data were selected for forty-five fluorine minerals and solution species which may play important roles in the fluorine chemistry of soils. Equilibrium reactions and stability constants for these minerals and species were calculated and used to develop stability diagrams in soils.

311 **Elsavage, R.E., Sexstone, A.J.,** 1989. Biodegradation of a dilute waste oil emmulsion applied to soil. J. Industrial Microbiol. 4(4): 289-298.

The use of land treatment for disposal of a dilute waste soil emulsion generated by an aluminum rolling industry was investigated. Major components of the waste were linear and branched (C_{12} - C_{25}) and fatty acid emulsifiers (primarily isomers of oleic acid). Hexadecane and pristane were readily biodegraded in vitro when added to soil collected from the waste disposal site. Hydrocarbons and fatty acids extracted from the waste were similarly biodegraded. The apparent half-life of resolvable waste hydrocarbons and fatty acids was 9.5 days in oil which had received waste applications averaging 24.4 lm^{-2}/week. In contrast, oil receiving either 50.8 lm^{-2}/week or no waste applications during summer 1987 apparent exhibited half-lives of 28.1 and 60.3, days, respectively. Waste components were restricted to the upper 48 cm of the soil cores collected from the disposal site. Core samples also provided evidence for biodegradation of hydrocarbons and fatty acids, as well as an accumulation of other compounds not readily resolvable by gas chromatography.

312 **Elseewi, A.A., Page, A.L., Bingham, F.T.,** 1978. Availability of sulphur in sewage sludge to plants, a comparative study. J. Environ. Qual. 7 (2): 213-217.

Alfalfa (*Medicago Sativa* L.) white clover (*Trifolium reports* L.) and turmip (*Bhassica rapa* L.) were grown on calcareous and acid soils low in available sulfur amended with sewage sludge and gypsum at rates equivalent to 0 and 80 ppm S for alfalfa and 0, 25, 50 and 100 ppm S for white clover and turnip. Addition of either sludge or gypsum corrected the S deficiency in the plants and significantly increased the dry matter yields. The S concentrations increased in the plant from deficiency levels (0.01 to 0.088%) to levels $\ngtr$ 0.2%. The average ratio of total S concentration in the sludge-treated plants to that in the gypsum-treated plants was 0.83 and the average S uptake and S recovery ratios were 1.09 and 0.95, respectively. Initial concentrations of NH_4-OAc-extractable SO_4-S in the soil were increased two to seven-fold by application of sludge. The ratio of post harvest SO_4-S in sludge and gypsum treated soils ranged from 0.39 to 2.27 with a mean of 0.95.

313 **Enell, M., Ryding, S.O., Wennberg, L.,** 1989. Nitrogen impact of agricultural activities on air and water. 'River basin Management- 5'. H. Laikari (Ed.), Internatl. Assoc. on Water Pollution Research and Control, London (U.K.) Pergamon Press, Oxford, 203-212.

An investigation has been made on the impact of agricultural activities on the atmospheric and aquatic environment. Factors responsible for nutrient losses from soils and nitrogen emission to the air are presented. Measures for decreasing nutrient losses from agriculture are discussed. The nutrient leakage from agricultural land is responsible for about 40% of the total Swedish nitrogen load into the sea, Sweden, as a whole, is however only responsible for 9% of the total discharge (1,170, 000 tonnes) to the surrounding sea areas. The phosphorus leakage from agricultural land is responsible for about 25% of the total Swedish discharge to the surrounding sea.

314 **Enfield, C.G., Walters, D.M., Wilson, J.T., Piwoni, M.D.,** 1986. Behaviour of organic pollutants during rapid-infiltration of waste water into soil: II Mathematical description of transport and transformation. Hazardous Waste Hazardous Material 3 (1): 57-61.

A compartmental screening model was developed to describe the movement of volatile and transformable organic chemicals in rapid-infiltration waste water treatment systems. The first compartment describes losses of the chemical from the infiltration basin when the basin is flooded with waste water; the second considers losses due to volatilization and transformation in near surface soils during period of drying and the third describes the transport and transformation of the remaining chemical to ground-water. The model was developed to consider an accidental spill of chemical into a treatment system or a constant input of chemical into a system. Laboratory data for 18 organic compounds from a microcosm designed to simulate a rapid-infiltration system were used to evaluate the model. Data used in the evaluation were obtained after quasi steady state had been achieved.

315 **English, C.J., Jr. Miner, J.R., Koelliker, J.K.,** 1980. Volatile ammonia losses from surface-applied sludge. J. Water Pollut. Control Fed. 52(9): 2340-2350.

Equilibrium constants describing the dissolution and dissociation of NH_3 were measured in anaerobically digested waste water sludge in a laboratory experiment. and compared with theoretically determined constants. Theoretical constants reasonably approximated equilibrium conditions in the sludge. Corrections for activity effects of ionic strength were necessary, but adjustment for the effect of sludge organic content was unnecessary. Sludge pH increased with time logarithmically; the increase was related to a decrease in dissolved CO_2 concentration. A CO_2 model was developed to describe volatile loss of NH_3 by convective mass transfer. The experimental results were used to formulate a procedure to predict volatile losses of NH_3 from waste water sludge applied to land.

316 **Epstein, E., Deane, D.B., Meisinger, J.J., Legg, J.O.,** 1978. Mineralization of nitrogen from sewage sludge and sludge compost. J. Environ. Qual. 7 (2): 217-221.

Digested and raw sludges and compost derived from these sludges were freeze-dried and applied to a silt loam soil at 0, to 1814 kg N/ha. The soil sludge mixtures were incubated at 35°C for various time intervals and periodically leached and analysed for total N, NH_4-N and NO_3-N. A separate study using $K^{15}NO_3$ was conducted to evaluate N transformations. Such sewage sludge and sludge compost differ markedly in their initial net mineralization patterns. Amendments high in available C (raw sludge) are biologically very active and significant quantities of NO_3-N can be lost by denitrification and immobilization soon after addition. The N in amendments that have been stabilized by removal of readily oxidizable C (digested sludge) gave net mineralization patterns similar to native soil-organic N although large amounts of N can be released from digested sludge. The N in amendments that have been stabilized by composting with wood chips is not easily mineralized. With time these initial differences among sources decrease and the mineralization rates become more alike-although the time needed to reach this point depends on the quantity of amendment added.

317 **Erel, Y., Patterson, C.C, Scott, M.J., Morgan, J.J.,** 1990. Transport of industrial lead in snow through soil to stream water and ground-water. Chemical Geology (Isotope Geosci. Section). 85(3): 383-392.

Combining measurements of isotopic composition of Pb in stream water, ground-water, soil and bed-rock with other geochemical and geological parameters allowed the use of isotope tracers to determine how Pb contained in snow is transported over and through soils and added to streams. This also permits its distinction from Pb weathered from bedrock.

318 **Erickson, J.E.**, 1989. The influence of pH, soil type and time on adsorption and uptake by plants of Cd added to the soil. Water Air Soil Pollut. 48: 317-335.

Adsorption of Cd by two soils and its uptake by perennial ryegrass (Lolium perenne) and winter rape (Brassica napus) as function of pH (pH 4 to 7) and the amount of Cd added to the soil (0 to 5 mg kg^{-1} soil) were studied in a 2 yr pot experiment. In the soils, the more soluble fractions of Cd increased as the pH was lowered. Increasing the pH from 5 to 7 by adding CaO invariably reduced the Cd-content of ryegrass plants, but this decrease was less consistent where the pH had only been increased to 6. In some cases, acidifying the soil with S to reach a pH of 4 also led to a decrease in plant Cd-content. The Cd-content of rapeseed plants was markedly higher at pH 4 than at pH 5. Plant damage at low pH was observed in this crop. Water-leachable and $CaC1_2$-extractable soil Cd levels as well as plant uptake were higher in the sandy than in the clay soil, whereas IM NH_4AcO (buffered at pH 4.8 and 7) extracted roughly equal amounts from both soils.

319 **Erickson, J.E.**, 1990. Effects of nitrogen containing fertilizers on solubility and plant uptake of cadmium. Water Air Soil Pollut. 49: 355-368.

In pot experiment, the effect of N fertilizers, differing in NO_3 and NH_4 on the extractability of soil Cd in 1 M ammonium acetate (pH 7) and on uptake of native and added Cd by winter rape were compared. With N fertilizers extractable soil Cd and plant Cd uptake was lowest with nitrate of lime treatment; highest, with ammonium sulphate treatment and intermediate with nitrochalk. The addition of 1 mg/kg DW Cd to the soil increased Cd levels but did not change the response pattern. In relation to pH the stronger the acidifying effect, the higher the Cd availability. Plant, uptake of Cd was greater from soil, receiving granular NPK with a high Cd content than from those receiving granular NPK low in Cd. More Cd was extractable from sand than from clay soil.

320 **Estan, M., Bolarin, M.C., Gullen, M.G.**, 1988. The effect of Ni on capsicum (*Capsicum annum* L.) Agrochimica, 32: 379-390.

Capsicums were grown in culture solutions containing Ni at 0, 3, 6, 12, 24, or 48, mg/l. Growth reductions were noted at concentrations of 12 mg/l and above. Data on macro- and micro-nutrient levels in different plant organs are tabulated. In the fruits, the Ni concentration was correlated positively with N, Fe, and Zn concentrations and negatively with Ca and Na concentrations.

321 **Evangelista, R.A., Zownir, A.P.,** 1989. Lead contamination removal by soil washing, 82. Annual meeting of the Air and Waste Management Association, Anahelm, CA.: 106.

The U.S. EPA performed bench-scale studies to determine the feasibility of soil washing with EDTA to remove lead contamination from soil at two abandoned battery reclamation sites, Lee Farm and Sapp Battery. Prior to washing, soils were classified into three-fractions: oversized, coarse and fine. For the Lee Farm coarse fraction, a total lead reduction of 9.10 to 97.1 per cent was achieved while meeting the EP Tox criterion, for the Sapp Battery coarse fraction a total lead reduction of 85.4 to 98.3 per cent was achieved, but the total lead criterion of 79 mg/l was exceeded.

322 **Evans, L.J.,** 1989. Chemistry of metal retention by soils. Environ. Sci. Technol. 23(9): 1046-1056.

This review considers speciation of metals in soil solutions; certain exchange reactions. Adsorption at mineral surface and by organic matter; the precipitation of metals as secondary minerals and their dissolution. The two major mechanisms involved in the retention of metals by soil are adsorption and precipitation. Approaches to predict the behaviour of metals added to soil are discussed.

323 **Falkeson, L.,** 1979. Interspecies calibration of heavy-metal concentrations in nine mosses and lichens: Applicability to deposition measurements. Water Air Soil Pollut. 11(2): 253-260.

A method for including 9 alternative moss and lichen species in heavy-metal air pollution surveys is described. Iron, Cu, Zn, Pb, Ni, and Cd concentrations were measured. Concentrations vary decidedly between species. The mosses frequently show higher concentrations than the lichens. The mosses use of different monitor species in a deposition survey without interspecies calibration is not advised. Calibration factors for concentrations in different species can be calculated from the mean concentrations in each species. With the help of the factors, concentrations in a species not found in a certain site can be estimated from concentrations measured in any of the other species sampled. The applicability of the reported calibration factors to surveys in other regions is discussed. Where these factors are not applicable, local calibration factors for indicator species of interest can be set up using the method presented.

324 **Fanning, D.S., Korcak, R.F., Gouin, F.R.,** 1979. Metal content of plants and soils in a tree nursery treated with composted sludge. J. Environ. Qual. 8(1): 63-68.

Digested sewage sludge compost from Washington, DC, was applied to a Downer sand at rates of 0, 56, 112, 224 and 448 dry t/ha. A fertilized control treatment was also utilised. Pearl millet (*Penniustum americanum*) was grown as a summer cover crop prior to fall tree seeding. Leaf samples of red oak (*Querecus ruba*) and black walnut (*Juglas nigra*) seedings were taken in the summer of the 1st growing season. The total metal contents of the compost were 2154 Zn, 517 Cu, 13.9 Cd, and 69 Ni (μg/g). No visual foliar effects were noted on the growth of pearl millet or tree seedlings from the increasing rates of compost; however, pearl millet tissue-Cd levels significantly increased with levels of compost from 0.40 to 1.62 μg/g. Metal contents of the tree seedlings were low and within normal levels. DTPA extractable soil Zn, Cd and Cu decreased and soil Ni tended to increase with time. Compost additions increased soil pH which was maintained throughout the experiment. Poor correlations were obtained between DTPA-extractable metals and metal concentrations of pearl millet, red oak, or black walnut.

325 **Farmer, W.J., Aochi, Y., Yanlee, Dar,** 1990. Sorption of napropamide on clay and soil in the presence of dissolved organic matter. J. Environ. Qual. 19(3): 567-573.

Dissolved organic matter (DOM) can affect the distribution of solute between solution and sorbed phases and the availability and environmental fate of the solutes. Batch sorption isotherm techniques were used to evaluate solute/solute and solute/sorbent interactions that control the effects of DOM on the sorption of a nonionic, moderately polar organic solute by solid sorbents. The sorption of napropamide (2 a naphthoxy-N N-diethyl propionamide) by Na, Cu and Al montmorillonite decreased when dissolved humic acid derived from peat (peat-DHA) was present in the slurry. For Na montmorillonite, the effect of DOM on sorption was reduced when a dialysis membrane prevented contact between the DOM and the clay. This suggests that competition for sorption sites on the clay between DOM and the pesticide contributed to decreased nepropamide sorption. The extent of the DOM effect was also dependent on the concentration and the source of DOM added.

326 **Farmer, J.G., Cross, J.D.,** 1978. Bromine in soil — an indicator of automobile exhaust lead pollution. Water Air Soil Pollut. 9: 193-198.

Soil Br concentrations, ranged from 'natural' levels of 11 to 18 ppm to values of up to five times as high in Glasgow roadside and park surface soil. Elevated Br concentration in soil is shown to be a useful quantitative indicator of automobile exhaust Pb pollution, although care must be exercised in sample selection to avoid erroneous interpretation of data.

327 **Federicke, L.L., Harris, R., Peterson, L., Kehrmeyer, S.,** 1988. Composting fishery waste, Proc. Annual Waste Conf. Madison, 11: 133-141.

It was shown that fishery compost could be produced profitably as a community and private partnership.

328 **Federle, T.W. Dobbins, D.C., Thornton, J.R., Jones, D.D.,** 1986. Microbial biomas, activity and community structure in subsurface soils.

Ground-Water, 24(3): 365-374.

Microbial biomass, community structure and activity were determined in the subsurface horizons of four soil types common to Alabama. In all soils, biomas and activity declined with increasing depth; however, the magnitude and pattern of this decline varied as a function of soil type. Biomass concentration in the lower Ap horizon ranged from 8.2 to 18.0 nmoles phospholipid/g dry wt. soil. In the deepest horizons the range was 0.0085 to 0.059 nmoles phospholipid/g dry wt. soil. The rate of FDA hydrolysis was highly correlated with biomass (r=0.90). Polyenoic fatty acids, which are present only in eukaryotic micro-organisms, were found in all horizons. However, their relative abundance differed as a function of soil type. Stepwise regression analysis revealed that soil characteristics could explain 89 and 82 per cent of the variation in biomass and activity, respectively.

329 **Fernandes, J.C., Henriques, F.S.,** 1989. Metal contamination in leaves and fruits of holm-oak (Quercus rotundifolia Lam.) trees growing in a pyrites mining area at Aijustrel Portugal. Water Air Soil Pollut. 48: 409-415.

Levels of Fe, Mn, Zn, Cu and Pb in leaves and fruits of holm-oak growing at the outskirts of the mining area, were measured. The trees showed pronounced stunting, reduced leaf size and extensive necrotic and chlorotic spotting, reduced leaf size and extensive necrotic and chlorotic spotting. The leaves had much higher concentrations of metals than the controls -ca. 50 times higher for Cu, 20 times for Pb and Zn, 10 times for Fe, and 2 times for Mn, but it is possible that part of the metals associated with the leaves are actually retained in the dense hair cover present on their lower surface.

330 **Fernandes, J.C., Henriques, F.S.,** 1990. Metal levels in soils and cattail (*Typha latifolia L.*) plants in a pyrite mine area at Lousal Portugal. Internatl. Environ. Studies 36(3): 205-210.

Levels of Fe, Mn, Zn, Cu and Pb were measured in both below and above grouped tissues of *Typha latifolia* as well as in the soils tracts supporting the plants in a pyritemine tailing derived, waterlogged soil. Salt concentration (excluding Mn) were found higher than in control soils showing relative enrichment of Cu and Pb of the order of 20 to 70 times, and 10 to 20 times, respectively. Plants growing in the contaminated soil also showed higher metal levels in their organs with the exception of Mn. Roots of *Typha latifolia* had iron contents often much higher than that in the soil, probably due to the formation of ferric hydroxide plaque at the root surface. *Typha latifolia* plants showed great capacity to accumulate Mn against a concentration gradient and to prevent potentially toxic metal levels from reaching the shoot selectively.

331 **Filipinski, M., Grupe, M.,** 1990. Distribution of lithogenic pedogenic and anthropogenic heavy metals in soils. Zeit. Pflanz. und Bodenkunde 153(i):

69-73.

Lithogenic heavy metals, showed uniform or stratified gradients in the profile with reduction in concentration in all direction from the centre of accumulation. Pedogenic processes influence the metal conc. in certain horizons. Lateral transport also causes increased heavy metals conc. in the low lying areas when compared to crests. Metals of anthropogenic origin are mainly accumulated in the top soil. The conc. of those emanating from dust deposition decreased marked by in the direction of the prevailing wind. Point source pollution could be traced according to property boundaries.

332 **Filipinski, M., Kuntze, H.,** 1990. Plant uptake and solubility of lithogenic, pedogenic and anthropogenic cadmium of an Ap-horizon from an Orthic Luvisols in loess. Zeits. Pflanzen. und Bodenkunde. 153(6): 403-407.

Cadmium uptake by ryegrass (*Lolium multiflorum*) and spinach (*Spinacea oleracea*) in an Ap-horizon of Orthic Luvisol from loess contaminated with Cd lithogenically (stone powder), pedogenically (soil from Ah- and Bv-horizon) and anthropogenically was determined. The concn. of Cd in the pots was adjusted to 1.5, 3 and 6 mg/kg soil. The total Cd concn. in the soil being at the same level, the plants tested took up at least twice as much of Cd of anthropogenic origin than of the Cd of pedogenic or lithogenic origin. A markedly greater solubility of the anthropogenic cadmium was noticed compared with the other sources. The DTPA solution showed these differences most clearly. The relative soluble part of the anthropogenic Cd was more than 60% of the total content, whereas it was lower by a factor of 2 to 3 in the pedogenic or lithogenic cadimium. In the 0.1 M $CaCl_{-2}$ and the acid (0.1 M HCl + 0.125 MH_2SO_4) – extraction these differences were not as marked. The DTPA soluble cadmium fraction and the Cd taken up by the plants tested showed the closest correlations.

333 **Fiskell, J.G.A., Neary, D.G., Comerford, N.B.,** 1990. Slash pine and understory interception of micronutrients mineralised from sewage sludge applied to a sandy acidic forest soil. For. Ecol. Manage. 37(1-3): 27-36.

An industrially enriched municipal sewage sludge was applied to an acid (pH 4.4) sandy spodosol in a 5-year old stand of slash pine (*Pinus elliotii Engelm*). with a gallberry (*Ilex glabra L. Gray*) and saw palmetto (*Serenoa repens (Bertram)*) small understory. The mean composition of a sewage sludge expressed as >gkg^{-1} was as follows: 59N, 33P, 1.88 Cr, 0.27 Cd, 0.57 Cu, 0.35 Mn and 0.88, Zn. The sludge was top-dressed at rates of 0, 5.5, 11, 22 t ha^{-1}. Five years later, multiple core samples of the sludge-amended soil were obtained from the Oi, A, E, Bh and Bc horizons at depths of 0-5, 5-15, 15-41, 41-53 and 53-64, cm, respectively. Recovery of all four metals was predominantly in the Oi horizon and ranged from 46.5% for Zn to 70.7 for Cr. Only Zn was accumulated to any appreciable extent in the slash-pine overstory or saw-palmetto/gallberry understory.

334 **Flanagan, J.T., Wade, K.J., Currie, A., Curtis, D.J.,** 1980. The deposition of lead and zinc from traffic pollution on two roadside shrubs. Environ. Pollut. (Ser. B: Chem. Physic.). 1(1): 71-78.

Leaves and twigs of bramble and rhododendron were collected beside a major road and washed in a variety of chemical of which the most efficient was ammonium ethylenediaminetetraacetic acid. Large amounts of Pb and Zn accumulated on the surfaces of the leaves, and bramble leaves collected much more of these metals than rhododendron leaves. Zinc was found on leaves and twigs in similar quantities to Pb.

335 **Fochat, D.D., Cheng, C.N.,** 1979. Production of arsine and methylarsines in soil and in culture. Applied. Environl. Microbiol. 38(3): 949-498.

Arsenate, arsenite, monomethylarsenate, and dimethylarsenate were added to 3 different soils, and the evolution of gaseous arsenical products was determined over 3 wk. Arsine was produced in all 3 soils from all substrates, whereas methylarsine and dimethylarsine were produced only from methylarsenate and dimethylarsenate, respectively. At least 3 times more arsine than dimethylarsine was produced in soil incubated with dimethylarsenate. Resting cell suspensions of pseduomonas and Alcaligeners produced arsine as the sole product when incubated anaerobically in the presence of arsenate or arsenite. No trimethylarsine was observed, nor was there any evidence of methylation of any arsenical substrate in soil or in culture. Reduction to arsine, not methylation to trimethylarsine, was the primary mechanism for gaseous loss of arsenicals from soil.

336 **Folkeson, L., Nyholm, Tyler, G..** 1990. Influence of acidity and other soil properties on metal concentrations in forest plants and animals. Sci. Total Environ. 96(3): 211-233.

The influence of acidity and other soil properties on the concentrations of 22 elements in *Fagus syivatica*, *Oxialis acetosella, Carex pilulifera, Carabus hortensisinemoralls, Clethnonomys glareous, Apodemus flavicollis* and *Ficedula hypoleuca* was investigated in 30 stands of European beech in Southern Sweden. Soil pH and metal ion saturation were positively correlated with Al, Ca, Fe and Mg in plant. They were negatively correlated with Rb in 10 of the 11 plants and animal materials and with Mn in all the plants but only in one animal material. Clay was positively correlated with Al and Ni in plants and negatively correlated with Rb in plants and animals. Soils organic matter showed weak correlations except for Rb in animals (positive). The strong relationship between soil acidity and biological accumulation of Rb was maintained over several trophic levels.

337 **Foner, H.A.,** 1987. Traffic lead pollution of some edible crops in Israel, in "Social issue: Highway pollution", Proc. of the Second Internl Symp.,

London, July 1986: 309-315.

Fruits, vegetables and other crops grown in areas of heavy traffic were sampled and analysed for lead. The maximum lead content in washed vegetables was found in lettuce which contained about 0.5 mg/kg (fresh weight). The low lead contents of the crops are partially due to the low lead contents of the soils on which they are grown. There appears to be no undue danger to health from eating crops tested.

338 **Frank, R.,** 1979. Metals in agricultural soils of Ontario. Can.J. Soil Sci. 59(2): 99-103.

Farm fields which had been treated with sludge were sampled at 228 locations across the agricultural belt of Ontario. In addition, 30 locations were selected where at least one sludge application had been made. At all sites soils was sampled to a depth of 15 cm and analyzed for Ag, B, Mo, Se and Sb. Normal farm practices did not affect the levels of these metals in the soils studied. Mean background levels of these elements in the soils were as follows: Sb, 0.24 μg/g; Se, 0.37 μg/g; Ag, 0.44 mg/g; and Mo, 1.65 mg/g.

339 **Frankenberger, W.T., Jr., Ali Tabaubai, M.,** 1981. Fate of amide nitrogen added to soils. J. Agric. Food Chem. 29(1): 152-155.

The fate of nitrogen in amides (formamide, acetamide, and propionamide) was studied in five soils. The amount of inorganic-N ion species and NH_3 produced from each compound were compared with those produced from soils treated with $(NH_4)_2SO_4$ or urea and incubated under aerobic conditions at 30°C for 14 days. Recovery of the inorganic N ion species and NH_3 produced was affected by the compound and soil used. More than 25% of the N added as formamide was evolved as NH_3 from one sandy soil. The nitrification rate of the amide N was the greatest with formamide, and those of acetamide and propionamide were similar to those of urea and $(NH_4)_2SO_4$. The total recovery of inorganic ion species of N and NH_3 produced in the five compounds and five soils studied ranged from 62 to 103%. The amounts of NH_3 volatilized from the amide and urea-treated soils were significantly but negatively correlated with cation-exchange capacity, organic C, and clay contents of the soils examined.

340 **Franz, D.A., Hadley, W.M.,** 1981. Lead in Albuquerque street dirt and the effect of curb paint. Bull. Environl. Contam. Toxicol. 27(3): 253-358.

In all the studies, the suggested source of the lead was automotive combustion of leaded gasoline and the erosion of curb paint can be a significant, non-vehicular source of lead in street dirts.

341 **Fresguez, P.R., Francis, R.E., Dennis, G.L.,** 1990. Sewage sludge effect on soil and plant quality in a degraded, semiarid grassland. J. Environ. Qual. 19: 324-329.

Dried, anaerobically digested sewage sludge was applied at three rates

(22.5, 45 and 90 Mg ha^{-1}) to a degraded semi-arid grassland site. Most nutrients, including soil N, P and K, increased linearly as a result of sludge amendment. Soil pH decreased linearly from 7.8 to 7.4 with the application of sludge after the second growing season, On the other hand, the levels of DTPA-extractable soil micro-nutrients (i.e., Cu, Mn, Sn) increased linearly with sludge rates to levels recommended for adequate plant growth. Total herbaceous plant yields increased significantly with sludge amendment, particularly at the 45 Mg ha^{-1} sludge rates, as compared with the control. Blue grama (*Bouteloua gracilis* (H.B.K.) Lag. ex study) yield increased two-to-three-fold in amended plots over the unamended control after two growing seasons. The forage quality of blue grama, galleta (*Hilaria Jamesii* (Torr.) Beth.) and bottlebrush squirreltail (*Sitamion hystrex* (Nutt). J.G. Sm.) improved significantly as the level of tissue N, P and K and crude protein increased linearly with sludge application. Levels of Cd and Pb in all plant tissues did not increase significantly by sludge amendment. All micro-nutrients increased to acceptable levels in deficient plant tissues.

342 **Friedland, A.J., Johnson, H.A., Siccama, T.G.,** 1987. Zinc, Cu, Ni and Cd in the forest floor in the North-eastern United States. Water Air Soil Pollut. 29:233-243.

Quantitative forest floor samples collected from 78 sites in 9 States in the North-eastern United States in 1978 and 1980 were analysed for Zn, Cu, Ni, and Cd. Differences in metal and organic matter concentrations and amounts among forest types were attributed to geographic location of specific forest types rather than to direct biotic influence. No element was strongly correlated with elevation for the entire sample areas. Regional patterns of elemental amounts showed that trace metal levels are slightly higher in the Southern part than in the Northern part of the study region. Regional variation of Zn, Cu, Ni, and Cd in the forest floor was not indicative of atmospheric deposition except near point sources of pollution.

343 **Fritze, H.,** 1991. Forest soil microbial response to emissions from an iron and steel works. Soil Biol. Biochem. 23(2): 151-155.

The influence of the emissions from an iron and steel works on soil respiration, fungal hyphal length, green needle litter decomposition and microbial biomass C and N, in the humus of Pinus, sylvestris (L.) forest were investigated. Twelve study sites were established in polluted area, 0.3-0.7 km from the plant. The same number of study sites were established in control area, 3.5-4 km from the plant. The industrial emissions were manifested in significantly higher amounts of soil extractable cations (Ca, Mg, Mn, Fe, Zn, A), higher soil pH and moisture, and lower total N and loss-on ignition. A principal component analysis of the chemical data extracted a pollution axis which significantly explained the increase in fungal hyphal length and soil respiration in the polluted study sites and the opposite reaction for microbial biomass C and N. The percentage mass loss of green needle litter was not affected by the emissions from the steel works. The result are discussed in relation to forest soil liming.

344 **Frost, J.P., Brewer, A.J.**, 1990. Sprinkler irrigation system for silage effluent and dirty water. Farm Building Engg. 7(2): 43-45.

Silage effluent dirty water and milking parlour wash water were pumped to an above ground tank in which 7,000 m^3 of water is collected. Settlement of some solids takes place in small tanks at the point of collection and in the large storage tank. 50m^3/ha were irrigated at 21 day intervals at an application rate of 5 mm/hr using a sprinkler irrigation system on a fixed grid. Specific details and parameters of the system are given.

345 **Fu, M.H., Tabatabhi, M.A.**, 1988. Tungsten content of soils, plants and sewage sludge in Iowa. J. Environ. Qual. 17: 146-148.

Results showed that the total W in 18 soil ranged from 0 to 2 mg kg^{-1}, with mean and median values of 0.89 & 0.88 mg kg^{-1}, respectively. The corresponding values for 22 plant materials ranged from 0 to 0.35 mg kg^{-1}, with mean and median values of 0.18 and 0.17 mg kg. Analysis of 44 sewage sludge samples showed that the concentrations of this element varied from 0.5 to 6.2 mg kg^{-1}, with mean and median values of 4.3 and 2.2 mg kg^{-1}, respectively.

346 **Fuge, R., Andrews, M.J., Clevenger, T.E., Davies, B.E., Gale, N.L., Paveley, C.F., Wixson, B.G.**, 1988. The distribution of chlorine and iodine in soil in the vicinity of lead mining and smelting operation Bixby area, S.E. Missouri, USA. Appl. Geochem. 3(5): 517-521.

Iodine and Cl are enriched in soils in the vicinity of the Magmont and Buick lead mines near Bixby, South-eastern Missouri. The enrichments, up to 5.6 ppm I, and 305 ppm Cl, are against regional backgrounds of 1.26 ppm I and 41 ppm Cl. The area of highest I and Cl is thought to reflect a zone of base metal sulphide mineralization occurring about 400 m below the surface. Iodine and Cl are also enriched in soils immediately adjacent to a tailings pond, hence these elements would appear to be leached from this source. A zone of enhanced I values (up to 2.65 ppm I) to the North of a lead smelter is superimposed on a much larger zone of lead enrichment (upto 12,000 ppm pb) and is thought to represent I released from sulphide ores on smelting.

347 **Fuge, R., Long, A.M.**, 1989. Iodine in the soil of North Derbyshire. Environ Geochem Health 11(1) : 25-29.

Derbyshire was one of the best known centres of endemic goitre in Great Britain. Some 160 km from the coast in the direction of the prevailing wind, toposoils in the area are generally low in Iodine (mean = 5.44 mg/kg). Weathered rocks and soils are richer in Iodine than the unweathered bed-rocks, with soils developed over limestones being richer than those over sandstones, shales and dolomites. Highest Iodine contents in soil profiles over limestones occur in the upper horizons while over sand stones, Iodine concentrates in the lower horizons. The major cause of endemic goitre in north derbyshire is likely to be relatively low levels of Iodine, while the calcium rich soils of the area may contribute by reducing plant iodine uptake.

348 **Fuhrer, J.,** 1983. Phytotoxic effects of cadmium in leaf segments of *Avena sativa* L. and the protective role of calcium. Experientia, 39(5) : 525-526.

It is shown that ethylene production can be stimulated in peeled oat leaf segments in the dark by cadmium at concentrations below 0.01 mM, and that cadmium concentrations cause membrane deterioration and inhibit ethylene production and senescence. These effects of cadmium are antagonized by calcium. This indicates a possible protection of plant cells against cadmium toxicity by calcium.

349 **Fujioka, R.S., P.C. Loh,** 1978. Recycling of water for irrigation : Persistence of entroviruses in sewage effluent and natural waters receiving the effluent. Water Air Soil Pollut. 9 : 213-226.

A virological analyses of a sewage treatment plant which provided chlorinated, activated sludge treated sewage effluent to irrigate a two year crop of sugarcane, was made. Viruses were recovered from 100% of the raw-sewages tested at concentration ranging from 27 to 19000 $PFUl^{-1}$ while 76% of the activated sludge treated effluent was positive for virus at concentrations ranging from 7 to 5222 $PFUl^{-1}$. After chlorination, 58% of the samples were positive for virus concentrations from 2 to 750 $PFUl^{-1}$. Human entroviruses were also isolated from shallow flowing streams at distances up to 5 km from the closest known sewage effluent discharge entering the harbor. The viruses most often isolated were echorirus-7, coxsachievirus B-4, B-5 and poliovirus 1, 2 and 3. Although activated sludge treatment plus chlorination remove approximately 90% of the virus from the raw sewage, the final treated sewage effluent, still contains a significant concentration of infectious viruses. Furthermore, the recovery of enter viruses from waterways at points distant from the sewage treatment plants indicate that sewage-borne virus persist in natural water environment.

350 **Fuller, W.H., Alesii, B.A.,** 1979, Behaviour of municipal solid waste leachates, II. In Soil. J. Environ. Sci. Health. Part A : Environ. and Engg. A 14(7) : 559-592.

The rate of movement of heavy metals and organic carbon, found in municipal solid waste (MSW) land fill leachates is correlated with certain measurable broad parameters of the leachate and soil. Usually the lower the pH and higher the concentration of the other constituents, the more rapid is the movement of the pollutants through soil. The behaviour of MSW leachate with respect to its influence on attenuation of heavy metal migration through soils is not the same generated from freshly deposited waste as from that deposited longer.

351 **Funderburg, S.W., Moore, B.E., Sagik, B.P., Sorber, C.A.,** 1981. Viral transport through soil columns under conditions of saturated flow. Water Res. 15:(6) : 703-711.

Movement of polivirus 1, reovirus 3, and bacteriophage OX174 was studied in 8 soils in acrylic cylinders, 10 cm in dia and 33, 66 and 100 cm in length. Sequential flooding of the columns with waste water and distilled water resulted in a cyclical pattern of viral release in column percolates. The total number of viruses detected in percolates differed among the soils tested.

352 **Furness, J.C., Hensley, D.L., Robel, R.J., Mulhern, D.W.,** 1989. Vegetation of waste disposal areas at a coal fired power plant in Kansas. J. Environ. Qual. 18(3): 285-292.

Field tests were conducted over a 3-yr period to determine if a vegetative cover could be established without first adding topsoil to waste sites. Seven herbaceous and six tree species were planted on scrubber sludge and bottom ash sites. These states were first amended with fertilizer and then hay woodchips (*Bos taurus*) or manure. The bottom ash was not capable of supporting vegetative growth, even with amendment. Tall wheatgrass, tall fescue and Japanese millet grew well on scrubber sludge, as did eastern cotton wood and eastern red ceder trees.

353 **Furr, A.K., Parkinson, T.F., Elfving, D.C., Bache, C.A., Gutenmann, W.H.,** 1981. Elemental content of vegetables and apple trees grown on syrscuse sludge-amended soils. Agric. Food Chem. 29(1) : 156-160.

Two successive crops of peppers, kohirabi, lettuce, peas, spinach, sweet potatoes, and turnips were grown in pots of control and municipal sludge-amended acid and neutral soils. Two commercial apple cultivars were also cultured. Cadmium, nickel, and zinc were usually higher in vegetable crops grown on the sludge-fortified acid soil. Copper was higher in the vegetables grown on the neutral soil-sludge mixture. Nickel and zinc generally decreased in concentration in sludge-grown vegetable crops and applied trees during the second year of growth. There was not a consistent varietal or soil pH effect as regards heavy metals in apple trees. Copper and zinc tended to concentrate in apple twings while nickel and lead concentrated in apple leaves. Metal residues in apple fruit were comparatively low.

354 **Gadded Subhas Chandra, M., Rodgi Shivas,** 1985. Effect of temperature on the growth and biochemical activities of the bacterium proteus vulgaris in sewage. Environ. Eco. 3(3): 414-417.

The bacterium *Proteus vulgaris*, isolated from a stabilization pond was grown in sterile sewage and maintained various temperatures ranging from 10 to 50°C to evaluate its growth and biochemical potentialities in term of utilisation of dissolved oxygen, release of ammonia, nitrogen, removal of biochemical oxygen demand, and activities of protease and catalase, for a period of 15 days. At 30°C the optimum growth and biochemical activities of the bacterium were recorded. At lower temperatures the activities were slower and at higher temperatures (50°C) the activities were inhibited to a great extent. The catalase activity was proportional to the viable cell count of the bacterium at lower temperatures and the protease activity was more pronounced during the stationary and declining phase of the bacterial growth.

355 **Gaggi, C., Chemello, G., Bacci, E.,** 1991. Mercury vapour accumulation in azalea leaves. Chemosphere. 22(9-10) : 869-872.

Experimental data on the accumulation and release kinetics of azalea leaves exposed to a constant vapour level of mercury is reported. The accumulation of mercury appears to be irreversible probably as a consequence of chemical transformation. Potential applications and implications on the biogeochemicals cycle of mercury are discussed.

356 **Gajghate, D.G., Saxena, E.R., Vittal Rao. M.,** 1990. Kinetics of adsorption of lead by active carbon from aqueous solution. Indian J. Environ. Sci. Health. 32(4) : 369-376.

The adsorption of lead from aqueous solution by active carbon has been investigated. The effect of concentration of lead, pH, particle size, surface area of carbon and the rate of adsorption have been studied. Desorption of lead from carbon have also been undertaken to understand the mechanism. The rate of adsorption of lead is controlled by rate of diffusion in the carbon pores, and adsorption is due to formation of complexes of $PbNO_3$+ species with surface functional groups of carbon.

357 **Gale, P.M., Gilmour, J.T.,** 1986. Carbon and nitrogen mineralization kinetics for poultry litter, J. Environ. Qual. 15(4) : 423-426.

An incubation study was conducted to evaluate the relationship between net C and net N mineralized during the decomposition of surface applied poultry litter. The two litters were passed through a 2 mm sieve and comparisons were made among the fine and coarse fractions, and a 50-50 mixture of these fractions. Carbon mineralization for the fine fraction, followed first-order kinetics. Three distinct phase of decomposition were observed. Rapid phase rate constants followed the Arrhenius equation for the 11 to 25°C temperature range, while slow and inter-mediates phase rate constants at 18 and 25°C were temperature independent. The fine fraction C mineration rate constant for the rapid phase were 0.018, 0.038 and 0.049 d^{-1} at temperatures of 11, 18 and 25°C, respectively. For the intermediate and slow phases rate constants at 25°C were 0.011 and 0.006d^{-1}, respectively. At 25°C the rapid phase rate constant for the course fraction was 0.41 d^{-1} and that of the mixture 0.046 d^{-1}. No effect due to size fraction was observed for the intermediate and flow phases. During the rapid phase, net N mineralization paralleled net C mineralization after an initial flush of N mineralization at 1 d.

358 **Gale, N.L., Wixson, B.G.,** 1979. Cadmium in forest ecosystem around lead smelters in Missouri. Environl. Health Perspectives. 28: 23-37.

Primary Pb smelters were identified as potential sources of Cd, Pb, Zn, and Cu. Sintering and blast furnace operations produced significant quantities of small particulates highly enriched in Cd and other heavy metals. At one smelter, samples of stack particulars emissions indicate that 0.21 lb of Cd may be released to the atmosphere per hour. This is accompanied by 0.44 lb Zn, 4.66 lb, Pb, & and 0.01 lb Cu/hr. These emissions contribute to a significant deposition of Cd in the surrounding forest and stream beds. Mobilization of heavy metals may be significantly increased by contact of baghouse dusts or scrubber slurries with acidic effluents emanating from acid plants designed to produce H_2SO_4 as a smelter by-product. Cadmium and other heavy metals accumulated in the forest litter and partially decomposed litter along stream beds. Greater solubility, lower levels of complexation with organic legends in the litter, and greater overall mobility of Cd compared with Pb, Zn, and Cu resulted in appreciable contribution of dissolved Cd to the watershed runoff.

359 **Galivlin, R.V., Pinskil., D.L.,** 1988. The effect of lead on dehydrogenase activity of Serozem-Meadow soil. Agrokhimiya, 6 : 93-99.

Interactive effect of lead (50 to 50000 mg/kg) and glucose (0.05 to 500 mg/1) was studied on a heavy loam. it was observed that upto 95% of lead (in solution) was absorbed within the first hour of interaction with the soil, the rest more slowly. The inhibiting effect of lead showed up after 6 minutes of incubation; at concentrations of 5000 and 50000 mg/kg and after 3 days at 500 mg/kg. A strong inhibiting effect of lead upon glucose break down was evident at 50 and 500 mg/l; there was no significant effect at 0.05 mg/l concentration.

360 **Galli, G., Parenti, A.,** 1990. Land applications of industrial residues. Biocycle : 31(6) : 64-65.

A soil amendment combining cement and gypsum factory wastes with refuse compost or sludge was tested for use in quarries and land fills in Italy. Grasses and lettuce grown on refuse compost and sludge amendments gave similar results, although the refuse compost treated plants showed less initial growth than those treated with sludge. The percolation did not reach 0.8 m depth indicating the suitability of gypsum waste amendment as a cover material for land fills.

361 **Garau, M.A., Daimau, J.L., Felipo, M.T.,** 1990. Nitrogen mineralization in soil amended with sewage sludge and flyash. Bio-Fertility Soil. 12(3) : 199-201.

The effect of fly ash on N mineralization in sewage sludge was studied during a 5 weeks aerobic incubation of soil-waste mixtures. Significant differences were found among different incubation periods and also between treatments. The net N mineralization expressed as percentage of organic N added in the sludge was drastically reduced when high rates (500 Mg/ha) fly ash was added while 50 Mg/ha did not significantly reduce N mineralization.

362 **Garcia, W.J., Blessing, C.W., Sandford, H.W., Inglett, G.E.,** 1979. Translocation and accumulation of seven heavy metals in tissues of corn plants grown on sludge-treated strip-mined soil. Agri. Food Chèm. 27(5) : 1088-1094.

Metal translocation studies for Zn, Mn, Cu, Pb, Cr, Cd, and Hg were conducted for corn plants grown on strip-mined soil in Illinois, amended with anaerobically digested sewage sludge (25 t/acre dry). Differential metal accumulation rates in the 7 tissues analyzed indicated that generally the highest metal concentrations occur in the leaves and roots, and the lowest in the grain and cob. With the exception of Mn and Hg, metal concentrations increased in tissues as a results of sludge application. The greatest increases were for Cd where mean tissue concentrations (ppm) for unamended and sludge-grown conditions, respectively, were as follows: roots-0.062, 3.63; lower stems-0.027, 0.204; and leaves-0.276, 1.52. Metal extractabilities for plant uptake were established for the soil samples adhering directly to the root system of the corn plants studied; these extractabilities were compared with the metal concentrations in the leaf and root tissues.

363 **Garcia, C., Hernandez, T., Costa, F.,** 1990. The influence of composting and maturation processes on the heavy metal extractability from some organic wastes. Biological Wastes. 31(4) : 291-301.

Seven mixtures from 4 organic residues- aerobic sewage sludge, refuse, peat residue and grape debris were prepared to study the extractability of heavy metal by DTPA and 0.05M$CaCl_2$ from the residues. Composting and maturity increased metal conc., and their solubility was also decreased. The extractants removed more metals from the raw composts rather than from the matured composts. $CaCl_2$ extractable metals did not correlate significantly with the metal contents of the composts. Only DTPA extractable Zn and Pb showed significant correlation between them. The load of Zn equivalent increased with the composting and maturation processes while the Cd/Zn decreased with these processes.

364 **Garnett, K., Kirk, P.W.W., Lestr, J.N., Perry, R.,** 1985. Effect of nitrilotriacetic acid on the solubilities of metals in soil sludge mixtures. J. Environ. Qual. 14(4) : 549-553.

Batch experiments were undertaken to determine the effect of nitrilotriacetic acid (NTA) on the solubilities of Cu, Mn, Ni. Pb and Zn in soil-sludge mixtures. Soil samples from Wye Coombe series (silt loam) and Essex Windsor series (clay-laom) were each mixed with anaerobically digested sewage sludge and influence of extraction time, NTA concentration, and pH on the solubility of NTA and metals was assessed. Removal of NTA from the liquid phase by soil/sludge colloids became constant after 8 h and was attributed in both soil/sludge mixtures with increase in NTA concentration from 0 to 0.212 mmolL^{-1}. Manganese was the least affected by the addition of NTA, and pH was shown to be the over riding influence on its solubility. In the Essex soil/sludge mixture increasing the NTA concentration from 0 to 0.005 mmolL^{-1} caused a sharp decrease in Cu solubility, with higher NTA concentrations having no further effect on soluble Cu levels.

365 **Garnett, K., Kirk, P.W.W., Perry, R., Lester, J.N.,** 1987. Nitrilotriacetic acid in sludge-amended soil : Mobility and effects on metal solubility. Environ. Pollut. 12 (2): 145-162.

Soil column studies were undertaken to determine the mobility of nitrilotriacetic acid (NTA) in agricultural top soil and its effect on the solubility of Cd, Cu, Mn, Ni, Pb and Zn following land application of sludge containing NTA. The total weight of NTA retained on the columns was > 99% of that applied, with the levels of leached NTA becoming undetectable after 56 days. The presence of NTA increased the solubility of all the six metals although the degree of solubilisation varied with the individual metal, NTA dose and sludge application rate.

366 **Gath, S., Frede, H.G.,** 1990. The heavy metal content of road run-off water using zinc, lead, copper and cadmium as examples. Mittelugen derdeutsch Boden Kundlichen Gesellschaft 61 : 85-88.

The pollution of urban soils and waste water by traffic-induced heavy metal was studied at a dual carriage-way near Giessen. The conc. of heavy metals in a run off water was greatest at the beginning of a rainfall period. The duration of the dry period between rainfall events had a significant effect on the heavy metal content of run off particularly for Cd. The annual loads in kg/ha were 10.6, 1.8, 0.5 and 0.1 for Zn, Pb, Cu, and Cd, respectively. Threshold values of the German waste water discharge act were exceeded at frequencies of 2% for Zn, 98% for Pb, 18% for Cu and 30% for Cd.

367 **Gatz, D.F., Baytlett, J. Hassett, J.J.,** 1981. Metal pollutants in Agricultural soils and the St. Louls urban rainfall anomaly. Water Air Soil Pollut. 15: 61-75.

Concentrations of Zn, Cd and Pb were measured and the role of the urban rainfall anomaly in their accumulation in potentially- affected soils were evaluated. Samples from three soil layers were collected from agricultural fields at 21 sites. The highest metal concentrations were observed near Granite City, Illinoism and coincided with an area of maximum of Zn deposition in rain found in an earlier study. Only slight increases of the metals over background were found in the area of rainfall anomaly. Present rates of atmospheric deposition can account for these slightly elevated metal concentrations.

368 **Gaudet, F.J., Qasim, S.R.,** 1985. Attenuation of heavy metal toxicity of the activated sludge process by treatment with ferric cloride. Internatl. J. Environ. Studies 25(1-2): 127-135.

Laboratory experiments were conducted to examine the use of ferric chloride acclimation for treatment against heavy metal toxicity of an activated sludge process. The oxygen uptake of acclimated and unacclimated seed was measured by respirometry to determine the inhibitory effects of Ag and Pb.

369 **Gautam, D.D., Bishnoi, S.,** 1990. Effect of Urmul dairy effluent on soil characteristics and plant growth in Avena Sativa Linn. Geobios. 17 (2 & 3): 2-3.

The effect of dairy effluent was studied on seed germination, plant growth and biomass of Avena Sativa Linn. The plants were moderately tolerant and exhibited better growth in diluted effluent.

370 **Gautam, D.D., Bishnoi, S.,** 1989. Studies on dairy effluent and its effect on soil characteristics and growth behaviour of *Cicer arietinum* Linn. Oikoassay, 6(2) : 61-65.

An attempt has been made to assess the impact of Urmul dairy effluent on soil, germination and growth behaviour of gram (*Cicer arietinum* Linn.) The value of BOD and COD of the effluent was higher as compared to ISI tolerance limit, whereas metallic components and basic nutrients were present within the limit. The pH of the effluent treated soil was slightly lowered and E.C. value raised. The basic nutrients of the soil were not changed. The pure effluent had significant inhibitory effect on seed germination and growth of gram. The inhibitory effect was minimised with the dilution of the effluent.

371 **Gaynor, J.D.,** 1978. Soil degradation of waste water sludges containing chemical precipitants. Environl. Pollut. 20(1) : 57-64.

Four sludges, 3 of which contained calcium hydroxide, ferric chloride, or aluminum sulfate for P removal, were compared as to degradation in soil. All sludges degraded rapidly but rates (25 mg/l) approached CO_2 evolution of untreated soil in 15 d while higher rates required 50 d. Each of the sludges contained lime which, at each addition, increased the soil pH. The Ca-sludge produced the greatest pH increase and evolved larger amounts of CO_2 than the Fe- and Al-sludges. The Ca-sludge evolved 52%, the untreated Al-sludge 20% and the Fe-sludge 5% of the sludge C. Calcium carbonate added to the soil increased the degradation of the Al-sludge, and no significant differences among sludges were noted in the percentage of sludge C evolved. The degradation of these sludges was more related to soil pH than to chemical treatment of the influent for P removal.

372 **Geeta, J. Pandey, G.S.,** 1991. Sedimented sludge of dress cleaning oil refuge : Determination of anthropogenic elements. Asian Environ. 13(1) :

69-7:13

A number of anthropogenic elements (Cu, Co, Ni, Pb, Zn, Mn, Ag, Bi, Cr, Sb and Cd), which owe their existence in the environment as a consequence of human activities, have been determined in the sludge of the dress-cleaning oil refuge of Bhilai and Raipur areas by atomic absorption spectrophotometry.

373 **Genevini, P.L.,** 1986. Considerations on agricultural valorization of sewage sludge and on inherent monitoring methods. Ing Ambient. 15: 413-425.

To evaluate the fertilizing and polluting potential of sludge and to establish whether the later is limiting the first one or not, and eventually to what extent, sludge must be characterized, application rates be chosen and sludge effects be monitored, according to the following steps; sampling; chemical analysis; phytotoxicity and bio-accumulation, bio-assay, back analysis sludge and soil; crop and leaching water monitoring.

374 **Geriste, R.G., Van Driel, W.,** 1984. Relationship between adsorption of trace metals, organic matter and pH in temperate soils. J. Environ. Qual. 13(2) : 197-204.

Distribution constant for Cd and Pb were measured for 33 temperate soils. The distribution constant were related to soil organic matter and pH at three different strengths of soil extractants. The soil extractants consisted of solutions of $CaCL_2$, NaCl and KCl and were taken to be representative of the compostion of the soil solution phases. For each ionic strength a significant log-log correlation was found between the distribution constants, related to organic matter content of the soil and the hydrogen ion concentrations of the soil extracts. Exchangeable or mobile fractions of Cd and Pb in the soil were calculated from the product of distribution constant and concentration in a soil extract. With the aid of adsorption data of previous work with other soils, assuming a similar relationship as found for Cd and Pb, comparable results were obtained for Cu and Zn. Exchangeable fractions were found to lie in a range of about 1 to 5% of total metal in the soils for Pb and about 10 to 50% for Cd, Zn and Cu.

375 **Gerstl. Z.,** 1990. Estimation of organic chemical sorption by soils. J. Contam. Hydrol. 6(4) : 367-375.

Sorption data for 400 compounds were collected and analyzed. Sorption coefficients on an organic carbon basis (Koc) were found to be log-normally distributed. Correlations between log Koc and log aqueous solubility (S), log Kow (octanol water partition coefficient) and molecular connectivity (MC) indices were calculated and their predictive ability determined with a set of test data not included in the original data set. It was found that the equations (Log Koc vs. either log S or log Kow) for individual chemical groups were preferred over the general equation for all chemicals but that a group correction term (Fe) added to the total equation gave similar results. The use of MC indices alone were inadequate for predicting sorption values with the exception of few homologous groups.

376 **Gesumaria, R.H.,** 1982. Industrial waste water sludge disposal on agricultural soils of northwest New Jersey. Diss. Abst. Int. Pt. B. Sci. & Eng. 42 (9) : 655.

Research was conducted in two parts: part I, Pilot-Scale Field Experiment and part II, Self-contained Lysimeter Experiment. The Pilot-Scale Field Experiment consisted of the application of aerobically digested, industrial sludge to two experimental plots. Principal variables of the research project were sludge application rate, soil system pH and surface cover. The fate of nitrogen and selected ions was monitored through extensive soil water and groundwater sampling. Samples taken by means of suction Lysimeters showed considerable inconsistency, necessitating periodic reassessment of sampling locations and frequencies.

377 **Geuenich, H.H., Mueller, H.E., Schretten-Brunner, A., Seeliger, H.P.R.** 1985. The Occurrence of different *Listerial* species in municipal waste water. Zentrabl. Bakteriol. Microbiol. Hyg. Abt. B 81(6): 563-565.

214 Listeria strains were isolated from purified municipal waste water. The differentiation was performed taking into account the newly described species within the genus Listeria. 92.5% of isolated Listeria strains belonged to *L. monocytogenes,* 4.2% to *L. innocua,* and 3.3 to *L. seeligeri.*

378 **Ghaly, A.F., Singh R.K., Burney, J.R.,** 1988, Land disposal of cheese whey. Can. Soc. Agri. Engg. (83), 1-24.

A laboratory experiment was carried out on transformation and transport of nitrogenous compounds in soils receiving high application rate of cheese whey. The experimental apparatus consists of 36 soil columns constructed of PVC pipes with 20 cm inside diameter. Three types of soil (sandy loam, loam and sandy clay loam) and three soil depth (60, 120 and 180 cm) were studied. Results indicated that all types had high removal efficiency of the nitrogenous compounds. The nitrate concentration in the leachate was very high at the beginning of the experiment which decreased with time. Therefore, continuous application of cheese whey at higher rates may result in ground-water contamination.

379 **Giashuddin, M., Cornfield, A.A.,** 1979. Effect of adding nickel (as oxide) to soil on nitrogen and carbon mineralisation at different pH values. Environl. Pollut. 19(1) : 67-70.

Nitrogen and C mineralization were measured after adding 50, 250, 1000 and 5,000 ppm Ni (as oxide) to a sandy soil at pH levels of 5.8, 6.9 and 7.6 and incubating aerobically for 6 wk at 30°C. Nitrification decreased to a greater extent with increasing Ni at pH 5.8 than at pH 6.9 and 7.6. Nitrogen mineralization decreased to about the same extent with increasing Ni at all pH levels. Carbon mineralization decreased with increasing Ni to about the same extent at pH 5.8 and 6.9 but to a lesser extent at pH 7.6.

380 **Gibson, D.T.,** 1989. Recent advances in the microbial degradation of aromatic hydrocarbons, in 'Biotechnology Applications in Hazardous Waste Treatment': Engg. Foundation, Newyork : 149-165.

Lab. studies were carried out to gain insight into the way in which micro-organisms degrade aromatic hydrocarbons, and ways in which recombinant DNA technology could be used to construct strains. capable of removing high concn. from polluted environments. The role of oxygen in the biodegradation of aromatic hydrocarbons and initial reactions in their oxidation by mammals and bacteria were examined. The bacterial degradation of toluene was used to examine new technologies which might find application in hazardous waste treatment.

381 **Giggey, M.D., Crites, R.W., Brantner, K.A.,** 1989. Spray irrigation of treated septage on reed canary grass. J. Water Pollut. Control Fed. 61 : 333-342.

Two plots (3 × 3 m) of reed canary grass were irrigated with effluent from a pilot plant that produced secondary treatment and nitrogen removal from septage. At hydraulic application rate of 18 to 36 mm per week and annual application of 450 kg N/ha, the plots provided more than 90% removal of BOD, TSS, N and P. Organic N was the main form of underflow N. The harvested grass had high protein content and normal levels of nutrients and metals.

382 **Gilbert, R.G., Lance, J.C., Miller, J.B.,** 1979. Denitrifying bacteria population and nitrogen removal in soil columns intermittently flooded with secondary sewage effluent. J. Environ. Qual. 8, (1): 101-104.

The effects of infiltration rates and carbon treatment on denitrifying bacterial population and N-removal in soil columns intermittently flooded with secondary sewage effluent (SSE) were determined. At low infiltration rates of 10 to 15 cm/day, N-removal by denitrification was > 80% and enrichment of the SSE with organic canbon did not further enhance N loss, even though the denitrifying bacteria populations were increased. However, at higher infiltration rates (15 to 40 cm/day), the physiologically active denitrifying bacteria populations were effective in net N-removal, and carbon enrichment of the SSE was essential for maintaining 80% N-removal. Continuous carbon treatments were more effective than 2-day pulse treatments for increasing the number of denitrifying bacteria and N-removal with continuous carbon treatments of 200 mg/litre, 80% N-removal was obtained at infiltration rates of 40 cm/day.

383 **Giller, K., McGrath, S.,** 1989. Muck, metals and microbes. New Scientist, 124 : 31-32.

Various aspects of heavy metals are reviewed. Effect of toxic metals on legume nodules and Rhizobium are outlined. it is not yet possible to assess the safe conc. of metals in the soil for microbes. Most metals have limited availability in soil: Zn and Cd are most readily adsorbed and accumulation of Cd in the food chain causes most concern.

384 **Gilmor, J.T., Clark, M.D.,** 1989. Nitrogen release from waste water sludge–a site specific approach. J. Water Pollut. Control Fed. 60(4):494-498.

An analytical computer simulation approach to the determination of plant available nitrogen (PAN) in waste water sludge was described and verified and then compared to the constant factor approach where an invariant percentage (usually 20%) of the organic N in sludge was assumed to contribute to PAN. The simulation approach estimated PAN values that varied with climate among sludges. The latter estimates were substantially larger than the constant factor approach and showed considerable variability that suggested that the constant factor approach would provide poor estimates of PAN under most conditions. Estimates of PAN using analytical computer simulation approach were related to sludge analytical data for 2 sludges.

385 **Giordano, P.M., Mays, D.A., Behel, A.D., Jr.** 1979. Soil temperature effects on uptake of cadmium and zinc by vegetables grown on sludge-amended soil. J. Environ. Qual. 8(2) : 233-236.

A field experiment was conducted during 1975-1977 to determine uptake of Cd and Zn by several vegetables from Sango Soil amended with 224 tons/ha of an anaeobically digested sewage sludge. Soils were heated to approximately 270°C using thermostatically controlled resistance cables placed 30 cm deep and 30 cm apart in the soil. Concentration of DTPA-extractable metals in soil increased with time. But these increases were not reflected in higher plant concentration. Soil heating significantly increased Cd and Zn concentrations in brocole and potato. Concentrations of Cd and Zn were not statistically significant. Liming reduced the concentrations of Zn & Cd in the crops but dilutions due to better growth may have accounted for a part of the reduction. Analysis of soil cores taken after cropping in 1977 indicated movement of Zn & Cd to a maximum depth of 20 to 30cm.

386 **Glordone, P.M., Mortvedt, J.J.,** 1976. Nitrogen effects on mobility and plant uptake of heavy metals in sewage sludge applied to soil columns. J. Environ. Qual. 5 (2): 165-168.

Columns of heavy metal-amended soil in plastic well casings were cropped with tall fescue (*Festuce arun dinacen Sehreb*) and leached three times with deionized water. Heavy metal concentrations above check values were not detected in leachates from any columns. Mobility of heavy metals from the inorganic sources was slightly greater than that from the sewage sludge. Nitrogen fertilization did not affect the down ward movements of Zn, Cd, Cr, Pb, or Ni in soil but enhanced uptake of these metals by fescue because of increased growth. Heavy metal contamination of ground-water is not likely in heavy textured soils when sewage sludge applications are accompanied by N fertilization at least for short periods of time.

387 **Giordano, P.M., Mortvedt, J.J.,** 1980. Zinc uptake and accumulation by agricultural crops. In "Zinc in the Environment. Pt. 2 : Health Effects. John Wiley & Sons, New York: 401-413.

Zinc uptake and accumulation vary widely in agricultural plants and are related to soil pH and texture, soil organic matter content, temperature and light intensity, crop species, and cultivars within a species. Interaction with other plant nutrients, especially P, N, and Fe, affect zinc uptake by plants. Both plant tissue analyses and oil tests can be used to diagnose zinc deficiencies in crops. A number of both inorganic and organic sources of zinc are effective in correcting zinc deficiencies in agricultural crops. Recommendations regarding sources, rates,and methods of applications should be followed for specific crops.

388 **Giulio, R.T., Ryan, E.A.,** 1987. Mercury in soils, sediments, and clams from a North Carolina peatland. Water Air Soil Pollut. 33: 205-219.

Mercury concentrations were measured in samples of peat soils, sediments and clams *(Raigia cuneate)* from a peatland region of North Carolina. Total Hg concentrations in peatcores ranged from 40 to 193 ng g^{-1}(dw); no depth-related trends were noted. Mercury concentrations in surface sediments from canals draining the peatlands and from the Pungo-River that receives this drainage ranged from 8 to 20 ng g^{-1} (dw). Selective extractions of these peat and sediments samples revealed that the bulk of the Hg was associated with organic matter-associated fractions. Total Hg concentrations in the soft tissues of clams from the Pungo River ranged from 25 to 32 ng g^{-1} (dw).

389 **Giusquiani, P.L., Patuirmi, M., Bushnell, M.,** 1989. Chemical composition of fresh and composted urban waste. Plant Soil. 116(2): 278-282.

Chemical, spectroscopic and molecular characteristics of humus extracted from urban waste before and after composting, are reported. The main differences are in the contents of acidic groups and straight alphatic chains which diminish in the composted material.

390 **Glenn, J., Riggle, D.,** 1989. Where does the waste go ? Biocycle. 30(4) : 34-39.

Data on Municipal solid waste (MSW) surveyed in USA in 1988, reveal that more than 80% of 250 million tons of MSW is disposed of in land fills. Only 3 states incinerate more than 30% of their wastes. With the remaining capacity of the land fills and availability of land decreasing, however, incererators are becoming more common. The data also reveal a trend to more recycling programmes and compositing of MSW. MSW generation, disposal methods costs and recycling or composting programmes are listed for each state.

391 **Glorioso, J.D.,** 1989. Combined sewage and lime sludge treatment process United States Patent No. 4852269.

A process is described for combining the disposal of sewage sludge and lime sludge by recalcing the lime sludge to produce lime for municipal water treatment and utilizing the excess heat from the recalcing process to dry and palletize sewage sludge or supplement the sewage sludge pellets and then produce in uniform sizes and have excellent value as a soil conditioner.

392 **Godwin, R.J., Werner, N.L., Hali, J.E.,** 1986. Soil injection of liquid waste. Soil Water 14(2) : 10-12.

The techniques for the disposal to agricultural land of either agricultural slurry or municipal sewage sludge are similar, and consist either of surface spreading or injecting the liquid waste below the soil surface. The soil injection technique has many advantages over surface spreading.

393 **Gohil, M.B.,** 1989. Soil chemical properties of sewage farms, Asian Environ 11(1): 61-71.

The impact of sewage irrigation on soil chemical properties and canal water irrigated farms of Gujarat State, in India, have been studied.

394 **Gohil, M.B., Aswani, P., Gohil, P.,** 1987. Land disposal of liquid industrial waste. National Seminar on Impact of Environment Protections on future Development in India. Tech. Papers II: 43-49.

Paper describes case studies of excellent land management of liquid industrial wastes generated from industries such as pulp and paper mill, food processing plant and dairy. Results indicate land treatment of these waste waters to be an attractive alternative cost-effective method. However, land disposal is by no means a panacea. The paper also describes some limitations associated with this technology.

395 **Gomah, A.H.M., Al-Nahid, S.I., Amer, H.A.,** 1989. Nitrogen mineralization in sludge-amended desert soil as affected by rate of sludge, salinity, and wetting and drying cycles. Arid Soil Res. Rehab. 3(4) : 417-429.

Three incubation experiments were conducted to determine the influence of sludge rate, N addition, salinity, and wetting and drying cycles on different N forms in sludge-amended calcereous silt loam soil. NH_4-N and No_3N were analyzed at intervals of 1, 2, 4, 8 and 12 weeks incubation at 30°C $\pm$ 1. The rate of sludge as well as N was found to significantly affect NO_3-N accumulation. The cumulative inorganic N at the end of 12 weeks incubation was dependent on sludge rate and slightly affected by N addition. Cumulative mineralized N at 0-, 40-, 80-, and 160-t/ha sludge treatments were 15.4, 83.7, 105.1, and 165.0 mg/kg soil, respectively. In case of sludge and N addition, these figures were 10.2, 99.6, 108.4 and 180.4 mg/kg soil. N-mineralization rate constant (K) increased from 0.214 in the control to 0.303, and 0.439, then decreased to 0.309/week in soil treated with 0, 40, 80 and 160 t/ha sludge, respectively. Mean K values decreased with N addition.

396 **Goodroad, L.L., Caidwell, A.C.,** 1979. Effects of phosphorous fertilizer and lime on the As, Cr, Pb, and V content of soils and plants. J. Environ. Qual. 8(4) : 493-496.

Two experimental sites-a Nicollet clay loam fertilized with 0, 1111, 2222, 4444 and 8888 kg/ha of concentrated super phosphate (CSP) and 20.2 t of lime, and a Port Byron slit loam fertilized for 19 yr with 99, 73, 82, and 352 kg/ha annually of CSP, calcium metaphosphate, phosphoric acid, and Southern rock phosphate, respectively, were sampled to determine if significant amounts of As, Cr, Pb, or V had been added from the use of these fertilizer materials. There was no indication of increased As, Cr, Pb, or V from the addition of P fertilizers to either the Nicollet or Port Byron soils. The addition to lime increased the Cr content of the Nicollet soil by 3 ppm, but there was no increase in As, Pb, or, V. There was no increase in As, Cr, Pb, V from addition of CSP in soils samples from below the Ap horizon to a depth of 47.5 cm. Corn *(Zea mays)* plant growth and grain yields were similar for all CSP and lime treatments.

397 **Gorbatov, V.S., Zyrin, N.G.,** 1988. Adsorption of Zn, Pb, and Cd soil and acid-base equilibrium. Moscow University Soil Sci. Bull. 43(3) : 21-25.

The change in the pH of solution in relation to adsorption of heavy metals by a native leached chernozem and calcic chernozem was investigated. It was established that in both cases the adsorption of metal is accompanied by a decrease of pH. Possible causes of this phenomenon are discussed.

398 **Gordeiko, V.A., Shustrova, N.M.** 1990. Yersinia in plants. Microbiol. Epidemiol. Immunobiol. 11: 16-19.

Plants collected on the plots of land formerly irrigated with sewage water from a sine breeding complex (in sewage and the soil, Yersinia had been earlier detected) were studied. In 4.9% of plant samples Yersinia were detected (*Y. enterocolitica* and *Y. Intermedia*). The isolated strains were biochemically and seriologically identical to those detected in sewage and the soil. No Yersinia were detected in washings from the surface of these plants, as well as in the study of control plants. These facts led to conclusion that Yersinia were present in plant tissues.

399 **Gotoh, S., Koga., H.,** 1985. Accumulation and distribution pattern of mercury in soil profile in Kyushu (Japan) as related to man's impact. Jarq. 19: 166-171.

Seven distribution patterns were detected for the total Hg content within the soil profiles. In general, soil contamination with Hg was limited to the upper horizons, and does not spread much downward. The total Hg in all the surface soil horizons combined ranged from 21-473 ppb with a mean of 173 ppb. Apparently, organic mercury-fungicides application in recent years was a principal factor above all regarding the establishment of the elevated Hg levels in the upper soil horizon under cultivation.

400 **Govindan, V.S., Devika, R.,** 1991. Studies on the heavy metal profiles of Adyar river and waste stabilization ponds. J. Ecotoxicol. Environ. Monit. 1(1) : 53-58.

The rate of leaching of heavy metals from the sediment to the water column as well as the associated physico-chemical parameters were investigated. The concentration of heavy metals leached from sediment to water column was inversely proportional to the pH of the water.

401 **Greene, J.C., Milier, W.E., Shiroyama, T. Maloney, E.,** 1975. Utilisation of algal assays to assess the effects of municipal, industrial, and agricultural waste water effluents upon phytoplankton production in the Snake river system, Water Air Soil Pollut. 4: 415-434.

Algal assays were conducted on waters of eighteen Snake river and tributory sites to: (1) determine if algal growth was consistent with results predicted from review of chemical·analysis for orthophosphorous and total soluble inorganic N: (2) determine if algal yields were limited by P, N, or some other nutrient essential to algal growth, and (3) predict the effect of N or P additions on algal productivity.

402 **Griffin, R.A., Chou, S.F.J.,** 1981. Movement of PCB's and other persistent compounds through soil. Water Sci. Technol. 13, 1153-1163.

The adsorption and mobility of polychlorinated biphenlys (PCBs, polybrominated biphenyls (PBBs), and hexachlorobenzene (HCB) were studied under laboratory conditions. The adsorption of PCBs, PBBs, and HCB by soils and by carbonaceous adsorbents from aqueous solutions and organic solvents could be described by the Freundlich adsorption equation. All three compounds were found to be strongly adsorbed by the carbonaceous adsorbents and by the soil materials. There was a very high direct correlation between the total organic carbon (TOC) content of the soils and the amounts adsorbed. No measurable adsorption of PBBs or HCB by soils occured from organic solvents; however, the compounds were strongly sorbed from the solvents by the carbonaceous adsorbent.

403 **Griffin, R.A., Schulter, R.M., Shimp, N.F., Shiley, R.H.,** 1980. Chemical and biological characterization of leachates from coal solid wastes. IL. Inst. Natural Resources. St. Geol Survey Div. Champaigh. II. 99.

Eleven coal solid wastes were characterized chemically and mineralogically. The wastes comprised three lurgi gasification ashes, mineral residues from the SRCC-I and H-Coal Liquefaction processes, two chars, two coal cleaning residues, and a fly ash and water-quenched bottom ash (slag) from a coal-fired power plant. Leachates that were generated from the solid waters at four pH levels and under two different gas atmospheres were analyzed for more than 40 chemical constituents. These leachates were also used in soil attenuation studies and in acute 96 hour static bioassays. Sixty constituents were determined in the solid wastes; the major elements among them were Al, Ca, Fe, K, Mg, Na, S, Si and Ti.

404 **Griffith, S.M., Ram, R., Ahmad, N.,** 1989. Humic substances from a petroleum-polluted tropical soil. Sci. Total Environ. 81-82: 511-519.
Humic materials were extracted with 0.5M NaOH under N_2 from three sites of Cromarty soil series (Entic pelluderts). Two of the sites, namely Kendell and Silver Stream, were petroleum-contaminated through intermittent flooding, whereas a third site was uncontaminated. Data obtained for the humic acid (HA) and fulvic acid (FA) fractions of soil at the contaminated and non-contaminated sites were compared for yields, functionality and the variability in patterns of infrared (IR) spectra and differential scanning calorimetric (DSC) thermograms.

405 **Grigoryan, K.V.,** 1990. Effect of irrigation waters polluted with industrial wastes on heavy metal concentration in soil and in certain crops. Soviet Soil Sci. 22(2) : 121-128.
Irrigation with polluted waters of Debed river, Armenia, USSR, led to increase in heavy metal conc. in soil and cultivated crops. A strong correlation was found mainly between the content of Cu, Pb, Ni and Mn in Cinnamon-brown forest steppe soil and in leaves of cultivated crops (r=0.51 to 0.97). A scale of heavy metal contamination of cultivated crops was devised.

406 **Gross, R., Schramel, P., Payer, H.D.,** 1987. Concentrations of lead, cadmium mercury and other in seeds of *Lupinus mutabilis* and of other legumes. J. Environ. Pathol. Toxicol. 7(3) : 59-65.
Several species of legumes and varieties of lupins were examined for their heavy metal content in the seeds. The heavy metal contents of legumes seeds of different origin and variety indicates a complex pattern of environmental and genetic factors that contribute to the specific metal contents of individual harvests. On the level of variations the environmental factors (climate, soil, geology, agricultural techniques) seem to exhibit more important influences on the specific accumulation of heavy metals than genetic factors. In contrast, on the level of species or genera, the accumulation of heavy metals seems to be dominated by genetic factors rather than by environmental influences.

407 **Grun, R., Pusch, F.,** 1989. Heavy metals in agro-ecosystems: heavy metals in the soil plant system after years of sewage sludge amendment on characteristic soils of the Weserems. area (FRG). Mitteil der Deuts Chem Bodenk. Gesellschaft 59(2) : 711-716.
The legal threshold values for heavy metals had not been reached at either site after years of sewage sludge application. Both soils (alluvial,

Podzol-psludogley) showed the highest contents of heavy metals in the top soil. Plant analysis showed the highest concentration of heavy metals in the roots of rye grass and wheat.

408 **Grupe, M., Filipinski, M.,** 1989. Availability and plant uptake of Pb in soil with high lithogenic heavy metal contents. Mittilungon Deutschen Bodenkundlichen Gesellschaft. 51(1) : 361-366.

The influence of lithogenic Pb content on, Pb, uptake of plants was studied under field and glasshouse conditions using soils with Pb contents of 900-6800 mg/kg. Results from field experiments showed that Pb contents of grass remained constantly under the 45 mg/kg threshold value required by the animal feed law. DTPA extractable Pb correlated well with Pb content of grass. For the pot experiments soils from Ah, Br, and Cr horizons were used and cultivated with wheat and barley. The Pb uptake of plants was strongly correlated with the soil horizons and pH of soils. The Pb content of wheat grains exceeded the legal threshold. A correlation with DTPA extractable soil Pb was only obtained for barley grain.

409 **Guedria, A., Trichet, J., Wilhelm, E.,** 1989. Behaviour of lead and zinc in calcrete-bearing soils around Bou Grine, Tunisia — its application to geochemical exploration. Geochemical Exploration 32(1-3) : 117-132.

The behaviour of Pb and Zn was studied in soils containing calcrete to determine the effects of calcrete formation on the surface expression of mineralization. Earlier investigations had shown that : (1) calcrete develops epigenetically within the soil from other minerals present in the horizon that is being encrusted; and (2) this epigenetic replacement is isovolumetric. One consequence of this process for geochemical exploration is that the development of calcrete can be compared to installing a screen that weakens the contrast of the anomaly. Another geochemical consequence is that the metals that were initially associated with various mineralogical phases in the parent rock ill-associate mainly with HCl (IN) soluble components in the calcrete horizons. In non-calcreted horizons, and in particular in the surficial layers, the metals are divided between carbonate and oxide phases, the latter being more or less well-crystallized.

410 **Gulbard, E.B., Thorton, I., Watt, J., Wheatlay, M., Moorcroft, S., Thompson, M.,** 1988. Metal contamination in British urban dusts and soils. J. Environ. Qual. 17(2) : 226-234.

The geometric mean concentrations of Pb, Cd, Cu and Zn was determined. Conc. of Pb in 5235 house dusts and 4650 garden soils collected in 53 locations in Great Britain are 580 and 298 mg kg^{-1}, respectively. Variation between locations are considerable with house dusts ranging from 205 mg kg^{-1} for Ayr in Scotland to 1870 mg kg^{-1} for an historic mining area located in Derbyshire, England. Lead concentrations in house dust are significantly and positively related to : (i) Pb concentration in garden soil, (ii) the area of exposed soil surrounding the house, (iii) the presence of high lead-containing points used inside the house and (iv) instances of recent redecoration. Concentrations are highest in the older homes.

411 **Gupta, A.P., Antil, R.S., Singh, A.**, 1986. Composition of some sewer water and their effect on soil properties, Proc. National Seminar on Environmental Pollution Control and Monitoring, October 1986.

The sewer water samples were collected from Hissar, Karnal, Panipat and Sonepat cities in Haryana to know their chemical composition. The soil samples from 2 depths (0-15, 15-30 cm), where sewer water was used for irrigation were also collected. The sewer water from different cities varied in their composition which was in accordance with the type of industries present in the area. The sewer water of Sonipat had the highest quantity of Ni, Zn, Fe and Mn. According to the parameters of water quality laid for irrigation purposes, these waters are fit for irrigation but the content of metal ions becomes a barrier for their use as potential source of irrigation around the cities.

412 **Gupta, M.S., Bhargava, D.S., Varshney, B.S.**, 1988. Removal of cadmium from wastes through adsorption on saw dust. J. Instn. Engrs. (India). Environ. Engg. 68(2): 69-72.

Locally available sawdust was used to study the removal of cadmium through adsorption from the waste water. In laboratory, batch-studies were made for different weights of sawdust in different concentrations of cadmium solutions. Sawdust was found to be a low-cost adsorbent to remove cadmium from waste water. The removal of cadmium was found to be dependent on the initial concentrations of the sorbent and the sorbat.

413 **Gupta, A.M.J., Bhargava, D.S.**, 1987. Removal of lead through adsorption on sawdusts of different woods. Res. J. Natl. Soc. Pollut.-free Environ. 1(1&2) : 14-19.

Based on laboratory studies for the adsorption of lead on the sawdust of several kinds of wood, it has been noted that the removal by bud is more than the other kinds of woods. The various woods in a decreasing order of effectiveness are found to be bud, *shisham, tun, aflatun, aam, padtal* and eucalyptus.

414 **Gupta, S., Blatter, A., Hani, H.**, 1988. Concentration of ionic copper in soil solution. Internatl J. Environ. Analyt. Chem. 34: 45-50.

Total metal concentration either in salt extracts of soils or saturation extracts, probably allows the best estimate of the deleterious effects of metals on soil micro-organisms and plants. In case of some metals like copper, the prediction of deleterious effect could be improved with the better understanding of competitive relationships of metal in contaminated soils and the consequences on soil micro-organisms and plants grown on them.

415 **Gupta, M.D., Chattopadhyay, N., Gupta, S.K., Banerjee, S.K.,** 1988. Studies on infrared spectra of humic acids of city waste compost. J. Indian Soc. Soil Sci. 36:349-351.

Infrared spectra of humic acids of city waste compost has been explained for total acidity and bond strengths.

416 **Gupta, G.C., Harrison, F.L.,** 1982. Effect of humic acid on copper adsorption by kaolin. Water Air Soil Pollut. 17(4) : 357-360.

Varying amounts of humic acid (na-salt; 0 to 10 ppm) were first equilibrated with a dilute suspensions of H^+ kaolin and then with spiked (high activity radioactive^{64} Cu) water. After filtration, through a .45 μm millipore membrane, the amount of radioactivity on the filter and filtrate was measured separately using a Gamma ray well counter. Adsorption of Cu (expressed as distribution coefficient Kd) was plotted against humic acid concentration values decreased sharply to 1 ppm humic acid concentration and thereafter remained constant up to 10 ppm.

417 **Gupta, U.C., Mcrae, K.B., Winter, K.A.,** 1982. Effect of applied selenium on the selenium content of barley and forages and soil selenium depletion rates. Can. J. Soil Sci. 62(1): 145-154.

Two separate field experiments were conducted on several crops to determine the effect of selenium (Se) applied to soils with pH levels between 5.7 and 6.6. Tissue Se levels after a single application of Se and lime, were monitored for up to six cropping years or until the tissue Se fell below 0.1 ppm, the level considered to be necessary for animal nutrition. For application of 1.12 and 2.24 kg Se/ha, the minimal tissue Se concentration (> 0.1 ppm) was maintained in barley for two cropping years, but with a a very sharp decrease for the first 3 yr. In the case of timothy (*Phleum pratense* L.) tissue levels greater than 0.1 ppm were maintained for 3 yr at the higher rate of Se without lime and up to 5 yr at high soil pH levels. At the applied rats of 0.28 and 0.56 kg Se/ha, the tissue Se levels above 0.1 ppm in timothy, red clover, (*Trifolium partense* L.) and alfalfa were maintained for one and two cropping years, respectively.

418 **Gupta, A.P., Narwal, R.P.,** 1988. Effects of sources and levels of nitrogen and sewage sludge on N transformation into ammonical and nitrate forms. J. Indian Soc. Soil Sci. 36: 352-355.

Nitrogen transformation from urea, CAN and Okhla sludge was studies upto 42 days at 60% saturation capacity and 25± 2 °C. NH_4-N regularly decreased and NO_3-N increased with time and level of nitrogen application. There was no adverse effect on sludge on nitrification.

419 **Gupta, A.P., Narwal, R.P., Antil, R.S.,** 1989. Effect of different levels of nitrogen and sewage sludge on wheat. J. Indian Soc. Soil Sci. 37 : 576-

578.

A greenhouse experiment was conducted by applying 0 to 1% sewage sludge and 0 to 120 ppm N as urea to wheat. Grain and straw yield increases both with N and sludge levels but their interaction is non-significant indicating that sludge supplements addition of N as urea.

420 **Gupta, P.K., Pant, M.C.,** 1983. Macro-benthos of lake Nainital, U.P., India with particular reference to pollution. Water Air Soil Pollut. 19 : 397-405.

The important attributes of macrobenthic community structure viz., species composition and number, population density,biomass and dominance and diversity indices were measured at different depths and discussed in relation to pollution of lake Nainital. The zone below 7 m depth, where anoxic conditions prevailed for most part of the year, showed complete absence of macrobenthos.

374 **Gupta, V.K., Potalia, B.S.,** 1990. Zinc-cadmium interaction in wheat. J. Indian Soc. Soil Sci. 38 : 452-457.

A pot culture experiment conducted on a Typic Ustipsamment consisting of 4 levels of Zn (0, 5, 10 and 20 ppm) and 5 levels of Cd (0, 12.5, 25.0, 50 and 100 ppm) revealed that application of Zn enhanced grain and straw yield while Cd resulted in drastic reduction in yields. The concentration of Zn and Cd in grain and straw increased with their respective application. Addition of Zn repressed Cd concentration in wheat grain, whereas Cd enhanced Zn concentration. Significant positive correlation was found between grain yield and Zn:Cd ratio. Grain contained more Zn and less Cd in comparison to straw.

422 **Haagvar, S., Abrahamsen, G.,** 1990. Micro-arthropod and Enchytraeidae (Ollgochaeta) in naturally lead-contaminated soils: A gradient study. Environl. Entomol. 19(5): 1263-1277.

The micro-arthropod and enchytrae fauna of a natural lead-contaminated soil in a Norwegian spruce, (*Picea abies* L). Karst, forest was studied in gradients from unpolluted soils to the middle of a vegetation free areas. Because of dissolved lead from the bedrock, about 50 m^2 of the forest floor lacked vegetation, and another 50 m^2 had weakly developed vegetation. The lead content in the raw humus was up to 10-15% dry wt. Increasing levels of lead gave a gradual reduction in species numbers among plants and micro-arthropods. Micro-arthropod species varied in their ability to live in lead-polluted soil, Four groups were recognized; (1) sensitive species associated with normal vegetation, (2) less sensitive species occurring even in areas with strongly reduced vegetation, (3) tolerant species extending their ranges into vegetation free areas, and (4) micro-arthropods favoured by strong lead pollution (Isotoma oilvacea tullberg among collembola and Nanorchestes Sp. among mites).

423 **Haertling, J.W.,** 1989. Trace metal pollution from a municipal disposal

site at Pan Nirtung North West Territories, Arctic. 42(1) : 57-61.

Although all trace metal concs. showed a considerable increase below the dump. Pb and Fe in water samples from the main collector ditch and below the dump exhibited excessive levels; with 6.1 and 53.3 ppm, respectively.

424 **Haghiri, F.**, 1974. Plant uptake of cadmium as influenced by cation exchange capacity, organic matter, zinc. and soil temperature, J. Environ. Qual. 3(2): 180-183.

The effects of several soil factors on cadmium accumulation by plants were determined. Cadmium concentration in oat shoots (*Avena Sativa* L.) was decreased by increasing the CEC of soil, while organic matter did not influence the concentration of Cd in oat shoots. The results indicate that the retaining power of organic matter for cadmium is predominantly through its CEC property rather than chelating ability. Cadmium concentration of soybean shoots increased with temperature. In the presence of 10 ppm of soil applied Cd, the addition of Zn from 5 to 50 ppm range, apart from raising the Zn concentration, significantly increased Cd concentration, was primarily due to decreased plant growth. A depression in Cd concentration of soybean shoots, relative to control, began to occur at the 100 ppm Zn level.

425 **Haghiri, F.**, 1976. Release of cadmium from clays and plant uptake of cadmium from soil as affected by potassium and calcium amendments. J. Environ, Qual. 5 : 395-397.

The effects of per cent K and/or Ca saturations on the release of Cd treated H clays (kaoline and illite) and on the Cd availability to plants from Cd treated field silt loam soil were determined. The concentration of Cd in the dialyzations from both kaolinute and illite clays increased as the per cent Ca or K saturation of the clays in the suspension decreased. The release of Cd from both clays was greater in the presence of Ca than K. In a separate experiment, the concentration of Cd in soybean shoots decreased with increasing per cent Ca or K saturation of the soil. The results indicated that Cd uptake by soybean shoots could be impaired to a great extent by K application.

426 **Haidouti, C.**, 1991. Soil mercury pollution in the area surrounding The State oil refinery of Aspropirgos, Greece. Catena 18(1) : 1-10.

The airborne contamination of soils with Hg was evaluated near the State oil refinery. High level of mercury enrichment were found in the upper 0-5 cm. The contamination is particularly heavy near the contaminating source and falls off with distance. DTPA, 0.5 N $NaHCO_3$ and IN HCl were used to determine available Hg, weakly organic bound Hg and strongly adsorbed Hg, respectively. The analysis showed that small amounts of mercury existed in an easily soluble state. Mercury occurs in soils mostly in the from of poorly soluble compounds. Particle size separations showed that more than 50% of the total mercury content is confined to separates 0.005 to 0.001 and <0.001 mm of diameter, and density gradient centrifugation indicated that mercury in soils is generally associated with organomineral fractions <2.8 g/cm^3.

427 **Halen, H., Garcia-Navarro, M. Bladel, R., Van, R.,** 1991. Adsorption capacity of cadmium in some calcareous soils of South-eastern Spain. Agronomie. 11(1): 35-44.

Toposoils of 12 calcareous soils in Spain were compared for their cadmium adsorption capacity. Data closely obey the Freundlich equation and indicate 2 distinct mechanisms of adsorption according to whether the cadmium in the bulk solution is present in trace or in the higher amounts. Some precipitation with a concomitant decrease in pH could occur at initial concn of Cd > 5mg/l. Statistical analysis demonstrates that the adsorbed amounts of Cd may be estimated from the CEC (ammonium acetate) values and the active calcium carbonate content. The agreement between the predictive values and the experimental ones is shown to be moderately good. The greater adsorption of Cd in comparison with non-calcareous soils is due to the reactivity of calcite surface (chemisorption and nucleation precipitation resp. at low and high rates of Cd) and also to the commonly high pH of the soils studied. Comparison of the adsorption isotherms measured in chloride and perchlorate media shows that adsorption of Cd is mainly determined by the activity of free Cd^{2+} in the soil solution.

428 **Halls, D.J., Mohl, C., Stoeppler, M.,** 1987. Application of rapid furnace programmes in atomic absorption spectrophotometry to the determination of Pb, Cr, Cu in digests of plant materials. Analyst, 112(2) : 185-189.

Following pressure digestion with nitric acid and pre-treatment with hydrofluoric acid for Cr in silica-containing materials Pb, Cr and Cu are determined in plant materials by graphite furnace programmes designed to keep the analysis time to a minimum, consistent with good accuracy and reproducibility.

429 **Hall, D.W., Sandrin, J.A., Mcbride, R.E.,** 1990. An overview of solvent extraction treatment technologies. Environ. Prog. 9(2) : 98-105.

This paper was prepared because of the lack of a compiled source of existing information on the alternative use of solvent extraction technology for treating soils contaminated with hazardous substances in a manner other than incineration.

430 **Hasselbach, G.,** 1990. Effects of long term application of domestic wastes on the heavy metal transfer from soil to plant. III Soil specific effect on the uptake and extraction of heavy metals. Verband, Deutscher Land wirtschaftlicher Unter-und Forsch., Reihe Kongress. 30 : 281-286.

Availability and uptake of Cd, Cu, Zn and Ni in relation to soil type and sewage sludge application were studied for 3 years in pots using ryeprass, spring wheat, and carrots and 4 soil types (sand, silty loamy sand; sandy silt loam, loamy silt). While grass and wheat grain showed no significant difference between soil types, carrots took up more heavy metals from sandy soils than from those with greater carbon or clay content. A long term application of sewage sludge did not markedly increase heavy metals uptake in the plants tested. Sludge reduced soil pH by one unit which enhanced metal uptake in all plants with maximum in carrots, and rye grass least. Copper uptake was not affected by pH variation. The addition of heavy metals salts increased heavy metals uptake of all plants. In combination with a lower soil pH, it led to significant yield losses with phytotoxic levels of Zn (737 mg/kg) in carrots. Threshold values for Zn also reached in wheat grain while the straw contained even higher levels at 745 mg per kg. Nutritional threshold values for Cd in wheat and carrots were often exceeded, even in relatively uncontaminates soils. In case of ryegrass the fodder threshold value for Cd was only reached in a small number of cases and exceeded only on the heavily contaminated treatment.

431 **Hana, A.A.K., Albassam, K.S.,** 1983. A survey of lead pollution in Baghdad. Water Air Soil Pollut. 19: 3-14.

Lead pollution in Baghdad city was studied. Several potential sources of Pb pollution as leaded gasoline, battery manufacturing, and printing press type were investigated. Blood samples from males and females and workers of different ages and professions, who were indirect contact with Pb materials, were examined. Samples of palm leaves were analysed from about twenty five different parts of Baghdad in 1978 and again in 1980. The results were compared with similar from less crowded city which show that Pb pollution exists.

432 **Handa, B.K., Kulkarni, V.S., Khanna, P.,** 1990. Ranking of technology options for municipal waste water treatment. Asian Environ. 12(3) : 28-40.

The paper presents a methodology for ranking of technology options for the municipal waste water treatment and validates it for real life situation.

433 **Handa, B.K., Seth, R.,** 1990. Waste management in distillery industry. J. Indian Assoc. Environ. Manage. 17(2) : 44-54.

Most of the distilleries are not treating their waste waters because of the non-availability of a proven process under India conditions. Amongst the various treatment alternatives anaerobic digestion seems to be the most attractive as it produced a needful byproduct-biogas. Anaerobic filter has been most widely used because of its stability, easy start-up and ease of operation.

434 **Hanks, R.J., Nielson, R.F., Cartee, R.L., Willardson, L.S., Long, R.E., Sorenson, R.B.,** 1984. Use of saline waste water from electric power plant for irrigation. Utah State Univ., Logan; UT; USA.

Research has been conducted involving the shared use of water from the

Utah Power & Light Company Huntington for irrigation. Water is partially "consumed" as it is recycled in the evaporation ending system of the power plant until the salinity reaches a high level, at which time it is disposed of as "waste" water. This saline waste water is used for irrigation to increase crop production and allow "consumption" by agricultural plants. Consumption of water by the plants causes part of the salt to be stored in the root zone. The salt is therefore not returned immediately to the basin water supply. This system has been found to not only by the best economic alternative for disposing of the waste water but it also minimizes the decreased crop production caused by using the water for power plant cooling rather than for irrigation. This covers the seventh year of this cooperative study. There have been no noticeable decreases in yield for forage crops caused by irrigation with salty irrigation water compared to normal fresh irrigation for the first six years. Decreases in crop yield were not noticed until the third year of the study. Corn, wheat, and barley have shown decreasing yields since the third year.

435 **Hansea, L.G., Hinesly, L.D.,** 1979. Cadmium from soil amended with sewage sludge. Effects and residues of swine. Environl. Health Perspectives, 28 : 51-57.

Liquid digested sewage sludge from a Chicago waste treatment plant was applied to experimental corn plots starting in 1968. The sludge averaged 200 ppm Cd (dry wt.) Corn grain harvested from the plots in 1974 was fed to growing swine for 56 d, and other swine were permitted to forage on the plots during the winters of 1976-77. The sludge fertilized corn contained higher concentrations of nutrient and toxic elements but did not interfere with swine performance. Minor changes in hepatic microsomal oxidases and red blood cells accompanied significant increases in renal Cd and decreases in hepatic Fe. Swine foraging on these plots ingested considerable amounts of sludge soil and accumulated significantly higher concentrations of renal Cd. At lower rates of sludge application the swine outperformed those foraging on control plots and those receiving heavy sludge applications in terms of weight gain, inutero pigiet survival, blood hemoglobin, and tissue Fe concentrations.

436 **Hargitai, L.,** 1989. The role of humus status of soils in binding toxic elements and compounds. Sci. Total Environ. 81-82 : 643-651.

According to the results of earlier investigations a new model and concept is outlined for characterization of polyfunctionally and chelating characteristics of humic substances. Both properties are outstandingly important in environmental protection through binding toxic elements and compounds on humic substances. Results were obtained in long-term experiments (10 years) carried out by treatment of soils with sewage sludge. Increasing doses of toxic heavy metals (Pb, Ni, Cd) have not increased their mobility in soils proportionally.

437 **Hargitai, L.,** 1990. The mobility to toxic heavy metals as effected by the

environment protection capacity of soils. Trans. 14th Internatl. Cong. Soil Sci. Vol. II: 102-107.

An area of sandy loam brown forest soil was treated with 3 rates of sewage applied for 1, 2 or 4 years. The contents of mobile Ni, Pb, Cd, and Zn in soil monitored during 10 yrs increased only 4.1, 5.7, 12.1, and 13.8 times, respectively over a 24 times increase in the rate of sludge. This is because the OM added in the sludge increased the 'environmental protection capacity' of the soil an index based on thickness of humus layer, humus content and humus quality. Ni and Pb were organophilic than Cd and Cr, and their mobility was reduced to a greater extent. Studies of soil profiles affected by heavy metal from power stations in West and North Hungary showed that most Pb and Ni accumulated in humic layers, while Cd and Mo were more mobile. Hg was always hydrophobic and accumulated in layers affected by ground-water.

438 **Harington, C.A., Debell, D.S.,** 1984. Effects of irrigation, pulp mill sludge, and repeated coppicing on growth and yield of black cottonwood and red alder. Can. J. For. Res. 14(6): 884-849.

Growth and yield of black cottonwood (*Populus trichocarpa* Torr) and gray and red alder (*Alnus Bong*), were measured at four successive 2 years coppices harvests. Three levels of amended pulp mill sludge (450, 250, and 0, t ha^{-1}) were applied before planting, and one half of the plots were irrigated during the 2 year establishment period prior to the first coppice cycle. Yields of black cottonwood were generally much higher than yields of red alder; maximum over dry yield obtained were 13.8 t ha^{-1} year for black cottonwood, and 7.1 t ha^{-1} for red alder. Growth and yield of black cottonwood was increased by the initial sludge application, but the reverse was true for red alder. The initial irrigation treatment had carry-over effects on the yields of subsequent growth cycles for both species. For all treatments the greatest yields were usually obtained at the first or second coppice harvest. On the average, red alder yields declined substantially between the third and fourth harvests; black cottonwood yields were generally more consistent between these two harvests.

439 **Harlin, C.C., Jr.,** 1979. Land treatment methods in perspective. Progress Water Technol. 114(4-5): 1-14.

In the USA, there is gradually developing a standard designation for 3 recognized types of land treatment systems: slow rate, rapid infiltration, and overland flow. Some of the positive attitudes towards land treatment utilization relate to economics, recycling and reuse of water and waste water constituents, energy conservation, and the use of natural process. Most negative aspects relate to public health, long term effects, land requirements, and public acceptance. Research in land treatment technology is being conducted in the following areas: health effects; infectious disease organisms; heavy metals; organic and toxic compounds, nutrient management and agricultural aspects, including crop and livestock production. The goal of most research is to develop design criteria to achieve the most efficient and cost-effective treatment and management of municipal waste waters.

440 **Harris, A.R.**, 1979. Physical and chemical changes in forested Michigan sand soils fertilized with effluent and sludge. in "Utilization of Municipal sewage effluent and sludge on forest and disturbed land" W.E. Sooper & S.N. Kerr, (Eds.), Pennsylvania State Univ. Press: 155-161.

Sludge applied to forested sand soils can improve the fertility of the soil. If the sludge is not directly plowed or disked into the soil, decomposition and incorporation into the system is much slower. Vegetation responses on surface-applied sludge plots indicate that many of the nutrients are used near or at the top of the soil surface. Before additional sludge applications are made, however, the sludge decomposition products should be accounted for. Threshold limits for sludge application rates in forested sand soil have yet to be determined.

441 **Harris, A.R.**, 1976. Sewage effluent infiltration in frozen forest soil. Forest Service, US Deptt. Agri. Minnisota.

Secondary treated sewage effluent applied at the rate of 1 and 2 inches per week, infiltrated a frozen Sparta sand soil forested with jack pine and scrub oak. Maximum frost depth in treated plots averaged 60 cm and in check plots averaged 35 cm. Nitrogen was mobile with some accumulation. Phosphorus was adsorbed.

442 **Harris, J.A., Birch, P.**, 1988. The effect of zeolite on the toxicity of lead to fungi. Environl. Pollut. 49(3): 235-241.

Botrytis cinerea was inhibited by 25% by 100 mg/dm^3 Pb in solid agar media and completely inhabited by 1000 mg/dm^3 Pb. *Fusarium culmorum* was completely inhibited. Aspergillusniger was 97% inhibited at 1000mg/dm^3 Pb. Addition of zeolite reduces Pb toxicity as Pb is adsorbed on it which reduced the availability of Pb to fungi.

443 **Harris, A.R., Urie, D.H.**, 1982. Water quality effects and growth benefits of entrenching sewage sludge in sandy forest soils. Proc. 5th Annual Madison Conf. Applied Res. and Practice on Municipal and Industrial Waste 475-493.

Sewage sludge with 10 per cent dry solids was entrenched at loading rates of 75 and 150 t/ha to measure its effects on water quality. Also, sludge cylinders 60 cm in diameter and 100 cm in depth with 10-, 15-, 20- and 40- per cent dry solids were buried in a hybrid popular nursery to measure rooting and other growth effects. Lateral leaching was minimal, and leaching from the bottom of the trench had minimal effect on groundwater quality because of dilution. In the nursery, concentrations of soluble constituents were directly related to dry solids content. Sludge constituents stayed bound tightly except for the soluble portion. pH increased in the soil. Growth response of hybrid polars was directly related to availability of sludge nutrients. The high sludge loading rate results in nitrate pollution of any underlying water table aquifers but surrounding natural ecosystems should be able to denitrify and/or to assimilate the additional nitrogen.

444 **Harris, A.R., Urie, D.H.,** 1983. Changes in a sandy forest soil under Northern Hardwoods after 5 years of sewage effluent irrigation. J. Soil Sci. Soc. Am. 47: 800-805.

The changes in a sandy forest soil under Northern Hardwoods after 5 years of sewage effluent irrigation were observed. Thinned and unthinned plots in a 50-year-old beech (Fagus sp.)-maple (Acre sp.) stand were irrigated with sewage lagoon effluent. After 5 years of effluent application at rates of 38 and 75 mm/week, litter weights were reduced, leaching was increased and forest floor humus weights were increased. Irrigation also resulted in decreased organic matter in the mineral soil. Nitrogen and P were leached from the litter; Ca, Mg and Na were retained in forest floor humus and mineral soil, greatly increasing the pH and base saturation. Nitrogen concentrations measured in leachate from the 120-cm soil depth were consistently below 10 mg. L^{-1}. Sodium was the predominant cation in the leachate. Irrigation over 5 years with waste water effluent has had such minimal effects that higher irrigation rates must be considered without posing serious environmental risks.

445 **Harris, A.R., Urie, H.D.,** 1987. Heavy metal storage in soils of an Aspen forest fertilized with Municipal sludge. in "The forest alternative for Treatment and Utilisation of Municipal and Industrial Wastes. D.W. Cole, et al. (Eds.), Washington Univ. Press: 168-176.

Municipal sewage was surface applied to aspen (populus grandidentata) on a simulated clear-cut, a six-year-old sapling stand, and a standard operational clearcut. The soil was a Montcalm loamy sand. Single applications of sludge were applied at the rate of 11.5 23, and 46 Mg/ha in the spring of 1976, 1977 and 1978. Some plots received a second application at 11.5 and 23 Mg/ha rate, the year following initial application. The aspen humus layer effectively immobilised a high proportion of the metals present in the sludge. Over a five-year period, most metal movement seemed to be limited to the upper 5 cm soil layer. The vegetation recycled heavy metals back to the humus layer. Repeated applications in the following year appear to increase leaching to the soil. Pretreatment history of the aspen determines to some extent the overall immobilisation of the heavy metals. More metals were lost from humus layer that had been recently disturbed after years of accumulation. Humus on plots receiving heavier dosage rates of sludge seemed more efficient in the storage of heavy metals. The mineral soil system does not, over a three to five year period, appear to play a major part in heavy metal storage or movement at the treatment rates used.

446 **Harris, A.R., Urie, D.H., Cooley, J.H.,** 1984. Sludge fertilization of Pine

and Aspen forests on sandy soils in Michigan. in Forest Soils and Treatments Impacts. E.L. Stone (Ed.): 193-206.

Raw paper mill waste water sludge, was applied on red pine at rates between 5 and 40 Mg ha^{-1}. Municipal sludge, was applied to aspen sprout stands, established in white and red pine plantations, and clearcut jeck pine sites at rates between 4.8 and 46 Mg.ha^{-1}. Biomass increase of both aspen sprouts and ground vegetation was related to sludge dosage. For all sludge treatments on aspen, biomass increased on an average of 78 per cent over controls in the first growing season. In white and red pine plantations, growth responses occurred in the ground vegetation and in the size and weight of pine foliage, but not in bole size at dbh. Sludge treatment increased naturally occurring understory vegetation 200 to 500 per cent in all tests. Foliage nitrogen increased in both trees and understory vegetation. Phosphorus concentrations increased in herbaceous species and pine foliage. Increased trace metal concentrations were found mostly in ground vegetation. The humus layer immobilised and stored most nutrients and trace metals either directly or after recycling through vegetation. Where humus was present, soil depths below 5 cm did not increase in measurable amounts of nutrients and metals. Where humus was not present, the organic matter in the soil immobilised sludge constituents. Nitrate-N in the soil water and groundwater was the limiting factor for sludge loading rate. Sludge additions resulted in nutrients enrichment of the soils and increased production of the forest ecosystems. On the soils studied, 5-15 Mg-ha^{-1} of sludge were applied without leachates or groundwater exceeding the nitrate standards of drinking water.

447 **Hart, J.E., Defore, R., Chiesa, S.C.,** 1986. Activated sludge control for seasonal nitrification. J. Water Pollut. Control Fed. 58(5): 358-363.

Seasonal nitrification in a step-feed activated sludge system was controlled by adjusting the aeration intensity in relation to the influent ammonia-nitrogen concentration and BOD loading. More air was required to initiate ammonia oxidation than to sustain it on a long term basis. Problems with high effluent nitrite-nitrogen concentrations arose when nitrification was induced at high liquid temperatures and projected steady state aeration intensities. Rapid startup could be achieved by maintaining a small nitrifier seed population in the activated sludge system during non-nitrifying periods.

448 **Hart, J.B., Nguyen, P.V., Urie, D.H., Brockway, D.G.,** 1988. Silvicultural use of waste water sludge. J. Forestry 8: 17-24.

In Michigan, sludge-applied nutrients substantially enhanced nutrient cycling, tree growth, wildlife habitat, and nutritional quality of forage plants in the forest. At appropriate application rates, these benefits were obtained while avoiding groundwater contamination & toxicant transmission in the food chain. Forestland application methods were shown to be technologically feasible and cost effective, providing the land manager with a valuable silvicultural option. Silvicultural use of waste water sludge be considered by land managers to not only benefit tree growth and wildlife habitat but also highlight the participation of forestry professionals in publicly supported environmental protection programmes.

449 **Hartenstein, Roy., Neuohausher, F.E., Narahara,** 1981. Effects of heavy metal and other elemental additives to activated sludge on growth of eisenia foetida. J. Environ. Qual. 10 (3): 372-376.

The approximate level at which added concentrations of certain elements would cause an activated sludge to induce a toxic effect upon the growth of eisenia foetida or a toxic was determined. During 43 trials on sludge samples obtained throughout one year of study, earth worms grew from 3 to 10 mg live wt. at latching to 792 mg± 18% (mean ±mean c.v.) in 8 weeks when sludge was 24°C and contained no additions. None of several elements commonly used in microbial growth media enhanced the growth rate of the earthworm. At salt concentrations upto about 66% on a dry wt basis, none of six anions tested was in and of itself toxic, while five of 15 cations-Co, Hg, Cu, Ni and Cd appeared specifically to inhibit growth rate of cause death. Manganese, Cr and Pb were innocuous even at the highest levels of application – 22000, 46000 and 52,000 mg/kg, respectively. Neither the anionic nor cationic component of certain salts, such as NaCl or NH_4Cl could be said to inhibit growth, which occurred only at high concentrations of these salts (about 3.3 and/or 6.6%) Below seven mmhos/cm, toxicity could not be correlated with EC though higher value may help to explain the non-specific growth inhibitory effects of salt like NaCl and KCl. Nor could toxicity ever be ascribed to hydrogen ion activity since sludge pH was not altered even at the highest salt dose. It is concluded that except under very extreme conditions, the levels of heavy metals and salts generally found in activated sludges will not have an adverse effect on the growth of E. foetida.

450 **Harter, R.D.** 1979. Adsorption of copper and lead by Ap and B_2 horizons of several Northeastern United States Soils. J. Soil Sci. Soc. Am. 43(4): 679-683.

Adsorption of Cu and Pb by surface and subsurface samples of 15 soils was determined. Soil adsorption maximum were derived from the reciprocal of the slope obtained by a least squares fit of "Langmuir" plots for each soil. The adsorption maxima were then regressed against various chemical and mineralogical properties of the soils to deduce adsorption mechanisms and to determine whether any commonly measured soil quantity could serve as an adsorption predictor. The best adsorption predictor by all samples was sum of bases, which explained 84 and 70% of the variation in Cu and Pb adsorption, respectively. In the subsurface horizons, the adsorption of Cu and Pb was significantly related to vermiculite content but sum of bases was still a better prediction for these horizons alone. Organic matter content had no significant relationship to adsorption by surface horizons.

451 **Hass, C.N., Horowitz, N.D.,** 1986. Adsorption of cadmium to kaolinite in the presence of organic material. Water Air Soil Pollut. 27: 131-140.
Kaolinite was equilibrated with Cd and with varying amounts of the individual compounds with EDTA, NTA, alginic acid, and humic acid. In experiments in which the Cd and kaolinite concentrations were held constant and the ligand concentrations allowed to vary, conditions under which ligand enhanced and inhibited Cd association with the solid phase were noted. Further experiments at constant Cd ligand confirmed that, for alginic acid and humic acid, enhancement of uptake occurred, while EDTA diminished uptake. These results were compared with the adsorption of ligand by clay in the absence of organic material. The enhancement of uptake is due to the formation of an adsorbed organic layer on the clay serving as a solid phase ligand.

452 **Hassett, D.J., Hassett, D.F., Brojorg, J.N.,** 1989. Control of trace element solubility in coal fly ash leachates Proc. Annual Madison Waste Water Conf. 11: 311-322.
Immobilization of trace elements was investigated with fly ash from a pulverized coal boiler and cyclone boiler. Iron compounds, sodium aluminate, lime, sodium carbonate and molecular sieves were used alongwith fly-ash. Results indicated that all of the additives had some potential to reduce leachability, but iron compounds were the most effective.

453 **Hattori, H.,** 1989. Influence of cadmium on decomposition of sewage sludge and microbial activities in soils. Soil Sci. Plant Nutr. 35(2): 289-299.
Investigations were conducted to evaluate the influence of cadmium (Cd) on the decomposition of sewage sludge, microflora and enzyme activities in soils. Cadmium and sewage sludge were mixed with 5 different types of soil at levels of 0.30 μmol/g and 20 mg/g, respectively. During a 8 weeks of soil incubation at 28°C, the mineralization of C was periodically measured. At the end of the incubation period, the soils were also analyzed to determine the amount of N mineralized, the numbers of bacteria, actinomycetes and fungi, the activities of β-glucosidase and proteinase, and the amount of Cd extracted with water, CH_3COONH_4, $Na_4P_2O_7$ and HCl. The amount of CO_2 evolved which decreased markedly with the addition of higher amounts of Cd, varied with the soils used. When the soil Cd concentration was based on the water-soluble form, the critical level for CO_2 evolution appeared to be identical about 1 μg/g for all soils.

454 **Heale, E.L., Ormrod, D.P.,** 1983. Effects of nickel and copper on seed germination and growth and development of seedlings of Acer ginnala,

Betula papyrifera, Picea abies and Pinus banksiana. Reclam. Reveg. Res., 2(1): 4-54.

Amur maple (Acer ginrela), Paper birch (*Betula papryifera*), Norway spruce (*Picea abies*) and jack pine (*Pinus banksiana*) seeds were germinated, and developing seedlings grown, in a controlled environment in silica sand treated with 2 or 10 mg Ni L^{-1}, or 4 or 20 mg Cu^{2+} L^{-1}, singly or in combination (2 and 4 mg L^{-1} or 10 and 20 mg L^{-1}). Exposure to toxic levels of Ni and Cu was associated with a very high degree of individual plant and species variation. Injury symptoms included marginal and inter-veinal leaf chloris, reddening of deciduous leaves, alteration of pigmentation of coniferous needles, increase leaf drop, a decrease in the amount of new leaf growth produced an influence on the orientation of seedling cotyledons and leaves. With increasing metal levels in the treatment solutions, fewer lateral roots developed.

455 **Heatwole, C.D., Diebel, D.L. Halstead, J.M.,** 1990. Management and Policy effects on potential ground-water contamination from dairy waste. Water Resource Bull. 26(1): 25-34.

This study provides both the environmental and economic effects of better management of dairy waste.

456 **Heckman, J.R., Angle, J.S., Chaney, R.L.,** 1987. Residual effects of sewage sludge on soybean: I. Accumulation of heavy metals. J. Environ. Qual. 16: 113-117.

The residual effects of sewage sludge after 9 years on heavy metal uptake by soybean was studied for 2 years at 2 locations. The concentrations of metals in soybean shoots varied according to sludge type, application rate, and soil pH. Metal uptake from low metal, limed sludge was similar to that of controls. Metal uptake was, however, increased by unlimed sludges that were high in metal content. Digested sludge linearly increased shoot metal concentrations of Zn, Cd, Cu, and Ni. Compared to the unamended control, soybean Zn increased from 24 to 165 mg kg^{-1} and Cd from 0.06 to 0.25 mg kg^{-1} at the 112 Mg ha^{-1} rate. The shoot Cd concentration was over seven times higher from Cd rich Nu-Earth sludge as compared to other sludges. Shoot Zn and Cd concentrations exhibited significant linear and quadratic relationship with rate of heat-treated and Nu-Earth sludge. There was a greater response of shoot Zn and Cd accumulation to sludge rate at low pH. At the 100 Mg ha^{-1} rate of Nu-Earth sludge, soybean Zn and Cd concentrations, respectively, were 59 and 1.75 mg kg^{-1} at soil pH 6.4, and 84 and 2.54 mg kg^{-1} at soil pH 5.8.

457 **Heckman, J.R., Angle, J.S., Chaney, R.L.,** 1987. Residual effects of sewage sludge on soybean-II. Accumulation of soil and symbiotically fixed nitrogen. J. Environ. Qual. 16 : 118-124.

Dry matter and N accumulation by non-nodulating soybean generally increased due to greater availability of soil N on the sludge plots. In nodulating soybean, dry matter production and N_2 fixation were enhanced by most sludges with the greatest increase occurring under moisture stress. In 1983, a dry year, dry matter of nodulating soybean and nitrogen fixation were increased by all sludges at Beltsville. Dry matter and amount of N_2 fixed increased from 16.5 g $plant^{-1}$ and 285 mg N $plant^{-1}$ (control) to 31.1 g $plant^{-1}$ and 706 mg N $plant^{-1}$ at the 672 Mg ha^{-1} limed compost sludge rate, respectively. In 1984, dry matter and N_2 fixation was moderately higher on sludge plots compared to control levels. Dry matter and N_2 fixation showed a quadratic response due to overliming by high applications of limed-digested and limed-raw sludges. Evidence for toxicity of sludge metals on N_2 fixation was not found at Beltsville sludge plots. However, a toxic effect may be suggested by high metal sludge at Fair land sludge plots. In addition to a decrease in the amount of N_2 fixed, non-nodulating plant dry matter increased with sludge, whereas nodulating plant dry matter decreased. Hence while sludge amended soil may enhance soybean growth, such beneficial results may be limited to sludges low in heavy metals.

458 **Hegemann, D.A.,** 1981. Algal availability of soil phosphorus. Diss. Abst. Int. Pt. B-Sci. and Eng., 42, (3): p. 229.

Laboratory and algal assays patterned after the Seleanastrum capricornutum Printz Algal Assay Bottle Test were conducted to assess algal available phosphorus in samples to algal cultures. Analysis of soil phosphorus loss during bioassay indicated that algal available phosphorus consisted of quantities that would otherwise be released to the nutrient medium plus a fraction of the phosphorus subsequently extracted with 0.1 N NaOH.

459 **Hegemann, D.A., Kennan, I.D.,** 1983. Bioassay techniques for soil-nutrient availability. Water Air Soil Pollut. 19: 259-276.

This research concerns the development of laboratory algal assay for evaluating the availability of soil P as an algal nutrient. Seleanastrum capricornutum is an acceptable test organism. Auto-claving soil samples does not result in a consistent, statistically significant change in algal available P. Maximum algal available-P is achieved with direct contact between soil and algae. Multiple incubation using fresh P - free medium results in significant increase in algal — available - P.

460 **Heitholt, J.J., Hodgson, R.H., Tworkoski, T.J.,** 1990. Toxicity and uptake of nitroguanidine in plants. Bull. Environl. Contam. Toxicol. 44(5): 751-758.

The toxicity of and to characterise the uptake of Ng in plants was tested.

461 **Helmake, P.A., Robarge, W.P., Korotev, R.L., Schombearg, P.J.,** 1979. Effects of soil-applied sewage sludge on concentrations of elements in earth worms. J. Environ. Qual. 8 (3): 322-327

Culture of earth-worms on soils treated with radio-active tracers shows that earthworms accumulate Cd, Co, Hg & Zn but not Hf, Sc and Tb. The results for the earthworms from the field plots are corrected for the effects of contamination by uneliminated casts with the use of interelements ratios. The concentrations of Hg and Cr in the casts increase with increasing rates of sludge application, but the constant concentrations of these elements in the earthworms show that these elements are not bioavailable. The concentrations of Cd, Cu and Zn in the earth-worms increase, while those of Se decrease with increasing rates of sludge application. The very high concentrations of Cd in the earth-worms, ranging from about 10 ppm in the control samples to over 100 ppm in the affected samples, show that earthworms efficiently accumulate Cd.

462 **Hensel, B.R., Griffin, R.A., Berg, R.C.**, 1988. Quantitative assessment of potential ground-water contamination from Municipal landfill leachate in Illinois. Proc. Annual Madison Waste Conf. 11: 28-46.

A numerical ranking of relative contaminant migration for 16 mapped hydrogeological sequences is presented. According to the model presented, area with aquifers, within 35 ft of ground surface, having hydraulic conductivity greater than about 10^{-4} cm/sec. have a high potential for contamination; areas where the largest hydraulic conductivity is from 10^{-6} to 10^{-4} cm/sec. have a moderate potential for contamination.

463 **Herms, U., Petterson, F.**, 1989. Heavy metal contamination of soils under power line pylons. Zeit. fur K'iltur. Landent. 31(2): 101-105.

Heavy metals conc. (Sn, Cd, Cr, Cu, Ni and Pb) in the vicinity of 14 pylons of various heights (20 to 80m) and ages (> 60 yr and 14 to 30 yr) were high in all cases. Zn was upto 372 mg/kg and Pb upto 400 mg/kg in the oldest pylon. HIgh Pb was attributed to the Pb content of primers used for the protection against rust. Contaminations of Cd, Cr, Cu and Ni were not detected. However Pb conc. decreased with increase of distance and almost no difference beyond 10 m distance from the pylon.

464 **Hershaft, A., Truett, B.**, 1981. Long-term effects of slow-rate and land application of Municipal waste water a critical summary. NTIS. Springfield: 100.

Long-term effects of applying partially treated municipal waste water to crop lands were examined at six locations in the Western U.S. All locations had received waste water for at least 10 years. The effects on soil, ground-water and crop tissues were measured and compared with measurements made at nearly control sites where crops were irrigated with water from wells or other conventional sources. Data for some 50 parameters measured at the six sites are summarized which indicate that the soli and plants effectively reduce the concentration of most pollutants in the waste water.

465 **Hertz, J., Angehrn-Bettinazzi, C.**, 1989. Inaccuracy of heavy metal analysis a problem of homogeneity. Bull. Bodenkund liche gesellschaft der

Schwetz 13: 81-92.

For different trees at each site the samples taken in the zone of infiltration showed the highest variations in Cd, Pb, Cu and Zn content, while the zone between the crowns was least variable. pH and OM were also variable. To compare heavy metals between sites, bulking of inter-grown samples from each site is recommended provided that at least 4 samples are taken at each site. Variance analysis showed that soil pH, was a major factor for Cd and Zn contents in the Ah horizon; OM content of the Ah horizon had very little influence. The month of sampling had quite large effects on the results; if all samples are taken from all sites in the same month, only 3 samples are required to provide for bulk sample.

466 **Hierold, W.,** 1990. Vertical distributions and special variability of heavy metals in contaminated soils of sewage farms. Arch IV for ancker und. Pflanzenban and Bodenkunde 34(5): 297-305.

The locations of heavy metals pollution were determined in soils of 90 years old sewage farms. Distribution of Cd, Ni, Pb, Cu, Zn & Cr in sandy and sandy loam soils are given. Results confirm that the application of sewage to land is limited by the concentrations of heavy metals. When determining the rate of applications, sorptive soil capacity showed be considered.

467 **Hill, D.C., Olson, B.H., Righy, M.G.,** 1981. Accumulation of cadmium and zinc in soil and vegetation from long-term application of waste water. Univ. Missouri, Columbia MO: 372-382.

The accumulation of Cd and Zn in soils and vegetation irrigated with treated sewage effluents was examined at 3 locations in Southern California. The Whittier Narrows site, a ground-water recharge test plot, received secondary effluent through intermittent flooding for approximately 14 years. Fountain valley, a forested site, was flood irrigated with both primary and secondary effluents for 16 yrs. The 3 Las Virgenes sites received various amounts of secondary effluent by spray irrigation for 8 yrs. Elevated levels of Cd and Zn were observed in the upper layers of soil at the Fountain valley and Whittier narrow sites. No metal accumulation from waste water application was found at Las Virgenes. However, Cd was elevated throughout the soil profiles which reflected the Cd-enriched underlying host rock.

468 **Hill, D.E., Sawhney, B.L.,** 1981. Removal of phosphorus from waste water by soil under aerobric and anaerobic conditions, J. Environ. Qual. 10, (3): 401-405.

Studies of the movement of fertilisers-P and P added to soils in waste water have shown that P movements is extremely slow. But in cultivated soils with tile drains it has also been observed that reducing conditions caused by flooding can increase P inability. To determine the movement of P under aerobic and anaerobic conditions, a simulated waste water containing 12 µg/ml P was added to an isolated soil block, two-three times a week for 25 years in a field experiment. The fine sandy loam soil was underlawn by bedrock at 72 cm and had a water table fluctuating between the 25 and 75 cm depths during the experiment. Analysis of the effluent from the weep holes at different depths suggested that the waste water moved along preferred pathways in heterogeneous soil, and produced break through of P to ground-water before all sorption sites were fully saturated with P. Also anaerobic conditions produced during periods of high water table enhanced the immobility of P, thus increasing the transport of P to ground-water in soils used for continued waste water treatment. Fonovati on of waste water own long periods of time reduces the P sorption capacity of a soil while periodic resting regenerates sorption sites and increases the potential for additional P sorption. Estimates of P retention based upon its concentration in influent and effluent solutions and bulk density of the soil show a reasonably good agreement with laboratory determination of P retained following waste water renovation. Data also show that most of the P retained is transformed into unavailable forms.

469 **Hillel, D,,** 1989. Movement and retention of organics in soil — a review and a critique of modelling In "Petroleum Contaminated Soils. Remediation Techniques and Environment Fate Risk Assessment". Vol. 1: 81-86.

Soils processes and soil characteristics influencing the movement and retention of organic contaminants in soil are briefly described to illustrate the complexity of time and space-variable factors involved. The possibilities and limitations of modeling such processes are then discussed.

470 **Hilleman, L.H.,** 1980, Composting agricultural residues. Compost, Science Utilization, 21(5): 49.

Excellent results were obtained with cotton gin trash compost for tomatoes, mums, and other plants. Research was also conducted on cotton, corn, forage sorghum, and snapbean production. Cotton trash compost applied in the row at 3t/acre gave a 1.02t increase yield of greenbeans, including a 1.97 increase in total biomass. A 6.70 t/acre increase in sorghum forage yield was obtained from 2t/acre cotton compost.

471 **Hindy, K.T., Abdal, Shafy, H.I., Farg, S.A.,** 1990. The role of the cement industry in the contamination of air, water, soil and plant with Vanadium in Cairo. Environl. Pollut. 66(3): 195-205.

The effects of atmospheric emission from a cement factory in Southern Cairo on the levels of vanadium in air water soil system was examined. It was concluded that the cement factory was the main source of Vanadium in the adjacent area. Continuous release of air borne dust from the factory will increase Vanadium levels in the surrounding environments.

472 **Hinesly, T.D., Ziegler, E., Barrett, G.L.,** 1979. Residual effects of ir-

rigating corn with digested sewage sludge. J. Environ. Qual. 8(1): 35-38.

The same corn hybrid was grown during the last 3 yr that Blount silt loam plots were irrigated with liquid, municipal sewage sludge and for the next succeeding 4 yr after termination of applications. During the last year in which sludge was applied, leaves from maximum sludge treated plots contained 112 mg Zn/kg and 7.1 mg Cd/kg. Four years after sludge applications were terminated, leaves from these plots contained 45 mg Zn/kg and 2.1 mg Cd/kg. Grain Zn concentrations decreased from 45 mg Zn/kg during the last year of sludge applications to 27 mg/kg in the 4th yr after termination of applications. Grain-Cd concentrations decreased from 0.44 to 0.07 mg/kg. During the 3rd and 4th yr after terminating sludge applications, grain from sludge-treated and control plots could not be distinguished by differences in Zn and Cd concentrations. Soil pH remained near neutral and was not affected by treatments. Except for the decrease during the 1st yr after sludge applications were terminated, total N and organic-C concentrations in previously sludge amended soil remained fairly constant at levels markedly higher than in control plots. The soil CEC increased in proportion to the amount of organic-C-remaining in the soil after termination of sludge applications.

473 **Hirai, N., Ker, K.C., Endo, T., Fujie, K., Shoda, K., Koibota, H.,** 1990. Method for monitoring the decomposition process in soil of organic waste waters with high strength and low C/N ratio: Soil Sci. Plant Nutr 36(3): 397-408.

Liquid extracts of pig manure and bornito processing waste water and the effluents after methane fermentation were studied in pot experiment with an alluvial and a volcanic ash soil. The stabilization period of these four waste waters in alluvial soil was 14 days for an effluent from methane fermentation of bornito processing waste water, 21 for an effluent from methane fermentation of pig manure extract (EMP) and bonito processing waste water (BWP) and 28 days for pig manure extract (SPM), Stabilization of all wastes occurred 1 week later in the alluvial than in the volcanic ash soil. Inspite of apparent stabilization inhibition of the growth of a 72 hr seedling of *Brassica composteris* was observed in EMP due to accumulation of NO_3-N especially in the aligo trophic alluvial soil.

474 **Hiroi, T.,** 1981. Vegetation in mining areas. in "Heavy Metal Pollution in Soils of Japan" Japan. Sci. Soc. Press: 219-231.

In general, the properties of vegetation are principally determined by climatic factors. Mining sites as plant habitats, however, are mainly characterized by edaphic factors. In many heavy metal mining areas the soil usually is contaminated by heavy metals. And in such sites abandoned metalliferous wastes also exist, often in great quantities. Heavy metal-contaminated soil and metalliferous wastes normally contain concentrations of toxic metals high enough to inhibit and restrict plant growth. Metalliferous wastes, especially, are deficient in nitrogen and phosphorus and often in various micronutrients. Deficiencies of these nutrients have adverse effects on the establishment of vegetation. The soil of mines exhibits considerable acidity. Especially in the sites adjoining smelters, the soil is strongly acidified due to sulfur dioxide gas that is produced in metallurgical processes. Such soil also hinders the growth of many plants.

475 **Hirsch, D., Banin, A.,** 1990, Cadmium speciation in soil solutions J. Environ. Qual. 19(3): 366-372.

Total Cd concentration was measured in the saturation extract of thee unpolluted arid zone forest soils to which Cd was added as Cd $(NO_3)_2$ solution (0.1 mg Cd kg^{-1} soil). The ratio of free to total Cd in the extracted soil solution was measured. A chemical equilibrium model including the major complexation reactions of Cd with anionic legends was used to estimate Cd speciation in solution and was validated by the agreement between the calculated and measured Cd^{2+}/Cd_T ratios. Free Cd and $CdHCO^+_3$ were each estimated to constitute 35 to 45 per cent respectively of total soluble Cd in the calcareous soil solutions studied, which had pH values between 7.5 and 8.5. Agreement between measured and calculated Cd^{2+}/Cd ratios improved slightly after destruction of organic matter by UV irradiation of the extracted solutions. Organo-Cd complexes were shown to be present in relatively minor amounts in these soils.

476 **Hsieh, Y.P., Douglas, L.A., Motto, H.L.,** 1981, Modelling sewage sludge decomposition in soil. I Organic carbon transformation J. Environ. Qual. 10(1): 54-59.

Mineralization of an activated and a digested sewage sludge in soil was studied in laboratory incubations. The activated sludge had a much higher mineralization rate of the digested sludge, mainly due to a larger portion of active organic carbon and stability of the organic matter. The amount of active organic carbon is a characteristic of sewage sludge, and is important in determining the aerobicity of the system. A regression model was developed in the form of an exponential function among the cumulative organic carbon mineralized and factors of time, sludge rate, and temperature.

477 **Hsieh, Y.P., Douglas, L.A., Motto, H.L.,** 1981. Modeling sewage sludge decomposition in soil. II. Nitrogen transformation. J. Environ. Qual. 10(1): 59-64.

Laboratory incubations were conducted to study N transformation in two sewage soil systems. The duration of the lag phase of nitrification was related to the organic C content and moisture level of the system. The N mineralization was found to be 30% and 38% of the organic N in the activated sludge and sludge respectively. The mineralization rate constant was 0.026 day^{-1} which corresponded to a half life of 27 days. Moisture levels of 0.06 and 0.33 showed no significant effect on the mineralization rate. Denitrification might be important pathway of N transformation in sewage sludge-soil systems.

478 **Ho, Y.B.,** 1979. Lead contamination in street dust in Hong Kong. Bull. Environl. Contam. Toxicol. 21(4-5): 639-642.

Lead levels were generally high in road-side dust samples collected from different sites throughout Hong Kong during winter 1977-78. Considerable differences in the concentration of Pb among these sites were detected but such differences bore no direct relationship to the traffic volumes of the sites from which the samples were collected. Different districts within the city varied widely in the mean concentration of Pb in their road-side dust samples.

479 **Ho, Y.B., Tai, K.M.,** 1979. Effect of rain on lead levels in roadside in Hong Kong. Bull. Environl. Contam. Toxicol. 23: 658-660.

The leaves of 2 species of plants growing within 3 m of the road curb were collected in 10 harvests between Jan. and Apr. 1979. Variations in Pb levels were compared with rainfall data from the same period. Data indicate that Pb levels in the leaves dropped in the occurrence of short, light rain periods, in one case from 240 to 80 ppm after 13 mm of rain. Between rainfalls, levels of Pb rose from 180 to 340 ppm during a period of 6 d in one species. Despite frequent and heavy rainfall at the end of the test period, a portion of the Pb in both plants remained resistant to washing. The nonwashable portion in *Alocasia odora* was 29 ppm, and 87 ppm for *Mikania gudco.*

480 **Hoitink, H.A.J., Kuter G.A.,** 1984. Role of composts in suppression of soilborne plant pathogens of ornamental plants. Biocycle, 25(4): 40-42.

Evidence for a role of mesophillic microbial antagonists in suppression was obtained by several types of experiments. For example, a batch of CHB prepared in a bioreactor (bin) and still undergoing thermophillic decomposition (thus not colonised by mesophillic microbes) was delivered to 10 different nurseries and greenhouses in Ohio. Media amended with this CHB became suppressive in some nurseries but remained conducive to Rhizotonia damping-off in others. On the other hand, CHB prepared in wind-rows near a forest at a nursery (field CHB) consistently became suppressive as it aged.

481 **Holopainen, J.K. Kainulainen, E., Oksanen, J., Wulff, A., Kaerenlampi, L.,** 1991. Effect of exposure to fluoride, nitrogen compounds and SO_2 on the numbers of spruce shoot aphids on Norway spruce seedlings. Oecologia 86(1): 51-56.

Development of spruce shoot aphid (*Cinara pilicornis Hartig*) populations was monitored in natural and artificial infestations of Norway spruce (*Picea abies Karst*), seedlings, exposed to air pollutants in an experimental field. The pollutants, applied both singly and in mixtures, were gaseous sulphur dioxide. NaF (30 mg/l F) and Ca $(NO_3)_2$ or (NH_4)

SO_4 in aqueous solutions (1200 mg/lN). At the beginning of the experiment aphid numbers did not differ between treatments. Aphid populations peaked in late June and July. All the pollutants and their combinations significantly increased the numbers of aphids per seedling. Four apterous females were transferred to spruce seedlings which were growing in containers in the same plots.

482 **Homann, P.S., Zasoski, R.J.,** 1987. Solution composition effects on cadmium sorption by forest soil profiles. J. Environ. Qual. 16:429-43.

Three mineral soil horizons from each of six western Washington state soil series were evaluated for their potential to sorb Cd. Horizons varied in pH from 3.6 to 6.4, in clay content from 100 to 470 g kg^{-1}, in organic carbon from 3 to 87 g kg^{-1} and in cation exchange capacity from 1.8 to 35.8 cmolc kg^{-1}. Batch equilibrium experiments were conducted in three background solutions (calcium nitrate, calcium sulphate, and sodium sulphate) that had ionic strengths of 0.016 and were maintained at pH values close to the natural soil pH. Between 4 and 97 per cent of the initial 10 μM Cd was sorbed by 1gm soil in 0.1 L background solution. Sorption varied among the horizons in each soil profile, but there was no consistent trend with depth among the six profiles. Sorption did not differ significantly between calcium nitrate and calcium sulphate solutions. However, it was significantly lower in calcium sulphate than sodium sulphate solution, supporting the hypothesis that calcium competition lowers Cd sorption. The amount of Cd sorbed, when a solution concentration of one μM free Cd^{2+} is maintained (Cd sorbed), decreased 81 per cent when free Ca^{2+} increased from 0.89 m M Ca^{2+} in sodium sulphate to 4.0 m M Ca^{2+} in calcium sulphate solution. The Cd sorbed increased with increased natural soil pH. A horizon had higher Cd sorbed than B horizons of similar natural soil pH, possibly due to their higher organic matter content.

483 **Homma, S.,** 1981. Yoneshiro river basin: soil pollution by heavy metals discharged from various mines in, "Heavy Metal Pollution in Soils of Japan", Kitagishi K.; Yamane, I. (Eds.). Japan Sci. Soc. Press, Tokyo: 137-148.

Two hundred mines exist including unused ones. Many of these mines are located in mountanous areas and heavy metals discharged from these mines and smilters into rivers have polluted farmlands along the river basin (especially paddy soils). In the area round smelters, not only has the growth of crops been damaged by heavy metals and sulfur dioxide discharged from their chimneys, but the soil and the crops have been polluted by heavy metals. Harmful effects on health, such as renal lesions, among people who have been eating crops harvested in the area are frequently observed. There are two large rivers in Akita Prefecture, the Yoneshiro River and the Omono River. Many mines are located on the tributaries of these rivers. Along the Yoneshiro River are found such famous mines as the Koska, Furutobe, Hanawa, Osarizawa, Hanaoka and Ani.

484 **Hook, J.E., Burton, T.M., 1979.** Nitrate leaching from sewage-irrigated perennials as affected by cutting management. J. Environ. Qual. 8(4): 496-502.

The effectiveness of various cutting treatments for controlling N leaching was evaluated. Secondary municipal sewage effluent was applied at 7.5 cm/wk during the growing season to Kentucky bluegrass (Poa praetensis) and at rates of 0, 5.0, and 10.0 cm/wk to indigenous vegetation in an abandoned field. The N concentration in the 120- to 150-cm depth was taken as a measure of N which escaped the root zone and which would reach to the groundwater. Soil-water from the 150-cm depth was taken as a measure of N which escaped the root zone and which would leach to the groundwater. Soil-water from the 150-cm depth in the Kentucky bluegras consistently contained < 10 mg/l of mineral N. Mineral N concentration of soil-water from the 150-cm depth did not differ significantly among the cutting managements. For the oldfield vegetation, there was no significant difference in mineral N concentration in soil-water at the 120-cm depth between the 5.0 and 10.0 cm/wk irrigation rates. The mineral N concentration at 120-cm under both irrigation rates was affected by time of year and by cutting treatments. The twice-annual harvest controlled N leachings were more effectively than not cutting. The once-annual harvest was more effective than not cutting for the 10-cm/wk rate but not for the 5.0 cm/wk rate. During the late summer and fall mineral N in the leachate increased to 10 mg N/l for the no cutting but not for the harvested oilfields.

485 **Hook J.E., Kardos, L.T.,** 1978. Nitrate leaching during long-term spray irrigation for treatment of secondary sewage effluent on woodland sites. J. Environ. Qual. 7(1): 30-34.

In the last 6 of 9 years of effluent treatment, 83 per cent of the 4.954 kg N/ha added leached from the site. Nitrate concentration in soil water at the 120-cm depth was generally 715 mg N/l. The hard wood forest was also in effective in keeping nitrate concentration below 10 mg N/l at the 120 cm depth when the 5-cm weekly application was split into two 2.5-cm irrigation or when it was lowered to 2.5 cm/week year round. An abandoned old field site planted with white spouce (*Piecea glovla* Moenely) and located on a well-drained clay loam soil was irrigated with effluent at 5 cm/week from Apr. through Nov. each year, beginning in 1963. Nitrate concentration at the 120-cm depth rarely exceeded 10 mg N/L and only 36 per cent of the 1246 kg N/ha applied leached during the 6th through the 9th year of this effluent treatment. In the 10 and 11th the years, when the application rate was increased to 7.5 cm/week, nitrate concentration exceeded 10 mg N/L at the 120 cm depth, and the amount of N which leached increased to 75 per cent of the amount applied.

486 **Horak, V.O.,** 1979. Lead uptake by plants. Bodenk. Jour. Landwirit, Forsch 30(2): 120-126.

Lead uptake experiments were carried out in a greenhouse with Zea mays, pisum satvum Dactylis glomerata and Trifolium pratense on different soils. From soils with added lead chloride (0, 100, 500, and 1,000 ppm Pb) considerable amount of Pb (≤ 470 ppm) were translocated to the vegetative above ground parts of the plants only at the 2 highest doses. Pea shoots grown on uncontaminated soils contained a very small amount of Pb, from which the greater part was derived from the air. On contaminated roadside soils with total amounts ≤ 1,100 ppm pb, peas took up, significantly more Pb, from which 2 to 3 ppm was derived from the soil. Lead contents of soil saturation extracts ranged between 3.8 and 42.5 ppb and showed a correlation to plant Pb contents. Plants grown on Pb-bearing mine tailings near Bleiberg-Kaernten contained from 25 to 487 ppm Pb.

487 **Horak, O., Rebier, R.,** 1979. Influence of different application rates of sewage sludge on the heavy metal content of plants in pot experiments. Oesterreichische Studiengesellschaft Fuer Atomenergie Sgae. Seibersdorf Berichte: 3048.

Pot experiments were conducted with brown soil and black soil amended with different amounts of air dried sewage sludge. At application rates of 40 and 80 t/ha, which are usual in practice, only the higher rate influenced the contents of some heavy metals in wheat and barley. Zinc and in part, Cu increased, and Mn decreased with sludge application. Strongly elevated rates of 320 and 640 t/ha had nearly no effect on the yield of corn, but markedly increased the yield of rape. The contents of Zn, Cu, Mn, and Mo increased with high sludge applications, whereas those of Pb, Cd, Co, Cr, and Ni were not affected.

488 **Horler, D.N.H.,** 1980. Effects of cadmium and copper treatments and water stress on the thermal emission from peas (Pisum sativum L.): controlled environment experiments. Remote Sensing Environ. 10: 191-199.

Pea plants were grown in hydroponic solution and in vermiculite in controlled conditions and were treated with various concentrations of Cd and Cu in the two types of rooting medium. Relative canopy temperature (T_1) were estimated from thermal images obtained with an AGA "Thermovision 680" inferred camera. Stomatal resistances (R), leaf temperature measures with thermocouples (T) and plant water potentials were also recorded. Metal-treated plants in hydroponic solution appeared to show a slight decrease in T_1 (about 0.2°C) relative to control plants, at concentrations upto 100 ppm Cd or Cu. At 200 ppm Cd or Cu, T_1 of treated plants was about 1°C higher than control, associated with visual toxicity symptoms. R in these plants was typically 5-10 sec cm^{-1}, compared with under 5 sec cm^{-1} in control plants, and probably limited evaporative cooling. Plants in vermiculite gave results consistent with those above.

489 **Hornbeck, J.W., Koterba, M.T., Pierce, R.S.,** 1979. Effects of sludge applications on soil water solution and vegetation in a northern hardwood

stand. J. Environ. Qual. 8(1): 72-78.

Dewatered and limed sludge from a primary treatment plant was applied at 25 and 125 wet t/ha (5.8 and 28.0 dry t/ha) on sand loam soils in a forest area in New England. Changes in soil water solution were assessed from water samples collected at 20 and 45 cm depths below the mineral surface. Application of 25 t/ha had little effect, but 125 t/ha increased the concentration of chloride, sulphate and calcium in soil water. Magnesium, Na, K, H, and NO_3 indicated maximum increases in concentration that averaged to 2 to 3-fold greater that control values of 0.5 mg/L. At 45 cm the increases in ionic concentrations following the heavy application were half of the increase that occurred at 20 cm. The concentrations of most ions returned to background levels within in June 1975 until the end of growing season in Oct, 1976, leaching losses for Ca and sulphate were estimated at 18 and 35 kg/ha for the control plots as compared with 39 and 64 kg/ha, respectively, from plots receiving the heavy application. No significant difference in basal-area growth among control and treated plots were observed for the first 2 growing seasons after sludge application. In the herb and shrub layer only 3 of the 31 commonly occurring species showed statistically significant changes in frequency.

490 **Hornburg, V., Brummer, G.,** 1989. Investigation on the mobility and availability of heavy metals in soils. Muttail-ungen der deutschen. Bodenk Gesellschaft. 59(2): 727-732.

Analysis for heavy metals was carried out on 158 top soil and 149 plant samples from a polluted sites on arable land, grassland, and forest. Fractionation of Cd, Mn, Zn and Cu was undertaken for water soluble $CaCl_2$, DTPA and EDTA extractable and $HNO_3/HClO_4$ digestion. Total metal contents correlated with EDTA extractable metals and pH was most correlated with EDTA extractable metal and pH was most influential to govern mobility and availability of metals. The pH dependent mobility of heavy metals below the element specific threshhold decreased from Cd > Mn > Zn > Cu > Pb.

491 **Horst, H., Brune, H., Sauerbeck, D., Hein, A.,** 1988. Estimation of plant-available Ni concentrations. Land Wirtschafilche Forshung, 41(3-4): 286-296.

Six extractants, 13 crop plants, five soils enriched with anthropogenic Ni by the addition of Ni-amended sewage sludge (6 to 40 ppm) and eight soils with naturally high levels (60 to 590 ppm) were used. Perennial ryegrass was most suitable as a test plant because it takes up high levels of Ni and because Ni concentrations in the plant are linearly related to extractable Ni in the soil. Soil pH and CEC affected Ni uptake; a formula for correcting the soil Ni values is given, as well as simplified correction factors. Clay, silt and C contents were not important.

492 **Hose, J.E., Barlow, L.A., Bent, S., Elseewi, A.A.,** 1987. Evaluation of

acute bioassays for assessing toxicity of poly-chlorinated biphenyl-contaminated soils. Regul. Toxicol. Pharmacol. 6:11-23.

Static 96-hr bioassays were performed using fathead minnows (Pimephales promelas), blacksmith (*Chronis punctipinnis*), and glass shrimp (*Palaemonetes Kadiakensis*), exposed to soil experimentally contaminated with up to 500 ppm polychlorinated biphenyal (PCB) capacitor fluid added to a concentration of 500 mgL^{-1}. Other bioassays were conducted with a 6-day mixing period prior to the bioassay or with acetone added to solubilize the PCB's. No mortality attributable to PCB toxicity was observed in definitive bioassays using the two fish and one invertebrate species. PCB levels leached from soil containing 500 ppm Aroclor 1242 ranged from 0.6 to 3.4 ppb in freshwater tests to 3.5 ppb in sea water bioassays. Using these data as the basis for waste classification, soils contaminated with upto 500 ppb PCBs during capacitor spills would be designated nonhazardous.

493 **Huang, J.C., Mccole, P.M.**, 1980. Pretreatment of sewage for heavy metal removals. Nat. Conf. Environ. Eng. ASCE. New York: 236-239.

An upflow expanded sand bed was used with lime feed to mix nuclear precipitation of metals, calcium carbonate and calcium hydroxylaptite on the sand grains. This new process could be used for pretreatment of municipal waste water ahead of conventional treatment to remove heavy metals into relatively small volume of granular precipitate, thus leaving the primary and secondary waste water treatment sludges with a lower metals content and making them more suitable for agricultural use.

494 **Hue, N.V.**, 1988. A possible mechanism for manganese phytotoxicity in Hawaii soils amended with a low manganese sewage sludge J. Environ. Qual. 17: 473-479.

A greenhouse experiment was conducted on three Hawaii soils: a Typic hyotrandept, a Typic Chromustert, and a manganiferous tropeptic Eutruston. Each soil received four rates (0, 20, 40 and 80 g kg^{-1}) of a low Mn municipal sludge, Lettuce was grown as a test crop. Manganese phytotoxicity unexpectedly occurred in all sludge amended treatments of the Oxisol and in the 80 g kg^{-1} rate of the vertisol as indicated by reduced dry matter yields and by high plant Mn concentrations which were all greater than 1000 mg Mn kg^{-1}. Soil solution Mn also increased. In the manganiferous Oxisol, where Mn toxicity was most serious soil solution Mn at transplanting significantly increased from 0.02 to 0.46, 5.57, and 7.26 mg Mn L^{-1} as sludge rate increased from 0 to 20, 40 and 80 g kg^{-1}, despite a concurrent increase in soil pH from 5.43, to 6.78, 7.91 and 8.10. Four weeks later (at harvest), soluble Mn increased even more drastically from 0.01 in the untreated soil to 5.7, 640 and 1160 mg Mn L^{-1} in the 20, 40 and 80 g kg^{-1} sludge rate, even though soil pH levels of all sludge treatments were essentially equal (pH = 5.0). These facts were virtually inexplainable by soil pH, redox conditions or the direct Mn contribution from the sludge. In contrast, Mn complexation by organic ligands e.g. tartric, pyruvic, protocatechoic acids which were found in considerable quantities in the soil solution of sludge amended soils, accounted for 76 to 99% of the soluble Mn, and adequately explained the high and phyto-toxic levels of Mn in soil solutions.

495 **Hue, N.V., Silva, J.A., Arifin, R.**, 1988. Sewage sludge soil interactions as measured by plant and soil chemical composition. J. Environ. Qual. 17: 384-390.

A green house experiment was conducted on three mineralogically different soils, a limed, volcanic ash-dried Andept an alkaline vertisol and a limed, manganiferous oxisol. Each soil received four rates (0, 45, 90 and 180 Mg ha^{-1}) of a Honolulu sewage sludge, and an NPK fertilizer treatment. Lettuce (*Lactuca sativa* L.) was grown as a test crop. Concentrations of plant Cu and Fe were not significantly affected by sludge rate. Plant Cd and Zn concentrations increased as sludge rate increased regardless of soil type. Plant N remained essentially constant as sludge rate increased in two of the soils, in the Oxisol, plant Ni increased with increasing sludge rate. Manganese in the soil solution drastically increased with sludge rate, and became phytotoxic. Plant Mn exceeded 700 mg kg^{-1}, level above which significant, yield reduction occurred) with increasing sludge addition in the Oxisol, and with 180 Mg ha^{-1} in the Vertisol. The Andept, with its high adsorption capacity, retained most of the heavy metals added by the sludge; this soil also retained phosphate so strongly that P was the growth limiting factor in all treatments as indicated by low dry matter yields low plant P 1.4 vs 4.0 mg kg^{-1} for maximum yield and by low soil solution P concentration (0.08 vs 0.40mg L^{-1}). In terms of heavy metals accumulation in plants, it appeared that the Andept could tolerate the highest sludge loading rate, and the Oxisol the lowest.

496 **Huebler, K.H.**, 1988. The new environmental issue: soil pollution. Environ. Prot. Eng. 12: 141-153.

A case study on soil pollution as well as the causes of this pollution in the Federal Republic of Germany are presented. There are also given perspective of a more active soil conservation in future.

497 **Huibregtse, K.R., Kastman, K.H.**, 1981. Development of a system to protect groundwater threatened by hazardous spills on land. NTIS, Springfield, VA: p. 43.

Direct grout injections enveloped spills to isolate them from groundwater and a mobile in-situ treatment unit was constructed and mechanically tested. Grouting procedures were most applicable in gravel, sand and some silty soils. Treatability agents added to four soils during flow-through tests showed 99 per cent detoxification.

498 **Humphries, R.N., Guarino, L.**, 1987. Soil nitrogen and the growth of birch and buddleia in abandoned chalk, quarries. Reclam, Reveg, Res., 6:

55-61.

Birch *(Betula pendula)* and buddleia *(Buddliea daviddi)* are amongst the earliest woody species to colonise abandoned chalk quiarries in South-East Britain. The development of birch scrub is slow, whereas that of buddleia is rapid. The possibility of a differential response to soil nitrogen level and form was tested in a pot experiment. At low soil nitrogen, buddleia had an ability to maintain leaf area irrespective of form, whereas birch did not. Maintenance of leaf area is proposed as means whereby some pioneer species are able to grow faster than other species on soils and spoils with low nitrogen level.

499 **Hunter, M., Stephenson, T., Lester, J.N., Perry, R.,** 1985. The influence of transient phenomena on the biodegradation of nitrilotriacetic acid in the activated sludge process-I: Variations in hydraulic loading and sewage strength. Water Air Soil Pollut. 25: 415-430.

The removal of nitrilotriacetic acid (NTA) following acclimatization in an activated sludge pilot plant has been studied during transient changes in operating conditions. These changes included increases in hydraulic loading and influent chemical oxygen demand (COD) and such phenomena in combination with transient temp. reductions. Short-term increases in hydraulic loading from 1 to 2 dry weather flow (DWF) had a very limited effect on NTA removal. Increasing the influent COD had a slight effect on NTA removal. Short-term increases in hydraulic loading combined with transient reduction in temperature significantly reduced NTA removal. The effect of these combined changes on NTA removal was synergistic, rather than additive. Increases in influent COD combined with transient temperature reductions also caused a significant reduction of NTA removal.

500 **Hurst, C.J., Gerba, C.P., Cech, I.,** 1980. Effects of environmental variables and soil characteristics on virus survival in soil. Applied. Environ. Microbiol., 40 (6): 1067-1079.

The objectives of this study was to measure the effects of various environmental variables on virus persistence. Test samples of soil were placed in vials, and the soil was wetted with suspensions of virus in either distilled water, unchroninated secondary sewage effluent, or mixtures of effluent and water. The ciruses used were coxsackteviruses. A9 and B3, echovirus 1, poliovirus 1, rotavirus Sa11, and bacteriophages T2 and MS2. The rate of virus inactivation was evaluated statistically with regard to conditions under which the vials were incubated and to the soil characteristics.

501 **Hutchison, F., Wai, C.M.,** 1979. Cadmium, lead, and zinc in reclaimed phosphate mine waste dumps in Idabo. Bull. Environl. Contam. Toxicol. 23(3): 377-380.

Two adjacent mines, Ballard mine and Henry mine, located 2 km NE of Soda Springs, Idaho, were studied in the summer of 1977. Soil samples consisting of the top 25 cm were collected randomly from each reclaimed waste dump at 10-15 sites. Alfalfa and grass species (brome, crested, orchard, and timothy) were sampled at each site when present. Heavy metal concentrations (Cd, Pb, and Zn) for soil and vegetation at the 2 mine reclaimed waste dumps are tabulated. Average Cd concentrations in soil from different reclaimed waste dumps vary from 14.5, 6.8 ppm to 38.8, 8.5 ppm. Zinc concentrations in soil of the waste dumps average 443, 210 ppm to 1,112 124 ppm. Average Pb concentrations in waste dump soil vary from 20.1, 5.2 ppm to 35.0, 2.5 ppm. Average Cd concentrations in vegetation from the reclaimed waste dumps vary from 1.1, 0.9 ppm in alfalfa and from 0.7, 0.3 ppm to 1.8, 0.6 ppm in grass. Cadmium levels in alfalfa grown on the waste dumps are 3-15 times higher than those in the control plot; grass shows a similar trend, with levels 7-18 times higher than the control plot. Zinc concentrations in vegetation from the dump sites are also high compared to the control plot. Lead in vegetation shows little differences between the dump sites and the control plot.

502 **Hutzler, N.J., Baillod, C.R.,** 1988. Biological reclamation of contaminated soils of a wood preserving site. Proc. Annual Madison Waste Conf. 11: 223-234.

Laboratory and field experiments were conducted to examine the feasibility of bio-degradation for reclamation of soil contaminated with pentachlorophenol (PCP) and polynuclear aromatic hydrocarbon (PHA). Results showed that PCP disappearance over 5 months ranged from 50% (low fertilizer application) to 92% (high temp, high fertilizer and high irrigation) in the lab. The PCP conc. decreased over 92% in the field value over a period of 4 months, PAH reduction ranged from 50 to 75% over the same period. Toxicity of the leachates was also reduced indicating no development of toxic by-products.

503 **Hutzler, N.J., Murphy, B.E., Gierke, J.S.,** 1991. State of technology review: Soil vapor extraction systems. J. Hazardous Mater., 26(2): 225-230.

Extracting vapor from soil is a cost-effective technique for the removal of volatile organic chemicals (VOCs) from contaminated soils. Among the advantages of the soil vapor extraction process are that it minimally disturbs the contaminated soil, it can be constructed from standard equipment, it has been demonstrated at pilot-and field scale, it can be used to great volumes of soil than can be practically excavated, and it has potential for product recovery.

504 **Hyde, H.C., Page, A.L., Bingham, F.T., Mahier, R.J.,** 1979. Effect of heavy metals in sludge on agricultural crops. J. Water Pollut. Control Fed. 53(10): 2475-2486.

Four years of field tests and a one year greenhouse tests were conducted to determine the effect of heavy metals in waste water sludge on agricultural crops in the Francisco Bay region. The total plant content of heavy metals increased but the corn-grain was not affected. The amount of plant-available forms of metals reach a "steady-state" condition or revert to less available forms after initial sludge applications. In the greenhouse and laboratory studies, sludge application to calcareous soils at 160 t/ha had minimal impact and resulted in plant tissue concentrations similar to those found in plants grown on acid soils unamended by sludge.

505 **Ibara, M., Lopez-Balmonte, F., Diez, M.A.,** 1988. Toxic effects of fluorine on the biological cycle of herbaceous dicotyledonous species and monocotyl. Anales. de Edafologia Agrobiologa 47: 683-706.

The effects of 10, 15, 30, 60 and 120 ppm F on growth and development in morphology and photosynthetic pigment content of Medicago Sativa and tobacco grown in solution were studied. Growth was simulated at 10 and 15 ppm F and carotenl and chlorophyll content were increased. At 15 ppm F, growth was reduced, with 70 and 100% of plants treated with 60 and 120 ppm F, respectively. Similarly in T. gesnerina 15 ppm F caused leaf necrosis and reduced growth while in sorghum F conc. 30 ppm did not affect plant growth. In both species 30 ppm F, reduced content of chlorophyll and carotenoids. At 60 and 120 ppm F, 80 and 100% plants died, respectively.

506 **Ibiebele, D.D., Inyang, A.D., Lawrence, C.H., Coleman, R.L., Pees, N.,** 1985. Some characteristics of the behaviour of indicator bacteria in sewage-amended soil. Environl. Pollut. 39 (2): 175-182.

The abundance, sensitivity to environmental conditions and growth recovery characteristics of faecal coliform bacteria and *Streptococcus faecalis* (indicator bacteria) were monitored in experimental plots receiving various quantities of undigested sewage sludge. The streptococci were less abundant in the sludge, but more abundant in the soil, than the faecal coliforms. Survival time of both groups of bacteria was not significantly different. The streptococcal numbers were not directly related to the quantity of sludge applied to the soil. Growth recovery was exhibited only by the *Streptococcus faecalis*.

507 **Idelovitch, E., Michail, M.,** 1980. Treatment effects and pollution dangers of secondary effluent percolation to groundwater. Water I. & Tech. 13(2): 949-966.

Percolation of secondary effluent from oxidation ponds to the groundwater aquifer, which was studied in a large-scale field operation acted as an efficient advanced waste water treatment system. The major process involved were slow sand filtration, biological degradation, nitrification, chemical precipitation, adsorption and ion exchange. Excellent removal was obtained by effluent passage through the soil aquifer system for several important pollutants, including; phosphorus, particulate organic matter, coliform bacteria, cadmium and chromium. Good removal was also obtained for soluble organics.

508 **Imandel, K., Razeghi, W., Samar, P.,** 1978. Tehran ground-water pollution by detergents. Water Air Soil Pollut. 9: 119-122.
Out of 3756 wells within metropolitan Tehran, 316 wells were selected according to simple random sampling without replacement. The conclusion asserted is that with a confidence limit of 95%, standard error of 2, and permissible error of ± 0.005, the average concentration of detergents in Tehran ground-water aquifer is within 0.1593 to 0.1163 mol^{-1} as MBAS.

509 **Inamori, Y., Matushige, K., Sudo, R., Kikuchi, H.,** 1987. Effect of organochlorine compounds on existence and growth of soil organisms in "Water Pollution Research and Control, Brighton" Part 5, L. Lijklema et al (Eds.), Pergamon, Oxford, 1887-1890.
This study was carried out to study the effect of organochlorine compounds on the existence and growth of organisms in soil ecosystems. The following organochlorine compounds, which have become a very serious problem recently and may be carcinogenic, were used: trichlorethylene, tetrachloreoethylene, and 1, 1, 1, trichloroethane.

510 **Inbar, Y., Chen, Y., Hadar, Y.,** 1991. Carbon, CPMAS. NMR and FTIR spectroscopic analysis of organic matter transformations during composting of solid waste from wineries. Soil Sci. 152(4): 272-282.
Composted solid waste from wineries were analysed for C/N, CEC and crude fibre. The man changes in the organic matter were (i) a decrease in C/N ratio both in skins and the combined samples but not in the seeds; (ii) an increase in CEC, (iii) a decrease in poly-saccharides, content, (iv) an increase in lignin and cellulose content. All methods showed that main changes took place in the skins while seeds changed slightly.

511 **Iqbal, M.Z.,** 1988. Deposition of air borne cations and anions in the vicinity of a polluted area. Indian. J. Ecol. 15(1): 1-6.
High deposition levels of sodium, potassium, calcium, magnesium and sulphur were recorded periodically in the soil and resin at a site which was polluted by the emission of oxides of sulphur and nitrogen and other industrial wastes from a fertilizer factory, an oil refinery, two power generating plants and burning of fossil fuels. The deposition of ions and cations were significantly higher in the polluted than the non-polluted site during winter months.

512 **Ireland, M.P.,** 1979. Metal accumulation by the earthworms Lumbricus rubellus, Dendrobaena Veneta and Eiseniella tetraedra living in heavy metal polluted sites. Environl. Pollut. 19(3): 201-206.
The earthworm (*L. rubellus*), takes up and retains Pb from soil containing a high concentration of Pb. Irrespective of the Cu, Zn, and Mn concentrations in the soil, these metals are apparently regulated in the

tissues. In soil containing high concentrations of Zn and Ca, there are species differences in tissue metal content. *L. rubellus* contained the highest amounts of Zn and Mn. *D. veneta* the highest concentration of Cd, and the highest mean Pb content was in *E. tetraedra*. The concentration of soil Ca and Cu, together with species differences in tolerance to heavy metals, are considered factors which may influence heavy metal accumulation. Earthworms concentrate Cd from environment at higher levels than any other metal studied.

513 **Irwin, K.C., Parish, H.J.,** 1989. Dynamic studies of naphthalene sorption on soil from aqueous solution. Chemosphere. 18(11-12): 2309-2312.

The thermodynamics and kinetics of naphthalene sorption from water on soil were examined over the temperature range of 5 to 50°C.

514 **Iskandar, I.K.,** 1978. The effect of waste water river in cold regions on land treatment systems. J. Environ. Qual. 7(3): 361-367.

The effect on ground-water quality and soils and vegetation of treatment and disposal of municipal/industrial waste water on land in cold regions was investigated using six outdoor test sites. Winter application of waste water was feasible even at very cold air temperatures (<0C) at the new Hampshire test site. High NO_3-N concentrations were observed in all treatments (5-15 cm/week) in both soils in early summer. Over the 12-mo period of study, removal of organic C, BOD, suspended solids, fecal coliform bacteria, and phosphorus by the soil types used (sandy loam and silt loam) was essentially complete. These had very little or no effect no ground-water quality. The principal mechanism for nitrogen removal was found to be plant uptake, which was seasonally dependent. Application of 15 cm of secondary effluent per week to a sandy loam soil was not feasible because of the presence of >10 mg/L NO_3-N in the leachate for > 9 mo/year. No efforts were made to apply waste water accordingly to plant need. Pre-application treatment is not necessary for the renovation of waste water by the soil-plant systems. Movement of applied heavy metals to a depth of 15-30 cm in the high treatment soil was thought to be a result of a drop in soil pH resulting from this treatment. In all other treatment, heavy metals were confined to the top 15 cm of the soil.

515 **Iskandar, I.K., Syers, J.K.,** 1980. Effectiveness of land application for phosphorus removal from municipal waste water at Manteca, California. J. Environ. Qual. 9 (3): 616-621.

The concentrations of dissolved inorganic phosphate in soil solution at 0.8 and 1.6 m in soils which had received municipal waste water for 4 and 13 years ranged from 7.3 to 13.9 μP/ml. In some cases, their concentrations were higher than that in the added waste water. Sorption studies indicated that the ability of soils from the control site to remove added P from solution was low. Waste water addition caused a substantial decrease in the P sorption capacity of surface soils and a marked change in the isotherm shape from a curvilinear to an essentially linear isotherm. Sorption capacity generally increased down the profile to 60 cm on the treated sites. Only a small proportion of the total P accumulated from waste water addition was in the organic form. Large amounts of P were extractable by 0.01M $CaCl_2$ particularly in the upper 45 cm of the profiles receiving waste water.

516 **Jackson, D.R., Ausmus, B.S.,** 1979. Effects of arsenic on nutrient dynamics of grassland microcosms and fields plots. Water Air Soil Pollut. 11(1): 13-21.

Grassland field plots were compared with 2 sizes of excised microcosms (15 and 30 cm diameter) and 30-cm diameter homogenized microcosms to assess the effects of As on soil-plant nutrient dynamics. All experimental units were treated with As, at rates of 0, 0.5 and 5.0 mg/cm, by superficial application of dissolved disodium arsenate. Calcium, PO_4-P, NO_3-N, dissolved organic carbon (DOC) and NH_4-N were determined in soil leachate and soil extracts. Greater loss of PO_4-P, NO_3-N, NH_4-N, DOC occurred via soil leachate from microcosms treated with the greatest level of As relative to untreated microcosms. Field plots were unaffected by As treatment. Excised microcosms were recommended for testing potentially hazardous chemicals.

517 **Jackson, D.R., Levin, M.** 1979. Transport of arsenic in grassland microcosms and field plots. Water Air Soil Pollut. 11(1): 3-12.

Arsenic was applied to each set of microcosms and the field plots, at rates of 0, 0.5, and 5.0 mg/cm. Arsenic was highly assimilated by grass, with a high concentration of 720 ppm. The microcosms represented the field plots in terms of As transport and offer several advantages over field testing of toxic substances.

518 **Jackson, D.R., Washburne, C.P., Ausmus, B.S.,** 1977. Loss of Ca and NO_3-N from terrestrial microcosms as an indicator of soil pollution, Water Air Soil Pollut. 8: 279-284.

An experiment was conducted using As-treated soil cores to develop a screening tool for toxic contaminants. Aqueous efflux of Ca and NO_3-N were tested as sensitive indicators of chemical stress on soil. Nutrient efflux from forest soil cores was increased at the highest As level (100 mg As cm^{-2}), while population parameters (i.e., microbial biomass and enzyme concentrations) were unaffected. These results indicate that nutrient efflux is more sensitive to chemical stress than population parameters. Nutrient losses from soils may be used as an early-warning device for assessing contaminants potentially toxic to terrestrial ecosystems.

519 **Jana, S., Choudhuri, M.A.,** 1984. Synergistic effects of heavy metal pollutants on senescence in submerged aquatic plants. Water Air Soil Pollut. 21: 351-357.

The effect of many combinations of toxic concentrations of heavy metal pollutants, viz., mercuric chloride, lead acetate, cadmium chloride, and cupric sulphate, on the senescene of isolated mature levels of submerged aquatic-plants, *Potamogeton pectinatus* L., *Vallisneria* L., and *hydrilla Verticillata* (l.f.) Royle were studied. All metal pollutants caused senescence in all three species by decreasing chlorophyll, DNA, RNA, protein and dry wt. and increasing free amino acid, tissue permeability, the activities of protease and RNise, and the ratio of acid to alkaline physophosphatase activity over control values. The effects were highest in Potamogeton and lowest in Hydrilla. The degree of senescene by combinations of toxic concentrations of heavy metal pollutants is much higher due to synergism than that by individual pollutants.

520 **Jana, S., Dalal, T., Barua, B.,** 1987. Effect and relative toxicity of heavy metals on *cuscuto reflexa*. Water Air Soil Pollut. 33: 23-27.

The effects of four concentrations (0.5, 1, 5 and 10 $\mu g\ mL^{-1}$) of the heavy metals (Hg, As, Pb, Cu, Cd and Cr) on some senescence variables of *Cuscuta reflexa* Roxb. were studied. All of the treatments, except 0.5 $\mu g\ mL^{-1}$, decreased Hill reaction activity, chlorophyll and protein contents and dry matter percentage in biomass and increased tissue permeability over control data. The harmful effects of the metals were best visible at 10 $\mu g\ mL^{-1}$. The general order of sensitivity was : As > Cd > Pb > Hg > Cu > Cr (Absolute metal concentration). *Cuscuta reflexa* shows tolerance to the heavy metals up to 0.5 $\mu g\ mL^{-1}$.

521 **Jane, S., Bhattacharjee, A.,** 1988. Effect of combinations of heavy metal pollutants on *Cuscuta reflexa*. Water Air Soil Pollut. 42: 303-310.

The effects of combinations of Hg, As, Pb, Cu, Cd and Cr on the variables of *Cuscuta reflexa* Roxb. in natural condition were studied. All of the combinations of heavy metals tested decreased Hill reaction activity, chlorophyll and protein contents; and increased tissue permeability over control values. The degree of inhibition or increase by combinations of heavy metals is much higher due to synergism.

522 **Jardim, W.F., Pearson, H.W.,** 1990. Toxicity of cupric ions to micro-organisms: Effects on ATP concentrations, Chemical Speciation and Bio availability 2(4): 155-156.

Toxicity of cupric ions to micro-organisms was investigated by measuring variations in the intracellular ATP concn. A laboratory-produced tolerant strain of Plectonema boryanum was grown to be less sensitive to cupric ions than was the nontolerant strain, which was affected by megal concn. below 10^{-9} M. The use of ATP as an indicator of both toxicity and biomass is evaluated.

523 **Jarrell, W.M., Page, A.L., Elseewi, A.A.,** 1980. Molybdenum in the environment. Residue Reviews: Residues of pesticides and other contaminue in the Sci. Total Environ., 74: (1) 43-60.

Molybdenum in the total environment is reviewed, specifically the supply of Mo, Mo cycle, importance of Mo in industry and agriculture, and the potential hazards which may result when excessive levels of Mo occur in the environment. In industry, Mo is used in a wide variety of metals and chemical compounds. The natural occurrence of Mo in minerals, rocks and other geological deposits. soils and water are considered. Molybdenum in plant, animal, and human mitrition are considered as to its essentiality and toxicity, plants grown in soils high in available Mo can accumulate excessive levels of Mo which, if they constitute a high proportion of the diet, they are toxic to ruminant animals. Therefore, the distribution of Mo in the environment must be carefully monitored to reduce the potential for toxicity to animals. The sources of Mo enrichment in the environment considered are release from industrial or sludge, in areas where Mo is added to soil in the form of fly ash, sewage sludge, high Mo waters, industrial wastes, or from the atmosphere. Forage grown on soil may contain levels of Mo considered unsafe for animal consumption.

524 **Jastrow, J.D., Koeppe, D.E.**, 1980 Uptake and effects of cadmium in higher plants. "Cadmium in Environ.", Pt. 1: Ecological Cycling" John Wiley & Sons, New York: 607-638.

Cadmium is readily taken up and accumulated by many plants; it gets into food chains via plant uptake, and it has profound toxic effects on plants when accumulated over a period of time. Further details regarding cadmium-resistant plants remain to be elucidated, as do the many complex interactions of soil and environmental variables with cadmium uptake. Since areas of high cadmium contamination are likely to occur in conjunction with high concentrations of other toxic trace elements, the interactions with other trace elements are important areas requiring further investigation.

525 **Jauhri, K.S.**, 1989. Evaluation of certain agro-industrial wastes as seed pelletants under adverse soil pH conditions. Biol. Wastes, 28(3): 233-236.

Rhizobium inoculation fails to respond favourably under adverse soil pH conditions. Among various agro-industrial wastes used to pellet the inoculated seed for ameliorating the effect of adverse soil pH, cow dung was found to be superior and improved nodulation and dry-matter yield of soybean in acidic soil of Palampur (pH 4-8). In sodic soil of Karnal (pH 9.5), neem leaf was found to improve nodulation and yield.

526 **Jedrczak, A., Drab, M.**, 1989. Soils and plants, pollution around the industrial wastes dump of Szczecin. Arch. Ochr. Spodowiska, No 3-4: 183-199.

Soil and plant samples taken from all directions and from various distances from the dump were analysed. There was high salinity and high micronutrient status: (Cu, Fe, Cd, Pb, Ni) and Co in soils near the dump. The soil samples which were taken from further distance were not polluted. In the plants near the wastes dump considerably higher Na, Cd and

Ni amounts were found. High salinity of the environment caused disturbances in the nitrogen cycle in plants. In the plant samples taken near the wastes dump, the total N amount were the lowest, and the plant samples from further distance contained much more nitrogen.

527 **Jenkins, S.H.,** 1979. Development in land methods of waste water treatment and utilisation : Conference Proc. Progress Water Technol. 11(4-5): 532.

Methods for the treatment, disposal, and utilization of sewage sludge and domestic waste waters are described. Included are overland flow, surface irrigation, and grass filtration. Agricultural and aquacultural uses are discussed alongwith the ecological and health hazards of heavy metals. Design of stabilization ponds, nutrients, N balance changes in soil, water movement and runoff, pH and oxidation are also considered. Several case studies are included.

528 **Jenne, E.A., Ball, J.W., Burchard, J.M., Vivit, D.V., Barks. J.H.,** 1980, Geochemical modelling: Apparent solubility controls on Ba, Zn, Cd, Pb and P in water of the Missouri Tri-State mining area. in "Trace Substances in Environ. Health XIV, Univ. Mo. Columbia: 353-361.

Aqueous speciation and disequilibrium solubility indices were computed, with the geochemical model. Good evidence exists for solubility controls on 3 elements. Ba, Zn and Cd) and possible controls were identified for 2 others (Pb and F). Barite ($BaSO_4$) appears to control the solubility of Ba in all the waters, including the storm drainage. All barite disequilibrium indices, except those from 4 undersaturated well waters, fall within the - 0.5 log unit error band. The carbonate salts appear to effectively place an upper limit on the dissolved levels of 2 toxic metals, (Zn and Cd), as well as that of Ca, in all waters except the acidic (pH 3. 5-4.8) drainage from the tailings piles themselves.

529 **Jenneman, G.E., McLnerney, M.J., Knapp, R.M.,** 1986. Effect of nitrate on biogenic sulfide production. Appl. Environ. Microbiol. 51(6): 1205-1211.

The addition of 59 mM nitrate inhibited biogenic sulfide production in dilute sewage sludge (10% (v/v) amended with 20 mM sulfate and either acetate, glucose, or hydrogen as electron donors. Similar results were found when pond sediment or oil-field brines served as the inoculum. Sulfide production was inhibited for periods of at least 6 months and was accompanied by the oxidation of resazurin from its colourless reduced state to its pink oxidized state. Lower amounts of nitrate (6 or 20 mM) and increased amounts of sewage sludge resulted in only transient inhibition of sulfide production. The addition of 156 mM sulfate to bottles with 59 mM nitrite and 10% (v/v) sewage sludge or pond sediment resulted in sulfide production. Nitrate, nitrite, and nitrous oxide were detected during periods where sulfide production was inhibited, whereas nitrate, nitrite, and nitrous oxide were below detectable levels at the time sulfide production began.

530 **Jin, Y., O'connor, G.A.**, 1990. Behaviour of toluene added to sludge-amended soils. J. Environ. Qual. 19(3): 573-579.

Laboratory experiments were conducted to study the behaviour of toluene in two soils in the presence and absence of municipal sludge. Sludge addition increased toluence adsorption in two soils because of increased organic C content. The source of organic C (soil or sludge) and soil clay content also influenced toluence adsorption. Toluene adsorption/desorption was reversible in one soil, but slightly hysteretic in the other soil. An air flow incubation system was used to evaluate toluene volatilization and degradation. The primary fate of surface, applied toluence in both soils was volatilization. Toluene volatilisation rates were independent of sludge treatments.

531 **Jindal, R., Verma, A.**, 1990. Heavy metal toxicity to *Dephnia pulex*. Indian J. Environ. Health, 32(3): 289-292.

Acute toxicity tests carried out, using heavy metals viz, cadmium, copper, mercury, nickel and zinc, on adult specimens of the cladoceran *Daphnia pulex*, revealed 48 hr LC_{50} values in the order of Hg > Cu > Cd > Zn > Ni. Mercury was found to be 3.58 times more toxic than cadmium, 3.25 times than copper, 37.14 times than nickel and 9.46 times than zinc. A significant ($P < 0.01$) linear correlation coefficient was observed between percentage mortality and the concentration of the metals.

532 **Jiunn, Fwulee, Crum, J.R., Boyd, S.A.**, 1989. Enhanced retention of organic contaminants by soils exchanged with organic cations. Environ. Sci. Technol. 23(11): 1365-1372.

The ability of soils to remove nonionic organic contaminants (NOCs) from water can be greatly enhanced by ion exchange reactions of organic cations for natural inorganic exchange ions. Soils exchanges with organic cations of the form $(CH_3)3\ NR)^+$, where R is C_9 C_{16} hydrocarbon, have significantly higher organic matter (OM) contents and display high sorptive uptake of common groundwater contaminants. Sorption coefficients (K values) of NOCs on hexadecyltrimethylammonium-(HDTMA) treated subsurface soil increased by ~200 times. The K values for HDTMA treated surface soil also increased significantly. When smaller organic cations. i.e., dodecyltrimethy ammonium (DDTMA) and nonyltrimethylammonium (NTMA), were used, the exchange reactions were less complete, and the increases in OM contents and K values were less. Organic matter derived from the exchanged organic cations appeared to form an effective partition medium for NOCs.

533 **John, D.L.**, 1980. Heavy metals distribution in particles from the flocculent sediments of Onondaga lake, NY. in "Trace substances in Environ. Health". XIV Unvi. MO Columbia: 489-499.

Onondaga lake, located in metropolitan Syracuse, NY, receives extensive industrially derived heavy metal loadings. Despite the diluting influence of high sedimentation rates, bulk analyses indicate that upper sediments are extremely contaminated with Cr, Ni, Cu and Zn. More than 10,000 particles from the upper flocculent sediments were analysed to identify and characterise heavy metal associations within the solid phase. The major chemical constituents were Si, Ca, Al, Fe and S. Only minor differences in the dominant chemical composition of the 4 heavy metal bearing populations were apparent.

534 **John, M.K., 1974,** Waste water renovation through soil percolation. Water Air Soil pollut. 3: 3-10.

Analysis of P in 22 leachate collections and distribution of both organic and inorganic P in column sections revealed the mechanism of p removal, the influence of differing soil properties, and the effect of continuous utilization. Renovation of effluent P was greatest with percolation through columns of acid Milner soil which contains abundant Al and Fe, and although Squilax soil removed more P from initial leachings due to its higher exchangeable Ca content, Glanmore soil was more suitable of these two alkaline soils over the long term. The leachate NO_3-N levels were lower than the original NO_3-N content of effluent for the first ten leachings but NO_3-N enrichment occurred for the last effluent percolations through all three soils. Analysis of Ca, Mg, K, and Na in leachates and soil columns indicated losses of exchangeable cations from the calcareous Squilax and Glenmore soils enriched effluent content and the accumulation of the cations in the acid soil reduced concentrations in effluent that passed through Milner soil.

535 **John, K. Cornelis, Van Laerhoken, J.,** 1976. Effects of sewage sludge composition, application rate and linė regime on plant availability of heavy metals. J. Environ. Qual. 5(3): 246-251.

Primary digested sludge from the metropolitan Vancouver sewage treatment plant and commercially available were applied to unlimed (pH 5.6) and limed (pH 6.4) silt loam at 0.5, 10, 25, and 100 g/kg in a growth chamber study involving ramaise lettuce (*Lactua sativa* L., *Val. longilocia*) and beets (*Beta vioganis* L.). Concentration of Cd, Zn, Pb, Cu, Ni, Mn and Fe in lettuce, but tops and beet tuber were not simply or solely dependent upon the resultant-sludge borne heavy metal contamination of the soil but a complexity of factors. Plant availability of the metals was influenced by the nature as well as the rate of sludge applied lime legime, their intraction, the increase in soil acidity associated with Milogranite application and metal adsorption and release from organic matter supplied.

536 **Johnels, A., Tyler, G., Westermark, T.** 1979. A history of mercury levels in Swedish fauna. Ambio. 8(4): 160-168.

Research regarding levels of Hg in Swedish fauna and flora is described. The increase of levels from the 19th century to the present (the last 150 yrs) caused by increased industrial activity is emphasized. The decrease since 1966, which is due to Fenno-Scandian (Finnish-Swedish) regulations and prohibitions in the use of Hg and its compounds, is also discussed.

537 **Johnsen, I., Pilegaard, K., Nymand, E.**, 1983. Heavy metal uptake in transplanted and in situ yarrow (*Achillea millefolium*) and eplphytic cryptogams at rural, urban and industrial localities in Denmark. Environl. Monit. Assess., 3(1): 13-22.

Yarrow (*A. millefolium* L.) and 3 cryptogamic epiphytes were collected from and transplanted to 10 various locations in Denmark. The spatial and temporal Variation in Pb and Cd concentrations of yarrow leaves and the cryptogams were determined. The physical structure of the plant parts, the mobility differences between the metals and the atmospheric fallout of metals at the growing site were believed to be important for the metal uptake. It was concluded, that yarrow leaves give a measure of the relative variation in deposition rates to surface of higher plants when collected at the end of a growth season, and that the geographic variation was revealed with similar accuracy by yarrow and the cryptogams.

538 **Johnson, S.W.**, 1990. Laboratory examination of soil venting for the recovery of volatile organic contaminants from unsaturated soil. Diss Abst, Int. Pt. B. Sci. & Eng. 51(1): 172.

Soil venting offers promise as a method for recovering volatile contaminants from unsaturated soil. This technique involves the withdrawal of air from a field of dry wells to recover pollutant vapors. Fieldscale venting applications have successfully recovered large quantities of volatile organics from contaminated soil. However, attempts to document recovery rates and final concentrations in pilot studies have met with limited success and previous laboratory studies have been restricted to artificial or modified soil.

539 **Johnson, V.R. Jr.**, 1975. Managing industrial wastes excluded from the sewer. Water Air Soil Pollut. 4: 201-207.

The 4 different disposal techniques for industrial waste disposal viz., treatment (usually chemical) followed by solar evaporation of the liquid from ponds; Incineration; biodegradation; and land disposal — usually burial or injection into soil or solid waste (garbage) are discussed.

540 **Johnson, K.R., Atwater, J.W.**, 1988. Role of saturated and unsaturated zone in soil disposal of septic tank effluent. Can. J. Civ. Engg. 15 (4): 709.

The guidelines for the use of the septic tank-soil absorption system (ST-SAS) in Province of British Columbia are very specific in regard to the separation distance between the ground surface and the ground-water table (minimum 1.2), and between the tile field and perimeter drains or ditches (minimum 3m). A pilot scale experiment employment waterproof channels filled with a saturated soil was used to evaluate the scientific basis for these guidelines. Septic tank effluent was applied to unsaturated columns, and samples were taken at different points in the channel. Measurements were made of total and fecal coliforms. chemical oxygen demand, ammonia, nitrate, and orthophosphate. Coliform reductions with the channels were at 30,000 fold with total coliform numbers generally lying below 200 coliforms/100 mL and fecal coliforms generally less than 50 coliforms/100 mL. and varying degrees of nitrification occurred in the unsaturated columns, resulting in relatively high concentrations of nitrate in some of the channel sections.

541 **Johnson, K.S., Harris, D.A.,** 1989. Prevention of water pollution in manufacture and use of agrochemicals. in "Annual Sympo. Institution of Water and Environmental Management", London, U.K.

The treatment of effluents from the formulation and manufacture of agrochemicals using a process of chemical flocculation and carbon filtration is briefly described. This process has adapted for use on farms to treat the washings from spraying machines and unused dilute spray liquids. The results showed that lindane, captafol, paraquat and pirimicarb were removed by carbon treatment to levels of < 0.001 < 0.01, < 0.01 and < 0.02 mg/L, respectively.

542 **Johnson, C.J., Kross, B.C.,** 1990. Continuing importance of nitrate contamination of ground-water and wells in rural areas. J. Industrial Medicine. 18(4): 449-456.

The contamination of ground-water and rural drinking water supplies by nitrates from livestock and human excrement, other organic waste, or chemical fertilizers is a potential hazard throughout the world. Infant illness and death from nitrate-induced methaemoglobinaemia is probably often misdiagnosed. Infant deaths resulting from misdiagnosis of this preventable, treatable intoxication were still occurring as recently as 1986 in South Dakota. In this State, about 39% of dug or bored wells were unsafe due to high nitrate content, compared with 22% of drilled wells and 16% of driven wells. Properly constructed wells more than 30 m deep are more likely to be safe. Groundwater concn. of nitrate may be unsafe for consumption and standards are needed to regulate such contamination. Such standards could serve as guidelines and could be enforceable.

543 **Johnson, W., Paone, J.,** 1982. Land utilisation and reclamation in the mining industry. NTIS, Springfield, VA, 28 pp.

The Bureau of Mines study indicates that land utilised by the mining industry for mineral extraction and processing from 1930 through 1980 amounted to 5.7 million acres, or 0.25 per cent of the land mass in the United States. Land reclaimed by the industry during the same period was 2.7 million acres, or 47 per cent of the land utilized. Land use by the mining industry includes surface land used for excavation or mining, for waste from underground mining, and for wastes from milling or processing operations. Data on land use for disposal of overburden waste from surface coal mines and on areas affected by sursidence associated with underground mining are included in the report for the period 1930-71 only.

544 **Johnson, D.W., Spalding, B.P.,** 1980. Zinc distributions and cycling in forest ecosystems. In "Zinc in the Environ". Pt. I. Ecological Cycling. John Wiley & Sons, New York: 419-437.

Pertinent literature concerning concentrations and distributions of zinc in vegetative and soil components of natural forest ecosystems has been reviewed.

545 **Jokela, E.J., Smith, W.H., Colbert, S.R.,** 1990. Growth and elemental content of slash pine 16 years after treatment with garbage composted with sewage sludge. J. Environ. Qual. 19(1): 146-150.

This study assessed tree growth and elemental tissue concentrations in a slash pine (Pinus elliottii Engelm). Plantation treated 16 yr previously with four rates (0, 112, 224, 448 Mg ha^{-1}) of municipal garbage composted with sewage sludge. Tree growth was significantly greater where garbage compost was applied. Stem biomass increased from 55.7 to 94.7 Mg ha^{-1} A 1.7 fold increase over the control for the heaviest garbage application rate. Annual tree basal area increment responses were also largest and most long-lasting (up to 9 yr) for the 4488 Mg ha^{-1} rate.

546 **Jones, R.,** 1983. Zinc and cadmium in lettuce and radish grown in soils collected near electrical transmission (hydro) towers. Water Air Soil Pollut., 19(4): 389-395.

Soil was collected from near hydro towers, to grow lettuce and radish in a glasshouse pot experiment. Plants grown in soil collected near a tower had concentrations of Zn 5 to 10 times higher than in plants grown in garden soil collected 10 and 90 m from a tower but concentrations were not high enough to have apparent toxic effects on growth, Concentrations of Cd in the soils, lettuce and radish plants indicated that the particular towers were not a source of Cd contamination.

547 **Jones, S.G., Brown, K.W., Deuel, L.E., Donnelly, K.C.,** 1979. Influence of simulate rainfall on the retention of sludge heavy metals by the leaves of forage crops. J. Environ, Qual. 8(1): 69-72.

Liquid digested sludges, containing 2 and 4% solids, were applied to greenhouse flats of common bermudagrass (*Cynodon dactylon*) and Bell rhodesgrass (*Chloris gayana*), equivalent to depths of 2.50 and 1.25 cm, respectively. Sludge-treated grasses were subjected to simulated rainfall equivalent to 2.5 cm/hr immediately following sludge treatments or after 24 hr of drying. Additional flats receiving the sludge treatments were sampled for 2 wk at regular intervals to determine the foliar retention of sludge in the absence of rainfall. The foliage of both grasses was visibly contaminated with sludge following application. The foliar concentrations of Cd, Cu, Pb, and Zn measured for each sludge treatment showed no preferential retention of any particular heavy metal. Bell rhodesgrass retained more sludge than common bermudagrass because of its larger leaf blades and overlapping sheathes. The sludge containing 4% solids was retained more by the foliage than sludge containing 2% solids. Sludge not allowed to dry on the leaves was removed by 1.25 cm of simulated rainfall, regardless of the grass species or sludge solids concentration. Sludge allowed to dry on the leaves, however, was not removed by 2.50 cm of simulated rainfall.

548 **Jones, K.C., Stratford, J.A., Waterhouse, K.S., Vogt, N.B.,** 1989. Organic contaminants in Welsh soil poly-nuclear aromatic hydrocarbons. Environl. Sci. Technol. 23(5): 540-550.

Soil samples from 49 locations were analysed for 14 polynuclear aromatic hydrocarbons (PAHs) to define typical range of PAHs in surface (0-5 cm) soil. The sum of 14 PAHs defined as Σ PAH varied by over 3 orders of magnitude. In general, soils show a constant, qualitative mixture of PAH components but marked differences in absolute values along the remote rural gradient. Soil OM has some controlling influence on PAH but not the other properties viz per cent clay, bulk density. The distinction between remote/rural and urban is made at < or > 60 μg of PAH/kg. Factors controlling PAH are also discussed.

549 **Joost, R.E., Olsen, F.J., Jones, J.H.,** 1987. Revegetation and minesoil development of coal refuse amended with sewage sludge and limestone. J. Environ. Qual. 16:65-68.

A study was conducted of deep incorporation of dried sludge and/or limestone to ameliorate acid coal refuse (gob) for establishment of three forage grasses. Dried sewage sludge and/or limestone were applied at 10 rates throughout the profile of trenches opened (30 or 60) cm by a cable trencher. Sub-plots of reed canarygrass, tall fescue and radtop were established. The organic matter applied in the sewage sludge decreased by 35% the plots were established, while the proportion of sand-size water-stable aggregates increased over in 2 years. The proportion of large pores increased in the high rate sewage sludge plots over that of lime-treated plots. Coal refuse pH increased from 2.7 in the unamended gob to 4.4 to 5.2 with all treatments but the two lower lime rates. All treatments maintained grass stands over 4 yr. with the exception of the 225 Mg sludge ha^{-1} plus 45 Mg limestone ha^{-1} mixture at 60 cm. Reed canary grass invaded adjacent plots and was more persistent than the other grasses. Mean herbage yield of the grasses exceeded 4.0 Mg ha^{-1} on all treatments. Tissue NO_3 levels were considered toxic for ruminants the first 3 yr, but decreased significantly over time.

550 **Joseph, H.,** 1984. Stoichiometric modelling of the activated sludge process. Water Air Soil Pollut. 23: 235-247.

A mathematical model of the activated sludge process is solved with consideration given to the waste water composition. Inclusion of waste water composition will lead to predictions where N or P may be limiting nutrients. The procedure presented is useful when designing or evaluating the operation of an activated sludge process.

551 **Joseph, K.O.**, 1989. Assessment of heavy metal pollution by analysis of sediments contaminated by industrial effluents. J. Indian Soc. Soil Sci. 37: 571-573.

Zinc and chromium pollution in aqualic environment by means of sediment analysis either alone or in combination with other water characteristics is a better tool for judging effects of pollution by industrial effluents.

552 **Joshi, S.R., Dutta, S.A.**, 1987. Studies on lignin removal by soil perfusion technique Water Air Soil Pollut. 36: 1-8.

Studies were carried out using a soil perfusion apparatus for the removal of lignin from waste water. It was observed that when a medium (pH 7.0) with lignin having about 1200 colour units was pursued through a soil column, perfusate contained only 250 to 300 colour units after three days to perfusion and pH was reduced to less than 5.0 with 70 to 80% reduction in total organic carbon (TOC). With a sterile soil column the colour was not removed and there was no change in TOC content. When the medium was buffered at pH 7.0, there was no reduction in colour units. When the pH of the perusate reduced to less than 5.0, it was also observed that the nitrate content had increased considerably. These results indicated that due to microbial activity lignin molecules might have been biotransformed and adsorbed on the soil column at lower pH. The major group of micro-organisms were also isolated from the soil.

553 **Jothikumar, N., Krishnamoorthi, K.D., Rao, D.M.R.**, 1986. Toxicity and biochemical responses of carp to dinitrobenzene plant effluent. Water Air Soil Pollut. 28: 117-126.

The effect of DNB (Dinitrobenzene) waste water on Cyprinus carp was found to be very toxic even at low concentration with 0.05% (v/v) at 96 hr LC_{50}. Various biochemical responses of carp such as O_2 consumption, NN_3 excretion, protein, glycogen and lipid contents were measured and statistically evaluated. The effect of this effluent on carp reduces O_2 consumption and NN_3 excretion and also interferes with the metabolism of the fish. The high toxicity of the effluent is attributed to the combined effect of a mixture of nitroaromatics present in the effluent.

554 **Joy, C.M., Balakrishnan, K.P.**, 1990. Effect of fluoride on axenic cultures of diatoms. Water Air Soil Pollut. 49: 241-249.

Algal bioassay studies on the effect of F concentrations on diatoms *Nitzschia palea* (fresh water) and *Amphora coffeaeformis* (Brackish water) were conducted in the laboratory. Significant enhancement of growth occurred in *N. palea* at F concentrations between 10 and 110 mg

L^{-1}. In *A. coffeaeformis* statistically significant stimulation occured at 70 mg L^{-1} and above 90 mg L^{-1}F the growth declined.

555 **Joy, C.M., Balakrishnan, K.P., Ammini Joseph,** 1990. Effect of industrial discharges on the ecology of phytoplankton production in the river Periyar (India). Water Res. 24(6): 787-796.

The ecology of phytoplankton production in the river Periyar, which receives continuous effluent discharge from a dozen industrial units, has been studied. Spatial variation of phytoplankton composition, chlorophyll pigments and physico-chemical features of water were observed for a period of 1 year. A multiple regression relationship was set up to determine the ecological factors that control phytoplankton production. The industrial zone was observed to have a high standing stock of phytoplankton during the premonsoon (summer), the causative factors of which are discussed.

556 **Jury, W.A., Winer, A.M., Shencer, W.F., Focht, D.D.,** 1987. Transport and transformations of organic chemicals in the soil-air-water ecosystem. Rev. Environl. Contam. Toxicol. 99: 120-164.

Mechanisms of transport and transformation of organic chemicals in soil, air, water system are reviewed extensively.

557 **Juste, C., Solida, P.** 1989. Changes in the cadmium, manganese, nickel and zinc bioavailability of a sewage sludge treated sandy soil as a result of ammonium sulphate, acid plant lime or iron compound addition. Agronomie 8(10): 897-904.

In pot experiment with grass, metals bioavailability was increased as a result of acidification due to NH_4 SO_4. Lime addition decreased metal availability in the plant for the first cut of the ryegrass, the fertilizing effect of ammonium nitrogen probably alleviated a possible detrimental effect, originating from the increase in metal bioavailability and thus enhanced grass yields. In contrast, Mn deficiency induced by $CaCO_3$ addition decreased dry matter production. Acid beet iron hydrogenoxide or steel shot addition to soil increased dry matter yield at the last cut of grass. This effect was correlated with lack of Cd and Ni in ryegrass.

558 **Juwarkar, A.S., Asha Juwarkar, Desh Bhrater, P.B., Bal, A.S.,** 1991. Exploitation of nutrient potential of sewage and sludge through land application, RAPA Report 7: 178-201.

Sewage irrigation increases yield or cereals, legumes, fodder, oilseed, fruit, cash crops and flowers. It supplements fertilizers requirement and improves soil physical condition. Heavy metal concentration in sewage sludges is also reported.

559 **Juwarkar, A.S., Shende, G.B.,** 1985. Interaction of cadmium-lead: Effect on growth, yield and content of Cd., Pb, in barley (*Hordeum Vulgare*). Indian J. Environ. Health. 28(3): 235-243.

A pot culture study with calcareous clay soil amended with varying rates of cadmium, lead and cadmium + lead was carried out with barely crop to evaluate the effect on growth, yield and content of cadmium and lead in plant tissue. The results showed that length of root, height of plants, length of earhead and grain yield were synergistically reduced due to the combined treatment of cadmium and lead in the range of 160 + 1600 and 320 + 3200 μg Cd + Pb/g of soil. Cadmium was translocated from root to shoot and got accumulated in grain tissue at all the concentrations studied whereas, even at the highest concentration of lead (3200 μg), there was no accumulation of lead in grains. High clay content, higher CEC and presence of calcium carbonate immobilised considerable amount of cadmium and lead in the soil and showed lesser phyto-toxicity to Cd and Pb in the present investigation as compared to that reported by others.

560 **Juwarkar, A.S., Subramanayam, P.V.R.,** 1986. Impact of pulp and paper mill waste water on crop and soil. Water Sci. Technol. 19: 693-700.
Exhaustive field and laboratory studies were carried out for 3 years using pulp mill waste water for crop irrigation. Anaerobically treated pulp mill waste water was found suitable for use on coarse textured soils with salt tolerant crops. Crops like maize, barely, wheat, kenaf and sesbenia were grown successfully. Waste water irrigation increases soil ESP upto 30 and even at this level there was no appreciable decrease in yield of crops and hydraulic properties of soil. Soil equilibrium studies showed that if the pulp mill waste water is diluted with chlorination and hypochlorite waste water in either 4:1 or 3:1 proportions, the resulting waste water can be successfully used on coarse to medium textured soils without the problem of sodicity.

561 **Kabata, A.P., Galczynska, B., Dudka, S.,** 1989. Baseline zine content of soils and plants in Poland. Environ. Geochem. Health. 11(1): 19-24.
Top soils from Poland were analysed for total and extractable zinc, and for a range of major elements. Plant samples form the same locations were also analyzed for zinc content. The geometric mean concentrations of zinc in samples were (mg/kg dry weight): soil total-Zn, 45.9; soil extractable-Zn. 3.1; grass, 30.0; dandelion-tops, 45.9; dandelion-roots, 23.2; oat-leaves, 20.0; oat grains, 29.7; lichens, 1115.5. Significant relationship were found for zinc in grass & extractable-Zn in soils as well as for zinc in lichens and both total and extractable Zn in soils. Zinc in soils varied for soil types and regions.

562 **Kadleg, R.H., Tilton, D.L.,** 1979. The use of fresh water wetlands as a tertiary waste treatment alternative. CRC Critical Reviews. in Environ. Control 9(2): 185-212.
Some wetland ecosystems are capable of removing P and N compounds, providing settling of SS, and handling large volumes of water. The physical and biological characteristics of wetland ecosystems are investigated. The abiotic factors discussed include hydrology, N, P, BOD,

COD, pH, Cl, SS, heavy metals, and soil. Biological factors of consideration in the use of the wetlands as disposal sites include viruses., bacteriology, vegetation, algae, inverterbrate and vertebrates. The social factors discussed include economics, regulatory considerations and aesthetics.

563 **Kahle, H., Breckle, S.W., Waisel, Y.,** 1986. Cadmium in *Fagus sylvatica* L. trees and seedlings : Leaching uptake and interconnection with transpiration. Water Air Soil Pollut. 29(4): 347-359.

^{115}Cd uptake by young beech trees (*Fagus sylvatica* L.) seems to be positively correlated with the concentrations of the applied solutions as well as with the duration of the exposure. Low environmental pH increase the rate of ^{115}Cd uptake. High or low transpiration had no apparent effect on root absorption of Cd, but exposure of beech trees to a Cd $(NO_3)_2$ solution reduced their rates of transpiration after very few days of treatment.

564 **Kaleta, M.,** 1989. The influence of emissions from iron mines on forest ecosystem. Ekologia, 7(2) : 213-224.

Foliar S contents were recovered from *Fagus sylroatica, Carpinas betulis,* and *betula pendula* leaves in stands 10-420 m from Nizna Slana mines and compared with those 60 km away. Although leaf S contents were often increased close to the mine, the increase (upto 222% of control) were not considered large enough to produce serious damage. Heavy metals increased in horn bean leaves and varied erratically with distrance from the mine, reaching upto 608, 1573, 1800, 542, and 2025% of control values for Fe, Mn, Cu, Zn and As. respectively.

565 **Kannan, K., Oblisami, G.,** 1990. Influence of paper mill effluent irrigation on soil enzyme activities. Soil Biol. Biochem. 22(7) : 923-925.

The practice of disposal of pulp and paper mill effluent onto the land adds large quantities of organic carbon and major essential elements to soils. A number of such soils had high organic matter contents and increased microbial populations, which were directly proportional to the periods of effluent irrigation. The application of effluent over a period of 15 years increased both the bacterial and the fungal populations in soil. There was an increase in amylase, phosphates and dehydrogenase activities in these soils as the period of effluent irrigation increased. The activities of cellulose and invertase were greater in submerged soils than in garden soils to which effluent had been applied.

566 **Kannan, K., Oblisami, G., Kalidaurai, M.,** 1990. Influence of paper mill effluent irrigation on the population dynamics of *Rhizobium* and *Azotobacter* in sugarcane rhizosphere. Zeitschrift fur Pflanzenernahrung und Bodenkunde, 153(5) : 421-424.

Application of paper mill effluent to sugarcane soils increased the populations of Rhizobium and Azotobacter for a time, but there was no further increased with increasing duration of irrigation. Prolonged irrigation of the effluent increased alkalinity and had a negative effect on the rhizosphere effect of these organisms. Populations of Rhizobium and Azotobacter were greater in the rhizosphere of effluent treated sugarcane and increased with the age of the crop in such soils.

567 **Karapana Giotis, N.K., Sterrit, K.M., Lester, J.N.,** 1990. Heavy metal binding by the polymeric organic fractions of sewage sludge. Environl. Pollut. 67(3) : 259-278.

Two organic fractions, bacterial extra cellular polymer and fulvic acid were extracted from mixed liquor and digested sewage sludge. The homo genesity of the extracts was verified. Organic fractions extracted from digested sludge demonstrated a greater capacity to complex metals over mixed liquor extracts. Copper formed stronger complexes than nickel with the mixed biomass, and cadmium exhibited the greatest affinity for digested sludge organic matter.

568 **Kardos, L.T., Hook, J.E.,** 1976. Phosphorus balance in sewage effluent treated soils. J. Environ. Qual. 5(1): 87-90.

Four field sites which have been irrigated with various levels of secondary treated effluent for 9 to 11 years have been examined for phosphorous content. Year round application of effluent including 2 years of effluent plus sludge to Reed canary grass on clay loam increased P status. In an abandoned field on clay loam where no P was removed by crops P concentrations were increased for the treated plot. Only the 15 cm depth had significantly higher P concentrations in the treated plot. A hardwood forest located on a sandy loam soil also showed increase phosphorus concentrations. Leaching losses were calculated from concentration of P in soil water at 120 cm from leaching volume which was rainfall plus irrigation minus potential evapotranspiration. Over 11 years of treatment, no site had leaching losses of > 3% of the total applied.

569 **Karlen, D.L., Vitosh, M.L., Kunze, R.J.** 1976. Irrigation of corn with simulated Municipal sewage effluent. J. Environ. Qual. 5 (3): 269-273.

A field study was conducted to evaluate the effects of applying 25, 50, 100 and 200 cm of simulated municipal sewage effluent to corn grown on a tile-drained loam soil. A soil water balance was determined by measuring rainfall, irrigation, evapotranspiration and tile flow. Deep percolation losses were estimated by difference. These effects of these annual loading rates were determined by measuring corn silage and grain yields. Sludge yield were maximized at the 50cm loading rate, however, the grain yields, were maximized at the 200 and 100 cm rates in 1973 and 1974, respectively. Nitrogen losses in the drainage water ranged from 0.1 to 18 kg/ha/year with maximum weekly losses of 3 kg/ha at 100 and 200 cm loading rates. The maximum Ploss was only 0.6 kg/ha/year and potassium losses ranged from 0.2 to 8.5 kg/ha/year. Nitrogen recovery through plant uptake at the 25, 50 and 100 cm loading rates exceed 40% of the N applied through effluent and starter fertilizer when the corn was harvested as silage. Nitrogen uptake in the grain at these loading rates exceeded 50% in 1973, but was much lower in 1974. When the entire plant was harvested, P uptake at the 25 and 50 cm loading rates exceeded the P applied, however, at the 100 and 200 cm rates or when only the grain was harvested, P uptake was less indicating a gradual build up in the soil. The K uptake exceeded 90% when the corn was harvested as silage, but was 40% if only the grain was removed. The distribution of NO_3 and Cl and the Cl/NO_3 ratios suggested that much of the unrecovered N was denitrified. Measurements of exchangeable K and Na indicated that if effluents which are low in K and high in Na, are to be renovated through land disposal, supplimental K must be applied.

570 **Karthikeyan, G., Appa Rao, B.V., Meenakshi, S., Umamaheshwari, N.,** 1990. Monitoring and control of environmental pollution due to effluents from tanneries located in Dindigul. J. Industrial Pollut. Control. 6(1) : 1-19.

Analysis of effluents from tanneries located in Dindigul indicated large presence of total solids, hardness, chlorides and BOD many times higher than the tolerance limits prescribed as per Indian standards. Analysis of groundwater samples collected from various villages within a distance of 6 km from the tanneries in the western direction revealed large excess of total solids, hardness, chlorides and BOD indicating severe pollution of ground-water sources of these areas due to tannery effluents; the amount of chromium, however, is not significantly higher. Tannery effluents make soils of neighbouring areas highly saline.

571 **Katterman F.R.,** 1981. Waste water chemical affects plant growth. Water Wastes Engg. 17(8): 33-35.

Municipal waste water when applied to cereal plants, increases the grain yield and protein content. An attempt was made to identify the chemical responsible for the observed effects. Previous studies suggest that the organic chemical is an altered form of a cytokinin present in human urine and Escherichia and that it exhibits cytokinin-like activity. Solubilized power obtained from samples of clarified municipal waste water effluent chromatographed and chlorophyll retention bioassays were performed. Spectral analysis of the compound indicate properties to that of a class of compounds known as ureido adenosines. More work is necessary to identify the compound's exact nature.

572 **Kaul, S.N., Pathe, P.P., Nandy, T.,** 1990. An overview of waste management in sugar industry. J. Indian Assoc. Environ. Manage. 12(2) : 55-78.

Sugar manufacture ranks fourth in the World. Details about manufacturing process along with water requirements, conservation and waste generated have been included. Cost estimates for five alternatives have been worked out. The treatment alternatives have been ranked based on the criteria of environmental, health and aesthetic risks, annualised cost, O

& M requirements, land requirements and reliability are presented.

573 **Kawabe, H., Yashiro, M., Kourai, H., Mamada, S.,** 1990. Mercury distribution in trees at a contaminated site in Japan. in "Internl. Conf. Environmental Pollution". B. Nath (Ed.): 381-387.

Mercury distribution among annual rings in trees of Japanese cedar (*Cryptomeria japonica D. Don*) in a contaminated site showed a good correspondence with the annual productions of acetaldehyde at a manufacturing factory nearby. On the other hand, a clear correspondence was not appreciated on other species i.e. a Pinus, a Quercus and a Magnolia species between them. The overall amount of mercury taken was by far the largest in trees of cedar, followed by pine and then 2 broad-leaved trees. Among components isolated from mercury containing samples, dioxane and Kiason lignin contained 2-2.5 times as much as wood and more than 30 times as much as residue of dioxane lignin extraction. On the contrary, *holocellulose* contained only 0.01, 0.07 ppm of mercury which is equivalent to 1 hundredth to 7 hundredth of that of wood.

574 **Kawansishi, T., Kawashima, H., Chihara, K., Suzuki, M.,** 1990. Effect of biological clogging on infiltration rate in soil treatment systems. Water Sci. Technol. 22 : 101-108.

The influence of biomass formation on soil hydraulic conductivity in trench soil and infiltration waste water treatment system was studied. The maximum allowable density of biomass corresponding to the minimum hydraulic conductivity of the clogging soil was estimated. Relationships among substrate concentrations, thickness of the clogged zone and percolation rates were established. A numerical model simulating biomass growth and change in permeability was developed and results compared with infiltration flow experiments.

575 **Kee, K., K.F., Huang, P.M.,** 1979. Surface reactivity of aluminium hydroxides precipitated in the presence of low molecular weight organic acids. J. Soil Sci. Soc. Am. 43(6) : 1107-1113.

The surface reactivities of aluminum hydroxides precipitated in systems at the initial Al concentration of 1.1×10^{-3}M and the OH:Al molar ratio of 3.0, in the individual presence of 0, 10^{-6}, and 10^{-4}M, respectively, of citric, L-malic DL-aspartic, and p-hydroloytic reactions of acids were investigated. The organic acids enhanced the specific surface of the precipitation products of hydrolytic reactions of Al through structural distortion. The development of surface charge and active sites for the retention of PO^{-3}_4 and Ca were thus promoted. The enhancement of the surface reactivities of the precipitation products of Al by the organic acids followed the sequence of the stability constants of the complexes of Al with the organic acids i.e. citric acid > malic acid > aspartic acid > P-hydroxybezoic acid. At the concentration of 10^{-4}M organic acids, deviation from the latter sequence occured in the development of positive surface charge and in the retention of PO^{-3}_4. Specific adsorption of anions, while favouring the retention of Ca, counteracted the promoting influence of high specific surface on the development of the net surface positive charge and on the retention of PO^{-3}_4 of the precipitation products of Al. Among the organic acids, used,with the exception of p-hydroxybezonic acid, a concentration of 10^{-4}M was sufficiently high to stabilize the high specific surface and PO^{-3}_4 retention capacity of the precipitation products of Al during aging.

576 **Kelly, J.M., Parker, G.R., McFee, W.W.,** 1979. Heavy meal accumulation and growth of seedlings of five forest species as influenced by soil cadmium level. J. Environ Qual. 8(3) : 361-364.

White pine (*Pinus strobus*), lobiolly pine (*P. taeda*), yellow poplar (*Liriodentdron tulipifera*), yellow birch (*Betula alteghanienisis*), and choke cherry (*Prumus virgainiana*) were grown from seeds in the greenhouse for 17 wk. Plainfield fine sand, with pretreatment Cd, Pb, Cu, and Zn concentrations of 0.6, 11.4, 2.0, and 20.6 ppm, respectively,was used as the growth medium. This soil was amended with cadmium chloride to produce Cd addition levels of 0, 15, and 100 ppm. Shoot elongation and root and shoot dry weights were reduced with increasing levels of soil Cd. All species exhibited increased Cd content in roots and shoots in response to increased soil Cd levels: however, content varied according to species. Roots and shoot accumulations of Cu, Pb, and Zn also varied with species as well as Cd concentration in the soil.

577 **Keltjens. W.G.,** 1990. Effects of aluminum on growth and nutrients status of Doglas fir seedlings grown in culture solution. Physiol. 6(2): 165-175.

Effects of Al on growth, nutrient uptake and protein efflux were studied in Douglas fir (*Pseudotsuga menziesii* (Mirb) Franco) seedlings grown for about nine months in culture solutions with a pH between 3.4 and 3.6 with both calcium and magnesium (Ca + Mg) at concentrations of 0.1, 0.5, or 2.5 mM. In the absence of Al, plant dry matter production and root development increased with increasing concentrations of (Ca+Mg) in the culture solution. At the low and intermediate (Ca+Mg) concentrations, optimal root and shoot development were observed. At the highest (Ca+Mg) conc. Al upto 4 mg/l did not affect growth, but at higher concentrations it significantly reduced both shoot and root growth.

578 **Kemp, M.S., Filip, D.S., George, D.B.,** 1979. Overland flow and slow rate systems to upgrade waste water lagoon effluent. Progress Water Technol. 11(4-5): 227-256.

Slow rate applications can result in a high degree of SS removal, but SS removal in the overland flow system used in the study was not sufficient to meet future discharge standards. Neither the slow rate system nor the overland flow system reduced organic pollutants. Phosphorus removal in the overland flow system was relatively low, and the removal in the slow rate system was much higher. Ammonia-nitrogen removal and conversion was high for both systems.

579 **Kenyon, D.J., Elfving, D.C., Pakkala, I.S., Bache, C.A., Lisk, D.J.,** 1979. Residues of lead and arsenic in crops cultured on old orchard soils, Bull. Environl. Contam. Toxicol. 22(1-1) : 221-223.

Edible portions of sweet corn, cucumbers, muskmelons, summer squash and tomatoes, grown on old orchard soil (pH 6.15) which had received application of Pb and As containing compounds for many years, were analyzed for Pb and As. Controls were grown on nonorchard soil. No significant differences were observed in metal concentrations. No phytotoxic effects were seen which could be attributed to residues in the soil.

580 **Kerndorff, H., Schnitzer, M.,** 1979. Humic and fulvic acid as indicators of soil and water pollution. Water Air Soil Pollut. 2 : 319-329.

A number of analytical characteristics were compared of humic and fulvic acids extracted from unpolluted and polluted soils and sediments. The main differences were that, per unit weight, polluted humic and fulvic acids contained more N, S and H but lower CO_2H groups, and were more aliphatic than unpolluted samples. Unusually high N and S contents of humic materials appear to be the most valid indicator of pollution. Humic acids are preferred to fulvic acids as indicators of pollution because the former are more readily separated and purified.

581 **Kerr, S.N., Sopper, W.E.,** 1980. Effects of spray irrigation of municipal waste water on trace metals in several crops and forest ecosystems. NTIS Springfield VA 33.

Since 1963 secondary treated municipal waste water has been spray irrigated on crops and forest land at various application rates at the Pennsylvania State University. In general, results have indicated that the waste water applications have been beneficial in terms of increasing crop yield and tree growth and that the waste water can be satisfactorily renovated for groundwater recharge. In 1975, soil and vegetation samples were collected from all control and irrigated plots for trace metal analysis. The highest application of waste water was at a rate of 5 cm per week.

582 **Kerry, E.,** 1990. Micro-organisms colonizing plants and soils subjected to different degrees of human activities including petroleum concentration in the Vestfod, hills and Macrobertson land, Antarctica. Polar Biology 10(6): 423-430.

Uncontaminated communities comprised relatively few fungal species. Oil contaminated soils contained more bacterial than fungi, and most contaminated bacteria which used hydrocarbons as their sole carbon source. Some of these bacteria showed a strong degradative potential,namely *Flavobacterium Corynebacterium* and *Bactllus* spp.

583 **Khalatkar, A.S., Ghosh, S.** 1979. Effect of polluted water on cytomorphology of C. bengalensis Linn. Indian J. Environ. Health 21(4): 377-380.

Cytomorphological studies were conducted of C. bengalensis, growing on the sides of a stream receiving overflow of waste water from various laboratories of Nagpur University. Effects of the polluted water on mitosis, vegetative and floral morphology, and pollen grains and seed size were examined. They displayed a high frequency of chromosomal aberration in mitotic anaphases, the latter of which resulted in high rats of pollen sterility. This was reflected in the low seed set 3.5 compared with 5.0 in control plants. The genetic disturbances observed are comparable to features induced by chemical mutagens.

584 **Khalid, R.A., Patrick, W.H., Jr., Nakano, Y.K.** 1979. Water movement in a land treatment system of waste water by overland flow. Progress Water Technol. 11(4-5) : 185-206.

A small-scale physical model of the overland-flow treatment system was used. Water movement in the system was primarily controlled by the application, the friction slope, the slope angle, the hydraulic characteristics of soils, and the evapotranspiration. The computer simulation of nonsteady flow satisfactorily predicts the rate of the total water recovered.

585 **Khan, S., Khan, N.N., Iqbal, N.**, 1991. Studies on the effects of some organic pollutants on the heavy metal transport in an Indian Soil. Environl. Pollut. 70(2): 109-115.

The translocation of Hg, Cd, Cu, Co, Ni and Zn, as affected by organic pollutants, (alcohols, aldehydes, ketones and cyclic compounds) was studied in an indian red soil (*Ultisol*) using thin layer chromatography. An increase in the concn. of organic compounds in the developer enhanced heavy metal mobility, except in the case of Cu and Hg. The results are discussed in relation to the physico-chemical characteristics of the soil and adsorption/desorption phenomena.

586 **Kiemnec, G.L., Jackson, T.L., Hemphill, Jr., D.D., Volk, V.V.**, 1987. Relative effectiveness of sewage sludge as a nitrogen fertilizer for tall fescue. J. Environ. Qual. 16: 353-356.

A 3-yr study was conducted to determine which sludge rates would give yields to tall fescue (*Festuca arunali-ancra shreb*, 'Alta') comparable to yields obtained from inorganic N application. Sludge and NH_4NO_3 were surface applied at annual rates of 0, 110, 220, 440 and 880 (sludge only) kg N/ha. Dry matter yields of tall fescue sludge treated soils was 36,56, & 50% of that on NH_4NO_3 treated soils. Sludge was 27, 41, and 44% as effective as NH_4NO_3 as a source of available N in 1976, 1977 and 1978, respectively. Ammonium-N in sewage sludge apparently provided most of the available N for fescue growth. Concentrations of Zn, Cd & Cu were higher and Mn lower in tall fescue grown on sludge treated soils with NH_4NO_3 and usually increased towards the end of the growing season. How ever, plant concentrations of these heavy metals never reached toxic levels at any time. Sewage sludge was an effective and safe nutrient source for tall fescue.

587 **Kilkeely, M.K., Harbert, H.P., Berg, W.A.,** 1981. Field studies on Paraho retorted oil shale lysimeters: Leachate, vegetation, moisture, salinity and runoff. NTIS Springfield, Va.: 98.

A disposal scheme for Paraho retorted shale utilizing lysimeters to simulate low-elevation (dry site) and a high-elevation (moist site) was constructed. Objectives of the study were to investigate: (1) vegetative stabilization of Paraho retorted shale, as affected by leaching and soil cover treatments; and (2) moisture and soluble salt movement through the soil/shale profile. After intensive management and four growing seasons, only a sparse (2% to 3%) cover of perennial vegetation resulted on the Paraho retorted shale. In contrast, good to excellent cover was established and maintained on the soil control and soil-covered reported shale treatments. Initial leaching and irrigation for plant establishment produced percolate from drains below the compacted shale zone.

588 **Kim, S.J., Chang, A.C., Page, A.L., Warneke, J.E.,** 1988 Relative concentrations of cadmium and zinc in tissues of selected food plants grown on sludge-treated soils. J. Environ, Qual. 17: 568-573.

Twelve selected food plants were grown in greenhouse pots to determine the relative concentrations of Cd and Zn in the plants grown in sludge-treated soils. The relative concentration of the metal was calculated as the quotient of the metal content in a plant and that in Swiss chard (*Beta vulgaris* subsp. *cicla* (L) Koch) grown under the soil conditions. The relative concentrations of Cd and Zn of food plants grown in several sludge treated soils were significantly different but the relative concentrations of these plants in one soils has the statistical characteristics (e.g. rang, mean, median, coefficient of variation etc.) as those in another soil.

589 **Kim, B.Y., So. K.H., Kim, K.S., Cho, J.K., Cho, i., H., Woo, K.D.,** 1990, Survey on the natural heavy meal contents in upland soil and crop grains in Korea. Research Reports of the Rural Development Admn. Soil Fertilizer 32(2) : 57-68.

The natural heavy metal content (Cd, Co, Cr, Cu, Pb, Zn, and As) of soils and crop grains were determined in regions regarded as unpolluted throughout Korea. 215 topsoil samples and 215 grain samples (barley, soyabean, maize) were taken. Average heavy metal contents for the soil and crop grain are presented.

590 **Kimmerer, R.W.,** 1989. Elemental determination of special pattern in the vegetation of Pb-Zn mines in South western Wisconsin. Amer. Midland. Naturalist 121(1) : 134-143.

Vegetation colonizing Pb-Zn mine waste in Wisconsin area was studied and reported.

591 **King, L.D.,** 1986. Design and management considerations in applying minimally treated waste water to land. In "Utilization, Treatment and Disposal of Waste on Land". (Workshop). E.C.A. Runge (Ed.), Soil Sci. Soc. Am. W., Madison, (USA). : 15-26.

Land has a capacity to treat waste water and that capacity should be considered first in system design so excessive pretreatment can be avoided. The general design process consists of determining the flow rate of the waste water and the concentration of solids, nutrients, heavy metals, COD, salts, toxic organics, etc., to determine if it is suitable for land applications. Treatment capacity of the proposed application site is then determined by estimating its assimilatative capacity for various constituents of the waste water. Using the waste water characteristics and the site assimilative capacity, the limiting constituents can be determined and the land area and required storage volume calculated.

592 **King, D.L.,** 1988. Retention of cadmium by several soils of the Southern United States. J. Environ. Qual. 17:246-250.

Cadmium nitrate was applied at rates supplying up to 1.25 mM Cd kg^{-1} (140 mg kg^{-1}) to soils from the A horizons and some B horizons of 10 mineral and three organic soils. The treated soils were incubated at 20°C and at the end of 2, 4 and 8 weeks samples were withdrawn and extracted with IMKCl, Mehlich. (MP), and 0.2 Mammonium oxalate (AO). Length of incubation had no effect of the quantity of Cd removed by the extractants. Extractability was related linearly to Cd application rate but the effect of soil type on slope was more pronounced with KCl (110% variation in slopes) and AO (27%) than the MP (27%). At the 1.25 mM Cd Kg^{-1} rate, KCl-extractable Cd decreased with increasing pH but differences among soils were large. Stepwise-multiple regressions was performed using sand; silt; clay; pH; exchangeable cations; organic matter; dithionate-extractable Al and Fe; and AO extractable Al, Fe, and Mn as independent variables. Exchangeable Cd and pH were important soil properties related to extractability with the three extractants but values of R^2 were <0.8 even for three variable models. Since pH was the dominant factor, the data were grouped into pH increments of 0.5 and regression repeated. Exchangeable Ca, CEC, and dithionate extractable Al were important factors related to extractability but values of R^2 were <0.6. Overall, the ability to estimate extractability from basic soil properties was low.

593 **King, L.D.,** 1988. Effect of selected soil properties on cadmium content of tobacco, J. Environ. Qual. 17: 251-255.

In a greenhouse study, limed and unlimed soil from the A horizon of six mineral soils and three organic soils of the South Eastern USA was amended with 0,1,2 and 4 kg Cd ha^{-1} as $CdCl_2$. Tobacco (Nicotiana tabacum L.) was grown until flower initiation (42d). The 2 and 4 kg Cd rates reduced dry weight on the Norfolk soil (Typic Paleuadult), but Cd had no effect on dry weight on other soils. Cadmium concentration was maximum in the lower leaves and decreased with leaf position up the stalk. At the 2kg Cd rate, liming reduced leaf Cd concentration in only three soils. Lack of liming effect in the other soils was thought to be a result of high organic matter, high initial pH or small pH changes affected by the lime. Lime reduced the effects of Cd loading rate and soil types on Cd concentrations and removal of Cd by tobacco harvest. When organic and mineral soils were considered together, leaf Cd and Cd removal were best related to the Cd sorptive capacity of the soils. When only the mineral soils were considered, inherent soil properties like sand content, ammonium oxalate-extractable Fe (Feo)., and pH dominated the regression models. With limed mineral soils (pH 5.7-7.0), models for leaf Cd and Cd removal contained pH, Feo and/or ammonium oxalate-extractable Cd. Model calculated values and actual values differed by only 4% so the models should be useful in ranking soils from the South Eastern USA for their capacity to retain salt sources of Cd. Soil cation exchange capacity did not appear in any of the models.

594 **King, L.D., Leyshon, A.J., Webber, L.R.,** 1977. Application of Municipal and liquid sewage sludge to agricultural land. J. Environ. Qual. 6(1): 67-71.

A lysimeter study was conducted using liquid sewage sludge and unsorted, pulverized municipal refuse. Refuse (R) at 188 tons/ha and a 2.3 cm depth of sewage sludge (S) were applied separately and in combination (RS). A double refuse-sludge rate (2 RS) and control treatment (C) receiving no additions were also used. Treatments sequence was winter fallow-corn (*Zea mays* L.), Winter fallow-spring barley (*Hordeum Vulgare* L.) Winter rye (*Secale cereals* L.)—corn. There was no effect of treatment on corn grain yields in 1972 but all treatments containing refuse increased grain yields in 1974. Treatment had little effect on levels of Cr, Fe, Mn, Ni and Pb in the corn grain and stover. Levels of Zn, Cu and Cd were increased mainly by treatments containing refuse. The 2 (RS) treatment resulted in stover Cd levels greater than the acceptable level of food stuffs. Nitrate leaching losses were greater for S and RS than C. Although NO_3-N leached from 2(RS) was low, the COD concentrations were high (> 1000 ppm), was 120 times that of the loss from C. The effect of treatment on C/N was inconclusive. Mixing sludge (C/N=49) with refuse (C/N=63) resulted in reduced NO_3 leaching from RS (C/N=41) as compared to that from S. However, refuse alone did not cause immobilization because NO_3-N losses from R were identical to those from C.

595 **King, L.D., Rudgers, L.A., Webber, L.R.,** 1974. Application of Municipal refuse and liquid sewage sludge to agricultural land : 1. Field study. J. Environ Qual. 3: 361-366.

The feasibility of using land for both waste disposal and crop production has been studied by applying pulverized municipal refuse and liquid sewage sludge of liquid manure to land which was later planted to rye (*Secale cercale* L.) and subsequently to corn. Refuse was applied at 188 t/ha singly (R) or in combination with either 2.3 cm of liquid sewage sludge (RS) or 1.4 cm liquid poultry manure (RM). Other treatments were a double waste rate — 376 t/ha of refuse +4.6 cm of sludge (2 RS), sludge alone (S) and a control (C) receiving no additions. Yield of rye forage was not affected by treatment. Highest corn grain yields were obtained with the R treatment while yields with S and 2(RS) treatments were significantly lower than yields with R. No treatments resulted in corn yields significantly different from the control treatment. Levels of Zn, Cu, Cd and Pb in the rye and corn tissue were usually increased by waste additions but were below levels toxic to the crops or to the animals that might consume the crops. Soil nitrate was increased by the various waste treatments. A considerable fraction of the nitrate lost from the soil profile during the winter could not be attributed to crop uptake.

596 **Kirk, P.W.W., Lester, J.N., Perry, R.,** 1983. Investigations into the fate of nitrilotriacetic acid in sewage sludge applied to agricultural land. Water Air Soil Pollut., 20(2) : 161-170.

The mobility of nitrilotriacetic acid (NTA) in agricultural soil was assessed in a soil/sewage sludge admixture and following surface applications using laboratory scale soil columns. Admixtures were found to retain NTA more effectively in the topsoil (0 to 200 mm) than surface applications, with up to 9.5% of the applied NTA passing through the topsoil following a surface application, when irrigated at average rainfall. Even at higher rates of irrigation a great proportion of the NTA was retained in a soil column containing topsoil and subsoil (200 to 300 mm). The adsorption capacity of the soil was determined in batch experiments and was found to be 17.5 μg NTA g^{-1} soil.

597 **Kirsch, S., Straeit, B.** 1989. Cadmium concentrations and accumulation by *Lumbricus rabellens* as influenced by various soil parameters in forest areas. Verhandlungen Gesellschaft fur Okologie. 18:403-407.

Analysis of soils and plant shows that accumulation of Cd in L. Rubellens is affected by organic matter and cleaning content as they reduce availability. Exposure of plant to different Cd concentrations in a sandy and a loamy soil resulted in markedly greater uptake of Cd in the sandy soil. The Cd concentration in the plant is related with the acetic acid extractable Cd in soil.

598 **Kishi, H., Kogure, N., Hashimoto, Y.,** 1990. Contribution of soil constituents in adsorption coefficient of aromatic compounds halogenated alicyclic and aromatic compounds to soil. Chemosphere 21(7) : 867-873.

The strength of adsorptivity of a chemical to soil Koc is the adsorption coefficient, Kd normalized by the organic carbon content in unit mass of soils, Coc. The Koc is expected to have a constant value for chemical in adsorption to soil, however, the Koc value of this chemical proved to be different in different kinds of soil. In this investigation, the relationship between Kd and Coc can be expressed as Kd = Koc. Coc+a for five kinds of soils and five kinds of chemicals, where Koc is defined as an "average" of the contribution of organic matter to K and intercept a expresses a fraction of adsorption by soil constituents other than organic carbons.

599 **Kistler, R.C., Widmer, F., Brunner, P.H.,** 1987. Behaviour of Cr, Ni, Cu, Zn, Cd, Mg and Pb during the pyrolysis of sewage sludge. Environ. Sci. Technol. 21(7) : 704-708.

Raw and digested sewage sludge samples were pyrolyzed in order to investigate the partitioning of selected heavy metals during anoxic thermal treatment. Cr, Ni, Cu, Zn and Pb were retained quantatiively in the char at temperature upto 750°C. Cd compounds were reduced to to Cd, which was volatilized at 600C. Mg was completely evaporated at the lowest investigated pyrosis temperature of 350°C. The metals contained in the char are highly immobile due the well buffered neutral to alkaline properties of the char.

600 **Kitagishi, K., Obata, H.,** 1981 Accumulation of heavy metals in rice grains. in "Heavy Metal Pollution in Soils of Japan". Sci. Soc. Press Tokyo: 95-104.

There are some reasons to believe that the mechanisms operating in rice plants to collect trace amounts of Zn and Cu from the transpirations stream and to transport them actively to the sink regions cannot discriminate Cd from Zn or Cu, thus contributing to the accumulation of nonessential Cd in rice grains. This is the main reason why investigations in this field have been restricted to Cd and Zn.

601 **Kitagishi, K., Yamane, I.,** (eds.) 1981. Heavy Metal Pollution in Soils of Japan. Sci. Soc. Press, Tokyo.

This monograph written by experts in their fields, presents a critical and comprehensive review of the studies carried out in Japan fields mainly during the last decade. The introduction provides some of the background features of heavy metal pollution in Japan. The main text is arranged into five parts: Part I is concerned solely with the basic aspects of heavy metal problems in Japanese soils, such as background levels, chemical forms and behaviour is soils. Part II is devoted to the response of rice plants to toxic levels of heavy metals and to the behaviour of heavy metals in rice plants. Part III, presents a critical review of case studies on the main polluted areas throughout Japan by heavy metals discharged from various sources.

602 **Klein, S.,** 1989. Input and distribution of heavy metals in surface water. in 6th internatl. Trace Element Symp. 5 : 1534-1544.

Elevated Pb and Cd contents in surface waters were found for samples taken in the vicinity of metal using factories.

603 **Kloke, A.,** 1990. Land use possibilities and reclamations of polluted soils. Verb. Deuts Land. Untes and Forsch. Reihe, Kong. 32: 51-56.

A three tier classification system for soil pollution in relation to land use is described: (1) soils without significant inputs from anthropogenic sources- this status should be preserved, (2) soils containing levels of substances not harmful to humans, animals or plants- tolerable status; (3) polluted soils, endangering humans, animals or plants- reclamation is necessary. While there is no restriction on land use for (1), the levels of (2) are related to use; the tolerance level for playgrounds is far below that of industrial sites.

604 **Kneip, T.J., Hazen, R.** 1979. Deposit and mobility of cadmium in a marsh-cove ecosystem and the relation to cadmium concentration in biota. Environl. Health Perspectives, 28 : 67-73.

The most contaminated aquatic sediments were dredged in 1972-73, but the resuspension of the sediments and recycle of water from the dredge spoil resulted in re-establishment of a large contaminated sediment bed with concentrations very similar to those observed before dredging. The stability of the sediment concentrations and shallow depth of the Cd in the sediments indicted that the deposit was relatively stable in agreement with the expectations based on the water chemistry of the system. Uptake occured in marsh and aquatic plants and all species of animal tested. Significantly elevated concentrations were observed compared with non-contaminated areas; however, edible portions of most fish apparently do not present a hazard. Crabs apparently present the most likely source of hazard to humans. The dredging removed »5.5t of Cd, 1/4 of that originally estimated to be present, but twice that amount was found in the cove sediments 3-4 yr after dredging.

605 **Knoetze, C., Davies, T.R., Wiechers, S.G.,** 1980. Chemical Inhibition of biological nutrient removal processes. Water SA. 6(4): 171-180.

The inhibiting effects of various heavy metal ion and organic inhibitions were studied using laboratory-scale activated sludge and biological rotating disc units. All the heavy metal ions were tolerable in raw sewage at concentrations below 1 mg L^{-1}. Oxidation of carbonaceous matter in the activated sludge units was unimpaired, even when nitrification and denitrification were severely inhibited and some of the mixed liquor suspended solids were killed and lost in the effluent. Given sufficient time to adapt, all the unit processes developed resistance to the inhibitors studied.

606 **Knudtsen, K., O'Connor, G.A.,** 1987. Characterization of iron and zinc in Albuquerque sewage sludge. J. Environ. Qual. 16 : 85-90.

Chemical forms of Fe and Zn present in anaerobically digested sewage sludge from Albuquerque, were identified and quantified. Water soluble

Fe and Zn were speciated based on charge and stability of metal complexes, and on their degrees of association with sludge organics. Chemical forms of Fe and Zn present in the solid phase of the sludge were characterised with a sequential extraction procedure. Soluble Fe was predominantly present as negatively slowly labile organic complexes of molecular weights >1000 daltons. Zinc was associated with negative and neutral species that were very or moderately labile. Iron was associated with a larger portion of sludge organics and with larger molecular weight fractions than Zn complexes. The percentage of total sludge Fe and Zn found in readily soluble forms was very small (< 1%). The amounts may nevertheless represent significant pools of metal forms available for plants. Zinc conc. was more than Fe in the potentially more labile, organic and carbonate fractions of the sludge.

607 **Knutinen, J., Palm, H., Hakala, H., Haimi, J., Huhta, V., Salimnen, J.,** 1990. Polychlorinated phenols and their metabolites in soils and earthworms of sawmill environment. Chemosphere, 20(6): 609-623.

Top soil and earthworms samples collected from 3 Finland sawmill environment were analysed for polychlorinated phenols and other metabolites. The total chloro-phenol conc. ranged from ca. 260 to 480 μg/g (DM) in soil and from ca. 140 to 3500 μg/g fat in earthworm. Chlorinated dihydroxy-benzenes were most important in soil. 2, 3, 4, 6-tetrachloroanisole and pentocholoroanisole were found at ppm level in the fat of earthworms.

608 **Kobus, J., Kurek, E.,** 1990. Effect of cadmium contained in plant residues on their microbial decomposition. Zent. Mikrobiol. 145(4): 283-291.

The effect of cadmium introduced to sand (2-9mg kg^{-1}) with polluted crop residues on the activity of microbes involved in their decomposition in controlled environment was examined. The decomposition of organic matter was carried out by native crop residues microflora or additionally by micro-organisms introduced to sand with garden or rhizosphere soil suspensions. Heavy metal contained in plant residues did not affect the total number of the native crop residues micro-organism, but however, decreased the number of celluloytic microbes. The bacteria actinomycetes and fungi introduced to sand with soil suspensions differed in their sensitivity to Cd. Heavy metal in plant material had inhibitory effect on ammonification and nitrification processes, but however, increased the amount of lost nitrogen from this system. Plant residues polluted with cadmium were more resistant to mineralisation than nonpolluted ones.

609 **Koe, T. De., Beek, M.A., Haarsma, M.S., Erns, W.H.O.,** 1991. Heavy metals and arsenic in grasses and soils of mine spolls in northeast portugal, with particular reference to some Portuguese goldmines, in International Conf. Environmental Pollution. B. Nath (Ed.): 373-380.

An overview is made of the soil pollution in the soil heaps of mostly inactive mines in North East Portugal. Heavy metals and arsenic concentrations have been analysed for soil and plant samples. The spoil heaps of the goldmines, almost without vegetation, contain high levels of heavy metals and arsenic in their soil samples. Spoils of the Fungsten mines present high concentrations of Cu and Cd. High levels of Mn have been found in the soil samples of Fungsten mines. The colonising grasses *Agrostis castellana, A. Delicatula* and *Hoicus lanatus* accumulate heavy metals and arsenic up to high levels in their tissues. Agrostis castellana, evolving resistant populations to heavy metals and arsenate, is evolving resistant populations to heavy metals and arsenate, is indicative of potential importance in revegetation experiments.

610 **Koeman, J.H.,** 1986. Review of environmental problems caused by the use of fertilizers and pesticides. in 'Environmental and Chemicals in Agriculture', F.P. Winteringham (Ed.). Elsevier Applied Sci. London: 19-26.

611 **Komai, Y.,** 1981. Heavy metal pollution in urban soils, in 'Heavy Metal Pollution in Soils of Japan', K. Kitagashi; I Yamane (Eds.) Sci. Soc. Press Tokyo : 193-217.

Investigations on the heavy metal (Zn Cu Mn Pb, Cd) status in urban soils, including park, arable land and paddy field soils, have been done in the cities of Sakai and Amagasaki since 1977.

612 **Kophalomoulos, S., Bionoli, G., Goetz, L.,** 1989. Finite element method to assess the impact on ground-water quality of trace metals released from a coal fly ash respository. in 'Groundwater Contamination; Use of Models in Decision-making', Jousma. G., Bear J., Haimes, Y.Y., Walter, F. (Eds.): 587-588.

A critical path model was compared to a finite element model for predicting Cr leaching from a fly ash deposit. The critical path approach was simpler, but did not take environmental variability into account. The finite element model described the environmental variability better, considers the heterogeneity of natural soil porous media, and can represent graphically the calculation of time-dependent isoconcentration contour levels.

613 **Korcak, R.F.,** 1985. Effects of coal combustions wastes used as lime substitutes in nutrition of apples in three soils. Plant Soil, 85:437-441.

A greenhouse experiment using apple seedlings, was carried out using fluidised bed combustion (FBM) Flyash (FA) and calcitic limestone applied at or up to twice the lime requirement on three soil materials. Seedling growth varied dependent upon the treatment-soil combination. Growth was reduced by 60% on the Manor soil from FA applied at twice the lime requirement and was attributed to the higher initial reactiveness of the FA compared to FBM or limestone. Leaf P, K, Zn, Cu and Al were not significantly affected by treatments over all soils while Ca and

N decreased and Mg varied dependent upon treatment. Soil pH was increased by all treatments. DTPA extractable Mn and Zn were good estimates of leaf Mn and Zn while DTPA-Cu and Fe were not.

614 **Korcak, R.F.**, 1988. Fluidized bed material applied at disposal levels : Effects on an apple orchard J. Environ. Qual. 17(3) : 469:473.
Fluidized bed material (FBM) was applied at two rates to the surface area within the rows of an established appled (*Malus domestica Borkh*), orchard containing four tree types. The rates were either 9.2 kg/m^2 (low rate), 36 kg/m^2 (high rate) or untreated control. Cumulative yields (kg/tree) were enhanced on three or four tree types over a period of 6yr. A 15% reduction in yield was noted for Redchief Delicious on M9/MM106 stocks at the high FBM rate. No nutritional related problems were noted for this or any other of the tree types used. Part of the yield reduction noted was due to fruit size differences and/or differential sensitivity of this interstock, rootstock combination to the altered soil chemical properties. Agricultural utilization of large volumes (up to 112 Mg/ha) of FBM, compared to past research where FBM was used as like substitute (2-6Mg/ha), appears to be feasible alternative. However, rootstock selection for apple may need to consider the resultant changes in soil chemical status from FBM additions.

615 **Korcak, R.F., Fanning, D.S.**, 1981. Interaction between high levels of applied heavy metals and indigenous soil manganese. J. Environ. Qual. 10(1): 69-72.
The importance of indigenous soil Mn level on plant Mn uptake from metal salt or sewage sludge amended soils was investigated using corn plant tissue. Mn levels increased with the application of Cd, Cu, Ni and Zn (in combination) as metal salts or as sewage sludge over the range of soil materials used. The amount of increase with a given increase in applied metals was greater for the unlimed than for the limed metal salt treatments. Elevated tissue Mn concentrations were positively and significantly correlated with indigenous levels of soil.

616 **Korenova, T.S., Goldrab, L.L., Turovskii, I.S.**, 1979. Agricultural value of the utilization of waste water sludges as fertilizer. Vodosnabzhenie I. Sanitaraia tekhnika 6: 4-6.
The use of sludges from the purification of municipal waste water as fertilizers increased the harvest of grain crops and the productivity of the soil. The thermally dried sludges are sanitarily disinfected, nitro-phosphorus, organo-mineral fertilizers, not inferior to basic fertilizers. Sludges obtained with preliminary dehydration in a vacuum filter of filter presses may be used as lime fertilizers. The sludge should be added to the soil periodically once every 5 years. The conditions for the use of sludges as fertilizers is subject to conformity with local sanitary-epidemiological regulations.

617 **Kortesharju, J., Savonen, K., Saeynaetkari, T.,** **1990.** Element contents of raw humus, forest moss and reindeer lichens around a cement works in Northern Finland. Ann. Bot. Fenn. 27(3): 221-230.

Nutrient elements (Ca, K, Mg, Na, N, P) and heavy metals (Cu, Fe, Mn, Pb, Zn) were studied in the surroundings of Kolari Cement Works. NW Finland, Elevated calcium concentrations were measured as far as 16 km from the works. The other elements clearly emitted by the works were magnesium and iron. The contents of calcium, magnesium and iron correlated well with the calculated depositions. The results show that mosses (*Pleurozium schreberi*) and lichens (*Cladina stellaris*) are preferable to raw humus in studies of atmospheric deposition. The element concentrations in Cladina lichens were much lower than in Pleurozium or raw humus. At distances of 0.5 to 1 km from the Cement Works, reindeer lichens were totally lacking. The distance from the cement works explained 85-90% of the variation in the calcium content of raw humus and Pleurozium, and the calcium concentration of the studies materials correlated significantly with the simulated particle fall-out of the preceding year.

618 **Kostecki, P.T., Calabrese, E.J., Horton, H.M.,** 1989. Review of present risk assessment models for petroleum contaminated soils. in 'Petroleum Contaminated Soils. Remediation Techniques and Environmental Fate Risk Assessment Vol. I: 263-300.

Seven risk assessment methodologies were evaluated as a preliminary means of developing a risk assessment methodology for petroleum contaminated soils. Criteria used to assess the strengths and weaknesses of the hazard, exposure, and risk analyses are discussed.

619 **Krause, R.,** 1987. Controlled land application of liquid manure and sewage sludge with tankers in 'Agricultural Waste Management and Environment Protection'. Welte.E, Szabolcs. I. (Eds.) 4th Internatl. CIEC Symp. 2: 275-284.

Rational utilization of natural resources and the necessity of environmental protection require improved application techniques for organic sludges. Pretreatment and upgrading can improve handling as well as the fertilizing effect. With adequate tankers and implements negative effects on the soil and plant can be minimized. A new approach using adequate sensors and electric, electronic and hydraulic components was suggested for improving the dosage as well as longitudinal and transversal distribution of sludges. The complete system was developed and investigated in laboratory and field experiments. By direct, shallow incorporation of sludges not only were the yield increased and the physical properties of the soil improved, but pollution was reduced.

620 **Kronfeld, J., Navrot., J.,** 1975. Aspects of trace metal contamination in the coastal rivers of Israel. Water Air Soil Pollut. 4: 127-134.

Nine trace elements of biological concern : Cr, Co, Cu, Cd, Ni, Pb, Hg,

Zn and Ag were investigated in the sediments of coastal streams in Israel. All of these are subjected to some degree of domestic and/or industrial sewage input with the consequent liability of contamination by trace elements. The Ayyalon, Gadura, Qishan and locally the Hadera rivers contain sediments exhibiting severe pollution effects. There is a danger of infiltration through the soils into the groundwaters as well as exposing nearshore fauna to sediments contaminated by possibly toxic trace elements. An increase of Pb and Zn levels occurs near major highways.

621 **Kruse, E.A., Barrett, G.W.** 1985. Effects of municipal sludge and fertilizer on heavy metal accumulation in earthworms. Environl. Pollut. 38(3): 235-244.

Comparisons were made of heavy metal concentrations of cadmium, copper, lead, and zinc in *Lumbricus rubellus* collected from a three year old field community in which replicate plots were treated five times annually for four years with either fertilizer, sewage sludge, or left untreated as controls. Concentrations of all four metals were significantly higher in the soil from sludge-treated plots than from fertilizer or control plots. Cadmium concentration was approximately nine-times greater in earthworms from sludge plots than in those from control or fertilizer plots. Although amounts of copper (20.7 $\mu g g^{-1}$) and lead (8.75 $\mu g g^{-1}$) were also significantly higher in earthworm tissue from sludge-amended communities as compared to fertilizer or control treatments, concentration factors were relatively low.

622 **Kuester, H., Kaa. R., Rehfuess, K.E.,** 1988. The utilization of beech forests and the deposition of Pb and Cd as reflected in peat profiles from the foothills of the Alps. Naturwissenchaften. 75(12) : 611-163.

There was a very early increase of Pb (Iron Age) and Cd (Early Middle Ages) concentration in a Southern Bavarian peat bog., which parallels a decline in beech pollen, both very likely reflecting increasing human activity.

623 **Kuhad, M.S., Malik, R.S., Singh, R., Anoop Singh,** 1989. Studies on mobility and accumulation of heavy metals in agricultural soils receiving sewer water irrigation. J. Indian Soc. Soil Sci. 37: 290-294.

Profiles were exposed at Ali, Sharan, Panipat and Sonipat to study the mobility and accumulation of heavy metals in agricultural soils receiving sewer water irrigation. Taxonomically, the soils are classified as Typic Ustorthent (Ali, Sharan and Sonepat) and Typic Ustilluvent (Panipat). Total Cd, Pb, Ni, Co, Zn,. Cu, Mn, and Fe content in soils ranged from 0.7 to 2.5, 12.5-225, 20-4750, 13.8-29, 13.3-2296, 55-2500, 119-288 and 21250-97500 ppm, respectively. The available Zn, Cu, Mn, Fe and Mo varied from 0.28-89.23, 1.2-150, 1.98-7.48, 0.28-2.37 and 0.13-0.42 ppm, respectively. Maximum accumulation of heavy metals was observed in Ap horizon of Sonepat profiles. The values of ratio of metal in

Ap versus C horizons indicate the tendency of metal accumulation in the surface horizon. No systematic metal distribution pattern was observed in Ali, Sharan and Panipat profiles but all the metals except Co decreased with depth in Sonipat profile.

624 **Kuhad, M.S., Malik, R.S., Anoop Singh, Dahiya, I.S.,** 1989. Background levels of heavy metals in agricultural soils of Indo-Gangetic Plains of Haryana. J. Indian Soc. Soil Sci. 37:700-705.

Background levels of some heavy metals (Fe, Mn, Ni, Co, Zn, Pb) in agricultural soils of three physiographic zones of Haryana were investigated. The values were found to be low and represent levels naturally occurring in uncontaminated soils. The contents of some of the metals were also found significantly correlated with soil properties.

625 **Kulshrestha, S.K., Adholia, U.N., Khan, A.A., Bhatnagar, A., Saxena, M., Manju Baghail,** 1989. Community structure of planktons and macrozoobenthos, with special reference to pollution in the river Khan (India). Internatl. J. Environ. Studies. 35 : 83-96.

Community structure of planktons and macrozo obenthos with special reference to pollution in the River Khan (India), changes in biotic communities were examined and explained with the help of a diversity index and showed a decrease in diversity values with increases in pollution. General tolerant to various degrees of pollution were also identified and the extent of pollution by heavy metals as Cu, Zn, Ni, Cd and Hg, has also been studied.

626 **Kulpa, C.F., Mcauliffum, K.S.,** 1989. Microbial perspectives on biodegradation. In 'Biotechnology Applications in Hazardous Waste Treatment'. Engineering Foundation, New York: 35-46.

Microbial processes used in the biodegradation of hazardous wastes are reviewed, with particular attention to bacteria. The usefulness of bacteria in the treatment of waste streams, leachates, soils and ground-water is related to the diversity, mutability and adaptability of the organisms concerned. An understanding of these properties in relation to mixed culture is considered essential to the application on bacteria in the bioremediation of contaminated environments of the treatment of waste streams.

627 **Kumar, Sanjiv,** 1989. Effect of seed treatment with Ni, Cd and Zn on seedling growth of two cultivars of *Hordeum vulgare*. Geobios, 16(1) : 15-20.

The seeds of two cultivars of Hordeum vulgare, viz BH-75 and BG-25, pretreated with 5×10^{-3} - M to 2.5×10^{-3}M of nickel sulphate, cadmium acetate and zinc sulphate separately, exhibit depression of organ specific seedling growth in decreasing order : Cd > Ni > Zn.

628 **Kung, H.T., Ying, L.G.,** 1990. Heavy metal concentration extractions in soils and crops of Baoshanwusong Area, Shanghai, China, Catena, 17(2) : 417-430.

Surface soils around Baoshanwusong area were more contaminated with heavy metals (Zn, Cd, Cr, Hg, F, Pb) than the surrounding agricultural areas. High correlation was found between soluble fraction of these metals with their conc. in wheat plant leaves and grains. Soil pollution mainly ocurred near the industrial areas covering about 20 sq km and was not wide spread. Metal conc. decreased with increase of distance from industrial area in a southeasterly direction.

629 **Kurek, E., Kobus, J.,** 1990. Effect of N nutrition on growth and cadmium accumulation by Trifolium incarnatum. Zentralbl. Mikrobiol 145(4) : 277-281.

Effects of Cd on the dry matter of plants and Cd accumulation in their tops and roots were investigated in pot experiments. *Trifolium incarnatum* fertilized with combined nitrogen or inoculated with Rhizobium trifolii was the test crop. Addition of Cd (1-10 mg kg^{-1}) to the sand decreased the dry matter of the plants. Reduction of plant tops dry matter was higher with mineral nitrogen fertilization than with inoculation of *R. trifolii* strains. The amount of accumulated Cd in the plant tops and roots was proportional to the amount of the element in the medium. Plants inoculated with *R. trifolii* accumulated less Cd than plants grown with mineral nitrogen fertilization.

630 **Kurihara, Y., Kikuchi, E., Ito, T., Shoji, S.,** 1989. Cultivation of upland rice in degraded estuarine lagoon spoils with emphasis on the chemical properties of the sediments. J. Environ. Manage. 29 : 115-128.

Dredged lagoon sediments from the Nanakite river polluted with 7000t carp pond effluent/day, with domestic waste and secondary treated waste water. 20 km upstream and with paddy soil and inorganic nutrients, were buried in a sand bar and upland rice was grown in trenches. The water content of the dredged material remained high for 5 months and was favourable for rice production. Upland rice grew well with or without (44 kg N, 88 kg P_2O_5 & 88 kg K_2O/ha). While the sediments contained high quantities of heavy metals, hardly any Cd was detected in husks and husked grain and only slight amounts of Cu and Zn were detected in polished grain.

631 **Kutukova, Yu. D., Lepneva, O.M.,** 1990. Heavy metal levels in plants and soils of the Central Botanical Garden, The USSR Academy of Science. Bulletin Glavnogo Botanicheskogo Sada. 156: 27-33.

Tree leaves and soil samples from surface (0-10cm) and deeper (up to 1 m) layers were analysed for heavy metals. The soil samples were shown to contain Pb and Cu at concn. 2-3 times higher than the 10 and 13 mg/kg respectively, recorded on the test plots outside Moscow. Concn. of Zn and Cd were 3-4 times and all at least one order of magnitude greater than those of control soils (37 and 0.05 mg/kg resp). Soil samples from selected portions of the Botanical Garden contained even greater concn. of heavy metals, with Zn levels 50 times those of the control plots. It is suggested that high level of local pollution was due to the use of composts contaminated with heavy metals. Coefficients of their accumulation by different tree species are reported.

632 **Kuziemska, I.,** 1980. Application of water extract of brown coal fly ash to phosphate precipitation from polluted waters. Water Res. 14(9): 1289-1293.

A method of phosphate precipitation from municipal water and the strongly polluted waters using water extract of brown coal fly and the Konin Power Plant is discussed. Phosphate precipitation occurs immediately after introduction of the coagulant and after a short and intensive mixing. Precipitation intensity depends mainly on the V coefficient (ratio of mass of alkalinity of in the extract to that in the water to be treated) and on the alkalinity of the treated water. Using a mathematical model of regression curve, which is described and applied, the degree of influence of each parameter on the process of phosphate precipitation, was determined.

633 **Lagerwerff. J.V., Biersdorf, G.T., Brower, D.L.,** 1976. Retention of metals in sewage sludge 1: Constituent heavy metals. J. Environ. Qual. 5: 19-23.

Sewage Sludge from Baltimore, Md. was compared to that of Washington, DC in terms of the tendency to release heavy metals under a variety circumstances. Total and 1.0 N HCl. extractable concentrations of Cd, Cu, Pb and Zn were determined. Fractionation of the metals by leaching columned samples of Baltimore sludge, with either a $CaCl_2$ solution or H_2O over extended periods of time, showed Cd and especially Zn, were more leachable than Cu and Pb. Except for Pb, leachability of the metals was much lower in the sludge from Washington, than in the Baltimore sludge. Regarding the sign of charge of Cu species as a function of the progression of leaching of Baltimore sludge, anionic and especially, amphoteric species increased, as catonic conc. deceased. When aqueous sludge leachates were stored for 13 months at 5°C, amphoteric Cu strongly increased while all other Cu species decreased. In contrast, nearly all Zn species in the leachates were cationic. When sludge samples were subjected to simulated weathering by striming with either H_2O_2 in a number of concentration, or H_2O followed by steam bath drying, the extractability of heavy metals with H_2O and 0.01N HCl increased. Extractability of Cu increased more than that of Cd, or Zn, suggesting that the stability of the amphoteric Cu species depended strongly on acidity. Because of the H_2O_2 treatments the cation exchange capacity of the sludges diminished by 15 to 25% depending on their organic, although no C was lost.

634 **Lagerwerff, J.V., Biersdorf, G.T., Brower, D.L.,** 1976. Retention of metal in sewage sludge II : Incorporated Radio-isotops. J. Environ. Qual. 5: 23-25.

Samples of digested sewage sludge from Baltimore, Md. and

Washington, DC were columned and leached for up to 240 hours with 0.06N $CaCl_2$, as well as with water, to study the release of trace amounts ^{85}Sr and ^{137}Cs introduced earlier. In percent of the radioactivity originally present, leaching with 0.06N $CaCl_2$ removed about 90 and 80% of ^{85}Sr, but about 9 and 16% of ^{137}Cs from Baltimore and Washington sludge, respectively. For leaching with H_2O, the corresponding values were 39 and 34% of ^{85}Sr and 4 and 3% of ^{137}Cs. Samples of sludge were subjected to treatments with H_2O_2, and steambath drying, followed by incubating with ^{137}Cs and ^{85}Sr, and either exhaustive leaching with H_2O (240 hours at 2 cm^3 cm^{-2} $hour^{-1}$), or equilibration for 1 hour with H_2O or 0.01N HCl. In percent of the radioactivity originally present, the pretreatment increased ^{137}Cs release by H_2O leaching from 9 to 18%, and from 7 to 10% with Baltimore and Washington sludge, respectively, depending on whether the sludge was pretreated with H_2O or with 3% H_2O_2. Corresponding ranges for ^{85}Sr were from 47 to 55% and from 41 to 48%. Incubation of Baltimore and Washington sludge for 44 months at room temperature slightly increased H_2O extractability of ^{137}Cs and ^{85}Sr when the incubated material was kept dry, rather than moist. This may have been due to smaller concentrations of complexing organic compounds, or to compounds with lesser complexing ability. When sludge was stored moist, the 0.01N HCl extractability of the isotopes sharply increased. This would also point to a greater abundance of organic complexes under moist conditions during storage, since a decrease in pH affects their stability.

635 **Lagerwerff, J.V., Biersdorf, G.G., Milberg, R.P., Brower, D.L.,** 1977. Effect of incubation and liming on yield and heavy metals uptake by rye from sewage sludged soil. J. Environ. Qual. 6(4): 727-731.

Rye was grown under controlled conditions on sandy loam soil amended with digested secondary sewage sludge with a purpose to measure plant yield and uptake of Cd, Cu, Pb and Zn as a functions of sludge applications rate (0 to 10% dry weight basis). Incubation time between mixing planting (0 to 7 weeks) and plant age (three clippings). Plant yield from successive clipping decreased as sludge application rates increased. Uptake of the four metals increased with sludge additions and with plant age. in the order : Zn > Cd > Pb ~ Cu. Metal uptake decreased in the order Zn > Cd > Pb > Cu with addition of lime. Incubation considerably diminished Cu and Pb uptake. all observations point to organic matter complex formation in the order : Cu > Pb > Zn > Cd. The relative uptake of HCl extractable Cd from soil was greater than that of Zn, especially upon liming, while the total uptake of these met as than decreased.

636 **Lahan, R.W.,** 1976. Molybdenum hazard in land disposal of sewage sludge. Water Air Soil Pollut. 6 : 3-8.

The application of sewage sludge to agricultural fields may result in the production of Mo-rich herbage, a cause of metabolic disorders in animals. An alternative to application of sludge to agricultural field, is sludge utilization in strip-mine reclamation. Oxidation of strip-mine spoil material causes accumulation of Mo-rich iron oxyhydroxide in stream beds and spoils piles. Strip-mine reclamation by sludge application may induce short-term increases in the concentration of Mo and other metals in waters discharged from the reclaimed area, because of pH dependent ion-exchange reactions and dissolution of Mo-bearing iron oxyhydroxides.

637 **La Mori, P.N.,** 1989. *In situ* hot air/steam extraction of volatile organic compounds. Solid. Sep. Waste. Manage and Product. : 385-396.

This paper presents the first detailed results on using a new technology for the in-situ removal of volatile organic compounds (VOCs) from soil. The technology injects hot air steam into soil through two 5-ft diameter counter rotating blades that air attached to drill stems. The soil is cleaned as the drill stems are advanced into the retracted from the ground. The evolved gases are trapped in a surface covering and contaminants are captured above ground via condensation and carbon adsorption. The recovered contaminants can be reprocessed or destroyed.

638 **Lance, J.C., Whistler F.D., Rice, R.C.,** 1976. Maximizing denitrification during soil filtration of sewage water. J. Environ. Qual. 5 (1): 102-108.

Two methods were developed to remove 80% of the nitrogen from secondary sewage effluent during soil filtration by using soil columns. No external energy source was needed to achieve denitrification with either method; and the volumes of water applied for exceeded irrigation rates for crop land. For the first method nitrogen removal was increased exponentially by decreasing the infiltration rate from 35 to 15 cm/day, which allowed nitrates formed during dry periods to mix with sewage effluent infiltrated during the succeeding flooding periods and provided C to NO_3-N ratio favourable for denitrification. In a second method, nitrogen was removed by collecting high-nitrate water after soil filtration, mixing it with sewage effluent, and recycling the mixture through the soil.

639 **Landry, E.F., Vaughn, J.M., Penello, W.F.,** 1980. Poliviras retention in 75-cm soil cores after sewage and rainwater application. Appl. Environ. Microbiol. 40(6): 1032-1038.

The adsorption rate of a quanidine-resistant strain of poliovirus LSC 2ab was measured in Long Island soils with in situ field cores (10.1 by 75 cm). The test virus was chosen because it exhibited woil adsorption and elution characteristics of a number of non-polioviruses. After the inoculation of cores with seeded sewage effluent at a 1-cm/h infiltration rate, cores were extracted, fractionated, and analyzed for total plaque-forming units per each 5-cm fraction. The results showed that 77% of the viruses were adsorbed in the first 5 cm of soil.

640 **Lane, C.L., Page, N.R., Smith, B.R., Shearin, A.T., Hegg, R.O.,** 1980.

Municipal sewage effluent application to soils bearing hardwood coppice and lobiolly pine stands. NTIS Springfield. VA: 24.

Treated municipal sewage effluent was spray irrigated on an area adjacent to the sewage treatment plant of the town of Clemson, South Carolina, A hardwood coppice and a 35 year old iobiolly pine plantation were irrigated with weekly treatments for two years. These treatments were zero, 2.5 and 5 cm and a variable rate that during the growing season was 11.5 cm equivalent irrigation per week. Two year biomass production on the coppice stand was proportional to treatment rates. There was no evidence of any groundwater or adjacent stream contamination at the rates applied.

641 **Langovan, K., Vivekanandan, M.,** 1990. Evaluation of crop resistance to aqueous oil pollution, Appl. Biochem. Biotechnol. 26(1) : 11-22.

Root and shoot tolerance indices and photosynthesis characteristics (CO_2 dependent-O_2 evolution; wholeleaf photosynthesis by infrared gas analyzer) indicted that ADT-36 and CR-1009 rice varieties were more tolerant than other varieties (IR50, R20 and Ponni). Vigna varieties (T-9 and Krishna) were most susceptible to aqueous oil pollution. Since the oil polluted soil contained a potentially toxic concentration of cadmium, tolerant (ADT 36) and susceptible (IR-50) varieties of Oryza were further analyzed for cadmium binding components. Higher accumulations of cadmium were found in the roots than in the leaves of both rice varieties.

642 **Larsen, V.J., Schierup, H.H.,** 1981. The use of straw for removal of heavy metal from waste water. J. Environ. Qual. 10(2) : 188-193.

The efficiency of barley straw in removing heavy metals from solutions was investigated. The efficiency of the straw was compared to that of activated carbon, pine saw dust, and $CaCO_3$. It was found that one g of straw was able to adsorb amounts of Zn, Cu, Pb, Ni and Cd ranging from 4.3 to 15.2 mg and pine sawdust from 1.3 to 5.0 mg, and from 1.6 to 19.8 mg of different metals were precipitated by $CaCO_3$.

643 **Lata, S.,** 1988. Differential influence of cadmium on growth of certain cucurbit seedlings treated after radicle emergence. Indian J. Ecol. 15(1) : 7-10.

Different cucurbit species (Cucumis sativus, *Cucumis melo* and *Leffa aegyptiaca*) were found to respond differentially to different concentrations of cadmium. On the basis of seedlings growth, *Cucumis sativus* cv "Faizabadi" appeared to be a resistant species and Luffa aegyptiaca cv. "Pusa Chikne" a sensitive species to cadmium. The findings emphasize the importance of using seeds with a equal size of radicle emerged and different conditions of light and dark for assessing the comparative resistance of crop species.

644 **Lawson, P.S., Sterritt, R.M., Lester, J.N.,** 1984. The speciation of metals

in sewage and activated sludge effluent. Water Air Soil Pollut. 21 : 387-402.

A gel filtration chromatographic technique was used to separate soluble species of Cd, Cu, Co, Mn, Ni and Tl in the influent and effluent of a laboratory scale activated sludge simulation operated at a range of sludge ages from 3 to 18 days. It was round that, whilst there was no general trend for all six metals; Cd and Mn associated mainly with low molecular weight fractions; Co, Cu, and Ni with a range of predominantly high molecular weight fractions; and Tl tended towards association with high molecular weight fractions which influenced metal solubility and appeared to be significant in determining metal removal. All metals exhibited high affinity for mixed liquor suspended solids (MLSS) and this affinity was strongest for Cu and Cd. Nickel, Co, Mn Tl appeared to show a high affinity for polymeric microbial products produced at longer sludge ages.

645 **Ledgard, S.F., Steele, K.W., Saunders, W.H.M.,** 1982. Effects of cow urine and its major constituents on pasture properties. Agric. Res., 25(1) : 61-68.

The effects of cow urine and equivalent nitrogen, potassium, and sulphur treatments on pasture yield, botanical composition, herbage chemical composition, and N_2 fixation by clovers were examined during winter and spring. Urine caused a large increase in ryegrass yield due entirely to its N component. The effect on yield lasted 2-3 harvests and was followed by a decrease in clover growth. The sulphur treatment (sodium sulphate) reduced the depressive effect of non-clover growth. Urine increased the N concentration of grass (particularly the nitrate fraction) and increased the potassium concentration of grass and clover. N_2 fixation by clover was markedly decreased by urine, particularly during the winter.

646 **Ledin, A., Petterson, C., Allard, B., Aastrup, M.,** 1989. Background concentration ranges of heavy meals in Swedish ground-water, from crystalline rocks-a review. Water Air Soil Pollut. 47:419-426.

Conc. of heavy metals (Zn, Cd, Cr, Cu, and Pb) in ground-waters are generally, at least qualitatively, related to concentration levels in the bed rock as well as to pH of water.

647 **Lee. C.R.,** 1979, Overland flow treatment of a municipal lagoon effluent for reduction of nitrogen, phosphorus heavy metals and coliforms. Progress Water Technol. 11(4-5) : 175-183.

Overland flow treatment of municipal facultative lagoon effluent was studied on research plots at Utica, Mississippi. The study evaluated the amount of waste water applied, length of application period, slope of treatment area, crop management, and reduction in BOD, SS, N, P, heavy metals and coliforms. Nitrogen reductions of 80% were achieved at application rates of 2.54 cm in 18hr for the warmer months of the year and 1.27 cm in 18 hr for the cooler winter months. Phosphorous reduction ranged from 40-60% at an application rate of 1.27 cm in 6 hr. However, addition to 80%. Fecal coliforms in undisinfected waste water were not reduced to 200 MPN/100 mL with 5-d/wk waste water application of waste water for 7 d/wk produced run-off coliform concentrations 200 MPN/100 mL. Overland flow effectively reduced heavy metals in applied waste water by 90%. Heavy metals accumulated in the biomass on the soil surface at the point of waste water application; elevated levels of heavy metals were found in the grass nearest the point of waste water application.

648 **Lee, E.W.,** 1989 Current options in treatment of agricultural drainage waste water. In 'Biotreatment of Agricultural Waste Water (Ed. M.F. Huntley): 33-45.

Targets for the reduction of trace elements in drainage water of California's Joaquin Valley and potential treatment are discussed. This presents major development problems, especially for selenium. Promising laboratory and pilot plant studies are reported, but their development to feasibility scale presents a major technical challenge.

649 **Lee, K.W., Keeney, D.R.,** 1975. Cadmium and zinc additions to Wisconsin soils by commercial fertilizers and waste water sludge application. Water Air Soil Pollut. 5 : 109-112.

Cadmium and Zn concentrations were determined in 21 commercial fertilizer samples. The cadmium concentration ranged from 1.5 to 9.7 mg kg^{-1}, (median 4.3 mg kg^{-1}). Zinc showed a much wider range. The Cd added to soil by fertilizer may be 2150 kg annually in Wisconsin, compared to a potential of 1700 kg if waste water sludges from all municipal sewage treatment plants in the state were disposed of on land. However, because of the higher application rates,sludge Cd on a soil concentration basis is a much more concentrated source of Cd than that from phosphate fertilizers.

650 **Lehrsch, G.A., Baker, D.E.,** 1989. Fly ash erodibility. J. Soil Water Cons. 44(6) : 624-627.

Fly ash erodibility was estimated by collecting sediments eroded by natural rainfall in the field from standard erosion plots (1.8 m wide and 22.1 m long on a 9% slope of exposed fly ash). The universal soil loss equation (USLE) was used with direct measurements on site to obtain estimates of the erodibility factor, K for fly ash. These estimates were then compared to an estimate obtained using a soil erodibility nomograph. The K factors measured in the field ranged from 0.11-0.13 Mg ha/h and averaged 0.122 Mg ha/h was recommended for erosion control. With this K factor and the USLE, the surface topography of vegetated fly ash disposal areas was designed to limit soil loss to a tolerance level of 4.5Mg (hay).

651 **Leinonen, K.P.,** 1989. The influence of soil preparation on the levels of aluminium, manganese, iron, copper, zinc, cadmium and mercury in *Vaccinium myrtillus.* Chemosphere, 18 : 1581-1587.

The levels of Al, Mn, Fe, Cu Zn, Cd and Hg in leaves of Vaccinium *myrtillus* growing in tilled and untilled clearcut forest and in untreated forest, all in the same locality on similar ground in Kuru, S-Finland were studied. Elevated levels of aluminium, manganese and mercury were noted in leaves growing on the tilled area.

652 **Leita, L., Nobili, M.De., Pardini, G., Ferrari, F., Sequi, P.,** 1989. Anomalous contents of heavy metals in soils and vegetation of a mine area in S.W. Sardinia, Italy. Water Air Soil Pollut. 48 : 423-433.

Samples of soils and vegetation from the mining area of South-West Sardinia (Italy) were analyzed for Pb, Zn, Cd, and C content. The land area (more than 100 km^2) is inhabited by many thousands of people; and utilization includes mainly grapes on some small plains and permanent sheep pasture on the hills. The levels of Pb, Zn, and Cd were found to be very high. Lead Conc. was up to 71,000 μgg^{-1} in the soils and 4000 μgg^{-1} in vegetation; Cd concentration was found upto 665 μgg^{-1} in soils and 26.5 μgg^{-1} in vegetation. The heavy metal content of some soil samples was highly variable. Data show that Pb is easily absorbed by plant roots and translocated to foliage. In spite of the high heavy metal level, no signs of toxicity were apparent in vegetation.

653 **Lemmon, W.A.,** 1982. Primary nicked industry and the environment. UNEP Indust. Environ. 5(1) : 14-15.

The recovery of nicked from the ores found in nature can, and often does, generate a number of significant environmental impacts. The use of modern process technology coupled with good planning of the facility and application of suitable environmental control technology can, and should avoid the adverse environmental impacts.

654 **Lewandowski, G.A., Abd-EL-Bary, M.F.,** 1979. Sludge applications: Remove heavy metals two ways. Water Sewage Works, 127(1) : 44-45.

Heavy metals can be eliminated from sludge at the municipal treatment plant by physicochemical means, following the primary settler, or treating the combined sludge prior to digestion. Heavy metals can also be removed at their source by activated carbon adsorption, adsorption on clay, ion exchange, cementation, or electrolysis. The most commonly used technique is chemical precipitation as an hydroxide, carbonate, or sulfide. The sequence for heavy metal precipitation generally involves equalization, precipitation, clarification, filtration, and land disposal of the filtered sludge or metals recovery. Since the volume of waste water is much smaller at the source than at a receiving municipal treatment plant, capital and operating costs for heavy metals removal are less at the source in most cases. The potential for metals recovery and reuse should be higher at the source of waste generation, and as disposal costs rise, recovery may become much more attractive.

655 **Lewin, V.H., Jones, P.W.,** 1981, Fate of bacterial pathogens in sewage treatment process. Water Pollut Control. 80(1): 42-53.

A survey of eight sewage treatment sites has been made for pathogenic bacteria. Although not exhaustive, this survey allows the following conclusions to be drawn. The presence of Salmonella is widespread in Sewage and sewage sludges. The concentrations of Salmonellae in settled sewage and untreated sludge are low and on average, less than 10^2/100 ml and 10^3/100 ml. respectively. Secondary treatment of settled sewage significantly reduces the numbers of Salmonellae present.

656 **Limura, K.,** 1981. Heavy metal problems in paddy soils. in 'Heavy Metal Pollution in Soils of Japan'. K. Kitagashi & I. Yamane (Eds.) Japan Sci. Soc. Press. Tokyo. 37-50.

The most characteristic difference of paddy soils from upland soils is the drastic shift in the oxidation-reduction state. Absorption of heavy metals by paddy especially Cd, is influenced seriously by the water management or oxidation-reduction state of the paddy soil. The article shows that the Cd concentration ratio (Cd conc. in brown rice/Cd conc. in soil) is less than 0.01 in the minimum case when the rice was grown under submerged conditions throughout the whole period of growth. While in the maximum case, in relatively coarse textural Tyama soil, it exceeds 2 when the submerging water was drained after the tillering stage (it should be remembered that the mean Cd content of paddy soils in Japan is about 0.45 ppm). The increase in absorption by rice due to draining of the submerged water after the panicle formation stage is most prominent for Cd, followed by Zn. For Cu and Pb, the increase due to draining is not so prominent except in the case of Pb in Fuchu soil.

657 **Lin, H.C.,** 1989. Utilization of municipal refuse in organic agriculture. in 'Organic Farming' (Eds. Hs-eih, S.C., Hseih C.F.). Dep. Agr. Chen. National Taiwan Univ., Taiwan.

Data are presented on the composition of municipal refuse and on the physico-chemical characteristics of sludges and composts. Attention is drawn to the need for sewage separation to minimize problem association with heavy metals.

658 **Lin, C., Chen, C.,** 1988. The compiling of water and soluble transport equations in studying the movement of heavy metal in sludge treated soil. J. Chinese Agri. Chem. Soc. 26(4) : 413-425.

A model for the transport of heavy metals in sewage treated soils was developed and tested against results obtained from column studies.

659 **Lin, C., Ke, C.K., Liu, T.S.,** 1988. Multifactor kinetics of heavy metal released from waste water sludge. J. Chinese Agri. Chem. Soc. 26(4) : 426-437.

Factors influencing the release of heavy metals from waste water sludge were studied from various industrial plants. Process related to pH, temp.: solid solution ratio and ionic composition were investigated. A model was developed to describe dynamics of heavy metal release from waste water sludges.

660 **Lindberg, S.E., Jackson, D.R., Huckabee, J.W., Janzen, S.A., Levin, M.J., Lund, J.R.,** 1979. Atmospheric emission and plant uptake of mercury from agricultural soils near the Almaden mercury mine. J. Environ. Qual. 8 : 572-578.

Surface soils collected near Almaden, Spain, Hg mine reflected increasing concentrations of Hg with proximity to the mine due to weathered mineral deposits and to atmospheric deposition of Hg from the smelter. Extractions with sodium bicarbonate or NH_4OAc removed small amounts of Hg from both control and mine site soils. A significant fraction of Hg was associated with a high-density mineral fraction, presumably cinnabar. Accumulation of Hg by alfalfa (*Medicago sativa*) suggested a dual mechanism of uptake; roots accumulated Hg in proportion to the soil levels, while aerial plant material absorbed Hg vapor directly from the atmosphere. Soil fertilization with and without liming significantly increased total Hg uptake, largely due to plant growth stimulation. Liming itself had no significant effect. The rate of volatilization of elemental Hg from both soils (0.13 and 0.33 $\mu g/m^2/hr$ at 25C, for control and mine site, respectively) exceeded reported background emission rates by factors of 4-10, increasing with surface temperature and Hg content and decreasing with increased plant cover.

661 **Il'in, V.B.,** 1988. Heavy metals in Western Siberian soils. Sov. Soil, Sci. 201, 88-96. Translation of Pochvoved., no. 6, 1987. : 87-94.

Many soils of Western Siberia differ considerably from the USSR soils as a whole in their content of heavy metals. INHCL extracted from Western Siberian soils, 30-40% of total nickel, lead, and manganese, about 20% of strontium, 4-10% of chronium, zinc, and copper. It is suggested that this mobile pool of heavy metals be regarded as the background level and taken into account when protecting soils against pollution.

662 **Lisk, D.J.,** 1988. Environmental implications of incineration of Municipal solid waste and ash disposal. Sci. Total Environ. 74:39-66.

Environmental aspects of municipal solid waste (MSW) incineration are reviewed. Metals were equilibrated for 6 d with 5-g samples of soil from the A horizons and some B horizons of 10 mineral and 3 organic soils (21 samples). The samples then were extracted with 1 M KCl to assess the quantity of non-exchangeable metal. The respective ranges of sorbed and non-exchangeable metal, expressed as a percentage of the total quantity of metal in the initial solution were Cd 0-90, 0-55; Co 15-39, 1-89; Cr 31-100, 22-100; Cu 36-100, 13-100; Ni 12-95, 5-82, Pb 31-100, 14-98; Sb 50-100, 42-99; Zn 13-98, 5-94. Stepwise multiple regression was performed (on mineral soils only) using sand, silt; clay, pH; cation exchange capacity; exchangeable cations; organic matter; dithionit-extractable Al and Fe; and ammonium oxalate-extractable Al, Fe, and Mn as independent variables and the quantity of sorbed or non-exchangeable metal as the dependent variable. Sorbed and nonexchangeable Cd, Co, Cu, Ni and Zn were related mainly to soil pH or dithionite-extractable Fe (Fed). Sorbed and non-exchangeable Cr, Pb and Sb were related mainly to Fed, ammonium oxalate-extractable Fe, sand or clay. Relative retention of metals by soil was in the order: Pb > Sb > Cu > Cr > Zn > Ni > Co > Cd. The study indicates that Fe oxides and clay content would be better parameters to use for soils of the Southeastern USA.

663 **Lisk, D.J., Furr, A.K., Parkinson, T.F., Wachs, T., Bache, C.A., Gutenmann, W.H., Wszolek, P.C., Pakkala, I.S.,** 1979. Multielement analysis of municipal sewage sludge ashes. Absorption of elements by cabbage grown in sludge ash-soil mixture. E S & T, 13(12) : 1503-1506.

An analytical survey of 42 elements and PCBs was conducted on municipal sewage sludge ashes from 10 American cities. The concentrations of specific elements in the ashes varied widely. Calcium and Fe content reflected the addition of lime and ferric chloride during sewage treatment. Elements such as Cd, Hg, N and Se were low, probably because of volatilization losses during incineration. PCBs were not detected in the ash samples. Although the total content of Ni and Zn in the ashes was high, absorption of these elements by cabbage (Brassica oleracea var. capitata) grown on ash-amended soil was surprisingly low.

664 **Lisk, D.J., Gutenmann, W.H., Pakkala, I.S., Churey, D.J., Kelly, W.C.,** 1979. Arsenic, brown molybdenum, and selenium in successive cuttings of forage crops grown on fly-ash amended soil. Agri. Food Chem. 27(6) : 1393-1395.

Alfalfa (*Medicago sativa*), birdsfoot trefoil (*Lotus corniculatus*), brome (*Bromos cultivar Saratoga*), orchard grass (*Dactylis glomerate*), and timothy (*Phleium practinse*) were grown on soil amended with 112.5. t/ha of coal fly ash and untreated soil. Five successive cuttings of each crop were analysed for As, B, Mo, and Se. Of the fly ash treated crops, B showed a consistent increase, mainly in the legumes, whereas Se increased mainly in the grasses. Molybdenum showed a consistent increase in all of the cuttings of all crops grown on fly ash. Arsenic increased mostly in the first cutting of the crops. Crop yields on the 2 treatments appeared comparable.

665 **Liu, D.,** 1980. Fate of petroleum hydrocarbons in sewage sludge after land disposal. Bull. Environl. Contam. Toxicol. 25; 616-622.

Petroleum hydrocarbons are fairly resistant to the biological treatment process in sewage plants; consequently, high concentration of petroleum hydrocarbons have been detected in various sewage sludges. Petroleum hydrocarbons are known to be toxic to plants and crops because of their damaging effect on the processes of translocation, transpiration and photosynthesis. The present study was intended to investigate the rate of petroleum hydrocarbons in digested sewage sludge after farmland disposal.

666 **Liu, Z.G.,** 1990. Capacity of waste water treatment of soil plant system and influence of waste water on soil property. Proc Internatl. Congress Soil Sci. 14(4): 204-209.

The treatment of waste water by several soil plant systems (soil-rice, soil-wheat, soil-grass) and its effect on the soil physical and chemical properties are discussed.

667 **Liu, D., Kwasniewska. K.,** 1980. Movement of sewage microorganisms in soils, in Trace Substances in Environ. Health XIV, Univ. Mo. Columbia: 464-469.

Three anaerobically digested, chemically treated sewage sludges (alum, iron and lime sludges) were applied to lysimeters containing silt loam or loamy sand. The individual cores were subsectioned and examined for population of heterotrophic bacteria, total coliform, fecal streptococcus and fungi. It was found that after one year of heavy sludge application 95% of the sewage micro-organisms were found still in the top 15 cm of soils. Thus it appears that sewage sludge land disposal would pose very little, if any significant contamination of underground water by sewage micro-organisms, provided by the land is not overloaded.

668 **Livine, M.B., Hall, A.T., Barrett, G.W., Taylor, D.H.,** 1989. Heavy metal concentrations during ten years of sludge treatment to an old field community, J. Environ. Qual. 18(4) : 411-418.

Heavy metal concs. were determined in an old field community treated for 10 consecutive years (1978-87) with sewage sludge. The study included sewage sludge, fertilizer and control. Cd concs. were highest in soils, vegetations, meadow vole (*Microtus pennsylvaincus*) livers and earthworms from sludge treated plots. Mean Cd conc. decreased in sludge and increased in soils and plant treated with sludge. No yearly increase in Cd content was observed in meadow vole liver or kidney. Cd conc. in earthworms was increased. Similarly data are presented for Cu, Pb and Zn in the soils, plants and earthworms which followed different trend for each metal with time.

669 **Loch, J.P.G., Lagas, P., Haring, B.J.A.,** 1981. Behaviour of heavy metals in soil beneath a landfill : Results of model experiments. Sci. Total Environ., 21 : 203-213.

Column experiments were set up in order to study the behaviour of heavy metals from landfill leachate in the soil. Special attention was given to the influence of fatty acids in the leachate on the mobility of the kind of soil material was investigated. At the end of the experiments, after 7 months, the soil was analysed for precipitates and adsorption of metals. In the presence of fatty acids, breakthrough of respectively nickel, zinc and lead took place, whereas copper accumulated in the soil. In the absence of fatty acids precipitation and adsorpiion of the metals took place.

670 **Lodenius, M.,** 1990. Environmental mobilization of mercury and cadmium. Report No. 13: 32.

The Finish environment has been studied for mobilization of Cd and Hg. Data on the effect of acidification and release have also been presented.

671 **Lodenius, M., Antio, S.,** 1989. Effects of acidification on the mobilization of cadmium and mercury from soils. Archives. Environ. Contam. Toxicity. 18: 261-267.

Sorption and mobility of Cd and Hg in two soils were studied in columns. Both metals were sorbed strongly to a peat-soil. The effects of 4 elements with different pH were studied at 20°C and 5C. Cd was released at low pH values. Strong leaching was also observed after treatment with a neutral salt solution with an ionic strength corresponding to a soil solution. The differences in leaching after different treatments and between the two temperatures were smaller for Hg. The leaching of Hg was slightly enhanced by decreasing the temperature.

672 **Lodenius, M., Kuusi, T., Laaksovirta, K.,** 1981. Lead, cadmium and mercury contents of fungi in Mikkeli SF Finland. Ann. Bot. Fennici., 18(2): 183-186.

Lead, cadmium and mercury contents of 59 samples of fruit-bodies of fungi wee determined. The dry wt concentrations ranged 0.5-16 mg Pb/kg, 0.2-130mg Cd/kg and 0.02-64 mg Hg/kg and were generally at the same level as reported earlier for unpolluted areas. High contents of cadmium (mean 32 mg/kg) and mercury (mean 11 mg/kg) were observed in Agaricus. The uptake of cadmium and mercury in fungi is highly species-dependent. As it is very difficult to identify the species of genus, the use of wild-growing Agaricus fungi for food should be limited. No correlation was found between the concentrations of these three metals.

673 **Lodenius, M., Laaksovirta, K.,** 1979. Mercury content of Hypogymnia physodes and pine needles affected by a chlor-alkali works at Kuusankoski, SE Finland. Ann. Bot. Fenici. 16(1): 7-10.

The Hg contents of the epiphytic lichen H. physodes and needles of Pinus, sylvestris were determined from 63 sites around a chlor-alkali works in Kuusankoski. The Hg content of the lichen ranged from 0.13 to 0.87 ppm and that of pine needles from 0.01 to 0.34 ppm. The concentration evenly decreased with increasing distance from the works, and the effect of the works could be noticed in the whole study area both in lichens and in needles.

674 **Lodenius, M., Seppaenen, A., Autio, S.,** 1987. Sorption of mercury in

soils with different humus content. Bull. Environl. Contam. Toxicol., 39(4): 593-600.

The strong sorption of mercury to humic matter in soil and in soil water has raised the question about the influence of organic matter of different soil types on the mobilization of mercury from soil. Mercury is normally bound to humic and fulvic acids, which may be released in connection with flooding, draining and ditching. High mercury contents in fish from man-made lakes have been reported mainly from temperate regions. The sorption and leaching of mercury in three different soils was studied in vitro using mercury concentration near the natural level.

675 **Loehr, R.C.,** 1979. Potential pollutants from agriculture an assessment of the problem and possible control approaches. Progress Water Technol. 11(6): 169-193.

Agriculture was identified as a potential source of water pollution as a result of the increasing intensity of many animal and crop producing operations. There are approaches that can be used to minimize any adverse effect that agriculture might have These include runoff and erosion control practices; better liming and use of pesticides, fertilizers, and manure applications; and soil and water conservation practices. Many of these approaches are being utilized and data on their effectiveness are available. Point and nonpoint potential agricultural pollutants are discussed in terms of sources, relative importance and types of pollutants, the magnitude of actual discharges; and approaches and practices that can be used for the control of specific pollutants.

676 **Logan, T.J., Cassler, D.E.,** 1989. Correcting widespread cadmium contamination. Water Environl. Technol. 1(2): 312-315.

Nineteen years after sludge application began, the community discovered that it had unknowingly created a serious soil cadmium contamination problem.

677 **Logan, T.J., Chang, A.C., Page, A.L., Gange, T.J.,** 1987. Accumulation of selenium in crops grown on sludge treated soil. J. Environ. Qual. 16: 349-352.

Uptake by barley years, Swiss chard and radish of Se from composted Los Angales Country sewage sludge applied to land was studied in a long-term field study. Sludge was applied at 0, 22.5, 45, 90 and 180 Mg/ha per year for 8 to 10 years and the data reported here are for the last year of the study. Total surface (0-15 cm) soil Se increased with the highest rate of sludge addition from 0.1 mg/kg in the control soil to 1.2 mg/kg. Only 13 to 25% of the sludge applied Se could be accounted for in the 0 to 15 cm depth of incorporation and there was no measurable Se (< 0.1 mg/kg) in the subsoil to 150 cm. There was little or no measurable uptake of Se by barley leaf and grain at the level of detection (0.–0.5 mg/kg) and there was also no significant increases in chard or radish Se concentrations with sludge addition. Selenium concentrations in chard (0.05 - 0.11 mg/kg) were severalfold lower than those in radish (0.17-0.26 mg/kg).

678 **Logan, T.J., Feltz, R.E.,** 1985. Plant uptake of cadmium from acid extracted anaerobically digested sewage sludge. J. Environ. Qual. 14(4): 495-500.

Approximately 80% of the Cd in an anaerobically digested sewage sludge was removed by acid extraction and dewatering. The acid extracted sludge was treated by (i) neutralization of pH 5.9 with $Ca(OH)_2$, (ii) addition of monocalcium phosphate (MCP) followed by $Ca(OH)_2$ neutralization to pH 5.9 and (iii) addition of rock phosphate (RP) followed by $Ca(OH)_2$ neutration to pH 5.9. The three treated sludges and the non acid-extracted sludge were applied to Spinks loamy sand at rates equivalent to 18.7 and 37.4 μmol Cd kg^{-1}. Swiss chard (Beta vulgaris) was grown in the green house for 56d. Cadmium, Fe, Ca, and P were measured in saturation extract of treated soil at 0, 4, 18, 39 and 60 d after sludge addition. Cadmium concentration in saturation extract will MCD sludge decreased below the detection limit at the 37.4 μmol Cd kg^{-1} application rate, while Cd concentrations in saturation extracts of the other sludge treatments were much higher throughout the study. Chard yields were higher in the control than in any of the sludge treatments, and the difference was attributed to greater N availability in the control. Cadmium concentration in Swiss chard tissue at harvest was significantly lower from the MCP sludge than from the other sludges. Cadmium concentration in chard tissue was also higher from the aerated sludge (11.9 mmol Cd kg^{-1}) than from the three acid-extracted sludges (2.58–3.29 mmol Cd kg^{-1}). No significant difference in the Cd concentration of chard was obtained for the 18.7 and 37.4 μmol Cd kg^{-1} rates of the MCP sludge, while Cd concentrations in chard increased linearly with Cd applied by the other sludges.

679 **Lubben, S., Rietz, E.,** 1989. The effects of long term application of domestic wastes on the heavy metals transfer from soil to plant. I Heavy metal contents and translocation in soils of long term field trials of domestic waste application. Verts. Dett. Land Unter und forsch. Rei Kongress.

At five locations long term studies with domestic waste were conducted in FRG. Normal application rates of sewage sludge or reuse of compost caused minor accumulation of heavy metals in top arable soil. With high dozes of excessively polluted sludges thresholds were reached for heavy metals or exceeded with in 20 yrs. only at one site sub-soil conc. of heavy metal was observed. The highest rate of accumulation was observed in silty loam soil. Increased heavy metal contents just below the tillage layer were attributed to root influences.

680 **Lund, L.J., Betty, E.E., Page, A.L., Elliott, R.A.,** 1981. Occurrence of naturally high cadmium levels in soils and its accumulation by vegetation. J. Environ. Qual. 10 : 551-556.

The relationship between parent materials and soil Cd contents for twenty four soils were analyzed after digestion in $4NHHO_3$. Residued soils developed from the shale parent materials had the greatest Cd concentrations, with a mean of 7.5 μg/g, whereas soils developed from sand stone and basalt had the lowest Cd concentrations, with a mean of 0.84 μg/g. Alluvial soils with parent materials from mixed sources had an intermediate mean Cd content of 1.5 μg/g. A more extensive survey of the dominant soil series of the area was carried out and the Millsholm series, mapped in 30% of the area, was found to have a mean Cd content of 7.3 μg/g. A greenhouse study conducted with seven soils showed that the Cd present naturally in these soils was absorbed by the vegetables in amounts sufficient to be of the public health concern.

681 **Lund, L.J., Page, A.L., Nelson, C.O.,** 1976. Movements of heavy meals below sewage disposal ponds. J. Environ Qual. 5(3): 330-334.

Concentrations of acid-extractable metals (4M HNO_3) were greater under disposal ponds than of control pits at both treatment plants. Metal (Zn, Cd, Cu, Cr and Ni) enrichment was evident upto 3m depth under some ponds. The depth and degree of metal enrichment depended on the specific pond type and the treatment plant. Metal concentrations were greater under anaerobically digested sludge holding ponds than effluent ponds. Concentrations of the metals in saturations extracts of soils beneath the ponds were greater than these typically found for California soils. The distribution of metals with depth were closely related to the changes in chemical oxygen demands of soil samples with depth. This suggest that the metals have moved as soluble metal organic complexes.

682 **Lund, L.J., Page, A.L., Nelson, C.O., Elliott, R.A.,** 1981. Nitrogen balances for an effluent irrigation area. J. Environ. Qual. 10 (3): 349-352.

An 8.5-ha pasture irrigated with secondary sewage effluent was studied to determine the fate of N applied in the effluent. Soils of the Corralitos series at nine plots were sampled twice to evaluate the spatial and temporal variations in the field water contents and NO_3-N and Cl concentrations in the unsatuated zone. Field water contents varied in space but not in time. Mean NO_3-N concentrations in soil solution ranged from 15.4 to 32.4 mg/l and varied significantly in space and time. Mean Cl concentrations varied in a similar manner. Average of N balances developed for three of the nine plots attributed 32, 60 and 90% of the N applied in the effluent to crop removal, leaching and gaseous losses, respectively.

683 **Lupi, C., Bucchi, A.R., Piccioni, A., Zapponi, G.A.,** 1988. The environmental behaviour of chemicals in soil: Atrazine as an example. Ecol. Environ. Saf. 16(2): 133-142.

A mathematical model has been developed and used to estimate the soil vertical distribution of Atrazine dispersed in the environment. Water transport rise due to capillarity, and partition among soil contained water, air and organic mater, as well as degradation processes, are considered. Nichois Walker Baker. Model has been extended to include a procedure which takes into account the atrazine mobility due to gravitational water flow. The organic carbon (OC) concentration gradient in soil was also considered in the evaluation when assessing partition processes. The degradation processes assumed to be first order, linearly related with OC content in soil. The application of this model to two sets of soil data demonstrated that Atrazine requires a long time (2 years or more, depending on soil features) in order to percolate at a depth comparable with those of a ground-water source.

684 **Macgregor, A.N., Tillman, R.W., Syers, J.K.**, 1979. Studies on the chemical and microbiological characteristics of soil filtered dairy shed effluent. Progress Water Technol. 11(6): 19-31.

The discharge from a drained pasture disposal site receiving milking shed waste water was sampled intensively over several 24-hr periods. The effluent was characterised in terms of nutrients (N and P forms), oxygen demand, coliform bacteria, solids, and pH. The efficiency of the disposal area in filtering the waste water was calculated and was relatively constant between runs, although with seasonal variations in antecedent soil moisture and rainfall, there were large differences in the volume of drainage water discharged. The pattern of flow and composition of the discharge were investigated and it was concluded that a sampling interval of no greater than 1 hr was required to provide estimates of loadings which were within 10% of the true values over all runs and all parameters.

685 **Mackay, D.**, 1988. The chemistry and modelling of soil contamination with petroleum, in Soils Contaminated by Petroleum: Environmental and Public Health Effects. John Wiley & Sons, New York: 5-18.

The mechanisms of oil migration in soil are reviewed and soil chemistry and the matrix approach briefly described.

686 **Madany, I.M., Ali, S.M., Akhter, M.S.,**, 1990. Assessment of lead in roadside vegetation in Bahrain. Environ. International 16(2): 123-126.

Leaves from the species of trees were sampled at 18 locations in Bahrain and were analyzed for lead. Lead levels in leaves from areas with high traffic density were generally higher than lead levels in leaves from area with low traffic density. The lead levels found in this study are in the range of 9 μg to 420 μg/g, which is low compared to values reported for leaves of trees along busy roads in developed countries. However, the concentration of lead is increasing.

687 **Madhavan, S., Roseman, D.D., Shehata, T.**, 1989. Lead in soil: recommended maximum permissible levels. Environmental Res. 49(1): 136-142.

From the aspect of public health, the proposed 'safe' level for lead in soil was 600 ppm. The maximum permissible for soil in areas where children do not play was 1000 ppm.

688 **Madhavendra, S.S., Satyakala, G., Kaiser Jamil, 1990.** Survey of vegetation in an industrial area. Indian J. Environ. Health 32(2): 113-123.

Vegetation of the industrial area of Balanagar, Hyderabad was surveyed for identification of pollution sensitive indicator and resistant species. Fifty one Angiosperm species were studied. Of them 3 indicators, 12 susceptible and 36 resistant species were identified. Defoliation, leaf chlorosis, necrosis, bronzing, withering, hyponasty and epinasty were observed in many of the plants in industrial areas.

689 **Madkour, S., Weinstein, L.H., 1987.** Effects of hydrogen fluoride on incorporation and transport of photoassimilates in soybean. Environl. Toxicol. Chem., 6(8): 627-634.

The effect of hydrogen fluoride (HF) on the translocation and partitioning of C between transport and nontransport photoassimilates from source leaves to sink regions was studied. Soybeans plants were fumigated continuously with HF at 0, 1, and 5 μgF m^{-3} for 8 to 10 d at three stages of development (vegetative, flowering and early fruit set, and pod filling). The second fully expanded trifoliate leaf of experimental plants was exposed to CO_2. In plants exposed to HF, there was an increased retention of C-labelled assimilates in foliage (source tissue), accompanied by a reduced export of these compounds to other plant parts (path and sink tissues). There was also a greater incorporation of C into nontransport ethanol-insoluble assimilates at the expense of the ethanol-soluble transport assimilates in source leaves. When compared with control plants, exposure to HF also increased the proportion of C incorporated into sugars in source leaves accompanied by a decrease in C-sugars in sink tissues.

690 **Magdoff F.R., Amadoji, J.F., 1980.** Nitrogen availability from sewage sludge. J. Environ. Qual. 9(3): 451-455.

Aerobically treated secondary liquid sewage sludge was applied to both corn and hay growing on Hadley sandy loam and Nellis loam soils. The nine treatments consisted of check, four ammonium nitrate levels (50, 100, 150 and 200 kg N/ha yr.) and four sludge levels (chosen to supply amounts of available, N similar to the ammonium nitrate rates). About 54% of the organic-N added to the sludge-amended corn soils was mineralised under laboratory conditions The amount of N mineralised was well correlated with a chemical test of N availability. While the corn and hay on the sludge amended Hadley soil out-yielded the N treatments, nitrate recovery to 1.2 m in the corn plots indicated that the available N supplied by the sludge treatments was no greater than that supplied by ammonium nitrate. Other factors, such as increased K supply to both corn and hay and residues N effect on the second year hay, probably caused the increased response of crops to sludge over N. There was little or no response of corn yields to sludge on N in the Nellis loam, which the hay responded more to N than sludge. Estimates of mineralisation of organic-N from sludge applied to corn and hay averaged 55% for the first year of applications. Recovery of N in the corn at harvest plus soil NO_3-N to a depth of 1.2 m was positively correlated with the estimated mineralisation of organic-N (from the N availability test) plus the inorganic N-added. The auto-claving test of N availability appears useful in predicting mineralisation of organic N from sludge under field conditions.

691 **Mahinthakumar, G., Vigneswaran, S.,** 1990. Solute transport through saturated soils: A study of the physical non-equilibrium model. Water Air Soil Pollut. 51(1-2): 161-180.

A two region physical non-equilibrium transport model incorporating mobile and immobile regions, originally developed by Van Genuchten and Wieringa (1976), was used to predict the movement of solutes through saturated soils. Freunditch's non-linear isotherms were coupled with this transport model to account for the absorption phenomena. A CSMP III (Continuous System Modelling Program) Program was used to solve this model numerically. The model was tested for 3 sets of experimental data having different soil and solute properties. The experimental curves were fitted by adjusting the 3 parameters, mass transfer coefficient (a) distribution factor for sorption sites in the mobile region (f), and the fraction of mobile water content (d). The model predicted well only for fairly conservative solutes. To predict the movement of highly reactive solutes such as Cd. The model needs further modification. Effects of disperson co-efficient (D), a.f. and f on the breakthrough curves were studied for highly reactive solutes.

692 **Mahler, R.J., Bingham, F.T., Page, A.L.** 1978. Cadmium-enriched sewage sludge application to arid and calcareous soils. Effect on yield and cadmium uptake by lettice and chard. J. Environ. Qual 7: 274-281.

Eight soils with pH values ranging from 4.8 to 7.8 were treated with sewage sludge amended with variable amounts of $CdSO_4$. The concentration of Cd in the soil ranged from 0.1 to 320 µg Cd/gm. and Swiss chard were grown to maturity in pot cultures on the treated soils to determine the effect of the soil pH on yield and Cd uptake. Fifty per cent yield decrements for acid and calcareous soils, respectively, were associated with the following concentrations of Cd in soils, lettuce 214 and 139 µg/gm; chard 175 and 250 µg/g. Tissue concentrations of Cd associated with for 50% yield decrement for acid and calcareous soils, respectively were as follow; lettuce 470 and 160 µg/gm; chard-714 and 203 µg/g. Multiple regression analysis of yields as a function of pH, CEC, $CaCO_3$, % organic carbon (OC), % sand - silt - clay, and Cd addition rate revealed a highly significant yield relationship with Cd addition rate, % OC, % clay and pH (Lettuce: $R^2 = 0.82$; Chard; $R^2 = 0.93$). Leaf Cd was significantly related to soil parameters as follows: lettuce-saturation extract Cd and CEC, $R^2 = 0.82$, chard-saturation extract Cd and pH, $R^2 = 0.89$.

693 **Mahler, R.J., Bingham, F.T., Sposito, G., Page, A.L.,** 1980. Cadmium enriched sewage sludge application to acid and calcareous soils; Relation between treatment, Cadmium in saturation extracts and cadmium uptake. J. Environ. Qual. 9: 359-364.

Four acid and four calcareous soils were treated with a unfirm amount of sewage sludge enriched with different amounts of $CdSO_4$ to yield soils Cd concentrations ranging from 0.1 to 160 μg Cd/gm of sludge amended soils. These treated soils were placed in plastic containers and cropped for approximately seven weeks with sweet corn tomato and Swiss chard. Shoot weights were obtained as a measure of yields. The concentration of Cd in the shoot (Cd uptake) was taken of a measure of Cd availability. Saturation extracts from each treated soil collected at harvest time were analysed for pH, ECe, soluble anions and cations, Cu, Cd, Ni and Zn. The chemical analyses of the saturation extracts were used as input data to calculate the concentration of free ionic Cd (Cd^{2+}), the activity of the Cd^{2+} (a Cd^{2+}) and the concentration of Cd complexes. These Cd parameters, along with the measured concentration of all Cd forms present in saturation extracts (Cd), were compared to Cd concentration in each of the test plant (μg Cd/g shoot). Result of these comparisons showed (i) Cd-was more available in acid than calcareous soils (ii) Cd uptake by the test plants correlated equally well with the concentration of Cdt, Cd^{2+}, or aCd^{2+}, and (iii) uptake of Cd was plant species dependent. Chard and tomato accumulated 2 to 3 times more Cd than corn when grown on the acid soils.

694 **Maiti, S.S., Mukhopadhyay, M., Gupta, S.K., Banerjee, S.K.,** 1990. Evaluation of fly ash as a useful material in agriculture. J. Indian Soc. Soil Sci. 38: 342-344.

Fly ash produced from coal fired power station may be useful for acid soils because of its alkaline nature and nutrient status (P and K).

695 **Majimel, J.** et al, 1989. Agriculture the threat of nitrates. Paysans. 196: 10-49.

A Collection of 6 articles is presented dealing with the dilemmas of pollution by agriculture.

696 **Malanchuk, J.C., Gruendling, G.K.,** 1973. Toxicity of lead nitrate to algae. Water Air Soil Pollut. 2: 181-190.

The fixation of radioactive C was used to measure toxicity of Pb $(NO_3)_2$ to five species of fresh water algae. Portions of unialgal cultures were inoculated into low salt medium and were used to test all species at 10, 20 and 30 ppm Pb. This medium approximated the salt concentration of natural aquatic environments. Three different cell weights were used for each concentration of Pb and for the control to determine a relationship between cell weight and toxicity. The concentration of Pb causing a 50% reduction of $^{14}CO_2$ fixation as compared to the control was called the ED_{50} (median effective dose). These values were extrapolated from graphs of ppm Pb vs dpm mg^{-1} dry cell weight. The ED_{50} for three of the species tested (Anabaena, Chlamydomonas, and Navicula) was between 15 and 18 ppm Pb. A desmid, Cosmarium, had an ED_{50} of 5 ppm. This species has a higher surface: volume ratio than the other species tested and this may account for its increased sensitivity. An ED_{50} for Ochromonas was not obtained. Throughout this experiment the fixation of $^{14}CO_2$ increased with increasing Pb concentrations and is not readily explained.

697 **Maliszeuska, W., Dec, S., Wierzbicka, H., Wozniakowska, A.,** 1985. The influence of various heavy metal compounds on the developments and activity of soil micro-organisms. Environl. Pollut. (A. Ecol. Bio.) 37 (3): 195-215.

The influence of various concentrations of metals on development and activity of soil microflora is presented. The relative toxicity of the compounds was in the order: Hg (metallic) > $CuSO_4$ > $HgC1_2$ > Hg_2C1_2 > HgO > As_2O_3 > $ZnSO_4$ > Na_2AsO_4 > Pb $(NO_3)_2$. Fungi and actionomycetes were the most resistant to all the metals used and Azotobacter Sp. and nitrifiers appeared to be the most sensitive.

698 **Mandre, M., Martin, J., Kangur, A., Kaur, L., Pihilakas, E.,** 1987. On physiological-biochemical aspects of the reactions of field crops on the industrial load. Proc. Acad. Sci. Estonian SSR, Biol., 35, 221-233.

Experiments with rye, barley and clover were carried out near the oil shale, cement and mineral fertiliser factories in small plots that were subjected to the influence of pollutants.

699 **Manoharan, M., Lakshmanan, K.K.,** 1987. Effect of tannery effluent on seed germination and early seedling growth of vigna Mungo (L). Heppel. Ann. Biol. 3(2): 68-70.

The effect of tannery effluent on seed germination and early seedling growth of black gram was studied.

700 **Manos, G.P., Eric, T.,** 1980. Chromatographic behaviour of humic materials extracted from Barberton sludge. Water Air Soil Pollut. 13: 373-377.

Humic and fulvic acids extracted from alkali treated municipal sludge contain higher molecular weight materials than from secondary waste water effluents. High molecular weight materials (> 30000) are more easily entrapped on the protoinaceous surface of the biomass. About 28% of the sludge COD is humic material. The humic acid fraction is of a higher molecular weight than the fulvic acid fraction. The value of the E_4: E_6 ratio indicates that humic materials of raw sludges are of recent origin.

701 **Marchwinska, E., Kucharski, R.,** 1987. The combined influence of SO_2 and heavy metal-containing particulates on beans, carrots and parsley. En-

viron. Monit. Assess., 8: 11-25.

Passely, beans and carrots were fumigated using SO_2 in concentrations ranging from (0.13 to 1.7 ppm) with and without lead/zinc/cadmium-containing particulate matter. A long-term exposure to low levels of SO_2, even without visible plant injuries, resulted in more significant crop losses than short-term, high concentrations. Measurements of root and leaf weight in carrot and passely fumigated in exposure chambers with SO_2 show that the ratio of root to leaf weight depends on the type and concentration of pollutants. A mathematical model describing the above phenomena might be a useful tool in the assessment of crop losses due to known concentrations of air pollutants during the growth period.

702 **Marfenina, O.E.,** 1989. The reaction of microfungi to soil pollution by heavy metals. Nauchnye Dokladyvysshei Shkoly Biologecheskie Nauki. 9:89-93.

The reaction of soil microfungi to heavy metal pollution is briefly reviewed.

703 **Markert, B., Thornton, I.,** 1990. Multielement analysis of an English peat bog soil. Water Air Soil Pollut. 49(2): 113-123.

Nineteen elements were determined in peat profiles in Ringinglow Bog. Derbyshire, England. For the elements Ba, Ca, Cd, Co, Cr, Fe, La, Mn, Ni, Ti and Zn and enrichment in the upper 5 cm of the peat bogs was found probably caused by anthropogenic influences. The elements Al, Be, Cu, & Pb showed a different distribution pattern with maximum concentration in the 5-15 cm layer. The elements Mg, Na, & Sr, showed no enrichment in the Upper 55 cm of the peat reflecting the constant input of these elements from the sea during the last few centuries. Upper parts leaves & stems of the plants investigated (*Calluna vulgaris* and *Enophorum vaginatum*) only represent higher values of Pb compared with the normal elements content in other plants compared with the results of peat profiles in Norwegian bog.

704 **Marshall, W.D.,** 1986. Determination of alkyllead salts in run-off soils, and street dusts containing high levels of lead. J. Environ. Qual. 15(3): 255-259.

A modified procedure has been developed in which alkyllead salts are selectively extracted complexo-metrically from samples which contain up to 1000 mg Pb^{2+} kg^{-1}. This procedure was applied to rainwater runoff, soils and street dusts from urban environments. Ethyllead salts but not methyllead salts were detected in all samples. Concentrations of these analysts were significantly correlated with levels of extractable Pb in these samples but not with total Pb.

705 **Martin, G.C., Larson, W.E., Clapp, C.E.,** 1980. Effects of Municipal waste water effluent on performance and feed quality of maize vs Reed canary grass. J. Environ. Qual. 9(1): 137-141.

Three soil treatments included a control (well water and mineral fertilizer) and two municipal waste water effluent levels (usually 5 or 10 cm/week), each applied to Reed canary grass and maize. In all except the first year, maize fodder was more digestible ($\bar{X}$ of 74.4%) than Reed canary grass ($\bar{X}$ of 68.9%) subjected to any soil treatment. Reed canary grass always contained much more crude protein ($\bar{X}$ of 17.5%) than did maize ($\bar{X}$ of 7.2%). Maize fodder yielded from 17 to 36% more dry matter and from 23 to 41% more digestible dry matter per ha than did Reed canary grass. These differences were progressively less as effluent application rate increased from 0 to @ 10 cm/week. Reed canary grass yielded from 30 to 52% more crude protein per ha than did maize. These differences were progressively greater as effluent application increased. Perennial grasses have superior capacity compared, to maize to remove N from soil treated with large amounts of waste water effluent. The grasses are also most likely to yield more protein per ha, but the least digestible dry matter in effluent treated systems.

706 **Mason, J.T. III, Liau, C.Y.P.,** 1985. Effects of pH on removing low-level chromium contamination in groundwater. J. Tenn. Aca. Sci. 60(3): 77-78.

In order to find the best pH for reducing the chromium contamination by adsorption, a series of tests varying adsorbent amount, flow rate, and pH showed that Duolite ES-392 worked best at a pH of about 5.6.

707 **Master, W.A., Zellmer, S.D.,** 1979. The effects of fertilizer made from flue gas and fly ash on selected crops and soils. Illnois Institute Natural Resources Document: 76/16.

A desulfurization process was developed to reduce stack emissions from a typical coal-fired boiler and to produce a new fertilizer product utilizing flue gases, fly ash, bottom ash, and materials added during the scrubbing process. The batches of fertilizer product received by ANL were analyzed for physical and chemical parameters, and 3 plant growth experiments were performed to determine the effects of the fertilizer products on soybeans (*Glycine max*), spring or winter wheat, and smooth bromegrass. The concentrations of elements varied widely between fertilizer batches. The single fertiliser product with bottom ash contained the highest concentrations of numerous trace elements. The growth experiments demonstrated that a single application equivalent to 224 kg N/ha of the fertilizer product will increase aerial biomass and crop yield as compared to unfertilized conditions. However, the ratio of harvestable grain to aerial vegetation may be reduced, and the development of root systems may be adversely affected.

708 **Mathur, S.P., Levesque, M.O., Desjardins, J.P.,** 1979. The relative immobility of fertilizer and native copper in an organic soil under field conditions. Water Air Soil Pollut. 11(2): 207-215.

Twelve cores were taken from a 2-ha field containing Cu from 0.01% to 0.03% in the top 0–10 cm layer from where Cu had been applied for 15 yr and 6 from areas not fertilized with Cu and examined for evidence of downward movement of Cu. The 30-50 cm layers in the profiles in both areas contained similar amounts of Cu, indicating a lack of vertical migration of the fertilizer metal under field conditions. A buried layer of humified material was found mostly between 50 and 60 cm depth. Of the mineral elements which enriched this layer during degradation and humification a few thousand years ago, Cu, Pb, and Mn were apparently retained more than Ca, Fe, Ni, Al, Mg, Zn and K.

709 **Mathys, W.**, 1980. Zinc tolerance by plants. In Zinc in the Environment, Pt. 2 Health Effects, John Wiley & Sons, New York. : 415-437.

A common characteristics of all species growing on zinc contaminated habitats is the evolution of zinc tolerant ecotypes. Zinc tolerance is one of the many possible tolerances against metals; resistance to aluminum, lead, copper, cadmium, nicket, chromium and other metals is also well known. Zinc tolerance is most intensively studied.

710 **Mayber, B.**, 1987. Results of preliminary investigations of Pb, Cd, S and F content in the soil of low land forests of the Kupcina basin. Sumarski. List. III: 19-27.

Analysis of samples showed that the area received air pollutants. Soil pH indicated the occurrence of acid rain and increased acidification of the pseudogley soil.

711 **Mayer, L.M., Schick, L.L., Rossi, P.M., Patterson, H.H., Chang, C.A.**, 1981. Analysis, Distribution and interactions of chromium in the aquatic environment. NTIS Springfield VA: 66.

Study was made downstreams of a Harland tannery on the Sebasticook River, and one in Saco on the Saco River just above its opening in the Gulf of Maine. Accumulation of Cr in Saco River sediments was found to occur in patterns controlled by hydrography and grain size. Pollutant impact assessment was made possible by textural normalisation using sediment specific surface areas. Oxidation of dissolved/particulate Cr (III) was shown not likely in the Saco estuary; and effluent dissolved Cr (III) is not likely retained, but rather flushed out to sea, bound to iron-humic colloids. Cr(III) sediment adsorption decreased with increasing salinity, and is not likely to be important, except in deposited sediments. Chemiluminescent analysis for sensitivity of free aqueous Cr (III) was enhanced by added halides, especially bromide, making possible the application of this technique to sea, water Cr analysis.

712 **Maynard, D.G., Germida, J.J., Addison, P.A.**, 1988. The effect of elemental sulphur on certain chemical and biological properties of surface organic horizons of a forest soil. Can. J. Forest Res. 16: 1050-1054.

Deposition of S has had a significant effect on the soil system close to the sulfur blocks. Elemental S has been oxidised to SO_4-S by the action of S-oxidising microorganisms, primarily *T. thiooxidans*. The oxidation of S has resulted in both direct chemical changes by lowering the pH and indirect changes through increased leaching of base cations and the solubilisation of Al and Fe. These chemical changes have, in turn, reduced the heterotrophic populations and the potential for C mineralisation. Plant responses to these chemical and biological changes have been dramatic and the understory vegetation has been virtually eliminated at the most contaminated site. Although the trees showed no outward response, the indirect effects of soil chemical and biological changes may only be detected with long-term studies.

713 **Mazcomini, A., Capel, E.D., Lichtensteiger, T., Brunner, D.H., Giger, W.,** 1989. Behaviour of aromatic surfactants and PCB's in sludge-treated soil and land fills. J. Environ. Qual. 18(4): 523-528.

All the aromatic surfactants demonstrated a very fast decrease in conc. (> 80% within a month) presumably due to biodegradation. But all of them exhibited a residual conc. in the soil after 320 days.

714 **McBride, M.B.,** 1989. Reactions controlling heavy metal solubility in soils. Adv. Soil Sci. 10: 1-56.

Heavy metals solubility is exhaustively reviewed.

715 **McBride, R.A., Gordon, A.M., Groenevelt, P.H.,** 1989, Treatment of land fill leachate by spray irrigation-an overview of research results from Ontario, Canada. II. Soil quality for leachate disposal. Bull. Environl. Contam. Toxico. 42(4): 518-525.

A study was initiated to evaluate leachate spray irrigation as a cost-effective, environmentally-sound, and longterm solution to the Muskoka Lakes sanitary landfill seepage problem. Given the nature of the local soils, the forest floor litter layer is the key to increasing the residence time of the waste water in the unsaturated zone and effecting a suitable level of renovation before the effluent reaches the ground-water table. High water table levels and shallow bedrock over much of spray area 1 and 2 greatly reduce this residence time and cause the formation of leachate breakouts in depressions. The waste water distribution system is currently less than satisfactory which gives rise to localized application rates far in excess of evapotranspirational demand and soil attenuation capacity. Pretreatment of leachate for Fe removal is necessary to avert major soil morphological changes with long-term spray irrigation.

716 **McCallister, D.L.,** 1982. Alteration of exchangeable cation distribution and associated chemical changes in acidifying surface mined soils. Diss. Abst. Int. Pt. B. Sci. & Engg. 42(7): 140.

Two mining areas of different ages, one mined in 1972 and the other in 1977, were sampled in June and July of 1978. Twenty-five 100 cm cores were taken from each area and subdivided into 10 cm segments. Material from each segment was analyzed for pH, SO_4-S, and total-S, while half the total of samples from each core were analyzed for CEC, base saturation percentage, and water extractable cations. General trends show lower pH, base saturation and total S in the 1972 minesoil, as well as higher SO_4-S and water extractable cations. The variability of the data is extremely high as indicated by the coefficients of variability, greater than 200% for some of the sulfur data. The effectiveness of the regression equation calculated to describe changes with depth and age is reduced by this variability, but the equations still suggest the presence of a weathered zone to the 20 cm depth in the 1977 minesoil.

717 **McGinnies, W.J., Nicholas, P.J.**, 1980. Effects of topsoil thickness and nitrogen fertilizer on the re-vegetation of coal mine spoils. J. Environ. Qual. 9: 681-685.

A field study was established at a coal mine site in northwest Colorado to measure the effects of 0-, 10-, 20-, 30-, and 46-cm depths of topsoil (a fine, montmorillonitic Typic Argiboroll) on establishment, per cent stand, and species composition of a seeded stand. A greenhouse study using topsoil and spoil from the same area evaluated the same topsoil depths with respect to their effects on herbage and root production of intermediate wheatgrass (*Agropyron intermedium*) and wheat (*Triticum destivum*). A 112 kg N/ha fertilizer treatment increased biomass (*herbage* and *roots*) of intermediate wheatgrass by 74% over similar unfertilized treatments. Yield of both crops increased linearly with increasing topsoil increases.

718 **McGrath, S.P., Lane, P.W.**, 1989. An explanation for the apparent losses of heavy metals in a long term field experiment with sewage sludge. Environl. Pollut. 60: 235-256.

Large losses of heavy metals applied to soil in metal contaminated sewage sludge have been reported. A two dimensional dispersion model (movement of soil due to cultivation) fitted well with the observed movements of metals during 1942 to 1961 and gave coefficients for movement of 0.24 and 0.31 m^2 per tillage operations in dimensions parallel or perpendicular to the direction of ploughing. respectively. The conc. measured in soils correlated with the predicted ways. The model was also used to estimate the proportion of the metal applied between 1942 to 1961 that remained in the 0.27 cm cultivated layer in 1985. About 80% accounted for detailed analysis of soil profile showed that $\simeq$1% of the metals applied had moved 3-5 cm below the plough layer or less; but there was no evidence of metals in deeper horizons down to 46 cm.

719 **Mcintyre, A.E., Lester, J.N.**, 1984. Occurrence and distribution of persistent organochlorine compounds in U.K. sewage sludges. Water Air Soil Pollut. 23: 397-415.

A total of 444 sewage sludge, samples from sewage treatment works in the U.K., were analysed for polychlorinated biphenyls (PCB) and the organochlorine insecticides r-Hexachlorhexane (r-HCH), aldrin, dieldrin and endrin. PCB, r-HCL and dieldrin were found to occur more frequently and at higher concentrations that aldrin and endrin. Three sewage treatment works were sampled at monthly intervals over an 18 months period. PCB, r-HCH and dieldrin were again the most frequently detected compounds. Concentrations of aldrin and endrin were only sporadically detected. The data acquired have been compared with the earlier results of similar work. The possible implications of the presence of persistent organochlorine compounds in sewage sludges which are disposed to the environments, are discussed.

720 **McLaughin, M.J., Champion, L.**, 1987. Sewage sludge as a phosphorus amendment for sesquloxic soils. Soil Sci. 143(2): 113-123.

Municipal sewage sludge and monocalcium phosphate (MCP) were applied to two soils-Griffin clay and Clovelly sandy clay loam at rates equivalent to 200, 500, and 10000 kg ha^{-1} P. Italian ryegrass (*Lolium multiflorum*) was grown in the soils using a split pot technique, and tops were harvested at 14, 35, 63, 97, 125, 153, 181, and 209 alter commencement of root soil contact. Yield and concentration of P, N, Ca, Mg, K and Na in the plant tissue were determined. Both soils exhibited responses to applied P, with P uptake from sludge treatments being significantly greater ($P < 0.05$) than MCP in one soil. In sludge treated soils rates of P uptake increased or decreased only slowly with increase of time. The relative efficiency of sludge P compared with MCP increased from 44 to 90% and over 64 to over 100% with time in the Clovelly and Griffin soils, respectively.

721 **McPherson, J.B.**, 1978. Land treatment of waste water at Werribee, past, present and future. Progress Water Technol. 11: 15-31.

Waste water from Melbourne Australia, has bee renovated by land treatment methods at the Board of Works Farm, Werribee, since 1897. Of the raw sewage, 30% of hydraulic loading and 75% of the BOD is contributed by tradewaste discharges, the balance coming from domestic sources. Average flow is 440 ML/d, BOD 570 mg/L and SS 620 mg/L. Land filtration, grass filtration, and lagooning are used for purifications depending on the season and the rate of flow. The soils and climatic conditions at Werribee favour land treatment methods for waste water renovation. The performance of the treatment system shows removal rates ≈ 95% BOD and SS. Nitrogen and P removal under grass filtration, the winter system is less effective than land filtration. The lagooning process is an efficient system for removal of BOD, N, and heavy metals. During the year 26% of flow is land filtered, 30% grass filtered, with 44% going through lagoons. The average seasonal operating hydraulic loadings grass imposed are 0.55 Ml/ha/d for land filtration and 0.18 ML/ha/d for grass filtration Analysis of herbage shows considerable increases in N, P and K, with very little increase in Ca and Mg levels. Heavy metals are within the acceptable range for most common grasses and legumes.

722 **McSweeney, G., Muller, F.B.,** 1979. Measurements of movement of some major plant nutrients through the New Zealand soil. Progress Water Technol. 11: 263-270.

Nutrient monitored in a series of experiments under field and glasshouse conditions indicate large movements of S and Ca to subsoil or subsurface water flows and much less of P and K. Preferential adsorption of P and K increases the mobility of the more loosely bound nutrients (S, Cl, Ca, Mg, Na). Movement of S can be reduced by granulation of the fertilizer or the use of elemental S.

723 **Mehra, M.C., Daigle, R.,** 1989. 2(p-iodopheny)-3-(p-nitrophenyl)-5-phenyl tetrazolium tetrakic (1-imidazoly) borate as a reagent for the determination of Ni, Zn, Co and Fe by flame atomic absorption spectrometry. Analyst, 114(8): 979-981.

The precipitated 2-(p-iodophenyl)-3-(p-nitrophenyl)-5-phenyl tetrazolium tetrakis between the respective chloride and sodium salts, was an excellent adsorbent for heavy metal ions in solution. A procedure is described for the in-situ solid-liquid chelate adsorptive separation and flame atomic obsorption spectometric determination of trace amounts of Ni, Zn, Co and Fe.

724 **Mehra, H.C., Frankenberger, W.T., Jr.,** 1989. Single-column ion-chromatographic determination of Cr (VI) in aqueous soil and sludge extracts. Talanta 36(9): 889-892.

Single column ion chromatography (SCIC) was investigated as a routine, rapid, precise and selective analytical method for the determination of Cr(VI) in aqueous extracts of soil and sludge. Chromatographic parameters were optimized for determination of Cr(VI), NO_3^- and SO_4^{2-}. The resolution between Cr(VI) and SO_4 was 2.8, the precision ranged from 0.9% for NO_3 to 2.0% for Cr. The SCIC results for Cr(VI) agreed closely with those obtained by inductively coupled argonplasma emission and spectrophotometry.

725 **Mehrotra, A., Mehrotra, I.T., Tandon, S.N.,** 1989. Speciation of copper and zinc in sewage sludge. Environ. Tech. Letters. 10(2): 195-200.

Species of Cu and zinc were identified in primary, secondary, digested and zinc spiked sewage sludges using a sequental extraction technique. Significant differences in the metal forms with the sludge type and zinc loading were not observed Correlation were found to exist between the major metal form and total metal present in each case.

726 **Mehrotra, R.C., Rai, A.K., Srivastava, V.S.,** 1989. Pollution status of soils beneath sewage disposal pond. Indian J. Environ. Health 31(4): 314-320.

Soil samples have been collected from sewage disposal pond (i.e. Jalmahal lake), Jaipur and their physico-chemical characteristics have been studied. The amount of total organic carbon (TOC) and its movements through the soil bed have also been determined.

727 **Meier, U.,** 1990. The cation exchange capacity as a basis for estimating the heavy metal migration in the soil. Acta Hydrochim Hydrobiol 19(1): 111-114.

The adsorption/desorption ratio is an important quantity of the displacement of heavy metals in the soil. Adsorption isotherms as control quantities are suitable for the development of a transport model, With the aid of the T value the sorption coefficients and distribution quotients can be determined for different soils. By two examples of summation the migration of Cd and Pb were calculated with soil samples of warp clay/gley and loam/parabrown earth. It was found inter all that with increasing time of input the concentration of dissolved a adsorbed heavy metals grows and that the added heavy metal ions are adsorbed in the uppermost layers already.

728 **Mekdaschi, R., Horiacher, D., Schulz, R., Marschner, H.,** 1988. Damage of trees along roadsides in Stuttgart by deicing agents and amelioration procedures. Angew. Bot. 62(5-6): 355-371.

An investigation of trees along roadsides in Stuttgart was undertaken to determine whether observed damage was due to the use of delcing agents. As the chloride concentrations of branches and leaves of linden trees (*Tillia* sp. and chestnut (*Aesculus* sp.) are highly correlated with the degree of leaf damage (chlorophyll content), the use of de-icing agents is regarded as the main reason for the damage to trees.

729 **Menser, H.A., Winant, W.M., Bennett, O.L., Lundberg, P.E.,** 1979. The utilisation of forage grasses for decontamination of spray-irrigated leachate from a municipal sanitary landfill. Environl. Pollut. 19(4): 249-260.

The lime (0.67t/ha), rock phosphate, and superphosphate (each at 11.2 t/ha) were applied in a randomized complete block design to reed canarygrass, tall fescue, orchardgrass, bromegrass, and bermudagrass. Leachate was applied by overhead rotary sprinklers in weekly 8-hr application for 6 months. The total application averaged 155 cm. Sprayed leachate contained 500 ppm of Ca, 150-200 ppm of Na, Fe, and Cl, 50-100 ppm of Mn, K, Mg, and N, 2-5 ppm of Al, Sr, Zn, P, and 0.5 ppm of Ni, Co, Cr, Cu, Pb, and Cd. COD decreased from 7,500 mg/L in water emerging from landfill drains to 5,000 mg/L in sprayed leachate. EC ranged from 3 to 4 mmhos/cm and pH from 5.3 to 5.5. Leachate irrigation appreciably increased Na, Fe, Mn, Cl, and S levels in all forages except orchardgrass. Lime significantly prevented Mn accumulation and benefitted forage grass persistence. Reed canarygrass generally contained the highest levels of most elements and along with Tufcote bermudagrass was more leachate-tolerant than other grasses. Seasonal factors affected the uptake of several elements, e.g. Na, Fe, Mn, Zn K, and Co were significantly lower in regrowth cuttings as compared with first cuttings of Midland bermudagrass and reed canarygrass. Superphosphate resulted in significantly higher Cl levels in forages. Heavy metal concentrations ranging from 0.1 to 0.3 ppm Cd. 1.0 to 1.5 ppm Ni and Cr, and < 1.0 ppm Pb and Co were below the toxicity limits for plants and animals.

730 **Merbach, W., Augustin, J., Mirus, E.,** 1990. Effect of aluminium on the legume-rhizobla-symbiosis. Zentralbl. Mikrobiol. 145(7): 521-527.

Alumium toxicity is an essential part of the harmfulness of low pH values on the legume-nodule-symbiosis, primary host damage, inhibition of infection and nodulation, restriction of nitrogenase activity, and immediate inhibition of rhizobia are supposed for causes. The importance of these single factors can vary in the individual case. An optimal supply with Ca and P as well as the selection of Al-tolerant lines of legumes and/or rhizobia are in consideration for corrective measures.

731 **Merkel, D.M., Hart, J.B. Jr., Nguyen, P.V., Carl, W.R.,** 1986. Municipal sludge fertilization on oak forests in Michigan: Estimation of long term growth responses in 'The Forest Alternative for Treatment and Utilization of Municipal and Industrial wastes'. Cole D.W. Herry C.L., Nutter W.L. (eds.): 292-300.

Relationship between mean annual increment (MAI) and total nitrogen and phosphorus contents in forest floor and 0 to 45 cm, soil samples were studied using regression methods. Twenty-nine forest stands were used with growths ranging from 1.19 to 4.26 m^3/ha per year. Nitrogen and phosphorus contents in the surface soil (A and E horizons), and nitrogen content in the fermentation and humus horizon (02), accounted for nearly 70% of the variation in MAI. Nutrient contents in surface soil and 02 layers from control and sludge fertilised plots were inserted in the regression equation. A 29% increase in growth (MAI) was predicted based on two year sludge effects on forest floor and soil nutrient contents. A three year, 44% increase in basal area growth was found using conventional fertiliser trial techniques on the same area. Long term responses of this magnitude would require that soil nutrient changes persist or can be maintained through treatment.

732 **Merry, R.M., Tiller, K.G., Alston, A.M.,** 1986. The effect of soil contribution with copper, lead and arsenic on the growth and composition of plant II. Effects of source of contamination, varying soil pH and prior waterlogging. Plant Soil. 95(2): 255-259.

The effects on radish (*Raphanus sativus*) and sugar beet (*Beta vulgaris*) were investigated in a greenhouse experiment with eight soils. The lead and copper concentration of the plants decreased with increasing soil pH, the effect being more marked in the more highly contamination soils. More Cu than Pb was translocated to the tops of the radish plants. Arsenic concentrations were less sensitive to changes in soil pH. Lower yields, lower copper concentrations in sugar beet and toxicity symptoms in some acid soil treatments were more likely to be due to Al and/or Mn than to excess Cu, Pb or As. Soils dosed with Cu, Pb and As did not always behave in the same manner as did soils contaminated with orchard sprays in the field and some toxic elements may be occluded in a mineral form that is not available to plants. The findings emphasize problems of interpretation of results obtained with freshly amended soils compared to soils contaminated in the field. Under some conditions in contaminated soils, DTPA extractions for Cu and Pb may be inappropriate, as the amounts extracted increased with increasing soil pH and plant uptake decreased.

733 **Merwe, C.G. Vander, Schoonbee, H.J., Pretorius, J.,** 1990. Observation on concentrations of the heavy metals zinc, manganese, nickel and iron in the water, in the sediments, two aquatic macrophytes (*Typha capensis* and *Arundo donax* L.) of a stream affected by goldmine and industrial effluents. Water SA. 16(2): 119-124.

Results show that with the exception of Fe, metal, deposition increased as the stream water flow because more alkaline and higher concs. of these metals were present in the tissues of both species *Adonex* and *T. capensis* which differed in their capacity to accumulate metals.

734 **Meshref, H., El-Arquan, M., Fawzi, I.,** 1989. Trace-elements in desert soils irrigated with Nile and waste water. Arid Soil Res. Rehab., 3(4): 405-416.

The present study was conducted to evaluate the status of trace elements (Cd, Cu, Fe, Mn, Ni, Pb, Zn) in soil and cultivated crops under a long-term irrigation with waste water and Nile water. The fractions of these elements extracted by ammonium acetate, DTPA, and ammonium oxalate were relatively higher in soil under irrigation with waste water than in that irrigated with Nile water. Generally, the amounts of DTPA-extractable Cd, Cu, Fe, Mn, Ni, Pb, and Zn in soils were below levels toxic to plants. The concentrations of trace elements in the tested fruits and juices of lemon and mandariti, bean seeds, and corn grain grown under continuous irrigation with waste water were below the standard critical levels of edible plant materials.

735 **Metson, A.J., Gibson, E.J., Hunt, J.L., Sauders, W.M.H.,** 1979. Seasonal variations in chemical composition of pasture. III. Silicon, aluminum, iron, zinc, copper and manganese. NewZealand J. Agril. Res. 22(2): 309.

Seasonal variations in the chemical composition of pastures, Si, Al, Fe, Zn, Cu, and Mn were determine in monthly sampling at 7 sites. Aluminum and Fe levels in grass and clover separates and Si in clover showed similar trends closely paralleling estimated soil contamination levels, with maximum levels during the period of lowest dry matter (DM) production in late winter. Uncorrected Si levels in grass were high throughout the year but corrected values showed a tendency to peak in summer. Of the trace elements, Zn showed high levels in "other species" (herbs) at the 1 site sampled, but grass and clover separates gave variable results with no clear seasonal trends. Low values were apparently associated with sites or periods of high DM production. Copper levels showed even less seasonal variation, but levels in clover were consistently a little higher than in grass. Manganese showed the greatest variability, seasonally and between sites. Similar seasonal trends in Mn levels wee observed in grass and clover separates, suggesting a soil effect on plant uptake; Mn in grass, but not in clover, was negatively correlated with topsoil pH. In general, the herbage analyses showed no evidence of deficiency of Zn, Cu, or Mn.

736 **Meyer, A., Chevallerie-Haaf, V., Dela, Henze, G.,** 1987. Determination of Zn, Cd, Pb and Cu in soils and sewage sludges by microprocessor-controlled voltammetry in comparison with atomic absorption spectrometry. Fresenius Zeitschrift fur Analytische Chemie 328(7): 565-568.

Zn, Cd, Pb and Cu can be determined in soils and sewage sludges by differential pulse polarography and differential pulse anodic stripping voltammetry. The use of a computer controlled polarograph allows simultaneous determination of these metals in one digestion solution unlike flame atomic absorption spectrometry.

737 **Miles, L.J., Parker, G.R.,** 1979. Heavy metal interaction for Andropogon scoparius and Rudbechin hirte grown on soil from urban and rural sites with heavy metals additions. J. Environ. Qual. 8(4): 443-449.

Little bluestem (*A. scoparius*) and black-eyed susan (*R. hirta*) were grown in 2 soils with all combinations of Cd, Zn, Pb, and Cu at 2 levels each for 12 wk. Germination and establishment were completely retarded by the addition of 2,000 μg/g Zn as zinc chloride. Neither Cd nor Cu additions affected germination. There was a slight decrease in germination for Pb additions of 900 μg/g. Cadmium at 10- and 20-μg/g addition rates did not affect top or root dry weight. Lead and Cu addition reduced shoot and root by weight yields of A. scoparius. Metal additions to the urban site soil did not reduce yields to the extent they did on the rural site soil. DTPA extraction levels of heavy metals were not well correlated to plant concentrations for comparisons between the 2 soils. DTPA soil extraction may not be acceptable for metal availability comparisons among soils of differing pH. Synergistic and antagonistic effects among the heavy metals were of a low level, no consistent response could be determined over species or soils.

738 **Miller, J.E., Hassett, J.J., Koeppe, D.E.,** 1977. Interactions of lead and cadmium on metal uptake and growth of corn plants, J. Environ. Qual. 6(1): 18-20.

Short term plant accumulation and growth effects of Pb and Cd added to soil separately and in combination were investigated with corn grown in a loamy sand under greenhouse conditions. A tendency for soil Pb to increase both the plant Cd concentration and the total Cd uptake of the corn shoots was observed. Conversely, soil Cd reduced the total Pb uptake and in some cases the lead concentration in the corn shoots. Both Pb (125 and 250 µg/g soil) and Cd (2.5 and 5 µg/g soil) reduced the vegetative growth of the corn shoots, and a positive interaction of the two metals on growth was noted.

739 **Miller, R.W., Honaryar, S.O., Hunsaker, B.,** 1980. Effects of drilling fluids on soils and plants: I. Individual fluid components. J. Environ. Qual. 9(4): 547-552.

The effects of 31 drilling fluid (drilling mud) components on the growth of green beans and sweet corn were evaluated in greenhouse studies. Yield was reduced of each crop.

740 **Miller, E., Joseph, Harsett, John, J., Koeppe, D.E.,** 1976. Uptake of cadmium by soybean as influenced by soil cation exchange capacity, pH, and available phosphorus. J. Environ. Qual. 5 (2): 157-160.

The accumulation of cadimum and its affect on vegetative growth of soybean in soils with a range in Cation exchange capacity, pH and available phosphorus were investigated in greenhouse experiments. Cadmium uptake decreased as soil pH and CEC increased while increasing available soil P was related to increased Cd accumulation. Cadmium extracted from the soil by Bray P_1 reagent, Bray P_2 reagent, 2N $MgC1_2$, and 0.01N EDTA was significantly correlated with plant Cd concentrations. The growth of the soybean shoots was generally depressed when tissue concentration reached. 3-5 µg/g dry wt. Cadmium uptake by soybean was correlated with the ratio of added Cd to the Cd sorptive capacity soil.

741 **Miller, W.P., Martens, D.C., Zelazny, L.W.,** 1987. Short-term transformations of copper in copper-amended soils. J. Environ. Qual. 16: 176-181.

Copper was added to three soils in the laboratory at a rate of 48 mg Cu kg^{-1} either as CuSO, or a swine manure (equivalent to) 100 Mg manure ha^{-1} containing 1060 mg Cu kg^{-1}). A sequential extraction methodology was used to determine types of soil-Cu association in samples taken 1, 4, 12 and 29 d after Cu additions to moist soils. Copper added as high-Cu manure substantially increased water-extractable Cu in all soils through the entire incubation period, while $CuSO_4$ additions resulted in higher exchangeable Cu levels through the days 4 to 12. Most of Cu added in both forms was recovered in "specifically adsorbed" forms, with 20 to 25 mg $CuSO_4$-Cu kg^{-1} being Pb extractable and 15 to 20 mg manure-Cu kg^{-1} being acetic acid-extractable. Significant amounts of Cu were also associated with soil organic matter ($K_4P_2O_7$ - extractable), more so when the Cu was added as high-Cu manure (10-15 mg Cu kg^{-1}) than as $CuSO_4$ (5 mg kg^{-1}). Some additional added Cu was associated with Mn oxides and noncrystalline Feoxides after 12 d of incubation, particularly in two soils containing higher amounts of these oxides.

742 **Miller, R.W., Pesaran, P.,** 1980. Effects of drilling fluids on soils and plants: II. Complete drilling fluid mixtures. J. Environ. Qual., 9 (4): 552-556.

Six typical drilling fluids (muds) and a drilling fluid base were mixed with six soils at ratios of 1:1 and 1:4 volumes of liquid mud/soil; these mixtures were tested for their effects on plant growth. Green beans (*Phaeolus vulgaris*) and sweet corn (*Zea mays.*) in pots in the greenhouse grew normally in a few mixtures but in most instances plants had reduced growth when compared to those growing in soil alone. High levels of soluble salts or ESP were the primary causes of reduced plant growth.

743 **Mineart, P., Salhotra, A.,** 1989. A sub-surface contaminant transport model for exposure assessment from land fills. Proc. Annual Madison Waste Conf. 12: 266-281.

Coupled unsaturated and saturated zone model was developed to estimate the amount of leachate generated from a land fill; simulate its flow and transport in the unsaturated and unconfined aquifer; and to quantify the effect of parameter uncertainty on model outputs.

744 **Mineyev, V.G., Kochetavkin, A.V., Nguyen, Van, B.,** 1990. Use of natural zeolites to prevent heavy metal pollution of soils and plants. Sov. Soil Sci. 22(7): 72-79.

Application of zeolites to pots already treated with heavy metals (Zn, Pb and Cd) decreased concentration of mobile zinc in the soil but did not significantly alter concentration of acid-soluble Cd and Pb. Lead, cadmium and especially zinc decreased the yield of barley grain. Addition of zeolite along with NPK fertilizers had a considerable effect on yield of barley but did not decrease the adverse effect of heavy metals. Accumulation of heavy metals in the above ground plant material and grain of barley and in the strawberries and cherries as well as the effect of zeolite, varied with plant species, levels of heavy elements in the soil and the degree of cultivation of the dermo-pod zolic soil.

745 **Mingelgrin, U., Biggar, J.W.,** 1986. Copper species in aqueous sewage sludge extract. Water Air Soil Pollut. 28: 351-359.

The Cu in the saturation extract of dried Davis sewage sludge was mainly in a complexed form. The adsorption coefficient for the complexed Cu on Yolo silt loam was 4 while for Cu added as $CuSO_4$ it was 90L kg^{-1} at relevant Cu concentrations in solution. Six fractions of positive, negative and neutral charge were isolated. The portion of Cu in the sludge which was water soluble increased significantly upon drying. The large percentage of complexed Cu and its relatively low adsorption on soil suggested that sewage sludge may, under certain conditions be a source of Cu contamination of plant systems and in extreme cases, of ground-water.

746 **Mirsatari, S.G., McChesney, M.M., Craigmill, A.C., Winterlin, W.L., Sieber, J.N.,** 1987. Anaerobic microbial dechlorination: an approach to on-site treatment of toxaphene contaminated soil. J. Environ. Sci. Health. 22(6): 663-690.

Enhanced microbial degradation of toxaphene by natural microorganisms occurred in soil and sediment amended with organic matter kept under anaerobic (flooded) conditions. Laboratory experiments yielded a dissipation half-life of approximately 3 and 1 week for soil and sediment, respectively, containing 10 ppm of technical toxaphene and a 1% alfalfa meal amendment. Dissipation was accompanied by an increase in early eluting peaks, indicating that dechlorination had occurred. Enhanced anaerobic dissipation also took place in soil containing 500 ppm of toxaphene, although a lesser rate than at 10 ppm, and when cotton gin waste was used as amendment in place of alfalfa meal. Sediment in a toxaphene contaminated pesticide waste disposal ditch was amended with 10% steer manure and flooded to ascertain field utility of the technique for on-site decontamination. Toxaphene residues were reduced from 63 to 23 ppm in 120 days, and some degradation activity still occurred up to 8 months after this single treatment.

747 **Mishra, G.P.,** 1990. Effects of industrial discharge on agricultural crops along the penalization gradient at ACC Kymore. Environ. Ecol. 8(1): 38-42.

The impact of industrial discharges on yield and other states of mature standing agricultural crops was studied. The crops were affected by way of soil and water pollution through biogeochemical cycling and the direct contact of exposed wastes from the cement works. The penalization index was recorded maximum (0.52122) and significant differences were found in the various crops along the penalization gradient.

748 **Mishra, L.C., Shukla, K.N.,** 1986. Elemental composition of corn and soybean crown on fly ash amended soil. Environl. Pollut. (Biochem. Phys.); 12(4): 313-321.

Corn and soybean were grown on sandy loam alluvial soil amended with fly ash at rates upto 25% by weight. Plant analysis data for 7 elements showed enhanced adsorption of B, Cu, Mn and Zn with increasing rates of fly ash applications. Phosphorus, potassium and calcium concentrations in the two crop were not affected by fly ash application.

749 **Mitchell, G.A., Bingham, F.T., Page, A.L.,** 1978. Yield and metal composition of lettuce and wheat grown on soils amended with sewage sludge enriched with cadmium, copper, nickel and zinc. J. Environ. Qual. 7(2): 165-171.

Lettuce and wheat were grown under greenhouse conditions on an acid and a calcareous soil amended with sewage sludge enriched with Cd, Cu,

Ni, or Zn to determine relative toxicities of the metals and uptake characteristics to the test plants. While the order of toxicities was not the same for all soil and plant species combinations, Cd, was in general most toxic followed by Ni, Cu and Zn. The latter three metals were about equally toxic to wheat grown in the calcareous soils; in the acid soil Cu was about four times and Ni about six-times more toxic to wheat than was Zn. Yield results indicated strong soils and plant species effects. Nickel was more phytotoxic to lettuce and wheat grown in the acid than in the calcareous soil whereas Cd, Ni, Zn toxicity dependent on plant species and metal concentrations range. At relatively low soi' 'reatments, Cu and Cd were more toxic to lettuce grown in the calcareous than in the acid soil. Both DTPA and water soluble metal concentrations were significantly correlated with metal uptake by plants. Water soluble concentrations of Cd, Cu and Ni better predicted plant uptake of these metals while Zn uptake was more closely correlated with DTPA soluble Zn.

750 **Mitchell, M.J., Hornor, S.G., Abrams, B.L.,** 1980. Decomposition of sewage sludge in drying beds and the potential role of the earthworm, Eisenia foetida. J. Environ. Qual. 9(3): 373-378.

Decomposition of sewage sludge in drying beds at Ley Creek (LC) and Meadowbrook Limestone (MB) Waste water Treatment facilities in Syracuse, New York, was monitored. LC and MB beds were from an anaerobically digested, primary sludge and an aerobically digested, activated sludge, respectively. Fluxes of O_2, CH_4 and CO_2 showed that at LC aerobic and anaerobic decomposition, and photosynthesis occurred constantly due to high moisture. At MB, both total decomposition rate and percentage of anaerobic decomposition (as indexed by CH_4, evolution vs. O_2 consumption,) decreased with time and were inversely related to sludge moisture content. Oxygen consumption rates, when standardized to 15°C, ranged from 10 to 80 µL/g dry wt. for both LC and MB sludge. Aerobic and anaerobic bacteria were abundant colonly-forming units/g dry wt), and dominant bacteria was not enteric. Nematode densities ranged from 7 to 814 individuals/g dry wt. A. computer simulation model on the role of macroinvertebrates in decomposition was used to analyze the direct effect of the earthworm, Esenia foetida. This oligochaete, introduced into onehalf of the MB cylinders accelerated decomposition and decreased the proportion of anaerobic decomposition if the sludge was 375% moisture dry wt and 40% anaerobic decomposition. This stimulation was also reflected in increased nematode density.

751 **Mitoff, S.D., Lewis, B.A.G.,** 1987. Phosphate fertilization of pyritic waste: Foliar versus ground application to soybean plants. Reclam. Reveg. Res. 6(2): 95-108.

Soybeans were grown on a P-fixing coal-cleaning waste and on an agricultural soil in an outdoor pot experiment to compare the effectiveness of foliar applications of P and application of P to the growth medium. The soil and waste were each limed to pH 6.5, fertilized with N and K and enough orthophosphate to make 20 p.p.m. extractable P. Three fertilizer treatments were compared: 0.4% P foliar sprays, 0.2% P foliar sprays (P supplied as ammonium pyrophosphate) and an additional 80 p.p.m. P (as orthophosphate) to the growth media. Plants were sampled three times throughout the growing season to determine yield and extent of nodulation. Plants from the second harvest (during podfill) were analysed for nutrient status.

752 **Mocking, M.B., Hocking, D., Smyth, T.A.,** 1980. Fluoride distribution and dispersion processes about an industrial point source in a forested coastal zone. Water Air Soil Pollut. 14: 133-157.

This preliminary survey comprises a collection of fluoride concentration data for air, water, soil, vegetation and marine samples.

753 **Modak, D.P., Singh, K.P., Ahmad, J., Ray, P.K.,** 1990. Trace metal ions in Ganga water systems. Chemosphere. 21(1-2) : 275-87.

Results indicate that Ganga river at Uluberia annually transports 0.00005 million tons (mt) of As, and Cd, 0.015, mt Cr, 0.007 mt Cu, 4.1, mt, Fe, 0.014 mt Pb; 0.056 mt Mn; 0.005 mt Ni and 0.014 mt of Zn. The quantity of trace metals depend upon the weathering of rocks and minerals, soil erosion, industrial activity and influxes from various tributaries. Most of the metals were highest during the peak flow. Trace metal composition of river Ganga is comparable to that of Rhine and less than the Amazon and the Mississippi.

754 **Mohapatra, A., Das, P.K., Panigrahi, A.K.,** 1990. Effect of mercury contained solid waste on the pigment content of a mulberry plant. J. Environ. Biol. 11(4): 355-363.

Changes in the pigment content of a mulberry plant exposed to solid waste of a chlor-alkali industry was reported. Initial appearance of brown patches followed by total browning of the leaf lead to fall of all leaves in the exposed plant. Drastic but significant decline in pigment contents in exposed plants were observed at higher concentrations of the solid waste and at prolonged exposure periods. However, an initial increases in the parameters wee also recorded.

755 **Mohapatra, P.K., Patnaik, L.N., Misra, G.,** 1990. Pollution due to textile industry — a case study. Asian Environ. 12(3): 57-66.

The quality of effluent from a textile mill at Choudwar that is discharged outside the factory premises, its potential effects on the surrounding agricultural field and ultimately on a small natural water stream that is used as a final refuse of the effluent, have been investigated. It is observed that the effluent quality which does not meet the prescribed standards with respect to several physicochemical parameters does eventually adversely affect the water quality of the stream rendering the downstream water unsuitable for drinking, irrigation and fish culture.

Some mitigating measures have been suggested.

756 **Moir, A.M., Thornton, I.,** 1989. Load and cadmium in urban allotment and garden soils and vegetables in the United Kingdom. Environl. Chem. Health. 11(3-4): 113-119.

In cities of England intake of Pb and Cd by carrots, lettuces spinach, broccoli, cabbages and parsmips was studied in plots in 94 gardens and allotments. The geometric means of Pb and Cd concentrations for the soil (n=94) were 217 μg. g^{-1} (varying from 27 to 1676 μg g^{-1}) and 0.53 μg g^{-1} (< .2 - to 5.9 μg g^{-1}), respectively. Compared with agricultural soils, the garden and allotment soils contained high level of Pb, but not of Cd. Pb concentrations in the vegetables ranged from < . 25 to 10.4 μg g^{-1} DW. Pb concentrations were higher than reported background levels although < 1% of the vegetables excessed the statutory limit for saleable food in U.K. (1 μg g^{-1} FW).

757 **Moller, C, Lepschv, J., Suss, A., Wurzinger, A.,** 1990. Atmospheric depositions in agroecosystems. Preliminary results of the Bavarian soil monitoring programme. Ver. Devt. Land. Unter. Und. Fors. Reihe Kongr. 32: 147-152.

Bulk precipitation deposition of N, S, Cl, Pb, Cd, Cr, Cu, Ni, Zn, Fe, Mn, P, K, Ca, Mg and Na was measured in 132 agricultural sites throughout Bavaria, Germany, since 1985 using the Bergerhoft method. The N input averaged 21 kg/ha annually, while 12 kg/ha SO_4-S were deposited per year. Heavy metal pollution was small in rural areas.

758 **Molnaa, B.A., Grubbs, R.B.,** 1989. Bioremediation of petroleum contaminated soils using a microbial consortia as inoculum, Aqua Water Internatl. 2(7): 26-35.

Bioremediation is an attractive alternative for cleaning up soil systems contaminated with petroleum and other hydrocarbons. A process was developed in which a consortia of microorganisms is introduced into the soil system to facilitate the bioremediation process and ensure consistency of results. Techniques to enhance the activity of the organisms and thus ensure the success of such programme are described. Several successful projects are described.

759 **Monn, L.,** 1989. Heavy metal leaching from catchment under different forests at the Schonbuch nature resource near Tubingen (FRG). Mitt. des Deutschen. Bodenk. Gesell 59(1): 429-432.

Most of the heavy metal leaching from plateau regions occurred by lateral movement as a result of soil water content exceeding field capacity. Heavy metals were transported with sediments in the low lands.

760 **Moore, J.N., Luoma, S.N.,** 1990. Hazardous wastes from large scale metal extraction: A case study. Environ. Sci. Technol. 24(9): 1278-1285.

The difficulties posed by large scale metal extraction are considered in terms of whether contamination of soil, air and water threatens ecological and human health. Waste associated with mineral extraction has been characterised as primary, secondary or tertiary contamination and the problems of remedial action on such waste is discussed.

761 **Moore, R.S., Taylor, D.H., Reddy, M.M.M., Sturman, L.S.,** 1982. Absorption of reovirus by minerals and soils. Appl. Environl. Microbiol. 44(4): 852-859.

Adsorption of (S) methionine-labeled reovirus by 30 dry soils, minerals, and finely ground rocks suspended in synthetic freshwater at pH 7 was investigated to determine the conditions necessary for optimum virus removal during land application of waste waters. All of the minerals and soils studied were excellent adsorbents of reovirus, with greater than 99% of the virus adsorbed after 1 h at 4°C. Thereafter, virus remaining in suspension was significantly inactivated, and within 24 h a three to five log reduction in titer occurred. The presence of divalent cations, i.e., Ca^{2+} and Mg^{2+} in synthetic freshwater enhanced removal, whereas soluble organic matter decreased the amount of virus adsorbed in secondary effluent. The amount of virus adsorbed by these substrates was inversely correlated with the amount of organic matter capacity to adsorb cationic polyelectrolyte, and electrophorptic mobility. Thus, adsorption of polyelectrolyte may be useful in predicting the fate of viruses during land application of sewage effluents and sludges.

762 **Moorhead, K.K., Graetz, D.A., Reddy, K.R.,** 1987. Decomposition of fresh and anaerobically digested plant biomass in soil. J. Environ. Qual., 16: 25-28.

Using water hyacinth for waste water revonation, produces biomass that must be disposed of. This biomass may be anaerobically digested to produce CH_4, or added to soil directly as an amendment. Fresh and anaerobically digested water hyacinth biomass, with either low or high N tissue content, were added to soil. Decomposition was evaluated by CO_2 evolution and N mineralization. After 90 days, approximately 20% of the added C of the digested sludges had evolved as CO_2 compared to 39 and 50% of the added C of the fresh plant biomass with a low and high N content, respectively. First-order kinetics were used to describe decomposition stages. Mineralization of organic ^{15}N to $^{15}NO_3$-N accounted for 8% of applied N for both digested sludges at 90 d. Nitrogen mineralisation accounted for 3 and 33% of the applied organic N for fresh plant biomass with a low and high N content, respectively.

763 **Moorhead, K.K., Reddy, K.R., Graetz, D.A,** 1988. Nitrogen transformations in a water hyacinth-based water treatment system J. Environ. Qual. 17: 71-76.

Fate of added $^{15}NH_4$-N and $^{15}NO_3$-N in water hyacinth waste water treatment system was evaluated under controlled conditions. Labelled ^{15}N uptake by waterhyacinth ranged from 57 to 72% of added $^{15}NO_3$-N and

70 to 89% for added $^{15}NH_4$-N. Both sediment and detritus were potential sources of N for water hyacinth. Water hyacinths cultured in sewage effluent removed 55% of the added NH_4-N and 14% of the added $^{15}NO_3$-N, respectively. Three to 44% added $^{15}NH_4$-N was lost through nitrification in the water column and subsequent denitrification in the underlying sediments, whereas 24 to 86% of the added $^{15}NO_3$-N was lost through denitrification. In a system without plants, 13 to 89% of the added NH_4-N and 48 to 96% of the added $^{15}NO_3$-N were lost from the system through a combination of nitrification, denitrification and ammonia volatilization.

764 **Morel, J.L.; Mench, M.; Guckert, A.,** 1987, Heavy metal dynamics in the rhizosphere: Role of root exudates. Rev. Ecol. Biol. Soc., 24(3): 485-492.

Interactions between root exudates and heavy metals have been studied using corn exudates produced from sterile hydroponic and field cultures. Equilibrium dialysis and potentiometric titrations showed that root exudates bind metals to an extent that depends on the ligand and the metal involved.

765 **Morishita, T.,** 1981. Watarase River basin: Contamination of the environment with copper discharged from Ashio mine. in 'Heavy Metals in Soils of Japan' Japan Sci. Soc. Press. Tokyo: 165-179.

The environmental pollution in the Watarase River basin caused by the mining activity of the Ashio Mine has held a symbolic position at every site during the rapid advance of mining and industrial activity in this century. Large number of the inhabitants in the vast area of the Watarase River basin have continued to suffer from the damage to agricultural crop yields and probably to animal or human health.

766 **Morishita, T.,** 1981. Jinzu River basin: Contamination of soil and paddy rice with cadmium discharged from Kamioka mine. in 'Heavy Metals in the Soils of Japan', Japan Sci. Soc. Press, Tokyo: 107-124.

Cadmium pollution problems in the Jinzu River basin have very important meaning, because the patients are certified as being victims of Itai-itai disease under the Relief Law and the Compensation Law only in this area. Meanwhile, there are also some characteristic peculiarities in the features of Cd pollution of soil and rice-plant systems. Empirical observations have proved, there is more frequent production of Cd-polluted rice in this basin. Further, a great deal of attention has been paid, because the area of polluted arable land and to protect improved soil from repollution. Fortunately, such more data on these problems from investigations has been accumulated for the Jinzu River basin area than for other polluted areas in Japan.

767 **Mortvedt, J.J.,** 1987. Cadmium levels in soils and plants from some long-term soil fertility experiments in the U.S.A. J. Environ. Qual. 16:

137-142.

Soil and plant tissue samples from nine long-term (> 50 yr) soil fertility experiments in the USA were analysed for Cd, P and other elements. Annual Cd rates were from 0.3 to 1.2 g ha^{-1}. Plant tissues analysed were corn, soybean and wheat leaves or grain, and timothy forage. Results have shown that plant uptake of Cd contaminants in P fertilizers containing < 10 mg Cd kg^{-1} is negligible. Adding Cd to soils as a contaminant in P fertilizers at rates from 0.3 to 1.2 g Cd ha^{-1} does not appear to result in increased Cd levels in plants.

768 **Mortvedt, J.J., Mays, D.A., Osborn, G.,** 1981. Uptake by wheat of cadmium and other heavy metal containments in phosphate fertilizers. J. Environ. Qual. 10 (2): 193-197.

A field experiment was conducted to determine uptake of Cd and other heavy metals by winter wheat from three diammonium phosphate (DAP) fertilizers containing 2.74 and 153 μg Cd/g. A phosphorus-deficient Paden silt loam (pH 4.7) was limed at two rates and treated with the DAP sources at a rate of 50 kg P/ha. Grain yields were higher at pH 5.9 than at pH 5.1, and were significantly increased by P applications and results were similar using all DAP sources. Concentrations of Cd in both grain and strain were significantly increased only with application of high Cd and DAP to the low lime soil. Cadmium concentrations in grain increased from 0.028 to 0.086 μg/g, and in straw from 0.067 to 0.118 μg/g (dry wt basis) with application of low Cd-DAP and high-Cd, DAP, respectively, and were lower on the high-lime soil. Concentrations of Cu, Mn, Ni and Zn in both grain and straw were not significantly affected by DAP sources. Results for a second year on the same plots limed to pH 5.8 and 7.0 and treated again with the same DAP sources were similar to those for the first year, except that heavy metal uptake was generally lower.

769 **Mosbaek, H., Tjell, J.C., Hovmand, M.F.,** 1989, Atmospheric lead input to agri-crops in Denmark. Chemosphere, 19: 1787-1799.

The plant uptake of lead from soil is reported for several edible crops species under field conditions using an isotopic dilution method. The species investigated acquire from soil 0.02-0.08 mg Pb/kg (drymatter). It is concluded that the remainder originates from the atmosphere. From the uptake determinations it is estimated that the soil supplies directly and indirectly only around 0.02 mg Pb/day per person in Denmark; the difference upto the daily intake (0.08 mg Pb/day per person) must come from the atmosphere, or other sources of contamination.

770 **Mueller, C.S., Thompson, R.L., Remelow, G.J., Beck, J.N., Langley, M.P., Young, J.C., Casserly, D.M.,** 1987. Distribution of Al, V, and Mn in lichens a cross Calcaslou Parish, Louisiana. Water Air Soil Pollut. 33: 155-164.

The lichen Ramalina stenospora was collected from 16 locations in Calcasieu Parish and from 2 locations in Cameron Parish in South-western Louisiana. The metals V, Mn, and Al were measured in lichen specimens collected during three seasons – fall 1983, winter and spring 1984. Vanadium was found to range in concentration from 2.1 to 10 mg kg^{-1}; and Al from 900 to 4500 mg kg^{-1}. Metal concentration was found to decrease exponentially with distance outward from the industrial corridor. The major industries included were an Al plant, two refineries and five chemical plants mostly related to plastics production.

771 **Mugwira, L.M.**, 1979. Residual effects of dairy cattle manure on millet and rye forage and soil properties. J. Environ. Qual. 8(2): 251-255.

Dairy cattle manure (0 to 270 t/ha dry wt.) was applied to a silty clay loam soil for 3 years (1971-1973). Pearl millet was grown in summer and clipped twice, and 'Wrens Abruzzi' rye Secale cereale was grown in winter. The residuals of 3 annual applications of 180 and 270 t/ha of manure were most effective in increasing millet and rye forage yields in 1974-1976 and total N and NO_3-N in 1974 and 1975. Phosphorus and, to some extent, Zn levels in millet were increased by the 22.5- and 45t/ha rates, leveling or decreasing at higher manure rates. The manure residuals increased the levels of K in 1974 and, generally, Mg in millet and K and Ca in rye and decreased Mn in millet add rye. Nitrogen limited plant growth in manured plots except at the 180- and 270-rates. At the higher rates there was significantly higher NO_3^-movement down the profile than the NPK check. Nitrogen mineralization from 3 consecutive annual manure applications of 22.5 t/ha was probably largely completed within the following 3 yr.

772 **Mulchi, C.L., Mastradone, P.J., Armbruster, J.A.**, 1990. Investigation of trace concentrations in crops and soils near a fossil-fuel power plant in Maryland. J. Air Waste Manage. Assoc. 40(2): 185-193.

Changes in atmospheric desposition rates for water soluble, Zn, Cu and Mn associated with a doubling of the generating capacity of a fossil fuel power station were compared with conc. of extractable metals in soils and in maize and soybean forage. 12 sites located at 1.6, 4.8 and 9.6 km were sampled monthly for 2 years before and after the expansion of generating capacity. Metal deposition decreased with distance. Significant differences in extractable Zn, Cu and Mn were observed between 12 sites and with distance. All sites combined, significantly higher levels of extractable Zn and Mn were found during post expansion mainly due to increase in acidity. Significant increases in foliar Cu and decrease in Mn in both crops from pre- to post expansion. Leaf Zn conc. declined in soybean but remained unchanged in maize after expansion. The increase in extractable Zn and Mn were associated with decrease in soil pH.

773 **Mulhern, D.W., Robel, R.J., Furness, J.C., Hensley, D.L.**, 1989. Vegetation of waste disposal areas at a coal-fired power plant in Kansas. J. Environ. Qual 18(3): 285-292.

Disposal of scrubber sludge and fly ash waste from coal-fired power plants is a costly problem for utilities. Current regulations call for the retired waste areas to be covered with topsoil, then seeded to produce a protective vegetative cap. We conducted field studies over a 3-yr period to determine if a vegetative cover could be established without first adding topsoil to waste sites. Seven herbaceous and six tree species were planted on scrubber sludge and bottom ash sites. These substrates were first amended with fertiliser, and then hay, woodchips, or cow (Bos taurus) manure. The bottom ash was not capable of supporting vegetative growth, even with amendment. Tall wheat grass tall fescue yellow sweet clover, and Japanese millet grew well on scrubber sludge, as did eastern cottonwood and eastern red cedar trees.

774 **Mulla, D.J., Page, A.L., Ganje, T.J.**, 1980. Cadmium accumulations and bioavailability in soils from long term phosphorus fertilisations. J. Environ. Qual. 9(3): 408-412.

Soils from citrus groves that had been fertilized with about 175 kg P/ha per year (as triple superphosphate TSP) over a 36 year period were analyzed for total Cd and Zn as well as water soluble P and Cd. Concentrations of total Cd in surface soil were highly correlated (r=0.89) with concentrations of total P. The concentration of Cd in surface soil receiving broadcast P for 36 years averaged 1.0 µg/g, and were considerably greater than those of controls which showed a mean concentrations of 0.07 µg/g. Phosphorus in soil saturation paste extracts ranged from 0.10 µg/mL (controls) to 8.87 µg/ml in P fertilised soils. Water soluble saturation extract Cd ranged from 0.008 µg/mL in controls to 0.017 µg/ml in fertilised soils and was not well correlated with water soluble P. Cadmium in barely grain and leaves grown in soil subject to long term heavy P fertilisation were not elevated above levels than on the control. Swiss chard was grown in the greenhouse on the above surface soils. Although Cd averaging 1.6 µg/g in plant tissue were significantly elevated than those on the control soil (0.26 µg/g); no yield depression was observed. Long term heavy application of TSP caused measurable increase in total Cd of surface soil; but the accumulated Cd burden per year was much lower than levels reported from application of sewage sludge. Cadmium accumulation in soils as a result of P fertilization seemed to be less available to swiss chard than Cd accumulations resulting from applications of sewage sludge.

775 **Mullen, M.D., Wolf, D.C., Ferries, F.G., Beveridge, T.J., Flemming, C.A., Bailey, G.W.**, 1989. Bacterial sorption of heavy metals. Appl. Environl. Microbiol. 55: 3143-3149.

Bacillus cerlus, B. subtills, Escherichia coli and *Pseudomonas aeruginosa* were examined for the ability to remove Ag, Cd, Cu and La from solution by equilibration methods. Cd and Cu sorption over the conc. of range (0.001 to 1 mM) was described by Freundlich isotherm. The affinity series for bacterial removal of these metals decreased in the order: Ag > La > Cu > Cd. These data show that bacterial cells are capable of binding large quantities of different metals. Adsorption equations may be useful for describing bacterium metal interactions with metals such as Cd and Cu. However, this approach may not be adequate when precipitation of metals occurs.

776 **Muntau, H., Croessmann, G., Schramel, P., Galiorint, M., Orvini E.**, 1987. Trace and nutrient element transfer from sewage sludge-amended soil to crop: A study on *Brassica Oleracea*. Fresenius'z, Anal. Chem, 326 (7): 634-635.

The cabbage, grown on sludge-amended soil was harvested and processed to a homogenous powder. The results of a preliminary test of homogeneity and a broad spectrum of element concentrations determined and reported. The soil around the plants was examined and estimates of uptake coefficients crop/soil are given.

777 **Muramoto, S., Nishizaki, H., Aoyama, I.**, 1990. The critical levels and maximum metal uptake for wheat and rice plants when applying metal oxides to soil. J. Environ. Health, Part B. (Pesti. Food Contam. and Agri. Wastes) 25: 273-280.

In pot experiments wheat and rice were grown in soil containing 0 to 10000 ppm, Cd, 1000 to 60,000 ppm Zn, 300 to 30000 ppm Pb; 100 ppm Cd + 500 ppm Zn or 1000 ppm Cd + 5000 ppm Zn. Cd reduced plant growth and yield parameters in both crops. Zn reduced wheat growth and grain yield where as 1000 ppm Zn increased rice grain yield and stem wt. although these were reduced at high conc. Pb reduced growth and yield of wheat but increased stem length and wt. and grain yield of rice at 10000 ppm. Wheat grain contained 141 μg/g at 10000 ppm soil conc. whereas rice contained 4.97 μg/g.

778 **Murdoch, A., Capobianco. J.A.**, 1979. Effects of treated effluent on a natural marsh. J. Water Pollut. Control Fed. 51(9): 2243-2256.

Long-term effects of poor-quality waste water treatment plant effluent on a natural marsh on the western shore of Lake Ontario were studied. The major contributor of N and P to the marsh area was the treatment plant discharge. Metal concentrations in the water were generally low. Increased concentrations of Pb, Cr, Zn, N, P, and organic C (300 μg/g, 90 μg/g, 210 μg/g, 2.34%, 1.10% and 0.87% of sediment dry weight, respectively) were found in the sediment vertical profile obtained from the marsh area. The shoot standing crop of the dominant plant species (*Glayceria grandis*) was associated with amounts of P, N and organic C in the sediments.

779 **Murillo, J.M., Hernandez, J.M., Barroso, M., Lopez, R.**, 1989. Production verses contamination in urban compost utilization. Annales de Edafologia Agro-Biologia. 48: 143-160.

Successive application of city waste compost increased yield of ryegrass, tomato and aubergine in the greenhouse. Available N, O.M. and CEC of top soil (0-22 cm) increased on applying 150 and 400t/ha compost. However, total and DTPA extractable heavy metals were also increased in this depth (0-10, 11-22 cm). Hence fertility is increased but increase of heavy metals is harmful.

780 **Murray, M.R., Baker, D.E.,** 1990. Monitoring and assessment of soil and forage molybdenum near an atmospheric source. Environl. Monit. Assess. 15(1): 24-33.

Forage and soil molybdenum (MO) were measured in the vicinity of a MO processing plant in Pennsylvania. Mo Conc. in red clover (*Trifolium pratense*) measured at 23 sites ranged from 1.1 to 56.6 mg/kg. 14 of the 23 samples had red clover plants with Mo Conc. over the thresh hold value of 6 mg/kg. Red clover Cu: Mo Conc. ratios were below the recommended ratio of 4 in 19 of the sites. The low, Cu: Mo ratio values along the high plant Mo Conc, indicates that there is a potential risk of Molybdenumsis in ruminant animals in this area. In acid digested (sorbed) soil, Mo conc. measured at 30 sites, ranged from 7 to 131 mg/kg. Using the Baker soil test (BST) extract, Mo conc. ranged from 0.01 to 3000 mg/kg. Regression equations were developed to predict plant uptake of soil Mo based on red clover soil extracts and soil pH date. R. squared values for predicting the plant uptake were 81.9% for the BST extract and 81.5% for the digestion extract plus soil pH.

781 **Murray, H.E., Beck, J.N.,** 1990. Concentration of synthetic organic chemicals in leachate from a Municipal land fill. Environl. Pollut. 67(3): 195-203.

A variety of potentially dangerous synthetic organic chemicals were recorded in the leachate from a Municipal land fill in Lousiana.

782 **Musgrove, S.D.,** 1989. The distribution of heavy metals in soil and metal uptake into vegetation at Beaum out Leys sewage Farm Leicester. Part II An assessment of the efficiency of remedial soil treatment. The weather brook respreading exercise. Part III. Analysis of cadmium, lead, and zinc in vegetables grown in a soil contaminated with sewage sludge, J. Assoc. Public Analysis 27(1): 1-33.

A former sewage farm has been developed into a residential area. Soil stripping and respreading has significantly lowered average contamination levels and reduced maximum metal levels. In vegetation grown in top soil previously contaminated with sewage sludge, the concentration of Zn, and Cd increased in parsnips but not in potatoes. Pb conc. did not exceed the statuary limit for Pb in food. However, lower metal conc. Can be expected in vegetables grown in local garden soils which generally contain < 3 mg/kg cadmium.

783 **Mutlak, S.M., Hamdi, M.A., Noup, N. Bakal, M.AL. Gazzaly, N. Ayar,** 1980. Sewage Farming in Iraq: A potential hazard for pollution. J. Environ. Qual. 9: 677-680.

A number of surface and subsurface soil and sewage samples were collected from a sewage irrigation farm near Baghdad and a bacteriological examination was made. The population of different bacteria progressively declined with time but the reduction in numbers was relatively greater in samples incubated at 37°C, than in those incubated at 10C. Salmonellae were detected after one week but disappeared thereafter. The potential hazard for pollution caused by sewage farming, as it practically threatens vegetables grown on the farms as well as ground and surface waters of the nearby area. Sewage farming may seriously affect the consumers. It is recommended that the conventional methods of treating the sewage effluents be adopted.

784 **Nag, P., Paul, A.K., Mukherji, S.,** 1989. The effects of heavy metals, Zn and Hg on the growth and biochemical constituents of mung bean (*Vigina radiate*) seedlings. Botanical Bull. Academica Sinica, Taiwan. 30(4) : 241-250.

Mungbean seeds were germinated for 48 hrs and then transferred to filter soaked in 10, 20 or 40 mM Zn SO_4 or 0.4, .6 or .8 mM $HgCl_2$ above or with 10^{-4} MGA or CAMP or 10 ppm kinetin. $ZnSo_4$ and $HgCl_2$ reduced seedling FW by 86-93% and 85-95%, respectively. GA_3 and CAMP reduced the growth inhibition except at the highest Zn and Hg Conc. Seedling respiration rate declined with increasing Zn and Hg.

785 **Naganawa, T., Kyuma, K., Yamamoto, H., Yamamoto, Y., Yokoi, H., Tatsuyama, K.,** 1989. Measurement of soil respiration in the field: Influence of temperature, moisture level, and application of sewage sludge compost and agrochemicals. Soil Sci. Plant Nutr. 35(4): 509-516.

Soil respiration data were obtained using a portable infrared gas analyzer by measuring the CO_2 concentration in a small chamber placed on the ground. The rate of respiration showed a geometrical mean of 11.4 ($mmol\text{-}h^{-1}\text{-}m^{-2}$) and ranged from almost 0 to about 80 ($mmol\ h^{-1}\ m^{-2}$) in the experimental field in the farm of Shimane University (103 plots, 1,081 data). The rate was stimulated strongly by the temperature (R^2 = 0.76) and weakly by the moisture level and input of organic matter. But the influence of agro-chemicals (standard and 5-fold dose of fenitrothion, chlorthalonil, and paraquat dichloride) was too small to be detected in the field.

786 **Nagele, D., Brunn, W.,** 1988. The improvement of chromium determination in soil extracts by means of atomic absorption spectroscopy. Zeitschrift fur flanzenernahrung und Bodenkimde, 15(1) : 55-56.

For nearly interference-free-detemination of Cr in soil analysis, a wavelength of 359.4 nm was recommended together with a blue air-acetylene flame which has a low fuel gas content or a N_2O/acetylene flame (approx. 5 cm high inner reduction zone).

787 **Namrata S., Pandey, G.S.,** 1991. Bio-degradation of some acid-dyes by sewage sludge. Indian J. Environ. Prot. 11(2) : 110-111.

The biodegradability of selected acid-dyes (methyl red, lissamine green, xylenol orange, phenol red, methyl thymol blue) by the sewage sludge has been investigated. Methyl red has been found to be most sensitive for biodegradation, followed by lissamine green, xylenol orange, phenol red and methyl thymol blue. The possibility of the removal of acid-dyes from contaminated effluents by using sewage sludge has been discussed.

788 **Nandy, T.N., Kaul, S.N., Pathe, P.P.,** 1988. Suspended growth systems a comparative study for treating municipal sewage. Indian J. Environ. Prot. 8(11) : 830-834.

A study was conducted on a laboratory scale to evaluate the feasibility of suspended growth system incorporating activated sludge and aerated lagoon for treating municipal sewage. The objective of this investigation was to compare the treatability performance of these two systems using the same municipal sewage and to determine the associated bio-kinetic parameters.

789 **Narasiah, K.S., Lemay, J.L.** 1986. Phosphorus removal from waste water using waste alum sludge from a water treatment plant. In 'Eastern Region Conference and of the Canadian Association on Water pollution Research and Control', Montreal (Canada), Nov. 1985: 6a, 6b.

In many water treatment plants, the alum sludge produced during coagulation-flucculation stage is wasted into the nearby stream or river. They contain however, high concentrations of aluminium and have a potential for reuse. The alum sludge from a filtration plant (60,000 m^3/d) is used to remove phosphorus in waste water effluent following secondary treatment. The efficiency of phosphorus removal is compared using pure alum solution one on hand and alum sludge on the other. The waste water treatment plant consists of aerated lagoons treating domestic wastes, having effluent total phosphorus concentration around 3 mg/L.

790 **Narwal, R.P., Bhandari, D.K., Mahendra Singh,** 1980. Chemical composition of sewage water in Haryana. Haryana Agric. Univ. J. Res. 10: 358-364.

Forty sewage water samples of 29 different cities of whole of Haryana State were analysed for pH, E C, N, P, K, S, B, Cl, CO_3 + HCO_3, Ca + Mg values. This was found to be a good source of nutrients like N, P, K, and S. The suitability of this water for irrigation, on the basis of RSC conductivity and SAR values was discussed and it was concluded that 40% of the total analysed samples did not require gypsum application while 5, 20 and 35% of the total samples required addition of 50 kg, 50 to 100 kg and > 100 kg gypsum/ha/irrigation, respectively.

791 **Narwal, R.P., Gupta, A.P., Singh, Anoop, Antil, R.S.,** 1990. Effect of FYM application on the growth and chemical composition of *methi (Trigonella Foenum Gracum)* plant grown in a polluted soil. Proc. Environ. Pollut.: 85-90.

A greenhouse experiment was conducted to study the effect of five levels of FYM (0, 0.25, 0.50, 1 and 2 per cent) on the growth and chemical composition of methi plants grown in an industrial effluent polluted soil collected from Sonepat. Increasing levels of FYM significantly increased dry matter yield of methi plant: concentration and uptake of macro- and micro-nutrients by plants and decreased toxic metals (Ni and Cd.) The methi plants contained Ni and Cd higher than those reported for plants grown on uncontaminated soils.

792 **Narwal, R.P., Gupta, A.P., Anoop Singh, Karwasra, P.S.,** 1990. Pollution potential of some sewage waters of Haryana. Proc. Environ. Pollut.: 121-126.

Analysis of sewer water samples collected from Faridabad, Ballabhgarh, Palwal, Gurgaon, Rohtak and Bahadurgarh revealed a wide variation in their physico-chemical characteristics (pH, EC, suspended soils, SAR, BOD), concentration of essential plant nutrients (N, P, K, Zn, Mn, Fe, Cu) and toxic metals (Pb, Ni, Cd). The Ballabhgarh water had lowest pH (1.1) and highest EC(34.0 dsm^{-1}), suspended solids (17000 mg L^{-1}), SAR (32.8) and BOD (768 mg L^{-1}) values. All the toxic metals were present both in insoluble and soluble phase in Ballabhgarh water. The variation in macro, micro and toxic elements concentration of sewer waters may be attributed to their sources of industrial effluents.

793 **Narwal, R.P., Mahendra Singh, Gupta, A.P.,** 1988. Effect of different sources of irrigation on the physico-chemical properties of soil. Indian J. Environ. Agri. 3: 27-34.

The changes in the physico-chemical properties of seven different profiles receiving irrigation through rain, dairy waste and sewer waters were studied at Military Farm, Ambala Cantt in Haryana. The results indicate that pH, EC, DTPA- and total Zn, Mn, Cu, Fe, Cd, Ni and Pb increased with the application of dairy waste and sewer waters. The increase in the above properties were more with sewer water application to that of dairy waste water application. The hydraulic conductivity of the soil decreased drastically with the application of dairy waste and sewer waters. Total Cd, Ni and Pb decreased with increasing soil depth in all the profiles studied.

794 **Nashikkar, V.J.,** 1989, Growth and uptake of nitrogen in wheat and maize grown on waste water effluents with varying BOD levels. Asian Environ. 11 : 44-76.

Wheat and maize were grown on domestic waste waters of varying BOD levels from 0 to 1000 mg/L. Irrigation with settled sewage having nitrogen concentration of 22-42 ppm and BOD about 150 mg/L, gave optimum results with respect to growth, yield and nitrogen uptake whereas irrigation with waste waters having higher levels of nitrogen tended to give relatively lower yields and uptake of nitrogen by both the crops.

795 **Nasu, Y., Kugimoto, M., Tanaka, O., Yanase, D.,** 1984. Physiological

toxicity of copper and cadmium to some plants. Proc. Tenth Symp. on Environmental Pollutants and Toxicology: p. 57.

The growth and multiplication rates of *Lemna* are extremely high compared with those of *Pharbitis* or *Triticum* seedling. The physiological changes accompanying the absorption of copper or cadmium, such as flowing and the inhibition of the frond multiplication of *Lemna* were not observed, in *Pharbitis* or *Triticum* seedlings, except for the inhibition of the lateral root formation by copper on *Pharbitis*. The absorption mechanism and made of of action of cadmium in plants seem to differ from those of copper.

796 **Navarre, J.L., Ronneau, C., Priest, P.,** 1980. Deposition of heavy elements Belgian agricultural soils. Water Air Soil Pollut. 14: 207-213.

A network of 19 rain gauges was set up over Belgium in agricultural zones. Determination of heavy metals content of water samples collected during 1 yr meteorological cycle allowed to estimate wet plus dry deposition rate of many toxic metals over the country. Soil contamination by deposition apparently contaminate through the use of chemical fertilizers.

797 **Ndiokwere, C.L.,** 1985. The dispersal of arsenic, chromium and copper from a wood treatment factory, and their effect on soil, vegetation and crops. J. Environl. Studies 24(3-4) : 231-234.

Substantial accumulations of As, Cr and Cu have been found in soil samples from a wood treatment factory, with average concentrations as high as 5312, 2552 and 2211 $\mu g\ g^{-1}$ for As, 3996, 2046 and 2005 $\mu g\ g^{-1}$ for Cr and 5424, 3460 and 3710 $\mu g\ g^{-1}$ for Cu at the solution mixing, treated wood storage and drainage sites, respectively. Average levels of 597 $\mu g\ g^{-1}$ As, 498 $\mu g\ g^{-1}$, 498 $\mu g\ g^{-1}$ Cr and 763 $\mu g\ g^{-1}$ Cu occurred at the sites within about 200 m of the factory. The metal levels in surface soils decreased significantly with distance from the treatment and storage sites. High levels of these metals were also found in vegetation as well as in vegetables and crops grown within the factory premises.

798 **Ndiokwere, C.L., Ezihe, C.A.,** 1990. The occurrence of heavy metals in the vicinity of industrial complex in Nigeria. Environl. International. 16(3): 291-295.

A high accumulation of Cd, Cr, Cu, Ni and Zn in soils, crops and plants as a result of industrial activities were observed from sites close to industrial emission sources and the levels decreased with distance away from the sources. Soil and crop contamination by the metals was generally higher in steel complex than the refinery. Cadmium and lead levels were particularly high in all the samples from both complexes.

799 **Neachamp, E.G., Soon, Y.K. Moyer, J.R.** 1979. Nitrate production from chemically treated sewage sludges in Soil. J. Environ. Qual. 8(4): 557-560.

Chemicals such as $Ca(OH)_2$, $Al_2(SO_4)_3$ and $FeCl_3$ are used to precipitate and prevent phosphorus from escaping in effluents from sewage plants. Since such chemicals affect the characteristics of anaerobically digested sludge, incubation experiments were conducted to determine if the nitrate production in soil treated with these sludges was also affected. Nitrate production of six anaerobically digested sewage sludges differed considerably when incubated with soil but not in a manner related to the chemical treatment of the sewage. Reduced nitrate production from whole sludge from one source was possibly attributable to relatively high lipid and petroleum hydrocarbons contents. With the exception of their sludge, 17 to 30% of the sludge N was nitrified in 16 weeks under laboratory conditions. Nitrate production lag periods of 2 weeks or more were observed with whole sludges. The lag period if present, when reconstituted sludges (ammonium and soluble organic N removed) were incubated with soil was 1 week with the exception of one sludge which probably had high lipid and petroleum hydrocarbon contents. Incubation of reconstituted sludges in soil resulted in 29 to 32% nitrification of the organic N during the first 16 weeks. Nitrate production was relatively rapid in the early part of the 49-week incubation period but slowed substantially later.

800 **Neelam, Sahai, R.,** 1985. Effect of fertiliser factory effluent on seed germination and growth behaviour of Vigna radiata. Environ. Ecol. 3(3) : 307-311.

In pulse crop Vigna radiata Linn, percentage germination and speed of germination index of seeds increased with increase in the effluent concentration up to 2.5 per cent. But the root and shoot lengths, pigment content, plant biomass and net primary productivity, and seed output increased up to 50 per cent effluent. Carotenoid content and soluble nitrogen were maximum at 30 per cent effluent, protein content of seed was maximum at 15 per cent effluent.

801 **Neera Singh, Wahid, P.A., Murty, M.V.R., Sethunathan, N.,** 1990. Sorption desorption of methyl parathion, fenitrothion and carbofuran in soils. J. Environ. Sci. Health. Part. B-25: 713-728.

Sorption/desorption of methyl parathion fenitrothion and carbofuran in four soils was studied. Organic matter was the most important single factor affecting the sorption/desorption of all the three insecticides. Freundlich K and specific organic sorption (Kom) of the three insecticides in a given soil distinctly varied, apparently due to the differences in their octanol water partition coefficient (KOW). Carbofuran with lowest Kow among the three insecticides was sorbed least. All the three insecticides desorbed less with increasing organic matter content of the soil.

802 **Neili, P.E.O., Jackson, T.J.** 1990. Observed effects of soil organic matter content on the microwave emissivity of soils. Remote Sens. Environ. 31(3): 175-182.

In order to determine the significance of organic matter content on the microwave emissivity of soils when emissating soil moisture, a series of field experiments were conducted in which 1.4 GHz micro-wave emissivity data were collected over test plots of sandy loam soil with different organic matter levels (1.8% 4.0% and 6.1%) for a range of soil moisture values. Analyses of the observed data showed only minor variation in microwave emissivity due to a change in organic matter content at a given moisture level for soil with similar texture and structure. Predictions of microwave emissivity made using a dielectric model for aggregated soils exhibited the same trends and type of response as the measured data when adjusted values for the input parameters were utilized.

803 **Nelson, P.O., Chung, A.K., Hudson, M.C.,** 1981, Factors affecting the fate of heavy metals in the activated sludge process. J. Water Pollut. Control Fed. 53(8) : 1323-1333.

Important factors that control the fate of heavy metals in the activated sludge process were studied in laboratory. Activated sludge bacteria were cultured on a soluble waste water substrate under constant growth rate conditions, whereas important inorganic or organic complexing ligands in the solution phase were either measured or estimated. An equilibrium chemical model incorporating conditional adsorption constants was successfully used to predict the distribution of metals between soluble chemical species and "Surface complexes". Biological solids retention time (0) and systems pH are factors that could be used to control the distribution of metals between solution and solid phases.

804 **Nemetz, P.N., Drechsler, H.D.,** 1978. The role of effluent monitoring in environmental control. Water Air Soil. Pollut. 10 : 477-497.

Composite sampling systems fail to provide the two key types of information required for effective environmental control: (i) a high representational accuracy of the effluent profile; and (ii) the detection of environmental consequences. In light of these conclusions, the authors make several recommendations concerning current and alternative sampling regimes.

805 **Neuhauser, E.F., Hartenstein, R.,** 1980. Efficiencies of extractants used in analyses of heavy metals in sludges. J. Environ. Qual. 9(1): 21-22.

A comparison of extractability was made for three solvents commonly used in estimating availability of heavy metals in soils to plants. Small, intermediate and large amounts of heavy metals were removed, respectively from an anaerobic digest of a sewage sludge with 2.5% actic acid, 0.1 NHCl. and 1.0 NHCl, respectively, with 10, 20, 30 and 40 mL HCl per gm sludge, approximately the same amount of each heavy metal was extracted during 1 hour of shaking, while for 0.1 NHCl and 2.5% actic acid increasing amounts were extracted at 10, 20, and 30 mL/gm, with somewhat higher or lower amounts being obtained at a ratio of 40 ml extractant per gm sludge. With 0.1 NHCl, an extraction period of 0.5 hour appeared to be suboptimal while periods longer than 1 hour did not yield significantly greater extractability except for Cd, extracted for 3 hours. Extraction of Ni for 5 hours and Pb for 5 or 7 hours resulted in significantly less metal than was obtained at 1 hour. Since it is highly likely that availability of heavy metals to plant will depend on numerous variables, it is proposed that until such factors are resolved, a standard extraction procedure be used by all workers on sludges and soils for comparisons of published data.

806 **Neuhauser, E.F., Malecki, M.R., Cukic, Z.V.,** 1985. Metal content of earthworms in sludge-amended soils; Uptake and loss. NTIS, Springfield, VA (USA): 7.

The study describes the content of five metals (Cd, Cu, Ni, Pb, and Zn) in one earthworks species, *Alloloobophora tuberculata,* as a function of varying soil metal concentration in the same soil type and the ability of the earthworms to bioconcentrate the five metals. The rate of uptake of the five metals in earthworms with initially low concentrations of metals placed in a soil with high metal concentrations was evaluated for a 112 days period. The rate of loss of the five metals in earthworms with initially high metal concentrations placed on soil with low metal concentrations was also examined.

807 **Ngugen, P.V., Hart, J.B., Jr., Merkel, D.M.,** 1986. Municipal sludge fertilization on oak forests in Michigan : Short term nutrient changes and growth responses in 'The Forest Alternative for Treatment and Utilization of Municipal and Industrial Wastes', Cole D.W., Herry C.L. and Nutter, W.L. (eds.): 282-291.

A research and demonstration project was initiated in 1981 in northern Michigan to explore the potential use of municipal water on forest lands. The forest stand was an upland mixed oak type with read oak (*Quercus cubra* L.), white oak (*O. alba* L.) and red maple (*Ace rubrum* L.). Sludge was applied on three 1.5 ha plots at the rate of 8 Mg dry solids/ha to provide 400 kg/ha of nitrogen from a liquid anaerobic source. Early results indicate the following responses : (1) There has been no tree mortality due to sludge application. (2) Tree growth was increased by sludge over a three year period: a significant increase of 63% in diameter growth over the control was observed for all species combined; basal area growth of all species combined exhibited a significant 44% increase over the control; a differential species response also occurred for diameter growth. (3) There were no effects on sapling diameter and basal area growth. (4) A large portion of the nonsoluble nutrients applied remained in the forest floor two years after applications. (5) There were no differences in chemical properties of surface and subsurface soils two years after sludge application. (6) Nitrate-N concentration in soil leachate increased five months after treatment, but the peak concentration was less than 3 mg and decreased to background level within one year after sludge application.

808 **Nichols, O.G., Michaelsen, D.V.** 1986. Successional trends in bauxite mine sites rehabilitated using three topsoil return techniques. For. Ecol. Manage. 14(3): 163-175.

In this study, successional trends of understory vegetation in 6-7 year-old bauxite minesites, revegetated using three topsoil return techniques, were examined. At ages 4 years and 7 years, the double stripping technique produced a vegetation community most similar in species composition to an unmined forest control. For all three topsoil return techniques there were no consistent trends in species richness or diversity from year 4 to year 7. This was indicted that both fresh topsoil return and seeding are important techniques for introducing a species which do not readily colonise mine stites.

809 **Nickless, G., Roberts, D.J., Kahokola, K.V.,** 1989. The use of experiment design and response surface in study of the influence of copper, arsenic and chromium on Lolium perenne seedings. Chemosphere, 19(12) : 1981-1987.

The effects of Cu, As and Cr on Lolium perenne seedlings were studied.

810 **Nikitin, A.P. Spirina, A.G.,** 1990. Protection of waters from pollution by fertilizer and pesticides by means of forest stands. Water Resource, 16(6) : 611-616.

Data on concentrations of N, P and K and of pesticide (herbicides and insecticides) residues in runoff, meltwater and sediment from farmland in the Volga forest-steppe are reviewed. The influence of plantation and natural stands on water quality is discussed. A method is proposed for calculating the area of protection forest necessary to purify runoff for various uses e.g. drinking water or irrigation.

811 **Nirmala, Devi, J., Janardhan, K.,** 1988. Effect of Sough India Viscose factory effluent on seed generation, seedling growth and chloroplast pigments content in five varieties of maize. Madras Agric J. 75 : 41-47.

An attempt is made to understand the effect of different concentrations of South India Viscose factory effluent on seed germination and seedling growth, parameters have shown an inverse relationship with increase in concentration of the effluent. Likewise, increasing concentrations of the effluent correspondingly decreased the fresh and dry weights of the treated seedlings.

812 **Nishizono, H., Kubota, K., Suzuki, S., Ishii, F.,** 1989. Accumulation of heavy metals in cell walls of *Polygonum cuspidatum* roots from metalliferous habitats. Plant Cell Physiol., 30(4): 595-598.

The distribution and accumulation of Cu^{2+}, Zn^{2+} and Cd^{2+} and ferrous and non-metalliferous habitats, were examined. About 90% of the metal ions was located in the cell wall fraction of roots of plants grown in either type of habitat. The metal-ion exchange capacity of the cell walls is not specific to the plants from metalliferous habitats, and there were no significant differences among plants from the various habitats. The capacity for Cu^{2+} ions was greater than that for Zn^{2+} or Cd^{2+} ions. Cu^{2+} ions have a high affinity for the cell wall and, thus, it appears that the cell wall is a barrier for the transportation of Cu^{2+} into the cytoplasm.

813 **Nriagu, J.O.,** 1980. Global cadmium cycle, In "Cadmium in Environment", Pt. 1: Ecological Cycling. John Wiley & Sons, New York: 1-11.

A tentative model of the global cadmium cycle is constructed. Such a model can be useful in identifying and evaluating any perturbations in the global cadmium systems attributable to cultural activities. The phenomenological model described here provides some relative measures of both the quantities of cadmium in the global systems and the importance of the various transport pathways in the cadmium cycle.

814 **Nurse, G.R.,** 1980. Denitrification with methanol : Microbiology and biochemistry. Water Res. 14(5): 531-537.

Denitrifiction with methanol results in a selective enrichment for bacterial belonging to the genus Hyphomicrobium. Based on current available biochemical knowledge of NO_3 reduction and assimilation, methanol oxidation and assimilation and the energy and requirement for these reactions, it is theoretically possible to develop an equation which describes the stiochiometry of denitrifiction with methanol.

815 **Nyangababo, J.T., Ichikuni, M.,** 1986. The use of cedar bark in the study of heavy metal contamination in the Nagatsuts area, Japan. Environl. Pollut. 11(3) : 211-229.

Analysis of cedar bark samples and deposition samples in the Nagatsuts area, Yokohama, Japan, shows that there is contamination by heavy metals, (Cr, Zn, Cu and Pb) as indicted by enrichment factor values, particularly in the parts adjacent to the highway. It is suggested that motor traffic is the major source. The soil is enriched with respect to these heavy metals by a factor of 2 to 361. It is suggested that this contamination occurs primarily by aerial deposition. A correlation between heavy metals levels and distance from the road was established and a power regression analysis, In Y = a + B In X, gave a fit (P = 0.001) indicating an exponential decay function.

916 **Obukhov, A.I., Lepneva, O.M.,** 1990. Biochemistry of heavy metals in urban environment. Sov. Soil Sci. 22 : 44-53.

The average values of heavy metals in grass strip soils of Moscow were 60, 230, 80 and 0.7 mg/kg for Pb, Zn, Cu, and Cd, respectively exceeding typical values of dermopodzolic soils in suburban park by 4 to 6 times. Despite of high heavy metals content in soils and leaves of apples trees from grass strips along high ways, heavy metal levels in fruit did not exceed acceptable concentrations.

817 **O'Connor, M.B.,** 1979. Yield and chemical composition of lucerne on a pumice soil as affected by regular application of secondary treated sewage effluent. Progress Water Technol. 11(6) : 427-432.

Pumice derived soils are physically well suited to the application of secondary effluent. At an application of 85 mm every 2 wk, lucerne (*Medicago sativa*) production was enhanced by 11% annum. Much of the effect was an irrigation response, but nutrient applications in the secondary effluent were considered more than adequate for crop requirements. The lack of response to applied nutrients could be attributed to the adequate previous fertilizer history of the site. Lucerne has two disadvantages for secondary effluent disposal poor winter growth leads to poor nutrient recovery, particularly of N and the spread of lucerne diseases such as bacterial wilt can be a problem. In this trial, plant number on effluent plots were reduced by 37% in 18 mo due to disease.

818 **O'Connor, G.A., Chaney, R.L., Ryan, J.A.,** 1991. Bioavailability to plants of sludge borne toxic organics. Rev. Environl. Contam. Toxicol. 121 : 129-156.

Various aspects of toxic organics as their content in sludges, plant uptake and volatilization have been reviewed extensively. Aromatic surfactants and their effects on plant metabolism are also discussed.

819 **O' Connor, O.A., Dewan, R., Goluzzi, P., Young, L.Y.,** 1990. Land fill leachate: A study of its anaerobic mineralisation and toxicity to methanogenesis. Archives Environl. Contam. Toxicol. 19(11): 143-147.

Results of two anaeboric bio-assays indicated that leachate conc. > 10% produced a significantly irreversible suppression of methanogenesis while conc. < 10% showed enhanced methane production above background levels.

820 **O'Connor, G.A., Kiehl, D., Eiceman, G.A., Ryan, J.A.,** 1990. Plant uptake of sludge borne PCB's. J. Environ. Qual. 19 : 113-118.

In a pot experiment, carrots and lettuce were grown in clay loam and sandy loam soils. In one experiment sewage sludge containing 52 μg polychlorinated biphenyls/kg was added to give 0, 0.5, 1.0 and 2.5 μg polychlorinated biphenyls/kg soil. Across all treatments and in all species poly-chlorinated biphenyls content was below the detection limit (20 μg/kg) except in carrot peels which reached a bioconcentration factor of 3.

821 **O'Connor, G.A., Knudtsen, K.L., Connell, G.A.,** 1986. Phosphorus solubility in sludge-amended calcareous soils. J. Environ. Qual. 15(3) : 308-312.

Sludge additions to calcareous soils increased water soluble and $NaHCO_3$-extractable P as well as plant uptake of P, whereas inorganic fertilizer P has often been ineffectual. Both greenhouse and field data, representing several croppings of amended soils were examined. Ancillary effects, primarily slight pH reductions, associated with sludge additions to the soils were apparently responsible for increased P solubility in amended soils.

822 **Odier, E., Janin, G., Monties, B.,** 1981, Pollar lignin decomposition by gram-negative aerobic bacteria. Appl. Environl. Microbiol., 41(2): 337-341.

Eleven gram-negative aerobic bacteria (Pseudomonadaceae and Neisseriaceae) out of 122 soil isolates were selected for their ability to assimilate poplar dioxane lignin without a cosubstrate. Dioxane lignin and milled wood lignin degradation rates ranged between 20 and 40% of initial content after 7 days in mineral medium, as determined by a loss of absorbance at 280 nm; 10 strains could degrade in situ lignin, as evidenced by the decrease of the acetyl bromide lignin content of microtome wood sections. No degradation of wood polysaccharides was detected. Lignin biodegradation by Pseudomonas 106 was confirmed by $^{14}CO_2$ release from labeled poplar wood, although in lower yields compared with results obtained through chemical analysis based on acetyl bromide residual lignin determination.

823 **Ogata, M., Kenmotsu, K., Hirota, N., Naito, M.,** 1981. Relationship between uptake of mercury vapor by mushrooms and its catalase activity. Bull. Environl. Contam. Toxicol., 27: 816-820.

This communication deals with the uptake of mercury vapor by mushroom (shitake) artificially grown on an oak tree and the uptake in vitro by catalase extracts prepared from mushroom, Hay bacillus and spinach.

824 **Ogawa, T., Usui, M., Yatome, C., Idaka. E.,** 1989. Influence of chromium compounds on microbial growth and nucleic acid synthesis. Bull. Environl. Contam. Toxicol. 43(2): 254-260.

The influence of $K_2Cr_2O_7$ and $CrCl_3$ on cell growth and nucleic acid content of microorganisms was measured with respect to the biological treatment of waste waters from the dying tanning industries. Both compounds inhibited DNA synthesis. This resulted in an increased generation span and decreased in cell division. A greater effect was produced by $K_2Cr_2O_7$ than by $CrCl_3$. The inhibitive factors of DNA synthesis may be grouped into two categories: (1) the interaction between the chromium compounds and DNA, (2) the inhibition of the DNA polymerase activity by the chromium compounds. The former, estimated by the measurement of the melting temperature of DNA and the equilibrium dialysis, was not responsible for inhibition of DNA synthesis. As chromium compounds and dyes co-exist often in the waste waters of the dyeing industries the effects of the mixed solution were measured. In the $K_2\ Cr_2O_7$-acid dye solution the formation ionic complex with $Cr_2O_7^{2-}$ and the dye cation seemed to mitigate the adverse effect of chromium.

825 **Okieimen, F.E., Okundaye, J.N.,** 1989. Removal of cadmium and copper ions from aqueous solutions with thiolated maize cob meal. Biol. Waste 30(3) : 225-230.

The sorption behaviours of cadmium and copper ions on maize cob metal modified by the incorporation of thiol groups was examined at 29C. The removal of the metal ions from solution by the thiolated material was markedly higher than the removal by the unmodified meal and Cd (II) ions were sorbed to a greater extent than Cu. The sorption data fitted the Langmuir isotherm equation, and saturation constants A, for sorption on thiolated maize cob meal of 4.53 mmol g^{-1} and 4.89 mmol g^{-1} were predicted for cadmium and copper ions, respectively. A rate equation based on the concept of linear driving force fitted the sorption rate data well, and gave a value of about 0.05 min^{-1} for the particle diffusion control rate coefficient for the sorption of the meal ions on thiolated meal.

826 **Okuno, I.A., Whitehead, J.A., Higgins, W.H., Savarie, P.J.,** 1979. A gas chromatographic method for determining residues of sodium cyanide in vegetation and soil. Bull. Environl. Contam. Toxicol. 22(3): 386-390.

Sodium cyanide was sprinkled directly by hand onto randomly selected 1. ft^2 plots of vegetation or soil. Each of 30 plots received 0.88 g. Soil samples were taken from 1 d to 67 wk after application, but vegetation sampling was discontinued after 2 d because the samples showed no residues. Residues in soil dropped rapidly within 2 d after application, but apparently leveled off. Levels of 0.5-6 ppm were found after 2 wk, and 0.1-0.6 ppm were found after 6 wk.

827 **Oleszkiewics, J.A., Sparking, A.B.,** 1987. Agricultural wastes. J. Water Pollut. Control Fed. 59(6) : 450-454.

The treatment and disposal of agricultural wastes are reviewed under sections on: 1) waste characterisation; 2) anaerobic treatment; 3) lagoons; 4) recovery and use; 5) miscellaneous treatment methods; 6) transport of slurries; 7) odour and land disposal.

828 **Olson, B.H. Hill, D.C., Rigby, M.C.,** 1983. Statewide evaluation of trace element accumulation from long term disposal of waste water. NTIS, Springfield: 133.

Twenty reuse sampling sites were selected on the basis of the following criteria: length of time the site has received water water, amount and manner of application, quality of waste water applied, and the availability of historical data on trace element content in waste water effluent. Both soil and vegetation samples were analyzed for Cd, Cu, Pb, Ni and Zn content. Results indicated that 9% of the fields investigated showed an accumulation of trace elements from reuse practices. Metal enrichment was confined to the upper layers of soil, but penetration into the soil column depending on soil type and rate of waste water application.

829 **Onianwa, P.C.,** 1988. Monitoring regional gradients in atmospheric heavy metal pollution : A comparative application of top-soil epiphytic moss and plant litter as indicators. Environl. Monit. Assess. 11 : 25-31.

Heavy metal levels in top soils, plant litter and mosses from uninhabited and polluted zones were compared. Though there was no correlation between different materials, metal concs. were higher in all indicator materials in zones of higher pollution. Highest concs. of metals were found in mosses within the lower and higher pollution zones. Pollution gradients were more visible in soils and plants.

830 **Onianwa, P.C., Ajayi, S.O., Osibanjo, O., Egunyomi, A.,** 1986. Accumulation patterns of heavy metals in forest mosses from the south-west region of Nigeria. Environl. Pollut., 12(1) : 67-78.

The accumulated levels of the metals, Pb, Cd, Cu, Ni, Zn, Mn, and Fe were determined in forest mosses from south-west Nigeria. Distinct gradients were observed only with Pb and Zn, and a small zone of contamination with Cu was identified in parts of the east and the south-east. This contamination was possibly a result of the use of copper-based fungicides and pesticides in cocoa farms in the area.

831 **Opydo, J.,** 1989. The determination of Zn, Cd, Pb and Cu in soil extracts by anodic striping voltametry. Water Air Soil Pollut. 45 : 43-48.

Simultaneous determination of Zn, Cd, Pb and Cu in soil extract by d, c anodic stripping voltammetry is described. These results are compared with those obtained by using other methods. The accuracy and precision of the presented methods are satisfactory. Iron, Al and Ti concentration of 1120, 5400 and 480 $\mu g\ g^{-1}$, respectively, do not present measurement difficulties.

832 **Otero, L., Ortega, S.F., Garcia, I.,** 1987. Influence of nickel industry effluents upon the drainage of water when applied to calcareous soils. Ciencias dela Agricultura 30: 102-145.

Application of nickel industry effluents (Moa liquor) to saline and non-saline calcareous soils in doses equivalent to 60 and 120 t/ha, did not significantly increase the trace element levels in drainage water from a 15 cm column.

833 **Ottolenghi, A.C., Kamparian, V.V.,** 1987. Multilayer study of sludge application of farm land; Prevalence of bacterial enteric pathogenic and antibody status of farm families. Appl. Environl. Microbiol., 53(5): 1118-1124.

The experience with the isolation of salmonellae from sewage sludge from four treatment plants of Ohio is described. Over 3 years, the authors isolated salmonellae 50 times from 311 sludge samples. Most isolations were made after enrichment in Selenite broth. The largest proportions of isolations came from the plant serving the population of columbus — a large metropolitan area. A significantly greater number of isolations from these plants were made during the first quarter of the year. Twenty-one different serotypes were isolated, alongwith five untypable strains. The most frequently isolated serotype was Salmonellal infantis. Five of the strains were multiple resistant to antibiotics. The authors also describe the prevalence of antibodies to salmonellae in members of the families residing on the farms in the study. It was found that antibodies to group C salmonellae predominated.

834 **Outridge. P.M., Hutchinson, T.C.,** 1990. Effects of Cadmium on integration and resource allocation in the *clonal fern Salvinia molesta.* Occologia. 84(2) : 215-223.

In clonal plants exposed to pollution, elements which are physiologically integrated may be less fit than ramels which are independent, it (a) translocation of toxins from contaminated ramels produced toxicity, or (b) toxicity in parent ramets reduced the degree of nutritional support to otherwise non-exposed daughters. These hypotheses were tested in the aquatic fern Salvinia molesta exposed to cadmium. Pre-treatment of parent ramel with cadmium decreased the number and biomass of daughter subsequently produced in a cadmium-free medium, because of reduced parental support of the first daughter generation. Second generation and later daughters were unaffected.

835 **Outridges, P.M., Noller, B.N.,** 1991. Accumulation of toxic trace element by fresh water vascular plants. Rev. Environl. Contam. Toxicol. 121: 1-66.

Various aspects of accumulation of trace elements and heavy metals by fresh water vascular plants have been reviewed including content in plants, physiological factors affecting element accumulation, food chain complications and toxicity of elements to vascular plants.

836 **Overman, A.R., Wolfe, D.W.,** 1986. Overland flow treatment of waste water at Florida State Prison. J. Water Pollut. Control Fed. 58(9) : 903-910.

The overland flow process is a proven waste water treatment technology. As more overland flow systems are brought into service, increasing amounts of performance data are becoming available. This information can be used to improve design and operation procedures. Treatment performance of the Florida State Prison overland flow system was monitored for 2 years. The system receives secondary effluent and consistently removes approximately 90% of 5-day bio-chemical oxygen (BOD_5) and total suspended solids (TSS). Operational and field management procedures were evaluated. The effects of season and plant upsets on treatment efficiency are discussed.

837 **Page, A.L., Bingham, F.T.,** 1981. Re-utilization of municipal waste water sludges-heavy metals and nitrate. J. Water Pollut Control Fed. 53 : 237-245.

Analysis of land application-related chemical characteristics of waste water shows that nitrogen and/or heavy metals are most likely to limit excessive usage of the sludges. In sludged soils heavy metals may accumulates through repeated applications to levels that may become phytotoxic. Even before detrimental effects to plants can be detected, elevated concentrations in the plant tissue may expose consumer to potentially hazardous trace metal element. Sludge-soil-plant interactions in a crop-land disposal system are discussed.

838 **Palazzo, A.J., Jenkins, T.F.,** 1979. Land application of waste water : Effect on soil and plant potassium. J. Environ. Qual. 8(3) : 309-312.

The removal of K by a forage grass mixture from soil that received applications of waste water over a 5-,r period was examined. The forages, which received waste water at a rate of 5.0 cm/wk, were grown on either Windsor sandy loam or Charlton silt loam soil. The waste water annually supplied from 231 to 433 kg/ha of N and 36 to 153 kg/ha of K. Plant removal of K increased as the amount of N applied or removed by the forage increased. During the initial 4 yr of the study, plant uptake of K exceeded the amount supplied by the waste water causing reduction in plant and soil concentrations of this element to low levels. Concentrations of K remained low in the soil solution and tended to decline with time. The inadequate supply of K was related to the low K/N ratio in the waste water applied. During the fifth year, K fertilization increased total plan yields and the concentration of this element in plants and soils to more nearly optimum levels. Since excessive K applications may also cause problems in plant or animal nutrition, total applications of K (waste water and fertilizer) should be adjusted to »90% of the amount of N expected to be removed by the crop.

839 **Pallah, B.S., Mittal, V.K., Sahota, H.S.** 1991. Correlations among trace elements and chemical parameters. Indian J. Environ. Prot. 11(2) : 124-128.

Twenty seven trace elements were detected and quantized whereas nine chemical parameters were measured in ground-water. All the 17 correlations among trace elements were observed to be positive. Only europium and bicarbonates showed a negative correlation ($r = -0.68$). Out of these correlations, in 9 cases the correlation co-efficient is highly significant, ($r \geq 0.7$).

840 **Palmer, C.D., With-brodt, R.P., Fish, W.,** 1990. Chromium mineral phase at a highly contaminated hard chrome plating site. EOS, Trans. Am. Geophys. Union. 71: (36) : 1068.

Chromium contamination of soils, ground-water and surface water at Conrvalis, Oregan, USA, is described. Cr. (VI) levels in a shallow aquifer at the site are 19 g/L; and 10mg/L in the ground-water of the lower aquifer. Cr (III) hydroxide precipitation with in streams increases the role of redox chemistry in Cr movement.

841 **Pandey, R.A., Animesh Kumar,** 1990. Heavy metals in coal carbonization waste water and their complexion-some observations. Water Air Soil Pollut. 50 : 31-50.

Effluents from low temperature carbonization, (LTC), high temperature carbonization and producer gas plants contain heavy metals. Phenols and organic bases present in the effluent can form organometallic complexes with metal ions present. Such complexes are of environmental significance being toxic, mutagenic and teratogenic in nature. Results show that LTC waste water forms complexes with Fe, Cu, and Co, however it does not form any complex with Mn and Zn.

842 **Pandey, D.D., Simba, A.K.,** 1990. Effect of cement kiln dust on chlorophyll in maize leaf. Geobios, 17(1) ; 40-41.

Effect of cement kiln dust on chlorophyll in maize leaf have been studied. The concentration of chlorophylls *a, b* and total chlorophyll in unit fresh weight in polluted leaves was always less than those in the controlled maize plants. In both control and polluted plants, the amount of chlorophyll *a* continued to increase with age till the plants were 60 days old and concentrations were 1.66 and 1.33 mg/g fresh leaf and similar results were also obtained in the case of chlorophyll *b*.

843 **Pandey, D.D., Sinha, C.S.,** 1991. Impact of coal dust pollution on grain characteristics of maize. Environl. Ecol. 9(2): 553-554.

Zea mays cultivated in the vicinity of coal field area of Dhanbad district of Bihar especially Jharia coal field was selected to know the response of grain characteristics of maize, number of grains per cob, weight and volume of 1,00 grains, moisture, protein, total ash, fat, crude fiber, total carbonhydrates, iron, phosphorus, calcium and calorific value to coal dust pollution. All characteristics of the polluted grains showed lower values compared to control except for carbohydrates, iron, phosphorus and calcium.

844 **Pandey, D.D., Verma, N.K.,** 1990. Impact of coal dust pollution on species composition, life-forms, biological spectrum and importance value index of grassland ecosystems of Bihar. Environl. Ecol. 8(3) : 959-964.

The study area was confined to the grassiands situated in the coal field area of Dhanbad district of the Bihar especially Jharia coal field dominated by *Aristida cyanantha* L. to know the effect of coal dust pollution on species composition, life, forms, biological spectrum and importance value index of grassland ecosystems of that area. The control grassland was away from the coal field area where the dust load was zero treated as control grassland. The species composition of control grassland was 19, 14 and 10 and 35, 27 and 21 on polluted grasslands in rainy, winter and summer seasons, respectively. The life forms class indicated a therohemi-cyptophytic flora on both types of grasslands. The chamaephyte hemicryptophyte and therophyte were more in polluted grassland compared to control grasslands. The percentage of therophyte was 3.64 and 4.40 control and polluted grasslands, respectively as compared to Raunklaer's normal spectrum.

845 **Pantelis, G., Ritchie, A.I.M.,** 1991. Macroscopic transport mechanisms as a rate-limiting factor in dump leaching of pyritic ores. Appl. Math. Model. 15(3) : 136-143.

The oxidation of mining heaps containing pyrite is modelled as coupling of macroscopic particle reaction kinetics. A numerical model is developed incorporating oxygen and heat transport based on the two major mechanisms of convection and diffusion. The authors examined separately the oxidation of single particles compared these rates with that of an entire heap to establish the rate limitation imposed by macroscopic transport.

846 **Papadopoulos, I., Stylianou, Y.,** 1988. Trickle irrigation of cotton with treated sewage effluent. J. Environ. Qual. 17:574-580.

The objectives of this 3 years field study, were to assess the effect of applying treated municipal effluent (ECw = 246 dsm^{-1} SAR 12.0) by trickle irrigation on soil N fertility, soil salinity and yield of cotton. Secondary treated effluent with 30 mg L^{-1} was compared with borehole water. Both waters were supplemented with 0, 30 60 and 90 mg NL^{-1}. The residual soil NO_3-N and NO_3-N concentrations in laminase and petoioles were in general greater in the effluent-irrigated crops. With both waters, excessive salt buildrup occured at the periphery of the wetting front. SAR was reduced beneath the dripper in the surface 15 and 30 cm depth with borehole water and effluent respectively. But below this depth the reverse occurred. Under the conditions effluent was generally superior to borehole water, particularly at the lower N levels in increasing yields. The seed cotton yield obtained in the first season was significantly greater in the effluent irrig. ted treatments supplemented with N upto 60 mg L^{-1}; in 1985 and 1986 seasons yield with treated effluent was significantly higher in comparison with borehole water.

847 **Parsons, J.D.,** 1977. Effects of acid mine wastes on aquatic ecosystems. Water Air Soil Pollut. 7: 333-354.

The Cedar Creek Basin was studied for the period June 1952 through August 1954 to observe the effects of both continous and periodic acid effluent flows on aquatic communities. The acid strip-mine effluent contained ferric and ferrous Fe, Cu, Pb, Zn , Al, Mg, titratable acid and elevated H ion concentration, and was toxic to many of the aquatic organisms. In the areas of Cedar Greek, subjected to continous acid flow, plants tonic and benthic species had become adopted to the severe conditions and varied in abundance and diversity. No fishes were observed in continous acid effluents area. Downstream, where periodic mineral acid conditions changed drastically during an excessive effluent flow, planktonic and benthic communities had high diversity but low density. The populations of fishes were variable in this stream reach. Physical, chemical and biological conditions of acid lakes formed by surface mining were reviewed. In addition to apparent physical and chemical differences in lakes, due in part to variable solar absorbance due to suspended oxides of Fe, chemical variability related to organic composition was reviewed. It is quite probable that degradation of such lakes can be reversed.

848 **Pascual, A., Riaza, A., Salgot, M., Cardos, J.,** 1986. Nutrient balance when treated waste waters are applied to lysimeters. in 'Corrosion in the Ambient Environment', J.M. Costa, P.L. Cabot, (eds.). Universitate De Barcelona, Barcelona (Spain): 257-262.

The authors describe the fate and balance of phosphorus and potassium contained in treated waste water and tap water when are applied to undisturbed soil cores with *Lolium perenne* contained in lysimeters. Relationships among treated waste water/soil/plant are discussed.

849 **Patel, C.B., Pandey, G.S.,** 1986. Alkalinization of soil through thermal power plant fly ash fallout. Sci. Total Environ., 57: 67-72.

Fly ash fallout rates in the vicinity of a thermal power station of 540 MW capacity were measured in tonnes per sq km. per month for 6 month of the post-rainy period from October to March. The concentrations of the alkali metals (Li, Na, K, Rb and CS) and alkaline earth metals (Be, Ca, Sr, and Ba) were determined in a number of fly ash samples collected at selected sites in the vicinity of the thermal power plant. These elements were also determined in soil samples collected from different depths to ascertain the leach profile, and also in samples collected from contamination-free areas. Conclusions with regard to the enrichment of alkali and alkalinearth metals in the soil horizon are discussed.

850 **Pathe, P.P., Kaul, S.N. Nandy, T.,** 1990. Physico-chemical treatment of domestic sewage. Asian Environ. 12(4) : 30-50.

In the present investigation an attempt has been made to determine the levels of coagulants required for treatment of domestic waste water.

851 **Patra, S.K., Padhi, A.K., Sahoo, B.K.,** 1989. Effect of paper mill sludges as liming amendment on the yield and economics of major rabi crops in acid soils. Environ. Ecol. 7(4): 871-873.

A field trial was conducted to study the response of five major rabi crops to different levels of lime application in the acid soils of Orissa. It was observed that all the five test crops responded positively to like application. At 0.25 LR value mustard showed the maximum response (90%) followed by bengal gram, wheat, garden pea and cauliflower while at 0.5 LR value bengal gram showed the maximum response (149%)) followed by cauliflower, garden pea and wheat over that of control. But no remarkable response was observed in mustard at 0.5 LR level. However, garden pea recorded the higher net return followed by cauliflower, wheat and bengal gram at 0.5 LR Value. On the contrary mustard obtained a positive net return only at 0.25 LR.

852 **Payne, M.R.,** 1982. Agriculture and Waste : 4-Pollution of Farms. Public Health Engg. 10(1): 31-34.

The effects of pollution on agriculture are seldom appreciated, and even today, while "acute" cases are all too obvious. As a result of the fragmented nature of the agricultural industry, together with a certain reluctance on the part of some authorities to take firm action where farms are polluted, there is a disturbing lack of protection for farms from pollution. This is not only against the national interest in terms of the import-saving role of home food production, but is resented by the farming community who experience increasingly strict control of their own activities by local and water authorities.

853 **Payne, M.R.,** 1989. Farm waste and nitrate pollution. In Agril. and the Environment. Proc. Institution of Water and Environmental Management. Annual Symp.: 27-33.

The paper considers future options for dealing with pollution from farm wastes and nitrate applications. Figures show the growth of reported farm pollution incidents; these are mainly attributed to cows and sliage. About 75% of the rising nitrate levels in rivers and ground-water originates from agril. land. However, this is due more to nitrogen mineralization from soil organic matter rather than loss of fertilizer nitrogen. The paper describes agril. restrictions that are likely to be introduced and comments on the desirability of incentives rather than penalties.

854 **Pearson, F., Chans, S.C., Gautier, M.,** 1980. Toxic inhibition of anaerobic biodegradation. J. Water Pollut. Control Fed. 52(3) : 472-482.

Preservative chemicals added to recreational vehicle waste holding tanks for odor control are toxic and inhibit biological waste treatment processes. Recreational vehicle waste were characterized, and the effect of toxicant dose on anaerobic biodegradation was evaluated. For formaldehyde, zinc sulfate, and phenol, the doses for 50% reduction in activity under shock loading were 200 mg/L, 400 mg Zn/L and 500 mg/L, respectively. Under acclimation loading, the doses of these 3 chemicals, and a quaternary ammonium compounds, were 100 mg/L, 700 mg Zn L, 700 mg/L and 50 mg organic N/L Preservatives at the concentrations found in recreational vehicle waste reduced the rate of anaerobic degradation by about two-thirds.

855 **Peereboom, Stegeman, J.H., Peereboom, Copius, J.,** 1989. The intake of cadmium in the Kempen, an area in the South of the Netherlands. Ecotoxicol Environ. Saf. 18(1) : 93-108.

This Kempen zone is polluted with heavy metals, especially cadmium (Cd) and zinc (Zn) emitted from metal factories in the Netherlands and in Belgium. Because of the high Cd in soil, vegetation grown in that area contain relatively high Cd concentrations. The Cd uptake by inhabitants of these areas especially individuals consuming vegetables from their own gardenst — herefore is considerably increased. The Cd intake is shown to be higher than the provisionally tolerated weekly uptake of Cd set by the WHO. The role of smoking in Cd intake is discussed.

856 **Pelzer, J.,** 1989. Effect of heavy metal concentration on the distribution of lead, cadmium and nickel in soil and solution. Archive. Fur. Acker. und pflazenbanund Bodenkunde 33(2) : 105-110.

Adsorption studies were conducted on six soils with Pb, Cd, and Ni. Distribution ratios permit the mathematical description of heavy metal distribution at the beginning of soil contamination. Langmuir and Freundlich isotherms can be used for greater contamination. Maximum sorption capacities and distribution ratios correlate with cation exchange capacity of soils.

857 **Perera, N.P.,** 1982. Environmental problems of copper mining and refining in Zambla. UNEP Inudstry Environ. 5(1) : 10-13.

This paper examines the methods of copper mining and processing and the nature of the waste material emitted and discusses the environmental consequences of such waste emissions and the measures taken to combat and minimize them.

858 **Pereira, W.E., Rostad, C.E., Steinheimer, T.R., Johnson, S.M.,** 1981. Characterization of organic compounds associated with weathered, surface-retorted oil shale. J. Environ. Sci. Health (A) 16(6): 571-587.

A sample of weathered, surface-retorted oil shale was analyzed for organic compounds using capillary gas chromatography/mass spectrometry/computer techniques. Various biological markers were identified including isorprenoid hydrocarbons, stearanes and terpanes, alongwith other classes of organic compounds including alkanes, fatty acids, alkylbenzenes, and polycyclic aromatic hydrocarbons. The origin and environmental significance of these compounds are discussed.

859 **Perez-Mateos, M, Gonzalez-Caredo, S.,** 1987. Effect of silver, cadmium and lead on soil enzyme activity. Revue d'Ecologie et de Biologie du Sol 24(1): 11-18.

Inhibition of the soil catalase activity by heavy metals (Ag, Cd and Pb) and the interactions between soil biological activity and Ag were studied. The biological activity was evaluated by means of soil catalase and dehydrogenase activities. Particle sizes < 50 μm, which contain well humified organic matter associated with enzymes, showed the greatest inhibition (80.1% inhibition).

860 **Petruzzelli, G.,** 1989. Recycling wastes in agriculture: heavy metal bioavailability. Agri. Ecosystems Environ. 27 : 493-503.

Recycling wastes in agriculture is an essential disposal method, and according to waste characteristics can produce supplementary organic matter resources (Sewage sludge-compost) for crop production or valuable soil amendments (coal flyash). This paper examines the extractability of heavy metals from water in relation to soil chemistry, and plant uptake bioassays as important diagnostic tools for metal bioavailability. The methods used together can significantly help in evaluating threshold levels for heavy metals, and allow the identification of differences between total and bioavailable heavy metal levels in the soil.

861 **Petruzelli, G., Lubramo, L., Guidi, G.,** 1981. Effect of sewage sludges and composts on the extractability of heavy metals from soil. Environ. Technol. Lett. 2, (10): 449-456.

In a field experiment heavy metals extractability from soil treated for two years with high rates of sewage sludges and composts was determined by a sequential extraction with H_2O, KNO_3 and DTPA. The extractable amounts of heavy metals showed a typical pattern over the two years with a maximum value at 30 days after each addition of sludges. Increases in the KNO_3 and DTPA extractable fractions were observed for Zn, Cd and partially for Pb.

862 **Petruzzelli, G., Szymura, I., Lubramo, L., Pezzarossa, B.,** 1989. Chemical speciation in different size fractions of compost from solid urban waste. Environ. Technol. Lett. 10(5) : 521-526.

Speciation of Cu, Ni, Cr, Pb, and Cd in a compost following extraction procedure (H_2O, KNO_3 EDTA) is discussed for different fractions (< 1, 1-2, >2 mm). The highest concs. of heavy metals were found in the finest fraction while most of the extractable Pb, Cu and Zn was extracted by EDTA. Cd and Ni showed a higher proportion extracted by KNO_3, and most of the Cr was water soluble.

863 **Phung, H.T., Lam, H.V., Page, A.L., Lund, L.J.,** 1979. The practice of leaching boron and soluble salts from fly ash-amended soils. Water Air Soil Pollut. 12(2) : 247-254.

The leachability of B and salts from 2 fly ash-amended soils was conducted in a column leaching experiment. Flyash was applied to the surface 3cm of a Baywood (acid) sand and an Arizo (calcareous) sandy loam at 5% by wt., the columns were continuously leached with Colorado River water at 2 different pH's. Boron from flyash was solubilized more readily in the Baywood than in the Arizo soil. Addition of flyash increased B levels in the leachates from 0.25 to 2.35 µg/mL (Baywood) and 0.93 µg/mL (Arozo). Acidified leaching water had no significant effect on B leaching patterns but resulted in leaching higher soluble salts. Approximately 348 and 161 cm of water for the Arizo and the Baywood soils, respectively, would be required to reduce the B concentration below a critical limit for B sensitive crops. Crops planted when fly ash is applied for disposal/recycling on land should be both salt and B tolerant.

864 **Piccardi, E.B., Cellini, P.L.,** 1978. Hydroxymethanesulphinate salts and related decomposition products in waste water. Water Air Soil Pollut. 9 : 301-307.

Hydroxymethanesulfinate (HMS) and its decomposition products such as HCHO, Zn and sulphites can be determined quantitatively in each other's presence by a polarographic method. In the alkaline medium, it is possible to have well defined and separated waves relative to the oxidation of HMS ion and to the reduction of HCHO and zincate ion. The quantitative determination of these compounds is carried out with standard addition methods since the concentration-current relationship is linear. The SO_2 is determined in $HClO_4$ 0.1 M and in the same sample it is possible to determine even HMS, HCHO and Zn after addition of NaOH upto 0.1 M. Moreover, a method of indirect determination of HMS is herein described. This is based on the determination of HCHO released by means of a weak oxidation of HMS which is stoichiometricaly proportional to the total HMS. The method is sensitive and is made specific for such of a waste water which come from textile industries.

865 **Piccolo, A.,** 1989. Reactivity of added humic substances towards plant available heavy metals. Sci. Total Environ. 81 & 82 : 607-614.

A solution (pH 7) of a purified humic acid was added to an organic and mineral soil to increase soil organic carbon by 1 to 2%. The samples were further treated with metals (Cd, Zn, Cu, Pb) to reach 0, 20 and 50 $\mu g\ g^{-1}$ conc. and incubated for one and two months and then extracted with 2.5% acetic acid for readily soluble and easily exchangeable forms of metals; DTPA (pH 7.3) and 1 $NHNO_3$. Results show that addition of humic acid immobilised the mineral soil. Retention capacity was directly related to the amount (OM) added and increased with time. The DTPA extractable metals were influenced by soil borne OM when the latter was present, its interaction with added humic materials reduced the metals extractability. Conversely in soils low in OM freshly added humic acid bound metals in readily accessible complexes which were then displaced with DTPA thereby enhancing their availability. Extraction with 1 N-HNO_3 followed by same mechanism. Effectiveness in decreasing metals extractability was of the same order found for stability contents of humic substances; Pb, Cu, Cd, Ni and Zn.

866 **Pick. F.E., De Beer, P.R., Van, L.P.,** 1986. Copper content of South African fruits and vegetables. Bull. Environl. Contam. Toxicol. 37(1) : 81-86.

The work reported here was to determine residue levels of copper in raw samples of fresh commercial fruit and vegetables and to see how these levels compared with the legal maximum permissible, residue limit of 20 mg/kg laid down for these products for local consumption and for export.

867 **Pichtel, J.R., Dick, W.A.,** 1991. Sulfur, iron and solid phase transformations during the biological oxidation of pyritic mine spoil. Soil Biol. Biochem. 23(2) : 101-107.

Spoil material composed of pyrite, coal and rock was ground and inoculated with spoils microflora and monitored for pH, SO_4, reduced S compounds, total soluble Fe and Fe(ii). A 7-day lag in production of both SO_4 and total soluble Fe was observed followed by a marked increase in concentration. Concentrations of SO_4, total soluble Fe and Fe (ii) after 28 days were 81, 91, and 59 mmol/kg spoil, respectively. Reduced S anions including thiosulfate, trithionate and tetrathionate were detected in the spoil at all samplings during a 28 day incubation. Final trithionate concentrations were greater (1.07 mmol/kg spoil). Scanning election micro scope observations of the pyrite revealed a gradual pitting and erosion of particle faces after prolonged incubation. Certain faces appeared to have been preferentially weathered.

868 **Pickering, W.F.,** 1980. Zinc Interaction with soil and sediment components. In 'Zinc in the Environment' pt.1. Ecological Cycling, John Wiley & Sons. New York: 71-112.

Soils and sediments differ greatly in composition, and it is preferable to observe zinc distribution using soils of different basic types. A few soils studied are also mentioned briefly to indicate the relevance and limitations of studies based on model or single adsorbent systems.

869 **Pickering, Q., Earle, D.O., Pilli, A. Willingham, T., Lazorchak, J.M,** 1989. Effects of pollution on fresh water organisms. J. Water Pollut. Control Fed. 61: 998-1042.

An annual review on the effects of pollutants including toxic elements and soil on fresh water fish, invertebrates, algae and duck weed is presented. Information is tabulated according to the chemical species,pollutant effect, duration and concentration.

870 **Pignatello,J.J., Cohen,J.J.,** 1990. Environmental chemistry of ethylene dibromide in soil and ground-water. Rev. Environ. Contam. Toxicol. 112: 1-48.

Various aspects of ethylene-dibromide in soils and ground-water are discussed.

871 **Pilotte, J.O., Winchester, J.W., Glassen, R.C.,** 1978. Detraction of heavy metal pollution in Estuarine sediments. Water Air Soil Pollut. 9: 363-368.

Anomalies in the concentration of heavy metals in estuarine sediments may not be reliably detected based on the measured concentration values or the ratios of metal concentrations to those of a reference element because of natural variations in both. However, the departure of a measurement from a regression line between metal and reference element concentrations may serve as a criterion for detecting an anomaly. The procedure has been applied to a suite of 34 sediments from a Flourida estuary.

872 **Pingitore, N.E.,** 1980. Zinc in the limestone cycle in 'Zinc in the Environment. pt.I: Ecological Cycling. John Wiley & Sons. New York: 267-295.

The path of zinc during the limestone cycle offers valuable insights into a variety of surfacial processes, ranging from oceanic chemical budgets through biogenic classifications to subaerial diagenesis. Zinc normally remains tied to its limestone host throughout the limestone cycle. The ultimate release of zinc from its limestone tomb comes only when gross dissolution occurs and the solution leaves the limestone terrace.

873 **Pinkowski, R.H., Rolfe, G.L., Arnold, L.E.,** 1982. A study of liquid Vestock waste disposal on forested watershed in Southern Illinois. V Effects on soil: Forestry Res. Rept. Agri. Expt. St. Illinois Univ. Bull. 82(9): 1-8.

This study showed the importance of monitoring the quantity of effluent discharged into a forested watershed. As long as its filtering capacity is not exceeded, a forested watershed can use the nutrients in feedlot runoff. If the watershed's filtering capacity is exceeded, however, salting in of the soil profile, decreased plant survival, and poor water quality may result.

874 **Pisanko, N.N.,** 1985. Sewage treatment in mining, metallurgical and oil-chemical industires. Environ. Prot. Engg. 11(3-4):31-39.

Mechanical processing of industrial wasterwater, utilization of sludges, and the recovery of water and its reuse in industry was studied. Some examples of solutions obtained at the Institute are given, i.e. vertical thickener of polyacrylamide solutions, utilization of secondary horizontal sedimentation tanks equipped with chambers for magnetic flocculation and separation of slags from ashes. A diagram of flows at the pulp thickening is also given.

875 **Piwoni, A.D., Wilson, J.T., Walters, D.M., Wilson, B.H., Enfield, C.G.,** 1986, Behaviour of organic pollutants during rapid-infiltration of waste water into soil: 1. Processes, definition, and characterization using a microcosm. Hazardous Waste Hazardous Materials. 3(1): 43-55.

A microcosm was constructed to study the behavior of organic pollution during rapid infiltration of municipal waste water into soil. The microcosm permitted a direct measure of the amount of volatilization and allowed calculation of the amount that degraded. The microcosms received 4.4+0.2 cm of waste water each day; an application was made every four hours. The waste water was amended with selected organic compounds at individual average concentrations of 0.2 to 32 μM/L chloroform, 1.1 dichlorethane, 1,1,1, trichlorethane, and tetrachloroethene extensively volatibized.

876 **Podoll, R.T., Irwin, K.C., Parish, H.J.,** 1989. Dynamic studies of naphthalene sorption on soil from aqueous solution. Chemosphere. 18(11-12): 2299-2312.

The thermodynamics and kinetics of naphthalene sorption from water on soil were examined over the temperature range of 15 to 50C.

877 **Prasad, B., Kumar, M.,** 1989. Visible absorption spectroscopic investigation in relation to molecular characteristics of fulvic acids extracted from organic wastes. J.Indian.Soc. Soil. Sci. 37: 655-660.

Fulvic acid fraction 'A' fractionated by gel permeation chromatography had higher E4/E6 and slope than those of higher molecular weight fractions. E4/E6 ratio and slope of different fulvic acids extracted from different organic wastes and their fractions increased as the pH was raised from 2 to 6. The values were maximum between pH 5.5 to 7.5 and then began to decrease gradually. At very high pH, E4/E6 ratio for the lower molecular weight fractions decreased significantly and tended to approach a common value indicating the formation of similar size particle. Transition measurements for fulvic acid fractions at various wavelengths, indicate that the absorption and slope decrease monotonically with increasing wavelengths.

878 **Prasad, B., Kumar, M., Prasad, J.,** 1989. Direct residual effect of organic wastes and zinc sulphate on zinc availability under cropping sequence of wheat rice in calcareous soils. Indian J. Agri. Sci. 59: 300-305.

Total Zn contents in biogas slurry, poultry manure composite, sewage sludge and press mud were 105, 160, 115 and 95 ppm, respectively. The relative order of Zn contribution of organic sources on yield and Zn uptake was: Poultry manure> composite> presumed biogas slurry> sewage sludge. Organic materials maintained higher levels of available nutrients.

879 **Prasad, B., Mehta, A.K., Sinha, M.K.,** 1990. Zinc fractions and availability of applied zinc in calcareous soil treated with organic materials. J. Indian Soc. Soil. Sci. 38: 248-253.

A field experiment was conducted to study transformation and availability of applied Zn in calcareous soil treated with organic materials viz., sewage sludge, municipal wastes, poultry manure, farmyard manure, pressmud. Most of zinc existed as residual zinc (41% of total Zn) and organically complexed Zn fractions (3%) in calcareous soil treated with organic materials. The organically bound Zn was significantly correlated with organic carbon. Most of the Zn fractions were correlated positively and significantly with DTPA extractable Zn and negatively with the soil pH. The data of path coefficient analysis showed that the major path by which Zn moved in the treated soil was organic complexed Zn. The organic complexed Zn for wheat and the organic complexed Zn and occluded Zn for rice are major sources of available Zn in organic materials amended calcareous soils.

880 **Preer, J.R., Murchison, G.B. Jr.,** 1987. A simplified method for detection of lead contamination of soil. Environl. Pollut. (B.Chem Phys.). 12(1): 1-13.

The rhodizonate spot test for Pb has been adapted to the detection of Pb contamination of soils.

881 **Preffer, J.T., Chang, Y., Chian, E.S.K.,** 1979. Comparative study of different iron compounds in inhibition of Sphaerotilus growth. Applied Eenvironl. Microbiol., 38(3): 385-389.

For both strains, 80% inhibition of the maximum respiration rate was obtained by the following levels of soluble. Fe concentrations at pH 6.0; iron citrate, 20mg/L. as Fe; iron cysteine. 5mg/L as Fe; and ferrous sulfate, 10mg/L. as Fe. At a pH of 6.7 with iron citrate (20mg/L as Fe),inhibition of both strains was 50%. Insoluble Fe compounds, i.e.iron hydroxides and ferrous carbonate, were much less effective than the soluble Fe compounds as inhibition of these 2 strains. Aged iron hydroxide (500 mg/L as Fe) produced a 70% inhibition in the maximum respiration rate, whereas fresh iron hydroxide (52 mg/L as Fe) and ferrous carbonate (500 mg/L as Fe) produced a 20% inhibition. Chemical analyses of the Fe-inhibited Sphaerotilus strains showed a close relationship between the inhibition of the organism's growth and the amount of Fe sorbed by the organisms.

882 **Pritchard, P.H.,** 1988. Fate of pollutants J. Water Pollut. Control Fed. 60(6): 983-999).

The degradation of chlorinated and non-chlorinated xenobiotic chemicals hydrocarbons, pesticides and heavy metals, in water and sediments is reviewed.

883 **Prochazkova, K., Krcmery, V., Jrfoltinova, J., Kapeller, K., Brezaniova, T.,** 1989. Indicators of quality of surface water in an industrially polluted country. Ekologia, CSSR, 8(3): 263-273.

The influence of industrial pollution from a Ni producing metal factory on surface waters in Czechoslovakia was studied. A comparison was made between a polluted lake and lake outside the contaminated locality. A significant change in most hydrobiological and microbiological properties was demonstrated in the lake near the factory.

884 **Procopiou, J., Wallace, A.,** 1982. Elements concentration of a native fern from Greece that grows in monoculture and of corn plants grown in the same soil with different levels of copper. Soil Sci. 134(1): 40-41.

Analysis of a native fern (*Pteridium aquilinum* L.) growing in large tracts of soil at about 1200 meters mean sea level in Greece indicated that it tolerated low levels of copper. Corn plants grown in potted soil from the area did respond slightly to Cu added to the soil.

885 **Pronk, J.T., Meulenberg, R., Hazeu, W., Bos, P., Kuenen, J.G.,**1990.

Oxidation of reduced inorganic sulphur compounds by acidophillc thiobacilli. in 'Adaptation of Microorganisms to Extreme Environments'. H.P. Duerre (Ed.). 293-306.

Acidophillic thiobacilli are at least partially responsible for the development of acid sulphate soils. The key reaction in the processes mentioned above is the biological oxidation of pyrite to ferric sulphate and sulfuric acid. Thiobacilius ferroxidans is widely used as a model organism to study the biological oxidation of pyrite. The growth yield of T. ferroxidans (expressed as the amounts of biomass produced per mol of electrons) is much higher on reduced sulphur compounds than on ferrous iron.

886 **Pussemier, L., Szabo, G., Bulman, R.A.,** 1990. Prediction of the soil adsorption coefficient Koc for aromatic pollutants. Chemosphere 21(10-11): 1199-1212.

The prediction of the adsorption factor Koc of eleven aromatic compounds has been made by using a multilinear relation with log Kow (Kow=octanol/water partition coefficient) and S (Hiidebrand's solubility parameter). Very significant relations could also be obtained using reverse phase HPLC retention factors instead of log Kow. The contribution of the S term is not constant and decreases when the polarity of the stationary phase increases.

887 **Pyatt, F.B., Lacy D.,** 1988. An appraisal of atmospheric pollution by aluminum fumes emanating from smelter works in Western Norway. Environ. Internatl. 14(5): 407-416.

Material including birch (betula) leaves, twigs, soil and grass (Agrostis, Festuca, deschampsla) was collected from nearby area of Aluminium smelter in Norway. The prevailing wind together with steep sided valleys controlled the fate of the pollutant, and the material was found to sediment out from the atmosphere in low land sites particularly to the north-east, north-west and east of the industrial complex. Most deposition occured within several km of the plants. Some effects of Al on plant surfaces are discussed.

888 **Quin, B.F.,** 1979. A comparison of nutrient removal by harvested reed canarygrass (Phalaris arundinacea) and ryegrass-clover in plots irrigated with treated effluent. New Zealand Agri. Res. 22(2): 291-302.

Harvested plots of reed canarygrass surface-irrigated at 3-wk intervals over 12 months with treated sewage effluent, produced similar dry matter yields, and removed similar quantities of nutrients, as plots of ryegrass-white clover. The higher spring production of reed canarygrass was offset by much lower production in autumn and winter. The reed canary grass maintained low NO_3-N levels (<3 mg/L) in the drainage water throughout the year, whereas levels under ryegrass-clover increased to < 18 mg/L in winter. The high levels under ryegrass-clover were caused by a continuation of mineralization of soil N, and nitrification of the effluent NH_4-N, at soil temperatures too low for herbage growth (<5°C). Reed canarygrass maintained low NO_3-N, at levels in winter by a continuing uptake of N by the plant's rhizome system. A corresponding decrease in Cl in drainage under reed canary grass suggested that N uptake during this period occurred as NH_4-N rather than as NO_3-N.

889 **Quin, B.F.,** 1979. Surface irrigation with sewage effluent in New Zealand : A case study. Progress Water Technol. 11(4-5): 103-126.

New Zealand's oldest existing sewage effluent irrigation scheme at Templeton, Christchurch, was investigated to determine the chemical compositions of the effluent; pasture production, and the nutrient and heavy metal status of pasture and soils; drainage loses of nutrients; and the effect of the drainage losses on ground-water quality. The effluent treated areas have a higher pH, and have high total N organic C, available P, and exchangeable Ca and Na levels compared to the control. No increases were observed in the total trace metal content of the soil. Chemical analysis data for the pasture from the 1958-1968, and irrigated control areas are tabulated.Twenty years of pasture irrigation with treated sewage and on pasture production, was 50% higher than that of non-irrigated land. Total drainage, calculated from evapotranspiration datataining 0.75 mg/kg poly chlorinated biphenyls., was 900 mm, which slightly exceeded the yearly effluent application. Annual losses of N in the drainage were estimated to total 180 kg/ha, giving a NO_3-N concentration in the deep drainage of 15-20 mg/L. The enforcement of a limit of 10 mg/L. NO_3-N for potable wasters may necessitate at least partial cropping of the area to increase nutrient removal.

890 **Quinn, N.W.T, Hachett, S.A., Swain, D.G.,** 1989. Evaluating policy options for management of selenium contaminated drainage related problems in Sanjoaquin Valley in "Toxic Substances in Agricultural Water Supply and Drainage." CID-USA: 401-4151.

A planning programme for current problems of selenium contaminated drainage system is presented.

891 **Radogana, V.M.,** 1990. Heavy metal accumulation in forest soils as an air pollution effect in Trans. 14th internatl. Cong. Soil Sci., Kyoto Vol. II: 84-89.

Zn, Cu, Ni, Cd, Cr, Pb and Cu were determined by progressive acidification, extraction or by sequential chemical extraction in the upper 10 cm of six soils under ash, oak, beech, *Pinus radiata, P. hale pensis* or *P. Ponderosa* at various distances from a smelting furnace in Italy. Results are discussed in relation to mobility and availability in soil.

892 **Raghu, D., Sieh, H.N.,** 1989. Origin, properties and disposal problems of chromium ore residue. Internatl. J. Environl. Studies 34(3): 227-235.

The generation of Cr waste, properties of Cr, Cr compounds, and the problems of chromium contamination in surface and ground were studied. Methods for control and treatment of Cr residues are outlined. The option of disposal of Cr ore residue are: (i) Disposal in a hazardous waste land fill-an expensive method, (ii) Removal of Cr by extraction at present economically unviable and (iii) Partial treatment of Cr contaminated ore and disposal in a special land fill which may be cheaper than option (i).

893 **Rai. L.C., Raizada, Meena,** 1989. Effect of bimetallic combinations of Ni, Cr, and Pb on growth, uptake of nitrate and ammonia, $^{14}CO_2$ Fixation and nitrogenase activity of *Nostoc muscorum*. Ecotoxicol. Environ. Saf. 7(1): 75-85.

The toxicity of Cr, Ni and Pb individually as well as in combination on growth, final yield, uptake of NO_3 and NH_4 photosynthesis nitrogenase activity of *Nostoc muscorum* has been studied. All test metals, when used individually, depicted toxicity against the above mentioned processes of test cyanobacterium. However, their interactive effect was found to be mostly of antagonistic type. Antagonism was more prevalent in those combinations containing nickel.

894 **Rakoczynski, R.W.,** 1988. Waste water treatment system for hazardous waste land fill leachate. Proc. Annual Madison Waste Conf. 11: 303-311.

Data are presented on the renewal and carbon adsorption of metals and organics biodegradation, secondary treatment of organics, and ion exchange treatment of metals in leachate.

895 **Ramachandran, V., D'Souza, T.J.,** 1990. Transformation of added chromium compounds in two soils. J. Indian Soc. Soil Sci. 38(3): 419-425.

Transformation of applied Cr compounds (III, VI) in Oxisol and a Vertisol, and also in soils treated with sewage sludge and municipal compost were studied. Soils were treated separately with 400 ppm of Cr (III) as $(Cr_2(SO_4)_3$. 15 $H_2O)$, Cr (VI) as $(Na_2Cr_2O_72H_2)$ and Cr-enriched sludge and compost and incubated. Sequential extraction after different intervals with deionised H_2O, IM NH_4Cl, 0.1M $CuSO_4$, 0.3M $(NH_4)_2C_2O_4$ and citrate-dithionite yielded water soluble, exchangeable, organic-bound, amorphous-precipitated and crystalline-precipitated Cr fractions, respectively. Appreciable amounts of Cr could be extracted with H_2O, NH_4Cl and $CuSO_4$ (Plant-available Cr) when Cr (III) was added to the Vertisol. Large amounts of plant-available Cr were extracted from soils treated with Cr (VI) and from soils mixed with Cr (VI) enriched compost. Soluble Cr compounds tended to become insoluble with time. While the Cr (III) addition reduced the pH, Cr (VI) addition increased the pH of both soils. Cr-enriched sludge amendments did not contribute to the extraction of significant amount of plant-available Cr in soils. The pH of the Oxisol increased and that of the Vertisol decreased with sludge amendments.

896 **Ramesh Kumar, K.T., Pramod Kumar, Patel, B., Pushpalatha, K.,**

1990. Effects of chemical factory effluent on germination and growth of Guar: Cyamopsis tetragonoloba L. Taub, Var. PNB., Adv. Plant Sci., 3(1): 34-42.

The study made to investigate the effect of the Saurashtra Chemicals effluent at 5, 10, 25, 15, 50 and 100% concentration on Cyamopsis tetragonoloba L. The root and shoot lengths, dry matter accumulation and crop productivity increased in 5, 10 and 15% of the effluent treated plants. There was no germination in undiluted effluent. At 25%, retardation in growth was observed. The highly toxic effluent can be used for irrigation after proper dilutions.

897 **Ransome, L.S., Dowdy, R.H.,** 1987. Soybean growth and boron distribution in a sandy soil amended with scrubber sludge. J. Environ. Qual. 16: 171-175.

Soybean plants were grown on plots amended with 0, 10, 20 and 40 Mg scrubber sludge ha^{-1}. Hot water extractable soil B was elevated from low (0.40 mg kg^{-1}) to sufficiency levels (> 1.0 mg kg^{-1}) by application of at least 20 Mg sludge ha^{-1}; such levels were maintained for two or three growing seasons. Soil water EC and B concentrations reached levels potentially detrimental to soybean production at the 40 Mg ha^{-1} rate. Soybean population decreased linearly with increasing rate of application- the first two growing seasons following application. Yield was significantly reduced in the first year but was enhanced in response to scrubber sludge applications the third growing season. Leaf B content was significantly increased all 3 yr: symptoms of B toxicity were visible only during the year of application. Seed B, although significantly affected by treatment, did not parallel leaf B or yield.

898 **Rao, S.N., Chaubey, R., Srinivasan, K.V.,** 1990. Ganga water quality in Bihar. Indian J. Environ. Health. 32(4): 393-400.

Studies carried out on the Ganga water quality in Bihar are discussed. The effects of city drains and effluents on the water quality are also presented.

899 **Rao, G.A.K., Viraraghvan, T.,** 1990. Removal of heavy metals in waste water treatment plants — a review. Indian J. Environ. Prot. 11(1): 1-10.

This paper reviews the various studies that have been undertaken for the removal of heavy metals in waste water treatment plants. Though most investigators conclude that suspended metals are better removed than dissolved metals, they differ in their findings that primary treatment process have better metal removal efficiencies than secondary treatment processes. Various analytical techniques available for detecting heavy metals are also briefly discussed.

900 **Rappaport, B.D., Martens, DC., Reneav, R.B., Jr. Simpson, T.W.,** 1987. Metal accumulation in corn and barley grown on a sludge-amended Typic Ochraqualf. J. Environl. Qual. 16:29-33.

A field experiment was conducted during the 1984-1985 in the Atlantic

Coastal Plain region to evaluate heavy metal accumulation in corn. grain and stover and in barley silage grown on a poorly drained, sludge-amended soil. The study was conducted using in situ controlled lateral flow plots (1.5 by 2.3 m) on Acredale silt loam. An aerobically digested sludge from a waste water treatment plant was applied initially at rates of 0, 42 and 84 dry Mg ha^{-1}. At the highest application rate, 1.8, 304, 17.2 and 248 kg ha^{-1} of Cd, Cu, Ni and Zn were applied, respectively. Cadmium conc. was < 0.01 mg kg^{-1} in the corn grain in both years. Sludge application increased Ni and Zn concentration while levels of Cd and Cu were unaffected in the corn grain for both years and Cu, Ni and Zn levels were increased in the barley silage. Levels of DTPA-extractable metal in the Ap horizon were increased and were 0.25, 60, 2 and 30 mg Cd, Cu, Ni and Zn kg^{-1} in the highest sludge treatment, respectively, The DTPA extractable Cd, Cu, Ni and Zn within the soil profile indicated no downward metal movement. On this poorly drained soil, phytotoxicity due to metals did not occur even where Cu was applied in excess of 280 kg ha^{-1}, which is a maximum amount of Cu that could be applied to the soil based on USEPA guidelines.

901 **Rappaport, B.D., Martens, D.C., Reneav, R.B., Jr. Simpson, T.W.,** 1988. Metal availability in sludge amended soils with elevated metal levels. J. Environ. Qual. 17: 42-47.

Field studied were conducted in 1984 with in situ controlled lateral flow plots to determine Cd, Cu, Ni, and Zn availabilities for corn grown on sludge amended soils. These plots were constructed in Bojac loamy sand, Davidson clay loam and Gross close silt loam located in the coasted plain, piedmont, and Ridge and valley provinces of Virginia, respectively. An aerobically digested sludge from a waste water treatment plant with major industrial inputs was applied to the soils at rates of 0, 42, 84, 126, 168 and 210 dry Mg ha^{-1}. The highest sludge rate supplied 4.5 kg Cd, 760 kg Cu, 43 kg Ni, and 620 kg Zn ha^{-1}. Corn grain and stover yields at the three locations increased linearly as a function of increased rate of sludge application (R = 0.92). Metal concentrations in corn grain and ear leaves from all treatments on the three soils were within normal levels. Nonsignificant relationship occured between levels of DTPA Cd, Cu, Ni and Zn and the respective metal concentrations in corn earleaves for data combined over the three soils. Amounts of DTPA extractable Cd, Cu, Ni and Zn in the Ap horizon of the three soils increased linearly (r = 0.76 to 0.88) with rate of sludge application. Maximum DTPA extractable metal levels in the soils were 0.6 mg Cd, 150 mg, Cu 4.0/mg Ni, and 75 mg Zn/kg. The order of DTPA extractable metal concentrations in the soils, Cu > Zn, > Ni, > Cd paralleled the amounts of metals applied via sludge application. Phytotoxicity did not occur in the corn grown on these diverse soils, even where Cu and Zn were applied in excess of USEPA guidelines.

902 **Rattan, R.K., Sehgal, D.,** 1989. Investigations on cadmium adsorption on

soils differing in physical and chemical characteristics, J. Indian Soc. Soil. Sci. 37: 284-289.

Adsorption behaviour of cadmium on soils differing widely in their physico-chemical characteristics and its predictability by linear, quadratic, Langmuir and Freundlich equations was investigated. The results show that quadratic equation was the most suitable in describing cadmium adsorption followed by the modified Langmuir equations containing square and square root terms. Fitting of adsorption data to the modified Langmuir and Freundlich equations, particularly in the acid soils, provided constant indication about the existence of more than one kind of population of sites on soil surface for cadmium adsorption. Multiple linear regression analysis data revealed that the Freundlich constant (K) was significantly correlated with pH, EC and CEC with all these parameters together accounting for 94.3 per cent variation in K values.

903 **Rauta, C., Carstea, S., Mihailescu, A.,** 1990. Impact of pollution on terrestrial ecosystem due to industrial emission in Romania. Trans. 14th Internatl. Congress Soil Sci. Kyoto Vol. II: 90-65.

The forms and extent of pollution arising from extraction and processing on non-ferrous metals, P fertilizer production, cement production and coal fire power station are reviewed.

904 **Raygor S.C., Mackay, K.P.,** 1975. Bacterial air pollution from an activated sludge tank. Water Air Soil Pollut. 5: 47-52.

Concentrations of air-borne coliforms and remaining 'other' bacteria were measured downwind of a sewage treatment plant activated sludge tank. The Gaussian plume diffusion equation adequately predicts concentrations of the 'other' bacteria; the diffusion equation must be modified by an extinction coefficient, equivalent to a half-life of about 7.45 to predict coliforms concentrations. Coliform concentration downwind of this tank did not present a significant health hazard, but the method is applicable to treatment plants of higher capacity and possibly greater emissions.

905 **Raza, S.H., Vijyakumari, N.,** 1989. Impact of distillery effluent "Spent Wash" on seed germination, morphological characters, yield and pigment concentration of *Trigonella foenum-graecum* L., Pollut. Res. 8(3): 109-116.

The effect of distillery effluent on growth of Fenugreek (*Trigonnella foenum-graecum* L.) Var. Desi in pot culture experiments was studied. Percentage germination of seeds and crop growth showed significant variation with the concentration of the effluent treatment. Root and shoot growth were retarded at higher concentration of the distillery effluent treatment beyond 10 per cent. However, increased dry matter production and pod yield was observed at one per cent dilute effluent treatment. Moreover, there existed a significant positive relationship between total chlorophyll content and effluent treatment at lower concentrations. Undiluted distillery effluent had a toxic effect on germination and growth, whereas 0.1 to 1% effluent concentrations had a growth promoting effect which was significantly better than control.

906 **Raza, S.H., Nirmala, B., Murthy, M.S.R., Fatima Nasreen,** 1987. Effect of industrial effluent on soil and natural vegetation of Nacharam industrial complex. Acta Ecologica. 9 (1&2): 28-33)

Paper describes the assessment of soil toxicity caused by the effluent and the physiological response of plants of Nacharam industrial area to saline toxicity of soils. Soils have become highly saline in nature due to open effluent discharges. The concentration of sulphates, chlorides, sodium and electrical conductivity was abnormally high. Physiological response of plants to salinity of soil was analysed in terms of chlorophyll, ascorbic and relative water content. Physiolotical' parameters have shown significant negative correlation with chlorides, sulphates and total salinity of soil. *Dactyloctenium aegyptium* was found to be resistant amongst all plants.

907 **Red, J.T., Muttler, W.L.,** 1986. Waste water renovation in a slash pine plantation subjected to prescribed burning. J. Environ. Qual. 15(4): 351-355.

Two experimental areas were established in the underdrained 16-yr-old slash pine (*Pinus elliothi* Mor.) plantation land treatment system receiving 2.5 cm/week of secondarily treated domestic waste water. One of the experimental areas was subjected to a prescribed burn as a forest management practice. A high degree of waste water renovation was achieved and the prescribed burn had no significant effect on waste water renovation. Forest floor storage of K, Ca, Mg, and P was significantly increased from pretreatment levels due to waste water irrigation. Prescribed burning had no effect on forest floor nutrient storage. Soil concentrations of total and available P, Ca, Mg, and K increased significantly in the surface soil horizon. Total P, Ca, Mg, and K concentration occurred due to burning. Waste water irrigation resulted in significant reductions in soil acidity and total-Kjeldahi N concentration in the surface horizon.

908 **Reddy, K.R., Graetz, D.A.,** 1981. Use of shallow reservoir and flooded organic soils system to waste treatment nitrogen and phosphorus transformation J. Environ. Qual. 10(1): 113-119.

Use of a shallow reservoir (with a marly clay loam bottom) and flooded organ soil (Histosol) for inorganic N and P removal from waste water (agriculture drainage effluent) was evaluated under simulated conditions. The results show the shallow reservoir and flooded organic soils could be effectively used for NH_4 and NO_3 N removal from the waste waters. For reservoir soil, about 70 and 76% the flood water P was removed under aerobic and anaerobic water column conditions, respectively.

909 **Reddy, G.B., Cheng, C.N., Dunn, S.J.,** 1983. Survival of Rhizobium japonicum in soil-sludge environment. Soil Biol. Biochem. 15(3): 343-345.

The number of R. japonicum (USDA 110) in treatment groups containing various soil-to-sludge ratio during incubation for 1, 21 and 42 days was investigation. Recovery of rhizobia from the soils was < 1% in all treatment groups after 42 days. However, for control, 13:1, 9:1, and 5:1 groups, the percentage recovery was higher in Enon sandy loam at 21 days. Recovery of Rhizobia in the 5:1 group from both soils was 7.9% after 1 days, whereas control values were 92%. However, the number of R. japonicum that survived to 21 days was $1.7 \cdot 10^5$ g^{-1} and $1.7 \times 10^6 g^{-1}$ for Mecklenburd clay and Enon sandy loam soils with highest sludge, respectively.

910 **Reddy, M.R., Jivendra Jain, S.C.,** 1981. Paper mills effluent for sugarcane irrigation. IAWPC Tech. Ann. 8:129-146.

Exhaustive experiments on four crops of sugarcane carried out for 8 years, separately with fresh water and effluent from an integrated Pulp and Paper Mill adopting sulphate process and high internal controls, indicate that the effluent can successfully be used for irrigation of sugarcane, especially on acidic coarse textured sandy/sandy loamy soils as available in Rayagada Region (Orissa) with about 20% increase in sugarcane yield without affecting the quality of cane or the soil.

911 **Reddy, K.R., Overcash, M.R., Khaleel, R., Vestermani, P.W.,** 1980. Phosphorus adsorption-desorption characteristics of two soils utilized for disposal of animal, wastes. J. Environ. Qual. 9 (1): 86-92.

In a laboratory 30d incubation study, Norfold soil was treated with beef, poultry wastes, and allowed to decompose and phosphorus adsorption-desorption characteristics of the soil were measured. Application of wastes decreased adsorption capacity of the soil and increased soluble P (in 0.01 M $CaCl_2$) acid-extractable P (0.05 N H Cl + 0.025 M H_2 SO_4), equilibrium P concentration (EPC) and P desorption (after swine four-1 hour extractions). In a field study, increased rates of swine lagoon effluent application over a period of 5 years to a Norfolk soil (site 1) and for 3 years to a Cacli soil (site 2) also increased soluble P (in 0.01 M $CaCl_2$), acid extractable P, P desorbed and EPC values and decreased the adsorption capacity. At high loading rates of swine lagoon effluent, soluble P movement occurred to a depth of 75 and 30 cm at site 1 & 2, respectively. Phosphorus adsorption increased with depth and EPC values decreased with increasing depths of soil profile. A significant relationship was observed between EPC values, and soluble and extractable P, P desorbed and EPC values and decreased the adsorption capacity.

912 **Regan, H.A., Mast. T.J.,** 1990. Cadmium inhalation and male reproductive toxicity. Rev. Environ. Contam. Toxicol 114: 1-22.

Source of cadmium in nature, its effect on organs and inhalation exposure are reviewed.

913 **Rettinger, S., Bischofsberger, W.,** 1990. Subsoil percolation of sewage-purification efficiency of unsaturated zone and mass balance of organic load. Water Sci. Technol. 22: 313-315.

Investigations were conducted using lysimeters and a full scale soil disposal system. Results on the variation of seepage water composition and mass balance are presented which enable the possible upgrading of soil disposal system to minimize pollution of soil and ground-water.

914 **Reuss, J.O., Dooley, H.L., William Griffis,** 1978. Uptake of cadmium from phosphate fertilizers by peas, radish and lettuce. J. Environ. Qual. 7 (1): 128-133.

Cadmium uptake from phosphate fertilizers by radish lettuce and garden peas was investigated in the greenhouse. Fertilizer in all treatments was applied at the rate of 100 μg P/g soil to pots containing 4 kg soils, when reagent grade mono-calcium phosphate was used as a P source on a coarse textured acid soil. Cd contents of edible radish roots and tops were < 0.4 μg/g dry weight, while the Cd content of lettuce and pea seeds and foliage was < 0.2 μg/g. The use of concentrated superphosphate (CSP) containing 17 μg Cd/g resulted in plant Cd levels of 2.4, 3.4, 6.3, 0.9 and 0.5 μg/g for radish roots, radish tops, lettuce, pea seeds and pea foliage, respectively. On a medium textured calcareous soil, the use of this CSP increased the Cd content of radish tops from 0.8 to 1.4 μg/gm, while in lettuce the increase was from 0.8 to 1.2 μg/g. The effect on radish roots from calcareous soil was non-significant. Pea seeds and foliage on this soil were below our Cd detection limit of 0.2 μg/g. Uptake on both soils was a linear function of the Cd content of the fertilizer. With the acid soil, uptake of Cd from CSP was essentially the same when the fertilizer was placed in a spot 5 cm below the seeds as when mixed with the soil. Di-ammonium phosphate (DAP) containing 157 μg Cd/g resulted in similar uptake to the CSP when mixed with the soil, but spot placement of DAP almost completely eliminated Cd uptake from the fertilizer. In the calcareous soil spot placement increased Cd uptake from the fertilizer. In the calcareous soil spot placement increased Cd uptake from the CSP fertiliser but slightly depressed uptake from DAP.

915 **Revis, N.W., Osborne, T.R., Holdsworth, G., Hadden, C.,** 1989. Distribution of mercury species in soil from a mercury-contaminated site. Water Air Soil Pollut. 45 (1-2): 105-113.

The distribution of mercury species was determined in soil from a site with Hg contamination. Mercury contamination was primarily confined to the top 40 cm of soil, and the concentration of total Hg ranged from 0.5 to 3000 μg Hg g^{-1}. Of total Hg present, 91% was inorganic 0.01% organic (as methyl Hg), and 6% elemental Hg. Furthermore, of total inorganic Hg present, 85% was in the insoluble mercuric sulfide form.

Thus, of total Hg present in soil at this contaminated site, 91% was in the relatively insoluble HgS and Hg forms.

916 **Revis, N.W., Osborne, T.R., Holdsworth, G., Hadden, C.,** 1990. Mercury in soil: A method for assessing acceptable limits. Arch. Environl. Contam. Toxicol. 19: 221-226.

The total conc. of Hg in soil site ranges from 0.5 to 3000 ppm. Of the total Hg present, 88% was HgS, 0.01% methyl mercury and 7% elemental Hg. Intenstrial absorptions in mice showed that 0.4% of the incubated dose was absorbed. An acceptable limit of Hg in soil was estimated at this site which was 22 ppm; and with a safety factory of 10, the limit would be reduced to above 12 ppm.

917 **Reynolds, J.H., Braun, M.O., Campbell, W.F., Miller, R.W., Anderson, I.R.,** 1970, Long-term effects of irrigation with waste water. J. Water Pollut. Control Fed. 42(4): 672-687.

A comparison between an agricultural site in Tooele, Utah, that received treated municipal effluent for 20 yr and a site that was irrigated with normal irrigation water conducted for 2-yr. While the secondary effluent was of significantly poorer quality than the normal irrigation water, it was of satisfactory quality for crop irrigation. No significant accumulation of N, Pb, Cu, Zn, Ni, Cr, or Cd could be attributed to the effluent irrigation. Available P in the soil was greater at the effluent irrigated site. No harmful accumulations of heavy metals on alfalfa grown at the site were noted.

918 **Rhoads, F.M., Oison, S.M., Manning, S.,** 1989. Copper toxicity in tomato plants. J. Environ. Qual. 18(2): 195-197.

Tomato plants were grown for approximately 6 wk in a greenhouse in pots of soil containing two levels of lime and six levels (0 to 2800 mg Cu/kg soil) of copper hydroxide in a factorial treatment arrangement. Tissue Cu concentrations was not a conclusive indicator of Cu toxicity in tomatoies. Near maximum Cu concentration in tomato tissue occurred at soil-Cu levels above 104 mg per kg, plant growth was reduced with soil Cu above 150 mg per kg and soil pH below 6.5. However soil Cu levels above 330 mg/kg were necessary to reduce plant growth with soil pH above pH.6.5.

919 **Richardson, J.A., Evans, M.E.,** 1987. Establishing trees and shrubs on magnesian lime-stone waste. J. Environ. Manage. 24 (2): 157-167.

Lists were made of trees and shrubs which were found in natural and semi-natural woodlands on the magnesian limestone tract in Country, Durham, and were colonizers of waste heaps at quarry workings. This information formed the basis of experimental plantations made to determine suitable species and cultivation methods for low-costs reclamation schemes. *Alnur glutinosa, A. incana,* Betula pendula, *Crategus monogyna, Fraxinus Excelsior, Populus alba* and *Salix caprea* were likely to succeed with only some modest ameleoration of the substrate.

920 **Riedel, G.F.** , 1985. The relationship between chromium (VI) uptake, sulphate uptake, and chromium (VI) toxicity in the estuarine diatom thalassiosira pseudomana. Aquat. Toxicol. 7(3): 191-204.

The uptake of hexavalent chromium and the effect of Cr(VI) on sulfate uptake by the diation Thalassiosira pseudomana were examined at varying salinities and sulfate ion concentrations. The uptake of Cr(VI) concentrations, were inversely proportional to external sulfate ion concentration. Concentration of Cr(VI) that inhibited growth also inhibited sulfate uptake.

921 **Riffaldi, R., Saviozzi, A., Levi Minzi, R.**, 1990. Retention of coumaric acid by soil and its colloidal components. Water Air Soil Pollut. 51(3-4): 307-314.

In this study of the behaviour of coumaric acid added to soil, the disappearance of the acid was found to be due to adsorption plus microbial degradation, and was influenced by the concentration and contact time. Adsorption experiments set up with soils varying widely in their chemical and physical properties, showed that the Freundlich fits the data quite well and that among the different soil factors. only the pH was closely and negatively correlated with coumaric acid adsorption. Approximately at pH = 7 no adsorption occurred, perhaps due to the repulsion between the negatively changes soil colloids and the dissociated acidic groups of coumaric acid. Adsorption experiments carried out with different adsorbents showed that the hydroxy-Fe compound was the most effective in retaining coumaric acid, followed by humic acid, illite, kaolinite and verminulite, in this order.

922 **Rippey, B., Murphy, R.J., Kyle, S.W.**, 1982. Anthropogenically derived in the sedimentary flux of Mg, Cr, Ni, Cu, Zn, Hg, Pb, and P in Lough Neagh, Northern Ireland. Environ. Sci. Technol. 16(1): 23-30.

The concentration-depth behaviour of Mg, Cr, Ni, Zn, Cu, Hg, Pb, and P in three sediment cores from a central side in Lough Neagh Northern Ireland, was examined for changes in the sedimentary flux of these elements. Two main periods of change were found, A change in the catchment erosion-leaching regime in the 17th century caused by widespread and comprehensive woodland clearance, produced increased sedimentary Mg, Cu, and Pb concentration. A second and larger change occurred after about 1880 A.D. Cr, Cu, Hg, Pb, P and to a lesser extent, Ni concentrations increased toward the sediment surface. Differing P and trace-metal profiles, a comparison of the estimated anthropogenic sedimentary flux with background atmospheric contributions, and a general comparison with other situations all suggest that background atmospheric sources make a substantial contribution to the more recent Cu, Zn, Hg, and Pb sedimentary contamination. The trace-metal contamination of Lough Neagh is part of a global pattern.

923 **Rittman, B.E., Johnson, N.M.,** 1989. Rapid biological clean-up of soils contaminated with lubricating oil. Pollut. Res. Control, Brighton, Part I: 209-219.

Large amounts of lubricating-oil-degrading bacteria could be grown in liquid culture, as long as a dispersant was applied to form and maintain an oil-in-water emulsion. Application of the oil-degrading bacteria significantly increased the initial rate of oil degradation in soil plots. Improved microorganism contact and dispersant effectiveness apparently were responsible for the rapid rates in slurry reactors. The increased rates demonstrated the potential value of adding a large, acclimated inoculum and providing good mixing and dispersion to make the oil more available to the microorganisms.

924 **Robert, L. Tale III; Richard, E. Terry,** 1980. Effect of sewage effluent on microbial activities and coliform populations of Pahokee Muck. J. Environ. Qual. 9 (4): 673-677.

To determine the effect of amendment with sewage effluent on microbiological properties of organic soils dehydrogenase, carbon metabolism by the microbial community and coliform survival were examined in field plots of Pahokee Muck. Test plots were amended at weekly intervals with sewage effluent at a rate of 5 cm/week. Control plot received water at comparable rates or were unamended. Dehydrogenase activities were increased approximately two-fold in the sewage and water amended soils over levels detected in the unamended soil. No significant variation in bacterial population was detected due to any treatment. Carbon metabolism in sewage and water amended soils was nearly equivalent and both activities were generally greater than those measured in unamended soils. Thus the increased microbial activity in sewage-amended plots resulted from augmented soil moisture and not the added nutrients of the sewage. Coliform (fecal and total) populations in the soil declined approximately 90% during the first 2 days following the addition of sewage affluent. Coliforms were detected to a 95-cm depth in soil columns receiving sewage effluent for 22 weeks. Hence survival of the coliforms is limited in Pahokee much, but that viable coliform, penetrated throughout the soil profile.

925 **Rochelle, B.P., Church, M.R., Daivid, M.B.,** 1987. Sulfur retention at intensively studied sites in the U.S. and Canada. Water Air Soil Pollut. 33: 73-78.

The authors compiled and summarized current literature on S input/output budgets for intensively studied sites and soil plots in the U.S. and Canada and found S retention to be related to both soil order and extent of the last glaciation. Zero net retention is associated with Spodosols and was found only at sites north of the limit of Wisconsian glaciation. Sites south of the limit of glaciation appear to be retaining from 20 to 90% of incoming S. These findings support the hypothesis that there exist regional variations in S retention in North America. Such variations are important in determining and predicting effects of acidic deposition on surface water chemistry.

926 **Romero, F., Elejaide, C.,** 1985. The uptake of metallic elements by plants from polluted soils. Toxicol. Environ. Chem. 10(3): 247-255.

Fiftyeight samples of five different species *(Poa, Trifolium repens, Plantago lanceolata, Diplotaxis* and *Pteridium aquilinum)* of wild plants were collected at seven points of Biscay. Statistically significant equations, relating most of metal uptake (i) to previously studied soil content and availability, (ii) to general soil characteristics and (iii) to position parameters could be obtained for all plants or individual species. Results are used as a basis to discuss uptake mechanisms of essential and heavy metals by plants collected from polluted areas.

927 **Romero, F., Elejalde, C.,** 1989. Distribution of metallic compounds between plants and soils. Toxicol Environ. Chem. 23(1): 143-152.

Distribution of metallic constituents between and aerial parts of wild plants has been discussed by using relative ionic impulsions. For calculation metals were divided into two groups leading to $^{I}_{MACRO}$ (K, Na, Ca, Mg and Mn, elements accumulted in aerial parts) and to $^{I}_{MICRO}$ (Fe, Cu, Zn, Co and contaminants accumulated in roots). Relative ionic impulsions may be attributed to an electric potential gradient and show if an active or passive uptake is happening. For macroelements linear relationships were obtained for Mg-K (global active uptake) and Na-Mn-Ca (global passive uptake) with inverse slopes. Passive ions seem to be used as counter ions for helping active assimilation Calculated potential gradient was close to 20 mV.

928 **Romero, F., Elejaide, C., Azpiazu, M.N.,** 1987. Metal, plant and soil pollution indexes. Water Air Soil Pollut. 34(4): 347-352.

Micro-constituent ionic impulsion, a parameter related to metal content and introduced to explain plant uptake, is now used to propose a plant global pollution index for industrialized areas. Plant toxic levels and previous analytical results (Pb, Co, Ni, Cr, Cd, Cu, Fe, and Zn) for five wild plant species and whole herbage from 14 sampling points with rural, industrial or urban character within Bilbao (Spain) zone, are used to calculate this index. On similar based a soil pollution index is also suggested, excluding Fe, as it is a natural and very variable macrocomponent. Comparisons between these two indexes are included; differences are discussed through leaf uptake or strong retention of metals on soils.

929 **Romero, F., Elejalde, C., Gomez, G.,** 1989, Monitoring of plant and soil pollution based on ionic impulsion. Water Air Soil Pollut. 44: 295-306.

Total pollution indexes for measuring heavy metal contamination of industrialized areas may be quickly estimated from selected metal partial indexes for soil (M-SPI) or plants (M-PPI). The best estimation (without distortion) for monitoring total plant pollution index is based on the sum of contributions of essential elements (Fe, Cu, and Zn). This fact suggests the existence of defense mechanisms of plants for balancing both the uptake of toxic metals and deficiencies of essential constituents. Finally total pollution indexes may be used for the estimation of the number of pollutants with toxic levels in plants or soils.

930 **Rosehart, G.R., Lee, J.Y.**, 1973. The effect of arsenic trioxide on the growth of white spruce seedlings. Water Air Soil Pollut. 2: 439-443.

In the smelting of arsenopyrite ores during the gold extraction process, substantial amounts of As_2O_3 are released into the environment. The potential effect of this fallout on the growth of white spruce trees is described. Several small trees were planted in soil containing various amounts of As_2O_3 and their growth was studied over an 11-month period. Substantial retardation of the growth of the trees with As containing soil was observed.

931 **Rossin, A.C., Sterritt, R.M., Lester, J.N.**, 1982. The influence of process parameters on the removal of heavy metals in activated sludge. Water Air Soil Pollut. 17: 185-196.

The behaviour of six heavy metals in an activated sludge pilot plant under conditions of normal and elevated influent metal concentrations has been studied. Percentage heavy metal removal at sludge ages of 4, 9 and 12d was more consistent when metals were added to the system, possibly as a result of lesser variation in heavy metal speciation in the settled sewage, and the greatest degree of accumulation of heavy metals by the biomass occured at the 12d sludge age. When shock loads of heavy metals were introduced into the system, their concentrations in the effluent did not immediately rise in proportion; however, heavy metal removal efficiencies were similar under steady state conditions of normal and elevated influent metal concentrations. Cd, Cu, and Ni were largely soluble in the effluent samples, but Cr, Pb and Zn were predominantly insoluble, indicating that particulate forms of these metals may escape removal in secondary sedimentation. The high degree of Ni solubility in the settled sewage and final effluent reflected its consistently poor removal in the process. The two most soluble metals, Cu and Ni, appeared to be associated to a large degree with high molecular weight substances in the settled sewage and final effluent, possibly influencing their availability for uptake by the biomass.

932 **Routson, R.C., Wildung, R.E., Bean, R.M.**, 1979. A review of the environmental impact of ground disposal of oil shale wastes. J. Environ. Qual. 8(1): 14-19.

Waste disposal methods for the major types of extraction processes, the potential environmental impacts of waste disposal to the ground, mitigation of environmental impacts of waste disposal to the ground, mitigation of environmental effects, and further research needs, are discussed.

Principal waste products of oil shale extraction constitute 125% of the original volume, and disposal may affect vast land areas. Principal wastes scheduled for ground disposal include the waters produced during retorting and subsequently separated from the shale oil and the spent shales remaining after extraction. Retort waters contain relatively high concentrations of complex, soluble organic components, and the spent shale contain potentially leachable salts and organic pyrolytic products. Spent shales have erosion potential when disposed on the surface. Shale management, emphasizing erosion control and shale as a growth medium, and revegetation methods for establishing salt and drought-tolerant plant species are discussed.

933 **Rump, H.H.,** 1980, Polynuclear aromatic hydrocarbons in trickling water and sewage. In 'Trace Substances in Environ.' Health XIV. Unvi. Mo. Columbia: 507-515.

Poly-nuclear aromatic hydrocarbons (PAHs) are an important class of organic compounds which can be found in the entire environment. The carcinogenic activity of some PAHs is very high so that thorough knowledge of their environmental behaviour is necessary. For investigations in aquatic systems, tricking filters filled with quartz and gavel were fed with a mixture of selected substances. Investigations of the behaviour of PAHs in surface and sewage water in some cases showed strong correlation to other parameters, e.g. the content of suspended matter. Analysis of PAHs was performed by high-pressure liquid chromatography and thin-layer chromatography.

934 **Russell, J.M.,** 1982. Interaction of slaughter house effluent protein with three New Zealand soils. Agric. Res. 25(1): 21-26.

Ability to sorb proteins of the type found in slaughterhouse effluents was assessed in three New Zealand soils. Bovine serum albumin was used as a representative protein. Significant adsorption of protein occurred within 2 hours at initial solution pHs typical of slaughterhouse effluent (pH 6-9). The amount of protein held is considerably increased by the presence of 0.005M $CaCl_2$ which compressed the charged double layer about the protein and soil particles. It is concluded that slaughterhouse effluent proteins will be held in the top layers of the soil under irrigation conditions.

935 **Saad, M.A.H., Ezzat, A.A., El-Rayis, O.A., Hafez, H.,** 1981. Occurrence and distribution of chemical pollutants in lake Mariut, Egypt, II Heavy metals. Water Air Soil Pollut. 16: 401-407.

The distribution of heavy metals in the water of polluted Lake Mariut, and their accumulation in Tilapia fish in this lake were studied. The concentration of the metals (Zn, Cu, Fe, Mn and Cd) in the lake water are mostly due to variations in the discharge rate of dumped wastes. The mean concentrations of these metals in different fish parts were much higher than those in the lake water.

936 **Sabey, B.R., Agbin, N.N.,** and **Markstron, D.C.,** 1977. Land application of sewage sludge: IV. Wheat growth, N content, N fertilizer value and N use efficiency as influenced by sewage sludge and wood waste mixtures. J. Environ. Qual. 6(1): 52-58.

Various combinations of sewage sludge and wood wastes were added at four rates ranging from the equivalent 22.4 to 224, tons/ha in a greenhouse study. Every mixture except 50% bark- 50% sludge caused an increase in wheat growth compared to the control. The highest application rates of 100% sludge, 25% wood- 75% sludge and 50% bark-50% sludge resulted in less growth than the next lower application rates. The addition of the equivalent of 134 kg/ha of N and 19.5 kg/ha of P with each organic material mixture and rate, generally caused an increase in growth compared to the organic material treatments without fertilizers but in most cases the increased was not great. The relationship between wheat growth and N and NO_3-N content in the plant tissue is quadratic. Correlations between wheat growth and N concentration or NO_3-N concentration in plant tissue were not as close as the above described relationships. The amount of total N, NH_4-N remaining in the greenhouse pots after harvest generally increased as the application rate of each treatment increases. Several approaches were used to determine the N use efficiency. It is estimated that from 2 to 22.7% of the initial N was taken up by plants during the 50 day growth period used in this study.

937 **Sabey, B.R., Evans, N.A.,** 1982. Application of the waste water effluent of a rural community to a Mountain meadow. J. Water Pollut. Control Fed. 54(1): 70-76.

The effects of sprinkler application of 7.5 cm/wk of effluent compared to 7.5 cm/wk of typical irrigation water used in the area on the water, plant, and soil characteristics of a mountain meadow were studied in 1977 and 1978. Also studied was the influence of drainage tiles compared to natural drainage. The addition of effluent caused a greater increase in the concentration of Cl and Na in soil solution samples than was caused by irrigation water. Application of effluent caused significant increases in plant yield, protein production, and Na and P uptake. Effluent application also significantly increased the ortho-P and the exchangeable Na and K of the soil surface. Some soil changes caused by a change in the type of irrigation system were observed.

938 **Sadana, U.S.,** 1987. Behaviour of toxic elements in the soil-plant system and associated hazards in intensive agriculture. Ann. Biol. 3(1): 1-14.

Toxic elements enter the soil-plant systems through a variety of sources. Sewage wastes and fertilizers are the major contributors . Once in the soil, these elements interact with organic and inorganic constituents. Transformations such as adsorption, chelation, dissolution-precipitation and methylation, control the availability of toxic elements to plants and consequently to humans and animals. The toxic effects of these elements are exhibited either through reduced plant growth or sick animal/humans. Among the various toxic elements, B and Ni are important in terms of their phytotoxicity. Cadmium, Pb and Hg though potentially hazardous to animals generally accumulate preferentially in leaves and roots rather than in grains. Phytotoxicity of Zn, Cu and Ni provides a barrier to their toxic levels in the food chain.

939 **Sadana, U.S., Singh, V.,** 1987. Effect of zinc application on yield and cadmium content of spinach (*Spinacea oleiacea* L.) Ann. Biol. 3(2): 59-80.

Cadmium ia s toxic heavy metal causing respiratory, photosynthetic and structural disorders in plant at relatively low concentrations. Due to geo-chemical kinship, zinc competes with Cd for absorption sites on the root surface of plants. Antagonistic effect of Zn on uptake or Cd by radish and bushbean had been reported though stimulation of Cd content of soybean by Zn has also been noted earlier. The possibility of reducing the Cd poisoning of spinach by soil application of Zn has been studied.

940 **Saeed, M., Rox. R.L.,** 1979. Influence of phosphate fertilization on zinc adsorption by tropical soil. J. Soil Sci. Soc. Am 43(4): 683-686.

Zinc adsorption isotherms were constructed for 5 soils from Hawaii. Equlibrating conditions were 25°C, 0.01 M $CaCl_2$ Zn ranged upto 600 μg/mL. Zn adsorption varies with the nature of charge on soil, as influenced by phosphates.

941 **Sahai, R., Shukla, N., Jabeen, S., Saxena, P.K.,** 1985. Pollution effect of distillery waste on the growth behaviour of phaseolus radiatus. L. Environl. Pollut. (A. Ecol. Biol.) 37: 245-253.

The impact of various concentrations of distillery effluent on the germination and growth behaviour of *phaseolus radiatus* L. was studied. The effluent was highly acidic with high BOD and N. The rate and germination percentage decreased with increasing effluent concentration. The respective length of the root and shoot, plant biomass, net primary productivity, seed output and chlorophyll content were considerably increased with when the plants were treated with 5% effluent. The carotenoid content increased at effluent concentrations up to 30% in the first and second harvests and up to 15 and 5% in the third and forth harvests, respectively. The soluble nitrogen and protein contents of the seed increased up to 5 and 15%, respectively.

942 **Sahai, R., Srivastava, Chetna,** 1988. Effect of fertilizer factory waste on seed germination, seedling growth and pigment contents of plants. J. Indian Botl. Soc. 67(3): 309-311.

The impact of various concentrations of fertilizer factory effluent on seed germination, seedling growth and pigment content of *Phaseolus vulgaris* Linn and *Momordica charantia* Linn was studied. With increase in effluent concentrations there was a gradual decrease in percentage germination, rate of germination and chlorophyll a and b. The effluent was toxic to seedlings at high concentrations, but was beneficial at 2.5 percent.

943 **Sahoo, S.K., Khopar, S.M.,** 1989. A novel method for separation of chromium (VI) from waste water by extraction chromatography. Indian J. Environ. Prot. 9(4): 241-244.

A novel method is developed for extraction chromatographic separation of chromium (VI) from water and waste water with Aliquat 336S as an extractant on silica gel column. Chromium (20 mg) was quantitatively extracted at pH 5.0 from 0.01 M citric acid. It was stripped from column with 2 M nitric or sulphuric acid or with 1M sodium hydroxide, sodium carbonate, ammonium hydroxide, sodium carbonate, ammonium hydroxide or ammonium nitrate. From the aqueous phase chromium was determined spectrophotometrically. Chromium was separated from a large number of elements normally associated with environmental samples. Several multicomponent separations of chromium involving copper, iron, lead, cadmium and bismuth were carried out. The method was extended for the analysis of chromium from samples, like, waste water and sediments.

944 **Sahu, S.K., Pal, S.S.,** 1987. Direct and residual effect of paper mill sludge and lime stone on crop Yield under three different crop rotations on an acid red soil. J. Indian. Soc. Soil. Sci. 35: 46-51

Significantly higher yields of crops was obtained with the application of paper mill sludge or limestone in crop rotations of pigeon pea (*Cajanus cajan Mill* sp.) plus black gram *(Phaseolus mungo Roxb.)*, wheat, little millet (*Panicum miliare* L), niger *(Giuizotia abysissinica cass)*, french bean (*Phaselus vulgaris* L) and finger millet *(Eleusine coracania Goertn)* rape seed (*Brassica Campestris.* L.) green gram *(Phaseolus aureaus Roxb.)* on an acid clay loam soil. Residual effect of liming was beneficial. lime dose at 0.25 lime requirement (LR) proved to be optimum dose and overliming at 1.5LR had detrimental effect on the crop yields. The yield increase may be due to increase in pH, exchangeable Ca^{2+} + Mg^{2+} and reduction of exchangeable H^{+} and Al^{3+} of the soils as observed in an incubation study.

945 **Sahu, K.C., Venkateswaran, D.,** 1989. Characterization of nickeliferous laterite of Sukinda in Cuttack District, Orissa. J. Geological Soc. India 33(2): 116-131.

Synthetic goethite and nickles containing solutions of various concn. were used in simulated weathering experiments to study the mechanisms of mobilization and the dispersion patterns of nickel in laterites. Amorphous hydrated iron-oxide scavenged Co and Ni from the precipitating solution, but Ni cations inhibited goethite crystallisation.

946 **Sakata, M.,** 1987. Relationship between adsorption of arsenic (iii) and

boron by soil and soil properties. Environ. Sci. Technol. 21(11): 1126-1130.

The distribution coefficients (K_d) for arsenic (iii) and boron in a linear adsorption isotherm were determined for 15 subsurface soils collected from different sites in Japan, and the relationship between those K_d values and soil properties was examined. The soils differed greatly in their chemical and physical properties. The K_d value for arsenic (iii) was significantly correlated with the dithionite-extractable Fe content in the soils (r = 0.90), whereas a high positive correlation was also found between the K_d value for boron and the oxalate-extractable Al content in the soils (r = 0.98).

947 **Saksena, D.N., Mishra, S.R.,** 1991. The water quality index and self-purification capacity of a sewage collecting channel, Morar (Kalpi) river at Gwalior, Madhya Pradesh. J. Freshwater Biol. 3(2): 169-175.

Water quality index and self-purification capacity of a sewage collecting channel, Morar (Kalpi) river were studied in different seasons at various stations during the period 1987-89. Abiotic parameters like DO_2, COD, total solids, sulphides and nitrites were considered for the assessment of self purification capacity of the river. The water quality indices were calculated in order to know the potability of water of the river for human consumption.

948 **Salafeigenbavm, A.G., Limoni, H.,** 1981. Volatelization efficiency of nitrogen from sewage effluent and fertilizer applied to corn plants growing in a clay soil. J. Environ. Qual. 10 (3): 284-287.

Effects of irrigation with secondary municipal sewage effluent on N availability in a fertilized soil were studied in a greenhouse using N as a tracer. Corn was grown in a clay soil with ammonium-N added as solid fertilizer, sewage effluent and a mineral solution. Between 55 and 69% of the ammonium sulfate ^{15}N was taken up by the corn plants. Between 21 and 32% of the fertilizer N was recovered as organic-N in the soil after 43 days, while negligible amounts of exchangeable NH_4 and NO_3 were detected. Losses of ammonium sulfate-N applied to the soil before seeding, probably through denitrification, ranged between 6 and 15%. Similar results were obtained whether the fertilized soil was irrigated with demineralized, water, sewage effluent, or a mineral solution simulating the mineral composition of the sewage effluent. About 61% of the tagged ammonium-N applied as sewage effluent was taken up by the corn plants and 14% was immobilized in the organic fraction of soil. About 24% of the effluent, tagged-ammonium-N was lost, apparently through both denitrification and volatilization.The corresponding loss from the mineral solution tagged-N was about 17%.

949 **Salim, R.,** 1986. Adsorption of lead on mud. J. Environl. Sci. Health, 21A, (6): 551-560.

The influence of few factors on lead adsorption as concentration, chemical form and drying of mud, has been studied. Desorption of lead from mud samples has been also looked into.

950 **Salkinoja-Salonen, M., Middeldorp, P., Briglla, M., Valo, R., Hag-gblom, M., Mcbain, A.**, 1989. A cleanup of old industrial sites, in 'Biotechnology and Biodegradation': 347-367.

The general problems of using micro organisms to remediate chemically contaminated soils is discussed. Lab and field experience are described for one category of chemically contaminated soils (wood preserving sites), where bioremediation under field conditions appeared possible. Chlorophenol degrading micro organisms were shown to detoxify the contaminated soils. Immobilized inoculant proved superior to liquid inoculum. Bioremediation was feasible for a wide range of concn. (1-9000 mg/kg) of chlorophenol. At older sites, range of a part of the chlorophenol was sometimes inaccessible to biodegradation by an unknown mechanism. Chlorophenoldegrading inoculants remained viable in soil a very long time so reinoculation was rarely needed. A gram-positive inoculant (*Rhodococcus*) was superior to a gram-negative inoculant (*Flavobacterium*) in survival and degradation capacity. Transforming reactions such as biomethylation of chlorophenol and its downstream metabolic intermediates were in some soils enhanced by external soil amendments. The response was unpredictable. Therefore testing for mineralization in the lab, is recommended for each soil before using soil amendments at field scale.

951 **Samiullah, Khan, Iqbal, N.**, 1988. Adsorption of Cu, Pb and Zn on saturated illite. Clay Res. 7: 50-53.

The adsorption Cu, Pb and Zn on Ca saturated illite was studied using Freundlich equation and thermo-parameters. The adsorption isotherm showed that the binary strength of metal ions, was in the order Cu > Pb > Zn and decreased with rising temperature. The Freundlish adsorption capacity constant followed the same order and the effect of temperature was identical but the intensity factor showed a reverse result. The thermodynamic parameters gave similar results.

952 **Samunder Singh, Pahuja, S.S., Singh, S.M.**, 1989 Effect of herbicides contaminated irrigation water on germination and seedlings growth of different crops. Internatl. J. Trop Agric. 7(3&4): 173-178.

The effect of the irrigation water contaminated with different concentrations of 2, 4 - D ester, glyphosate and paraquat was studied on the germination, root and shoot lengths and seedling weights of pearlimillet, green gram, cowpea, maize, toria, cluster bean and pigeon pea. Among the three herbicides, 2 4-D was the most deleterious and paraquat the least. The higher concentration was more harmful than the lower one.

953 **Sangalang, J.B.**, 1985. The breeding of sweet potato (*ipomoea batatas* L). Lam. for tolerance to aluminum toxicity. Diss Abst Int. Pt. B. Sci. & Engg.

46(5).

Results of a field test conducted in a silt loam at Orange Virginia demonstrated that yield of sweet potato was not significantly affected by the application of sulphur (pH = 4.2) or lime (pH = 5.4). The relative marketable yield (RMRY), which is the ratio of the marketable yield in the sulphur treatment to that in the lime treatment confirmed the greenhouse classification of the clones into tolerant and susceptible groups. The tolerant group had greater RMRY than the susceptible group.

954 **Sant, H.R., Jha, M.N.**, 1986. Effect of chemical factory effluents on germination of finger millet seeds. Agric. Biol. Res. 2(1-2): 44-48.

The effect of a chemical factory effluent on seed germination and seedling growth of finger millet was studied. The seeds were treated with different concentrations of effluent viz. 0, 2.5, 5, 10, 25, 50 and 100 per cent. Results on mortality, percentage seed germination, quantitative changes and seedling growth reveal that best seed germination and seedling growth occurred in 2.5 to 5.0% effluent concentration. Reverse results were observed at 10 per cent and above effluent concentration.

955 **Sarkunan, V., Misra, A.K., Nayar, P.K.**, 1988. Effect of factory effluents on germinability and growth of rice. Oryza 25: 323-324.

The chemical characteristics of the effluents discharged by paper mill and a rayon factory were assessed. The effect of these effluents on the germinability and growth of rice (Cr. IR 8) was determined. Both the effluents were however, low in metal contaminants barring Al in the paper mill effluent. The effluents had no effect on the germinability of rice seeds., but showed adverse effect on seedling growth. Root and shoot growth of rice seedlings was inhibited to an extent of 50 and 28 per cent, respectively, by the paper mill effluent in contrast to 13 and 3 per cent inhibition caused by rayon factory effluent.

956 **Sarkunan, V., Misra, A.K.; Nayar, P.K.**, 1989. Interaction of Zn, Cu and Ni in soil on yield and metal content of rice. J. Environ. Sci. Health. Part A. Env. Sci. and Engg. A 24 (5): 459-466.

A pot culture experiment was conducted under flooded conditions using an alluvial soil (Haplaquept) with the rice cultivare Ratna, treated with a 3^3 factorial combination of Zn (200, 400 and 800 mg/kg soil), Cu (50, 100 and 200 mg/kg soil) and Ni (25, 50 and 100 mg/kg soil). Significant metal interactions for Zn-Cu, and Zn-Cu-Ni were observed both for grain and straw yield. Stepwise multiple regression analysis indicated that the prediction values for grain yield increased significantly when DTPA extractable metals were taken into consideration rather then the metal addition rate. The relative metal contents both in the grain and straw were in the order Zn > Cu > Ni. The mean values of DTPA extractable metals in the post harvest soil were 23, 22 and 16% of the added levels for Zn, Cu and Ni, respectively. The metal interaction effects in soil, particularly of

Zn-Cu, was reflected in the yield as well as metal contents of grain and straw.

957 **Sato, K., Sada, K., Asakura, K.,** 1988. Effect of emissions from a coal-fired power plant on soil trace element concentration. NTIS Springfield: 38.

A coal-fired power plant that has been operated for 25 years was selected for this study. The effect of trace elements (As, Cd, Cr, Cu and Hg) in the flue gas emitted from the plant on the soil environment has been evaluated through the soil observations and diffusion estimation. The element concentrations in soils in the vicinity of the plant roughly coincided with those observed at background regions. The enrichment discrimination factors (EDF) for the 5 elements were also within the range of those observed at background regions. As a result, increases in EDF caused by deposition of elements for 25 years were estimated to be less than 0.2. This value was within the range of the scatter at background regions.

958 **Sattar, M.A., Morshed, G.S.,** 1989. Effects of urea pesticide combinations on ammonification and nitrification in soil. Chemosphere 18(11-12): 2329-2337.

The combined uses of dichlorvos ureas or dieldrin+urea greatly influenced the ammonification and nitrification in Red Brown Terrace soils. A t-test and a linear regression were applied to the results.

959 **Savey, B.R., Barbarick, K.A., Evans, N.A.,** 1981.

Soil filtration of sewage effluent of a rural Area. NTIS, Springfield, Va.: 115.

The treatment performance of irrigation using primary lagoon treated municipal sewage is compared to normal stream or ditch water irrigation when applied to mountain meadows and crops in a high altitude climate during summer months. The two irrigation waters are applied at different rates to plots that have both natural drainage and tile underdrains. A special winter operation is evaluated for applying primary lagoon treated municipal waste water to ridge and furrow basins after they have been been covered with an insulating sheet of ice and snow. Development of winter operations allow capital cost of constructing winter storage to be drastically reduced for small rural treatment facilities.

960 **Saviozzi, S., Levi-Minzi, R., Riffaldi, R.,** 1983. How organic matter sources affect cadmium movement in soil. Biocycle, 24(3): 29-31.

This research indicated that adding organic residues to soil can restrict heavy metal movement and that various organics behave in different ways.

961 **Sawarkar, N.J., Dikshit, P.R.,** 1990. Use of oxalic acid industry waste as a source of sulphur and its effect on availability of rock phosphate. J. In-

dian Soc. Soil Sci. 38: 333-335.

Oxalic acid industry waste water increased yield of maize and soybean while phosphorous had no significant effect mainly due to presence of sulphur in water.

962 **Sawhney, B.L.,** 1987. Movement of organic chemicals through land fill and hazardous waste disposal sites. J. Soil Sci. Soc. Am. 22: 447-474.

Out of about 250 constituents of the USEPA's target compound list (TCL), 126 are organic chemicals - 35 volatiles, 65 semivolatiles, and 26 pesticides and PCBs. Analyses of leachates from a number of landfills have revealed the presence of both volatile and semi-volatile organics, Similarly, soil, water and container samples from hazardous waste dump sites have been found to contain many of the TCL organic chemicals. Some sites contain large concentrations of these chemicals. Movement of organic chemicals is governed not only by the capacity of the soil to retain the chemical, but also by the soil environment, non-equilibrium interactions, and hydrogeology of the site. Effects of the soil environment and the non-equilibrium interactions on movement of organic chemicals are illustrated by reactions of phenol under aerobic and anaerobic conditions and persistence of volatile hydrocarbon 1, 2-dichloropropane, respectively. Movement of organic chemicals in relation to hydrogeological features is illustrated from examples of groundwater analysis near landfill and chemical waste-disposal sites.

963 **Sawyers, D.E., Dental, S.L.,** 1990. Analysis of in situ landfill leachate chemistry. Resource Manage. Technol. 18(3-4): 123-128.

Chemical data on leachate obtained in situ from a municipal solid waste site were collected for a study on landfill-age, with or without leachate recirculation. Results indicated the laboratory procedures and experimental apparatus maintained in situ characteristics.

964 **Saxena, S.K., Chatterji, P.C.,** 1988. Mining activity and creation of wastelands in western Rajasthan. In Wastelands Development and their Utilization. Scientific Publishers: Jodhpur, India 41-61.

The various mining activities in western Rajasthan, India, and their effects on land degradation, reduction in agricultural land, land subsidence, salinization, and vegetation degradation are described. Methods of reclamation, such as soil conservation and revegetation of mine spoils and the use of water filled pits for fish farming, are outlined.

965 **Schaedle, M., Thornton, F.C., Raynal, D.J., Tepper, H.B.,** 1989. Response of tree seedlings to aluminium. Tree Physiol. 5(3): 337-356.

This review focuses on the mechanisms underlying aluminum toxicity in trees. The major topics discussed include the uptake and localization of Al, effects of Al on growth and composition, factors determining the response to Al, proposed mechanisms of Al resistance and the occurence of Al phytotoxicity under field conditions.

966 **Schaedle, M., Thornton, F.C., Raynal, D.J.,** 1989. Tolerance of red oak and American and European beach seedlings to aluminum. J. Environ. Qual. 18(4): 541-545.

The effect of aluminum on the growth of red oak (Quercus rubra L.), American beech (Fagus grandifolia Ehrh.) and European beech (Fagus sylvatica L.) seedlings was studied in solution culture containing from 0 to 3000 μM Al at pH 4.0. Aluminum had no detrimental effect on biomass of shoots or red oak and American beech. Shoot biomass of European beech was significantly reduced by Al, with greater reduction measured for seedlings grown in lower ionic-strength media. Root biomass of species did not decline with increasing Al, and actually increased in some Al treatments. Generally, Ca, Mg, and P tissue concentrations of leaves and roots decreased with increasing Al for all three species.

967 **Schafelford, C.D.,** 1991. Laboratory diffusion testing for waste disposal – A review. J. Contam. Hydrol. 7: 177-217.

A summary of effective diffusion coefficients from the literature suggests that the major physical factor affecting the value of the measured diffusion coefficient is the degree of saturation of the soil, with D - values for nonreactive and reactive solutes in saturated soils being as much as 10-20 times higher than the corresponding values in unsaturated soils. Most of the other physical factors only become important in soils which are highly unsaturated. In addition, the diffusive transport rates or reactive solutes subject to reversible sorption reactions can be as much as 5000 times lower than those of nonreactive solutes in saturated soils and from 20 to 630,000 times lower in unsaturated soils.

968 **Schafelford, C.D., Daniel, D.E.,** 1991. Diffusion in saturated soil, I Background, II Results for compacted clay. J. Geotechnical Engg. 117(3): 467-484; 485-506.

Both steady-state and transient equations describing the diffusive transport of inorganic chemicals are presented. Several factors affecting diffusion coefficients are identified. The definition for the diffusion coefficient for diffusion in soil (effective diffusion coefficient, D) is shown to vary widely. In general, variations in the definition of D result from consideration of the different factors that influence diffusion of solutes in soil and the different ways of including the volumetric water content in the governing equations. The effective diffusion coefficients, D of three anions (Br, Cl, and I) and three cations (Cd^{2+}, K^+ and Zn^{2+}) diffusing in two compacted clay soils, kaolinite and Lufkin clay are measured. The effects of molding water content and method of compaction on the measured D values are evaluated for kalinite. The calculated D values varied between $4 \cdot 10^{-10}$ m^2/s and 2×10^{-9} m^2/s and based on the results for chloride diffusion in kaolinite, are relatively insensitive to molding water content and compaction method. The measured D values for Cl and Br in kalinite are in excellent agreement with previous studies, High D values for the cations are attributed to nonlinear adsorption behaviour at relatively high concentrations and to the possibility of chemical precipitation of the heavy metal species (Cd^{2+} and Zn^{2+}). Also, D values determined from reservoir concentrations typically are higher than D values determined from soil concentration profiles.

969 **Schafelford, C.D., Daniel, D.E., Liljestrand, H.M.,** 1989. Diffusion or inorganic chemical species in compacted clay soil. J. Contam. Hydrol. 4(3): 241-273.

The diffusion of inorganic chemicals in compacted clay soil was studied. The effective diffusion coefficients (D) of anionic (Cl, Br and I) and cationic (K, Cd^{2+} and Zn^{2+}) species in a synthetic leachate were measured. The two soils were compacted and pre-soaked to minimize mass transport due to suction in the soil. The D values for Cl reported in this study are in excellent agreements with previous findings for other types of soil. The D values for the metals (K^+, Cd^{2+} and Zn^{2+}) are thought to be high (conservative) due to: (1) Ca^{2+} saturation of the exchange complex of the clays: (2) precipitation of Cd^{2+} and Zn^{2+}; and (3) nonlinear adsorption behaviour.

970 **Schalscha, E.B., Vergara, I., Schirado, T., Morales, M.,** 1979. Nitrate movement in a Chilean agricultural area irrigated with untreated sewage water. J. Environ. Qual. 8(1): 27-30.

Nitrate concentrations in soils and drainage and well waters were determined in a 15-ha field representing about 4,000 ha of Agricultural land irrigated exclusively with raw sewage water for > 25 years. Analysis of the percolating water below the root zone indicated that the leached NO_3-N was about 350 kg/ha per year. The transit time for water to move through the unsaturated zone to the saturated zone at a depth of 2 to 2.2 m was < 1 year, and the leaching fraction was estimated as 0.63. Concentrations of NO_3-N ranged from 20 to 35 mg/L in the percolating water of the unsaturated zone; whereas two well waters contained 9 and 14mg/L.

971 **Shier, G.A.,** 1985. Response of red spruce and Dalsam fir seedlings to ammonium toxicity in nutrient solutions. Can. J. For. Res. 15(1): 29-33.

Red spruce picea rubens Sang. and Dalsam fir (*Abies balsamea* (L). Mill). were grown in nutrient solutions containing 1, 25, 50, 100 and 200 mg/L aluminium (Al) at pH 3.8. Seedlings died only when placed directly in solutions containing Al without first being conditional to growth in a hydroponic system. In preconditioned seedlings, no evidence of Al injury was noted in the tops of seedlings at any level of Al except for small reductions in shoot growth. Aluminium toxicity symptoms in roots, however, were well developed, though spruce showed less tolerance than fir, inhibition of root growth in both species was first evident at 50 mg/l Al, root length decreasing with increasing concentrations of Al. Spruce seedlings at Al concentrations of 100 mg/l and higher were characterised by thickened, stunted, dark brown roots. Roots deterioration was caused by Al-induced destruction of epidermal and cortical cells. Although root elongation was severely restricted in spruce and fir, root dry weight was not significantly reduced. Aluminium decreased seedling uptake of most mineral elements, manganese, magnesium, and zinc were affected most, and boron and phosphorus least.

972 **Schinner, M.,** 1980. The distribution of lead emissions over a wide area in an east Alpine basin. Environl. Pollut. Ser. A: (Ecol. Biol.) 22 (4): 247-258.

Determination of the Pb concentrations in spruce needles and twig axes showed that the Pb contents of sites located in the area around Innsbruck, Austria, varied significantly. Sites within the town area showed the highest Pb concentration. With increasing altitude the Pb accumulation decreased, both at sites on the northwest slope of the Patscherkofel and at those on the southeast slope of the Nordkette mountain. Comparison of different samples revealed that 2- and 3-yr old twig axes are best suited for illustrating slight differences in Pb concentration. The Pb contents of the younger twig axes and those of the needles differ significantly. The possible causes of the increased Pb content of the needles and twig axes are considered.

973 **Schitzer, M., Kerndorff, H.,** 1980. Effect of pollution on humic substances. J. Environ. Sci. Health. Part B, Pesticides. Food Contaminants and Agril. Wastes, 15(4): 431-456.

Humic acids (HAS) and fulvic acids (FAS) were isolated from unpolluted and polluted soils and sediments. Following purification the HAS and FAS were characterized. Polluted HAS and FAS contained more N and S but less O and were richer in all metals and Si than were unpolluted ones. IR spectra showed that polluted humic materials were enriched in COO-groups, secondary noncyclic amides, and possibly also in SO_3H groups. DTA curves indicated that the polluted HAS and FAS were more thermostable than unpolluted HAS and FAS. Unusually high N, S, Cu, Cr, Zn and Hg contents of humic materials are apparently useful indicators of soil and sediment pollution.

974 **Schmitt, H.W., Sticher, H.,** 1989. Competitive behaviour of binary and ternarymetal systems in soils. Mittell der Devts. Bodenk Gesell 59(1): 473-476.

To describe transport of heavy metals-soil, Langmiur equations which take changing proportions of metals into account, are described. The competition of Cd and Zn in various ratios and that of Cd, Pb and Cu are discussed using competitive Langmuir equations.

975 **Schoen, R.S., Winterlin, W.L.,** 1987. The effects of various soil factors and amendments on degradation of pesticides mixtures. J. Environ. Sci.

Health 22(3): 347-377.

Atrazine, captan, carbaryl, 2, 4-D, diazinon, fenitrothion, and trifluralin were studied under varying laboratory conditions of soil type, pH, moisture content, organic matter content, microbial activity, and pesticide concentration. Of the variables investigated, pesticide concentration was the single most important factor with degradation rates much slower at high (1000 ppm) levels of fortification than moderate (100 ppm) levels. Under most conditions, chemical degradation was at least as significant as microbial degradation. Effects of other factors varied considerably and were pesticide dependent.

976 **Schonhard, G., Laar, C. Von, 1990.** The heavy metal content of horticultural and agricultural soils in the overcrowded area of Berlin. Gesunde Pflanzen 42 (10): 361-368.

The concentration of the population of west Berlin causes a corresponding concentration of water, soil, and air pollutants. About 1100 samples from small allotments and 500 from agricultural soils were analysed for their Pb, Cd, V, Cr, Co, Ni, Zn and Cu content. The garden soils had greater contents on average, as most were within the area of concentrations whereas the agricultural soils were outside. The heavy metal content of 284 manure samples were also determined. About 15% of these had contents (2 M HCl extracts) above permissible values.

977 **Schramel, P., Lillg, G., Seif, R., 1987.** A complete HF digestion method for element and trace element determination in soils, sediments, sludges and other similar samples using a closed system. Fresenius'z Anal. Chem. 326(2): 135-138.

978 **Schuller, E., 1989.** Enzymic activities and microbial biomass in old land fill soil with long term metal pollution. Verhandlungen Gessellschaft fur Ekologuia. 18: 339-348.

The effects of heavy metal pollution on the biomass of bacteria and fungi, and on the enzyme activities of amylase, dehydrogenase and phosphates were studied. Soil samples were obtained from an old zinc smelter an old landfill site which had received wastes from a copper smelter and from an urban beech forest. There was no significant effect of heavy metal contamination on microbial biomass, while fungal biomass production was inhibited by high concentrations of Cd and Cu. There were highly significant correlations between heavy metal concentrations (log transformed) and enzymic activities. Pb was most inhibiting compound for dehydrogenases, while amylase and acid phosphatase were most adversely affected by Cd, and Cd and Zn, respectively.

979 **Schuman, G.E., Rauzi, F., Howard, G.S., 1987.** Vegetation responses to soil surface modification in mined land reclamation Reclam. Reveg. Res., 6(1): 49-54.

Three surface modification treatments (pitting, furrowing and soil ridges) were imposed on topsoiled uranium mine spoil to evaluate their effect on forange production. Coasted wheat grass (*Agropyron desertorum* (Fisch) *Schult.*) production was greater for all three treatments when compared to the control in 5 of the 6 years evaluated. Precipitation was only 49% of the annual average for the year in which the treatment did not exhibit any benefits. The greater production of the surface modification treatments is attributed to improved water infiltration, increased slow trapping and reduced evaporation.

980 **Schwedt, G., Jahns, G.,** 1987. Scheme for the analysis of lead distribution within and upon contaminated plants. Fresenius Zeits chrift fur Analytische Chemie. 328(1-2): 83-88.

The solubility of lead on contaminated *Decylis glomerata* was determined by stepwise extraction with n-butanol, water and 0.1 or 1 M HCl. Compartmentation of lead in leaves between cellular walls, vacuole liquid (and soluble proteins) and cellular organelles was obtained by filtration and centrifugation. Cellular walls and organelles were also analysed by stepwise extraction. This scheme of analysis provides the following distribution of lead (average total lead was 14 ppm in 10 samples): 64% upon the surface of leaves (of which 66% was soluble in water), 28% within the cellular walls 5% within the vacoule liquid and 3% mainly as phytotoxically active.

981 **Schwer, C.B., Clausen, J.C.,** 1989. Vegetative filter treatment of dairy milkhouse waste water. J. Environ. Qual 18(4): 444-445.

Comparison of this study with earlier ones suggests that hydraulic loading rate governs the effectiveness of filter strip treatment.

982 **Scialdone, R., Scognamiglio R., Ramunni, A.U.,** 1980. The short and medium term effects of organic amendments on lead availability. Water Air Soil Pollut. 13(3): 267-274.

The effect of 6 organic amendments on Pb solubility and availability was studied from May to Sept., 1978 in a sandy soil low in organic matter. Three extractants were used to assay the Pb solubility-barium chloride 0.5 M, ammonium acetate 2.5% at pH 7 and EDTA 0.05 M at pH 7. During the aging process both increases and decreases of Pb solubility were observed in manured soils with respect to the control. Only in the soil treated with cow manure was a decrease of Pb solubility in NH_4ACO always noted. From regression lines of Pb concentration on soil solution ratio, it was observed that only the soil treated with cow manure showed a significant decrease of slope of regression line when it was dispersed in NH_4ACO solution. The regression lines of Pb concentration on organic matter extracted by NH_4ACO and, especially EDTA showed that these reagents extract mainly Pb complexed with organic compounds. A physiological test on Pb availability showed that only in the presence of cow manure was the Pb assimilation greatly decreased.

983 **Scott, T.M.**, 1979. Removal of pollution in the overland flow (grass filtration) system. Progress Water Technol. 11(4-5): 301-313.

In the overland flow system at Melbourne, Australia, the sewage is given primary sedimentation and passed to irrigation areas. A design hydraulic loading on the system of 0.23 ML/ha/d can be achieved with corresponding BOD and TOC decayed in exponential from mean levels of 507 mg/L and 350 mg/L to 24 mg/L and 65 mg/L. respectively with TOC approaching a non-decaying residual of 56 mg/L. Suspended solids reduction was of an exponential nature with a residual of 22 mg/L. Methylene blue Active Substances showed a similar decay. The removal of N was complex and to some extent unexplained. The main N losses could be attributed to plant uptake and stripping of NH_3 from the waste water. Organic N loss followed a linear regression. Small amounts of NO_3 appeared late in the system. The overall reduction in N concentration was 30%. Little P removal was evident, with the system exhibiting as apparent increase and then a decrease to about the original level. Precipitation of heavy metal as surfides in the anaerobic section of the system was rapid generally linear with very small residuals of unknown organic complexes. The overland flow system is effective in the removal of BOD, SS, and heavy metals but only moderately efficient in the removal of nutrients.

984 **Scott, D.S.**, 1980, Removal and recovery of metals and phosphate from Municipal sewage sludge. Municipal Environ. Res. Lab. Off. R&D USEPA: 34

The technical and economical aspects of acid extracting heavy metals and phosphates from municipal chemical sludges and subsequently recovering them by lime neutralization were examined. Such a process was found to be technically feasible, but the cost of the process was economically unattractive. The results should be valuable in assessing similar technology for removing heavy metals from municipal sludges.

985 **Seaker, E.M., Sopper, W.E.**, 1988. Municipal sludge for minespoil reclamation I. Effects on microbial population and activity J. Environ. Qual. 17: 591-597.

A field study of five coal surface mine sites reclaimed with sewage sludge and one site reclaimed by conventional methods was conducted to assess the effects of sludge amendments and time on population of bacteria. fungi, and actinomycetes, and on microbial respiration and organic matter decomposition. The sludge amended sites ranged in age from 1 to 5 yr, following sludge application, at rates of 120 to 134 Mg ha^{-1} (dry wt. basis). All sites were planted to grass and legume cover. Population of aerobic heterotrophic bacteria, fungi and nitrobacter and soil respiration, rate, were highest.

986 **Seaker, E.M., Sopper, W.E.**, 1988. Municipal sludge for minespoil

reclamation II. Effects on organic matter. J. Environ. Qual. 17: 598-602.

A field study of five coal stripmine sites reclaimed with sewage sludge and one site reclaimed with chemical fertilizers was conducted to determine the effects of sludge amendments and time on dry matter yields, detritus accumulations root growth, organic matter content, and soil organic C and N content. The reclaimed sites ranged in age from 1 to 5 yrs following reclamation with sludge at rates of 120 to 134 Mg ha^{-1} (dry basis). The fertiliser amended site was 5-yr old. All sites were planted in grass and legume cover. On the sludge amended sites, yield detritus, root growth, and organic matter were positively correlated with site age, increasing from the 1yr to 3-yr old site. On the 4 or 5 yr old sites values were greater than or equal to the 2-yr old site, and no indication of the site deterioration was evident. Organic C significantly increased from the 1yr old to the 2-yr old site, and was highest for the 5-yr old site. Total N remained constant on all sites.

987 **Sekar, T., Bhattacharya, A.K.,** 1982. Effects of sewage effluents on carbon and nitrogen mineralisation of a soil in 'Waste Treatment and Utilisation'. Vol. 2. Murray Moo-yong et al (Eds.) Pergamon Press N.Y.: 447-459.

Raw sewage and sewage effluents from a domestic sewage treatment plant serving Delhi were analysed for their physical, and chemical characteristics in view of evaluating their suitability for irrigation to agricultural lands. In laboratory experiments, these effluents were added to a soil and incubated at 30 $\pm$ 1°C. Microbial populations, CO_2- evolution and NH_4 - N and NO_2 + NO_3-N concentrations were determined at 10 day intervals for a period of sixty days and were compared with tap water treatment. Chemical properties of the soil applied with sewage were also determined after 60 days of incubation. Sewage addition caused significant increase in soil bacterial, fungal and Azotobacter populations. CO_2 production rates of the soil were enhanced by raw sewage and effluents both without and with glucose amendment. Raw Sewage and effluent treatment resulted in significant increases in ammounium and (nitrite + nitrate) nitrogen concentrations of the soil with respect to the control. Raw sewage treatment increased NO_2 + NO_3 -N levels in soil over the effluents also. Soil pH was not found to be altered while sewage application caused substantial changes in electrical conductivity, CEC, organic matter and available nitrogen.

988 **Selim, H.M., Amacher, M.C., Iskandar, I.K.,** 1989. Modelling the transport of chromium (VI) in soil columns. J. Soil Sci. Soc Am. 53(4): 996-1004.

Miscible displacement experiments were conducted to described Cr (VI) mobility and interactions in six different soils. For Calciorthid, Webster, and Norwood soils Cr breakthrough curves (BTCs) indicated that the interactions with the soil matrix were similar to those for a non-reactive solute where no or small retardation of the equilibrium type was observed. These observations are in support of earlier kinetic batch results where little retention was observed for a wide range of Cr concentrations in these (high pH) soils. The BTCs from Olivier, Cecil, and Windsor soils indicated high Cr retention capacities as indicated by increased retardation, low peak concentration, irreversible sorption and extensive effluent tailing during desorption (leaching). A non-linear retention/release model is proposed for describing Cr (VI) reactions during transport in soils. The model is incorporated into the convection dispersion transport equation for reactive solute in uniform soils. The model was capable of providing a good description of the Cr BTC's for all soils where model parameters were obtained using a non-linear least squares (best-fit) parameter optimization scheme. The model grossly under-estimated effluent concentrations for Olivier, and Windsor BTC's when independently measured retention/release rate coefficients from the batch data sets were used. Model predictions over-estimated the amount irreversibly retained by Cecil soils, Model predictions indicated that a unique set of independently measured rate coefficients was not capable of providing an adequate description of Cr BTCs for these soils.

889 **Semu, E. Singh, B.R., Selmer Oisen, A.R.S.,** 1986. Adsorption of mercury compounds by tropical soils. I. Adsorption in soil profiles in relation to their physical, chemical and mineralogical properties. Water Air Soil Pollut. 27: 19-27.

Mercury adsorption of $HgCl_2$ and 2-methoxyethyl mercury chloride (Aretan) (100 mg HgL^{-1}) was measured for three soil profiles from Morogoro, Arusha, and Dar-es-Salaam in Tanzania. The adsorption was investigated for the physical, chemical and mineralogical properties of the soils. All soil samples showed greater capacity for adsorption of Aretan than for $HgCl_2$ in the Morogoro profile. Hg adsorption decreased with depth but in the other two soils, the minimum adsorption occurred in the third horizon and increased both, upwards and downwards. In the Morogoro profile, aretan adsorption correlated well with pH. Adsorption of both Aretan and $HgCl_2$ correlated well with the distribution of organic C and cation exchange capacity of the soils. In the Arusha and Dares Salaam profiles, Hg adsorption was not significantly correlated with any of the soil properties tested.

990 **Sen, A.K., Nitya Mondal, G.,** 1990. Removal and uptake of copper (II) by Salvinia natans from waste water. Water Air Soil Pollut 49: 1-6.

The plant *Salvinia natans* L., was found to be very useful in the removal of Cu (II) from waste water. Maximum accumulation was noted within one day and maximum removal (about 90%) was recorded below 50 mg/L. of Cu (II). Copper was successfully removed from the waste water of Hindusthan Copper Limited (HCL), Bihar.

991 **Senesi, N.,** 1989. Composted materials as organic fertilizers. Sci. Total Environ. 81-82: 521-542.

This review paper is divided into three sections: the first section briefly discusses on input., transformation and loss of native and added organic matter in soil and on principal effects of fresh organic matter addition on soil properties. The second section focuses on organic waste composting process, substrate materials and products of compostation, i.e. composts. The third section discusses extensively on the most commonly used criteria and parameters for the evaluation of compost quality as organic fertilizers, including various proposed "Humidification degree" indies and compositional, structural and functional properties of humic-like substances in compost.

992 **Senesi, N., Sposito, G., Bradford, G.R., Holtzclaw, K.M.,** 1991. Residual metal reactivity of humic acids extracted from soil amended with sewage sludge. Water Air Soil Pollut. 55(3-4): 409-425.

Copper, Fe and Mn were used as probes to investigate residual metal reactivity for humic acid (HA) samples extracted from a loam soil, either non-amended or amended with anerobically digested sewage sludge for 4, 5, 6, or 7 yr at 90 t/ha/yr. Irrespective of their origin, the HA complexes significant amounts of metal, in forms stable against intense water leaching in the order Fe > Cl > Mn. Sludge amended soil HA adsorbed and retained Fe in amounts greater than HA extracted from non-amended soil. Metal adsorption occurred mainly by cation-exchange from non-amended soil. Metal adsorption occurred mainly by cation exchange replacement of metals previously bound to HA. Water stable Fe^{3+}-HA complexes prepared in the laboratory were partially stable against H and metal ion exchange reactions, whereas Cu^{2+} and Mn^{2+} in laboratory prepared, water stable HA complexes were desorbed almost completely by these two reactions.

993 **Sharma, H.C., Thakre, R.A., Ramteke, D.S., Moghe, C.A., Aggarwal, A.L.,** 1985. Biomonitoring of refinery emissions. Proc. Natl. Semin. Polln. Contl. Environ. Manag, Nagpur: 200-217.

The findings reveal that plants near by refinery and 10 km in the down wind are adversely affected. The leaves show signs of severe injury and premature aging. The seasons have shown comparatively higher rate of sulfate accumulation.

994 **Sharpley, A.N., Smith, S.J., Stewart, B.A., Mathers, A.C.,** 1984. Forms of phosphorus in soil receiving cattle feedlot waste. J. Environ. Qual. 13: 211-215.

Cattle feedlot waste (FLW) was applied to irrigated continuous grain sorghum grown on Pullman clay loam over an 8-yr period. The FLW applications increased the total, inorganic, and available P content and decreased the P sorption index of surface soil. Amounts of P in the surface soil were highly correlated with the total amount of FLW-P applied and time since the last application. The proportion of total P as inorganic P increased with large FLW applications. Increases in the amounts of surface soil inorganic and organic P with FLW applications were due mainly to increases in labile fractions of these P forms. When FLW applications were stopped, however, soil organic P contents decreased to pretreatment levels more rapidly than organic P contents as a result of labile organic P mineralization. Increased P contents of surface soil following FLW applications will increase the potential for soluble and sediment-bound P to be transported in runoff.

995 **Shayegan, J., Sanai, M.,** 1980. Land disposal of waste water from a beet sugar factory and its effect on soil. Environl. Pollut.: Ser. B: Chem. Physic. 1(1): 61-70.

Experiments on the long-term effects of land application of effluents from a beet sugar processing plant are described. Non-soluble compounds such as calcium and magnesium carbonates are filtered by top layers of soil while more soluble salts are carried to much lower depths. Despite the apparent damage caused to upper soil layers because of accumulation of various constituents during the past 10 yr of continuous operation, these soils may still be cultivated after a relatively simple treatment has been carried out. Based on extensive chemical analyses of composite soil samples collected from various depths, the leachate ultimately recharging the groundwater reservoir is essentially purified and will thus enhance the potential supply of clean water in the region.

996 **Sheaffer, C.C., Decker, A.M., Chaney, R.L., Douglass, L.W.,** 1979. Soil temperature and sewage sludge effects on corn yield and macronutrient content. J. Environ. Qual. 8(4): 450-454.

The effect of soil temperature on sewage sludge nutrient release was evaluated. Corn was grown in a sandy (Typic Hapludult) soil amended with 0, 56, or 112/t ha^{-1} of anaerobically digested sewage sludge in field experiments during 1975 and 1976. Soil temperature regimes of 16, 27°, 35C or ambient (22°C) were applied to plots each year from planting to harvest. Increases in soil temperature increased germination and maturation rates of corn. A 16C soil temperature significantly decreased stover and grain yields both years. In 1975, temperatures above ambient did not result in higher grain or stover yields, but in 1976 grain and stover yields increased as soil temperature rose to 35°C. Sewage sludge application had no significant effect on 1975 stover yield, but at a 16C soil temperature grain yields were significantly higher for the 112-t/ha sludge plots. Nitrogen P and K levels in corn ear levels were higher at 35°C than 16C in both years, but Ca was lower. Higher ear leaf levels of N, P, Ca, and Mg occurred with 112 t/ha sludge than the check both in 1975 and 1976.

997 **Sheaffer, C.C., Decker, A.M., Chaney, R.L., Douglass, L.W.,** 1979. Soil temperature and sewage sludge effects on metals in crop tissue and soil. J. Environ. Qual. 8(4): 455-459.

Effects of soil temperature and sewage sludge application on plant and soil Zn, Cu, Cd, Ni, and Pb levels, soil pH, and soil organic matter were determined in a field experiment in which corn was grown for 2 yr in a sandy soil amended with 56, and 112 t/ha of sewage sludge. Soil temperature regimes of 16°, 27, 35°C, and ambient (22C) were applied to sludge treatments from May to Oct. each years. Following removal of corn, oats (Avena sativa), wheat *(Triticum destivum)*, rye *(Secale cereale)*, crimson clover *(Trifolium incarnatum)*, and arrowleaf clover *(Trifolium vesiculosum)* were grown until the following spring. Sewage sludge application resulted in significant increases in soil organic matter, pH, and DTPA extractable Zn, Cu, Cd, and Ni. Soil heating to 35°C significantly reduced pH for all sludge rates compared to 16C and ambient (22°C) temperatures by the end of experiment. Concentrations of Zn, Cu, Ni, and Cd were increased in corn, legume, and small grain tissue by sludge treatments. Corn seedling Zn and Cu concentrations exceeded that in ear leaves, stover, and grain; lowest metal concentrations were in the corn grain. Increasing soil temperature did not consistently affect Cu, Ni, Cd, or Pb concentrations in corn tissue.

998 **Shelef, G.**, 1991. The role of waste water reuse in water resources management in Israel. Water Sci. Technol. 24: 2081-2089.

Waste water reuse is a vital water resource in Israel with an annual flow of 420 million m^3 planned for the year 2010 constituting 19% of the total water supply and about one third of that allocated to the agricultural sector. The trend is for less crop restriction and wider crop rotation and thus greater effluent quality requirements. Economical considerations are favourable even with the need for seasonal storage and extra treatment. A brief description of the major waste water reuse schemes is given.

999 **Sheppard, S.C., Gibb, C.L., Hawkins, J.L.**, 1989. Fate of contaminants during utilisation of peat materials. J. Environ. Qual. 18(4): 503-506.

If peats are used in industry, their metal contents should be studied in relation to their conc. in the produce.

1000 **Sheppard, M.I., Thibault, D.H., Mitchell, J.H.**, 1987. Element leaching and capillary rise in sandy soil cores: Experimental results. J. Environ Qual. 16(3): 273-283.

This study examines both the leaching and capillary rise of Rc, I, Np, U, Th, Cs, Cr and Mo through a sandy soil. Eighty undisturbed soil cores from a forest floor were contaminated, half were contaminated 10 cm from their base to simulate contact with contaminated groundwater (groundwater cores), and the other half were contaminated below the litter layer to simulate soil surface deposition (leaching cores). Cups at the base of the cores served as receptacles for groundwater or for leachate. The cores were placed in the ground with their surfaces exposed to natural rainfall. After I yr, half of the cores were exhumed. Soil moisture and temperature conditions in the cores reflected the trends of moisture and temperature at the coring site. Leachate analyses and exhumation data of the leaching cores indicated element mobility as Tc, I, Mo, Cr, U, Np, Cs, Th, with Tc the most mobile, and Th the least mobile. Only Tc,

I, Mo and Cr passed through the cores in the leachate in the first year. The groundwater cores showed that Tc, I, Mo and Cr are most likely to reach surface soils from contaminated groundwater based on one year of data. Partition coefficient (Kd) value for Tc, I and U from batch sorption experiments were compared with Kd values obtained from the exhumation porewater and soil, by soil horizon.

1001 **Shinde, D.B., Trivedy, R.K.**, 1983. Effects of distillery waste water irrigation on agronomical characteristics of Abelmoschus esculentus and Zea mays at germination stage. Environ. Ecol., 1(2): 109-111.
High concentration of distillery waste (25 to 50%) inhibited germination and reduced seedling height and dry matter production of Abelmoschus esculentus and Zea mays. But 10% of the waste in the irrigation water proved to be beneficial. Reduction in root length was observed with all dilutions. Zea mays was found to be more tolerant to distillery waste than Abelmoschus esculentus.

1002 **Short, T.M. Black, J.A., Birge, W.J.**, 1990. Effects of acid mine drainage on the chemical and biological character of an alkaline head water stream. Archives Environl. Contam. Toxicol. 19: 241-248.
Metal levels in water and sediments remained elevated in regions of biological recovery and consequently down stream communities were composed predominantly of metal tolerant texa. Metal conc. of Al, Cu, Fe, and Zn increased 2 to 3 orders of magniride in the receiving water which decreased with down steam distance.

1003 **Shukla, J.B., Freedman, H.I., Pal, V.N., Misra, O.P., Agarwal, M., Shukla, A.**, 1988. Degradation and subsequent regeneration of a forestry resource – a mathematical model. Ecol. Modelling 44(3-4): 219-229.
A dynamical model to assess the effects of industrialisation on the degradation of forestry biomass in a given region is presented. It is shown that increasing industrialization may lead to eventual extinction of the forest. However, incorporating reforestation into the model may allow one to sustain the forestry biomass at its carrying capacity. Motivation for this model is the effect of industrialisation of the Doon Valley in India.

1004 **Shuman, L.M.**, 1980. Zinc in soils, in 'Zinc in the Environment pt 1. Ecological Cycling'. John Wiley & Sons, New York: 39-69.
Zinc in soil-plant system is reviewed. By the late 1960s, 39 states in the United States recommended that zinc be applied to major field, forage, vegetable, fruit and nut crops. Emphasis has been placed on deficiencies, and possible zinc toxicity problems due to increasing concern as on land disposal of high-metal content sludges.

1005 **Siccama, T.G., Smith, W.H., Mader, D.L.**, 1980. Changes in lead, zinc, copper, dry weight, and organic matter content of the forest floor of white

pine stands in central Massachusetts over 16 years. E.S.& T. 14(1): 54-56.
Lead, Zn, Cu, dry weight, and organic matter content of the litter, fermentation, and humidified layers of the forest floor were measured in 10 white pine stands in central Massachusetts in 1962 and again in 1978, to provide quantitative estimates of these parameters at 2 points in time. Total Pb content increased significantly. Average Pb concentration increased in all layers, but the increases were not statistically significant, due primarily to the dilution effect of the concurrent increase in the mass of the forest floor. The observed net increase in Pb of 30 $mg/m^2/Yr$ is » 80% of the estimated total annual input of this element via precipitation in this region during the 16-yr period. There wee no statistically significant changes in total Zn and Cu content of the forest floor.

1006 **Siderle, T.W., Dobbins, D.C., Thornton, J.R., Jones, D.D.,** 1986. Microbial biomass, activity, and community structure in subsurface soils. Ground-Water 24(3): 365-374.
Microbial biomass, community structure and activity were determined in the subsurface horizons of four contrasting soil types common to Alabama. In all four soils, biomass and activity declined with increasing depth, however, the magnitude and pattern of this decline varied as a function of soil type. Biomass concentration in the lower Ap horizon ranged from 8.2 to 18.0 nmoles phospholipid/g dry wt soil. In the deepest subsoil horizons the range was 0.0085 to 0.059 nmoles phospholipid/g dry wt soil. The rate of FDA hydrolysis was highly correlated with biomass ($r = 0.90$). Polyenoic fatty acids, which are present only in eukaryotic microorganisms, were found in all horizons. However, their relative abundance differed as a function of soil type. Stepwise regression analysis revealed that soil characteristics could explain 89 and 82% of the variation in biomass and activity, respectively.

1007 **Sidle, R.C., Hook, J.E., Kardos, L.T.,** 1976. Heavy metals application and plant uptake in a land disposal system for waste water. J. Environ. Qual. 5 (1): 97-102.
Municipal sewage effluent with sludge injected and effluent alone were spray-irrigation on seed canary grass and corn, respectively. In the maximum level (10 cm/week) reed canary grass treatment application rates for Cu, Zn, Cd, and Pb were 15.5, 25.5, 0.162 and 9.1 kg/ha in 1972 and 7.7, 13.2, 0.135 and 7.8 kg/ha in 1973. Rates of application for Cu, Zn, Cd and Pb in the maximum level (7.5 cm/week) cornfield treatment were 0.6, 2.0, 0.029 and 1.1 kg/ha in 1972 and 0.6, 2.4, 0.032 and 2.4 kg/ha in 1973. Reed Canary grass was irrigated year round, while corn was irrigated only during the growing season. Copper and Zn concentrations and total uptake in the treated reed canary grass area were generally higher than in the control for all cuttings of 1972 and 1973. Total uptake of heavy metals in the corn area control was usually as high or higher than in the treated area. Copper and Zn concentrations and uptake in the effluent irrigated corn area were lower than in the treated reed canary

grass area. Data show a relative exclusion of Cd by Zn in the plant material, since Cd/Zn ratio in the harvested crops are lower than in either the applied waste water or the 0.1N HCl extractable fraction of the treated soils. Accumulation of applied heavy metals in the treated soils > 93% of the amounts applied in 1972 and 1973 for all heavy metals in the reed canary grass area and slightly less in the corn area.

1108 **Sidle, R.C., Kardos, L.T.,** 1977. Transport of heavy metals in sludge treated forested area, J. Environ. Qual. 6(4): 431-437.

Plots in a mixed hardwood forest received two separate applications of anaerobically digested sewage sludge in fall 1974 and spring 1975. Total solids loading in the low and high treatments were 12.71 and 26.96 tonnes/ha, respectively. Copper, Zn and Cd loadings in the high treatment were 24.50, 28.49 and 0.253 kg/ha respectively. Calculated amounts of percolate Cu, Zn and Cd moving out of the 120 cm depth in the high treatment were 0.3, 3.2 and 6.6% of the total applied levels, respectively, indicating the order of relative mobility in soil as Cd > Zn > Cu. Relative levels of 0.1 N HCl extractable vs total soil Cu, Zn and Cd sampled before and after sludge application indicated that Cu applied in the sewage sludge was more extractable than the native soil Cu, Zn was only slightly more extractable and Cd was less extractable. Of the other heavy metals (Cr, Pb, Co and NI) analysed in 0.1 N HCl extracts, only Cr and Ni increased in the 0 to 7.5 cm depth following sludge application.

1009 **Sidle, R.C., Kardos, L.T.,** 1977. Aqueous release of heavy metals from two sewage sludges. Water Air Soil Pollut. 8: 453-459.

Two anaerobically digested sewage sludges were extracted several times with water to determine the levels of readily available Zn, Cu, and Cd Generally, the quantity of metal released in the aqueous extracts was between 1 to 7% of the total content with Cu and Zn being released to a greater extent than Cd. The proportion of relatively mobile, non-cationic heavy metals in the aqueous extract differed in the two sludges and ranged from < 1% for Zn and Cd in one sludge to 56.2% for Cd in the other sludge.

1010 **Sidle, R.C., Sopper, W.E.,** 1976. Cadmium distribution in forest ecosystems irrigated with treated Municipal waste water and sludge. J. Environ. Qual. 5 (4): 419-422.

Treated municipal waste water was irrigated in an abandoned old field area from 1964-1974 and in a mixed hardwood area (old gamelands) from 1964-1974. Total applications of Cd in the old field and old gameland areas were 0.47 and 0.61 kg/ha, respectively. White sprace and wild straw berry foliage, sampled from the old field showed no increase in Cd concentrations due to effluent irrigation while goldenrod had lower Cd levels in the treated area than in the un-irrigated control area. Foliage sampled from red maple white oak and wild sarraparilla, in the old gamelands, showed no increase in Cd as a result of waste water irrigation. Soil Cd levels were not significantly affected by waste water irrigation in either area, except for the increase in soil Cd in the 0-5 cm depth of old gameland land. The Cd/Zn ratios of the vegetation foliage were not significantly different between the treated and control area.

1011 **Siegel, S.M., Eshieman, A.**, 1975. Chlorine bleaches: A significantly long term source of mercury pollution. Water Air Soil Pollut. 4: 461-463.

Products of industrial eledrolysis of brine-NaOCl based bleaches and NaOH yielded 17 to 1290 ppb of Hg and compared with current U.S. rejection value of 5 ppb for potable waters, the above levels seem sufficiently high.

1012 **Siegel, S.M., Siegel, B.Z.**, 1986, *Equisetum* and the cycling of mercury at Mount St. Helens: Plant-Soil relations, 1980-1984. Water Air Soil pollut. 27: 441-444.

The Hg content of Equisetum shoots at six stations near Mount St. Helens rose to a peak value in July 1982, 26 months after the great eruption of May 1980. The July 1982 peak in plant Hg content was followed by a continual decline in plant tissue Hg at six stations as measured in September 1982 and August 1984. During this 2 yr period, soil Hg levels declined at only three of the six stations, While remaining essentially unchanged at two stations and increasing nearly 20-fold at one station. Therefore, soil Hg behaved independently with respect to plant Hg at least at three of the six sites. This follow-up study at Mount St. Helens supports the notion of a major source of atmospheric mercury which is taken up directly by plants.

1013 **Siegel, S.M., Siegel, B.Z.**, 1988. Temperature determinants of plant-soil-air mercury relationships. Water Air Soil Pollut. 40(3-4): 443-448.

Using the Arrhenus thermodynamic equation, which relates rates of processes to temperature through the quantity E_a, the Heat (or energy) of Activation, we have evaluated the thermal relationships for several parameters of Hg cycling. It is shown that release from isolated leaves (shoots) of Hg° is a two step process with a higher E_a Values below 21C than above (28 vs 14 kcal mol^{-1}). Open field air Hg measurements over a mixed stand of grasses and other plants in volcanic soil show strikingly similar behaviour to detected organs. Mercury release from volcanic soil was uniform over a wide temperature range, resembling plant and open field emissions above 18 to 21 > °C with an E_a value of 13 kcal mol^{-1}.

1014 **Siegel, S.M., Seigal, B.Z., Barghigiani, C., Aratani, K., Penny, P., Penny, D.**, 1987. A contribution to the environment biology of mercury accumulation in plants. Water Air Soil Pollut. 33: 65-72.

Data support the hypothesis that specific local environmental factors strongly influence the accumulation of Hg in plants even when the immediate soil concentrations are same. Findings show that some plants contain concentrations of total Hg as high as 5,500 to 14,000 μg kg^{-1} (dw).

1015 **Siegel, S.M., Siegel, B.Z., Sheldon, L., Yaeger, E., Chang, D.**, 1986. Mercury antagonists: protection of plants against vapor injury by thiamine and other compounds. Water Air Soil Pollut. 27(3-4): 243-246.

Mercury vapor-induced abscission of coleus cuttings was prevented by thiamine, other organo-S (Se) compounds and selenits, but not by common sugar metabolites, amino acids, non-auxin growth regulators and selenate. Protection was also afforded to other plants including ferms and gymnospherms. Thus the compounds that protect plants against Hg intoxication correspond to the Hg antagonists known in animals including man.

1016 **Siegrist, R.L.**, 1987. Soil clogging during subsurface waste water infiltration as affected by effluent composition and loading rate. J. Environ. Qual. 16: 181-187.

The soil clogging effects of waste water effluent composition and loading rate were investigated in pilot scale infiltration cells installed in situ in the structured silty clay loam subsoil of a Typic Argiudoll. Over a 70-month period domestic septic tank effluent (DSTE), graywater septic tank effluent (GSTE) and tapwater (TW) were intermittently applied in an average of 5.2 cm/d to yield daily loading rates of 1.3, 2.6, and 5.2 cm/d. Soil clogging was negligible in all TW treatments and in GSTE treatments at 1.3 and 2.6 cm/d. In the GSTE treatments at 5.2 cm/d and in all DSTE treatments, severe soil clogging led to continuous ponding of the soil infiltrative surfaces. A logistic model fit to the experimental data confirmed that soil clogging development was highly correlated with the cumulative mass density loadings of total biochemical oxygen demand and suspended solids. After 62 and 70 months of loading, soil properties were determined with depth. Clogged infiltrative surface zones exhibited significant accumulations of organic materials at the infiltrative surface and within the first few mm of the soil matrix.

1017 **Sigleo, A.C., Means, J.C.**, .1990. Organic and inorganic components in Estuarine colloids: Implications for sorption and transport of pollutants. Rev. Environ. Contam. Toxicol. 112: 123-147.

The content of inorganic and organic components in estuarine collides have been described. The behaviour of soil collides in transport of pollutants is reviewed and future research needs are indicated.

1018 **Sikora, F.J., Wok, J.**, 1986. Effect of cadmium-and zinc-treated sludge on yield and cadmium-zinc uptake of corn. J. Environ. Qual. 15(4): 341-344.

Sludge obtained from a regional waste water treatment plant in Tennessee was factorially treated with four levels each of Cd and applied to Statler sandy loam surface soil sown to corn in a greenhouse experiment. The higher Cd and Zn additions (75.1 and 759 mg kg^{-1}) respectively, results in dry weight decreases of 19 and 25%, respectively, for corn tops, 47 and 56%, respectively, for corn roots. The 19% dry weight reduction was attributed to a lower Cd availability due to Cd precipitation or binding in the sludge. Zinc effectively competed with Cd in uptake as evidenced by a decrease in Cd content of roots with increased Zn additions. On the contrary, Cd content of tops was consistently decreased with increased Zn application. An increase in the Zn levels of sludge was also found to increase the solubility of Cd in the sludge and soil.

1019 **Silviera, D.J., Sommers., L.F.** 1977. Extractability of Cu, Zn, Cd and Pb in soils Incubated with a sewage sludge. J. Environ. Qual. 6: 47-52.

Soils amended with sewage sludge were incubated in the laboratory and analyzed periodically by a seqential fractionation procedure for the accounts of Cu, Zn, Cd, and Pb that were H_2O soluble, KNO_3 exchangeable, and DTPA and HNO_3 extractable. The H_2O) soluble and exchangeable metals comprised a small percentage of the total metal concentration in the sludge and in the soil sludge mixtures incubated for 7 to 28 days. The proportion of total Cu, Zn, and Cd extracted by DTPA increased with time while this fraction remained constant with time for Pb.

1020 **Simon, J.J.,** 1987. Waste water application to soils : Hydraulic and nitrogen considerations. Diss. Abst. Int. Pt. B. Sci. & Eng., 47(6) : 167.

A textile waste water containing high concentrations of organic N was spray-irrigated to tall fescue (Festuca arundinacea) to determine optimum N application levels. Nitrogen balances were determined at each N level and the potential for predicting the leaching competent of the excess N applied was investigated. The relations between soil properties, hydraulic performance of OSWDS, and N distribution around OSWDS are evaluated.

1021 **Sims, J.T.,** 1990. Nitrogen mineralization and elemental availability in soils amended with the composted sewage sludge. J. Environ. Qual. 19: 669-675.

Nitrogen mineralization studies, conducted for 20 wk with three soils amended with 22 Mg/ha of each CCSS type (total 250 to 398 kg N/ha.) indicated that immobilization of N could be a serious problem with these composts. Negative values, ranging from 7 to 39 mg/kg, were obtained for net N mineralization (N mineralized adjusted for inorganic N added in the CCSS and mineralized soil N). Additionally, wheat plants grown in the greenhouse for 8wk with the same CCSS applied at rates of 0,11,22 and 44 Mg/ha, and supplemented with 100 mg/kg of N as NH_4 NO_3 exhibited N defninciency symptons, reduced dry matter production and lower plant N concentrations. Only slight differences in plant and soil (Mehlick-I extractable) concentrations of P, K, Ca, Mg, Cu, Cd, Cr, Ni and Pb were noted among CCSS types in the greenhouse study. The CCSS rate also had little influence on plant and soil concentrations of these elements. Soil pH, however, was increased by a lime-amended CCSS resulting in significant decreases in plant concentrations of Mn and Zn. These results suggest that, when applied at agronomic rates, these composts can produce satisfactory plant growth, if adequate amounts of supplemental N fertilizers are applied, and that increases in soil and plant concentrations of nonessential heavy metals should be a limiting factor in compost use.

1022 **Sims, J.T., Boswell, F.C.,** 1980. The influence of organic wastes and inorganic nitrogen sources on soil nitrogen-yield and, elemental composition of Corn. J. Environ. Qual. 9: 512-518.

Treatments consisted of equivalent rates of N (224 kg/ha) as NH_4NO_3 urea, sewage sludge, sewage sludge fortified with urea, leather tankage (LT) and organiform (Leather tankage chemically fortified with urea formaldehyde). Soil levels of NH_4-N, NO_3-N and total N indicated that the organic waste materials provided adequate amounts of available N for crop growth. Fortified and nonfortified wastes resulted in similar amounts of mineral and total N on the soil, indicating that fortification could reduce application problems associated with high loading rates of organic wastes. Accumulations of mineral N at the end of the corn growing season suggest that the loading rates used in this study may have been excessive. While this excess available N would be beneficial for subsequent crops, it could also provide a source of contamination for surface and ground-waters. Organic wastes consistently produced yield and plant tissue N levels equal to or greater than yields and N levels obtained with ammonium nitrate of urea. The treatments increased Zn in plant tissue and on plots receiving sewage, and Mn and Cr accumulations in the tissue of plant grown on leather tankage treated plots. Except for the LT-treated plots at the early growth stage, crop growth and yield were uninhibited.

1023 **Sims, J.L., Sims, R.C., Mathews, J.E.,** 1990. Approach to bioremediation of contaminated soil. Hazardous Waste Hazardous Materials 7(1): 117-149.

Biological processes, including microbial degradation have been identified as critical mechanisms for attenuating organic contaminants during transit through the Vadose zone to the groundwater. On site soil remedial measures using biological processes can reduce or eliminate ground-water contamination, thus reducing the need for extensive ground-water monitoring and treatment requirements. On site remedial systems that utilize the soils as the treatment system accomplish treatment by using naturally occurring microorganisms to treat the contaminants. Treatments often may be enhanced by a variety of physical/chemical methods, such as fertilization, tilling, soil pH adjustment, moisture control, etc. The development of a bioremediation programme for a specific contaminated soil system includes: (1) a thorough site/soil/waste characterisation: (2) treatability studies; and (3) design and implementation of the bioremediation plan.

1024 **Singh, K.N,.** 1979. Sorption and release of cadmium in some Canadian soils. Can. J. Soil Sci. 59(2) : 119-130.

Adsorbed Cd is correlated to the cation exchange capacity (CEC) of soils in a linear regression, however, the numerical value of a intercept in the regression equation indicates that soil properties other than cation exchange are also important. A major portion of adsorbed Cd is neutral salt-extractable, and the Cd not released (fixed Cd) in NaCl solution is correlated to CEC, pH, and organic content of soils. The fixation reactions of Cd do not have priority over adsorption reactions in these soils. The sequences of application of saturated calcium hydroxide solution to soil influence the quantity of the fixed Cd.

1025 **Singh, A.K., Gaur, J.P,** 1991. Inhibition of NO_3, NH_4 uptake in *Anabaena doliolum* exposed to a petroleum oil. Ecotoxicol. Environ. Saf. 21 : 103-108.

The aqueous extract of Assam crude inhibited the uptake of NO_3, NH_4 and PO_4 in anabaena doliolum and the response was essentially concentration dependent. Inhibition was most severe for the uptake of NH_4 followed in decreasing order by PO_4 and NO_3. Uptake of nutrients was competitively inhibited as in all the cases oil extract did not change I_{max}, however apparent K_{max} was increased. The nature of oil components competing with nutrient ions is not certain at present. Oil-induced inhibition of nutrient uptake in cyanobacteria might be reversed in eutrophic waters rich in nutrients.

1026 **Singh, K.K., Mishra, L.C.,** 1987. Effect of fertilizer factory effluent on soil and crop oroductivity. Water Air Soil Pollut. 33 : 309-320.

The impact of various concentrations (2.5, 5, 10, 25 & 50%) of fertiliser factory effluent on physico-chemical properties of soil, and germination, growth, photosynthetic pigments, and dry matter production of corn and rice was studied. The effluent treatment to soil resulted in a significant increase in the water soluble salts, EC, CEC, pH, N, Ca, Na, and Cl content of the soil for effluent concentrations of the 10% and above. The effluent of 2.5 and 5% conc. enhanced the growth and development of corn and rice. Higher concentrations of effluent (10% and above) however, inhibited the percentage of seed germination and caused deterious effects on the dry matter production, yield and the photosynthetic pigments of both test crops.

1027 **Singh, S.P., Nayyar, V.K.,** 1990. Accumulation characteristics of cadmium and its upper critical levels in selected vegetable species. Internatl. J. Environl. Studies 36(3) : 199-204.

In a greenhouse experiment, five vegetable species belonging to four families, i.e. *Chenopodiacese, Leguminosae, Umbelliferae* and *Crucifere* were grown on a coarse texture soil amended with different rates of Cd

(0 to 100 mg kg^{-1} soil). Yields versus Cd addition rate relations exhibited significant yield reductions at addition rates exceeding 10 mg Cd kg^{-1} soil in almost all the vegetable crops under study. The Cd content of aerial parts of the plants (tc) was correlated with the DT PA extractable soil Cd level (sc) in a double logarithmic relationship. log (tc) = a + b log (Sc.) The regression coefficients a and b were estimated for each species. Based on a values, plant families were divided into three categories, (1) low accumulators, Legminosae; (2) moderate accumulators, Umbelliferae and (3) high accumulators, Chenopodiaceae and Cruciferae. For characterisation of Cd accumulation, a values proved more descriptive than the values of b.

1028 **Singh, S.N., Rao, D.B.,** 1980. Growth of wheat plants exposed to cement dust pollution. Water Air Soil Pollut. 14: 241-249.

A field study was conducted at different locations in the environment of Churk Cement factory in Mirzapur district, U.P. Plant samples were collected at 100, 500, 1000, 1500, 2000, and 4000 m northeast of the factory, at three successive stages of plant growth. The plant samples of 4000 m distance were treated as control, as there was no apparent deposition of cement dust on their surface. The samples were analysed with respect to foliar injury symptoms, chlorophyll concentrations and phytomass accumulation. Only plant closest to the factory displayed symptoms of foliar injury. The results reveal that wheat plant at polluted sites contained decreased concentration of chlorophyll in their leaves and had reduced accumulation of phytomass, as compared to control. The grains obtained from affected sites showed quantitative and qualitative deterioration. Physico-chemical properties of the soils at polluted sites also underwent some undesirable changes. These effects had negative correlation with the distance from the factory.

1029 **Singh, A.K., Rai, B.,** 1990. Effect of cement dust treatment on some hylloplane fungi of wheat. Water Air Soil Pollut. 49 : 349-354.

The per cent frequency and number of colonies cm^{-2} leaf area of all the test fungi decreased significantly at the higher doses of cement dust during both pre-and post inoculation treatments. However, the population of some fungi increased at the low dose only. Stimulatory as well as inhibitory effect of cement dust on colony growth of the test fungi were observed at different concentrations of cement dust (500, 1000, 1500, and 2000 μmg/mL).

1030 **Singh, M., Singh, N., Relan, P.S.,** 1981. Adsorption and desorption of selenite and selenate selenium on different soils. Soil Sci. 132(2) : 134-141.

Adsorption on soils of selenite and selenate selenium and desorption by sulfate and phosphate was studied. Initial selenium solutions contained 500 μ mole P or S/g soil. All soils sorbed variable amounts of selenite and selenate in the order: high organic carbon soil > calcareous soil >

normal soil > saline soil > alkali soil. Adsorption of both selenite and selenate forms of selenium was influenced positively by organic carbon, clay content, $CaCO_3$ and CEC and negatively influenced by high salt content, alkalinity K and pH. langmuir curve analysis of Eadie-Hofstee was valued in normal and calcareous soils for selenite and in calcareous and saline soils for selenate. The analysis of Syers et al, did not fit well in any case. The adsorption of selenite and selenate showed differential behaviour and indicated that a part of both selenite and selenate is adsorbed on differential qualitative sites. Selenate was always sorbed in higher amounts than selenite. The desorption of selenite selenium showed on preference for sulfate or phosphate, but selenate, was more effectively desorbed by phosphate than sulfate in all soils.

1031 **Sinton, L.W.,** 1986. Microbial contamination of alluvial gravel aquifers by septic tank effluent. Water Air Soil Pollut. 28 : 407-425.

The effect of two methods of septic tank effluent disposal on the microbial quality of alluvial gravel aquifers were investigated at an experimental site in the Danterbury plains, New Zealand. The movement of feacal coliform bacteria 9 m from a 5.5 deep soakage pit into an uncomfined aquifer, and 42 m from an 18 m deep injection bore into a confined aquifer was recorded, Partial sealing of the soakage pit sidewalls was evident, but approximately 80% of the effluent appeared to percolate rapidly into the unconfined groundwater through a permeable pathway in the unsaturated zone. There was evidence of groundwater mounding beneath the soakage pit and around the injection bore and the consequent radial spread of leachate from both disposal structures. In both the confined and unconfined aquifers, the most heavily contaminated bore exhibited marked diurnal fluctuations in fecal coliforms concentrations in response to periods of effluent discharge. First arrival velocities of a rifamphycin-resistant Escherichia coil tracer of approximately 15 m day^{-1} in the inconfined groundwater and 151 m day^{-1} in the confined groundwater were recorded.

1032 **Sirms, G.K.,** 1990. Biological degradation of soil. Adv. Soil Sci. 11: 289-330.

Effects of microbial degradation of soil has bee reviewed in relation to heavy metals in mining operation and pollution.

1033 **Sivaswamy, S.N.,** 1990. Effect of pollutants on the nutrient status of field soils. J. Indian Soc. Soil Sci. 38(4) : 663-666.

Changes in microbial populations and nutrient status of soils treated with tan-liquor (a tannery effluent) and tannin were studied. Treatment with tan-liquor resulted in an increase in the Azotobacter population, but a decrease in the fungal and bacterial populations as a whole. Levels of nitrogen and zinc also decreased but levels of P, K, Cu, Fe and Mn increased. In tannin treated soils bacterial and fungal population increased although the Azotobacter population decreased, as did levels of Cu and

Fe. Levels of N, P, K, Zn and Mn increased however.

1034 **Slavek, J., Pickering, W.F.,** 1989. Extraction of metal ions sorbed on Mn (IV) oxides and $CaCO_3$ ion exchange resings. Water Air Soil Pollut. 45: 63-75.

The ability of ion exchange resins to promote release of metal ions (Cu, Pb, Cd or Zn) presorbed on different structural forms of Mn (IV) oxide or $CaCO_3$ has been investigated using exchangers possessing different types of functional groups and charged in either the H^+ or Na^+ form. The exchange uptake reflected the degree of soluble salt or labile complex displaced from the substrate surface, and its magnitude varied with metal ion involved, exchanger type and initial counter ion (i.e. H^+ forms retrieved more than Na^+ forms). With Mn (IV) oxides substrate structure was important, with $CaCO_3$ a major factor was desolation of the matrix. The amount of calcite dissolved was controlled by the number of exchange sites introduced, and exchanger type. The "labile metal" levels determined by the exchanger technique did not directly correlate with bonding fraction category values obtained using a series of chemical extractant solutions.

1035 **Smith, A.G.,** 1979. Nitrification-denitrification of waste water using a single-sludge system : Canada Ontario Agreement on Great Lakes Water Quality Research Report, Vol II, 96: 67.

A full scale evaluation of the split return made for nitrification – denitrification of a combined domestic/industrial waste water is described. The factors investigated were the effect of ferric chloride addition on p removal; the effect of solids retention times and sludge ages on N reactions at various temperatures; hydrogen peroxide addition and the use of screen centrifuge on mixed liquor conditioning; and the suitability of the system for solids control and for maintenance of consistent N removal under different temperature conditions. The single-sludge, split-return gave excellent removal with minimal methanol application. Control of soils in both aeration and denilrification basings was easily accomplished by adjusting the return-split. On site monitoring of the process was also easily accomplished. The lack of clearly defined temperature effect on N metabolism was attributed to the long sludge retention time inherent in the system.

1036 **Smith, J.M., Hayden, C.W.,** 1980. Treatment and disposal of sugarbeet processing waste water by irrigation. U.S. Dept of Agri. Conse. Report, 25: 55.

Irrigation with sugarbeet processing waste water was studied at 3 Idaho locations for 2 or 3 yr where perennial grass and alfalfa were irrigated at intervals of 1, 2 or 4 wk. This scheduled as maintained for the first year until the weekly irrigated plots were discontinued because of excessive loading. Waste water was sampled twice weekly from the sugar factories, and water samples were extracted from the soil at depths of 15-

150 cm each time the fields were arrogated. Soil water and plants were also analyzed for selected constituents; the following levels were noted for experimental plots and fields, respective N 280-4, 200 kg/ha and 277-1425 kg/ha, P 5-50 kg/ha and 11-43 kg/ha; K, 195-6 350 kg/ha and 490-3410 kg/ha. Water applications were 28-201 cm/yr, and COD applications were 8-140 t/ha. Nitrates found in water samples extracted from 150 cm in the soil were mostly <10 ppm N with few samples higher. Irrigation with sugarbeet processing waste works well in the field.

1037 **Smith, S.J., Scheppers, J.S., Porter, L.K.,** 1990. Assessing and managing agricultural nitrogen losses to the environment. Adv. Soil Sci. 14: 1-43.

The following topics are discussed : (a) contribution to N input : (b) N loss processes; (c) practices to ameliorate N losses or increase N use efficiency; (d) N research tools; and (e) research needs.

1038 **Soikkeli, S.S., Tuovinen, T.,** 1979. Damage in mesophyll ultrastructure needles of Norway sprace in two Industrial environments in central Finland. Anna. Bot Fen. 16(1) : 50-64.

The observations were made on material taken near a pulp mill and a fertilizer factory during the 2nd yr of the needles, from summer 1976 to summer 1977. In summer 1976, the injuries in the needles from the 2 areas were the same. Early in 1977 injured cells became more frequent and in spring healthy cells were rare. From January 1977 the injuries differed with the origin of the material. Needles taken near the pulp mill, which mainly emits sulfur dioxide (SO_2), the chloroplasts were rounded and the grana reduced. Later in spring the chloroplast envelopes broke, the lamellae swelled, the cytoplasm was destroyed, and the whole cell finally collapsed. In needles taken near the fertilizer plant, whose emissions included SO_2 and fluorides, the chloroplast envelopes became stretched, and the lamellae swelled, or curled: the 2 types of injury seen near the pulp mill also occurred but were rare. No evidence of the true recovery of single cells was found during the study period.

1039 **Somashekar, R.K., Ramaswamy, S.N., Arekal, G.D.,** 1982. Studies on the trace metal accumulation in grasses and sedges. Internatl. J. Environl. Studies 19(1): 69-70.

Results of a two-year study on the trace metal accumulation in grasses and sedges growing in a polluted area fed with electroplating wastes discharged by an automobile factory are presented. An accumulation of comparative accumulation rates were found to be higher in sedges than in grasses.

1040 **Sommers, L.E., Nelson, D.W., Silviera, D.J.,** 1979. Transformation of carbon, nitrogen, and metals in soils treated with waste materials. J. Environ. Qual. 8(3) : 287-294.

Intact soil cores were used to evaluate decomposition, NH_3 volatilization, N transformations, and metal movement in soils treated with sewage sludges and antibiotic processing wastes. Soil cores were leached monthly with water and incubated for 1 yr. Less than 1% of the NH_4-N applied was lost through NH_3 volatilization. The addition of wastes to 5 soils established that soil properties did not influence decomposition. However, appreciable differences in decomposition were observed when different wastes were added to the same soil. Significant amounts of NO^-_3-N were leached from soils treated with antibiotic wastes, while essentially no NO_3 leaching occurred in soils receiving sewage sludge, suggesting that denitrification and/or immobilization are major N loss mechanisms in soils treated with sewage sludge. Minimal amounts of P and metals were leached from sludge-amended soils. Soil analysis indicated that the majority of the added Zn, Cu, Cd, Ni, and Pb remained in the zone of sludge incorporation (7.5 cm) with minimal or no movement into the 7.5- to 15-cm soil depth.

1041 **Sommers, A.E., Tabatabai, M.A., Nelson, D.W.,** 1977. Forms of sulphur in sewage sludge. J. Environ. Qual. 6 (1): 42-46.

This study was conducted to determine the forms of S and their relationships to other components in sludge. Analysis of sludge produced by 11 Indiana cities showed that total S concentrations ranged from 0.7 to 2.1% and that from 1 to 27% of the total sludge S was inorganic S extractable with 0.1 M LiCl expressed as a percentage to total S, the sludge samples contained from <1 to 35% sulfide S, from 18 to 53% in organic non-sulphate S, from 18 to 56% carbon bonded S, from 0 to 35% ester sulphate S and inorganic sulphate S, and from 0 to 42% unidentified organic S. Analysis of seven sludge samples obtained over a 2-year period from the same treatment plant indicated that the forms of S vary with time. Non-consistent relationships were found between the amount of organic C, N, S and P in sludges while Pb and Zn were significantly correlated with sulfide S and that Cd was significantly correlated with organic S, ester sulfates and with 0.1M LiCl extractables. No significant relationships were found for other metals and the various S fractions.

1042 **Soon, Y.K., Bate, T.E., Beavchamp, E.G., Moyer, J.R.,** 1978. Land application of chemically treated sewage sludge: I. Effects on crop yield and nitrogen availability. J. Environ. Qual. 7 : 264-269.

Anaerobically digested sewage sludge resulting from treatment of sewage with Ca $(OH)_2$, Al_2 $(SO_4)_3$ or $FeCl_3$for phosphorus removal were applied to land on which corn and bromegrass were grown. Sludge applications provided 200 to 1800 kg N/ha each year for 3 years and NH_4NO_3 supplied 0 to 400 kg N/ha. Yields were increased by sludge upto 800 kg N/ha and NH_4NO_3 up to 400 kg N/ha. There was an appreciable residual effect of sludge nitrogen on the grass yield. The highest rate of sludge produced hazardous levels of NO_3 in the grass in the third year. On the loam and clay loam soils, there was no further increase in the yield of corn with sludge in excess of 200 kg N/ha or NH_4NO_3 above

100 kg N/ha. On the clay loam, the Ca-sludge appeared to benefit the corn most. There was no yield response to sludge or NH_4NO_3 on the loamy sand. Nitrate concentration in corn stover was increased by high rates of either NH_4NO_3 or sludge and in 1975 on the loamy sand soil approached levels hazardous to live stock. In both the corn and grass experiments 800 kg N/ha from sludge resulted in as much NO_3 in the top 15 cm of soil as 400 kg N/ha from NH_4NO_3. High concentrations of NO_3 were present in the soil to 90 cm depth in the grass experiment after 3 years of sludge application at rates supplying 800 kg N/ha but not at 400 kg N/ha. With corn on the loam & loamy sand high NO_3 concentrations were present in the soil to about 75 cm depth after 3 years of sludge application at rates supplying 400 kg N/ha.

1043 **Sopper, W.E.,** 1989. Revegetation of a contaminated zinc smelter site. Landscape urban Plann. 17(3) : 241-250.

Over 800 ha of forest vegetation are dead on Blue Mountain at Palmerton, Pennsylvania. The major cause was emissions of Zn, Cd, Cu, Pb, and SO_2 from a zinc smelter operating since 1898. In 1985 a research effort was initiated to develop a remedial action programme to mitigate the environmental damage. Field plot studies were conducted to determine the feasibility of using mixtures of dewatered municipal sludge and fly ash as amendments to facilitate the establishment of vegetation on the highly contaminated soil. Three mixtures of sludge and fly ash were evaluated. After two growing seasons, results indicate that all three sludge-fly ash mixtures were successful in facilitating vegetation establishment.

1044 **Sopper, W.E., Kerr. S.N.,** 1980. Maximizing forest biomass energy production by municipal waste water irrigation in "Energy From Biomass and Wastes IV". 115-133: Inst. Gas Tech. Chicago.

Energy plantations were established to evaluate the growth and development of hybrid poplar cuttings planted at densities of 0.09, 0.19, 0.37 m^2 of growing space per tree. Treated municipal waste water was used to irrigate half of the plantations during the growing season (April to October) at the rate of 5 cm per week. Waste water irrigation significantly increased diameter and total height growth. There is a common relationship between the two concepts of land treatment of municipal waste water ad silvicultural energy farms, and that the combination of the two concepts provides for a beneficial cost-effective solution.

1045 **Sopper, W.E., Kerr, S.N.,** 1980. Cadmium in forest ecosystems. In "Cadmium in Environent. Pt. 1 ; Ecological Cycling : John Wiley & Sons. New York: 655-668.

Data have been presented showing levels of cadmium in forest vegetation and soils subjected to waste water irrigation for 16 years. In the old field areas while spruce, goldenrod, and wild strawberry showed no increase in cadmium levels due to waste water irrigation. Cadmium concentration in all species were lower in the waste water-irrigated area than in the control area because of the greater biomass production resulting from the irrigation. Under low cadmium applications in a waste water disposal system the actual cadmium concentration of some herbaceous vegetation may be decreased. None of the species sampled in the Old Gamelands area showed a significant increase in cadmium levels as a results of the waste water irrigation. Soil cadmium status was not significantly affected by waste water irrigation in either area, except for the increase in cadmium concentrations at the 0 to 5 cm depth in the irrigated Old Gamelands area. Cadmium levels decreased with depth in the soil profile in both treated and control areas.

1046 **Spain, J.C., Haigler, W.E., Nishino, S.,** 1990. Development of bacteria for biodegradation of chloroaromatic compounds, in "Biotechnology Applications in Hazardous Waste Treatment." Engineering Foundations, New York : 129-147.

Selective enrichments were carried out for aerobic bacteria able to use the dichlorobenzenes (DCB) as a source of carbon and energy. Cultures were inoculated with soil and activated sludge from various sources and supplied with low conc. of ortho-or para-DCB in the vapour phase. A Pseudomonas str. (Js6), able to degrade para. DCB was found int he enrichment culture after a year of selection. Another strain (JS100) capable of ortho-DCB degradation was isolated after 1.5 yr of enrichment.

1047 **Spooner, E.T.C., Gale, N.H.,** 1982. Pb-isotopic composition of ophiolitic volcanogenic sulfide Deposits. Troodos Complex, Cyprus. Nature, 296, No. 5854: 239-242.

The volcanogenic sulphide ore deposits in the ophiolitic rocks of the Troodos Massif, Cyprus, are thought to be ~ 80 Myr old analogues of the metal sulphide accumulations actively being deposited from ~ 350C water at a depth of 2.6 km on the East Pacific Rise. In both cases, mineralization is thought to be a consequence of heat transfer by convective seawater circulation within the oceanic crust. The isotopic composition of Pb was examined as a geochemical tracer to clarify the origin of one of the metals contained in the sulphide concentrations in the Troodos Complex. Isotope ratios suggest that the lead is actually a mixture,and also contains an important component derived from seawater.

1048 **Spooner, J., Wyatt, L., Berryhill, W.S., Lanier, A.L., Brichford, S.L., Smolan, M.D., Coffey, S.W., Bennett, T.B.,** 1989. Non-point sources. J. Water Pollut. Control Fed. 61 : 911-924.

Literature on nonpoint source pollution during 1987 and 1988 in USA is reviewed with respect to policy, economics, water quality, management monitoring and modelling.

1049 **Sposito, G., Holtzclaw, K.M., Levesque-Madore, C.S.,** 1979. Cupric ion complexion by fulvic acid extracted from sewage sludge-soil mixtures. J.

Soil Sci. Soc. Am. 43 : 1148-1155.

The complexes formed between Cu-fulvic acid extracted from sewage sludge were investigated by potentiomietric titration of K/H fulvate with cupric perchlorate at pH 5 and 25°C in an ionic medium of 0.1M potassium perchlorate. Formation functions, giving the number of moles of Cu bound per mole of K/H fulvate, were calculated from the titration data and plotted against the molar concentration of Cu with the concentration of K/H fulvate being a fixed parameter for each plot. These functions were analysed by the Scatchard plot method and were interpreted as evidence of a relatively strong 1:1 complex formed between Cu and the most acidic functional groups in fulvic acid and a weaker set of complexes formed between Cu and the more weakly acidic functional groups acting as unidentate and bidentate ligands.

1050 **Sposito, G., Leclair, J.P.; LeVesque, C.S., Senesi, N.,** 1984. Methodologies to predict the mobility and availability of hazardous metals in sludge-amended soils. NTIS, Spring field, VA.

Sequential extraction of field soil samples with KNO_3, H_2O, NaOH, sodium EDTA, and HNO_3 was shown to provide reliable estimates of trace metals solubility and uptake by barely, irrespective of soil texture, rate of sludge application or time during a three year study period in arid-zone soils receiving sewage sludge or effluents. The total conc. of trace metals Ni, Cu, Zn, Cd and Pb accumulated in two sludge amended soils during the project period were comparable with the amounts of these metals sorbed by untreated soils at soil solution concentrations below 100 parts per million. At these low metal conc. i.e; below sorption isotherms often exhibited a sigmoid shape that precludes interpretation of terms of conventional distribution function techniques. Organic forms of the trace metals, particularly copper, were found to increase in importance with sludge application rate. These organic-metal compounds could be characterized conveniently by electron spin resonance spectrometry.

1051 **Sridhar, M.K.C., Bammeke, A.O.,** 1986. Heavy metal contents of some solid wastes in Ibadan, Nigeria. Water Air Soil Pollut. 29 : 51-56.

The heavy metal contents of some solid wastes produced in residential areas, a market, a cafeteria and the composts in Ibadan, were measured. The solid wastes produced in low density areas with higher per capita income showed higher levels of heavy metals. The cafeteria waste showed low levels of some of these metals.

1052 **Srikanth, R., Reddy, S.R.P.,** 1991. Lead, cadmium and chromium levels in vegetables grown in urban sewage sludge-Hyderabad, India. Food Chem. 40(2) : 229-234.

The present paper examines levels of metal contamination of vegetables grown on urban sewage sludge. Vegetable samples of spinach, amaranthus and cabbage, were collected along the cultivated sites of the River

Musi, which carries the urban sewage load of Hyderabad city. Lead, cadmium and chromium levels of these metals were detected in both soil and food crops indicating possible health hazard for consumers.

1053 **Shrivastava, J.P.,** 1987. Status of selected trace elements in some common vegetables. Indian J. Air Pollut. Control. 7(1) : 19-24.

Iron, copper, zinc and manganese are essential to men, while mercury, cadmium and lead are toxic and act as cumulative poisons even in trace amounts. The industrial discharges and uncareful processing of food, deposit large quantity of these elements in food stuff. Study suggests that vegetables such as guwar, suran and cauliflower should not be taken daily in diet because of high proportion of lead and cadmium.

1054 **Srivastava, R.K.,** 1991. Effect of paper mill effluent on seed germination and early growth performance of radish and onion. J. Ecotoxicol Environ. Monit. 1(1): 13-18.

Effect of paper mill and chlor-alkali plant, effluent was studied on the seed germination and early growth performance of *Raphanus sativus* and *Allium cepa seeds.* It was found that chlor alikali plant effluent was highly deterious for germination and early growth performance of seeds as compared to paper mill effluent. Co-efficient of correlation "r" was calculated between germination, early growth performance and increasing concentration of effluents; all the values showed negative correlation. The relative toxicity of effluents to both the seeds was; chlor-alkali > Paper mill.

1055 **Srivastava, S.C., Jha, A.K., Singh, J.S.,** 1989. Changes with time in soil biomass CN and P of mine spoils in a dry tropical environment. Can. J. Soil. Sci. 69(4) : 849-855.

Soil biomass C, N and P were determined for a native forest site, an unmined deforested site and an age-series of adjacent coal mine spoils (5, 10, 12, 16 and 20 yr). Biomass C ranged from 209 to 867 μ/g soil and P from 7 to 29 μg/g soil. Biomass C, N and P were linearly related to each other. Biomass C was also related to the root biomass. Biomass N with a mean C:N ratio of 11.8 accounted for 2.2-4 % of the total soil N and was positively related to the mineral N of soil. Biomass C:P ratio ranged from 27.6 to 31.0. The biomass P was significantly related to the bicarbonate soluble soil P. Soil microbial biomass was characterized by a mean C:N:P ratio of 29:3:1. Soil microbial C, N and P were positively related with age of mine spoils, the values for the youngest spoil (5 yr old) being about four times lower compared to native forest soil. Total soil N was also positively related with age of spoil. The data suggest that microbial biomass can be taken as a functional index of soil redevelopment.

1056 **Srivastava, R.K., Mathur, K.C.,** 1987. Germination and seedling growth of *Raphanus sativus* seeds treated with chlor alkali plant effluent. Environl. Ecol. 5(2): 352-354.

The effect of chlor-alkali plant (CAP) waste water on the seed germination and early growth performance of *Raphanus sativus* was studied. The CAP waste water produced marked deleterious effects on the germination and seedling growth, specially at higher concentrations. Their values showed negative correlation.

1057 **Srivastava, L.L., Mishra, B., Srivastava, N.C.,** 1988. Recycling of organic wastes in relation to yield of wheat and rice and soil fertility. J. Indian Soc. Soil. Sci. 36: 693-697.

A field experiment to study the effect of incorporation of organic waste was conducted at Kanke, Ranchi. The treatments consisted of three levels of organic waste (0, 2.5, 5.0 Mg ha^{-1}) as rice straw and water hyacinth (50:50) alone and in combination with 3 levels of N (0,50 100 kg N ha^{-1}) as urea. The crop yield of wheat-rice showed an increasing trend with the corresponding increase in the application of organic waste and a moderate level (2.5 Mg ha^{-1}) gave good response as compared with maximum level. Soil analysis indicated a trend similar to yield, vis-a-vis rich straw and water hyacinth additions.

1058 **Srivastava, N., Sahai, R.,** 1987. Effects of distillery waste on the performance of *Cicer arietinum,* Environl. Pollut. 43(2) : 91-102.

The impact of distillery effluent in various concentration (1, 2.5, 5, 10, 25, 50, 75 and 100%) on the seed germination, speed of germination index, growth behaviour, leaf area, biomass, net primary productivity, pigment content, reproductive capacity, seed output, seed weight, seed density and the seed protein content of *Cicer arietinum* L. plants was investigated. The percentage and speed of germination of seeds were increasingly retarted with increase in effluent concentrations and at 100% concentration there was no germination. The seedlings exhibited maximum shoot length at 5% concentration and maximum root length at 2.5 concentrations.

1059 **Staiger, K., Machelett, B., Podlesak, W.P.,** 1985. Comparison of mineralization and extraction methods for the determination of copper, zinc, cadmium lead and nickel concentrations in soils of different anthropogen contamination. Bodenkultur 36(2): 99-107.

Mineralization techniques for determining total amounts of the heavy metals, Cu, Zn, Cd, Pb and Ni in agricultural soils were tested with the help of rock and soil standard samples. Various extraction methods, aqua regia; boiling 1.5N HNO_3; 1 N HCl and 0.025 MEDTA were employed to determine the proportions between extractable and total metals in 80 soils. Mineralization by H_2F_2/HNO_3 in platinum crucibles proved to be a suitable method to investigate total amounts of heavy metals. As a screening method, to assess the metal contamination of soils, the extraction by boiling 1.5 N HNO_3 is proposed. The proportions of metal extracted by HNO_3 were as follows : Cu 80%, Zn‡ 70%, Ni 50%, Cd 100%.

Pb ≥ 70%.

1060 **Stamley, J.S.,** 1981. Investigations of trace elements and organic ligands in oil shale wastes. Diss. Abst. Int. Pt. B. Sci. & Eng. 52(4) : 182.

The waste waters from oil shale retorting operations are complex mixtures of hydrophobic and hydrophilic organic solutes, inorganic salts, and trace elements. Following adsorbent separations of the organic constituents, measurement of dissolved organic carbon showed the proportions of acid, base and neutral subfractions that comprise the hydrophilic solutes are very different for three different processes and sources of oil shale waste waters. The organic compounds that have been identified by high resolution fused silica capillary chromatography included phenol, ortho-meta-and paraphenol, alkyl substitute phenols. NC_6C_{12} carboxylic acids, methylpyridines, dimethlpyridines, trimethy-lpyridines, aniline, substituted quinolines. The use of fused silica capillary columns provided separations with high resolution and excellent peak shapes for polar compounds like underivatized carboxylic acids and the aromatic amines. Many of the organic compounds identified are good complexing ligands.

1061 **Stark, S.A., Clapp, C.E.,** 1980. Residual nitrogen availability from treated with sewage sludge in a field experiment. J. Environ. Qual. 9 : 505-512.

The residual nitrogen availability from sewage sludges applied to a Hubbard sandy loam soil was studied. In study I, three sludge types-anaerobically digested (119, 237 and 466 t/ha) or aerobically digested (493 t/ha) were applied over a 3 year period for maize. Soil samples were collected 2 years after the final sludge application. In study II samples were obtained from the plots in which an aerobically digested sludge had been applied (63, 125 and 200 t/ha) 4 years earlier for sorghum and sudangrass. Several biological and Chemical characteristics were examined as indexes of N availability. For study I N availability, in general, reflected the quantity of sludge added. The sludge application rate was more important than the sludge type in affecting N mineralization. Each index was useful in determining relative differences of N availability for this soil having received greatly differing organic N treatment from sewage sludge. The chemical indexes of N availability were as reliable as more time-consuming incubation procedures for determining the N-supplying capacity of soils.

1062 **Stark, J.M., Redente, E.F.,** 1990. Plant uptake and cycling of trace elements on retorted oil shale disposal piles. J. Environ. Qual. 19(3) : 495-501.

This study considers some of the environmental hazards posed by high trace element concentrations in plants growing on retorted oil shale disposal piles and the potential for surface accumulation of trace element via biocycling. Arsenic, B, Cu, F, Mo and Se concentrations in plants growing on six disposal piles were determined 7yr following site construction. Disposal treatment consisted of leaving paraho retorted shale exposed at the surface, leaching exposed retorted with 760 mm of water, covering retorted shale with 30, 60 or 90 cm of soil, or a 30 cm rock capillary barrier and 60 cm of soil. These treatments plus a disturbed soil reference plot were seeded in 1977 with three mixtures of native and introduced plant species in 1983. Mo was present in plants at high enough levels to cause molybdenosis in ruminants. Molybdenum, F, As and Se concentration in plants decreased as depth of replaced topsoil increased leaching only slightly reduced concentration in plants.

1063 **Stark, J.M., Redente, E.F.,** 1990. Copper fertilization to prevent molybdenosis on retorted oil shale disposal piles. J. Environ. Qual. 19(3) : 502-504.

Plants growing on retorted oil shale disposal piles often have Mo concentrations high enough and Cu/Mo ratios low enough to cause molybdenosis in grazing ruminants. High Mo concentration are present is some plant species in spite of 90 cm of top soil Cover. Copper sulfate was broadcast at rates of 0, 8, 16 and 32 kg Cu ha^{-1} on plots with 30 and 90 cm of topsoil over Parho retorted oil shale to determine if Cu fertilization can increase Cu/Mo ratios in plants so that molybdenosis is no longer a hazard. Of the plant species studied winterfat, *A. desertorum (Fisch*). Schult, *A. intermedium* (Host Beauv), and *Bromus biedersteinii* Roem and Schult, all except alfalfa showed increased tissue Cu concentration, however, only winterfat under high fertilization rates developed Cu/Mo ratios sufficient to prevent molybdenosis (i.e>2.0). By the end of the second growing season, increase in Cu concentrations due to fertilization had declined approximately 30 per cent.

1064 **Starken-Burg, W., Van Luim, A.B.** 1989. Heavy metals in industrial waste waters. in "Protection of water quality from harmful emissions with special regard to nitrate and heavy metals." Proc. 5th Internl. Symp. of CIEC E. Welter, I. Szabolcs (Eds.) 365-367.

The presence of Hg, Cd, As Cr, Zn, Cu, Pb, Ni and Ag, in effluents from 25 different types of industrial plants in the Netherland is reported: Hg, Cr, Cu and Zn were present in almost all samples.

1065 **Steinhilber, P.M.,** 1982. Fate of sewage sludge derived zinc relative to soil fractions and plant utilization. Diss. Abst. Int. Pt. B. Sci. & Eng. 42(8): 79.

Several experiments were conducted to determine the nature of Zn compounds derived from sewage sludge and the effect of sludge-borne Zn on selected soil fractions and bioavailability. The first experiment involved the chemical fractionation of indigenous soil Zn via a sequential extraction procedure, in anticipation of applying the fractionation scheme to sludges and sludge-treated soils. In the second experiment, aerobic sewage sludges from Winder and Norcross, Georgia, were subjected to elemental analysis to determine their suitability for land application, chemical fractionation to elucidate the nature of sludge-borne Zn and infrared spectroscopic analysis to investigate water-soluble and insoluble light sludge organic components. In the final experiment, Norcross and Winder sludges were applied to a Cecil soil under north greenhouse and field conditions to determine the face of sludge-borne Zn relative to soil fractions and plant availability using rye and soybeans as indicator crops.

1066 **Steinnes, E., Solberg, W., Petersen, H.M., Wren, C.D.,** 1989. Heavy metal pollution by iong range atmospheric transport in natural soils of Southern Norway. Water Air Soil Pollut. 45(3-4) : 207-218.

Natural surface soils in Southern Norway are strongly contaminated by metals from atmospheric deposition. Except from local pollution with Cu, Ni and to limited extent Pb around the town of Kristians and Pheric. This large scale contamination can be ascribed to long range atmospheric transport from other parts of Europe. Zinc, As Cu, and Pb are all found in excessive concentrations in the surface layer of natural soils throughout the region and in particular within a zone of about 20 to 40 km from the coast. In this zone the element appeared at the following concentrations of higher in the Ao layer (typical in parentheses). Zn, 120(3) mg kg^{-1}, As 4(0.5) mg kg^{-1}, Cd 2(0.2) mg kg^{-1}, Pb 160(15) mg kg^{-1}. Possible harmful effects to soil biological processes of this contamination cannot be excluded.

1067 **Tenstrom, M.K., Poduska, R.A.,** 1980. The effect of dissolved oxygen concentration on nitrification. Water Res. 14(6) ; 643-649.

The effect of DO concentration on the rate of nitrification was investigated using both pure and mixed cultures, and cultures found in waste water treatment systems. The maximum growth rate of both nitrification reactions are reported to be affected by DO concentrations over the range of 0.3 mg/L. to 4.0 mg/L. In some instances a DO concentrations of 4.0 mg/L/ is required to achieve maximum nitrification rates, while in some cases only 0.5-1.0 mg/L is required. Several factors are responsible for the wide range of reported nitrifications rates with varying DO concentrations. Among these are the effects of 0_2 diffusion influx, variation between measured results due to steady-state and dynamic measuring techniques, and double-substrate limited kinetics. The nitrification literature with respect to the effects of DO concentrations is reviewed, and it is shown that double-substrate limiting kinetics could account for the variation in the reported results.

1068 **Stephenson, N.T., Perry, R., Lester, J.R.,** 1985. The influence of transient phenomena on the biodegradation of nitrilotriacetic acid in the activated sludge process II. Variation in influent metal and NTA concentrations. Water Air Soil Pollut 25: 431-450.

The removal of Cd, Cr, Cu, Pb, Ni and Zn in an activated sludge pilot plant acclimatized to nitrilotriacetic acid (NTA) has been compared with an identifically operated plant receiving no NTA. During steady state operating the removal of Pb and Ni was reduced in the presence of NTA but there was no detectable difference in mixed liquor metal concentrations. Transient changes in the influent metal concentration of an order of magnitude had only a slight influence on NTA removal, Ni had the greatest effect, Cd and Cu some effect and Pb a negligible effect. Short term variation in influent NTA concentrations had no effect on NTA removal. A transient increase in influent NTA concentration caused a slight decrease in NTA removal. Transient increase in Ni concentration combined with reductions in temperature to 10 and 7.5 had a slight adverse effect on NTA removal. This effect did not appear to be additive or synergistic. Combinations of transient increase in influent NTA concentrations and reduction in temperature caused a significant decrease in NTA removal. The effect was synergistic rather than additive.

1069 **Sterritt, R.M., J.N., Lester,** 1980. Concentration of heavy metals in forty sewage in England. Water Air Soil Pollut. 14 : 125-131.

Samples of forty sewage sludges taken in England during 1979 were analyzed for ten heavy metals. For all metals, the mean concentration were influenced by a small number of sludge containing exceptionally high concentration. Typically the concentration ranges showed approximately a 100-fold spread. Calculations based on U.K. guidelines for limiting the addition of toxic metals in sludge to agril. soils indicated that application rate would theoretically be limited for more than 75% of the sludges by the concentration of Zn, Cu, and Ni, expressed aditively as the Zn equivalent. Calculations of the theoretical maximum quantities of sludges which could be applied to land on an annual basis suggested that a significant proportion of the sludges would be unsuitable for application to agricultural land at rate of more than 2 t ha^{-1} yr^{-1}.

1070 **Sterritt, R.M., Lester, J.N.,** 1981. Influence of sludge age on heavy metals removal in the activated process. Water Res. 15(1) : 59-65.

In a laboratory simulations of the activated sludge process ten heavy metals were added continuously to the system which was allowed to equilibrate at six sludge ages between 3 and 18d. Cobalt, manganese and molybodenum removals were poor and were unaffected by changes in the sludge age. The highest removal efficiencies for the other metals occurred at the 15d sludge age, Chromium (Trivalent) and Cadmium had the highest removal efficiencies, typically greater than 50%. The behaviour of the majority of the metals which were removed to a significant extent was related to one of the parameters influenced by sludge age. The metals which were poorly removed showed little affinity for the activated sludge.

1071**Steven, B.G., Charles, R.J., Edward, Z.E., Cothern, R.C.** 1979. The use of zonal configuration in delineating trade elements distributions in sewage sludge from the Dayton-Ohio. Area. J. Environ. Qual. 8(3): 416-422.

The distributions of Cd, Cu, Pb, Ni, and Zn in the sludge fractions were determined. Seventy-five weight per cent of the total trace elements in the sludges are contained in low density (1.60-2.10 gm/cm^3) organic rich fractions. A small portion of the total trace element in sludge is also associated with minerals such as sulfides and sulfates in high density fractions. Most of the trace elements are located in organic compounds in the sludges applied.

1072 **Stvenson, F.J., Welch, L.F., 1979.** Migration of applied lead in a field soil. E S & T 13(10) : 1255-1259.

Field plots amended with variable amounts of Pb were resampled after 6.5 yr to ascertain the extent to which the applied Pb had moved from the application zone. The soil, Drummer silty clay loam, effectively bound Pb in nonexchangeable forms over the range at which Pb had been applied (0-3200 kg/ha). Downward movement of Pb occurred (to 90 cm) and was attributed to leaching as soluble chelate complexes with organic matter, transfer of soil by earthworms and other faunal organisms, translocation in plant roots, or a combination of these. Significant horizontal movement also occurred, due primarily to physical transfer of soil through tillage operation. Evidence was obtained for migration of trace amounts of Pb as wind-blow soil or plant particles.

1073 **Stewart, L.W., Reneau, R.B. Jr., 1988.** Shallowly placed, low pressure distribution system to treat domestic waste water in soils with fluctuating high water tables. J. Environ. Qual. 17:499-504.

Soils with seasonal fluctuating high water tables are common in the Atlantic Coastal Plain and are considered to be unsuited for conventional on site waste water disposal systems (OSWDS). This study was conducted to monitor the performance of a shallowly placed, low pressure OSWDS in a Typic Ochraquult. Changes in water table levels, effluent distribution, and movement of fecal coliforms and selected chemical contaminants in ground-waters were monitored in situ from December 1980 through May 1982. An unsaturated zone was present beneath the OSWDS during the entire study except for the period from January through May of 1982. During this period the water table intersected the OSWDS, for some time interval (<24h), on 36d primarily following large rainfall events. Movement of fecal coliforms and P were restricted both horizontally and vertically. Nitrate concentrations were highest beneath the OSWDS during periods of rising water tables following prolonged periods of time when the water table was deeper than 1.5 m. Following the accumulations of NO_3-N in the upper portion of the water table, NO_3-N concentrations decreased rapidly. The observed decrease in NO_3-N was attributed to denitrification and was supported by NO_3-N/Cl ratios, approximately 90%, of the NO_3-N could not be accounted for with increased distance from the OSWDS.

1074 **Stokes, P.M.,** et al 1988. Manganese in the Canadian environment. NRCC Pub : 26193: 177.

This publication contains sections on: i) Environmental chemistry of

Mn, ii) The GPO-chemical cycle iii) manganese and terrestial plants, iv) Effects of manganese on aquatic biots, and v) Manganese and human health.

1075 **Stones, T.**, 1980. The oxygen demand of sewage. Effluent Water Treatment J. 20(9) : 437-440.

The oxygen demand of sewage is used as a basis for the determination of its strength which reflects its pollution character and also for the assessment of the loading and performance of sewage treatment plants. Other arbitrary criteria which have been adopted as parameters for assessing the strength of sewage give partial measures of the carbonaceous oxygen demand, e.g. BOD & the permangnate value (PV). One method for calculating the approximate value of the absolute strength of sewage indirectly is based from the use of factors in which the first stage BOD was calculated from its ratio with the PV. Any practicable method to provide a satisfactory measure of the carbonaceous oxygen demand of sewage must depend upon the expeditious and complete oxidation of the carbonaceous matter. COD fulfills these requirements. The ratio of BOD to COD gives the fraction of the total carbonaceous oxygen demand which is satisfied biochemically during a 5-d period, and thus given a rational indication of the amenability of a sewage to treatment.

1076 **Stott, D.E.**, 1982. Stabilization in humus and incorporation into biomass of a wide variety of organic compounds during biodegradation in soil. Diss Abst. Int. Pt. B. Sci. & Eng., 43 (1): 106.

The effect of soil type and incubation period on the biodegradation, incorporation into biomass and stabilization of humus of specific carbons of ferulic, p-hydroxycinnamic and benzoic acids; of ^{14}C-labeled cornstalk and/or wheat straw lignin, polysaccharide, and protein fractions and whole wheat straw : of ^{14}C-labeled catechol, 4-chlorocatechol, and 4, 5 dichlorocatechol, free and linked into model humic acid polymers, and 2, 3, 4, D, glucose and a fungal melanin were followed over one year. Biomass was estimated by the fumigation methods. The rate and extent of degradation depended upon the substrate, the concentration, and the soil.

1077 **Street, J.J., Lindsay, W.L., Sabey, B.R.**, 1977. Solubility and plant uptake of cadmium in soils amended with cadmium and sewage sludge. J. Environ. Qual. 6 (1): 72-77.

Adsorption and precipitation of Cd^{2+} in soil suspensions were investigated as possible factors controlling Cd^{2+} levels in soils. Both adsorption of Cd^{2+} onto soils surface and possible precipitation of cadmium minerals were evident in this study. At low cadmium levels solubility relationship in soils are best described by adsorption and fit the empirical Freundlich adsorption isotherm. Based on current thermodynamic data the solid phases $CdCO_3$ (log K_{SP} = -12.7) and $Cd_3(PO_4)_2$ (log K_{sp} = - 32.61) most likely limit Cd^{2+} activities in soils. Under alkaline conditions, Cd^{2+} actively decreased approximately 100-fold for each unit increase in pH. In this study, $CdCO_3$ precipitated in sandy soils, having low CEC, low organic matter and pH values > 7.0. DTPA-extractable cadmium levels in soils were highly correlated (r - 0.96) with Cd concentrations in corn seedlings grown on soils amended with Cd solutions, sewage sludge or Cd-spiked sewage sludge. Increasing Cd additions to the soil increased plant Cd regardless of the form of Cd added. Addition of inorganic Cd to the soil increased Cd concentrations of corn seedlings more than equivalent Cd additions in the form of sewage sludge or Cd-spiked sludge.

1078 **Street, J., Sabey, B.R., Lindsay, W.L.** 1978. Influence of pH, phosphorus, cadmium, sewage sludge and incubation time on the solubility and plant uptake of cadmium. J. Environ. Qual. 7 (2) 286-290.

Corn was grown in the greenhouse on a loamy sand amended with cadmium, cadmium-spiked sewage sludge and sewage sludge. Soil pH was adjusted to approximately 5.7, 6.7 and 7.8 and phosphorus was applied at 0,200 and 400 µg/gm soil. Soil treatments were applied 0, 8 and 16 weeks prior to planting, and the plants were grown for 5 weeks. Increasing the pH of the soil amended with inorganic $CaSO_4$) decreased the Cd concentration of corn seedlings by approximately 67%. The Cd concentration was reduced approximately 47% for a similar increase in pH on soil amended with Cd-spiked sludge. The Cd concentration of corn seedling was significantly reduced by the addition of P. Increasing incubation time decreased the availability of added inorganic Cd, but increased the availability of Cd applied with sewage sludge. Increasing the amount of Cd added to the soils increased the Cd concentration of the corn seedlings regardless of the form of Cd used. Cadmium concentrations in the corn seedlings were significantly correlated with DTPA-extractable soil Cd. Solubility measurement of Cd in the acidified soils showed under saturation with respect to all known Cd mineral's whereas in soils above pH 7.25 the Cd solubility was limited by $CdCO_3$ at CO_2 level of 0.003 atm. or higher and showed the expected hundredfold decrease in solubility for each unit increase in pH.

1079 **Stroo, H.F., Jencks, E.M.,** 1985. Effect of sewage sludge on microbial activity in an old, abandoned minesoil. J. Environ. Qual. 14(3) : 301-304.

The effect of lime, fertilizer, and sewage sludge (50 and 100 kg ha^{-1}) upon microbial activity and growth of sparsely distributed tall fescue (*Festuca arundinaceae* Schreb) on an old acidic infertile sandy, loam minesoil was evaluated. Respiration rate and activities of amylase, urease, and phosphatase were used an indices of microbial activity. When compared with the control, lime significantly increased respiration rate and amylase activity, but significantly decreased ureare activity. Phosphates activity was not affected by fertilizer applications. Lime plus fertilizer significantly increased respiration rate and amylase activity, had no affect upon phosphatase activity while it drastically reduced urease activity.

1080 **Stuart, R.C., James, A.M.,** 1984. Bacterial pollution of groundwater – a review. Water Air Soil Pollut. 22 : 67-83.

Contamination of groundwater resources from bacterial laden waste water and effluents poses a great threat to the potability and use of these water resources. Major factors affecting the quantity and velocity at which bacteria are able to migrate through soil can be classified as (1) soil factor including particle size distribution, structure, clay content, pore size distribution and moisture regime, and (2) biological factors responsible for bacterial die-off including pH, temperature, moisture content, and nutrient supply. Past bacterial pollution problems have been shown to be localized and restricted to wells utilizing near-surface waters. The following problem areas exist and must be given special consideration in planning and development : (1) use of septic disposal systems in unsuitable soils, (2) drainage waters from waste water application areas utilising artificial drainage systems, (3) waste applications in areas underlain by fractured crystalline rock or channelized bedrock; and (4) bacterial contamination induced over great distances by groundwater pumping.

1081 **Subrahmanyam, P.V.R.,** 1990. Water management in pulp and paper industry. J. Indian Assoc. Environ. Manage. 17(2) : 79-94.

Various processes involved in pulp and paper making using different raw materials and chemicals are described. The sources and quantum of pollution in a mill are presented. Methods of controlling pollution from both large and small paper mills are elaborated and cost estimates for the treatment alternatives worked out. Discharge standards for effluents have been given.

1082 **Subhadra, A.V., Nanda, A.K., Behera, P.K., Panda, B.B.,** 1991. Acceleration of catalase and peroxidase activities in Lemna Minor L. and Allium cepa. L. in response to low levels of aquatic mercury. Environl. Pollut. 69: (2&3) 169-179.

The growth of fronds of duckweed (Lemna minor) or onion roots (Allum cepa) and the production of catalase and peroxidase in both plants were studied following 96-h exposure to mercuric chloride ($HgCl_2$) or methyl mercuric chloride (Me $HgCl_2$). $HgCL_2$ and $MeHgCl_2$ were lethal to L. Minor at concn. of 4 and 0.01 mg/ L respectively. The results suggest that assays of catalase and peroxidase in Lemna and Allium could be used for toxicity testing and biomonitoring of particularly low levels of mercury and other heavy metals in the aquatic environment.

1083 **Sundblad, K., Wittgren, H.B.,** 1989. *Glyceria maxima* for waste water nutrient removal and forage production. Biol. Wastes. 27: 29-42.

Potential biomass yield, nutrient uptake capacity and forage quality of Glyceria maxima was tested in four field lysimeters (I-IV) receiving municipal waste water. Waste water was applied during 3 years at different frequencies in order to achieve maximum N-reduction in the system. Accordingly lysimeters III and IV were ponded for part of the week. Harvesting (in June and August) progressively favoured competing terrestrial species in the non-ponded lysimeters (I and II). In year 3 the other species accounted for 65-70% of the harvested biomass in these lysimeters. In the ponded lysimeters reduction conditions in the soil probably prevented species from establishing.

1084 **Sutton, A.L., Nelson, D.W., Mayrose, V.B., Nye, J.C.,** 1978. Effects of liquid swine waste applications on corn yield and soil chemical composition. J. Environ. Qual. 7 (3): 325-333).

Liquid swine waste (1.8 to 3.0 dry matter) was applied annually at rates of 45, 90 and 134 t/ha. The high rate provided in average of 378 kg N, 113 kg P, 163 kg K and 42 kg Na per ha. Check and inorganic fertilizer (168 kg N/ha, 56 kg P/ha, 112 kg K/ha) treatments were included. Soils Na, nitrate-N, and extractable P concentrations increased with increasing waste application rates. Soil ECe was not affected by waste. The effects of dietary salt levels and waste handling systems on the chemical composition of the soils were inconsistent. There was evidence for down ward movement of N, K and NO_3 in all soil profiles. Downward movement of NO_3 was observed greater in fertilizer than in the waste plots. 2 years of waste application had no detrimental effects on the chemical composition of the two loam soils. Soil application of waste resulting from different dietary salt levels and waste holding systems resulted in similar corn yields and leaf chemical composition. Yields were higher from plots treated with waste and inorganic fertilizer compared to the check plot. Corn yields increased with increasing rates of waste application up to the 90 tons/ha rate, then leveled off.

1085 **Swaminathan, K., Arjunan, J., Guruswamy, R.,** 1989. Effect of glucose factory effluents on seed germination and seedling development of groundnut (*Arachis hypogea*). Proc (Vol. 2) Seminar "Environment Impact" held at Loyola College, Madras : 81-87.

The glucose factory effluent contained high amount of total solids, dissolved solids, chlorides, sulfates, calcium, magnesium and iron. BOD and COD values were also very high. While the pure effluents retarded seed germination, hypocotyl development, speed of germination and seed vigour of groundnut seeds, the dilute effluents (up to 50%) favoured these factors. Similarly the seedling growth and seedling biomass were also favoured by diluted effluents. The seedlings irrigated with diluted effluents contained high amounts of photosynthetic pigments, carbohydrates and proteins when compared to seedlings irrigated with water and pure effluents. This simulation in seed germination and seedling growth was attributed to micronutrients in proper concentration in diluted effluents.

1086 **Sweazy, R.M., Wells, D.M., Whetstone, G.A.,** 1979. Long term experiences with effluent reuse. J. Water Pollut. Control. Fed. 51(II): 2641-2648.

Municipal effluent produced in the high plains of west Texas, was reused for agricultural and industrial purposes in a routine manner for at least 50 yr. The treated effluent from ≈ 80 municipalities is reused for irrigation, and all or part of the effluent from most of the cities in the areas reused for industrial purposes. Much of the effluent generated by industrial operation. e.g., slaughter houses is reused, for irrigation. While several government agencies are apparently discovering reuse for the first time, multiple reuse of waste water is becoming common place. The city of Odessa's waste water is reused for process, cooling, and boiler makeup in a petrochemical complex; then that complex's waste water is reused again for secondary oil recovery. Part of the city of Lubbock's waste water is reused for cooling water and boiler makeup water in a power plant. The power plant's boiler and cooling tower blow down water is diluted with waste water and then reused a second time for irrigation.

1087 **Sweeney, D.W., Graetz, D.A.,** 1988. Chemical decomposition characteristics of anaerobic digester effluents applied to soil. J. Environ. Qual. 17: 309-313.

A study was conducted to determine the elemental concentrations of an effluent that resulted from the anaerobic digestion of rum distillery by products (also called molasses residue) and decomposition characteristics in soil. Two additional effluents from the anaerobic digestion of swine wastes and borine wastes were included. The carbon content of oven-dry molasses residue and swine waste effluents were both approximately 250 g kg^{-1}. where as the borine wastes was 152 g kg^{-1}. An analysis of variance performed on total CO_2-C evolved after 20d as well as at the end of experiment (117d) indicated an interaction between effluent source and rate. This was caused by the low amount of CO_2 evolved from soil amended with the borine waste effluent regardless of application rate. At day 20, cumulative CO_2 evolution was higher with the molasses residue effluent than with the swine waste effluent; however by day 117, only at the high application rate was CO_2 evolution higher with the molasses residue. Lower application rate allow for proportionally more short term decomposition of the molasses residue and swine waste effluents than at higher rates. Although effluent sources result in different amounts of total evolution, between the 40 and 50% of the total CO_2 evolved may occur in the first 20d.

1088 **Tabakov, D., Dimitrov, R.,** 1989. Environmental pollution and its effect on the soil. in "The scientific technical revolution era status and problem." Sels. Kosto Panska Nauka 27(6) : 29-37.

Soil is contaminated by erosion, industrial emission of SO_2, agri. chemicals and non-ferrous metals. Data on pollutant concentration in Bulgaria are presented and methods of environmental pollution control suggested.

1089 **Tabatabia, M.A., Chae, Y.M.,** 1991. Mineralization of sulfur in soils amended with organic wastes. J. Environ. Qual. 20: 684-690.

This study was conducted to compare the mineralization of S in soils amended with various types of sewage sludges, animal manures and plant materials. Field-moist amended with organic waste materials at a 50-Mg-ha^{-1} rate were mixed with glass beads, packed in leaching columns, leached with 5 mM $CaCl_2$ to remove the mineral S, and incubated at 30C. The leaching procedure was repeated every 2 wk for 26 wk. The leachates were analyzed for SO_4^{2-}-S. The rate of $SO^{2-}{}_4$ release from sewage sludges was rapid during the first 6 wk, followed by a slow linerar release. The release of $SO^{2-}{}_4$ from animal manures was linear with time of incubation. With the exception of alfalfa (*Medicago sativa* L.) which showed a rapid SO_4^{2-} release within the first 2 wk and a subseqent linear release with time up to 26 wk, the additon of all other plant materials resulted in net S immobilization. The total net S mineralized from the organic waste materials varied considerably, depending on the type of soil and the C/N/S ratio of the organic waste material. The amount of S mineralized in soils amended with sewage sludges and animal manures ranged from 99 to 345 mg S kg^{-1} and from 32 to 52 mg S kg^{-1} soil, respectively. The total S mineralized in soils amended with plant materials ranged from 15 to 57 mg S kg^{-1}. Expressed as a percentage of total organic S added to soils, the S mineralized ranged from 41 to 97% for sewage sludges and from 62 to 127% for animal manures. The percentage of organic S mineralized in the plant materials ranged from 510% for cornstalk (*Zea mays* L.) to 87% for alfalfa. Soil types have marked effects on the mineralizable S(S_o) pool and first-order rate constants (k).

1090 **Tadesse, W., Shuford, J.W., Taylor, R.W., Adrianc. D.C., Sajwan, K.S.,** 1991. Comparative availability to wheat of metals from sewage sludge and inorganic salts. Water Air Soil Pollut. 55(3-4) : 397-408.

A greenhouse experiment was conducted to evaluate the availability of metals from sewage sludge and inorganic salts, and the effect of pH and soil type on yield and metal (Zn, Cu, Cd and Ni) uptake by wheat. Soils used in this study were sandy loam and silty clay loam. Two treatments of sewage sludge containing metals were applied at the rate of 20 and 100 t/ha, inorganic salts of Zn, Cu, Cd and Ni were applied (as sulfate salts) at concentrations equivalent to those found in the 20 and 100 t/ha sludge. One treatment consisted of inorganic metals plus sewage at the 20 Mg/harate. Two soil pH levels, one at field pH (below 6.0) and another pH adjusted between 6.5 and 7.0 were used. Wheat plants were harvested four weeks after germination. Two more subsequent harvests were made four weeks intervals. For each harvest, dry matter yield increased as the rate of sludge application increased for both soil types.

1091 **Takala, K., Olkkornem, H.,** 1981. Lead content of an epiphytic lichen in the urban area of Kuopio, East Central Finland. Ann. Botanici Fennict. 18(2) : 85-89.

The epiphytic lichen hypogymnia physodes (L) Nyl. growing on birch and pine, was analysed for lead by the Pu-238 excited Si(Li) semiconductor detector X-ray fluourescence method. The lead content of the lichen varied between 14 and 308 ppm. The background lead concentration was 14 to 31 ppm. The zone with lichen lead contents over 90 ppm and the zone with contents of 40-90 ppm were determined by the image reconstruction methods. The lead content of the lichen correlated with the traffic density. Lead accumulation in the lichen was considered in relations to the distance from the nearest road or street, the shelter effect, the phorophyte species and the level of sulphur dioxide.

1092 **Tam, N.F.Y., Wong, Y.S., Wong, M.H.,** 1989. Effects of acidity on acute toxicity of aluminium waste and aluminium contaminated soil. in Environmental Bioassay Technoloqies and their Applications: 385-395.

The total heavy metal concentration of Alwaste and Al-contaminated soil were many times higher than that found in the control soil, which might pose toxic effects on nearby ecosystems under acidic condition. The present study aimed to detect the amount of Al, Cu, Zn, Mn, Pb, Ni, and Cd extracted by distilled water and ammonium acetate at pH, 3.8, 4.8, 5.8, 6.8, & 7.8. The acute toxicities of after extracts were assessed by two bioassays. Results showed that concentrations of heavy metals, especially Al, were the highest in extracts from Al-contaminated soil extracted with NNH_4OAC, followed by Al-waste. The control displayed relatively low levels of metals. More heavy metals were extracted at acidic pH than at neutral pH.

1093 **Tarmura, R., Fukzaki, N., Hirano, Y., Mizushima, Y.,** 1985. Evaluation of mercury contamination using plant leaves and humus as indicator. Chemosphere 14 : 1687-1693.

Plant leaves and humus were collected from three areas with and without mercury emission sources. Mercury in these samples, were determined by cold flameless atomic absorption spectromery. A part of mercury emitted from the source into the atmosphere is absorbed by plant leaves and moved to humus through fallen leaves. Consequently plant leaves are able to be used as an indicator for the evaluation of mercury in air at present. Humus is useful for the evaluation of mercury contamination through the air from the past to present.

1094 **Tanji, K.K.,** 1989. Chemistry of toxic elements (As, B, Mo, Se) accumulating in agricultural evaporation ponds in 'Toxic Substances in Agricultural Water Supply and Drainage, ICID, USA : 109-121.

A multi-cell evaporation pond facility in which water flows by gravity from cell to cell in series, and each cell receives more concentrated water than the one before due to evaporation. Boron accumulated in the cells in direct proportion to the evaporation factor while As remained as low conc. because of 42 to 88% removal from water column by sink mechanisms removed 5 to 51% of these metals. The main sink mechanisms are adsorption to pond sediments (for As and Mo), volatilization along methylated forms (for As and Se) reduction to elemental forms (for Se) and complexation to organic constituent (for Mo).

1095 **Tanji, K., Valoppi, L.,** 1989. Ground-water contamination by trace elements. Agril. Ecosystem Environ. 26 (3-4) : 229-274.

Heavy metal cations are accumulated by soil and do not increase metal conc. to a large extent in ground-water except in coarse soil with shallow soil profile and large water fluxes. However oxyanions are more mobile and accumulate in ground-water. A case study with application of sewage sludge heavy metals, (Cd, Cr, Cu, Zn, Pb) to cropped soils indicated that metals were accumulated within 15 cm depth by clays, hydroxides of Fe and Mn, complexation with organic matter and precipitation as inorganic minerals. In case of shallow ground-water problems, Se is correlated with salinity in ground-water. It is accumulated upto 4200 μg/L due to leaching of soil Se. Irrigation has aggravated the toxic element problem by mobilising Se.

1096 **Tate, R.L.,** 1979. Municipal waste water reutilization on cultivated sol. J. Water Pollut Control. Fed. 51(1) : 85-88.

Secondary waste water effluent was added to intact cores of pahokee muck to determine efficiency of assimilation of nutrients. Less than 6% of added orghophosphate and 30% of added inorganic nitrogen were leached through cores amended with effluent at rates of 2.5 to 5.0 cm/week. Nearly 75% of added inorganic nitrogen drained through cores amended at the rate of 7.5 cm/week. This indicates that this rate would be too great for effective waste water renovation. Nutrient loadings of drainage water was significantly greater from waste water effluent amended cores than those amended with pond water or deionized water. Raising the depth to water table from 75 to 45 cm increased nutrient retention soil cores. These studies demonstrate that drained cultivated organic soils could be effectively used for waste water renovation.

1097 **Tate, R.L., Terry, R.E.,** 1980. Effect of sewage effluent on microbial activities and coliform populations of Pahokee much. J. Environ. Qual. 9(4) : 673-676.

To determine the effect of amendment with sewage effluent on microbiological properties of organic soils, dehydrogenase, carbon metabolism by the microbial community, and coliform survival were examined in field plots of Pahokee muck. Test plots were amended at weekly intervals with sewage effluent at rate of 5 cm/week. Dehydrogenase activities were increased approximately two-fold in the sewage and water amended soils over levels detected in the unamended soil. No significant variation in bacterial population was detected due to any treatment. Data indicate that the increased microbial activity in sewage amended plots resulted from augmented soil moisture and not the added nutrients of the sewage.

1098 **Taylor, G.J.,** 1983. The physiology of aluminum phytotoxicity in metals lons in biological system, Vol. 24. Aluminum and its Role in Biology. H. Sigel; A-Sigel (Eds.) Marceldekkar, New York p 123-163.

The potential stress injuries include the effects of Al on membrane structure and function, DNA synthesis and mitosis, cell elongation, and mineral nutrition and metabolism. Before addressing these potential stress injuries, the expression of Al phytotoxicity and the uptake, transport and distributions of Al have been reviewed.

1099 **Taylor, J.M., Sikora, L.J., Tester, C.F., Parr, J.P.** 1978. Decomposition of sewage sludge compost in soil. II Phosphorus and sulphur transformations. J. Environ. Qual. 7:119-123.

Incubation studies were conducted in which sewage sludge compost was incubated at 22 C with three soils-loamy sand, silty clay loam and silt loam and a sand, at rates of 44.8, 89.6 and 134.4 ha^{-1} of the dry weight,. Extractable P in the compost sand mixtures ranged rom 48 to 81% of the total P. The Euesbora compost sand mixtures showed in initial high P mineralization trend followed by a slight immobilization trend at 54 days. Both P and S were sufficient for plant growth at 44.8 t/ha sludge.

1100 **Taylor, R.W., Thangudu, P.R., Duseja, D.R.** 1981. Effect of sewage sludge and manure on soil available calcium magnesium, and potassium. J. Environ. Sci. Health, A16 (6): 589-604.

Beef cattle feedlot manure at 0, 6.7, 20.2, and 40.4 t/ha and anaerobically digested municipal sewage sludge at 0, 11.2, 33.6, and 67.2 t/ha were applied and incorporated into an acid (pH 5.6) Byler loam soil for two consecutive years. Corn and sorghum were grown. Available calcium, magnesium and potassium (in $NH_{4.}$ acetate extractable, pH 7) were increased.

1101 **Tepper, B.T., Yang, C.S., Schaedle, M.,** 1989. Effect of aluminium on growth of root tips of honey locust and loblolly pine. Environ. Exp. Bot. 29: 165-173.

Honey locust (*Gleditsia triacanthos* L.) and loblolly pine (*Pinus taed* L.) were grown in solution culture with 150-1500 µM Al. In both species Al reduced primary root elongation, but more severely in honey locust. The decrease was most evident in the 2nd mm root segment after 24 hr. The decrease in elongation was not accompanied by a decrease in cell size. Al drastically reduced mitotic activity in honey locust which was not reversed with time. These observations plus the appearance of necrotic lesions in honey locust suggest: (1) that honey locust is more sensitive to Al than loblolly pine and (2) that Al more probable exerts its growth effect through a nuclear rather than cell wall synthesis mechanism.

1102 **Terry, R.E., Nelson, D.W., Sommers, L.E.,** 1979. Decomposition of anaerobically digested sewage sludge as affected by soil environmental conditions. J. Environ. Qual. 8:342-347.

The effects of soil characteristics, sludge management procedures,, and environmental conditions on the decomposition rate of sewage sludge in soils were determined. Synthetic sewage sludge was prepared by anaerobically digesting a mixture of C-labelled Candida utilis cells and inorganic salts. The sludge prepared was similar in composition to anaerobically digested Municipal sludges. After incorporation into soil, decomposition of sludge was rapid during the first 28d, but the decomposition rate was low and relatively constant for the remainder of the incubation period. At the end of 336 days of incubation, 46% of synthetic sludge organic C was evolved as CO_2 suggesting that one fraction of anaerobically digested sludge was readily decomposable when added to an aerobic soil. However, the major portion of sludge organic matter was resistant to decomposition. Factors such as soil texture, pH, and moisture content had little effect on sludge decomposition rates. Decomposition was greatest in soil samples receiving surface-applied sludge and in samples incubated at high temperature (30C) as compared to samples having sludge incorporated for incubated at 21°C.

1103 **Tester, C.F., Sikora, L.J., Taylor, J.M., Parr, J.F.,** 1977. Decomposition of sewage sludge compost in soil : 1. Carbon and nitrogen transformation. J. Environ. Qual. 6: 459-463.

Freezedried compost made from undigested sewage sludge was mixed with three soils (loamy sand, silt loam, silty clay) and a sand at rates of 0.2, 4 and 6% of the dry weight. The mixtures were incubated at 22C in a constant atmosphere of CO_2 and NH_3 free air. Rates of mineralization and decomposition were determined. Cumulative CO_2 evoluation was linearly related to the rate of sludge compost applied. Approximately 16% of the compost C evolved in 54 days of incubation. Nitrogen mineralization was lowest in the silt loam compost treatment. In the sand-compost mixture, mineral N was immobilized during incubation. Ammonia volatilization from all other treatments was minimal. Approximately 6% of the compost N in loamy sand composite treatment had mineralized after 54 days incubation. Interlattice fixation of NH^+_4 may have occurred in the silt loam and silty clay loam soils.

1104 **Tester, C.F., Sikora, L.J., Taylor, J.M., Parr, J.F.,** 1979. Decomposition of sewage sludge compost in soil: III. Carbon nitrogen, phosphorus transformations in different sized fractions. J. Environ. Qual. 8 : 79-82.

Three fractions of compost (> 6, 1-6, and < 1 mm) were mixed with a loamy sand at a rate of 89.6 t/ha (dry wt) and incubated at 25°C. Decomposition of the compost fractions, as determined by CO_2 evolution, directly related to the amount of C in the compost-soil mixtures. Cumulative CO_2

evolution was lowest from the compost that passed the <1-mm sieve. About 8% of the compost-C from all fractions evolved as CO_2 in 45 d of incubation. The quantity of N mineralized ranged from 3 to 13% for the different fractions, and the extent of N mineralization was inversely related to the C-N, ratio. Ammonia evolution paralleled N mineralization in these mixtures. The amount of extractable P was nearly the same for all fractions and did not change during incubation. Although the <1-mm fraction contained a greater amount of total P than the other 2 fractions, it contained a smaller amount of extractable P. When the pH was adjusted to 6.6 decomposition of the native soil C increased 82%, but neither soil N mineralization nor the amount of extractable P was affected.

1105 **Thangudu, P.R., Taylor, R.W., Duseja, D.R.**, 1981. Available phosphorus status of an acid soil treated with sewage sludge and farm manure. J. Environ . Sci. Health, A16 (6): 611-621.

Anarobically digested sewage sludge at 11.2, 33.6, and 67.2 t/ha and farm manure at 6.7, 20.2, and 40.4 t/ha rates were applied annually for two consecutive years to an acid Byler loam soil cropped to corn and sorghum. A recommended NPK check was included. Available P (1% $(NH_4)_2SO_4$ in 0.05 NH_2SO_4 extractable) levels in the soil were determined after crop harvest in the ensuing spring, each of the two years. Levels of available P in the organic amended plots did not increase significantly in the surface soil (0-20 cm) layer in the fist year. Some movement of P into the subsurface soil (20-40 cm) layer was observed, however.

1106 **Thergaonkar, V.P., Thakre, O.B., Tarafdar, P.K., Thakre, R.A., Ramteke, D.S.**, 1981. Series suspension and their coagulation. IAWPC Tech. Ann. 8: 161-167.

Fly ash and six soil samples were suspended in tap water and their analysis, and Cation Exchange Capacity (C.E.C) determinations were done. Soils could be catagorized in four groups on the basis of their CEC (meq/100 g soil) viz., (i) with 0 or negligible (Flyash) (ii) less than 10 (iii) between 10 and 20 and (iv) between 20 and 100. Soil suspensions were coagulated with alum at 5 pH ranges including highly acidic, original soil suspension pH and highly alkaline pH. Jar tests were used to plot coagulation curves. It was found that optimum dose recognized to get a residual turbidity of 50 NYU increases with the CEC of subsoils for all the pH values studied. The experiments indicated correlation between CEC and pH of suspension and the alum requirement.

1107 **Thornton, J. XU.**, 1985. Arsenic in garden soils and vegetable crops in Cornwall, England: Implications for human health. Environ. Geochem Health 7(4): 131-133.

Total concentrations of arsenic in surface garden soils in the historical mining area of Hayle-Camborne-Godolphin, Cornwall, England are large and range widely. Amounts of water soluble and acid fluoride extractable soil arsenic are significantly correlated with total content. Examination of 6 salad and vegetable crops grown in 32 gardens has shown arsenic concentrations in the edible tissues to be only slightly elevated. There were strong correlations between arsenic in beet-root, lettuce, onion, and peas and soil arsenic. Regression equations have been calculated. ridge regression analysis applied to test the importance of other soil variables has shown both iron and phosphorus to influence the uptake of arsenic. Arsenic in all the vegetables sampled was below the statutory limi' of the U.K. of 1 mg/kg fresh weight. Implications for health should be assessed in relation to other exposure routes viz. water, air and directly ingested dust and soil.

1108 **Thukral, A.K.,** 1989. Effect of tailings water irrigation on the biomass of some crop plants. J. Environ. Biol. 10(4) : 337-342.

A study was undertaken to determine the effects of tailing water discharged from Khetri Copper Complex, Khetrinagar on the biomass of some crop plants. A decrease in plant dry weight-was observed on regular irrigation with tailings water in all the crops. However no complete suppression of growth was observed in any of the crops.

1109 **Tiller, K.G.,** 1989. Heavy metals in soils and their environmental significance. Adv. Soil Sci. 9 : 113-142.

Various aspects of soil pollutants in relation to heavy metals are reviewed. This includes effect of heavy metals on soils, crop and animal system. Uptake by crops, prediction by soil test methods and guidelines for regulatory content of pollution of Agricultural land.

1110 **Tirsch, F.S., Baker, J.H., Digiano, F.A.,** 1979. Copper and cadmium reactions with soils in land applications. J. Water Pollut. Control Fed. 51(11) : 2649-2660.

The fate of heavy metals found in municipal and industrial waste waters is important in determining the useful life of a land application site. Soil binding of Cu and Cd in 5×10^{-4} and 2×10^{-3} M cadmium chloride salt solutions was evaluated and compared with soil bindings of Cu and Cd in raw, primary clarified, tricking filter, and extended aeration effluent waste waters. Cation competition, pH effects, and complexation with organic compounds gave rise to poor binding of Cu and Cd from the waste waters as compared to the salt solutions. PH, a soil property that can be controlled if necessary, probably has the greatest influence on Cu and Cd removal from solution.

1111 **Toell, J.C., Hovamand, M.F., Mosback, H.,** 1979. Atmospheric lead pollution of grass grown in a background area in Denmark. Nature, 280: 425-426.

The uptake of Pb by plant roots was determined by measuring specific activity in soil labeled with ^{210}Pb and comparing the specific activity in soil with the specific activity in the plants. A pot experiment was conducted involving 3 different soils and a crop of Italian rye-grass (Lolium multiflorum). Pots were fertilized with normal amounts of N,P, and K at the beginning of the season to give a normal growth rate. During the growing season the bulk precipitation of Pb and the content of Pb in the ambient air around the experimental station were measured. The total Pb concentration in the plant material exposed to the atmosphere varied from 0.6 to 8 ppm dry matter for plants grown in the summer, while concentrations were considerably greater for those grown during the winter. Deposition of atmospheric Pb on the plant surface was responsible for 90-99% of the total Pb content in the grass in the typical background area in Denmark.

1112 **Toivonen, P.M.A., Hofstra, C.U.,** 1979. The interaction of copper and sulphur dioxide in plant injury. Can. J. Plant Sci. 59(2): 475-479.
The most SO_2-sensitive barley cultivar (*Laur ier,*) was used to study the effects of Cu in the rooting medium on plant growth. Copper stunted growth, especially of the roots, and induced leaf injury starting at the leaf tips. The cultivar, grown in a medium watered with 0, 10, 50, and 100 ppm Cu as cupric sulfate pentahydrate, was exposed to 1.0 - 0.1 ppm SO_2 for 6 and 7 hr on 2 consecutive d. Less injury due to SO_2 was observed at the higher Cu concentration. The higher levels of Cu greatly increased stomatal resistance, thereby reducing SO_2 uptake.

1113 **Tong, S.T.Y.,** 1990. Roadside dusts and soils contamination in Cincinnatt Ohio, USA. Environ Manage 14(1) : 107-113.
Roadside dusts and soils were collected from various non-industrial districts in Cincinnati, Ohio, USA and analyzed for lead and copper contents. Results showed that the recent lead phase-down action has reduced the level of lead, but the concentrations of both metals are still higher than the background levels for normal soil. Elevated concentrations of copper in heavily travelled highways were noted, suggesting that much of the copper pollutants is probably of automotive origin. The concentrations of lead was found to vary with housing age, and higher levels of contamination in the older neighbourhoods were observed. This result is probably ascribable to the accumulation of residues from leaded gasoline and lead based point in the past and the use of coal fire for space heating in older houses.

1114 **Torrents, A., Stone, A.T.,** 1991. Hydrolysis of phenyl picolinate at the mineral/water interface. Environl. Sci. Technol. 25(1): 143-149.
Hydrolysis of a pesticide-like compounds, phenyl picolinate (PHP) was examined in aqueous suspensions of amorphous silica (SiO_2), Γ-aluminium oxide (Al_2O_3), anatase (TiO_2), haematite (Fe_2O_3), and goethite (FeOOH) in the absence of light. TiO_2 and FeOOH caused a significant increase in PHP hydrolysis rate. As the oxide loading increased a corresponding increase in the rate of hydrolysis was observed. SiO_2, Al_2O_3 and Fe_2O_3 exhibited no surface-catalyzed hydrolysis. Although the

extent of PHP adsorption was small (less than 5% of total PHP), adsorption was necessary for surface-catalyzed hydrolysis to occur. Hydrolysis of the isomer phenyl isonicotinate was not promoted by any of the oxide surfaces, examined. These results indicate that adsorption of PHP occurs through chelate formation with surface metal centres involving the heterocyclic nitrogen and the carbonyl oxygen. Surface chelate formation is not possible for phenyl isonicotinate. Surface chelate formation involving PHP activates the carbonyl carbon towards hydrolytic attack in a way similar to metal non-catalysis observed in homogeneous solution.

1115 **Trapp, S., Matthies, M., Scheunert, I., Topp, E.M.,** 1990. Modelling the bioconcentration of organic chemicals in plants. Environl. Sci. Technol. 24(8): 1246-1252.

Uptake of several organic chemicals by growing barely was investigated in a closed laboratory model ecosystem (volume 9.4 L). to discriminate between root and foliar uptake, the soil was divided into test soil contaminated with 2 mg/kg ^{14}C labeled chemicals and unpolluted control soil. Air was exchanged at a rate of 10 mL/min. Concentrations of ^{14}C chemicals in air, soil roots, and shoots and bioconcentrations factors were simulated with a mathematical model based on fugacity. Bioconcentration in the plant is dependent on transfer rates and the ratio of Kow and Koc values. Uptake into foliage is mainly from air for chemicals with a high Kow and a Henry's law constant high enough for volatilization.

1116 **Tripathi, B.D.,** 1989. Physico-chemical and biological properties of effluent-affected soil at Varanasi, India. Environ. Conserv. 16(3): 263-266.

The present investigation has been undertaken around the Hari fertilizer factory near Varanasi, India, for soil pollution.

1117 **Tripathi, B.D., Dwivedi, R.K., Tripathi, A.,** 1990. Influence of industrial wastes on physico-chemical properties of soil and germination and mineral composition of wheat. Water Air Soil Pollut. 49(1-2) 107-112.

The effect of chemical effluents discharged from a chemical and fertilizer factory on physico-chemical properties of soil and germination and mineral composition of wheat was studied at Varanasi, India. Forty times higher concentration of Na was observed in the effluent than that of the nearby well water. It showed a positive (significant) correlation with Na and a negative (significant) with K and Ca of the soil. Cation exchange capacity, porosity and water holding capacity were reduced by effluent of affected soil. The germination percentage of wheat was negatively correlated with the the Na of effluent and Na+Mg/Ca of the soil. A significant (positive) correlation existed between Na of effluent and Na content of plants, while calcium percentage exhibited a reverse trend.

1118 **Tripathi, B.D., Shukla, S.C.,** 1991. Biological treatment of waste water by selected aquatic plants. Environl. Pollut. 69(1) : 69-78.

Sewage of Varanasi city, mixed with the effluents of about 1200 small scale industries, was used for the tests. The investigation was performed in three stages i.e. a water hyacinth culture, followed by an algal culture, and finally a second water hyacinth culture. For the first water hyacinth culture, 10 water hyacinth plants were grown in a tank of waste water with 15 days' retention time. In the second stage, algal species were cultured in the treated waste water for 5 days, whilst in the third stage, water hyacinth plants were again grown for further treatment of the waste water for 9 days. This three stages aquaculture resulted in very high reductions of BOD (96.9%), suspended solids (78.1%), total alkalinity (74.6%), PO_4-P (89.2%), NO_3-N (81.7%), acidity (73.3%), NH_4-N (95.1%), COD (77.6%), hardness (68.6%) and coliform bacteria (99.2%). An increase in the concentration of dissolved oxygen (70%) was also observed.

1119 **Truby, P.,** 1988. Distribution of lead in forest trees at sites with different levels of pollution. Ange Wandte Botanik 62 : 93-104.

Trees on sites in West Germany with soil pollution (nine spoils), air pollution (near a motor way) or with little pollution were studied for Pb uptake. *Doughas firs* and silver firs growing on nine spoils took up enough high Pb. Max. Pb content in silver fir wood exceeded 100 $\mu g\ g^{-1}$ DM. Heart wood contained more Pb than sap wood. Pb was immobilised in heart wood. The inner bark of trees on mine spoils, contained relatively high Pb contents, even higher than those on slightly polluted areas, while Pb content of outer bark of both sites was similar. The wood and inner bark of *querucus robur* trees near motor way had very low Pb content. However, the outer bark was highly polluted.

1120 **Tsutsumi, M.,** 1981. Arsenic pollution in arabic land. in Heavy metals in the soils of Japan. Japan Sci. Soc. Press. Tokyo: 181-192.

Apparent As pollution in arable land has been found almost exclusively in paddy fields in Japan. This may be fundamentally attributable to the ease with which paddy fields receive As pollutants transported by irrigation water from sources such as mines. Paddy rice is especially susceptible to As toxicity as compared with upland crop plants. This is in fact due to the increase in both the availability and toxicity of As under the reductive conditions of submerged soil in paddy fields, where soluble ferrous arsenate is produced from insoluble ferric arsenate, and the resultant arsenite is much more toxic to general organisms, including higher plants than arsenate.

1121 **Tuin, B.J. W, Tels, M.,** 1990. Removing heavy metals from contaminated clay soils by extraction with hydrochloric acid, EDTA or hypochlorite solutions. Environl. Technol. 11: 1039-1052.

The efficiency of removal of six heavy metals (Cd, Cr, Cu, Ni, Pb, and Zn) from contaminated clay soils was measured in batch extractions. Between 80 and 90% of Cd, Cu, Pb and Zn was extracted by hydrochloric acid (HCl) treatment (repeated extractions with 0.1 N or a single one with 2 N). Ni extraction percentages varied between 45 and 80%. A concn. >0.01 N HCl is necessary to restore the contaminated clay soils to maximum tolerable metal levels. This caused severe damage to the original soil structure. A successful extraction with EDTA required a suspension pH below 4. Only Cd and Pb were removed to levels comparable with the HCl treatments. Chromium was scarcely extracted by HCl or EDTA. Treatment with a hot 0.46 sodium hypochlorite solution at pH 8.5 gave the greatest chromium release (70-85%) compared to other extractants.

1122 **Tuin, B. J.W., Tels, M.,** 1990. Extraction kinetics of six heavy metals from contaminated clay soils. Environl. Technol. 11 : 541-544.

The rate of extraction of Cu, Zn, Pb, and Ni from artificially polluted and water site clay soil was determined in 0.1 NHCl solution. A two way reaction model was developed. The influence of temperature on the extraction rate of Ni was measured over 5 to 80°C temperature.

1123 **Tuin, B.J.W., Tels, M.** 1990. Distribution of heavy metals in contaminated clay soils before and after extractive cleaning. Environl. Technol. 11: 935-948.

A sequential extraction procedure (Tersler, et al.) was carried out to compare the distribution of metals (Cd, Cr, Ni, Cu Pb and Zn) in contaminated soil, clay, before and after extractive cleaning with 0.1 N HCl or 0.1 MEDTA. The metals were preferentially bound to soil fractions. For example Cd was found in the exchangeable fraction; Cr and Pb in the residual fraction and Cu in the organic/sulfide fraction. Extraction of these meals became more difficult in the order: Carbonate < Fe/Mn oxides<organic/sulfide < residual. Extraction from the residual fraction was harder than from any other with only a 33% extraction efficiently for HCl and 27% for EDTA. Hence removal of remaining pollutant would be difficult without the destruction of soil components.

1124 **Turner, R.R., Bogle, M.A., Baes, C.F.,** 1985. Survey of lead in vegetation, forest floor, and soils of the Great Smoky Mountains National Park, NTIS, Springfield, Va (USA): 117.

Samples of vegetation, forest floor, and soil were collected at the five spruce-fir and two hardwood sites in the park in 1982. Forest floor lead concentrations were generally less than values reported for similar sites in the north eastern United States and Western Europe. As expected, lead concentrations generally increased (1) with increasing age of spruce and fir foliage, (2) with increasing degree of decomposition of forest floor materials, and (3) with increasing elevation for foliage and forest floor materials.

1125 **Turner, R.S., Johnson, A.H., Wang, D.,** 1985. Biogeochemistry of lead in Mc Donalds Branch Watershed New Jersey pine Barrens. J. Environ. Qual. 14:305-313.

Lead concentrations, fluxes and storage were measured in the vegetation, forest floor, and acid sandy-mineral soil of a forested watershed in the New Jersey Pine Barrens. Total Pb content of the forest floor was 7.6 kg $ha.^{-1}$ with an accumulation rate of 100 g ha^{-1} yr^{-1} (1980-1982), or 1.3% of the forest floor pool. Estimated mean residence time of Pb in the forest floor was 220 yr. About 35g Pb moved out of the forest floor in solution through the E horizon and was correlated strongly with dissolved organic matter. Approximately 20 g Pb ha^{-1} yr^{-1} accumulated in the B and C soil horizons. Less than 1 g Pb ha^{-1} yr^{-1} percolated past a depth of 2 m. Lowland muck soils and vegetation accumulated 98% of incoming Pb, with only 3.2 g Pb ha^{-1} yr^{-1} exported in the stream.

1126 **Turner, R.S., Johnson, A.H., Wang, D.,** 1985. Biogeochemistry of aluminium in McDonalds Branch Watershed, New Jersey Pine Barrens. J. Environ. Qual. 14: 314-323.

Aluminum concentrations, fluxes, and storage were measured in the vegetation, forest floor,and acid, sandy mineral soil of a forest watershed in the New Jersey Pine Barrens. Volume-weighted mean Al concentration in solution increased as water passed through the upland ecosystem, from 0.012 mg L^{-1} in bulk precipitation to 0.14 mg L^{-1} in throughout fall to 0.45 mg L^{-1} in the C horizon. Weighted mean Al concentration of the stream water was 0.15 mg L^{-1}. Solution Al concentration in different compartments of the ecosystem were related to the magnitude of moisture flux, dissolved organic carbon concentration and pH. Soil solution and stream water Al concentrations were high in the winter and spring and low in the summer and fall, inversely following solution pH.

1127 **Turski, R. Wojcikowska-Kabusta,** 1987. A Lead balance in soils differently fertilized and watered in lysimetric experiment. Pamietruk Pulawski, 89 : 173-183.

Lead in soils and plants was measured for 4 years (1978-81). Industrial pollution through emissions was the source of Pb and Pb addition through fertilizer was small. Analysis of Pb balance in the soils showed that annual inflow of Pb in precipitation water and in fertilizers considerably exceeded the out flow of Pb through leaching. The out flow was 6.7% of the inflow. Maximum Pb was retained by loess soil.

1128 **Twiss, M.R.** 1990, Copper tolerance of *Chlamydomonas acidophila* (Chlorophyceae) isolated from acidic, copper contaminated soils. J. Physol. 26(4) : 655-659.

Cells of *Chlamydomonas acidophila* Negoro, isolated from three soils with different available copper contents (74, 80 and 87 μg/g), were assayed for their responses to copper. Soil pH ranged from 3.3 to 3.9. Responses were evaluated using algistalic assays involving five day exposure to copper concentrations from 0.1 to 100 mg/L at pH 3.8 and 6.6 in defined liquid media. Interspecies and intraspecies comparisons were made between the soil isolates and laboratory strains of C. reinhardtill and C. acidophila, respectively. Algistatic copper concentrations of soil isolates were 20-125 times greater than those of the laboratory strain of *C. reinhbardtii.* Concentrations of 0.1 mg Cu/L. or greater killed the laboratory strain of C acidophila Soils isolates of C. acidophila appeared to be copper tolerant; however, there was no conclusive evidence to indicate that the level of copper tolerance in the soil isolates was positively correlated with the level of available copper in the soil.

1129 **Tyler, G.,** 1990. Bryophytes and heavy metals : A literature review, Bot. J. Linn. Soc. 104(1-3) : 231-253.

The literature on the heavy metals in bryophytes is reviewed, including mechanisms of metal uptake, retention, toxicity and tolerance. Interspecies differences in particular are discussed, including the development of extreme tolerance encountered in certain taxa. The use of bryophytes in monitoring heavy metals deposition is considered and comparisons are made with direct deposition measurements.

1130 **Tyler, L.D., Mcbride, M.B.,** 1982. Mobility and extractability of Cadmium, copper, nickel, and zinc in organic and mineral soil columns. Soil Sci. 134(3) : 198-205.

The relative mobility of Cd, Cu, Ni and Zn added to several soils and the simultaneous desorption and leaching of metals were determined by eluting soil columns with 0.01 M $CaCl_2$ and analyzing the metals in leachates and soils. Although soil chemical properties generally had a larger effect on the mobility of metals than did the properties of the metals themselves, Cu moved least readily through all soil columns. The least mobility of metals was observed in a mineral soil with a relatively high pH, CEC, and exchangeable base content. The liming of an acid mineral soil reduced metal mobility, but not to the extent expected from the very low mobility observed for a naturally non-acid mineral soil. The order of mobility of the metals in the soils was : Cu > Zn > Ni > Cd. These metals were almost completely extractable from a non-acid mineral soil and an organic soil. The effect is attributed to partially irreversible binding of the metals in organic matter, phenomenon inhibited by the presence of Al on organic complexation sites.

1131 **Udosen, E.D., Udoessien, E.I., Ibok, U.J.,** 1990. Evaluation of some metals in the industrial wastes from a paint industry and their environmental pollution implications. Nigerian J. Technological Res. 2(1): 71-77.

Effluent and sludge samples, as well as their precipitates, from the paint industry in Nigeria were analysed for Zn, Pb, Cd, Cu and Cr. Soil samples were also analysed in the immediate vicinity of the factory. Concentrations of the metals were very high in the precipitates, and soil receiving paint wastes compared with those in the effluent and sludge samples. Correlation coefficients of metals between pairs of samples were also computed and used to establish relationship between the metals in different samples.

1132 **Ueda, K., Kobayashi, M., Takahashi, E.,** 1988. Effect of anionic heavy metals on ammonification and nitrification in soil. Soil Sci. Plant Nutr. 34(1) : 139-146.

Several experiments were carried out to analyze the effect of anionic heavy metals and chromium chloride on the activities of micro-organisms. *Azotobacter* and *Fusarium* were cultured in a liquid medium containing 5 and 25, μ M of each heavy metal and the changes in the optical density in relation to microbial growth were analyzed. Alluvial soil containing ammonium sulfate or urea, was treated with each heavy metal at the levels of 10, 100 and 1,000 ppm. After the soil was incubated at 30C, the process of nitrification and ammonification was analyzed by determining the content of ammonium-N and nitrite + nitrate – N. The growth of *Azotobacter* and *Fusarium* was affected by chromate at the level 25 μM and *Azotobacter* was affected more than *Fusarium*. Tungstate did not reduce the growth of *Azotobacter* at all but inhibited considerably the growth of *Fusarium* at a level of 5 μM. Nitrification was prevented at the 10 ppm level for chromate and at the 1,000 ppm level for chromium chloride. Vanadate also affected nitrification at the 1,000 ppm level.

1133 **Uhnak, J., Rippel, A.,** 1990. Content of metals in vegetables grown in the neighbourhood of nickel works. Rostlinna vyroba 36(4): 387-394.

Carrots, parsley, potato, onions, lettuces cabbages savory cabbages cucumbers, tomatoes and capsicum grown at distances of 1.8 km from a nickel plant were analysed for Pb, Cu, Cr, Co, Cd, Zn, Mn and Ni in 1981-82. Results are discussed in relation to data available. Growing vegetables for fresh consumption near nickle works, is not recommended.

1134 U.K. Department of the Environment, 1982. Cd, Cr, Cu, Pb, Ni, and Zn in sewage sludge by atomic absorption spectrophotometry following digestion with nitric acid. Her Majesty's Stationery Office London, U.K.: 13.

This method was designed for rapid analyses on a routine basis of typical sewage sludges. The performance characteristics, hazards, sources of error and concentration ranges of the six elements for which it is suitable, are presented.

1135 U.K. Department of the Environment, 1981. Chromium in raw and potable waters and sewage effluents. Her Majesty's Stationary Office, London: 21.

Two tentative methods for the determination of Cr in water are described. The first is based on concentration of evaporation followed by AAS and is suitable for raw and potable waters and sewage effluents. The second is based on spectrophotometry of the Cr diphenyl carbazide complex and is suitable for raw and potable waters. Interferences, hazards, sources of error and accuracy are covered.

1136 **Undberg, S.E., Jackson, D.R., Huckabee, J.W., Janzen, S.A. Leun,**

M.J., Lund, J.R., 1979. Atmospheric emission and plant uptake of mercury from agricultural soiis near the Almaden Mercury Mine. J. Environ. Qual. 8 (4): 572-578.

Surface soils collected near the Almaden, Spain, Mercury mine reflected increasing concentrations of mercury with proximity to the minedue to weathered mineral deposits and to atmospheric deposition of Hg from the smelter. Extractions with Na-HCO_3 or NH_4OAc removed small amounts of Hg from both control (20 km from mine; total Hg = 2.3 μg/g) and mine site soils (1 km; total Hg = 97 μg/g). Density gradient centrifugations indicated a significant fraction of the Hg to be associated with a high density mineral fraction presumably cinnabar. Accumulation of Hg by alfalfa suggested a dual mechanism of uptake; roots accumulated Hg in proportion to the soil levels, while plant material absorbed Hg Vapor directly from the atmosphere. Soil fertilization with and without liming significantly increased total Hg uptake, largely due to plant growth stimulation Liming itself had no significant effect. The rate of volatilization of elemental Hg from both soils (~ 0.13 and 0.33 μg/m^2) per hour at 25°C for control and mine site, respectively) exceeded reported back ground emission rates by factors of 4 to 10, increasing with surface temperature and Hg content, and decreasing with increased plant cover.

1137 **Upadhyay, V.P.,** 1988. Effect of naphthalene on decomposition of oak leaf litter in a pine mixed broadleaf forest in the Himalaya. Indian J. Ecol. 15(1) : 11-15.

The effect of naphthalene on the rate of decomposition (weight loss) of leaf litter of oak (*Quercus gluca Thunbs*) was studied in a Kumaun Himalayan pine mixed broadleaf forest for one annual cycle. The samples treated with the naphthalene balls (to exclude micro-arthropods) had slower decomposition rates (71%) compared to the untreated control (100%). However, in the rainy season there was no marked difference in weight loss between the two sets.

1138 **Urie, D.H., Harris, A.R., Colley, J.H.,** 1984. Forest land treatment of sewage waste water and sludge in the Lake states. Res. & Development Conf.: 101-110.

Lagoon-treated waste water and secondary municipal and raw paper mill sludge were applied to several tree species, both hardwood and softweed, on nutrient-poor sandy soils. Lagoon waste water is low in nutrients with a range of total nitrogen between 2.5 and 15 per cent. Up to 90 per cent of the nitrogen was removed by young, growing forest. Survival and height growth increased in irrigated Christmas trees. Populous tripled in height and other species more than doubled. Sludge-treated forests responded equally well. Biomass increased in both aspen sprouts and the ground vegetation and was related to sludge dosage. Foliar nitrogen increased in all vegetation. Increased metal concentrations were found mostly in surface contaminated understory vegetation. The surface humus layer immobilised and stored most nutrients and trace metals either directly or after recycling through vegetation. On the soils studied, 5-15 t/ha of sludge were applied without leachates or ground exceeding the nitrate standards of drinking water.

1139 **Vaisman, I., Shalhevet, I., Kipnis, T. Feigin, A.** 1981. Reducing ground-water pollution from municipal waste water irrigation of rhodes grass grown on sand dunes. J. Environ. Qual. 10 (4): 434-439.

During 1978 and 1979 an effluent-irrigation field experiment was carried out on a sand dune established with Rhodes grass (*Chloris gayana* Kunth). The municipal effluent used had received secondary treatment. Irrigation of Rhodes grass with waste water on sandy dune soil may be considered an appropriate method for the treatment of secondary effluent. The method obtained at one and the same time, high production and the avoidance of ground-water pollution, especially by nitrate and phosphorus.

1140 **Valentine, G.E., Ross, C.C., Harper, Ş.R.,** 1990. Agricultural wastes research. J. Water Pollut. Control. Fed. 62(4) : 467-73.

The characteristics, effects on soil fertility and soil properties , recycling treatment and environmental impact of agricultural wastes are reviewed.

1141 **Van Assche, C., Uyttebroeck, P.,** 1980. Heavy metals in soils and their neutralisation. Agril. Wastes 2(4) : 279-291.

A field experiment was conducted to check the influence of selective cation exchangers on the growth of various edible crops in a soil contaminated with Pb, Cu, and Zn, in the vicinity of a metallurgical plant in Beerse, Belgium. Experiments were also conducted on soils from coniferous forests, certain types of peat, sludge and sewage. Experiments also investigated the influence of cation exchangers on the possible infection of susceptible host plants by pathogenic soil fungi, particularly the relationships between Rhizoctonia solani and Phaseolus vulgaris and between Fusarium oxysporum and Solangum iycorpersicum. The influence of the heavy metals in an abiotic fermented, domestic waste compost is also illustrated. The application of cation exchangers to a contaminated soil and/or substrate shows that a positive influence on plant growth restores soil fertility, microbial activity and production capacity.

1142 **Vandenbergh, P.A., Gonzalez, C.F., Wright, A.M., Kunka, B.S.,** 1983. Iron-chelating compounds produced by soil pseudomonads : Correlation with fungal growth inhibition. Appl. Environl. Microbiol.46(1) : 128-132.

Strains of pseudomonas putida, Pseudomonas sp., and Pseudomonas aeruginosa were examined for their ability to grow in the presence of the iron chelator, ethylenediamine-di-(o-hydroxyphenylacetic acid). In vitro fungal inhibition assays showed that the isolates varied in their ability to inhibit the growth of representative fungal plant pathogens. Fungal inhibition in vitro was superior to that of previously reported pseudomonas sp. Studies with Fusarium oxysporum forma sp. lycopersici and a susceptible tomato cultivar demonstrated that Pseudomonas putida PPU 3.1 was able to significantly reduce wilt disease.

1143 **Vanloon, J.C., Lichwa, J., Ruttan, D., Kinrade, J.,** 1973. The determination of heavy meals in domestic sewage treatment plant wastes. Water Air Soil Pollut. 2 : 473-482.

It is recommended that reference standards and internal laboratory control samples be used to allow some assessment of the validity of results. Sewage treatment plant products both liquid and solids were analysed and results give for samples representing a wide range of sewage input patterns.

1144 **Van Riemsdkjk, W.H., Beek. J., Dehann, F.A.M.,** 1978. Phosphates in soils treated with sewage water : IV. bonding of phosphate from sewage water in sand columns containing aluminium hydroxide. J. Environ. Qual. 8(2) : 207-210.

The long term reaction of P (0.5 mM/L) and X-ray amourphous Al $(OH)_3$ was not detected at pH 8. To columns of quartz sand mixed with Al $(OH)_3$ domestic sewage water (pH = 8) was added during 10 months once every 2 weeks. The phosphate retention in these columns was much higher than could be expected from the pure Al $(OH)_3$ system experiments, indicating the occurrence of a long term reaction. Negligible Ca-P was formed. Electron microscopy and X-ray analysis showed quartz particles, Al-containing particles with no detectable P, and particles containing Al, P and Ca. Formation of the Al-P-Ca particles contribute to the capacity of soils to retain P.

1145 **Van Riemsdkjk, W.H., Weststate, F.A., Beek, J.** 1977. Phosphates in soils treated with sewage water : III Kinetic studies on the reaction of phosphate with aluminium compounds. J. Environ. Qual. 6 (1): 26-29.

The reaction of phosphate with aluminum hydroxide and $_aAl_2O_3$ was studied at an initial phosphate concentration level of 0.35 mM/L and a temperature of 20 C°. Solution of KH_2PO_4 and synthetic inorganic sewage water were used as phosphate sources. In all experiments involved, a marked change of the reaction rate was found after about 1 day in $Al(OH)_3$ and about 4 days in the case of $_aAl_2O_3$ the formation of a solid aluminium phosphate is initiated and this new phase was later identified as sterettite by means of electron microscope, electron diffraction, and X-ray diffraction.

1146 **Van Schoor, O., Class, I., Deelstra, H.,** 1986. Chromium content of European wines. Belg. J. Food Chem. Biotechnol. 41(3): 59-61.

Chromium and nickel content of 95 European wines were determined. The mean chromium concentration was 85.4 ppb (range 13-186 ppb); means nickel concentration was 51.7 ppb (range 14-360 ppb). There was a significant correlation between Cr and Ni concentration. The Cr/Ni ratio in wine was 0.68; this agreed well with the ratio of released Cr/Ni by stainless steel in wine. The amount of released Cr and Ni however was too small to explain the high levels of these elements found in wine. The calculated daily chromium intake by wine was 1.7 μg in Belgium 1.6μg in the Netherlands, 8.0 μg in Spain. 8.7 μg in Italy and 11.2 μg in France.

1147 **Vasil'Eva, G.K., Surovtseva, E.G., Ivoilov, V.S.,** 1990. Soil adaptation of the chloroaniline-utilizing Pseudomonas diminuta strain INMIKS-7. Microbiology 59(3) : 326-332.

Pseudomonas diminuta INMIKS-7 was able to adapt to grey forest soil when inoculated in quantities ranging from a few cells to several million cells per gram. The presence of 3,4-dichloroaniline (DCA) was required for multiplication and stabilization of the cell population at a level of 10^4- 10^7 cells/g. Addition of DCA to soil is followed by the formation of residues bound irreversibly to the soil, which are virtually inaccessible to degrading microorganisms. Thus, DCA is most effectively degraded when added to soil containing an already adapted strain, and when it is in direct content with the bacteria.

1148 **Verloo, M., Eeckhout, M.,** 1990. Metal species transformation in soils; An analytical approach. Internatl. Environ. Analy. Chem. 39(2) : 179-186.

The use of different analytical techniques to determine and speciate metals in soil system is discussed. Separative techniques such as ion exchange chromatography and get permeation chromatography allow species estimation based on charge characteristics of molecular size of water soluble metal compounds. Electrochemical techniques such as potentiometry with ion selective electrodes and polarography provide more detailed information about complex formation and stability.

1149 **Verloo, M., Wilaert, G., Cottenie, A.,** 1986. Determination of the upper critical levels of heavy metals in plants and soils. Proc. 5 International Conf. Chemistry for Protection of the Environment. L. Pawlowski, G. Alaerts, W.J. Lacy (Eds.) Elsevier Sci. Pub. Amsterdam: 207-215.

A procedure is developed to determine the upper critical levels of the concentration of heavy metals in plants and soils. Experimentally it has been shown that the soil type affects the upper critical (Phytotoxic) level of zinc and cadmium for maize and spinach. Phytotoxicity of Zn and Cd is observed on maize when the concentration in the plant reach 600 and 56 mg/kg respectively when grown on a sandy-loam soil. On a sandy soil, toxicity occurs at plant concentrations of 225 and 7.2 mg/kg respectively. The availability of Zn and Cd in a heavy clay soil is very low, so that this soil type generally has a high critical soil level when compared to light soil types.

1150 **Verriopoulas, G., Moraitou, A., Postolopoulou, M., Milliou, E.,** 1987.

Combined toxicity of four toxicants (Cu, Cr, oil, oil dispersant). Artemia salina. Bull. Environl. Contam. Toxicol. 38(3) : 483-490.

For a realistic approach to pollution effects it is essential to estimate the combined toxicity of two or more chemicals. There is a need to understand the mechanisms and quantity the effects of multiple toxicity in order to provide responsible authorities with rational estimate of the effects of chemical mixtures. Thus the potential toxic effects of mixtures of toxicants has recently become a subject of growing scientific interest. In this paper the authors have tried to estimate the joint toxicity of some pollutants commonly found in nearshore polluted waters; two metals, copper and chromium; an oil (Tunisian crude oil zarzaitine type); and oil dispersant (Finasol OSR-2).

1151 **Vestergaard, N.K., Stephansen, U., Rasmussen, L., Pilegaard, K.,** 1986, Airborne heavy metal pollution in the environment of Danish Steel Plant. Water Air Soil Pollut. 27(3-4) :363-377.

A survey of heavy metal deposition was carried out in the vicinity of a Danish steel plant. Bulk precipitation and transplanted lichen (*Hypogymni physodes* L). NYl were sampled at 12 stations in the environment before & after the production had been converted from open heath furnaces to a electric arc. The samples were analyzed for Cd, Cr, Cu, Fe, Mn, Pb and Zn. The results show that a heavy metal pollution from the steel works still is severe and that if follows a decreasing power curve when the distance to the steel works is increased. However, a reduction in the deposition of heavy metals close to the steel works has been observed pointing to the conclusion that the change from a situation of emission through a 46m stalk without any filter to emission from the electric arc furnaces equipped with bag filters has lead to changes in the emission. At the sampling stations with the highest deposition levels measured in bulk precipitation the corresponding concentrations in the lichens were relatively lower indicating a change in the particle size distribution. Within each station there was a direct proportionality of metal concentrations in lichens and atmospheric fallout measured in bulk precipitation.

1152 **Vian, A., Mirada, F., Rodriguez, J.J.,** 1985. Copper, zinc and nickel effects on activated sludge. J. Environ Sci. Health Pt. A. 20A (7) : 823:835.

This paper presents a study on the effects of Cu, Zn and Ni in activated sludge, focussing on their influence in COD removal efficiency. Experiments have been done at different heavy meals-concentrations varying from 1 to 25 mg/L. Cu exhibits the higher detrimental effect, followed by Zn and Ni. Mixtures of these heavy metals show a less than additive effect.

1153 **Viraraghavan, T., Simon, H.,** 1986. Trace organics in septic tank effluent. Water Air Soil Pollut. 28 : 299-308.

The presence and the level of certain trace organics in waste water samples collected from a septic tank in an individual households, from a lift station, and from a waste treatment lagoon, near Regina, Canada, is described. Out of 11 priority pollutants analyzed, 6-priority pollutants – chloroform, bromodichloromethane, toluene, benzene, methylene chloride and tetrachloroethylene were detected in the samples. The trace organics in the septic tank and lagoon effluent at these comparatively low concentrations may not pose any significant risk either to aquatic life or to public health, taking into account the attentuation capacity of the soil and the dilution usually available.

1154 **Visscher, K., Brinkman, J., Soczo, E.R.,** 1989. Biotechnology in hazardous waste management in the Netherlands in Biotechnology and Biodegradation, Gulf Pub. Com. Houston: 389-403.

Research in the Netherlands has resulted in important applications including treatment processes for industrial waste water, processes for cleaning contaminated soil and polluted air purification. However, more research is necessary in order to apply present and future microbiological knowledge to specific environmental problems.

1155 **Vogel, J., Breimer, R.F., Ottow, J.C.G.,** 1989. Fluoride pollution of soils, vegetation and soil fauna in the vicinity of an emitter. Verhandlungen Gesellschaft for Okologia 17 : 619-625.

Fluoride analysis (total, water soluble and HCl extractable F) of different soils, vegetation samples and soil fauna in a polluted area showed F accumulations in all samples. Two contaminated zones around the emitting industry could be identified. In the calcareous soils leaching of fluoride seemed to be insignificant because of a strong F immobilisation as CaF_2. Fluoride content in the washed levels of *Heder a Helex* and in decaying grass reached levels of 306 and 997 µgF/g, respectively. *Saprophagous* soil arthropods contained high fluoride levels upto 732 µF/g in *Armadillidium vulgare.*

1156 **Voos, G., Sabey, B.R.,** 1987. Nitrogen mineralization in sewage-sludge-amended coal mine spoil and topsoils. J. Environ. Qual. 16 : 231-237.

A 16-week incubation was conducted to determine the rate of net N mineralization in sewage sludge-amended coal mine spoil, two topsoils, a 1:1 mixture of the spoil with each topsoil, and a quartz sand. Sewage sludge was added at rates of 0 to 120 Mg ha^{-1} which added 0 to 4890 kg N ha^{-1}. The total amount of inorganic N accumulated was increased significantly with the rate of sewage sludge addition in all materials tested. However the rate of sludge addition did not have a similar effect on the amount of NO_3 accumulated in any of the sand treatment samples and only small amounts were produced in the spoil. Ammonium-N increased with increasing rates of sewage sludge in all materials examined. The rate of ammonification was more stable after the 8-weeks sampling interval in most cases. Mineralization of organic N added with the sewage sludge varied between 10 to 34%. At all rates of sludge addition, more organic N was mineralised in stock piled topsoil than in the other materials. A nonlinear least squares regression equation for N mineralization as first-order kinetics slightly overestimates N mineralization in the 4 to 8 week interval and slightly underestimated N mineralized through 16 weeks.

1157 **Vuori, E., Vaeaeriskoski, Hartikainen, H., Vakkilainen, P., Kumpulainen, J., Nilnivaara, K.,** 1989. Sorption of selenate by Finnish agricultural soils. Agric. Ecosyst. Environ. 25, (2-3): 111-118.

The sorption of added selenate in 18 different types of cultivated Finnish soils was studied. In a 7-day incubation trial the sorbed fraction varied from 3.6 to 24.6% from the added amount of 5000 μg Se kg^{-1} soil. Sorption correlated positively with the clay%, iron content and surface area of the soils and negatively with sulphuric and extractable phosphorus. Thus in Finnish soils the sorption tendency is higher in fine textured soils and increases with weathering.

1158 **Vyrodova, L.P., Vorobyeval, L.A., Korobeinikova, L.G.,** 1990. The valence status of chromium in soil (model experiment). Moscow University Soil Sci. Bull. 45(1) : 31-35.

Adsorption of chromium by soil samples was observed in a laboratory experiment when potassium bichromate was added to samples of dermopodzolic and grey forest soils. Cr (VI) was stable in Southern chernozem. Cr(VI) was found in water extracts from chernozem; the amount of Cr(VI) increased with increase in the time of incubation of soil samples with chromium nitrate. The thermodynamics of chromium transformation is discussed.

1159 **Wagner, D.J., Bacon, G.D., Knocke, W.R., Switzerhaum, M.S.,** 1990. Changes variability in concentration of heavy metals. Environl. Technol. 11(10) : 949-960.

The heavy metal concentrations of sewage sludge increased during composting for Cd, Cr, Pb and Zn and decreased for Cu and Ni. Cd and Pb were the most variable of the metals, Cu and Zn the least. Variability within a batch was small (4-12%) but variability attributable to batch to batch differences was larger (4-30%). The variability of sludge entering the batch process and of compost existing the process, were similar for each metal.

1160 **Wallace, A.,** 1982. Additive, protective and synergistic effects on plants with excess trace elements. Soil Sci. 133(6): 319-323.

Bush bean plants were grown 15 days in solution culture to test whether or not multiple trace elements that result in little or no apparent stress when applied alone would result in more or less stress when applied together. Prior experience had indicated these possibilities, and the matter is of considerable concern in establishing threshold levels for excess of some trace elements in the environment. Levels of cadmium (5x10-

^{7}M,) copper (10^{-5}M), zinc ($5x10^{-5}$M), manganese (10^{-4}M), cobalt (10^{-6}M), and nickel (10^{-6}M) were applied singly : Cadmium, copper, and zinc together; manganese, cobalt and nickel together; and all six combined. Little or no stress was expected for some of the single elements; the yield depression in dry weight of trifoliate leaves for the experiment was zero per cent for Cd, 2 per cent for Cu, 43 per cent for Zn, 32 per cent for Mn, 0 per cent for Co, and 4 per cent for Ni. For Cd, Cu and Zn together, the depression was 46 per cent; for Mn, Co, Ni, 23 per cent and for all six 85, per cent. Additive, protective, and synergistic effects were involved, although induced iron deficiency complicated the results for all six elements combined. The results indicate that even if the concentration of at east some elements is too low to have any visual effects, they can have important consequences if other trace element stresses are simultaneously present.

1161 **Walsh, C.E., Alexander, S.V.,** 1980. A marine algal bioassay method: results with pesticides and industrial wastes. Water Air Soil Pollut. 13 : 45-55.

A simple marine bioassay method is described for short-and long-term studies on pesticides and industrial wastes.

1162 **Wang, L.K., Poon, C.P.C., Wang, M.,** 1977. Control tests and kinetics of activated sludge process. Water Air Soil Pollut.8 : 315-351.

Basic activated sludge processes kinetics of: (1) complete-mix reactor without sludge recycle; (2) complete-mix reactor with sludge recycle; and (3) plug-flow reactor with sludge recycle, are summarized and illustrated. Some related operational tests and control parameters, such as biodegradability, oxygen uptake rate, sludge acclimation, solids and residuals, sludge settings, depth of sludge blanket, sludge units, and substrate utilization rate, are presented and discussed.

1163 **Wanhassel, J.H., Ney, J.J. Garling, D.L.,** 1979. Seasonal variation in the heavy metal concentration of sediments influenced by highways of different traffic volumes. Bull. Environl. Contam. Toxicol. 23(4-5): 592-596.

Two study sites, one averaging 15,000 vehicles/d and a 2nd averaging 6,500 vehicles/d were located in Back Creek near Raonoke, Virginia. A 3rd site upstream of all traffic was selected as a reference point. Sediment samples were collected at each site during each of the 4 seasons over 1 yr. During normal flow periods, heavy mental concentrations in streamwater were very low. Sediments loads of Pb, Ni, and Zn, however, were highly correlated to traffic volumes. Lead and Zn concentrations were highest is the spring, but seasonal variations in Ni and Cd were not significant.

1164 **Watson, J.E., Pepper, I.L., Fuller, W.H., Watson, J.E.,** 1985. Yields and leaf elemental composition of cotton grown in sludge-amended soil. J. Environ. Qual 14(2) : 174-177.

A 3-yr field study was conducted to determine the effects of land application of anaerobically digested, air-dried sewage sludge on growth of upland cotton. Cotton lint yields obtained with sludge rates from 20 to 80 Mg/ha were comparable with those obtained by areas farmers employing conventional fertilizer practices. Rates of 80 Mg/ha had no significant effect on limit yields, although lint/seed ratios tended to decreases with increased sludge rate for all years. After 3 yr of sludge application, the leaf and seed concentrations of Cd, Zn, Ni and Cu were not significantly different from those on the fertilized check plots. Leaf concentrations of Cd were higher than seed concentrations, but the reverse trend was true for Zn, indicating that Zn may not be directly usable as a model for Cd behaviour in cotton.

1165 **Weaver, J.N., Hanson, A., Mcgaughey, J., Steinkruger, J.E.,** 1974. Determination of heavy metals in municipal sewage plant sludges by neutron activation analysis. Water Air Soil Pollut. 3:327-335.

The results of neutron activation analysis (NAA) for the content of Hg, Se, Sr, Sb, Co and Fe are described in sludges from six North Carolina cities that represent the spectrum of rural to heavily industrialized pollution sources. Trace metal content variations and possible meanings for these variations are presented alongwith the precision and potential of NAA for trace metal scanning.

1166 **Webber, L.R., Beauchamp, E.G.,** 1979. Cadmium concentration and distribution in corn (*Zea mays* L.) grown on a calcareous soil for three years after annual sludge applications. J. Environl Sci. Health. Part B; (pesti, food contam. and agri. wastes) 14(5) : 459-474.

The levels of Cd in corn grain and stover for 6 yr—3 yr with sludge applied annually and for 3 yr after sludge applications were terminated, are presented. The rates of sludge applications are equivalent to 0, 1.25, 2.5 and 5.0 cm/ha. The highest concentration of Cd in corn grain was 0.12 µg/g and occurred following 2 applications of sludge at the highest rate. Since termination of sludge application, the Cd, content of corn grain the tended to decrease with all treatments. The Cd concentration in corn grain from the yr 6 was similar to values found in corn grown on non-sludge plots. In corn stover from treated plots the Cd concentration was greater than from untreated plots. Phytotoxic levels of Cd did not exist even though elevated levels occurred in the corn stover. Data demonstrating the leachability of Cd in calcareous soil are also presented.

1167 **Weber, W.J.,** 1981. Application of adsorption of waste water treatment. Indust. Water Engg. 18(4) : 19-25.

This article considers the availability and significance of data regarding the adsorbability of some of the more common of the 144 organic priority pollutants, typical differences in capacities among different activated carbons, the potential effects of solution conditions and the presence of competing organic compounds, and finally examples of the application of modeling techniques for adsorber predictions and parameter sensitivity analysis.

1168 **Weber, A.S., Sherrard, J.H.,** 1980. Effects of cadmium on the completely mixed activated sludge process. J. Water Pollut. Control Fed. 52(9): 2378-2388.

A laboratory study was conduced to measure the effect of Cd on COD removal efficiency, degree of nitrification and the kinetic coefficients Y max. (the maximum yield coefficient) and b (the microorganism maintenance coefficient). Data were obtained from the operation of bench scale reactors which were fed, 0.5, 15 and 9.98 mg/L solutions of Cd. Mean cell residence time was used as the primary operational control parameter, and values between 3 and 15 d were used to obtain data. COD removal efficiencies of all reactors were independent of the mean soil cell residence time for the range studied. The COD removal efficiencies for the reactor containing Cd were slightly less than those obtained for the control reactor. No distinguishable difference was obtained for the kinetic coefficients, Y max and b. Nitrification however, was significantly altered in the presence of Cd. The degree of nitrification decreased as Cd concentrations increased at a given mean cell residence time.

1169 **Wei, Q.E., Lowery, B., Peterson, A.E.,** 1985. Effect of sludge application on physical properties of a silty clay loam soil. J. Environ. Qual. 14(2) : 178-180.

This study was conducted to elucidate the long term effect of dewatered sludge application on a silty clay loam soil which possesses poor permeability and other undesirable physical properties. Bulk density, infillration, hydraulic conductively and aggregate stability were measured 5 yr after application. The bulk density decreased over the control. Improved soil permeability was due to the enhancement of aggregate stability, which increased relative to the control by 3.3, 9.4 and 11.9% with the 44.8, 112.0 and 134.4 Mg ha^{-1} treatment, respectively. The in situ volumetric moisture content of the sludge treated soils was always higher than the control, especially after a prolonged period of evaporation. At 33.3 kPa or less, more water was released from soils treated with high rates of sludges. This indicated an increase in the volume of larger pores, which resulted in the higher hydraulic conductivities.

1170 **Wei-ChunMa,** 1989. Effect of pollution with metallic lead pellets on lead bioaccumulation and organ/body weight alternations in small mammals. Arch. Environl. Contam. Toxicol. 18, (4): 617-622.

Using small mammals as bioindicators, the bioavailable status and ecotoxicity of lead was investigated in an acidic sandy soil environment polluted with metallic lead pellets from shotgun ammunition. Average concentrations of lead in kidney, liver and bone tissue of wood mice (*Apodemus sylvaticus*), bank voles (*Clethrionomys glareolus*), and shrews (*Sorex araneus*) were strongly elevated, compared to tissue levels of conspecifics collected from an adjacent unpolluted range exceeded the critical renal Pb concentration of 25 μg/g dry weight, considered diagnostic of lead intoxication in mammals. The geometric mean renal Pb concentration in shrews was 270 μg/g dry weights, with an upper range of more than, 1,000 μg/g. The population of shrews and bank voles from the shooting range also showed a significantly increased average relative kidney weight (Kidney-to-body weight ratio), which is indicative of lead poisoning.

1171 **Weis, I.M., Barclay, G.F.,** 1985. Distribution of heavy metals and organic contaminants in plants and soils of Windsor and Essex Country, Ontario. Great Lakes Research. 11(3) : 339-346.

Concentrations of Pb and Cd in county soils were not significantly greater than accepted provincial background levels; average conc. were 12 mg kg^{-1} and 0.38 mg kg^{-1} dry soil for Pb and Cd, respectively. The Pb concentration in tissue of crop plants was less than 0.25 of that in adjacent soil while Cd conc. was similar. Concs. of both metals were significantly higher with in the city. Soil Pb averaged 44.8 mg kg^{-1} and soil Cd 0.62 mg kg^{-1} dry soil. These conc. correlated with traffic volume on nearby streets. In roots of chenopodium, averages were 18.1 mg kg^{-1} for lead and 0.60 mg kg^{-1} for Cd.

1172 **Weisenfeld, P.,** 1989. The cadmium and lead pollution of earth worms in cultivated soils near industrial areas at Berlin-Verh and Lengen. Gesellschaft fur Okologie 18 : 285-287.

Earthworms from the distant site showed significantly higher heavy metal accumulation. This was due to high organic matter content at the site close to the emission area as shown by correlation analysis. There was correlation between heavy metal content and the age of the earthworm.

1173 **Weiss, B., Larink, O.,** 1991. Influence of sewage sludge and heavy metals on nematodes in an arable soil. Biol. Fert. Soil 12 : 5-9.

Abundance of nematodes was studied in a field soil with control, sewage sludge (300 m^3/ha/year or 12t dry matter) and sewage sludge + heavy metals (Pb, Ni, Cd, Cr, Cu, Zn). Total numbers of nematodes were highest with sludge and heavy metals. In the mycophagic and bacteriophagic mematoes, numbers increased with the amount of sludge, especially in the sites with a higher heavy metal content, and the family Rhabditidae was the most numerous group in the sludge plus heavy metals. In contrast the omnivorous mematodes were the rare in the sludge treated plots and were totally absent in sludge + heavy metal treatment whereas predatory mematodes were numerous only after the sludge treatment.

1174 **Welch, J.E., Lund, L.J.,** 1987. Soil properties, irrigation water quality,

and soil moisture level influences on the movement of nickel in sewage sludge-treated soils. J. Environ. Qual. 16:403-410.

An air dried, anaerobically digested sewage sludge was mixed into the top 15 cm of soil at a rate of 300 Mg ha^{-1}. The columns were maintained at moisture levels of saturation and unsaturation (16.7 K Pa tension) and leached with two waters of different quality. Irrigation water quality did not affect the amount of Ni leached from the sludge amended soil layer nor the depth of Ni movements. Mass balance calculation showed that on average of 3.3% of sludge applied Ni leached from the sludge amended soil layer of the saturated columns compared to 10.7% for the unsaturated columns. For the saturated columns an average of 74.9% of sludge applied Ni leached form the sludge amended soil layer was accumulated in the 0 to 30 cm soil interval compared to 4.65% for the unsaturated columns. Nickel movement below the sludge amended soil layer for the saturated columns ranged from 3 to 15 cm with an average of 9 cm compared to a range of 3 to 45 cm and an average of 18 cm for the unsaturated columns. Correlation and regression analysis indicated that pH and soil texture were the soil properties that best predicted the depth of Ni movements.

1175 **Whelan, B.R.,** 1986. Mineral phosphate precipitates from septic-tank effluent. Perth Geoderma, 39(2) : 125-139.

The layer formed in soils at the base of four soak wells and leach drains discharging septic-tank effluent was removed and examined for discrete mineral phosphate precipitates using spot tests, a scanning election microscope and an electron microprobe. Phosphate minerals were found only in the two septic systems over 10 years old that treated the waste water from the toilet alone. The pH of the slime layer of these systems was between 7 and 8. The precipitates were iron- and calcium-phosphates with composition that did not correspond precisely to any well-known phosphate mineral. Although the composition differed among grains, any given phosphate grain was homogeneous. No discrete aluminium phosphates were found. Attempts to determine the identify of phosphate minerals from solubility product measurements were inconclusive. Precipitation of phosphate from solution increases the capacity of soils with low adsorption characteristic to retain phosphate from waste water.

1176 **Whelan, B.R., Titamnis, Z.V.,** 1982. Daily chemical variability of domestic septic-tank effluent. Water Air Soil Pollut. 17 : 131-139.

Effluent from the septic tanks of five households was sampled daily for 15 days. Temperature, redox potential, conductivity and biochemical oxygen demand (BOD_5) were measured and samples were analysed for N, P, Ca, Mg, Na, K, Zu, Cd, Cr, Pb, Mg and linear alkylate sulphonate (LAS). Samples differed in the values obtained but the differences were small. The effluent was in a reduced and anaerobic conditions with almost all the N and P occurring in the inorganic forms in the solution.

The effluent concentrations N was about 100 mgL^{-1} and fP about 15 mgL^{-1}. The mean annual N and P loading in the effluent over the five households was 3.8 kg N/head yr and 0.6 kg P/head yr. Copper and Zn only were of any significant and their concentrations were less than in tap water. The chemical composition of the effluent was very similar to that found in New Zealand, Canada and USA.

1177 **White, R.K., Perry, J., Brown, R.E.** 1981. Applying Municipal sludge cake to Ohio crop land. Ohio Rept. 66(1) : 5-8.

More than 80 Ohio cities are currently applying sewage sludge to cropland. An EPA demonstration project is also underway in the state. Article describes how two major cities- Columbus and Toledo – apply sludge cake to agricultural land.

1178 **Wiechers, H.N. S.,** 1986. Chemical phosphate removal from Municipal waste waters: Current practice and recent innovations. Water S.A. 12(4) : 197-202.

The advantages, limitations and disadvantages of conventional chemical phosphate removal processes are reviewed. The need to minimize the costly disadvantages of these processes by optimization is stressed. Process parameters which lend themselves to optimization are identified. Attention is focussed on several innovative processes which overcome some of the inherent disadvantages of the conventional processes. The following innovative processes are reviewed: Calcium phosphate crystallization, magnesium ammonium phosphate precipitation, flocculation filtration and biologically induced chemical phosphate precipitation.

1179 **Wild, S.R., Waterhouse, K.S., McGrath, S.P., Jones, K.C.,** 1990. Organic contaminants in an agricultural soil with a known history of sewage sludge amendments and poly-nuclear aromatic hydrocarbons (PAH). Environl. Sci. Technol. 24(1) : 1706-1711.

The PAH content of soils from a long term experiment that received 25 separate sewage sludge applications (1942 to 1981) is presented alongwith control and a plot that received repeated applications of FYM. Samples were analysed for 1942-84. Soil ΣPAH conc. increased between 1942 and 1960 on the sludge amended plot and subsequently showed a decline. By 1984 the sludge amended plot contained over 3 times more s PAH than the corresponding control plot soil. By 1960 about 70.1% of the Σ PAH load added in the sludge was unaccounted for: this had increased to nearly 85% by 1984. Generally the high molecular weight PAHs have been more persistent. It is argued that biodegradation and transboundary transfers due to ploughing are the two main loss mechanisms.

1180 **Wilhelm, R.C., Martens, D.C., Hallock, D.L., Collins, E.R., Kornegay, E.T.,** 1980. Characterization and agricultural utilizations of swine waste lagoon effluents. Water Air Soil Pollut. 14 : 443-450.

The elemental composition of effluents from three aerobic swine waste lagoons and one aerobic swine waste lagoon are determined, and the effects of effluent application on growth of corn evaluated. Wide variation occurred in the elemental composition of effluents among the four lagoons and among four sampling dates from each lagoon. Effluent application increased corn grain yield on a Woodstown loamy fine sand.

1181 **Wilke, B.M.,** 1990. Effects of different abiotic soil properties on the microbial toxicity of zinc. Agribiol. Res. 43(4) : 309-318.

Effects of different abiotic soil properties on the microbial toxicity of zinc were investigated in laboratory perfusion experiments. Effects of zinc on microorganisms were measured by means of the dehydrogenase activity test. Experiments were carried out on A-horizon of 10 agricultural and preserve area soils, respectively. Zinc additions of 500 mg Zn/kg soil inhibited the dehydrogenase activity of 13 soils significantly. Statistical analysis of data showed Zn-concentrations of perfusion liquids to correlate significantly with the inhibitions of dehydrogenase activity. Thus close correlations were also detected for pH, CEC, clay and Fe content, which were correlated with the Zn concentration. The main abiotic factor responsible for the different degrees of inhibition was the clay content of soils.

1182 **Wilke, B.M.,** 1991. Effects of single and successive additions of cadmium, nickel and zinc on carbon dioxide evolution and dehydrogenase activity in a sandy loam Luvisol. Biol. Fert. Soils 11(1) : 34-37.

The effects of single and successive additions of Cd, Ni and Zn on CO_2 evolution and dehydrogenase activity in a sandy loam Luvisol were investigated in batch experiments under laboratory conditions. Successive additions of Cd, Ni and Zn before the same amount of metals had been added. Split additions of all metals reduced dehydrogenase activities in all soils to a lesser degree until the 28th day. Thereafter both modes of metal addition had the same effect throughout although the last addition was on the 35th day. It is assumed that the relatively greater effect, especially on CO_2 evolution, of successive addition during the first period was due to short-term increases of metal concn. in the soil solution after each application.

1183 **Williams, A.J.,** 1991. Evaluating policy options for controlling nitrate pollution from agril. International Conf. on Environ. Pollu. (B. Nath, J.P. Robinson. (Eds). 553-562.

This paper outlines the structure and functioning of a model designed to fulfil these tasks. The results of studies on enforced land use change the introduction of fertilizer quotas, and the applications of a fertilizer tax are considered in some detail. The implications of recent farm based research work, which pay close attention to nitrate leaching and the principles of which would form the core of a new code of "Best Farm Practice", are also investigated. This shows much promise and deserves active support both at the research and extension level.

1184 **Williams, R.T., Sisk, W.E., MacGillivray, A.R.** 1989. Degradation of nitroguanidine waste water components in soil. Environ. Toxicol. Chem. 8(6) : 469-475.

The degradation of nitrogunidine (NQ) waste water components was studied using continuous-flow and perfusion soil columns. After 271 d of operation of the continuous flor columns and 84 d of operation of the perfusion columns, only some components of NQ waste water were completely or partially removed. Guanidine nitrate and sulfate were the most readily transformed. NQ however, was only partially removed. Carbon supplements enhanced the transformation of both sulfate and NQ. Transformation products included nitrosoguanidine and ammonia, but not cyanoguanidine or kelamine. Microbial adaptation to waste water components was not demonstrated. Based on test data, land application of untreated waste water is not recommended.

1185 **Williamson, J.C., Johnson, D.B.,** 1990. Mineralisation of organic matter in topsoils subjected to stockpiling and restoration at open cast coal sites. Plant. Soil. 128(2) : 241-247.

Topsoil stockpiled for 4 years resulted in an accumulation of NH_4N at depths of 1m or more in mound, as measured by an ammonia gas sensing electrode. When leached with water these soils were also found to contain high concentrations of dissolved organic C below im. Both NH_4N and DOC were products of microbial mineralisation of soil organic matter that accumulated under anaerobic conditions. When these soils were resorted a flush of decomposition took place, fuelled by labile organic matter and soluble nitrogen. Stockpiled soil which underwent an ammonium rich perfusion regime in the laboratory indicated that in mound soils rapidly attained greater nitrification potential than surface mound soils and also had greater potential for further mineralisation of organic matter to NH_4-N. this further production was seen as a contribution from the bacterial flush, stimulated by the large labile-C pool already present.

1186 **Williman, B.P. Peterson, G.W., Fritton, D.D.,** 1981. Renovation of septic tank effluent in sandy clay mixtures. J. Environ. Qual. 10 (4): 439-444.

Limestone, sandstone and shale sands were used with clay added to give 0, 3, 6 and 12% clay. Septic tank, effluent was applied at the rate of 1.5 cm/day to the surface of each sandy clay mixture for 2-3 weeks. The effluent was analyzed at regular intervals before and after flowing through 60 cm of the sand for the following 16 chemical and biological variables: pH, chemical oxygen demand (COD) fecal coliforms, fecal streptococi total N, NH_4-N, NO_2-N, NO_3-N (NO_3-NO_2)-N, PO_4-P total, P, Cl, Ca, Na, K and specific conductivity. All the sand-clay combinations (including the 0% clay samples) removed over 99% of the fecal coliforms and streptococes. The removal of P and COD and the transformation of N were highly efficient in the limestone and shale sands regardless of clay content. Renovation in the sandstone sand, which is a relatively inert material, was increased by the addition of small amounts of clay. It was concluded that sand type influences the renovation of effluent and is more important than the amount of clay. The results indicate that limestone is the most desirable sand type, although long-term dissolution may be a problem, followed by sandstone with a small percentage of clay and then by shale. Although shale was a relatively efficient renovates of effluent over the time period studied, it is anticipated that the susceptibility of shale to weathering would lead to early clogging.

1187 **Winant, W.M., Menser, H.A. Bennett, D.L.,** 1981. Effect of sanitary landfill leachate on some soil chemical properties. J. Environ. Qual. 10:318-322.

Approximately 100 cms of leachate from a sanitary landfill was applied over a 6 month/period. After which soil samples were collected to a depth of 60 cm. At a soil depth of 0-5 cm Ca, Mg, Na, K and Sr levels of ammonium acetate extracts markedly increased, while leachate irrigation did not significantly change Fe, Zn, P and K-jeldahel N concentrations. Leachate irrigation increased soil pH from 4.7 to 5.8 at 0-5 cm depth and from 4.5 to 5.7 at the 15 to 30 cm depth. Most elements were attenuated to some extent by the soil but lime and fertilizer addition did little to influence soil adsorption capacity.

1188 **Winchester, J.W., Nifong, G.D.,** 1971. Water pollution in lake Michigan by trace elements from pollution aerosol fallout. Water Air Soil Pollut. 1: 50-64.

A partial inventory of air pollution emissions for 30 trace elements is presented for the Chicago, Milwaukee, and northwest Indiana metropolitan areas. The inventory is then compared with actual stream inputs measured for Zn, Cu and Ni and with estimates of preindustrial unpolluted stream inputs for 28 elements. Evidence indicates that the atmosphere may now be a major source of Zn in lake Michigan, and atmosphere inputs of Cu and Ni may also be considerable.

1189 **Winter, J., Zeliner, G.,** 1990. Thermophilic anaerobic degradation of carbohydrates-metabolic properties of microorganisms from the different phases. in 'Adaptation of Microorganisms to Extreme Environments' H.P. Duerre (Ed.): 139-154.

Organisms that might participate in an aerobic themophilic degradation of carbohydrates to methane and CO_2 and their metabolic properties are shortly reviewed in this paper. More than 20 thermophilic species of classical, fermentative bacteria and of archaebacterial methane bacteria from thermophilic ecosystems have been described and thermophilic acetogenic butyrate — and acetate thermophilic degrading consortia have been enriched. Pure cultures of thermophilic fermentative bacteria can degrade a variety of different sugars and polysaccharices, irrespective of their origin which was either sewage sludge, soil or a soltataric environment. The sewage sludge organisms, *Acelomicrobium flavidum* and *Acetothermus paucivorans* fermented giucose via the EMP-Pathway to 2 acetate, 2 CO_2 and 4 H_2.

1190 **Wisemen, J.T., Zibilske, L.M.,** 1988. Effect of sludge application sequence on carbon and nitrogen mineralization in soil. J. Environ. Qual. 17:334-339.

A laboratory experiment was conducted to determine the effect of an initial sludge amendment on C and primarily N mineralization of a second sludge amendment. A municipal sludge containing Cr-tanning effluent, and a domestic sludge with little metal contamination were added to a sandy loam soil at rates of 6.65 g domestic sludge kg^{-1} soil and 9.75 g municipal sludge kg^{-1} soil. Sludge were reapplied 40d later at the same rates in all sequence combinations. Respiration and nitrification were increased in sludge amended soil. Atleast 70% of the total C mineralized from both sludges within the first 11 d initial sludge applications. Nitrogen mineralized from a sludge-amended soils during the initial 40 d of incubation was linearly related to time. A second applications of sludge did not change the liner nature of N mineralization in all but one treatment. Ammonium N rapidly decreased and was negligible 2 weeks after sludge addition. Nitrite nitrogen levels were negligible throughout the experiment. By the end of the incubation period, the quantity of nitrate produced in all sequences of sludge additions was similar. Results indicate little effect of initial sludge addition on C and N mineralization of a second sludge amendment, even if the initial sludge applied contained a high concentration of Cr.

1191 **Wixson, B.G.,** 1988. Lead in soil : Issue and guidelines, Trace Substances in Environmental Health-XXII. Univ. Mo. Columbia: 349-356.

At the present time there are no recognized guidelines in the United States of America for lead in soil. The most current scientific knowledge and data were discussed, case studies of soil lead abatement programmes presently used in the U.S. and other countries were evaluated, and possible approaches to be used for the development of criteria and guidelines were suggested. It included assessment of human exposure pathways and indices.

1192 **Wixson, B.G., Ghazifard, A., Davies, B.E.,** 1987. Industrial wastes and soil lead concentrations as a basis for remedial or other action. In 'Proceedings of the Industrial Waste Conference' Purdue University (Ed. J.M. Bell.): 798-791.

Based on soil lead guidelines used to protect human health in Britain and Canada, levels of 1,000 µg/g soil lead for industrial (Open spaces or parks) purposes and 500 µg/g lead for soils which are used for growing vegetables for consumption are proposed where maximum contact exposure to children might occur, such as in residential areas. Guidelines must take pertinent factors into account, such as a soil pH above 6.5., the influence of organic matter, the presence of chelating compounds and site specific geological conditions that might affect metal mobility. The use of soil lead sample patterns to determine possible areas for remedial action is illustrated by a case study on a former landfill site near Kansas City, Missouri.

1193 **Wolfe, T.A., Demirel, T., Baumann, E.R.** 1986. Adsorption of organic pollutants on montmorillonite treated with amines. J. Water Pollut. Control Fed. 58(1) : 68-76.

The present study explores addition of the hydrochloride salts of propylamine, dodecylamine, and deodecyldiamine to sodium montmorillonite (a smectite) to improve its capacity for adsorbing organic pollutants from water and waste water. The amine ions were exchanged for charge-compensating sodium ions in the montmorillonite structure to further separate the montmorillonite unit layers and expose the large interlamellar clay surfaces. The interlamellar surfaces thus became available for adsorption of organic pollutants from the aqueous phase.

1194 **Wollan, E., Beckett, P.H.T.,** 1979. Changes in the extractability of heavy metals on the interaction of sewage sludge with soil. J. Environl. Pollut. 20(3) : 215-230.

On first mixing digested sewage sludge with soil, the proportions of the Cu and Zn in the sludge that are extractable to conventional extractants fluctuate considerably. Thus, Cu extractable from sludge alone shows a marked initial fall to a minimum at 8-29d and then rises to rear its initial value; from a sludge-soil mixture there is a less marked decrease-(over 8-16d), and the extractable Cu returns to near its initial value over 90-100d. The Zn extractable from sludge alone falls to a minimum at 8-16d and then rises to near the initial value, but the Zn extractable from sludge-soil mixtures rises sharply over 2-4d and then falls to near the initial value over 50-100d. There appears to be little further change in the extractable Cu, Ni, or Zn during the next 600d. although the metals in the sludge are still relatively more extractable than those "native" to the soil. It is likely that similar processes operate under field conditions, but more slowly.

1195 **Wolnik, K.A., Firdke, F.L., Capar, S.G., Meyer, M.M., Satzger, R.D., Bonnin, E., Gaston, C.M.,** 1985. Elements in major raw agricultural crops in the United States. 3 Cadmium, lead and eleven other elements in carrots, field corn, onions, rice spinach and tomato. Agric. Food Chem. 33(5) : 807-811.

Six raw agricultural crops were collected from major U.S. growing areas uncontaminated by human activities other than normal agricultural practices. Handling, preparation, and analysis of the 1215 samples were performed. Cd, Pb, Ca, Cu, Fe, K, Mg, Mn, Mo, Na, Ni, P and Zn were estimated. Mean Cd concentration in carrots, field corn. onions, rice, spinach, and tomatoes were 0.028, 0.012, 0.011, 0.012, 0.065 and 0.017

μg/g (wet weight) respectively, and mean Pb concentrations in these crops were 0.009, 0.022, 0.005, 0.007, 0.045 and 0.002 μg/g (wet weight), respectively.

1196 **Wolt, J.D.,** 1985. Utilization of organic water on agricultural soils of Tennessee. Agri. Expt. Stat. Bull. Univ. of Tennesse. 638: 30

The data presented in this bulletin serve to indicate the value of diverse types of organic wastes as sources of N for crops. Furthermore, they provide an estimate of TKN loadings required to achieve maximum yields when organic wastes are applied to forage crops (corn silage, wheat and rye haylage, and bermudagrass) over relatively short periods of continued application (three years or less). Waste generators and crop producers wishing to land-apply organic waste must be aware of the many factors that allow for waste disposal/utilization on corp land in an environmentally sound manner.

1197 **Wong, K.H., Chan, K.Y., Ng, S.L.,** 1979. Cadmium uptake by the unicellular green alga cholorella salina Cu-I from culture media with high salinity. Chemosphere : 8(11-12) : 887-891.

The growth behaviour and the Cd uptake phenomena of algae found to grow well in sewage effluent with salinities of 0-16 parts per trillion (ppt) in Cd-contaminated culture media which have different salinities was examined. Sodium chloride can greatly suppress Cd uptake by the algal cells. In 0.1 ppm Cd-contaminated media, the contents of Cd in the algal cells was 124 ppm in medium without added NaCl; 58 ppm in medium with 5 ppt NaCl; 18 ppm in medium with 10 ppt NaCl; and only 7.6 ppm in medium with 15 ppt NaCl. Similar declines in Cd uptake were observed for media containing 0.001, 0.005, 0.01, 0.05 ppm Cd with different salinities C. Saline is well suited for serving the dual functions of waste water purification and recycling through the production of algal protein. Sodium chloride can suppress the Cd uptake in the algal cells and therefore reduce the amount of Cd accumulated in higher trophic levels of the food chain.

1198 **Wong, M.H., Chu, L.M.,** 1985. Yield and metal uptake of Cynodon dactylon grown on refuse-compost amended soil. Agric. Ecosyst. Environ. 14(1-2): 41-52.

In a glasshouse trial refuse compost was mixed with a loamy sand at rates equivalent to 0, 10, 25, 50 and 75 t ha^{-1} before planting seeds of Bermuda of grass. Adding compost to the soil increased the concentrations of various heavy metals. The yield of bermuda grass was greater with the highest rate of compost application, probably because of the combined effect of enhanced germination and improved growth. The second cut also yielded more than the cut at the heaviest levels of composting. With the exception of Pb, Mn, and Cd, metal contents of bermuda grass were increased by compost application. In general, the root portion contained higher levels of metals than the aerial part. It was found that contents of Cd, Mn, and Zn were higher in the foliage of the second harvest than the first.

1199 **Wong, M.H., Lay, C.C.,** 1980. Comparison of soy-bean wastes, used tea-leaves and sewage sludge for growing Chloriella Pyrenoidosa. Environl. Pollut. 23(4) : 247-259.

A preliminary experiment was conducted to search for the most suitable concentration of each culture medium for the growth of C. Pyrenoidosa. The following concentration of the waste material were chosen for the subsequent cultivation: sludge 2%, used tea leaves, 1% and soybean residue 2%. It was discovered that 2% soybean residue extract produced the highest growth rate, followed by 2% sludge and Bristol medium, with the used tea leaves producing the lowest.

1200 **Wong, M.H., Lau, M.W.,** 1985. Root growth of *Cynodon dactylon* and *Eleusine Indica* collected from motorways at different concentrations of lead. Environ. Res. 36(2) : 257-267.

An ecological survey was conducted on the roadside vegetation, a three different sites: Tai Po, a commercial and residential areas. *Cynodon dactylon* and *Eleusine indica* were the two most dominant species recorded. The Tai Po had higher Pb contents in both soil and plant, followed by shek O, and then Wu Kai Sha. Tillers of *C. dactylon* and *E. indica* from the three sites were subjected to a series concentrations of $Pb(NO_3)_2$. By comparing their indexes of tolerance and values of 14-days EC_{50} (effective concentration reducing the normal root growth by 50%), roadside populations of the two grasses collected from Tai Po and Shek O, especially the former one, were more tolerant to elevated levels of Pb compared with those collected from Wu Kai Sha.

1201 **Wong, M.H., Wong, J.W.C.,** 1989. Germination and seedling growth of vegetable crops in fly ash-amended soils. Agric. Ecosyst. Environ. 26. (1): 23-25.

The soil amendment effects of fly ash, were examined during germination tests of two vegetable crop species. Fly ash samples contained a high total content of various trace element including Cd, Pb and other meals such as Co, Cu, Fe, Mn, Mo, Ni and Zn. Fly ash was applied at rates of 0.3, 6, 12 and 30% of (dry weight basis) to a sandy and a sandy loam soil. After application of fly ash, germination of *Brassica parachinensis* and B. *chinenis* seeds in 3 and 6% treated sandy soil was enhanced, while those in 12 and 30% treated sandy soil and 30% treated sandy loam showed a significant reduction. Value of EC_{50} of fly ash for both plants on seed germination were higher in sandy soil than in a sandy loam.

1202 **Wu, L., Kruckeberg, A.L.** 1985. Copper tolerance in two legume species from a copper mine habitat. New Phytol. 99(4) : 565-570.

Lupinus bicolor Lindl and *Lotus purshianus* (Benth). Clem. and Clem.

plants growing on copper mine waste in northern California exhibited considerably greater copper tolerance at 0.2 mg CuL^{-1} in nutrient solution than plants from an adjacent meadow. Effectively nitrogen fixation in the copper enriched soils is suggested from acetylene reduction assays.

1203 **Wyatt, L., Sponner, J., Berryhill, W., Brichford, S.L., Lanier, A.L.,** 1988. Non-point sources J. Water Pollut. Control. Fed. 60 : 925-933.

Nonpoint source (NPS) pollution is reviewed under: 1) NPS policy, economics and planning, 2) water quality and water resources, 3) best management practices, for NPS control and 4) NPS monitoring modelling and analytical methods.

1204 **Xian, X,** 1989. Effect of chemical forms of cadmium, zinc and lead in polluted soils on their uptake by cabbage plants. Plant Soil, 113(2) : 257-264.

Seven soils which had been polluted with heavy metals from a zinc smelter were sequentially extracted so that Cd, Zn and Pb could be partitioned into five operationally defined chemical fractions. exchangeable, bound to carbonate, bound to Fe-Mn oxide, bound to organic matter, and residual. Cabbage was planted in the soils to examine the effects of concentrations and chemical from of the metal in soil on their uptake. The exchangeable fraction contained 55, 13, and 6%, and carbonate fraction 11, 10 and 6% of the total Cd, Zn, and Pb, respectively. Thé highest amount of Zn (42%) was detected in residual, and Pb (43%) in organic fraction. Metal levels in plant were in accord with their levels in soil.

1205 **Xiaobing, Yu, Xiaoping Wang, Bartha, R., Rosen, J.D.,** 1990. Supercritical fluid extraction of coal tar contaminated soil. Environ Sci. Technol. 24(11) : 1732-1738.

A coal tar contaminated soil containing over 0.1% polycyclic aromatic hydrocarbons (PAH) was treated by supercritical fluid extraction with carbon dioxide/methanol.A 7-h extraction period resulted in removal of 92% of the PAH and other contaminants. This was reflected in the virtual elimination of toxicity and mutagenic activity as measured by two short term assays. Shorter extraction periods gave lesser, but still significant, toxicity and mutagenic activity reductions.

1206 **Xuexoun Zhang, Linhai Guo,** 1990. Studies on the heavy metals pollution of soil and plant in Tlanjin waste water. Ekologia (SCFR) 10(1) : 87-97.

In Tianjin aquatic soil area, the soil is polluted by heavy metals after waste water irrigation. In this paper, through studies of migration and distribution of heavy metals in soil as well as study of relationship between content of available heavy metals in sol and in crop, the critical values of six heavy metal elements in soil are; Hg 0.5 ppm; Cd 1.2 ppm, Pb 20 ppm, Cu 160 ppm, Zn 500 ppm, and Ni 30 ppm. The evaluation of pollution was carried out according to the soil pollution index.

1207 **Yadav, K.,** 1990. Nature of Phenolic compounds in soils treated with sugarcane trash and rice straw. J. Indian Soc. Soil Sci. 38(3) : 531-533.

Samples of a Calcifluvent and a Haplustalf were mixed with sugarcane trash and rice straw and incubated for 60 days at 30 - 1 C° at the moisture level of field capacity. The phenolic compounds were extracted with 4% NaOH (w/v) and 1% NaSH and their relative amounts determined by comparing the intensity of the colour of the chromatographic zones developed by suitable reagents. Orsionl, pyrocatechol, P-hydroxy benzoic acid, protoatechoic acid and vanillic acid were defected in both materials in the Calcifluvent. Orselline acid in the Haplustalf, both in the control and the treated soil incorporation of trash and straw significantly increased the number and amounts of phenolic compounds in both soils; the amounts were greater with sugarcane trash.

1208 **Yadav, K., Jha. K.K.,** 1988. Nature of amino acids in soils incubated with poultry manure and sewage sludge under field capacity and submergence. J. Indian Soc. Soil Sci. 36 : 791-793.

Incubation studies were conducted with poultry manure and sewage sludge (30 Mg ha^{-1} each) on two soils under field capacity and submergence (5 cm to - 1 cm) for 130 days at 30±1.c. In sewage treated soils out of 14 amino acids glycine, aspartic acid, glutamic acid, methionine were detected in humic acid extract and only alanine, lysine, threonine, glutamic acid and metheomine were found in fluvic acid hydrolysate. Leucine was found in sewage sludge under submergence. In general higher number and amount of amino acids were detected under submergence in humic and acid hydrolysate of sewage treated soil. Sulfur containing amino acid was only detected in humic acid and fulvic acid hydrolysate of sludge treatment. This indicates higher availability of N and S in sewage treated soils under submergence.

1209 **Yadav, K., Jha, K.K., Jha, K.,** 1989. Microbial decomposition of poultry manure and sewage sludge in soil J. Indian Soc. Soil. Sci. 37 : 301-305.

Different genera of bacteria and fungi were isolated from soils treated with poultry manure and sewage sludge. Pseudomonas dominated in the Pusa Soil *(Calcifluvent)* and Flavo bacterium in the Ranchi soil *(Haplustaff)*. Escherichia was only detected in sewage sludge treatment. Aspiergillus candidus, A. Terreus, Alternaria, alternata, Cu rvularia spp. C, Lunata, Fusarium oxysporium, Mucor plumbeus, penicillium digiatum, P. funiculosa trichoderma spp were identified. The cellulolytic activities of the fungi isolated at 130 days of incubation were measured on modified Richard's nutrient agar and in Reese and Mandels medium with paper strips, Maximum and minimum cellulolytic activity were shown by trichoderma spp (35.1) and curvularia lunata (7.3), respectively.

1210 **Yadav, K., Jha, K.K., Prasad, C.R., Sinha, M.K.,** 1989. Kinetics of carbon mineralization from poultrymanure and sewage sludge in two soils at field capacity and submergence moisture. J. Indian Soc. Soil Sci. 37:240-243.

The kinetics of carbon mineralization in calcareous soil and red loam soil mixed with poultrymanure and sewage sludge under field capacity and submergence were investigated under laboratory conditions. At field capacity 46 to 56 per cent, and under submergence only 30 to 38 per cent added carbon was mineralized as CO_2 in 25 days of incubation and the biodegradation of the organic materials during total period of 130 days involved first order reactions. Mineralization potential in the poultry manure treatment was higher than in the sewage sludge. The rates of decomposition of sewage sludge treatment were approximately two times at field capacity and 2.5 times under submergence greater than those of poultry manure treatment.

1211 **Yanful, E.K., Nesbitt, H.W., Quigley, R.M.,** 1988. Heavy metal migration at a landfill site, Sarnia, Ontario, Canada-1. Thermodynamic assessment and chemical interpretations. Appl. Geochem. 3(5) : 523-533.

The transition metals Fe, Cu, Zn and Pb have diffused only 10-20 cm into the clay barrier at the Confederation Road landfill compared to 130 cm for porewater chloride. Other major dissolved species, including the alkali and alkaline earth metals, have also defused out of waste landfill and into clay subsoils more rapidly than the metals. Redox potentials, E_h indicate strongly reducing conditions (E_h = -130 mv) in the clayey soil at the subsoil/waste interface and increase to +50 mv at a depth of 45 cm below the slightly lower values (7.8-8) near the interface may result from production of organic fatty acids during degradation of the waters. Thermodynamic analysis of subsoil pore waters indicates that Fe, Cu, Zn, and Pb exist primarily as metalhydroxy complexes of the forms $(MeOH)^-$ and $Me(OH)^0_2$ although a complex of $(PbCl)^+$ may be significant but not predominant. The analysis also demonstrates that the dissolved transition metal concentration of the subsoil pore waters are controlled at carbonate mineral saturation levels, whereas Fe concentrations in leachate solutions associated with the wastes are controlled at FeS_2 saturation levels.

1212 **Yaron, B., Sutherland, P., Galin, T., Acher, A.J.,** 1989. Soil pollution by petroleum products. II Adsorption-desorption of 'kerosene' vapours on soils. J. Contam Hydrol. 4(4) : 347-358.

Adsorption/desorption of vapour hydrocarbons from the synthetic 'kerosene' on different soils was studied. Kerosene contained 20% aromatic compounds and 80% aliphatic compounds. Soil moisture was most important parameter for adsorption processes. The highest adsorption values were on arid brown loessial silty loam soil, having the following order of adsorption: n-decane > m-xylene > ps-cumene> n-butylbenzene > n-dodecane. Fastest desorption. rate was of m-xylene and the lowest of n-dodecane in all the 3 soils.

1213 **Yeoman, S., Sterritt, R.M., Rudd, T., Leaster, J.N.,** 1989 Particle size fractionation and metal distribution in sewage sludges. Water Air Soil Pollut. 45 : 27-42.

A sequential step filtration technique has been used to investigate the different size particles of suspended solids in several raw, activated and digested sewage sludges. Liquid sludge was passed through filters with increasing pore sizes (0.2 μm to 10μm). Results showed that there was greater proportion of larger particles with raw and activated than digested sludges. Generally in the activated sludge, the metals (Cd, Ni, Pb, Cu, and Zn) tended to be associated with large particles (> 100 μm), whereas in raw and particularly digested sludges the metals were found in the smaller particle size fraction from 20 to 2.5 μm. Calculating specific associations in terms of mg/kg the 8 to 20 μ size range appears important in complexing metals. Generally distributions were more widespread when results were expressed as mg/kg as opposed to mg/L.

1214 **Yimbo, P.O.,** 1986. Cadmium and lead at two selected roadside sits in Texas : A field and laboratory appraisal of concentration and growth effects. Diss. Abst. Int. Pt.B., Sci & Engg. 47(1).

Concentration of lead and cadmium in roadside soils and bermudagrass from Dallas and Hopkins Rains countries, Texas were determined. Generally no significant differences for metal levels at these two sites, and levels found are much lower than those reported for many regions of the USA and Dallas county. Uptake of Cd and Pb by bermudagrass was investigated through greenhouse experiments using Kervin sandyloam and Houston black clay soils treated with 0-3000 ppm Pb $(NO_3)_2$ or 0-1000 ppm Cd $(NO_3)_2$. Little of the added metals were found in the above-ground plant portions. Visual observation of the plants over a three month growing period did not reveal any delerterious effects for poor germination and stunted growth at 1000 and 3000 ppm Cd and Pb treatment levels, respectively.

1215 **Yonge, D.R., Keinath, T.M.,** 1986. The effects of non-ideal competition on multi-component adsorption equilibria. J. Water Pollut. Control Fed. 58(1) : 77-81.

Increased concern over hazardous and toxic compounds in waste waters and drinking water supplies has led to interest in development of suitable removal technologies. Adsorption on activated carbon has proven to be one of the most technically feasible means of removing the majority of toxic organic materials from potable water suppliers. The mechanism of competitive adsorption on activated carbon, however, is not well understood and, therefore, is not adequately considered by existing multisolute equilibrium models. This can lead to inaccurate adsorber performance predictions.

1216 **Yong, R.N., Warkentin, B.P., Phadungchewit, Y., Galver, R.,** 1990. Buffer capacity and lead retention in some clay materials. Water Air Soil

Pollut. 53(1-2) : 53-67.

The link between buffer capacity and the ability of clays to retain Pb in interactions between Pb contaminant leachate and the clays, was studied, using a natural clay from Quebee and laboratory-prepared clays (kaolinite, illite, and smectite). The retention of Pb in the clay suspensions as they received increasing amounts of acid was investigated, and the results examined in terms of the buffer capacity of the clays. As the clays receive increasing amounts of acid (e.g. akin to addition of acid leachate) high amounts of Pb can be retained if the buffer capacity prevents the pH from dropping to values where precipitation mechanisms are not operative. The high carbonate content in the illite gave it higher buffer capacity than the smectite and natural clay, and permitted to to retain high amounts of Pb. High Pb uptake by the clays can affect the buffer capacity and the Pb retention capacity.

1217 **Youssef, R.A., Chino, M.,** 1989. Root induced changes in the rhizosphere of plants II. Distribution of heavy metals across the rhizosphere in soils. Soil Sci. Plant. Nutr. 35(4) : 609-621.

Three experiments were carried out using the rhizobox system to determine the distribution of heavy metals (Cu, Zn, Mn, and Fe) across the rhizosphere of barley (*Hordeum vulgare* L. var. Dorirumugi). The movement of ^{65}Zn, ^{54}Mn and ^{59}Fe within the rhizosphere was also investigated. The solubility of heavy metals was evaluated by using double acid (H_2SO_4 + HCl) extractant. The results indicated that the rhizobox system provides quantitative information on the area of rhizobox concerning the heavy metal distribution. The increase of the pH in the vicinity of the roots tended to decrease the amount of soluble Cu and Zn. In spite of the increase of the pH, the solubility of Mn and sometimes of Fe was increased in the rhizosphere.

1218 **Yuanlee, Dar, Farmer, W.J., Acchi, Y.,** 1990. Sorption of napropamide on clay and soil in the presence of dissolved organic matter. J. Environ Qual. 19(3) : 567-573.

Dissolved organic matter (DOM) can affect the distribution of solutes between solution and sorbed phases and the availability and environmental area of fate of the solutes. Batch sorption isotherm techniques were used to evaluate solute solute and solute sorbent interactions that control the effects of DOM on the sorption of a nonionic, moderately polar organic solute by solid sorbents. The sorption of napropamide by Na^+, Cu^{2+} and Al^{3-} montmorillonite decreased when dissolved humic acid derived from peat (peat-DHA) was present in the slurry. For Na-montmorillonite, the effect of DOM on sorption was reduced when a dialysis membrane prevented contact between the DOM and the clay. This suggests that competition for sorption sites on the clay between DOM and the pesticide contributed to decrease napropamide sorption. The extent of the DOM effect was also dependent on the concentration and the source of DOM added.

1219 **Zaciara, J.M., Ainsworth, C.C., Cowan, C.E., Resch, C.T.,** 1989. Adsorption of chromate by subsurface soil horizons. J. Soil Sci. Soc. Am. 53(2) : 418-428.

Chromate adsorption was measured with and without reactive consolutes on four subsurface soil horizons differing in pH and mineralogy and on clay fractions from two of the oxide containing subsoils. Chromate adsorption was greatest in lower pH materials enriched in kaolinite and crystalline iron oxides. Over a range in pH, chromate adsorption to subsoil was similar to that observed for pure-phase oxides. Chromate binding was reversible to pH and was depressed in the presence of SO_4^{2-} and dissolved inorganic C, which competes for adsorption sites. A surface site density for crystalline Al-substituted iron-oxides in the subsoil was estimated from chromate adsorption on the clay fractions using the model FITEOL and outer sphere surface coordination constants from Al-goethite. The estimated density for soil crystalline iron oxides was well below that of clean oxides, suggesting surface saturation by indigenous soil ions. The calculated site density and surface binding constants for Al-goethite were used in the Triple Layer Model to calculate the effect of ionic strength, consolutes, solids concentration and sorbate concentration on $CrO^{2-}{}_4$ adsorption. Model calculations were in good qualitative agreement with experimental results.

1220 **Zachritz, W.H.** 1986. Modelling the nitrogen dynamics of a water hyacinth- Azolla-freshwater prawn polyculture waste water treatment system. Diss. Abst. Int. Pt. B- Sci. & Engg. 46(12) : 246.

A two-stage polyculture waste water treatment system, using water hyacinth, Eichhormia crassipes, in the first — stage and a combination of Azolla and the fresh water prawn, Macrobrachium rosenbergii, in the second stage, was developed at the pilot plant scale to provide tertiary treatment to municipal waste water. A three-compartment dynamic nitrogen model was also developed to stimulate the first stage of the system. The results of the analysis of the first stage water hyacinth system indicated that for NH_3-N loadings ranging from 11.6 to 76.1 kg NH_3N/ha-d, NH_3N removals averaged 76.8 percent over the study period. Nitrate and ORG-N removals ranged from 24 to 80 per cent and 75 to 95 per cent, respectively. The first stage effluent NH_3-N, NO_3N and ORG-N concentrations ranged from 0.3 to 25.0 mg/L, 0.5 to 2.3 mg/L, and 0.3 to 0.8 mg/L, respectively, over the sample period. The second stage Azolla-prawn system results indicated that at NH_3-N loadings between 115 to 10,360 gm-N/ha-d, system performance for NH_3-N varied between a 14% increase to a 90% removal. Nitrate and ORG-N removals in the Azolla-prawn system were highly variable through the system.

1221 **Zayed, J., Andre, P., Kennedy, G.,** 1991. Variation of aluminum levels in black spruce (*Picea mariana*). Water Air Soil Pollut. 55(3-4) : 337-344.

The aim of this work is to evaluate black spruce (*Picea mariana*) as an historical indicator of Al deposition from the atmosphere. The territory studied extends to a radius of 10 km around the Alcan aluminum refinery at Jonquere, Quebec, Canada. The sampling strategy was designed to determine the variability within an individual free and to determine local and regional differences. Using an incremental crore, xylem samples were taken from trees at six sites at 5 and 10 km from the refinery.

1222 **Zee, S.E.A.T.M., Van Der, Ferdinandus, H.N.M., Bockhold, A.E., Haan F.A.m. De** 1990. Long term effects of fertilization and diffuse deposition of heavy metals on soils and crop quality in "Plant Nutrition, Physiology and Applications" (Ed. Beusichem B.L.Van).
Calculation of the balance between input and acceptable removal indicate that current emission rates of Cd and Pb are on the average too high to preserve good soil quality in the long term in Netherlands.

1223 **Zibilske, L.M., Wagner, G.H.,** 1982. Bacterial growth and fungal genera distribution in soil amended with sewage sludge containing cadmium, chromium and copper. Soil Sci. 134(6) : 364-370.
The effects of three concentrations were studied on micrograms per gram of soil, of sludge-borne cadmium (111, 1, 0.1), chromium (556, 44, 1 and copper (556, 78, 11) on bacterial numbers, ATP content, and distribution of major fungal genera in an agricultural soil suited for the disposal of sewage sludge. Bacterial were stimulated initially in the 78 and 11μg/g Cu treatments and in the 1μg/g treatments. Restriction of bacterial growth occured in the 556 μg/g Cu and 556 μg/g Cr treatments. Cadmium treatments exhibited counts similar to controls initially, but were reduced after two weeks incubation. After 25 days, bacterial counts in controls were higher than in all but two metal treatments. Fungal intergenus relationship were altered in all but Cr treatments. ATP estimates indicated that biomass increased initially but by 1 week, was reduced in Cu treatments. ATP in Cr paralleled the initial stimulation, but by 2 weeks, gave lower estimates than controls. Cadmium treatments showed similar trends in bacterial counts and measured ATP. Metal-laden sewage sludge affected soil microbial populations quantitatively or qualitatively, which could influence the capacity of these soil population for nutrient cycling.

1224 **Zirschky, J., Abernathy, A.R.,** 1988. Land application of waste water. J. Water Pollut. Control Fed. 60(6) : 857-868.
The application of waste water to land is reviewed.

1225 **Zirschky, J., Crawford, D., Norton, L., Deemer, D.,** 1989. Metal removal overland flow. J. Water Pollut. Control Fed. 61(4) : 470-475.
Metals removal from advanced secondary quality waste water was evaluated for 1 year. Application rates (0.17 to 0.57 m^3/min) were tested. Only Cu and Zn were consistently removed at all applications rates. Over land flow is not recommended as a heavy metal removal process

without pilot testing.

1226 **Zoettl, H.W.,** 1985. Heavy metal levels and cycling in forest ecosystems Experientia: 41 (9): 1104-1113.

Any estimate of the impact of environmental pollution depends on a reliable knowledge of input levels and the element turnover in the particular ecosystem. Ten years ago a biogeochemical inventory including measurements of element turnover in forest ecosystems near the "Baethalde" (Black forest) was initiated and continued for upto five years. This paper present several results of this study concentrating on input, output, storage, and turnover of five selected elements in these forest ecosystems.

1227 **Zoller, U., Ashash, E., Ayali, G., Shafir, S., Azmon, B.,** 1990. Environl. Internatl 16(3) : 301-306.

Streams polluted by sewage and six adjacent water wells were analyzed for nonionic detergent concentrations in Israel. Ground-water was contaminated by nonionic synthetic detergents (0.1 to .8 mg/L) the origin of which are the adjacent surface water bodies, polluted by sewage. The mean velocity of movement of the detergent pollution front in the soil was found to be about 0.4 metre/day.

1228 **Zommer, S., Urbanska, Kukinski, M.,** 1985. Lead level in certain vegetable and fruits raised in the range of emission of lead compounds by the Irena Glass works inowroclaw. Rocz. Pranst. Zakl. Hig. 36(4) : 298-303.

1229 **Zuckerman, L.S., and Kirkham. M.B.,** 1978. Cadmium and zinc availability in soil irrigated with sludge containing a cationic conditions. Water Air Soil Pollut. 9 : 467-473.

Tomato plants grown in 15 cm diameter plastic pots were irrigated for 15 weeks with liquid sewage sludge containing a liquid cationic conditioner to determine its effect on Cd and Zn available. Half of the plants received 50 ml week^{-1} sludge containing 0.25 ml conditioner and half of the plants received 50 ml week^{-1} liquid digested sludge with no conditioner. Plants were harvested 3, 6, 9, 12 and 15 weeks after sludge treatments began. Dry weights of plant grown with conditioned sludges were similar to those grown with the non-conditional sludge. Plants with conditioner flowered and fruited one and two weeks earlier, respectively, than plants without conditioner. Six weeks after treatments began when the plants had grown to their greatest height. Cd concentrations in sludge crusts, soil and roots receiving conditioner were 2.0, 1.5, 2.1, times greater, respectively, than without conditioner, respectively. After the six weeks sampling time, shoots of plants grown with conditioner had 2.6 times more Cd than shoots of plants grown without conditioner. Cadmium concentration in shoots from both treatments were similar at treatment at all sampling times. Zinc content of roots, shoots, fruits, soil and sludge crusts was not affected by the conditioner. Results showed that a cationic conditioner, added to sludge, increased the availability of Cd, but not of Zn, for tomato plants until maximum height was reached.

1230 **Zurera, G., Arcos, F., Rincon, F., Rozo-Lora, R.,** 1986. Mercury content in mushroom species in the Cordova area. Bull. Environl. Contam. Toxicol. 36 (5): 662-667.

Data on the levels of mercury contents in mushroom species collected in the Cordova area (Spain) are presented.

1231 **Zvera, V.J., Danneberg-Rg, O.H.,** 1979. The influence of high sewage sludge doses on yield-development and nutrient uptake. Bodenk. Jour. Fuer. Lardwirik Forscr. 30(2) : 127-133.

In a pot experiment carried out in the greenhouse, the effect on high application rates of dry sewage sludge on dry matter production of barley, peas and spinach was tested. Plants were also analyzed for N, P, K, Ca, Mg and Na uptake. Rates ≤106.6 g/pot, corresponding to 320 t/ha, resulted in increasing yield of barley; higher rates depressed the yield. With peas and spinach, the highest yield was achieved with sludge rates of 53.2 g/pt (160 t/ha). Spinach was most sensitive to higher application rates. The N and Na content of all plants increased with increasing sewage sludge application. The P content remained constant in all plants: K-, Ca- and Mg-contents differed with increasing sludge rates, depending on the plants.

1232 **Zvyagintsev, D.G., Cuzev, U.S., Levin, S.U., Seletskiy, G.I., Oborin, A.A.** 1989. Diagnostic signs of differences in level of petroleum pollution of Soil. Sov Soil Sci. 21 : 104-109.

The effect of petroleum pollution was studied in USSR by 5 microbial methods. 12 levels of petroleum (0.1 to 500 ml/kg soil) were studied. Results showed 4 levels of petroleum were important: 1) The homoeostasis one with conc. of petroleum up to 0.7 ml/kg soil composition were virtually unchanged, 2) The stress zone, from 0.7 to 50 ml/kg soil with a marked decrease in the proportion of dominant organisms in the control soil, 3) The resistant zone from 50 to 300 ml/kg soil in which there is a sharp decline in species diversity and a change in the composition of the microbial population and, 4) the repression zone with above 300 ml/kg soil which showed a strong suppression of microbiological activity in the soil.

1233 **Zwarich, M.A., Millis J.G.,** 1979. Effects of sewage sludge application on the heavy metal content of wheat and forage crops. Can. J. Soil Sci. 59(3) : 231-239.

A growth chamber experiment was used to investigate the effects of digested sewage sludge application on the heavy metal content of wheat and brome-alfalfa forage crops. Samples of wheat were obtained from farm fields which had received heavy applications of sludge. No adverse effects on yields or appearance of crops were noted. The tissue levels of Hg, Cr, and Pb were unaffected by sludge treatment. Copper levels in wheat kernels and straw were only slightly increased, but Cu levels in the forage crop were elevated by the sludge treatment. There was a considerable increase in the Zn content of all crops, but levels were not excessive. Sludge treatment produced » 6-fold increase in the Cd content of the forage crop. The increased Cd levels are undesirable. but can be controlled by restricting the sludge application rate. Little or no effect of sludge treatment on Cd levels in wheat straw was observed.

SUBJECT INDEX